Lecture Notes in Computer Science 8712

Commenced Publication in 1973
Founding and Former Series Editors:
Gerhard Goos, Juris Hartmanis, and Jan van Leeuwen

T0213754

Mirosław Kutyłowski   Jaideep Vaidya (Eds.)

Computer Security – ESORICS 2014

19th European Symposium
on Research in Computer Security
Wrocław, Poland, September 7-11, 2014
Proceedings, Part I

 Springer

Volume Editors

Mirosław Kutyłowski
Wrocław University of Technology
Wrocław, Poland
E-mail: miroslaw.kutylowski@pwr.edu.pl

Jaideep Vaidya
Rutgers, The State University of New Jersey
Newark, NJ, USA
E-mail: jsvaidya@business.rutgers.edu

ISSN 0302-9743   e-ISSN 1611-3349
ISBN 978-3-319-11202-2   e-ISBN 978-3-319-11203-9
DOI 10.1007/978-3-319-11203-9
Springer Cham Heidelberg New York Dordrecht London

Library of Congress Control Number: 2014947642

LNCS Sublibrary: SL 4 – Security and Cryptology

Typesetting: Camera-ready by author, data conversion by Scientific Publishing Services, Chennai, India

Printed on acid-free paper

Springer is part of Springer Science+Business Media (www.springer.com)

Preface

These volumes contain the papers selected for presentation at the 19th European Symposium on Research in Computer Security (ESORICS 2014), held during September 7–11, 2014, in Wrocław, Poland. ESORICS has a two-decade-old tradition of bringing together the international research community in a top-quality event that covers all the areas of computer security, ranging from theory to applications.

In response to the symposium's call for papers, 234 papers were submitted to the conference from 38 countries. The papers went through a careful review process and were evaluated on the basis of their significance, novelty, technical quality, as well as on their practical impact and/or their level of advancement of the field's foundations. Each paper received at least three independent reviews, followed by extensive discussion. We finally selected 58 papers for the final program, resulting in an acceptance rate of 24.79%. The authors of accepted papers were requested to revise their papers, based on the comments received. The program was completed with invited talks by Moti Yung from Google Inc. and Columbia University, Stefano Paraboschi from Università di Bergamo, and Shlomi Dolev from Ben Gurion University of the Negev. A special talk on privacy protection was given by Wojciech Wiewiórowski, Inspector General for Personal Data Protection in Poland.

An event like ESORICS 2014 depends on the volunteering efforts of a host of individuals and the support of numerous institutes. There is a long list of people who volunteered their time and energy to put together and organize the conference, and who deserve special thanks. We are indebted to Jacek Cichoń, the general chair of this symposium, for his continuous support. Thanks to all the members of the Program Committee and the external reviewers for all their hard work in evaluating the papers. We are also very grateful to all the people whose work ensured a smooth organization process: the ESORICS Steering Committee, and its chair Pierangela Samarati in particular, for their support; Giovanni Livraga, for taking care of publicity; Małgorzata Korzeniowska for management of the local arrangements, Kamil Kluczniak for the technical work of putting the proceedings together; and the local Organizing Committee, in particular Przemysław Kobylański, Maciej Gebala, and Wojciech Wodo, for helping with organization and taking care of local arrangements. We would also like to express our appreciation to everyone who organized the workshops (BADGERS, DPM, QASA, SETOP SIoT, STM, Smart ConDev S&P, UaESMC) co-located with ESORICS. A number of organizations also deserve special thanks, including Wrocław University of Technology for acting as host, National Cryptology Centre as a partner institution, and the ESORICS sponsors.

Finally, we would like to thank the submitters, authors, presenters, and participants who, all together, made ESORICS 2014 a great success. We hope that the papers in these volumes help you with your research and professional activities and serve as a source of inspiration during the difficult but fascinating route toward an on-line world with adequate security and privacy.

September 2014   Mirosław Kutyłowski
                                                                      Jaideep Vaidya

Organization

Program Committee

Masayuki Abe	NTT Secure Platform Laboratories, Japan
Gail-Joon Ahn	Arizona State University, USA
Mikhail Atallah	Purdue University, USA
Vijay Atluri	Rutgers University, USA
Michael Backes	Saarland University, Germany
Kun Bai	IBM T.J. Watson Research Center, USA
Giampaolo Bella	Universitá di Catania, Italy
Marina Blanton	University of Notre Dame, USA
Kevin Butler	University of Oregon, USA
Zhenfu Cao	Shanghai-Jiao Tong University, PR China
Srdjan Capkun	ETH Zurich, Switzerland
Liqun Chen	Hewlett-Packard Laboratories, UK
Xiaofeng Chen	Xidian University, PR China
Sherman S.M. Chow	Chinese University of Hong Kong, SAR China
Veronique Cortier	CNRS, LORIA, France
Marco Cova	University of Birmingham, UK
Laszlo Csirmaz	Central European University, Budapest, Hungary
Frederic Cuppens	TELECOM Bretagne, France
Nora Cuppens-Boulahia	TELECOM Bretagne, France
Reza Curtmola	New Jersey Institute of Technology, USA
Ozgur Dagdelen	Technische Universität Darmstadt, Germany
Sabrina De Capitani Di Vimercati	Università degli Studi di Milano, Italy
Roberto Di Pietro	Università di Roma Tre, Italy
Claudia Diaz	KU Leuven, Belgium
Josep Domingo-Ferrer	Università Rovira i Virgili, Catalonia
Wenliang Du	Syracuse University, USA
Simon Foley	University College Cork, Ireland
Philip W.L. Fong	University of Calgary, Canada
Sara Foresti	Università degli Studi di Milano, Italy
Keith Frikken	Miami University, Ohio, USA
Dieter Gollmann	Hamburg University of Technology, Germany
Dimitris Gritzalis	Athens University of Economics and Business, Greece
Ehud Gudes	Ben-Gurion University, Israel
Thorsten Holz	Ruhr University Bochum, Germany

Yuan Hong   University at Albany, SUNY, USA
Xinyi Huang   Fujian Normal University, PR China
Sushil Jajodia   George Mason University, USA
Sokratis Katsikas   University of Piraeus, Greece
Stefan Katzenbeisser   Technische Universität Darmstadt, Germany
Florian Kerschbaum   SAP, Germany
Kwangjo Kim   KAIST, Korea
Marek Klonowski   Wrocław University of Technology, Poland
Wenke Lee   Georgia Institute of Technology, USA
Adam J. Lee   University of Pittsburgh, USA
Helger Lipmaa   University of Tartu, Estonia
Peng Liu   The Pennsylvania State University, USA
Javier Lopez   University of Malaga, Spain
Haibing Lu   Santa Clara University, USA
Emil Lupu   Imperial College, UK
Mark Manulis   University of Surrey, UK
Krystian Matusiewicz   Intel Technology Poland
Christoph Meinel   Hasso-Plattner-Institut, Germany
Refik Molva   EURECOM, France
David Naccache   Ecole Normale Suprieure, France
Stefano Paraboschi   Università di Bergamo, Italy
Gunther Pernul   Universität Regensburg, Germany
Indrakshi Ray   Colorado State University, USA
Christian Rechberger   Technical University of Denmark
Kui Ren   University of Buffalo, SUNY, USA
Ahmad-Reza Sadeghi   Technische Universität Darmstadt, Germany
Rei Safavi-Naini   University of Calgary, Canada
Pierangela Samarati   Università degli Studi di Milano, Italy
Andreas Schaad   SAP, Germany
Basit Shafiq   Lahore University of Management Sciences,
                                 Pakistan
Radu Sion   Stony Brook University, USA
Shamik Sural   IIT, Kharagpur, India
Willy Susilo   University of Wollongong, Australia
Krzysztof Szczypiorski   Warsaw University of Technology, Poland
Mahesh Tripunitara   The University of Waterloo, Canada
Michael Waidner   Fraunhofer SIT, Germany
Lingyu Wang   Concordia University, Canada
Yang Xiang   Deakin University, Australia
Xun Yi   Victoria University, Australia
Ting Yu   Qatar Computing Research Institute, Qatar
Meng Yu   Virginia Commonwealth University, USA
Rui Zhang   Chinese Academy of Sciences, PR China
Jianying Zhou   Institute for Infocomm Research, Singapore

Table of Contents – Part I

Table of Contents – Part II

Detecting Malicious Domains
via Graph Inference

Pratyusa K. Manadhata[1], Sandeep Yadav[2], Prasad Rao[1], and William Horne[1]

[1] Hewlett-Packard Laboratories
[2] Damballa Inc.
{pratyusa.k.manadhata,prasad.rao,william.horne}@hp.com,
sandeepvaday@gmail.com

Abstract. Enterprises routinely collect terabytes of security relevant data, e.g., network logs and application logs, for several reasons such as cheaper storage, forensic analysis, and regulatory compliance. Analyzing these big data sets to identify actionable security information and hence to improve enterprise security, however, is a relatively unexplored area. In this paper, we introduce a system to detect malicious domains accessed by an enterprise's hosts from the enterprise's HTTP proxy logs. Specifically, we model the detection problem as a graph inference problem—we construct a host-domain graph from proxy logs, seed the graph with minimal ground truth information, and then use belief propagation to estimate the marginal probability of a domain being malicious. Our experiments on data collected at a global enterprise show that our approach scales well, achieves high detection rates with low false positive rates, and identifies previously unknown malicious domains when compared with state-of-the-art systems. Since malware infections inside an enterprise spread primarily via malware domain accesses, our approach can be used to detect and prevent malware infections.

Keywords: belief propagation, big data analysis for security, graph inference, malicious domain detection.

1 Introduction

This is the age of big data. Organizations collect and analyze large datasets about their operations to find otherwise difficult or impossible to obtain information and insight. Big data analysis has had an impact on online advertising, recommender systems, search engines, and social networks in the last decade, and has the potential to impact education, health care, scientific research, and transportation [1]. *Big data analysis for security*, i.e., the collection, storage, and analysis of large data sets to extract actionable security information, however, is a relatively unexplored area.

Organizations, especially business enterprises, collect and store event logs generated by hardware devices and software applications in their networks. For example, firewalls log information about suspicious network traffic; and hypertext

M. Kutyłowski and J. Vaidya (Eds.): ESORICS 2014, Part I, LNCS 8712, pp. 1–18, 2014.

transfer protocol (HTTP) proxy servers log websites (or domains) accessed by hosts in an enterprise. Enterprises collect and store event logs primarily for two reasons: need for regulatory compliance and post-hoc forensic analysis to detect security breaches. Also, availability of cheap storage has facilitated large scale log collection. Such logs generated by both security products and non-security infrastructure elements are a treasure trove of security information. For example, if hosts in an enterprise network are infected with bots, then the bots may contact their command and control (C&C) server over domain name system (DNS) and may exfiltrate sensitive data over HTTP. Hence both DNS logs and HTTP proxy logs will contain information about bot activities. Developing scalable and accurate techniques for detecting threats from logs, however, is a difficult problem [2]; we review related work in Section 5. In this paper, we introduce a big data analysis approach to detect malicious domains accessed by hosts in an enterprise from the enterprise's event logs.

1.1 Malicious Domain Detection

Malware infections spread via many vectors such as drive-by downloads, removable drives, and social engineering. Malicious domain access, however, account for majority of host infections [3]. Malware installed on hosts may be involved in pilfering sensitive data, spreading infections, DDoS attacks, and spamming. Legal issues and loss of intellectual property, money, and reputation due to malware activities make security a pressing issue for enterprises. Hence to contain malware, enterprises must prevent their hosts from accessing malicious domains.

Reliable and scalable detection of malicious domains, however, is challenging. Many enterprises use both commercial and freely available domain blacklists, i.e., list of known malicious domains, to detect and prevent malicious domain access; such lists, however, incur a significant delay in adding new domains as they rely on many manual and automated sources. Moreover, the techniques used to generate the lists are resource intensive. For example, malicious domain inference using DNS and network properties such as a domain's IP addresses and BGP prefixes requires data collection from sources with specialized vantage points. Similarly, machine learning techniques, e.g., analyzing a domain's lexical features, or a related IP address's structural properties, requires large feature data sets and accurately labeled training sets; hence these techniques are computationally expensive and may suffer from increased delay in detection.

In this paper, we present a scalable malicious domain detection approach that uses event logs routinely collected by enterprises and requires no additional data collection, and uses minimal training data. We model the detection problem as an *inference* problem on very large graphs. Our graph inference approach utilizes inherent malware communication structure, e.g., all bots in an enterprise contact the same command and control server. We first construct a *host-domain graph* by adding edges between each host in the enterprise and the domains visited by the host. We *seed* the graph with ground truth information about a small fraction of domains obtained from domain blacklists and whitelists, i.e., we label a small fraction of domains as malicious and benign, and label the rest of the domains as unknown. We then adapt *belief propagation* to estimate an unknown domain's likelihood of being malicious [4,5]; if the likelihood is more than a threshold, we identify the domain to be malicious. We chose belief propagation because it is a fast and approximate estimation algorithm that scales well to large graphs, and also takes structural advantage of malware communication (Please see Section 2 for details).

We applied our approach to 7 months of HTTP proxy data collected at a large global enterprise. Our results show that with minimal ground truth information, e.g., with only 1.45% nodes in the graph, we achieve high true positive rates (TPR) of 95.2%, with low false positive rates (FPR), for 0.68%. A benign node labeled as malicious by our approach is a false positive (FP) and a correctly identified malicious node is a true positive (TP). Our approach takes the order of minutes to analyze a large-sized enterprise's day long data, and identifies previously unknown malicious domains.

1.2   Contributions and Roadmap

We make the following contributions in this paper.

- We demonstrate that we can extract actionable security information from enterprise event logs in a scalable and reliable manner.
- We model the malicious domain detection problem as a graph inference problem and adapt belief propagation to solve the problem. Our approach does not require additional data beyond event logs, does not compute features, and uses minimal data from existing blacklists and whitelists.
- We apply our approach to event logs collected at a global enterprise over 7 months and show that our approach scales well and identifies new malicious domains not present in the blacklists.

The rest of the paper is organized as follows. We introduce our graph inference approach in Section 2. We describe our data set and analysis setup in Section 3. We present and discuss our experimental results in Section 4. We compare our work with related work in Section 5 and conclude with a discussion of future work in Section 6.

2   A Graph Inference Approach

In this section, we describe our approach to detect malicious domains. We assume that we have an enterprise's *host-domain graph*, i.e., we know the domains accessed by the enterprise's hosts. We construct the graph by adding a node for each host in the enterprise and each domain accessed by the hosts and then adding edges between a host and its accessed domains. We can construct the graph from multiple enterprise event log datasets, e.g., HTTP proxy logs and DNS request logs.

We also assume that we know a few nodes' *states*, e.g., malicious or benign. A domain present in a domain black list or a domain white list is known to be

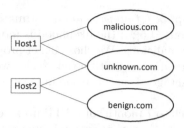

Fig. 1. A host-domain graph containing a malicious domain, *malicious.com*, a benign domain, *benign.com*, and an unknown domain, *unknown.com*

malicious or benign, respectively. Similarly, a malware infected host is known to be malicious whereas an uninfected host is known to be benign. The known nodes constitute our *ground truth* data set; the rest of the graph nodes are *unknown* nodes. We note that a small fraction of the graph's nodes are present in the ground truth data set. We show an example host-domain graph in Figure 1. The graph contains a malicious node, *malicious.com*, a benign node, *benign.com*, and three unknown nodes, *Host1*, *Host2*, and *unknown.com*.

Given the host-domain graph and the ground truth information, our goal is to *infer* the states of the unknown domains in the graph. For example, in Figure 1, we would like to infer the state of *unknown.com*. Formally, we would like to compute a node's *marginal probability* of being in a state, i.e., the probability of the node being in a state given the states of other nodes in the graph. We will then label the nodes with high marginal probability of being malicious as malicious nodes and benign otherwise.

In principle, our approach can detect both malicious domains and infected hosts in the enterprise. For example, in Figure 1, we can infer the states of *Host1* and *Host2*. In this paper, however, we focus on malicious domain detection.

Marginal probability estimation in graphs is known to be NP-complete [5]. Belief propagation (BP), introduced in the next section, is a fast and approximate technique to estimate marginal probabilities. BP's time complexity and space complexity are linear in the number of edges in a graph; hence BP scales well to large graphs. A typical enterprise host-domain graph has millions of nodes and tens of millions of edges. Hence we chose BP as our inference technique due to its scalability and its successful application in diverse fields such as computer vision [6], error correcting codes [7], fraud detection [8], and malware identification [9].

BP relies on ground truth information and *statistical dependencies* between neighboring nodes to reliably estimate marginal probabilities. The dependencies are derived from our domain knowledge. For example, user activities on benign hosts result primarily in benign domain accesses and occasional unintended malicious domain accesses, e.g., via phishing. Hence we may assume that benign hosts are more likely to visit benign domains than malicious domains. Similarly, a benign domain's neighbor is more likely to be a benign host than a malicious host. Malicious hosts may visit benign domains due to user activities; however, they are more likely to visit malicious domains as malware tend to contact many malicious domains. Intuitively, *Host 1* in Figure 1 is more likely to be malicious as it has a malicious neighbor. Similarly, *Host 2* is more likely to be benign, and *unknown.com* is equally likely to be either.

2.1 Belief Propagation

In this section, we summarize the BP algorithm; please see Yedida et al. for details [5]. Judea Pearl introduced the BP algorithm for trees [4]. BP is an efficient technique to solve inference problems on graphical models. Given an undirected graph, $G = (V, E)$, where V is a set of n nodes and E is a set of edges, we model every node $i \in V$ as a random variable, x_i, that can be in one of a finite set, S, of states. A graphical model defines a joint probability distribution, $P(x_1, x_2, ..., x_n)$, over G's nodes. The inference process computes the marginal probability distribution, $P(x_i)$, for each random variable, x_i. A node's marginal probability is defined in terms of sums of the joint probability distribution over all possible states of all other nodes in the graph, i.e., $P(x_i) = \sum_{x_1} .. \sum_{x_{i-1}} \sum_{x_{i+1}} .. \sum_{x_n} P(x_1, x_2, ..., x_n)$. The number of terms in the sum is exponential in the number of nodes, n. BP, however, can approximate the marginal probability distributions of all nodes in time linear in the number of edges, which is at most $O(n^2)$.

BP estimates a node's marginal probability from prior knowledge about the graph's nodes and their statistical dependencies. A node, i's, belief, $b_i(x_i)$, is i's marginal probability of being in the state x_i. $b_i(x_i)$'s computation depends on *priors* of the graph nodes. A node, i's, prior, $\phi_i(x_i)$, is i's initial (or prior) probability of being in the state x_i. In our model, a node's priors indicate the node's initial likelihood of being in malicious and benign states. We estimate a node's priors using our ground truth information. $b_i(x_i)$'s computation also depends on *edge potential* functions that model the statistical dependencies among neighboring nodes. The edge potential, $\psi_{ij}(x_i, x_j)$, between two neighboring nodes, i and j, is the probability of i being in the state x_i and j being in the state x_j.

BP achieves computational efficiency by organizing global marginal probability computation in terms of smaller local computations at each node. This is done via *iterative* message passing among neighboring nodes. Consider a node, i, and its neighbors, $N(i)$. In each iteration of the algorithm, i passes a *message vector*, m_{ij}, to each of its neighbors, $j \in N(i)$. Each component, $m_{ij}(x_j)$, of the message vector is proportional to i's perception of j's likelihood of being in the state x_j. i's outgoing message vector to its neighbor j depends on i's incoming message vectors from its other neighbors and is computed as follows.

$$m_{ij}(x_j) = \sum_{x_i \in S} \phi_i(x_i)\psi_{ij}(x_i, x_j) \prod_{k \in N(i) \setminus j} m_{ki}(x_i) \qquad (1)$$

The order in which messages are passed is not important as long as all messages are passed in each iteration. Malware communication, e.g., bots communicating with C&C servers, provides a structural advantage in using BP as messages can propagate over multiple hops. In a *synchronous* update order, i's outgoing messages in iteration t is computed from i's incoming messages in iteration $t - 1$. In an *asynchronous* update order, incoming messages are used as soon as they are available. We chose to use a synchronous update order for its simplicity. The iterations stop when the messages converge within a small threshold, i.e., messages don't change significantly between iterations, or when a threshold number of iterations is reached. We then compute a node, i's, belief values from i's incoming messages in the converged or the last iteration.

$$b_i(x_i) = C\phi(x_i) \prod_{k \in N(i)} m_{ki}(x_i) \tag{2}$$

C is a normalization constant to ensure that i's beliefs add up to 1, i.e., $\sum_{x_i \in S} b_i(x_i) = 1$.

In the case of trees, BP always converges and the beliefs represent accurate marginal probabilities. But if a graph has loops, then belief propagation on the graph may not converge or may converge to inaccurate marginal probabilities [10]. In practice, however, belief propagation has been successful on graphs with loops: it converges quickly to reasonably accurate values [11].

3   HTTP Proxy Data Analysis

In this section, we describe our approach's application on an enterprise HTTP proxy data set. An HTTP proxy acts as an intermediary between an enterprise's hosts and the domains accessed by the hosts. Hence we can determine the domains visited by the hosts from proxy logs and construct an enterprise's host-domain graph.

3.1   Data Set and Graph Generation

We collected proxy logs over a 7 month period from August 2013 to February 2014 from 98 proxy servers in a global enterprise's worldwide locations. Each entry in the log represents an HTTP request and contains the requesting host's IP address, the domain requested, a time stamp, an HTTP header, and the request status. If we see an HTTP request from an IP address, I, for a domain, D, then we create two nodes, I and D, in the host-domain graph, and add an edge between I and D.

We follow standard terminology and note that given a domain, *www.hp.com* (or *www.hp.co.uk*), *hp.com* (or *hp.co.uk*) is the *second-level domain (2LD)* and *com* (or *co.uk*) is the *top-level domain* (TLD). The TLD is also known as a *public suffix*. We use only 2LDs in our graph– collapsing domain nodes in this manner increases the number of paths in the graph, making paths between nodes more likely and hence information propagation between nodes more likely. Such a choice also reflects our assumption that usually 2LDs are responsible for their domain's and sub-domains' security. If a proxy log contains an IP address instead of a domain name as the destination, we add the IP address as a graph node.

We represent hosts by their IP addresses in our graph. Since IP addresses are transient in nature, a single host may be represented by multiple graph nodes.

Table 1. Data and graph description. Each row in the table represents a time period, and the columns show the time period, the number of events in the time period, the number of nodes and edges in the graph constructed from the events, the number of known malicious nodes and benign nodes in the graph, and the number of known nodes as a percentage of all graph nodes (B = billion, M = million, and K = thousand).

Time Period	Events	Nodes	Edges	Malicious Nodes	Benign Nodes	Ground truth (%)
01-16-2014	1.29B	2.80M	27.8M	21.6K	19.7K	1.45
01-17-2014	1.19B	2.58M	25.3M	21.5K	19.8K	1.60
01-18-2014	0.40B	0.80M	5.33M	10.8K	9.41K	2.51
01-19-2014	0.36B	0.70M	4.17M	10.7K	9.45K	2.88
01-20-2014	1.02B	2.46M	22.0M	21.4K	19.7K	1.67
01-21-2014	1.26B	2.81M	27.9M	21.6K	19.8K	1.47
01-22-2014	1.00B	2.35M	23.2M	21.3K	19.7K	1.73
1 Week	6.52B	10.5M	85.2M	104K	103K	1.98
3 Hours-1	0.20B	0.78M	6.95M	5.62K	4.66K	1.32
3 Hours-2	0.22B	0.76M	7.27M	5.80K	4.65K	1.38
6 Hours-1	0.31B	1.08M	8.90M	8.76K	7.65K	1.52
6 Hours-2	0.41B	1.21M	12.1M	9.06K	7.59K	1.38

We, however, observe that IP address assignment in enterprise networks is stable over periods of days and even months.

Table 1 shows the summary of one week's data collected from January 16th, 2014 to January 22nd, 2014. For each day (column 1), we show the number of log events (column 2, in billions), and the numbers of nodes (column 3, in millions) and edges (column 4, in millions) in the graph constructed from the day's logs. The 7th row in the table shows the numbers for the graph constructed from the week's data. January 18th and 19th were weekend holidays; hence the numbers of events collected on those days are much less than the numbers on weekdays.

3.2   BP Parameters

We obtained blacklists of known malicious domains and IP addresses from a commercial blacklist and seventeen freely available lists including *OpenBL.org* and *malwaredomains.com* projects. Since domain blacklists change frequently, we obtained blacklists from the same time period as the logs. We use Alexa's popular domain list as our whitelist [12], where we chose top K entries to be benign domains to maintain a balance between malicious and benign domains. Table 1 shows malicious nodes (column 5, in thousands) and benign nodes (column 6, thousands) in each graph. These nodes represent our ground truth information; column 7 shows ground truth as a percentage of all graph nodes. Since our focus was on detecting malicious domains, we did not use any ground truth information for the host nodes.

We assign priors to graph nodes according to our ground truth data. For example, we assign a prior, $P(malicious) = 0.99$, to the nodes present in the

Table 2. Priors assigned to a node according to the node's state

Node	P(malicious)	P(benign)
Malicious	0.99	0.01
Benign	0.01	0.99
Unknown	0.5	0.5

blacklist. We do not assign a probability of 1 to account for possible errors in our ground truth data. Table 2 shows the prior assignments according to whether a node is known malicious, known benign, or unknown. We assume that an unknown node is equally likely to be malicious or benign.

We introduce an edge potential matrix to reflect the statistical dependencies among neighboring nodes. We assume a *homophilic* relationship, i.e., two neighboring nodes are more likely to be of the same state than different states. For example, a malicious host and a malicious domain are more likely to be neighbors than a benign host and a malicious domain. The relationship is based on our intuition that hosts that visit benign sites are likely to be benign and hosts that visit malicious sites are likely to be infected. Table 3(a) shows our edge potential matrix. We explore more parameter choices in Section 4.2.

Table 3. Edge potential matrices

(a)

x_i \ x_j	Benign	Malicious
Benign	0.51	0.49
Malicious	0.49	0.51

(b)

x_i \ x_j	Benign	Malicious
Benign	0.75	0.25
Malicious	0.49	0.51

3.3 Experimental Setup

We implemented the BP algorithm in `Java` and ran our experiments on a 12-core 2.67 GHz desktop with 96GB of RAM. Since our graph has many high degree nodes, e.g., degree $> 100K$, and the incoming messages are less than 1, multiplying all incoming messages results in underflow, i.e., multiplication results in 0. We handled underflow in two ways. First, we used `Java's` *BigDecimal* data type to perform arbitrary precision operations; we, however, pay a performance penalty. Second, we *normalize* outgoing message vectors, i.e., we ensure that a vector's components add up to 1. For example, instead of sending a vector, (0.0023, 0.0023), we normalize the vector to (0.5, 0.5). The larger normalized numbers help avoid underflow.

We constructed our graphs off-line, i.e., we stored the logs in compressed format on disk and then uncompressed them in memory to create the graphs. Graph construction from a week day's compressed data took an average of 5 hours with peak memory usage of 9GB. In practice, however, graph construction will be done online: as and when event logs are generated, new nodes and edges will be added to the graph as needed. Hence at any point in time, the day's graph will be up-to-date. If we need to store historical data, we can store the graphs and not the event logs. A weekday's graph requires an average of 426MB of disk space.

The peak memory usage during BP's iteration phase was 53GB. The average iteration time was 7.8 minutes on a weekday's data and 1.25 minutes on a weekend day's data. The BigDecimal data type's use was a major contributor to iteration time and memory usage.

We used *message damping* to speed up convergence [13]. If m_{ij}^{t-1} is the outgoing message from a node, i, to its neighbor, j, in $t-1^{th}$ iteration, then the outgoing message in the tth iteration is $m_{ij}^t = \alpha m_{ij}^{t-1} + (1-\alpha)\bar{m}_{ij}^t$, where $\bar{m}_{ij}^t$ is the outgoing message in the tth iteration as computed by Equation 1 and α is a damping factor in the range [0,1]. We experimented with a range of values for α and empirically determined that $\alpha = 0.7$ produces the best performance.

We ran each experiment till either BP converged or 15 iterations were completed. We then computed the belief values as defined in Equation 2.

3.4 Result Computation

Following standard practice, we use *K-fold cross validation* to compute our malicious domain detection performance, i.e., we divide the ground truth data into K folds, mark one fold as *test* data and the remaining *K-1* folds as *training* data. We seed the host-domain graph with the training data, reset the priors of the nodes in the test data to unknown priors, run belief propagation, and then compute beliefs following the procedure described in the previous subsections. We then compute our detection performance on the test fold. We repeat the process for each of the K folds and report our average performance over the K folds. We describe the process of selecting K in the next section.

We present our malicious domain detection results as Receiver Operating Characteristics (ROC) plots, i.e., plots showing false positive rates and true positive rates. Since low FPRs are essential in enterprise settings, we chose ROC plots instead of overall classification accuracy. We obtain an ROC plot by *thresholding* a node's malicious belief value. For example, given a threshold, t, if a node, n's, malicious belief, $b_n(malicious) > t$, then we predict n as malicious; else, n is benign. We then use n's ground truth state and predicted state to label n as false positive, true positive, false negative, or true negative. For example, given a malicious node, n, in ground truth, if we predict n as malicious, then n is a true positive; else n is a false negative. Similarly, given a benign node, n, in ground truth, if we predict n as benign, then n is a true negative; else n is a false positive. We then repeat the process for all nodes in the test fold to compute the FPR and the TPR at threshold t. We then vary t uniformly in the range [0,1] to obtain an ROC plot. Network administrators can pick an operating point on the plot according to their risk profiles. For example, they may choose a high threshold to reduce FPs or a low threshold to increase detection at the risk of increasing FPs.

4 Results and Discussion

In this section, we first present our experiments on BP's parameter selection and then present our malicious domain detection results. We also demonstrate our ability to detect new malicious domains that are unlikely to be present in externally sourced blacklists.

4.1 K-Fold Cross Validation

We conducted an experiment to compare our performance under 3 different values of K: 2, 3, and 10. We constructed a host-domain graph from January 16th's event logs, seeded the graph using the day's blacklist and whitelist, used BP parameters described in Section 3.2, and then performed K-fold cross validation. We show the ROC plots in Figure 2. The areas under the ROC curves (AUC) are 98.53%, 98.72%, and 98.80% for $K = 2$, 3, and 10, respectively. The higher the AUC, the better the classification result. Hence, $K = 10$ produces the best classification result. Also, 10-fold cross validation is the standard practice in classification tasks. Hence we use $K = 10$ in our subsequent experiments.

When $K = 10$, we use $9/10^{th}$ of the ground truth data as training data whereas we use only half the ground truth data as training data when $K = 2$. Hence the result confirms our intuition that everything else being equal, more training data leads to better detection results.

4.2 Parameter Sensitivity Analysis

We conducted parameter sensitivity analysis on January 16th's graph to study priors' and edge potentials' impact on our results. We experimented with different priors values, e.g., {0.95, 0.05} for malicious nodes, instead of the values shown in Section 3.2 for known nodes; our performance did not change. We also assigned priors to unknown nodes according to the nodes' attributes. For unknown domains, we assume that popular domains are likely to be benign. Hence we assign a *sigmoid* function, $1/(1 + \exp(-d))$, of an unknown domain node's degree, d, as the benign prior. We also assume that malware infected hosts make large number of HTTP requests, e.g., bots trying to contact their command and control server. Hence we assign a sigmoid function of an unknown host node's HTTP request count as the malicious prior. The sigmoid prior's ROC plot is marginally inferior to Figure 2; hence we omit the plot due to space limitation.

We also experimented with the edge potential matrix shown in Table 3(b); we assume the prevalence of beneficence and assign a lower probability to spread of malware. Our FPR and TPR does not change from Figure 2. Hence our approach is robust with respect to our parameter choices and we use the parameters shown in Section 3.2 for our subsequent experiments.

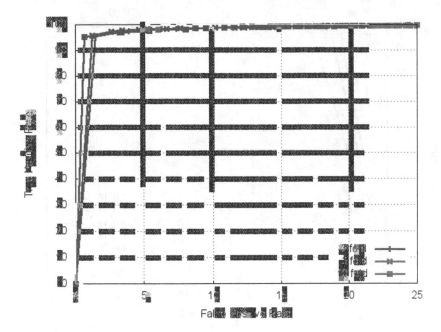

Fig. 2. ROC plots for different K-fold cross validations. For clarity, the X-axis ends at FPR = 25%. $K = 10$ performs the best.

4.3   Malicious Domain Detection

We present our malicious domain detection results on data collected on 7 consecutive days in January 2014. For each day, we constructed a host-domain graph from the day's logs, seeded the graph from the day's whitelist and blacklist, used parameters described in Section 3.2, and then performed 10-fold cross validation. We show the ROC plots in Figure 3.

The plots show that our approach can achieve high detection rates with low false positive rates using minimal ground truth information. For example, on January 16th, the host-domain graph has only 1.45% nodes in the ground truth data; yet we achieve a 95.2% TPR with a 0.68% FPR.

The results obtained on weekdays' data are similar to that of January 16th. The results on weekends, however, are inferior. For example, on January 18th, we achieve a 96.7% TPR at a high FPR of 5.6%. The AUC on January 16th is 98.80% compared to 96.12% on January 18th.

The number of events on the weekend days is smaller than the weekdays due to less activity in the enterprise over the weekend; hence the graphs on weekend days have fewer edges (Table 1). January 18th's average domain degree is 8.47 compared to 11.45 on January 16th. Hence the weekend's graphs do not include complete node behavior and have fewer paths in the graphs for information propagation. These two reasons may have caused the inferior performance.

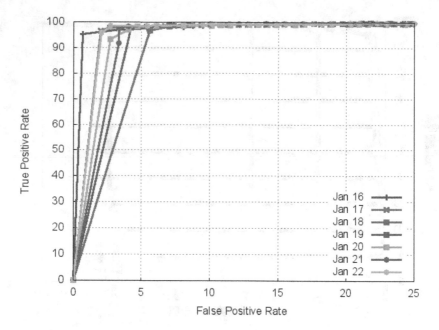

Fig. 3. ROC plots for 7 days in January 2014. Our approach performs better over weekdays than weekend days.

4.4   More Event Logs

Given the discussion above, we naturally examined the question of whether more event logs collected over a time period longer than a day, leads to better performance. Intuitively, we believed that more event logs will capture more complete node behavior. Hence we constructed a single host-domain graph from the logs collected over the 7 days in January. We also combined the blacklists and whitelists over the 7 days to a single whitelist and a single blacklist. Figure 4 shows the ROC plot for the graph and the combined whitelist and blacklist. The results are counterintuitive.

Our performance on 7 days data is inferior to its performance on a single day's data. For example, we achieve a TPR of only 90.2% at the FPR of 3.09%. Two key reasons contribute to the poor performance. First, the combined graph's average domain degree is less than those of the graphs constructed from single days' data. This is due to the fact that the enterprise's hosts visited many new domain nodes every day; these domains were not present in the previous days' logs. Second, combining the blacklists and whitelists may have introduced errors in the ground truth information. For example, a domain may have been malicious the first day and might have been cleaned up later. But our approach will consider the domain as malicious for the entire 7 day period.

Furthermore, the average iteration time on the combined graph was 31.0 minutes. Hence we do not recommend our approach over longer time scale data.

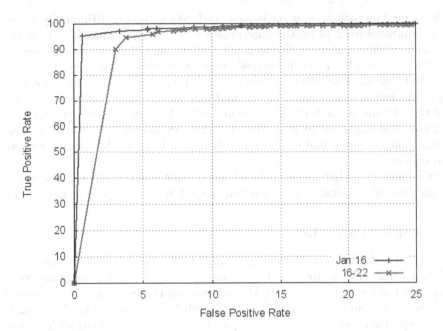

Fig. 4. Our performance on a week's data is inferior to a single day's data

4.5 Detection Details

In this section, we examine our false positives and true positives. Most of our
FPs, i.e., benign domains identified as malicious by our approach, are of low
degree. Though these domains are in Alexa's popular list and are globally popular, e.g., an Indian matrimonial site, very few hosts in the enterprise access
them. If an administrator blocks access to such domains, they will not impact
business activities. However, blocking access to popular domains such as *shop-
ping.hp.com* and *google.com* will be catastrophic. Our approach didn't commit
any such mistake in our experiments.

We also examine new malicious domains identified by our approach. These are
not present in the blacklist and hence are unknown domains in the host-domain
graph. BP assigns high malicious beliefs to these domains and classifies them as
malicious. We show a few such domains in Table 4.

Table 4. Our approach identifies new malicious domains

luo41cxjsbxfrhtbxfubxaqawhxjshsjx.info
awhvkvkzk17fxa67e51pvp42ozmyiqhvfwp12.info
etn30aqjxf12e61d30hxkxhxgvktmqaqkqdu.info
f32pxntk37gxgxmqn30bzhqpqavovbqgtk67.ru

These random looking domain names are likely to be algorithmically generated by malware resident on the enterprise's hosts. For example, bots typically generate new domains every day to contact their command and control server. Externally sourced blacklists are unlikely to contain these domains for three reasons. First, the list generation process may not be aware of the domains; even if the process had access to malware, the malware may generate different domains every time it runs. Second, the domains are active for a short time period, e.g., a few hours, and might not exist by the time they are added to lists. Third, there are many such domains and adding all of them will increase the list size without much benefit.

Our results show that we can take advantage of the externally sourced blacklists and identify previously unknown malicious domains not present in the lists.

4.6   Near Real Time Detection

Our system implementation's average completion time for 15 iterations on a day's data was 115 minutes. Hence, we can construct the host-domain graph online and run our approach every 115 minutes. In the best case, our approach can detect a domain 115 minutes after the domain's first access. This delay might be unacceptable in some sensitive settings. Hence we experimented with smaller data sets. We divided January 16th's data into 3 hours and 6 hours blocks, constructed a host-domain graph from each block, and then applied BP. Due to space limitation, we show a few representative graphs in Table 1's last 4 rows and ROC plots in Figure 5. Our detection performance on smaller datasets is marginally inferior to a day's data. The time gain, however, is compelling. For example, 15 iterations took 16.6 minutes for completion on 3 hours' data and 37.5 minutes for 6 hours' data. Hence in principle, our approach can run every 17 minutes and detect previously unknown domains.

4.7   Seven Months' Data

Finally, we demonstrate that our detection results over 7 days in January 2014 are not due to extraneous reasons. We randomly chose 7 days from the 7 months, one day from each month, and applied BP on the host-domain graphs obtained from each day's event logs. Figure 6 shows the ROC plots. The plots are similar to the plots obtained from data collected in the days in January.

5   Related Work

In this section, we compare our work with related work in big data analysis for security and malicious domain detection. Yen et al. analyze HTTP proxy logs to identify suspicious host activities– they extract features from the logs and then use clustering to find outlying suspicious activities [14]. Their approach, though carried on smaller scale data, is complimentary to ours; they focus on host activity detection and we focus on malicious domain detection. Giura et al.

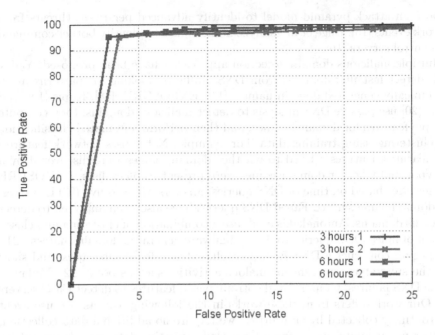

Fig. 5. Few ROC plots for 3 hours' and 6 hours' data. The results are marginally inferior to a day's data.

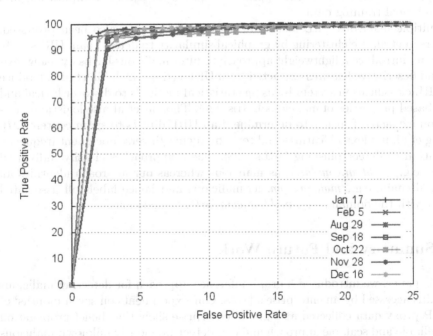

Fig. 6. ROC plots for 7 days' data, one randomly chosen from each of the 7 months, are similar to Figure 3

propose an attack pyramid model to identify advanced persistent threats from network events [15]. Bilge et al. analyze netflow data to identify botnet command and control servers [16].

Multiple malicious domain detection approaches have been proposed. Yadav et al. detect fast flux domains from DNS traffic by looking for patterns in algorithmically generated domain names [17]. EXPOSURE [18], Kopis [19], and Notos [20] use passive DNS analysis to detect malicious domains: they compute multiple features for domains names, and then perform automated classification and clustering using training data. For example, Notos uses network features, zone features, features related to whether domain names were discovered by a honeypot and whether domain names were present in black lists. EXPOSURE uses features based on time of DNS queries, answers, time-to-live (TTL) values, and domain name syntax. Failed DNS queries have also been analyzed to detect malicious domains. Antonakakis et al. use a combination of clustering and classification of failed DNS queries to detect malware generated domains names [21]. Jiang et al. construct a DNS failure graph, extract dense subgraphs, and show that the subgraphs represent anomalous activities such as bots [22]. Yadav et al. use DNS failures' temporal and entropy based features to detect C&C servers [23]. Our work differs from these works in the following aspects: we use event logs routinely collected by enterprises; we require no additional data collection, whether passive data, e.g., zone information, or active data, e.g., honeypot interaction data. Also, extensive feature computation may be prohibitive in large enterprise settings. Hence our approach requires no feature computation and uses minimal training data.

Multiple malicious URL identification approaches have also been proposed. Anderson et al. use clustering by graphical similarity to detect spam URLs [24]. Lin et al. introduce a lightweight approach to filter malicious URLs by using lexical and descriptive features extracted from URL strings [25]. Ma et al. introduce an URL classification system by using statistical methods to discover lexical and host-based properties of malicious URLs [26]. Thomas et al. use logistic regression on extracted features to determine if an URL directs to spam content [27]. Zhang et al. use lexical features and term frequency/inverse document frequency algorithm to detect phishing URLs [28]. These approaches classify individual URLs, e.g., *maldom.com/url1*, as malicious whereas our approach identifies an entire domain, e.g., *maldom.com*, as malicious and hence labels all associated URLs with the domain, e.g., *maldom.com/url**, as malicious.

6   Summary and Future Work

In this paper, we introduced a graph inference approach for detecting malicious domains accessed by an enterprise's hosts. Our experiments on seven months' of HTTP proxy data collected at a global enterprise show that belief propagation is a reliable and scalable approach and can detect previously unknown malicious domains. Our work is an example of big data analysis for security, i.e., analyzing enterprise event data to extract actionable security information. In the future, we plan to extend our work to track the spread of malware infections inside an enterprise network. We also plan to explore big data analysis approaches for other types of enterprise event logs such as DNS logs and firewall logs.

Acknowledgments. The authors thank Marc Eisenbarth, Stuart Haber, and A. L. Narasimha Reddy for helpful discussions and feedback at various stages of the research.

References

1. CRA: Challenges and opportunities with big data (2012),
   http://cra.org/ccc/docs/init/bigdatawhitepaper.pdf
2. Cardenas, A.A., Manadhata, P.K., Rajan, S.P.: Big data analytics for security. IEEE Security & Privacy 11(6), 74–76 (2013)
3. Symantec internet security threat report (2011),
   http://www.symantec.com/content/en/us/enterprise/
   other_resources/b-istr_main_report_2011_21239364.en-us.pdf
4. Pearl, J.: Reverend bayes on inference engines: a distributed hierarchical approach. In: Proceedings of the National Conference on Artificial Intelligence (1982)
5. Yedida, J., Freeman, W., Weiss, Y.: Understanding Belief Propagation and its Generalizations. Exploring Aritificial Intelligence in the New Millennium (2003)
6. Freeman, W.T., Pasztor, E.C., Carmichael, O.T.: Learning low-level vision. International Journal of Computer Vision 40(1), 25–47 (2000)
7. Mceliece, R., Mackay, D., Cheng, J.: Turbo decoding as an instance of pearl's belief propagation algorithm. IEEE Journal on Selected Areas in Communications (1998)
8. Pandit, S., Chau, D.H., Wang, S., Faloutsos, C.: Netprobe: a fast and scalable system for fraud detection in online auction networks. In: World Wide Web Conference (2007)
9. Chau, D., Nachenberg, C., Wilhelm, J., Wright, A., Faloutsos, C.: Polonium: Terascale graph mining and inference for malware detection. In: SIAM International Conference on Data Mining (2011)
10. Murphy, K., Weiss, Y., Jordan, M.: Loopy Belief Propagation for Approximate Inference: An Empirical Study. Uncertainity in Artificial Intelligence (1999)
11. Frey, B.J., MacKay, D.J.C.: A revolution: Belief propagation in graphs with cycles. In: Neural Information Processing Systems (NIPS) (1997)
12. Alexa: Top Sites, http://www.alexa.com/topsites
13. Pretti, M.: A message-passing algorithm with damping. Journal of Statistical Mechanics: Theory and Experiment 2005(11), P11008 (2005)
14. Yen, T.F., Oprea, A., Onarlioglu, K., Leetham, T., Robertson, W., Juels, A., Kirda, E.: Beehive: Large-scale log analysis for detecting suspicious activity in enterprise networks. In: Proceedings of the 29th Annual Computer Security Applications Conference, ACSAC 2013, pp. 199–208. ACM, New York (2013)
15. Giura, P., Wang, W.: A context-based detection framework for advanced persistent threats. In: International Conference on Cyber Security (2012)
16. Bilge, L., Balzarotti, D., Robertson, W., Kirda, E., Kruegel, C.: Disclosure: Detecting botnet command and control servers through large-scale netflow analysis. In: Proceedings of the 28th Annual Computer Security Applications Conference, ACSAC 2012, pp. 129–138. ACM, New York (2012)

17. Yadav, S., Reddy, A.K.K., Reddy, A.N., Ranjan, S.: Detecting algorithmically generated malicious domain names. In: Proceedings of the 10th ACM SIGCOMM Conference on Internet Measurement, IMC 2010. ACM, New York (2010)
18. Bilge, L., Kirda, E., Kruegel, C., Balduzzi, M.: EXPOSURE: Finding Malicious Domain Using Passive DNS Analysis. In: Proceedings of the Network and Distributed System Security Symposium (NDSS) (2011)
19. Antonakakis, M., Perdisci, R., Lee, W., Vasiloglou II, N., Dagon, D.: Detecting malware domains at the upper dns hierarchy. In: 20th USENIX Security Symposium (2011)
20. Antonakakis, M., Perdisci, R., Dagon, D., Lee, W., Feamster, N.: Building a Dynamic Reputation System for DNS. In: USENIX Security Symposium (2010)
21. Antonakakis, M., Perdisci, R., Nadji, Y., Vasiloglou, N., Abu-Nimeh, S., Lee, W., Dagon, D.: From throw-away traffic to bots: Detecting the rise of dga-based malware. In: 21st USENIX Security Symposium (2012)
22. Jiang, N., Cao, J., Jin, Y., Li, L.E., Zhang, Z.L.: Identifying Suspicious Activities Through DNS Failure Graph Analysis. In: IEEE Conference on Network Protocols (2010)
23. Yadav, S., Reddy, A.L.N.: Winning with DNS failures: Strategies for faster botnet detection. In: Rajarajan, M., Piper, F., Wang, H., Kesidis, G. (eds.) SecureComm 2011. LNICST, vol. 96, pp. 446–459. Springer, Heidelberg (2012)
24. Anderson, D.S., Fleizach, C., Savage, S., Voelker, G.M.: Spamscatter: Characterizing internet scam hosting infrastructure. In: 16th USENIX Security Symposium (2007)
25. Lin, M., Chiu, C., Lee, Y., Pao, H.: Malicious URL filtering- a big data application. In: IEEE BigData (2013)
26. Ma, J., Saul, L.K., Savage, S., Voelker, G.M.: Beyond Blacklists: Learning to Detect Malicious Web Sites from Suspicious URLs. In: Proceedings of the ACM SIGKDD Conference on Knowledge Discovery and Data Mining (KDD) (June 2009)
27. Thomas, K., Grier, C., Ma, J., Paxson, V., Song, D.: Design and Evaluation of a Real-Time URL Spam Filtering Service. IEEE Security and Privacy (2011)
28. Zhang, Y., Hong, J., Cranor, L.: Cantina: A content-based approach to detecting phishing web sites. In: World Wide Web Conference (May 2007)

Empirically Measuring WHOIS Misuse*

Nektarios Leontiadis and Nicolas Christin

Carnegie Mellon University
{leontiadis,nicolasc}@cmu.edu

Abstract. WHOIS is a publicly-accessible online directory used to map domain names to the contact information of the people who registered them (registrants). Regrettably, registrants have anecdotally complained about their WHOIS information being misused, e.g., for spam, while there is also concrete evidence that maliciously registered domains often map to bogus or protected information. All of this has brought into question whether WHOIS is still needed. In this study, we empirically assess which factors, if any, lead to a measurable degree of misuse of WHOIS data. We register 400 domains spread over the five most popular global top level domains (gTLD), using unique artificial registrant identities linked to email addresses, postal addresses, and phone numbers under our control. We collect, over six months, instances of misuse targeting our artificial registrants, revealing quantitative insights on both the extent and the factors (gTLD, domain type, presence of anti-harvesting mechanisms) that appear to have statistically-significant impact on WHOIS misuse.

Keywords: WHOIS, misuse, security, privacy.

1 Introduction

WHOIS is an online directory that primarily allows anyone to map domain names to the registrants' contact information. Based on their operational agreement with ICANN [2], all global Top Level Domain (gTLD) *registrars* (entities that process individual domain name registration requests) are required to collect this information during domain registration, and subsequently publish it into the WHOIS directory; how it is published depends on the specific *registry* used (i.e., entities responsible for maintaining an authoritative list of domain names registered in each gTLD). While the original purpose of WHOIS was to provide the necessary information to contact a registrant for legitimate purposes (e.g. abuse notifications, or other operational reasons), there has been increasing anecdotal evidence of misuse of the data made publicly available through the WHOIS service. For instance, some registrants[1] have reported that third-parties used their publicly available WHOIS information to register domains similar to the reporting registrants', using contact details identical to the legitimate registrants'. The domains registered with the fraudulently acquired registrant information were subsequently used to impersonate the owners of the original domains.

---

* This paper is derived from a study we originally conducted for ICANN [1].
[1] http://www.eweek.com/c/a/Security/
  Whois-Abuse -Still-Out-of-Control

M. Kutyłowski and J. Vaidya (Eds.): ESORICS 2014, Part I, LNCS 8712, pp. 19–36, 2014.
© Springer International Publishing Switzerland 2014

While such examples indicate that legitimate registrants may suffer from misuse of their WHOIS data, registrants of malicious domains often use bogus information, or privacy or proxy registration services to mask their identities [3].

This sad state of affairs brings into question whether the existence of the WHOIS service is even needed in its current form. One suggestion is to promote the use of a structured channel for WHOIS information exchange, capable of authenticated access, using already available web technologies [4,5,6]. An alternate avenue is to completely abandon WHOIS, in favor of a new Registration Data Service. This service would allow access to verified WHOIS-like information only to a set of authenticated users, and for a specific set of *permissible purposes* [7].

The present paper attempts to illuminate this policy discussion by empirically characterizing the extent to which WHOIS misuse occurs, and which factors are statistically correlated with WHOIS misuse incidents. This research responds to the decision of ICANN's Generic Names Supporting Organization (GNSO) to pursue WHOIS studies [8] to scientifically determine if there is substantial WHOIS misuse warranting further action from ICANN.

We generalize previous work [9, 10] with a much more comprehensive study using 400 domains across the five largest global top level domains (*.COM*, *.NET*, *.ORG*, *.INFO* and *.BIZ*) which, in aggregate, are home to more than 127 million domains [11]. In addition, we not only look at email spam but also at other forms of misuse (e.g., of phone numbers or postal addresses).

We validate the hypothesis that public access to WHOIS leads to a measurable degree of misuse, identify the major types of misuse, and, through regression analysis, discover factors that have a statistically-significant impact on the occurrence of misuse.

The remainder of this paper is organized as follows. In Section 2 we provide an overview of the related work. We discuss our methodology in Sections 3 and 4. We present a breakdown of the measured misuse in Section 5, and the deployed WHOIS anti-harvesting countermeasures in Section 6. We perform a regression analysis of the characteristics affecting the misuse in Section 7, note the limitations of our work in Section 8, and conclude in Section 9.

2   Related Work

Elliot in [12] provides an extensive overview of issues related to WHOIS. Researchers use WHOIS to study the characteristics of various online criminal activities, like click fraud [13, 14] and botnets [15], and have been able to gain key insights on malicious web infrastructures [16,17]. From an operational perspective, the Federal Bureau of Investigation (FBI) has noted the importance of WHOIS in identifying criminals, but the presence of significant inaccuracies hinder such efforts [18]. Moreover, online criminals often use privacy or proxy registration services to register malicious domains, complicating further their identification through WHOIS [3].

ICANN has acknowledged the issue of inaccurate information in WHOIS [19], and has funded research towards measuring the extent of the problem [20]. ICANN's GNSO, which is responsible for developing WHOIS-related policies, identified in [9] the possibility of misuse of WHOIS for phishing and identity theft, among others. Nevertheless, ICANN has been criticized [12, 21] for its inability to enforce related policies.

Table 1. Number of domains under each of the five global Top Level Domains within scope in March 2011 [11]

gTLD	.COM	.NET	.ORG	.INFO	.BIZ	Total
# of domains	95,185,529	14,078,829	9,021,350	7,486,088	2,127,857	127,694,306
Proportion in population	75.54%	11.03%	7.06%	5.86%	1.67%	100%

A separate three-month measurement study from ICANN's Security and Stability Advisory Committee (SSAC) [10] examined the potential of misuse of email addresses posted exclusively in WHOIS. The authors registered a set of domain names composed as random strings, and monitored the electronic mailboxes appearing in the domains' WHOIS records for spam emails, finding WHOIS to be a contributing factor to received spam. Our work adopts a similar but more systematic methodology, to measure a broader range of misuse types and gTLDs, examining five categories of domain names, over a period of six months.

3 Methodology

To whittle down the number of possible design parameters for our measurement experiment, we first conducted a pilot survey of domain registrants to collect experiences of WHOIS misuse. We then used the results from this survey to design our measurement experiment.

3.1 Constructing a Microcosm Sample

In November of 2011 we received from ICANN, per our request, a sample set of 6,000 domains, collected randomly from gTLD zone files with equal probability of selection. Of those 6,000 domains, 83 were not within the five gTLDs we study, and were discarded. Additionally, ICANN provided the WHOIS records associated with 98.7% (5,921) of the domains, obtained over a period of 18 hours on the day following the generation of the domain sample.

Out of these nearly 6,000 domains, we created a proportional probability microcosm of 2,905 domains representative of the population of 127 million domains, using the proportions in Table 1. In deciding the size of the microcosm we use as a baseline the 2,400 domains used in previous work [20], and factor in the evolution in domain population from 2009 to 2011.

Finally, we randomly sampled the domain microcosm to building a representative sample of $D = 1,619$ domains from 89 countries. (Country information is available through WHOIS.)

3.2 Pilot Registrant Survey

We use the domains' WHOIS information to identify and survey the 1,619 registrants associated with domains in D, about their experiences on WHOIS misuse. Further details on the survey questions, methodology, and sample demographics are available in the companion technical report [1].

Despite providing incentives for response (participation in a random drawing to be eligible for prizes such as iPads or iPods) we only collected a total of 57 responses, representing 3.4% of contacted registrants. As a result, this survey could only be used to understand some general trends, but the data was too coarse to obtain detailed insights.

With the actual margin of error at 12.7%, 43.9% of registrants claim to have experienced some type of WHOIS misuse, indicating that the public availability of WHOIS data leads to a measurable degree of misuse. The registrants reported that email, postal, and phone spam were the major effects of misuse, with other types of misuse (e.g. identity theft) occurring at insignificant rates.

These observations are based on limited, self-reported data, and respondents may incorrectly attribute misuse to WHOIS. Nevertheless, the pilot survey tells us that accurately measuring WHOIS misuse requires to primarily look at the potential for spam, not limited to email spam, but also including phone and postal spam.

3.3 Experimental Measurements

We create a set of 400 domain names and register them at 16 registrars (25 domains per registrar) across the five gTLDs, with artificial registrant identities. Each artificial identity consists of (i) a full name (i.e. first and last name), (ii) an email address, (iii) a postal address, and (iv) a phone number.

All registrants' contact details are created solely for the purpose of this experiment, ensuring that they are only published in WHOIS. Through this approach, we eliminated confounding variables. From the moment we register each experimental domain, and the artificial identity details become public through WHOIS, we monitor all channels of communication associated with every registrant. We then classify all types of communication and measure the extent of illicit or harmful activity attributed to WHOIS misuse targeting these registrants.

Given the wide variety of registrars and the use of unique artificial identities, the registration process did not lend itself to automation and was primarily manual. We registered the experimental domains starting in the last week of June 2012, and completed the registrations within four weeks. We then monitored all incoming communications over a period of six months, until the last week of January 2013. All experimental domains were registered using commercial services offered by the 16 registrars; we did not use free solutions like DynDNS.

4   Experimental Domain Registrations

We associated the WHOIS records of each of the 400 domains with a unique registrant identity. Whenever the registration process required the inclusion of an organization as part of the registrant information, we used the name of the domain's registrant. In addition, within each domain, we used the registrant's identity (i.e. name, postal/email address, and phone numbers) for all types of WHOIS contacts (i.e., registrant, technical, billing, and administrative contacts).

Figure 1 provides a graphical breakdown of the group of 25 domains we register per registrar. Every group contains five subgroups of domains, one for each of the five

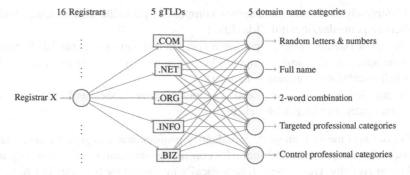

16 Registrars   5 gTLDs   5 domain name categories

Registrar X →

.COM → Random letters & numbers
.NET → Full name
.ORG → 2-word combination
.INFO → Targeted professional categories
.BIZ → Control professional categories

Fig. 1. Graphical representation of the experimental domain name combinations we register with each of the 16 registrars

gTLDs. Finally, each subgroup contains a set of five domains, one for each type of domain name, as discussed later.

4.1 Registrar Selection

We selected the sixteen registrars used in our measurement study as follows. Using the WHOIS information of the 1,619 domains in D, we first identify the set R of 107 registrars used by domains in D. Some registrars only allow domain registration through "affiliates." In these cases we attempt to identify the affiliates used by domains in D, by examining the name server information in the WHOIS records.

We then sort the registrars (or affiliates, as the case may be) based on their popularity in the registrant sample. More formally, if $D_r \subset D$ is the set of domains in the registrant sample associated with registrar r, we define r's popularity as $S_r = |D_r|$. We sort the 107 registrars in descending order of S_r, and then select the 16 most popular registrars as the set of our *experimental registrars* that allow:

- The registration of domain names in all five gTLDs. This restriction allows us to perform comparative analysis of WHOIS misuse across the experimental registrars, and gTLDs.
- Individuals to register domains. Registrars providing domain registration services only to legal entities (e.g. companies) are excluded from consideration.
- The purchase of a single domain name, without requiring purchasing of other services for that domain (e.g. hosting).
- The purchase of domains without requiring any proof of identity. Given our intention to use artificial registrant identities, a failure to hide our identity could compromise the validity of our findings.

4.2 Experimental Domain Name Categories

We study the relationship between the category of a domain name, and WHOIS misuse. Specifically, we examine the following set of name categories:

1. Completely random domain names, composed by 5 to 20 random letters and numbers (e.g. unvdazzihevqnky1das7.biz).
2. Synthetic domain names, representing person full names (e.g. randall-bilbo.com).
3. Synthetic domain names composed by two randomly selected words from the English vocabulary (e.g. neatlimbed.net).
4. Synthetic Domain names intended to look like businesses within specific professional categories (e.g. hiphotels.biz).

To construct the last category, we identify professional categories usually targeted in cases of spear-phishing and spam, by consulting two sources. We primarily use the "Phishing Activity Trend" report, periodically published by the Anti-Phishing Working Group (APWG) [22]. We identify the professional categories mostly targeted by spam and phishing in the second quarter of 2010 with percentages of more than 4% in total. These categories are: (i) Financial services, (ii) payment services, (iii) gaming, (iv) auctions, and (v) social networking. We complement this list with the following professional categories appearing in the subject and sender portions of spam emails we had previously received: (i) medical services, (ii) medical equipment, (iii) hotels, (iv) traveling, and (v) delivery and shipping services.

In addition, we define a control set of professional categories that are not known to be explicitly targeted. We use the control set to measure the potential statistical significance of misuse associated with any of the previous categories. The three categories in the control set are : (i) technology, (ii) education, and (iii) weapons.

4.3 Registrant Identities

We create a set of 400 unique artificial registrant identities, one for each of the experimental domains. Our ultimate goal is to be able to associate every instance of misuse with a single domain, or a small set of domains.

A WHOIS record created during domain registration contains the following publicly available pieces of registrant information: (i) full name, (ii) postal address, (iii) phone number, and (iv) email address. In this section we provide the design details of each portion of the artificial registrant identities.

Registrant Name. The registrant's full name (i.e. first name-last name) serves as the unique association between an experimental domain and an artificial registrant identity. Therefore we need to ensure that every full name associated with each of the 400 experimental domains is unique within this context.

We create the set of 400 unique full names, indistinguishable from names of real persons, by assembling common first names (male and female) and last names with Latin characters.

Email Address. We create a unique email address for each experimental domain in the form *contact@example.com*. We use this email address in the domain's WHOIS records, and we therefore call it *public email address*.

However, any email sent to a recipient other than *contact* (e.g. **foo**@example.com), is still collected for later analysis under a *catchall* account. We refer to these as *unpublished email addresses*, as we do not publish them anywhere, including WHOIS.

Mail exchange (MX) records are a type of DNS record pointing to the email server(s) responsible for handling incoming emails for a given domain name [23]. The MX records for our experimental domains all point to a single IP address functioning as a proxy server. The proxy server, in turn, aggregates and forwards all incoming SMTP requests to an email server under our control. The use of a proxy allows us to conceal where the "real" email server is located (i.e., at our university); our email server functions as a spam trap (i.e., any potential spam mitigation at the network- or host-level is explicitly disabled).

Postal Address. We examined the possibility of using a postal mail-forwarding service to register residential addresses around the world. Unfortunately, and, given the scale of this experiment, we were unable to identify a reasonably-priced and legal solution.

In most countries (the US included) such services often require proof of identification prior to opening a mailbox,[2] and limit the number of recipients that can receive mail at one mailbox. Moreover, we were hesitant to trust mail-forwarding services from privately owned service providers,[3] because the entities providing such services may themselves misuse the postal addresses, contaminating our measurements. For example, merely requesting a quote from one service provider, resulted in our emails being placed on marketing mailing lists without our explicit consent.

We eventually decided to use three Post Office (PO) boxes within the US; and, randomly assigned to each registrant identity one of these addresses. Traditionally, the address of a PO box with number *123* is of the following format: *PO Box 123, City, Zip code*. However, we utilize the US Postal Service's (USPS) *street addressing* service to camouflage our PO boxes as residential addresses. Street addressing enables the use of the post office's street address to reach a PO box located at the specific post office. Through this service, the PO box located at a post office with address *456 Imaginary avenue*, is addressable at *456 Imaginary avenue #123, City, Zip code*.

In addition, PO boxes are typically bound to the name of the person who registered them. However, each experimental domain is associated with a unique registrant name, even when sharing the same postal address, different than the owner of the PO box. We evaluated possible implications of this design in receiving postal mail to a PO box addressee not listed as the PO box owner. We originally acquired five PO boxes across two different US states, and sent one letter addressed to a random name to each of these PO boxes. We successfully received letters at three of the PO boxes indicating that mail addressed to any of the artificial registrant names would be delivered successfully. The test failed at the other two PO boxes—we got back our original test letters marked as undeliverable—making them unsuitable for the study.

Phone Number. Maintaining individual phone numbers for each of the 400 domains over a period of six months would be prohibitively expensive. Instead, we group the 400

---

[2] For example USPS form 1583: *Application for Delivery of Mail Through Agent* in the US.

[3] Also known as "virtual office" services.

domains into 80 sets of domains having the same gTLD and registrar, and we assign one phone number per such group. For example all .COM domains registered with GoDaddy share the same phone number.

We acquire 80 US-based phone numbers using Skype Manager[4] with area codes matching the physical locations of the three PO boxes. We further assign phone numbers to registrant identities with area codes matching their associated PO box locations.

5   Breaking Down the Measured Misuse

In this section we present a breakdown of the empirical data revealing WHOIS-attributed misuse. The types of misuse we identify fall within three categories: (1) *postal address misuse*, measured as postal spam, (2) *phone number misuse*, measured as voice mail spam, and (3) *email address misuse*, measured as email spam.

5.1   Postal Address Misuse

We monitor the contents of the three PO boxes biweekly, and categorize the collected mail either as *generic spam* or *targeted spam*. Generic spam is mail not associated with WHOIS misuse, while targeted spam can be directly attributed to the domain registration activity of the artificial registrant identities.

When postal mail does not explicitly mention the name of the recipient, we do not associate it with WHOIS misuse, and we classify it as generic spam. Common examples in this category are mail addressed to the "PO Box holder", or to an addressee not in the list of monitored identities.

In total, we collected 34 pieces of generic spam, with two out of the three PO boxes receiving the first kind of generic spam frequently. Additionally, we collected four instances of the second type of generic spam, received at a single PO box. A reasonable explanation for the latter is that previous owners of the PO box still had mail sent to that location.

Postal mail is placed in the targeted spam category when it is addressed to the name and postal address of one the of the artificial registrant identities. We observed targeted spam at a much lower scale compared to the generic spam, with a total of four instances.

Two instances of targeted postal spam, were sent to two different PO locations, but were identical in terms of (i) their sender, (ii) the advertised services, (iii) the date of collection from the PO boxes, and (iv) the posting date. The purpose of the letters, as shown in Figure 2a, was to sell domain advertising services. This advertising scheme works with the registrant issuing a one-time payment for $85 USD, in exchange for the submission of the registrant's domain to search engines in combination with search engine optimization (SEO) on the domains. The two experimental domains subjected to this postal misuse were registered using the same registrar, but under different registrant identities, and gTLDs.

The purpose of the third piece of targeted postal spam (Figure 2b) was to enroll the recipient in a membership program that provides postal and shipping services. Finally,

---

[4] http://www.skype.com/en/features/skype-manager/

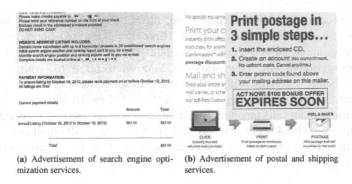

(a) Advertisement of search engine optimization services.

(b) Advertisement of postal and shipping services.

Fig. 2. Targeted postal spam attributed to WHOIS misuse

the fourth piece of postal mail spam was received very close to the end of the experiment and offered a free product in exchange for signing up on a website.

Overall, the volume of targeted WHOIS postal spam is very low (10%), compared to the portion classified as generic spam (90%). However, this is possibly due to the small geographical diversity of the PO boxes.

5.2 Phone Number Misuse

We collected 674 voicemails throughout the experiment. We define the following five types of content indicative of their association (or lack thereof) to WHOIS misuse, and manually classify each voicemail into one of these five categories:

WHOIS-attributed spam. Unsolicited calls offering web-related services (e.g. website advertising), or mentioning an experimental domain name or artificial registrant name.

Possible spam. Unsolicited phone calls advertising services that cannot be associated with WHOIS misuse, given the previous criteria. (e.g. credit card enrollment based on random number calling)

Interactive spam. Special case of possible spam with a fixed recorded message saying "press one to accept".

Blank. Voice mails having no content, or with incomprehensible content.

Not spam. Accidental calls, usually associated with misdialing, or with a caller having wrong contact information (e.g. confirmation for dental appointment)

Two of these categories require further explanation. First, in the case of *possible spam*, we cannot tell if the caller harvested the number from WHOIS, or if it was obtained in some other way (e.g., exhaustive dialing of known families of phone numbers). We therefore take the conservative approach of placing such calls in a category separate from WHOIS-attributed spam. Second, calls marked as *interactive spam* did not contain enough content to allow for proper characterization of the messages. However, the large number of these calls—received several times a day, starting in the second month of the experiment—suggests a malicious intent.

Of the 674 voicemails, we classify 5.8% as WHOIS-attributed spam, 4.2% as possible spam, 38% as interactive spam, and 15% as not spam. Finally, we classify 36.9% of voicemails as blank due to their lack of intelligible content.

Of the 39 pieces of WHOIS-attributed spam, 77% (30) originated from a single company promoting website advertising services. This caller placed two phone calls in each of the numbers, one as an initial contact and one as a follow up. These calls targeted .BIZ domains registered with 5 registrars, .COM domains registered with 4 registrars, and .INFO domains registered with 6 Registrars. In total, the specific company contacted the registrants of domains registered with 11 out of the 16 registrars.

The remaining spam calls targeted .BIZ domains registered with 4 registrars, .COM domains registered with 4 registrars, and .INFO, .NET, and .ORG domains associated with 1 registrar each. In one case we observed a particularly elaborate attempt to acquire some of the registrant's personally identifiable information.

5.3 Email Address Misuse

We classify incoming email either as solicited or spam, using the definition of spam in [24]. In short, an email is classified as spam if (i) it is unsolicited, and (ii) the recipient has not provided an explicit consent to receive such email. For this experiment, this means that all incoming email is treated as spam, except when it originates from the associated registrars (e.g., for billing).

The contract between registrar and registrant, established upon domain registration, usually permits registrars to contact registrants for various reasons (e.g. account related, promotions, etc.). We identify such email by examining the headers of the emails received at the public addresses, and comparing the domain part of the sender's email address to the registrar's domain.

However, under the Registrar Accreditation Agreement (RAA) [2]), ICANN-accredited registrars are prohibited from allowing the use of registrant information for marketing, or otherwise unsolicited purposes. Nevertheless, we acknowledge the possibility that some registrars may share registrant information with third parties that may initiate such unsolicited communication. We do not distinguish between registrars that engage in such practices and those that do not, and we classify all communications originating from a party other than the registrar as spam.

Throughout the experiment, published email addresses received 7,609 unsolicited emails out of which 7,221 (95%) are classified as spam. Of the 400 experimental domains, 95% received unsolicited emails in their published addresses with 71% of those receiving spam email. Interestingly, 80% of spam emails targeted the 25 domains of a single registrar.

In an effort to explain this outlier, we reviewed the terms of domain registration for all 16 registrars. We discovered that four registrars (including the registrar that appears as an outlier) mention in their registrant agreements the possibility of use of WHOIS data for marketing purposes. Since this is only a hypothesis, we do not factor it into the regression analysis we propose later. It is, however, a plausible explanation for the outlier.

We classified all 1,872 emails received at the unpublished addresses as spam, targeting 15% of the experimental domains. Since the unpublished addresses are not shared in any way, all emails received are unsolicited, and therefore counted as spam, including some that may have been the result of the spammers attempting some known account guessing techniques.

Table 2. Breakdown of measured WHOIS-attributed misuse, broken down by gTLD and type of misuse. Per the experimental design (Section 4), each gTLD group contains 80 domains.

Type of misuse	gTLD of affected experimental domains					Total
	.COM	.NET	.ORG	.INFO	.BIZ	
Postal address misuse	1 domain	1 domain	1 domain	1 domain	–	4 domains
Phone number misuse	5.0%	1.3%	1.3%	7.5%	10.0%	5.0%
Email address misuse	60.0%	65.0%	56.3%	77.5%	93.8%	70.5%

Two domains received a disproportionate amount of spam in their unpublished mailboxes. We ascribed this to the possibility that (i) these domains had been previously registered, and (ii) the previous domain owners are the targets of the observed spam activity. Historical WHOIS records confirm that both domains had been previously registered (12 years prior, and 5 years prior, respectively), which lends further credence to our hypothesis.

We examine the difference in proportions of email spam between published and unpublished addresses. Using the χ^2 test, we find that the difference is statistically significant considering the gTLD ($p < 0.05$), and the registrar ($p < 0.001$), but not the domain name category ($p > 0.05$).

Attempted Malware Delivery. We use VirusTotal [25] to detect malicious software received as email file attachments during the first 4 months of the experiment. In total, we analyze 496 emails containing attachments. Only 2% of emails with attachments (10 in total) targeted published email addresses, and they were all innocuous. The 15.6% of emails (76 in total) containing malware, targeted exclusively unpublished addresses, and VirusTotal classified them within 12 well-known malware families. As none of the infected attachments targeted any published email address, we do not observe any WHOIS-attributed malware delivery.

5.4 Overall Misuse per gTLD

In Table 2 we present the portion of domains affected by all three types of WHOIS misuse, broken down by gTLD and type of misuse. We find that the most prominent type of misuse is the one affecting the registrants' email addresses, followed by phone and postal misuse. Due to the small number of occurrences of postal misuse, we present the absolute value of affected domains. For both phone and email misuse, we present the misuse as the portion of affected domains, out of the 80 experimental domains per gTLD. Clearly, email misuse is common; phone misuse is also not negligible (especially for .BIZ domains).

The stated design limitations, especially the limited number of postal addresses we use, potentially affect the rates of misuse we measure. We nevertheless find that misuse of registrant information is measurable, and causally associated with the unrestricted availability of the data through WHOIS. We acknowledge though that this causal link is only valid based on the assumption that all ICANN-accredited registrars comply with the relevant RAA provisions (e.g., no resale of the registrant data for marketing purposes), as discussed in Section 5.3.

6   WHOIS Anti-Harvesting

WHOIS "anti-harvesting" techniques are a proposed solution deployed at certain registrars to prevent automatic collection of WHOIS information. We next present a set of measurements characterizing WHOIS anti-harvesting implemented at the 16 registrars and the three thick WHOIS registries.[5] Later on we use this information to examine the correlation between measures protecting WHOIS, and the occurrence of misuse.

More specifically, we test the rate-limiting availability on port 43, which is the well-known network port used for the reception of WHOIS queries, by issuing sets of 1,000 WHOIS requests per registrar and registry, and analyzing the responses. Each set of 1,000 requests repeatedly queries information for a single domain from the set of 400 experimental domains. We use different domain names across request sets. We select domains from the .COM and .NET pool when testing the registrars' defenses, and from the appropriate gTLD pool when testing thick WHOIS gTLD registries.

In addition, we examine the defenses of the remaining 89 registrars in the registrar sample. In this case we query domains found in the registrant sample instead of experimental domains. In three occasions, all domains associated with three out of the 89 registrars had expired at the time we ran this experiment. Therefore, we exclude these registrars from this analysis.

The analysis of WHOIS responses reveals the following methods of data protection:

Method 1: Limit number of requests, then block further requests.
Method 2: Limit number of requests, then provide only registrant name and offer instructions to access complete the WHOIS record through a web form.
Method 3: Delay WHOIS responses, using a variable delay period of a few seconds.
Method 4: No defense.

In Table 3 we present in aggregate form the distribution of registrars and registries using each one of the four defense methods. We find that one of the three registries does not use any protection mechanism, while the remaining two take a strict rate-limiting approach. For instance, one registry employs relatively strict measures by allowing only four queries though port 43 before applying a temporary blacklist.

Only 41.6% of the experimental registrars employ rate-limiting, allowing, on average, 83 queries, before blocking additional requests. Just two registrars in this group provide information (as part of the WHOIS response message) on the duration of the block, which, in both cases, was 30 minutes. The remaining registrars either use a less strict approach (Method 2, 18.8%), or no protection at all (Method 4, 37.5%)

---

[5] *Thick WHOIS* registries maintain a central database of all WHOIS information associated with registered domain names, and they respond directly to WHOIS queries with all available WHOIS information. From the five gTLDs under consideration, the three registries maintaining the .BIZ, .INFO, and .ORG zones are thick registries.

Table 3. Methods for protecting WHOIS information at 104 registrars and three registries

Tested entities	Total #	Type of WHOIS harvesting defense			
		Method 1	Method 2	Method 3	Method 4
Thick WHOIS registries	3	2 (66.6%)	–	–	1 (33.3%)
Experimental registrars	16	7 (43.7%)	2 (12.5%)	1 (6.3%)	6 (37.5%)
Remaining registrars	89	37 (41.6%)	1 (1.1%)	3 (3.4%)	48 (53.9%)

One registrar would not provide responses in a timely manner (method 3), causing our testing script to identify the behavior as a temporary blacklisting. It is unclear if this is an intended behavior to prevent automated queries, or if it was just a temporary glitch with the registrar.

The remaining 89 registrars (not in the experimental set) follow more or less the same pattern as our experimental set. The majority does not use any protection mechanism, and a relatively large minority uses Method 1.

7 Misuse Estimators

We finally examine the correlation of a set of parameters (i.e. estimators) with the measured phone and email misuse, attributed to WHOIS. These estimators are descriptive of the experimental domain names, and of the respective registrars and (thick) WHOIS registries. We do not examine postal address misuse, as the number of observed incidents in this case is very small and unlikely to yield any statistically-significant findings.

More specifically, we consider the following estimators:

- β_1 : Domain gTLD.
- β_2 : Price paid for domain name acquisition.
- β_3 : Registrar used for domain registration.
- β_4 : Existence of WHOIS anti-harvesting measures at the registrar level for .COM and .NET domains (thin WHOIS gTLDs), and at the registry level for .ORG, .INFO, and .BIZ domains (thick WHOIS gTLDs).
- β_5 : Domain name category.

We disentangle the effect of these estimators on the prevalence of WHOIS misuse through regression analysis. We use logistic regression [26], which is a generalized linear model [27] extending linear regression. This approach allows for the response variable to be modeled through a binomial distribution given that we examine WHOIS misuse as a binary response (i.e. either the domain is a victim of misuse or not).

In addition, using a generalized linear model instead of the ordinary linear regression allows for more relaxed assumptions on the requirement for normally distributed errors. In this analysis, we use the iteratively re-weighted least squares [28] method to fit the independent variables into maximum likelihood estimates of the logistic regression parameters.

Our multivariate logistic regression model takes the following form:

$$logit(p_{\text{DomainEmailMisuse}}) = \beta_0 + \beta_1 x_1 + \beta_2 x_2 + \beta_3 x_3 + \beta_4 x_4 + \beta_5 x_5 \qquad (1)$$

$$logit(p_{\text{DomainPhoneMisuse}}) = \beta_0 + \beta_1 x_1 + \beta_2 x_2 + \beta_3 x_3 + \beta_4 x_4 \qquad (2)$$

Equation 2 does not consider β_5 as an estimator, since the experimental design does not permit the association between measured misuse and the composition of the domain name.

We considered the use of multinomial logistic regression (MLR) for the analysis of phone number misuse, given the five classes of voicemails we collected. Such regression models require a large sample size (i.e. observations of misuse in this case) to calculate statistically-significant correlations [29]. However, in the context of our experiment, the occurrence of voicemail misuse is too small to analyze with MLR.

Therefore, we reverted to using a basic logistic regression by transforming the multiple-response dependent variable into a dichotomous one. We did this by conservatively transforming observations of possible spam into observations of not spam. In addition, we did not consider the categories of interactive spam and blank, as they do not present meaningful outcomes.

All estimators, except β_2, represent categorical variables, and they are coded as such. Specifically, we code estimators β_1, β_3, and β_5 as 5-part, 16-part, and 5-part categorical variables respectively, using deviation coding. Deviation coding allows us to measure the statistical significance of the categorical variables' deviation from the overall mean, instead of deviations across categories.

We code WHOIS anti-harvesting (β_4) as a dichotomous categorical variable denoting the protection of domains by any anti-harvesting technique. While the 16 registrars, and 3 thick WHOIS registries employ a variety of such techniques (Section 6), the binary coding enables easier statistical interpretation.

7.1 Estimators of Email Misuse

In Table 4 we report the statistically-significant regression coefficients, and associated odds characterizing email misuse. Overall, we find that some gTLDs, the domain price, WHOIS anti-harvesting, and domain names representing person names are good estimators of email misuse.

Domain gTLD. The email misuse measured though the experimental domain names is correlated with all gTLDs but .INFO. Specifically, the misuse at .BIZ domains is 21 times higher than the overall mean, while domains registered under the .COM, .NET, and .ORG gTLDs experience less misuse.

Domain Price. The coefficient for β_2 means that each \$1 increase in the price of an experimental domain corresponds to a 15% decrease in the odds of the registrants experiencing misuse of their email addresses. In other words, the more expensive the registered domain is, the lesser email address misuse the registrant experiences.

The reported correlation does not represent a correlation between domain prices and differentiation in the registrars' services. Even though we did not systematically record the add-on services the 16 registrars offer, we did not observe any considerable differentiation of services based on the domain price. Most importantly, we did not use

Table 4. Statistically-significant regression coefficients affecting email address misuse (Equation 1)

Estimator	coefficient	odds	Std. Err.	Significance
Domain gTLD (β_1)				
.COM	-1.214	0.296	0.327	$p < 0.001$
.NET	-0.829	0.436	0.324	$p = 0.01$
.ORG	-1.131	0.322	0.318	$p < 0.001$
.BIZ	3.049	21.094	0.566	$p < 0.001$
Domain price (β_2)	-0.166	0.846	1.376	$p < 0.001$
Lack of WHOIS anti-harvesting (β_4)	0.846	2.332	0.356	$p = 0.01$
Domain name composition (β_5)				
Person name	-0.638	0.528	0.308	$p = 0.04$

any such service for any of the experimental domains we registered, even when such services were offered free of charge.

What this correlation may suggest is that higher domain prices may be associated with other protective mechanisms, like the use of blacklists to prevent known harvesters from unauthorized bulk access to WHOIS. However, such mechanisms are transparent to an outside observer, so we may only hypothesize on their existence and their effectiveness.

WHOIS Anti-Harvesting. The analysis shows that the existence of WHOIS anti-harvesting protection is statistically-significant in predicting the potential of email misuse. The possibility of experiencing email misuse without the existence of any anti-harvesting measure is 2.3 times higher than when such protection is in place.

Domain Name Category. We identify the category of domains denoting person names (e.g. randall-bilbo.com) as having negative correlation to misuse. In this case, the possibility of experiencing email address misuse is slightly lower than the overall mean.

This appears to be an important result. However, we point out that all the domain names in this category contain a hyphen (i.e. -), contrary to all other categories. Therefore, it is unclear whether the reported correlation is due to the domain name category itself, or due to the different name structure.

7.2 Estimators of Phone Number Misuse

The gTLD is the only variable with statistical significance in Equation 2. Table 5 presents the 3 gTLDs with a significant correlation to the measured WHOIS-attributed phone number misuse. Domains under the .BIZ and .INFO gTLDs correlate with 7.4 and 5.1 times higher misuse compared to the overall mean, respectively. On the other hand, .ORG domains correlate with lower misuse, being close to the mean.

There is no verifiable explanation as to why gTLD is the sole statistically-significant characteristic affecting this type of misuse. A possible conjecture is that domains usually registered under the .BIZ and .INFO gTLDs have features that make them better targets.

Table 5. Statistically-significant regression coefficients in Equation 2

Estimator	coefficient	odds	Std. Err.	Significance
Domain gTLD (β_1)				
.INFO	1.634	5.124	0.554	$p = 0.003$
.ORG	-2.235	0.106	0.902	$p = 0.01$
.BIZ	2.000	7.393	0.661	$p = 0.002$

8 Limitations

Specific characteristics of the experimental design (e.g., cost limits) result in some limitations in the extent or type of insights we are able to provide.

In particular, we were not able to use postal addresses outside the United States, due to mail regulations requiring proof of residency, in most countries. In addition, "virtual office" solutions are prohibitively expensive at the scale of our experiment, and, as discussed earlier, could introduce potential confounding factors. Therefore, we were not able to gain major insights on how different regions, and countries other than the US are affected by WHOIS-attributed postal address misuse.

Similarly, we were not able able assign a unique phone number to each of the 400 artificial registrant identities. Instead, every phone number was reused by five (very similar) experimental domains. This design limits our ability to associate an incoming voice call with a single domain name, especially if the caller does not identify a domain name or a registrant name in the call. Nevertheless, we were able to associate every spam call with a specific [registrar, gTLD] pair.

9 Conclusion

We examined and validated through a set of experimental measurements the hypothesis that public access to WHOIS leads to a measurable degree of misuse in the context of five largest global Top Level Domains. We identified email spam, phone spam, and postal spam as the key types of WHOIS misuse. In addition, through our controlled measurements, we found that the occurrence of WHOIS misuse can be empirically predicted taking into account the cost of domain name acquisition, the domains' gTLDs, and whether registrars and registries employ WHOIS anti-harvesting mechanisms.

The last point is particularly important, as it evidences that anti-harvesting is, to date, an effective deterrent with a straightforward implementation. This can be explained by the economic incentives of the attacker: considering the type of misuse we observed, the value of WHOIS records appears rather marginal. As such, raising the bar for collecting this data ever so slightly might make it unprofitable to the attacker, which could in turn lead to a considerable decrease in the misuse, at relatively low cost to registrars, registries, and registrants.

Acknowledgments. This research was partially funded by ICANN. Input from the anonymous reviewers, from the participants to the WHOIS Misuse Webinar, and from several members of the ICANN community contributed significant improvements to this manuscript. We are also grateful for numerous discussions with Lisa Phifer, Liz Gasster, Barbara Roseman and Mary Wong, which led to considerable refinments in the design of the experiments. Finally, Tim Vidas provided invaluable support in setting up and maintaining our email infrastructure, Ashwini Rao assisted with some of the early testing scripts and documentation, and Patrick Tague helped us with testing some of the postal boxes.

References

1. Leontiadis, N., Christin, N.: WHOIS misuse study (March 2014), http://whois.icann.org/sites/default/files/files/misuse-study-final-13mar14-en.pdf (last accessed July 3, 2014)
2. ICANN: 2013 Registrar Accreditation Agreement (2013), https://www.icann.org/resources/pages/approved-with-specs-2013-09-17-en (last accessed July 3, 2014)
3. Clayton, R., Mansfield, T.: A study of Whois privacy and proxy service abuse. In: Proceedings of the 13th Workshop on Economics of Information Security, State College, PA (June 2014)
4. Newton, A., Piscitello, D., Fiorelli, B., Sheng, S.: A restful web service for internet names and address directory services, pp. 23–32. USENIX; login (2011)
5. Sullivan, A., Kucherawy, M.S.: Revisiting WHOIS: Coming to REST. IEEE Internet Computing 16(3) (2012)
6. Hollenbeck, S., Ranjbar, K., Servin, A., Newton, A., Kong, N., Sheng, S., Ellacott, B., Obispo, F., Arias, F.: Using HTTP for RESTful Whois services by Internet registries (2012)
7. Expert Working Group on gTLD Directory Services: A next generation registration directory service (2013), https://www.icann.org/en/groups/other/gtld-directory-services/initial-report-24jun13-en.pdf (last accessed July 3, 2014)
8. ICANN. Generic Names Supporting Organization: Motion to pursue WHOIS studies, http://gnso.icann.org/en/council/resolutions#20100908-3 (2010) (last accessed July 3, 2014)
9. ICANN. Security and Stability Advisory Committee: Advisory on registrar impersonation phishing attacks (2008), http://www.icann.org/en/committees/security/sac028.pdf (last accessed July 3, 2014)
10. ICANN. Security and Stability Advisory Committee: Is the WHOIS service a source for email addresses for spammers (2007), http://www.icann.org/en/committees/security/sac023.pdf (last accessed July 3, 2014)

11. ICANN: gTLD–specific monthly registry reports (February 2011), http://www.icann.org/sites/default/files/mrr/[gTLD]/[gTLD]-transactions-201102-en.csv (last accessed July 3, 2014)
12. Elliott, K.: The who, what, where, when, and why of WHOIS: Privacy and accuracy concerns of the WHOIS database. SMU Sci. & Tech. L. Rev. 12, 141 (2008)
13. Dave, V., Guha, S., Zhang, Y.: Measuring and fingerprinting click-spam in ad networks. In: Proceedings of the ACM SIGCOMM 2012 Conference on Applications, Technologies, Architectures, and Protocols for Computer Communication, pp. 175–186. ACM (2012)
14. Christin, N., Yanagihara, S., Kamataki, K.: Dissecting one click frauds. In: Proc. ACM CCS 2010, Chicago, IL, pp. 15–26 (October 2010)
15. Yarochkin, F., Kropotov, V., Huang, Y., Ni, G.K., Kuo, S.Y., Chen, I.Y.: Investigating dns traffic anomalies for malicious activities. In: 2013 43rd Annual IEEE/IFIP Conference on Dependable Systems and Networks Workshop (DSN-W), pp. 1–7. IEEE (2013)
16. Li, Z., Alrwais, S., Xie, Y., Yu, F., Valley, M.S., Wang, X.: Finding the linchpins of the dark web: a study on topologically dedicated hosts on malicious web infrastructures. In: IEEE Symposium on Security and Privacy, pp. 112–126. IEEE (2013)
17. Leontiadis, N., Moore, T., Christin, N.: Measuring and analyzing search-redirection attacks in the illicit online prescription drug trade. In: Proceedings of the 20th USENIX Security Symposium, San Francisco, CA, pp. 281–298 (August 2011)
18. United States Congress. House Committee on the Judiciary. Subcommittee on Courts, the Internet, and Intellectual Property: Internet Domain Name Fraud: The U.S. Government's Role in Ensuring Public Access to Accurate WHOIS Data. H. hrg. U.S. Government Printing Office (September 2003)
19. WHOIS Task Force 3: Improving accuracy of collected data (2003), http://gnso.icann.org/en/issues/whois-privacy/tor3.shtml (last accessed July 3, 2014)
20. NORC: Proposed design for a study of the accuracy of WHOIS registrant contact information (2009), https://www.icann.org/en/system/files/files/norc-whois-accuracy-study-design-04jun09-en.pdf (last accessed July 3, 2014)
21. Watters, P.A., Herps, A., Layton, R., McCombie, S.: Icann or icant: Is whois an enabler of cybercrime? In: 2013 Fourth Cybercrime and Trustworthy Computing Workshop (CTC), pp. 44–49. IEEE (2013)
22. Anti-Phishing Working Group: Phishing attack trends report - Q2 2010 (Janurary 2010)
23. Mockapetris, P.: Domain names – Implementation and specification (RFC 1035). Information Sciences Institute (1987)
24. The Spamhaus Project: The definition of spam, http://www.spamhaus.org/consumer/definition/ (last accessed July 3, 2014)
25. VirusTotal: Free online virus, malware and URL scanner, https://www.virustotal.com/ (last accessed July 3, 2014)
26. Hosmer Jr., D.W., Lemeshow, S.: Applied logistic regression. John Wiley & Sons (2004)
27. Nelder, J.A., Wedderburn, R.W.M.: Generalized linear models. Journal of the Royal Statistical Society. Series A 135(3), 370–384 (1972)
28. Del Pino, G.: The unifying role of iterative generalized least squares in statistical algorithms. Statistical Science 4(4), 394–403 (1989)
29. Ye, F., Lord, D.: Comparing three commonly used crash severity models on sample size requirements: multinomial logit, ordered probit and mixed logit models. Analytic Methods in Accident Research 1, 72–85 (2014)

EncDNS: A Lightweight Privacy-Preserving Name Resolution Service

Dominik Herrmann, Karl-Peter Fuchs, Jens Lindemann, and Hannes Federrath

University of Hamburg, Computer Science Department, Germany

Abstract. Users are increasingly switching to third party DNS resolvers (e.g., Google Public DNS and OpenDNS). The resulting monitoring capabilities constitute an emerging threat to online privacy. In this paper we present EncDNS, a novel lightweight privacy-preserving name resolution service as a replacement for conventional third-party resolvers. The EncDNS protocol, which is based on DNSCurve, encapsulates encrypted messages in standards-compliant DNS messages. User privacy is protected by exploiting the fact that a conventional DNS resolver provides sender anonymity against the EncDNS server. Unlike traditional privacy-preserving techniques like mixes or onion routing, which introduce considerable delays due to routing messages over multiple hops, the EncDNS architecture introduces only one additional server in order to achieve a sufficient level of protection against realistic adversaries. EncDNS is open source software. An initial test deployment is available for public use.

Keywords: anonymity, obfuscation, confidentiality, encapsulation, DNSCurve, nameserver, DNS proxy, encryption, third-party DNS, open source.

1 Introduction

The Domain Name System (DNS) is a globally distributed name resolution service that is used to translate domain names like www.google.com to IP addresses. Clients offload most of the work to so-called "DNS resolvers" that query the authoritative name servers, which store the mapping information, on behalf of users. Due to their central role, DNS resolvers are a preeminent entity for behavioral monitoring as well as for access control. Numerous nations and regimes have made efforts to prevent access to websites that they deem inappropriate, among them the United States (cf. the SOPA and PIPA bills [1]), Germany [2], Pakistan [3], Turkey [4] and China [5].

In some cases users can circumvent the filtering by switching to a different resolver [5]. Apart from well-known offers like Google Public DNS and OpenDNS, there is a huge number of name servers operated by NGOs and individuals (cf. http://public-dns.tk), some of them claiming to offer high availability and confidentiality as well as low latencies. Unfortunately, switching to a freely available resolver inevitably discloses one's online activities to the DNS provider. This

M. Kutyłowski and J. Vaidya (Eds.): ESORICS 2014, Part I, LNCS 8712, pp. 37–55, 2014.
© Springer International Publishing Switzerland 2014

gives rise to privacy concerns [6]. Neither the DNS protocol nor the DNSSEC security extensions account for privacy [7]. Therefore, the resolver can log the IP addresses of its users and the domain names they are interested in. Some experts believe that the discussions about limiting traditional tracking via cookies will result in DNS queries becoming the next target for tracking and profiling [8].

Previous work on improving confidentiality of DNS, namely DNSCurve and DNSCrypt (cf. Sect. 3), only provide link encryption, i. e., these proposals focus on protecting messages while in transit. However, link encryption is not sufficient for users who want to issue DNS queries without disclosing the desired domain names to the DNS provider. If the DNS provider learns the desired domains, privacy may be at risk even when the provider has good intentions and makes sincere commitments. This is exemplified by the case of "Lavabit", an e-mail service that has been legally obliged to disclose personal information to the authorities without being allowed to announce that breach in public [9].

This paper introduces a solution to protect confidentiality against attacks perpetrated by both eavesdropping outsiders *as well as* the DNS provider. Previous research efforts on such a privacy-enhanced DNS have not resulted in readily available systems so far. We believe that this is due to compatibility issues, high complexity as well as the penalty on latency (cf. Sect. 2). In contrast, we aim for a lightweight solution that is compatible with existing infrastructure and can be set up by a single party. Our approach is in line with a recent avenue of research, studying privacy solutions that sacrifice the objective of providing anonymity from strong adversaries in favor of low overhead and latencies [10,11].

The **contribution of this paper** is to propose EncDNS, a novel approach to provide a low-latency, privacy-preserving DNS resolution service. We describe the EncDNS architecture, the corresponding protocol as well as the message format. We have implemented a prototype of EncDNS and demonstrate via empirical evaluation that EncDNS offers low-latency name resolution. Initial tests also indicate that EncDNS is compatible with the majority of the name server implementations currently deployed on the Internet.

The paper is structured as follows. In Sect. 2 we review the Domain Name System, related work and outline the general requirements of a privacy-preserving name resolution service. After that we describe the design of EncDNS, its architecture, the name resolution process and the message format in Sect. 3. In Sect. 4 we carry out a security analysis of the proposal before we provide results from a performance evaluation in Sect. 5. Further, we assess the compatibility of EncDNS with the existing DNS infrastructure in Sect. 6. Limitations are discussed in Sect. 7 before we conclude the paper in Sect. 8.

2   Fundamentals, Related Work and Requirements

2.1   Domain Name System

The Domain Name System (RFCs 1034 and 1035 [12,13]) is used by clients to resolve human-readable domain names into IP addresses. Applications on a client computer use a *stub resolver* to send DNS *queries* to a *recursive name server*,

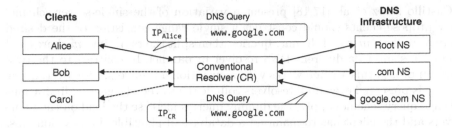

Fig. 1. Architecture of DNS

which is either operated by a user's ISP or by a third party. For reasons of clarity we will refer to the already existing recursive name servers as "Conventional Resolvers" (CRs) in this paper (cf. Fig. 1). The conventional resolver looks up incoming queries in its cache and, in case of a cache miss, retrieves the desired DNS resource record on behalf of the stub resolver from the appropriate *authoritative name servers* (Root NS, .com NS and google.com NS in Fig. 1). Once it has obtained the desired resource record, the conventional resolver will send a DNS *reply* to the stub resolver on the client. DNS messages are delivered via UDP, i. e., each DNS transaction consists of a single query and reply datagram.

The authoritative name servers collectively make up the distributed DNS infrastructure (cf. Fig. 1). An authoritative name server is responsible for a dedicated part of the DNS namespace, which is called a *zone*. The zones form a hierarchy with the so-called root zone at the top and the zones corresponding to so-called top-level domains (e. g., "com", "net", and "org") at the second level. Authoritative name servers can delegate the responsibility for a subtree in the namespace to other servers.

2.2 Related Work

In the following we will review existing proposals to provide privacy-preserving name resolution. Previous work has followed two different approaches: query obfuscation and sender anonymity.

The concept of "range queries" hides a query within a set of dummy queries. Zhao et al. [14] propose a straightforward solution: $n - 1$ randomly generated dummy queries q_i are submitted together with the desired query q_{desired} to a single conventional resolver. Depending on the choice of the security parameter n, this scheme may significantly increase the load of the resolver. Zhao et al. also present a more efficient scheme [15], which is inspired by private information retrieval [16]. The principal idea consists in sending two sets of queries Q_1 and Q_2 to two different servers with $Q_1 = q_1, q_2, \ldots, q_n$ and $Q_2 = Q_1 \cup q_{\text{desired}}$. Each of the two servers j collects all IP addresses, combines them using the XOR operation and sends the result as a reply r_j to the client. The client can then obtain the desired IP address: $r = r_1 \oplus r_2$. However, this scheme requires two special resolvers, which must not collaborate. Moreover, a passive observer can trivially determine q_{desired}, because the ranges are not encrypted.

Castillo-Perez et al. [17,18] present a variation of the single-server scheme. They propose clients should construct a single range consisting of the desired query as well as $(m \cdot n) - 1$ dummy queries, then split the range into m shares and send each share to a different DNS resolver in parallel. In contrast to the two-server approach this scheme works with conventional resolvers. Moreover, query privacy is preserved even if all resolvers collude. However, the general limitations of range query schemes apply: the dummy queries increase the load on the name servers and the client has to maintain a database of plausible dummy domains.

Lu and Tsudik propose PPDNS [19], a privacy-preserving DNS system, which is built on top of CoDoNS [20], a next-generation DNS infrastructure based on distributed hash tables (DHT) and peer-to-peer technologies. In PPDNS clients issue a range query by retrieving all records whose hash value matches a *hash prefix*, which is obtained by truncating the hash value of the desired domain. While PPDNS is a promising approach, we do not expect that it will be widely adopted in the near future due to the need for a completely different DNS infrastructure and its high computational complexity, which requires special hardware.

More relevant for our work are proposals that aim for *sender anonymity*. General-purpose anonymizers like Tor could be used to hide DNS queries, but they introduce significant delays. Response times are reported to be 45 times higher, if queries are resolved via Tor, with delays reaching up to 15 s [21].

In an earlier work we suggested to implement a special purpose mix cascade that provides unlinkability between queried domain names and the identity of the sender [22]. Although [22] is specifically tailored for DNS messages, relaying messages over multiple mixes has a significant impact on performance. The median response time was 171 ms when three mixes were used; name resolution via mixes takes more than twice as long as without mixes. In order to reduce the effect of high latencies we proposed to push the resource records of popular domain names to clients. This allows clients to resolve queries for popular names with zero latency. Keeping the records of the 10,000 most popular domain names up-to-date on the client requires a bandwidth of 1.5 MB/h. A fundamental limitation of [22], which may hinder deployment, is the fact that query privacy relies on a number of additional servers that have to be run by non-colluding providers.

2.3   Requirements

In the following we briefly outline the properties a privacy-preserving name resolution service should exhibit. First of all, such a service has to ensure that the conventional resolver cannot observe the domains contained in the queries of a user. More generally, no single entity in the final design should be able to link the identity of the sender with the contents of the queries or replies.

Secondly, the design of the service must not introduce significant delays into the resolution process. Currently, DNS queries are resolved within 10–100 ms [23]. A privacy-preserving resolution service will have to achieve a comparable performance in order to be accepted by users.

Thirdly, the name resolution service has to be compatible with the existing DNS infrastructure. Fundamental changes to the DNS are deployed only very

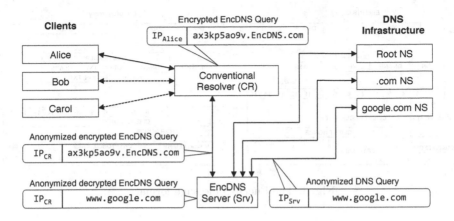

Fig. 2. Architecture of EncDNS

slowly, as exemplified by DNSSEC, which has been standardized more than ten years ago, but is still not widely available [24]. If the privacy-preserving name resolution service required changes to the DNS, it would not see widespread adoption in the near future. Moreover, the design should ensure that barriers for providers that want to offer the service as well as for users who want to use it are low. As a consequence, the service should offer a standards-compliant interface that can be accessed transparently by existing applications.

Fourth, as name resolution is a commodity service on the Internet, relaying and processing queries has to be efficient and scalable. Therefore, computational complexity on servers should be low, the protocols should be stateless and message sizes should be small.

None of the previous proposals meets all of these requirements. In the following we will outline the design of EncDNS, which aims to fulfill these requirements.

3   The EncDNS Design

We propose EncDNS (short for *Encapsulated DNS*) as a novel lightweight approach to enable anonymous usage of the DNS. The main idea of the EncDNS design is depicted in Fig. 2. Instead of using a *conventional resolver* (CR) for name resolution directly, the CR is utilized as a simple proxy that forwards DNS queries in encrypted form to an additional node, the *EncDNS server*. The encryption of queries is performed by clients to prevent the CR from learning the desired domain names.

Encrypted queries are standards-compliant DNS messages for a specially crafted domain name that consists of two parts: prefix and suffix. The prefix of this domain name contains the original query of the client, which is encrypted and integrity-protected. The suffix of the domain name (*EncDNS.com* in Fig. 2) is the domain name for which the EncDNS server is authoritative, i. e., it contains

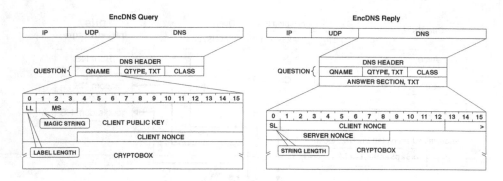

Fig. 3. The EncDNS message format

the *routing information* for the CR. Replies from the EncDNS server are delivered within standards-compliant DNS messages that contain a TXT resource record with the original DNS reply in encrypted and integrity-protected form.

The EncDNS server takes over the tasks carried out by CRs in conventional DNS, i. e., the EncDNS server performs the actual name resolution. While it is able to decrypt queries and thus learns the desired domain names, the EncDNS server cannot learn the client's IP address, since the queries are coming from the IP address of the CR.

In essence, the EncDNS design avoids a single point of trust (i. e., CRs in conventional DNS) by establishing a two-hop sender anonymous tunnel. However, only the second hop is introduced by EncDNS itself; existing conventional DNS resolvers are utilized as first hops. Thus, in EncDNS we have to address two challenges: Firstly, we have to design a message format that is **compatible with DNS**, i. e., it must be encapsulated within standard DNS messages. Secondly, EncDNS **must not introduce significant overhead** in terms of message sizes, reply times, and computational complexity. In the remainder of this section, we will describe how these challenges are addressed in EncDNS.

3.1 Encapsulation

Encapsulation of EncDNS messages in standard DNS messages is required for compatibility with CRs, which are not aware of the EncDNS protocol, but are supposed to forward EncDNS messages.

EncDNS encapsulates **encrypted queries** within the *question name* field of a standard DNS query in binary form. The question name field is the only suitable part of a DNS query for transmitting data to the EncDNS server. Binary query names comply with the DNS protocol specification: While [12, pp. 7–8] notes that "domain name comparisons [...] are done in a case-insensitive manner, assuming an ASCII character set, and a high order zero bit", it also states that implementations "should preserve [the] case" of a received domain name, because "full binary domain names for new services" may someday be needed. More concretely, RFC 2181 specifies "any binary string whatever can be used as the label of any resource record" [25, p. 13]. A limitation of using the query name field is its maximum length of 255 octets [13, p. 10]. This restriction has implications for the choice of the cryptographic primitives (cf. Sect. 3.2).

Encrypted replies are encapsulated within the data section of a TXT resource record. Although TXT records are designed to hold so-called "character-strings", their contents are not limited to the ASCII set of characters. According to RFC 1035 character-strings are treated as binary information [13, p. 13]. While the query name can only carry a limited amount of information, there are no specific length restrictions for TXT records, apart from the general constraints of DNS or EDNS(0) messages [26].

Although our encapsulation is standards-compliant, we cannot assume that all implementations of CRs will be able to forward EncDNS messages. We evaluate its compatibility with common implementations in Sect. 6.

3.2 Cryptography

As shown in the previous section EncDNS messages, especially queries, are subject to space restrictions due to encapsulation in standard DNS messages. Thus, we have to design a message format that introduces low overhead in terms of message sizes, while still providing confidentiality and integrity of messages. Moreover, computational overhead for message processing should be kept to a minimum, so that a single server can handle a sufficiently large number of clients.

These requirements are addressed by using a message format inspired by DNSCurve [27]. DNSCurve employs a hybrid cryptosystem based on elliptic curve cryptography (Curve25519), the Salsa20 stream cipher and the Poly1305 message authentication code [28,29,30]. The encrypted output of these three cryptographic primitives is referred to as the *cryptobox*.

In the following we outline the construction of queries and replies in the EncDNS protocol. A detailed overview of the cryptographic operations involved in obtaining the cryptobox is given in [31,32].

Each EncDNS client and EncDNS server has a Curve25519 key pair. Whenever an EncDNS client is about to send an **encrypted query**, it uses its *private key a* and the *public key of the EncDNS server B* (which has been obtained out-of-band) in order to calculate a message-independent shared secret key k_{aB}. The secret key is used in conjunction with a *client nonce* in order to create the cryptobox from the original DNS query. The format of EncDNS queries is depicted in Fig. 3. We focus on the part that is encapsulated in the question name of a DNS query. An EncDNS query starts with a magic string (a constant protocol identifier), the (current) public key of the client and the client nonce. The next block is the cryptobox containing the original query. Finally, the client appends the domain name of the EncDNS server, in order to allow the CR to forward the message to its destination. Note that the EncDNS client includes its public key in every query, i.e., the EncDNS server can process messages in a stateless fashion, which is one of the central properties of DNS. This is affordable because Curve25519 public keys consume only 32 octets.

When the EncDNS server receives an encrypted query, it decrypts the cryptobox. To this end, the server derives the secret key k_{Ab} from *its private key b* and the *public key of the client A*, which is equivalent to the secret key obtained by the client, i.e., $k = k_{aB} = k_{Ab}$. Using k and the *client nonce* the EncDNS server decrypts the cryptobox, obtains the plaintext DNS query of the client, and resolves the desired domain name.

Once the EncDNS server has obtained the resource record from the authoritative servers, it will construct an **encrypted reply** as follows: The EncDNS server chooses a *server nonce*, which is used in conjunction with the *client nonce* and the shared secret key k to create a cryptobox from the plaintext DNS reply. The format of EncDNS replies is depicted in Fig. 3. The reply is encapsulated in a TXT record and contains the client nonce, the server nonce and the cryptobox.

When the EncDNS client receives an EncDNS reply, it determines the corresponding query based on the value of the client nonce field, which serves as transaction identifier. If there is no unanswered query, the reply will be dropped. In order to decrypt the contents of the cryptobox the client uses the shared secret key k, the client nonce and the server nonce.

Key Pair Re-use and Secret Key Caching. An EncDNS client can re-use its key pair and the derived shared secret key k for multiple queries (see Sect. 4 for security implications of key re-use). Thus, the EncDNS server will obtain the same shared secret key every time it receives a query from this specific client. A straightforward optimization consists in caching k in the EncDNS client as well as in the EncDNS server. This spares client and server from repeatedly performing the same asymmetric cryptographic operations, reducing the overall computational effort. The practice of caching k effectively creates an anonymous tunnel between EncDNS client and server.

3.3   Open Source Prototype and Test Installation

We have implemented an EncDNS client as well as an EncDNS server in the gMix Framework [33] with the Java programming language. For cryptographic operations the implementation uses a Java Native Interface (JNI) binding to "libsodium", which is a platform independent port of the NaCL library, providing fast implementations of the Curve25519, Salsa20, and Poly1305 algorithms.[1]

We have released the EncDNS server and client implementation as open source. Source code as well as pre-compiled binaries for Linux and Windows systems are available at https://svs.informatik.uni-hamburg.de/gmix/. Moreover, for further field tests we have set up a publicly available open resolver, which runs an EncDNS server. We have made this server authoritative for the domain name *enc1.us.to*. It can be accessed by EncDNS clients to test compatibility with various CRs on the Internet. Setup instructions and the public key of *enc1.us.to* can be obtained from the mentioned website. We encourage readers to try out the EncDNS client and server and report any issues observed.

---

[1] Homepages: `https://github.com/jedisct1/libsodium` and
`http://nacl.cr.yp.to`

4   Security Analysis

In the following we will analyze the security properties of EncDNS in terms of query privacy, query integrity and availability.

4.1   Query Privacy and Attacker Model

Query privacy is protected if an adversary does not learn the IP address *and* the desired domain name for a given query. EncDNS provides query privacy against the CR as well as against the EncDNS server. It also provides query privacy against observers eavesdropping either on the link between the EncDNS client and the CR or on the link between the CR and the EncDNS server.

EncDNS does *not* offer query privacy if the provider of the CR colludes with the provider of the EncDNS server. If these two servers share their knowledge they can correlate the individual queries along the route, thus linking sender IP addresses with the desired domain names. We point out that other low-latency anonymization services, like Tor and AN.ON are subject to this limitation as well: Entry and exit nodes can correlate incoming and outgoing messages by timing and tagging attacks [34,35].

After a client has obtained an address record via EncDNS, it will usually establish a TCP connection to the target host, exchanging packets that contain the source IP address of the user as well as the destination IP address of the target host. A quite obvious limitation of EncDNS is that the desired domain names cannot be disguised from an adversary that operates the target host or is able to observe the network link between the user and the target host, i. e., a user cannot disguise the websites he visits from the operator of the web servers.

Furthermore, query privacy is not protected, if the CR is also authoritative for a specific DNS zone. If the user issues a query for a domain name in that zone, the provider of the CR will be able to link the plaintext DNS query of the EncDNS server to the corresponding encrypted query of the EncDNS client based on the timing of these two queries. In other words: if a user relays EncDNS queries using the CR of his own organization, he should not expect to be able to resolve domain names of his own organization privately using EncDNS.

Another privacy issue stems from the fact that encrypted messages can be linked as long as the EncDNS client uses the same key pair. Therefore, the EncDNS server can track the activities of a (anonymous) user, even if the user is issuing queries using different IPs and different CRs. To achieve query unlinkability EncDNS clients can be configured to use **ephemeral keypairs**, i. e., at runtime they create new key pairs in regular intervals. For maximum protection clients can be configured to use each key pair for a single query only. However, query unlinkability comes at a cost: it conflicts with key caching (cf. Sect. 3.2).

4.2   Message Integrity

The EncDNS protocol provides message integrity protection between the EncDNS client and the EncDNS server, i. e., manipulation of messages by CRs can be detected. EncDNS does not offer end-to-end integrity, i. e., a malicious EncDNS server could forge the IP addresses in its replies (DNS spoofing). This is not a specific limitation of EncDNS; users of existing third-party DNS resolvers have to trust the operators as well.

However, while "professional" operators may refrain from tampering with responses facing loss of reputation, the risk of poisonous replies may be higher for voluntarily provided EncDNS servers (cf. the issues with malicious exit nodes in Tor [36,37]). Once DNSSEC is deployed on a large scale, end-to-end integrity protection will be available. A temporary solution would consist in extending the implementation of the EncDNS client, so that it issues queries to multiple EncDNS servers in parallel in order to detect forged replies. This approach resembles CoDNS [38] and is also being investigated to detect faked web server certificates used in man-in-the-middle attacks [39]. However, asking multiple servers introduces new challenges: Content delivery networks reply with various IP addresses, the choice of which depends on the location of the EncDNS server.

4.3 Availability

Finally, we analyze availability aspects. On the one hand there is the risk of a denial of service attack against an EncDNS server. On the other hand, an EncDNS server could be used to leverage an amplification attack.

We start out by considering *denial-of-service attacks* against EncDNS servers. In contrast to DNSSEC, which uses offline signing of messages, EncDNS uses online encryption, which means that an adversary may be able to induce a significant load on the EncDNS server by sending EncDNS messages to it. In the following we analyze the effectiveness of potential mitigation techniques.

First of all, EncDNS messages contain a *magic string*, which allows the EncDNS server to identify EncDNS messages immediately upon receipt. Messages without the magic string, e. g., standard DNS queries, which are seen on EncDNS servers due to bots that probe the Internet for open resolvers, are dropped immediately. However, the magic string cannot protect against denial-of-service attacks by dedicated adversaries, who create a valid EncDNS query once and repeatedly send it to the EncDNS server. Identically replayed messages could be detected by the EncDNS server due to the fact that they contain identical client nonces. However, the adversary could easily vary the client nonce (as well as any other part of the query).

Denial-of-service attacks are a general problem of proxy services that do not require authentication. In future work we plan to adapt the EncDNS protocol so that EncDNS servers can demand that clients include a proof-of-work (client puzzle) in their queries, which can be verified efficiently by the EncDNS server.

In an *amplification attack* the adversary exploits the fact that he can induce a DNS resolver to send out a large reply with a comparatively small query [40]. This traffic amplification effect can be used to carry out a reflected denial-of-service attack against a victim. To this end the adversary will send a large number of small DNS queries containing the IP address of the victim in the source IP address field to (multiple) DNS resolvers, asking for a large resource

Table 1. Scalability evaluation of EncDNS server (Experiment 1, key caching enabled)

	EncDNS		Baseline	
Queries/sec	Failures [%]	CPU load [%]	Failures [%]	CPU load [%]
2000	0.00	23.6	0.00	13.9
4000	0.00	47.9	0.00	22.3
6000	0.00	63.9	0.00	30.9
8000	11.82	75.4	0.00	41.6

record, which will effectively result in overloading the victim. EncDNS servers are of little use for amplification attacks, because the amplification factor is smaller than in conventional DNS due to larger size of encrypted queries.

5 Performance Evaluation

In this section we evaluate the performance of EncDNS. We consider two distinct scenarios. The first scenario (Setup 1: Lab Environment) is used to assess the scalability of the EncDNS components, i. e., we want to determine the number of concurrent users that can be serviced by a single EncDNS server. In the second scenario (Setup 2: Emulated Environment) we want to determine the effective user-perceived latency for name resolution via EncDNS. To this end, we extend Setup 1 by using the network emulator *netem* [41,42] that simulates real-world latencies between the individual components. In both scenarios, the evaluation environment consists of a local network (1 Gbps) with off-the-shelf desktop machines (Intel Core i5-3100 quad cores, 8 GB RAM, CentOS 6).

5.1 Experiment 1: Scalability Assessment

In order to assess the scalability of EncDNS, we start out with experiments in the lab environment (Setup 1). To this end, we deploy load generators on multiple machines. Each load generator sends encrypted EncDNS queries towards a single EncDNS server (bottleneck). The server decrypts the queries and constructs encrypted replies that are sent back to the load generator. The load generator tracks its queries and the corresponding replies. When the EncDNS server becomes overloaded, it will not be able to receive all incoming queries any more, i. e., the load generators will not observe a reply for each query (resolution failure due to overload). In order to determine the maximum achievable throughput, we increased the query rate incrementally from 2000 to 8000 queries/sec.

The results of this set of experiments are shown in Table 1 (EncDNS columns). For up to 6000 queries/sec, all queries are processed. The CPU loads, which are denoted in the table, increase in a linear fashion with the query rate, because due to the EncDNS design every query can be processed independently from all other queries. At 8000 queries/sec, 11.82 % of queries remain unanswered due to

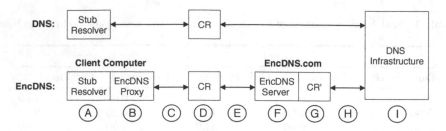

Fig. 4. Components and connections involved in (Enc)DNS name resolution

overload of the EncDNS server. At this point the average CPU load (averaged over all four cores) is 75.4 %. Further analysis has shown that CPU loads cannot approach 100 % due to context switches between the EncDNS server and resolver components running on the machine under test. The baseline measurements shown in Table 1 (same experiment without cryptographic operations) indicate that the cryptographic operations account for roughly 50 % of the load.

5.2   Experiment 2: User-Perceived Latency

In the following we extend the setup of Experiment 1 to resemble a real-world deployment of EncDNS. The goal is to assess the impact of EncDNS on query latency from a user's perspective. Figure 4 shows the components and connections involved in the resolution process. The effective latency is the sum of individual latencies introduced by network connections (labeled with C, E and H in Fig. 4) and the components A, B, D, F, G and I. We focus on the delay introduced between A and G, because this part of the system replaces the conventional name resolution process. We exclude the latency introduced by H and I, because this part of the resolution process is not affected by the use of EncDNS and lookup latencies vary heavily depending on the performance of the authoritative name servers [43]. To this end CR' (label G in Fig. 4) is configured to be authoritative for all queries issued during the experiment.

We consider three configurations: (1) a baseline measurement, which routes messages through EncDNS client, CR, and EncDNS server *without any encryption*, (2) EncDNS with key caching disabled, and (3) EncDNS with key caching enabled. During all experiments the client uses a single key pair for all queries.

By comparing the results for configurations (1) and (2) we can observe the impact of the asymmetric as well as the symmetric cryptographic operations. The performance of configuration (2) is to be expected when clients use a new ephemeral key pair for every single query (worst case; assuming that key pairs are pre-generated by the client). Comparing configurations (2) and (3) allows us to specifically observe the time needed for the asymmetric operations, i. e., we can evaluate the utility of the key caching mechanism (best case).

In order to observe the computational delay without any bias we start out by excluding network delays (connections C and E) from the measurements. Later on we employ a network emulator to incrementally increase network delays,

Table 2. Response times in Experiment 2 for various emulated delays between CR and EncDNS Server

Measurement	Delay (ms)	P_{25}	P_{50}	P_{75}
(1.1) Baseline	$C + E = 0$	1.36	1.39	1.41
(1.2) EncDNS	0	1.77	1.80	1.84
(1.3) EncDNS + cache	0	1.61	1.65	1.68
(2.1) Baseline	30+10	41.97	42.00	42.02
(2.2) EncDNS	30+10	42.50	42.53	42.56
(2.3) EncDNS + cache	30+10	42.13	42.17	42.19
(3.1) Baseline	30+50	81.98	82.00	82.03
(3.2) EncDNS	30+50	82.48	82.51	82.54
(3.3) EncDNS + cache	30+50	82.16	82.19	82.22
(4.1) Baseline	30+100	132.01	132.04	132.06
(4.2) EncDNS	30+100	132.45	132.49	132.52
(4.3) EncDNS + cache	30+100	132.13	132.16	132.19

which allows us to study the performance under more realistic conditions. We measure the **response time**, which equals the duration of a DNS lookup from a user's perspective: To this end we issue queries via a single EncDNS client (A) at a fixed rate (30 ms interval between queries). The response time consists of the time span between issuing a query and receiving the corresponding reply. To obtain significant results we issued 10,000 queries in each experiment. Based on the observed response times we calculated the 25th (P_{25}), 50th (P_{50}, the median) and 75th percentile (P_{75}). The results are shown in Table 2.

In the baseline configuration (1.1), we observe a median latency of 1.39 ms, which is caused by forwarding the query and reply between A and G. Enabling cryptographic operations (1.2) increases median latency by 29 % to 1.80 ms. When the key caching mechanism (1.3) is enabled, median latency decreases by 8 % to 1.65 ms, i. e., the median latency is only 19 % higher than in the baseline measurement. The values for P_{25} and P_{75} are very close to the median value.

The remaining experiments take network latencies into account. For connection C we set the round-trip time to a fixed value of 30 ms (latency of 15 ms in each direction), because we assume that the CR is operated by the ISP of the user or the user has selected a CR, which is geographically close. As the effective latency between the CR and the EncDNS server depends on the distance between them in practice, we simulate various typical conditions found on the Internet by varying round-trip times between 10 and 100 ms (cf. Table 2). The results indicate that the overhead introduced by EncDNS is constant and independent of the network delay. In practical deployments we expect that network delays and lookup latency (labels H and I in Fig. 4) will dominate the user-perceived latency. As anonymization services that rely on distributing trust need to forward traffic over at least two hops, some additional network delay is inevitable. The delay caused by message encryption is much smaller and is expected to be negligible in practice.

Table 3. Results of compatibility tests for popular CR implementations

Software	Version	Binary labels	Binary TXT records
BIND	9.7.3	✓	✓
MaraDNS	1.4.03	✓	✓
Unbound	1.4.6	✓	✓
PowerDNS	3.2	✓	✓
dnscache	1.05	✓	✓
Windows Server	2012 R2	×	✓

6   Compatibility Assessment

As explained in Sect. 3.1, encrypted EncDNS queries are encapsulated within the query name field of standard DNS queries in binary form using octets in the range from 0x00 to 0xff. Some CRs and intermediate DNS forwarders may not expect binary domain names. They might mangle the query name or discard the encrypted queries altogether. In order to assess the practicability of our encapsulation scheme, we have relayed EncDNS queries over commonly used recursive name server implementations in their default configuration.

The results of our compatibility tests are depicted in Table 3. The table indicates whether the respective implementation can handle binary labels (needed for transportation of encrypted queries) and binary data in TXT records (needed for transportation of encrypted replies). According to the results almost all popular implementations forward EncDNS queries and replies without interference. Only the name server of Windows Server 2012 R2 fails to relay EncDNS traffic: While it forwards our encrypted queries, it fails to link the encrypted replies to them; it reports a SERVFAIL error to the EncDNS client instead.

While this result look promising, we point out that all CRs that use the "0x20 encoding" security mechanism [44] *will* interfere with the encrypted query names. When a CR is configured to employ the 0x20 encoding scheme, it performs a random ad-hoc modification of the capitalization of each letter in the query name before forwarding the query to the authoritative name server (i. e., the EncDNS server). This measure is supposed to increase the entropy within DNS queries to foil cache poisoning attacks. In a 2013 survey only 0.3 % of the evaluated DNS resolvers used 0x20 encoding [45]. If its use becomes more widespread in the future, the EncDNS message format will have to be adapted (cf. Sect. 7).

7   Discussion and Future Work

In the following we will discuss limitations and open questions regarding the security analysis (Sect. 4), the performance evaluation (Sect. 5) and the compatibility assessment (Sect. 6). Additionally, we will point out possible deployment issues and how they can be overcome in future work.

We outlined the privacy properties of EncDNS in the **security analysis**. EncDNS prevents the CR from learning the queried domains. However, the current implementation does not incorporate *message padding*. This may allow the CR to infer the queried domains from the size of the encrypted payload. As the majority of the domain names is short, we conjecture that inference attacks have only limited effectiveness. In future work we will study the utility of various padding schemes and their impact on performance. Our preliminary tests indicate that message sizes have only a negligible effect on user-perceived latencies.

The results from the **performance evaluation** indicate that EncDNS is sufficiently scalable. Given the result of [22], who found that a user issues 0.05 DNS queries/second on average, the results of our scalability assessment (Experiment 1) suggest that a single EncDNS server, which can handle 6000 queries/second according to our scalability assessment, would be able to serve up to 120,000 concurrent users. However, this extrapolation is inadmissible, because DNS queries are neither evenly distributed among users, nor are they sent at a constant rate. DNS traffic typically contains bursts of queries, which occur when a browser retrieves a website that contains content from multiple web servers. In future work, we plan to assess the scalability of the EncDNS server with trace-driven simulations in order to provide a more realistic account of its scalability. The initial results presented in this paper indicate that a single EncDNS server will be able to create a sufficiently large anonymity set.

In Experiment 2 we measured the user-perceived latency and found that the overhead of the EncDNS components is almost constant and independent of network latency. This is mainly due to our design decision to relay EncDNS messages statelessly with UDP. Therefore, EncDNS is not subject to issues found in TCP-based overlay networks such as *head-of-line blocking* [46,47,48] or *cross-circuit interference* [49,48]. These effects result from the combination of TCP congestion control with multiplexing and have been shown to have a significant impact on the performance of systems like Tor.

According to the results of the **compatibility assessment** EncDNS queries and replies are forwarded by common name server implementations. If it turns out that implementations have difficulty with the binary message format, we could switch to a more conservative encoding such as Base32 [50]. Additionally, the message format could be extended to support message fragmentation in order to handle large queries and replies.

Future work will also have to consider some **deployment issues**: Firstly, the EncDNS design does not contain a directory service, i.e., techniques for server discovery are out of the scope of our proposal. Initially, a central bulletin board on a website may be sufficient for this purpose. Closely related to server discovery is the matter of key distribution: EncDNS clients need an authenticated copy of the public key of their EncDNS server. In the long run, DANE [51] could be used for authenticated key storage and distribution.

Finally, we remark on a practical privacy issue: If users configure their operating system to use the EncDNS client as DNS resolver, this will relay *all DNS queries* to the EncDNS server. This is undesirable in scenarios where users are in a local network with a *split-horizon* or hybrid DNS server that functions as recursive name server, but is also authoritative for some internal domain names (e. g., *database-server.corp.local*). Queries for internal domain names will be forwarded to the EncDNS server, which will be unable to resolve them, because they are not part of the public DNS namespace. As a result users may be unable to reach internal services. Moreover, private information (internal hostnames, for instance) may be disclosed to the EncDNS server. A straightforward countermeasure consists in a blacklist within the EncDNS client that explicitly denotes the domain names that should not be forwarded to the EncDNS server. Note that other drop-in anonymization services that use a proxy on the user's machine are subject to this privacy issue as well.

8   Conclusion

In this paper we have presented EncDNS, a lightweight open source name resolution service that leverages existing DNS resolvers to protect the privacy of its users. We have described the EncDNS architecture, the protocol and the message format. DNS queries are encrypted by the EncDNS client software, which runs on the machine of a user, and forwarded to the EncDNS server via a conventional DNS resolver. The EncDNS server decrypts incoming queries, obtains the desired resource records and responds with an encrypted reply. As EncDNS relies on conventional resolvers, encrypted messages are encapsulated in standards-compliant DNS queries and replies. According to our experiments EncDNS provides low-latency DNS resolution and is compatible with almost all popular DNS resolvers. We encourage researchers and users to evaluate the EncDNS prototype and to report on any issues found in practice.

References

1. Lemley, M., Levine, D.S., Post, D.G.: Don't Break the Internet. 64 Stan. L. Rev. Online 34 (2011)
2. Kleinschmidt, B.: An International Comparison of ISP's Liabilities for Unlawful Third Party Content. I. J. Law and Information Technology 18(4), 332–355 (2010)
3. Nabi, Z.: The Anatomy of Web Censorship in Pakistan. CoRR abs/1307.1144 (2013)
4. Verkamp, J.P., Gupta, M.: Inferring Mechanics of Web Censorship Around the World. In: 2nd USENIX Workshop on Free and Open Communications on the Internet. USENIX Association (2012)
5. Zittrain, J., Edelman, B.: Internet Filtering in China. IEEE Internet Computing 7(2), 70–77 (2003)
6. Goodson, S.: If You're Not Paying For It, You Become The Product. Forbes.com (2012), http://onforb.es/wVrU4G
7. Arends, R., Austein, R., Larson, M., Massey, D., Rose, S.: DNS Security Introduction and Requirements. RFC 4033 (2005)
8. Conrad, D.: Towards Improving DNS Security, Stability, and Resiliency (2012), http://www.internetsociety.org/ towards-improving-dns-security-stability-and-resiliency-0

9. Poulson, K.: Edward Snowden's E-Mail Provider Defied FBI Demands to Turn Over Crypto Keys, Documents Show. Wired, http://www.wired.com/2013/10/lavabit_unsealed/

10. Hsiao, H.C., Kim, T.H.J., Perrig, A., Yamada, A., Nelson, S.C., Gruteser, M., Meng, W.: LAP: Lightweight Anonymity and Privacy. In: IEEE Symposium on Security and Privacy (S&P 2012), pp. 506–520. IEEE (2012)

11. Jansen, R., Johnson, A., Syverson, P.F.: LIRA: Lightweight Incentivized Routing for Anonymity. In: 20th Annual Network and Distributed System Security Symposium (NDSS 2013). The Internet Society (2013)

12. Mockapetris, P.: Domain Names: Concepts and Facilities. RFC 1034 (1987)

13. Mockapetris, P.: Domain Names: Implementation and Specification. RFC 1035 (1987)

14. Zhao, F., Hori, Y., Sakurai, K.: Analysis of Privacy Disclosure in DNS Query. In: International Conference on Multimedia and Ubiquitous Engineering (MUE 2007), pp. 952–957. IEEE (2007)

15. Zhao, F., Hori, Y., Sakurai, K.: Two–Servers PIR Based DNS Query Scheme with Privacy–Preserving. In: International Conference on Intelligent Pervasive Computing (IPC 2007), pp. 299–302. IEEE (2007)

16. Chor, B., Goldreich, O., Kushilevitz, E., Sudan, M.: Private Information Retrieval. In: Proceedings of the 36th Annual Symposium on Foundations of Computer Science, Milwaukee, Wisconsin, pp. 41–50. IEEE (1995)

17. Castillo-Perez, S., Garcia-Alfaro, J.: Anonymous Resolution of DNS Queries. In: Meersman, R., Tari, Z. (eds.) OTM 2008, Part II. LNCS, vol. 5332, pp. 987–1000. Springer, Heidelberg (2008)

18. Castillo-Perez, S., García-Alfaro, J.: Evaluation of Two Privacy–Preserving Protocols for the DNS. In: 6th International Conference on Information Technology: New Generations (ITNG 2009), pp. 411–416. IEEE (2009)

19. Lu, Y., Tsudik, G.: Towards Plugging Privacy Leaks in the Domain Name System. In: IEEE 10th International Conference on Peer-to-Peer Computing (P2P 2010), pp. 1–10. IEEE (2010)

20. Ramasubramanian, V., Sirer, E.G.: The Design and Implementation of a Next Generation Name Service for the Internet. In: SIGCOMM 2004 Conference on Applications, Technologies, Architectures, and Protocols for Computer Communication, pp. 331–342. ACM (2004)

21. Fabian, B., Goertz, F., Kunz, S., Müller, S., Nitzsche, M.: Privately Waiting – A Usability Analysis of the Tor Anonymity Network. In: Santana, M., Luftman, J.N., Vinze, A.S. (eds.) 16th Americas Conference on Information Systems (AMCIS 2010), p. 258. Association for Information Systems (2010)

22. Federrath, H., Fuchs, K.P., Herrmann, D., Piosecny, C.: Privacy-Preserving DNS: Analysis of Broadcast, Range Queries and Mix-Based Protection Methods. In: Atluri, V., Diaz, C. (eds.) ESORICS 2011. LNCS, vol. 6879, pp. 665–683. Springer, Heidelberg (2011)

23. Ager, B., Mühlbauer, W., Smaragdakis, G., Uhlig, S.: Comparing DNS Resolvers in the Wild. In: Allman, M. (ed.) SIGCOMM Conference on Internet Measurement 2010 (IMC 2010), pp. 15–21. ACM (2010)

24. Wander, M., Weis, T.: Measuring Occurrence of DNSSEC Validation. In: [52], pp. 125–134

25. Elz, R., Bush, R.: Clarifications to the DNS Specification. RFC 2181 (1997)

26. Vixie, P.: Extension Mechanisms for DNS (EDNS0). RFC 2671 (1999)

27. Dempsky, M.: DNSCurve: Link-Level Security for the Domain Name System. Internet Draft draft-dempsky-dnscurve-01, RFC Editor (2010)

28. Bernstein, D.J.: The Poly1305-AES Message-Authentication Code. In: Gilbert, H., Handschuh, H. (eds.) FSE 2005. LNCS, vol. 3557, pp. 32–49. Springer, Heidelberg (2005)

29. Bernstein, D.J.: Curve25519: New Diffie-Hellman Speed Records. In: Yung, M., Dodis, Y., Kiayias, A., Malkin, T. (eds.) PKC 2006. LNCS, vol. 3958, pp. 207–228. Springer, Heidelberg (2006)

30. Bernstein, D.J.: The Salsa20 Family of Stream Ciphers. In: Robshaw, M., Billet, O. (eds.) New Stream Cipher Designs. LNCS, vol. 4986, pp. 84–97. Springer, Heidelberg (2008)

31. Bernstein, D.J., Lange, T., Schwabe, P.: The Security Impact of a New Cryptographic Library. In: Hevia, A., Neven, G. (eds.) LATINCRYPT 2012. LNCS, vol. 7533, pp. 159–176. Springer, Heidelberg (2012)

32. Bernstein, D.J.: Cryptography in NaCl. Technical report, Department of Computer Science (MC 152). The University of Illinois, Chicago, IL (March 2009), http://cr.yp.to/highspeed/naclcrypto-20090310.pdf

33. Fuchs, K.P., Herrmann, D., Federrath, H.: Introducing the gMix Open Source Framework for Mix Implementations. In: Foresti, S., Yung, M., Martinelli, F. (eds.) ESORICS 2012. LNCS, vol. 7459, pp. 487–504. Springer, Heidelberg (2012)

34. Levine, B.N., Reiter, M.K., Wang, C.-X., Wright, M.: Timing attacks in low-latency mix systems (extended abstract). In: Juels, A. (ed.) FC 2004. LNCS, vol. 3110, pp. 251–265. Springer, Heidelberg (2004)

35. Pries, R., Yu, W., Fu, X., Zhao, W.: A new replay attack against anonymous communication networks. In: International Conference on Communications (ICC 2008), pp. 1578–1582. IEEE (2008)

36. McCoy, D., Bauer, K.S., Grunwald, D., Kohno, T., Sicker, D.C.: Shining Light in Dark Places: Understanding the Tor Network. In: Borisov, N., Goldberg, I. (eds.) PETS 2008. LNCS, vol. 5134, pp. 63–76. Springer, Heidelberg (2008)

37. Winter, P., Lindskog, S.: Spoiled Onions: Exposing Malicious Tor Exit Relays. CoRR abs/1401.4917 (2014)

38. Park, K., Pai, V.S., Peterson, L.L., Wang, Z.: CoDNS: Improving DNS Performance and Reliability via Cooperative Lookups. In: 6th Symposium on Operating System Design and Implementation, pp. 199–214. USENIX Association (2004)

39. Wendlandt, D., Andersen, D.G., Perrig, A.: Perspectives: Improving SSH-style Host Authentication with Multi-Path Probing. In: USENIX Annual Technical Conference, pp. 321–334. USENIX (2008)

40. Kambourakis, G., Moschos, T., Geneiatakis, D., Gritzalis, S.: Detecting DNS Amplification Attacks. In: Lopez, J., Hämmerli, B.M. (eds.) CRITIS 2007. LNCS, vol. 5141, pp. 185–196. Springer, Heidelberg (2008)

41. Linux Foundation: Netem (2009), http://www.linuxfoundation.org/collaborate/workgroups/networking/netem

42. Nussbaum, L., Richard, O.: A Comparative Study of Network Link Emulators. In: Wainer, G.A., Shaffer, C.A., McGraw, R.M., Chinni, M.J. (eds.) Proceedings of the 2009 Spring Simulation Multiconference. SCS/ACM (2009)

43. Liang, J., Jiang, J., Duan, H.X., Li, K., Wu, J.: Measuring Query Latency of Top Level DNS Servers. In: [52], pp. 145–154

44. Dagon, D., Antonakakis, M., Vixie, P., Jinmei, T., Lee, W.: Increased DNS Forgery Resistance Through 0x20-bit Encoding: Security via Leet Queries. In: Ning, P., Syverson, P.F., Jha, S. (eds.) Conference on Computer and Communications Security (CCS 2008), pp. 211–222. ACM (2008)

45. Schomp, K., Callahan, T., Rabinovich, M., Allman, M.: Assessing DNS Vulnerability to Record Injection. In: Faloutsos, M., Kuzmanovic, A. (eds.) PAM 2014. LNCS, vol. 8362, pp. 214–223. Springer, Heidelberg (2014)
46. Karol, M., Hluchyj, M., Morgan, S.: Input versus output queueing on a space-division packet switch. IEEE Trans. on Communications 35(12), 1347–1356 (1987)
47. Nowlan, M.F., Wolinsky, D., Ford, B.: Reducing Latency in Tor Circuits with Unordered Delivery. In: 3rd USENIX Workshop on Free and Open Communications on the Internet. USENIX Association (2013)
48. Reardon, J., Goldberg, I.: Improving Tor using a TCP-over-DTLS Tunnel. In: USENIX Security Symposium, pp. 119–134. USENIX Association (2009)
49. AlSabah, M., Goldberg, I.: PCTCP: per-circuit TCP-over-IPsec transport for anonymous communication overlay networks. In: Sadeghi, A.R., Gligor, V.D., Yung, M. (eds.) Conference on Computer and Communications Security (CCS 2013), pp. 349–360. ACM (2013)
50. Josefsson, S.: The Base16, Base32, and Base64 Data Encodings. RFC 4648 (2006)
51. Barnes, R.: Use Cases and Requirements for DNS-Based Authentication of Named Entities (DANE). RFC 6394 (2011)
52. Roughan, M., Chang, R. (eds.): PAM 2013. LNCS, vol. 7799. Springer, Heidelberg (2013)

Ubic: Bridging the Gap between Digital Cryptography and the Physical World

Mark Simkin[1], Dominique Schröder[1], Andreas Bulling[2], and Mario Fritz[2]

[1] Saarland University
Saarbrücken, Germany
[2] Max Planck Institute for Informatics
Saarbrücken, Germany

Abstract. Advances in computing technology increasingly blur the boundary between the digital domain and the physical world. Although the research community has developed a large number of cryptographic primitives and has demonstrated their usability in all-digital communication, many of them have not yet made their way into the real world due to usability aspects. We aim to make another step towards a tighter integration of digital cryptography into real world interactions. We describe Ubic, a framework that allows users to bridge the gap between digital cryptography and the physical world. Ubic relies on head-mounted displays, like Google Glass, resource-friendly computer vision techniques as well as mathematically sound cryptographic primitives to provide users with better security and privacy guarantees. The framework covers key cryptographic primitives, such as secure identification, document verification using a novel secure physical document format, as well as content hiding. To make a contribution of practical value, we focused on making Ubic as simple, easily deployable, and user friendly as possible.

Keywords: Usable security, head-mounted displays, ubiquitous cryptography, authentication, content verification, content hiding.

1 Introduction

Over the past years, the research community has developed a large number of cryptographic primitives and has shown their utility in all-digital communication. Primitives like signatures, encryption schemes, and authentication protocols have become commonplace nowadays and provide mathematically proven security and privacy guarantees. In the physical world, however, we largely refrain from using these primitives due to usability reasons. Instead, we rely on their physical counterparts, such as hand-written signatures, which do not provide the same level of security and privacy. Consider the following examples:

Authentication. In practice, most systems, such as ATMs or entrance doors, rely on the two-factor authentication paradigm, where a user, who wants to authenticate himself, needs to provide a possession and a knowledge factor. At

M. Kutyłowski and J. Vaidya (Eds.): ESORICS 2014, Part I, LNCS 8712, pp. 56–75, 2014.

an ATM, for instance, the user needs to enter his bank card and a PIN in order to gain access to his bank account. Practice has shown that this type of authentication is vulnerable to various attacks [1,2,3], such as skimming, where the attacker mounts a little camera that films the PIN pad and a fake card reader on top of the actual card reader that copies the card's content. Here, the fact that users authenticate with fixed credentials is exploited to mount large scale attacks by attacking the ATMs rather than specific users.

Hand-written signatures. Physical documents with hand-written signatures are the most common form of making an agreement between two or more parties legally binding. In contrast to digital signatures, hand-written signatures do not provide any mathematically founded unforgeablility guarantees. Furthermore, there is no well-defined process of verifying a hand-written signature. This would require external professional help, which is expensive, time consuming, and therefore not practical.

Data privacy. Todays workplace is often not bound to specific offices or buildings any more. Mobile computing devices allow employees to work from hotels, trains, airports, and other public places. Even inside office buildings, novel working practices such as 'hot-desking' [4] and 'bring your own device' [5] are employed more and more to increase the employee's satisfaction, productivity, and mobility. However, these new working practices also introduce new privacy threats. In a mobile working environment, potentially sensitive data might be leaked to unauthorized individuals, who can see the screen of the device the employee is working on. A recent survey [6] of IT professionals shows that this form of information theft, known as *shoulder surfing*, constantly gains importance. 85% of those surveyed admitted that they have at least once seen sensitive information that they were not supposed to see on somebody else's screen in a public place. 80% admitted that it might be possible that they have leaked sensitive information at a public place.

In this work, we present Ubic, a framework and prototype implementation of a system that allows users to bridge the gap between digital cryptography and the physical world for a wide range of real world applications. Ubic relies on *head-mounted displays* (HMDs), like Google Glass[1], resource-friendly computer vision techniques as well as mathematically sound cryptographic primitives to provide users with better security and privacy guarantees in all of the scenarios described above in a user-friendly way. Google Glass consists of a little screen mounted in front of the user's eye and a front-facing camera that films the users view. It supports the user in an unobtrusive fashion by superimposing information on top of the users view when needed.

1.1 Contributions

To make a contribution of practical importance, in this work we focus on providing a resource-friendly, easy-to-use system, that can be seamlessly integrated into the current infrastructures. Ubic offers the following key functionalities:

---

[1] https://www.google.com/glass/

Authentication. We use a HMD in combination with challenge-response protocols to allow users to authenticate themselves in front of a device, such as an ATM or a locked entrance door. In contrast to current solutions, the PIN is not fixed but generated randomly each time. Neither does an attacker gain any information from observing an authentication process, nor does he gain any from compromising the ATM or the bank, since they can only generate challenges, but not solve them. Copying the card does not help the attacker, since it does not contain any secret information, but merely a public identifier.

Content Verification. We enable the generation and verification of physical contracts with mathematically proven unforgeability guarantees. For this purpose, we propose a new document format, VeriDoc, that allows for robust document tracking and optical character recognition, and contains a digital signature of its content. Using the HMD, a user can conveniently and reliably verify the validity of the document's content.

Two-Step Verification. Based on the signature functionality described above, we introduce *two-step verification* of content. During an online banking session, for instance, a user might request his current account balance. This balance is then returned along with a signature thereof. Using the HMD, we can verify the signature, and therefore verify the returned account balance. In this scenario, an attacker would need to corrupt the machine that is used for the banking session and the HMD at the same time in order to successfully convince the user of a false statement.

Content Hiding. We provide a solution for ensuring privacy in the mobile workplace setting. Rather than printing documents in plain, we print them in an encrypted format. Using the HMD, the user is able to decrypt the part of the encrypted document that he is currently looking at. An unauthorized individual is not able to read or decrypt the document without the corresponding secret key. Companies commonly allow employees with certain security clearances to read certain documents. We use predicate encryption to encrypt documents in such a way that only employees with the requested security clearances can read them.

1.2   Smartphones vs. Head-Mounted Displays

It might seem that all of the above scenarios could also be realized with a smartphone. This is not the case. In the content hiding scenario, we rely on the fact that the decrypted information is displayed to the user right in front of his eye. A smartphone is still vulnerable to shoulder-surfing and would therefore not provide any additional privacy guarantees. Realizing the authentication scenario with a smartphone is also problematic because a loss of possession is hard to detect and therefore an attacker might gain access to all secret keys as soon as he obtains the phone. Requiring the user to unlock the phone before each authentication process does not solve the problem, since the attacker might simply observe the secret that is used to unlock the phone.

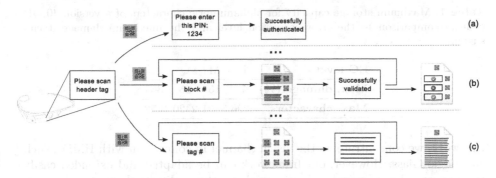

Fig. 1. Overview of the Ubic processing and interaction pipeline for the different operation modes: identification (a), content verification (b), and content hiding (c). The user starts each interaction by scanning the header 2D-barcode (indicated in gray). Ubic then guides the user through each process by providing constant visual feedback.

Ubic overcomes this problem by using the so-called *on-head detection* feature of the Google Glass device[2]. The device is notified whenever it is taken off and at this point, Ubic removes all keys from the memory and only stores them in an encrypted format on internal memory. HMDs are considered to be companions that are worn the whole day and only used when needed. When a user puts on the device in a safe environment, he has to unlock it once through classical password entry. Future versions might be equipped with an eye tracker, which would allow gaze-based password entry [7].

2   The Ubic Framework

The key aim of Ubic is to provide a contribution of practical importance that bridges the gap between digital cryptography and real world applications. We put emphasis on making our solutions as simple as possible and only use well researched and established cryptographic primitives in combination with resource friendly computer vision techniques to allow for easy deployment and seamless integration into existing infrastructures.

The general processing and interaction pipeline of Ubic is shown in Figure 1. Each interaction is initialized by the user scanning the header 2D-barcode (indicated in gray). The header code is composed of the framework header and an application specific header. The former contains the framework version as well as the mode of operation, e.g. identification, content verification, content hiding; the latter is an application specific header, containing information that is relevant for the given application.

Assumptions. The general setting we consider is a user who communicates with a possibly corrupted physical token over an insecure physical channel. In

_____

[2] https://support.google.com/glass/answer/3079857

Table 1. Maximum storage capacity for alphanumeric characters of a version 40 QR code in comparison to the error correction level and the maximum damage it can sustain

EC level	L	M	Q	H
Max. damage (%)	7	15	25	30
Max. characters	4296	3391	2420	1852

this work, we concentrate on the visual channel in connection with HMDs, such as Google Glass. However, our framework can be adapted and extended easily to support other physical channels, such as the auditory channel, if needed. The visual channel is very powerful and key to the vast majority of interactions that humans perform in the real-world. HMDs are personal companions that, in contrast to smartphones, sit right in front of the user's eyes. Google Glass comprises an egocentric camera that allows us to record the visual scene in front of the user, as well as a display mounted in front of the user's right eye. While the developer version that we used could still allow an observer to infer information about the content shown on the display by looking at it from the front, we assume that this is not possible in our attack scenarios. We consider this to be a design flaw of some of the first prototypes, which can be solved easily. Since the display only occludes a small corner of the user's field of view, it could simply be made opaque. We further assume that HMDs are computationally as powerful as smartphones. In practice, this can be achieved by establishing a secure communication channel between the HMD and the user's smartphone.

An *encoder* E = (ENCODE, DECODE) is used to transform digital data from and to a physical representation. We will not mention error-correcting codes explicitly, since we assume them to be a part of the encoder. In particular, our framework uses two-dimensional barcodes, called QR codes [8]. These codes are tailored for machine readability and use Reed-Solomon error correction [9]. Depending on the chosen error correction level, the barcode's capacity differs. Table 1 provides a comparison of their storage capacity for alphanumeric characters and their robustness.

3   Authentication

Our goal was to design an authentication mechanism that allows a user to authenticate himself in front of a token, such as a locked door or an ATM, without revealing his secret credentials to any bystanders who observe the whole authentication process. In addition, even a malicious token should not be able to learn the user's secret credentials. We focused on providing a solution, which is easy to deploy into the current infrastructures, i.e. merely a software update is required, and is as simple and user-friendly as possible.

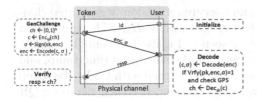

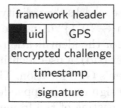

Fig. 2. Visualization of a identification scheme using an optical input device

Fig. 3. The identification header composed of the framework and application header

3.1 Threat Model

We consider two different types of adversaries for the authentication scenario. An *active* adversary is able to actively communicate with the user and impersonate the token. He has access to all secrets of the token itself. His aim is to learn a sufficient amount of information about the user's credentials to impersonate him at a later point in time. Note that security against active adversaries implies security against *passive* adversaries, who are only able to observe the data that the user passes to the token during the authentication process. Passive adversaries represent the most common real world adversaries, who can mount attacks like shoulder surfing and skimming. A *man-in-the-middle* adversary is able to misrepresent himself as the token. He is able to communicate with the user and a different token and forward possibly altered messages between the two parties. He does not have the token's secret keys. His aim is to authenticate in front of a different token, while communicating with the user.

Insecurity of current approaches. Clearly, the most common widely deployed solutions, such as those used at ATMs, do not provide sufficient protection against such adversaries. During an authentication process the user's fixed PIN and card information is simply leaked to the adversary, who can then impersonate the user.

3.2 Our Scheme

Let $\Pi_{\mathsf{pke}} = (\mathsf{Gen}, \mathsf{Enc}, \mathsf{Dec})$ be a CCA2 secure public-key encryption [10] and $\mathsf{DS} = (\mathsf{Kg}_{\mathsf{Sig}}, \mathsf{Sig}, \mathsf{Vf})$ a digital signature scheme secure against existential forgery under an adaptive chosen message attack (EU-CMA) [10], where $\mathsf{Kg}_{\mathsf{Sig}}$ is the key generation algorithm, Sig is the signing algorithm, and Vf, the verification algorithm. We assume that the token has knowledge of the user's public key. In the case of an ATM, the key could be given to the bank during registration. Our protocol is a challenge-and-response protocol that we explain with the help of Figure 2. The entire communication between the user and the token uses a visual encoder, which transforms digital information to and from a visual representation. The user initiates the protocol by sending his identifier *id* to the token. The challenger retrieves the corresponding public key from a trusted database, checks the validity of the key, and encrypts a randomly generated challenge ch $\leftarrow \{0, 1\}^n$ using the public-key encryption scheme Π_{pke}. The application header for the identification scenario can be seen in Figure 3. It contains a token identifier (tid), a user identifier (uid), the encrypted challenge, a timestamp, and the token's GPS location. The application header is signed with DS by the token and the signature is appended to the application header. It then generates a QR code consisting of the framework, and the application header.

The resulting QR code is displayed to the user, who decodes the visual representation with his HMD, parses the header information, checks the validity of the signature, the date of the timestamp, whether his location matches the given location, and decrypts the encrypted challenge to obtain ch. The user sends back ch to the token to conclude the authentication process. In the case of an ATM or a locked door, the last step can be done via a key pad. Choosing the length of the challenge is a trade-off between security and usability.

Security Analysis. Due to page constraints, we only provide an informal reasoning, showing that none of our three adversaries can be successful. Note that security against the active adversary already implies security against a passive adversary. Since we assumed that $\Pi_{\mathsf{pke}} = (\mathsf{Gen}, \mathsf{Enc}, \mathsf{Dec})$ is secure against chosen-ciphertext attacks, an adversary is not able to infer any information about the plaintext, i.e. the encrypted PIN, from the given ciphertext, even if he is able to obtain encryptions and decryptions for messages of his choice. This ensures that an (active) adversary can only guess the challenge, since he effectively plays the CCA2 game. To prevent man-in-the-middle attacks, we use an idea called authenticated GPS coordinates, recently introduced by Marforio, Karapanos, and Soriente [11]. We assume that the man-in-the-middle attack is perfomed on two tokens that are at different locations. Recall that each token signs its challenges along with its own GPS location. An adversary is not able to simply forward these challenges between two tokens, since the user, upon receiving a challenge, verifies the signature of the challenge and compares its own location to the signed location. Hence, such an adversary would need to break the unforgeability of DS to be able to forward challenges that will be accepted by the user.

4   Content Verification

The goal of our content verification functionality is to enable the generation and verification of physical documents, such as receipts or paychecks, with mathematically proven unforgeability guarantees. In particular, the validity of such documents should be verifiable in a secure, user-friendly, and robust fashion. The combination of physical documents with digital signatures is a challenging task for several reasons. Firstly, the document's content

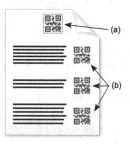

Fig. 4. The *VeriDoc* document format

Algorithm 1: Signing	**Algorithm 2:** Verify
input : m, sid, sk, layout **output**: Header token TOKEN$_H$ and ; side tokens TOKEN$_1, \ldots,$ TOKEN$_\ell$	**input** : Document D **output**: Valid or Invalid

$H_f \leftarrow$ GenFrameworkHeader(Verification)
 choose a random did $\leftarrow \{0,1\}^n$;
 parse $m = 1, \ldots, m_\ell$;
 set $h_H \leftarrow H(H_f, \text{sid}, \text{did}, \ell, \text{layout})$;
 set $\sigma_H \leftarrow$ Sig(sk, h_H);
 set TOKEN$_H \leftarrow$ ENCODE(H_f, sid, did, ℓ, layout, σ_H);
	Verify the document header
	 $(H_f, \text{sid}, \text{did}, \ell, \text{layout}) \leftarrow$ DECODE(TOKEN$_H$);
	 set $h_H \leftarrow H(H_f, \text{sid}, \text{did}, \ell, \text{layout})$;
	 set vk $\leftarrow$ PKI(sid);
	 return 0 if Vf(vk, $h_H, \sigma_H) = 0$;

Compute QR codes for each message block
 for $i = 1, \ldots, \ell$ **do**
     $h_i \leftarrow H(\text{did}, m_i, i)$;
     $\sigma_i \leftarrow$ Sig(sk, h_i) ;
     TOKEN$_i \leftarrow$ ENCODE(i, σ_i);
	Verify each message block
	 for $i = 1, \ldots, nb$ **do**
	     $m_i,$ TOKEN$_i \leftarrow$ OCR(b_i) //see Section 6;
	     $h_i \leftarrow H(\text{did}, m_i, i)$;
	     $i, \sigma_i \leftarrow$ DECODE(TOKEN$_i$);
	     return 0 if Vf(vk, $h_i, \sigma_i) = 0$;

return TOKEN$_H$, TOKEN$_1, \ldots,$ TOKEN$_\ell$	return 1

Fig. 5. The signing algorithm   **Fig. 6.** The verification algorithm

must be human-readable, which prevents us from using machine-readable visual encodings like QR codes. Secondly, we must be able to transform the human readable content into a digital representation such that we can verify the digital signature. Here, we apply techniques from computer vision such as optical character recognition (OCR). However, OCR has to be performed without any errors and from a practical point of view OCR is very unlikely to succeed without any errors when reading a whole document with an unknown layout. Observe that error-correction techniques cannot be applied, since a contract that says *"Alice gets $100"* is very different from one that says *"Alice gets $1.00"*. Using error-correction one could transform a wrong document into a correct one, which would result in a discrepancy between what the user sees and what is verified. To overcome the aforementioned problems and provide a practical and useable solution, we developed a novel document format, called VeriDoc (see Figure 4). This document facilitates robust document tracking and optical character recognition by encoding additional layout information into it. The layout information is encoded in a header QR code (a) and signatures for each block are encoded into separate QR codes (b).

4.1 Threat Model

Based on the standard EU-CMA notion for digital signature schemes, we consider the following adversary: In the first phase, the query phase, the adversary is able to obtain a polynomial number of (signed) VeriDoc documents for documents of his choice from some user Alice. In the second phase, the challenge phase, the adversary outputs a VeriDoc document D and wins if D verifies under Alice's public key and was not signed by her in the first phase.

4.2   Our Scheme

Let $\mathsf{DS} = (\mathsf{Kg_{Sig}}, \mathsf{Sig}, \mathsf{Vf})$ be a signature scheme secure against EU-CMA and H a collision-resistant hash function.

CONTENT SIGNING: A formal description of the signing algorithm is depicted in Figure 5. It takes the signer's private key sk, his identifier sid, the message $m = m_1, \ldots, m_\ell$ consisting of ℓ blocks as input and the layout information layout. First, the algorithm computes the document header TOKEN_H, which comprises of the framework header and the application header. The application header contains the signer's id sid, a randomly generated document id did, the number of message blocks ℓ, and layout. This header is signed and the signature σ_H is appended to the header itself. In the second step, each message block m_i is signed along with did and it's position i. All generated signatures are encoded into QR codes and printed onto the document next to the corresponding message blocks (see Figure 4).

CONTENT VERIFICATION: The content verification algorithm, depicted in Figure 6, is given a signed document D consisting of blocks b_i and verifies its validity. The extraction of a message block, the corresponding signature, as well as the underlying computer vision techniques that are used are simplified to $\mathrm{OCR}(\cdot)$ in this description. A description of $\mathrm{OCR}(\cdot)$ will be provided in Section 6. In the first step, the document header TOKEN_H is parsed by the computer vision system. Using the signer's id sid, the corresponding public key vk is obtained from a PKI. Afterwards, the verification algorithm checks the validity of each block. To do so, the algorithm first reads the message block along with its signature $(m_i, \mathrm{TOKEN}_i) \leftarrow \mathrm{OCR}(b_i)$, it computes the hash value $h_i \leftarrow H(\mathsf{did}, m_i, i)$, extracts the signature from the corresponding QR code, i.e. $(i, \sigma_i) \leftarrow \mathrm{DECODE}(\mathrm{TOKEN}_i)$ and outputs 0 if the signature is invalid, i.e., if $\mathsf{Vf}(\mathsf{vk}, h_i, \sigma_i) = 1$. If all checks are valid, then the verification algorithm outputs 1.

Security Analysis. We assume that the underlying signature scheme $\mathsf{DS} = (\mathsf{Kg_{Sig}}, \mathsf{Sig}, \mathsf{Vf})$ that is used to generate the VeriDoc documents is secure against EU-CMA. This means that an adversary is allowed to obtain signatures on messages of his choice adaptively and he is not able to generate a valid signature for a new message that was not queried to the signing oracle before (except with negligible probability). Furthermore, we assume that the hash function is collision-resistant, meaning that an efficient adversary finds two distinct messages m_0, m_1 that map to the same image $H(m_0) = H(m_1)$ only with negligible probability. In the query phase, the adversary obtains signed tokens for messages of his choice. Note that for each signed token a new random document id $\mathsf{did} \in \{0,1\}^n$ is generated and the header also contains the number of blocks ℓ. This document id prevents so called mix-and-match attacks, where a new valid document is generated by mixing message blocks from other valid documents. Since the id is n-bit long, where n is the security parameter and we consider poly-time adversaries, the probability of two documents having the same id is negligible in n.

Since the signed document header contains the number of message blocks and all blocks are enumerated according to their ordering in the layout, an adversary can neither rearrange, nor remove any message blocks without breaking the unforgeability of the signature scheme. Thus, the resulting VeriDoc document is also existentially unforgeable under chosen message attacks.

4.3   Two-Step Verification

Over the past years a constant increase in digital crime, such as identity theft, has been observed. To counteract these developments, companies like Facebook, Google, Yahoo, and many others allow users to use a technique known as two-factor authentication [12], when using their services. During such an authentication process, an additional layer of security is introduced by requiring a second authentication factor, e.g. a physical token, along with the password. In a similar vein we introduce the *two-step verification technique* that introduces a second step into the process of verifying retrieved content. Consider, for example, a user, who requests his account balance during an online banking session. If the machine that is used is untrusted and possibly even compromised, then the user cannot verify the correctness of the returned balance. To overcome this problem, we use our content verification technique described in Section 4, meaning that in our banking example the account balance is returned together with a visually encoded signature thereof. Using the HMD we parse the signature and the account balance and verify its correctness. An adversary, who wants to convince a user of a false statement, would need to compromise the machine, that is used by him, and the HMD simultaneously, which is considerably harder to achieve in practice. Due to the simplicity of the two-step verification technique, it could easily be integrated into many existing systems immediately.

5   Content Hiding

Motivated by the increasing existence of mobile workplaces, we introduce our content hiding solution. Our goal was to allow users to read confidential documents in the presence of eavesdroppers. HMDs are situated right in front of the user's eye and only he is able to see the displayed content. Confidential documents are printed in an encrypted format and using the HMD an authorized user decrypts the part he is looking at on-the-fly. Applications using this technique are not limited to paper-based documents or tablet computers. Consider an untrusted machine through which a user might want to access some confidential data. Using our content hiding technique, he could obtain the information without leaking it to the untrusted machine. For the sake of clarity and brevity, we describe our technique using public key encryption schemes. In Section 5.3 we show how to realize more complex access structures, such as security clearance hierarchies in office spaces, using predicate encryption schemes.

Algorithm 1: Encryption

input : m, ek
output: Header token TOKEN_H and ;
           ciphertext tokens $\text{TOKEN}_1, \ldots, \text{TOKEN}_\ell$

$H_f \leftarrow \text{GenFrameworkHeader(Hiding)};$
choose a random key $k \leftarrow \mathcal{G}(1^\lambda);$
compute $\text{key} \leftarrow \text{Enc}(ek, k);$
set $\text{TOKEN}_H \leftarrow \text{ENCODE}(H_f, \text{key});$

Compute encoded ciphertext blocks
$m_1, \ldots, m_\ell \leftarrow \text{split}(m)$;
for $i = 1, \ldots, \ell$ **do**
  $c_i \leftarrow \mathcal{E}(k, m_i);$
  $\text{TOKEN}_i \leftarrow \text{ENCODE}(i, c_i);$

return $\text{TOKEN}_H, \text{TOKEN}_1, \ldots, \text{TOKEN}_\ell$

Algorithm 2: Decryption

input : $\text{TOKEN}_H, \text{TOKEN}_1, \ldots, \text{TOKEN}_\ell, dk$
output: message m

Decode the header
$(H_f, \text{key}) \leftarrow \text{DECODE}(\text{TOKEN}_H);$

compute $k \leftarrow \text{Dec}(dk, \text{key});$

Decrypt the ciphertext
for $i = 1, \ldots, \ell$ **do**
  $(i, c_i) \leftarrow \text{DECODE}(\text{TOKEN}_i);$
  $m_i \leftarrow \mathcal{D}(k, m_i);$

return $m = m_1, \ldots, m_\ell$

Fig. 7. The encryption algorithm   **Fig. 8.** The decryption algorithm

5.1   Threat Model

In this scenario we basically consider the adversary from the standard CCA2 security notion. The adversary is allowed to obtain a polynomial amount of encryptions and decryptions for messages and ciphertexts of his choice from some honest user Alice. At some point the adversary outputs two messages, Alice picks one at random, and encrypts it. The adversary wins if he can guess which message was encrypted with a probability of at least $\frac{1}{2} + \epsilon(n)$, where ϵ is a non-negligible function and n is the security parameter.

5.2   Our Scheme

Let $\Pi_{\text{pke}} = (\text{Gen}, \text{Enc}, \text{Dec})$ be a CCA2 secure public key, and $\Pi_{\text{priv}} = (\mathcal{G}, \mathcal{E}, \mathcal{D})$ a CCA2 secure private key encryption scheme. To obtain public key encryption scheme with short ciphertexts, we use a hybrid encryption scheme [13]. The basic idea of such a scheme is to encrypt a randomly generated key $k \leftarrow \mathcal{G}(n)$ with the public key encryption scheme and store it in the header. The actual plaintext is encrypted using Π_{priv} with k.

ENCRYPTION: The encryption algorithm is depicted in Figure 7 and works as follows: At first, a randomly chosen *document key* k is encrypted with a public-key encryption scheme under the public key ek of the recipient. A header QR code TOKEN_H is created, which contains the framework header, the encrypted document key. The actual body of the document m is split into message chunks $m_1, \ldots, m_\ell$ and each chunk is encrypted separately using the document key and is then encoded, along with the block id, into a QR code TOKEN_i.

DECRYPTION: The decryption algorithm is depicted in Figure 8. Upon receiving a document, the receiver decodes the header QR code, obtains the encrypted document key key. Using his secret key dk, the algorithm recovers the document key $k \leftarrow \mathcal{D}(dk, \text{key})$ and it uses the key to decrypt the document body.

The advantages of representing the document as a sequence of encrypted blocks is twofold. Firstly, it allows the user to only decrypt the part of the encrypted document body that he is currently looking at without the need to scan the whole document first. Furthermore, the encrypted documents are robust to damage, meaning that even if a part of it is broken or unreadable, we are still able to decrypt the remaining undamaged ciphertext blocks as long as the document header is readable. Choosing the size of the message blocks is a trade-off between space and robustness. The bigger the message blocks are, the more plaintext is lost once a single QR code is not readable anymore. The smaller they are, the more QR codes are required, hence the more space is needed to display them.

Security Analysis. It is well known that using the hybrid argument proof technique [10] the CCA2 game, where the adversary outputs two distinct messages in the challenge phase, is equivalent to a CCA2 game where the adversary outputs two message vectors of polynomial length. The security of our scheme directly follows from this observation.

5.3 Extending Content Hiding to Support Fine-Grained Access Control

Using public-key encryption in our content hiding scheme allows us to encrypt documents for certain recipients. In companies or organizations, however, it is more desirable to encrypt documents, such that only employees with certain security clearances can read certain enrypted documents. Ubic allows to encrypt documents, such that only users with certain security clearances can read them. Therefore, we replace the public-key encryption scheme by a *predicate* encryption scheme [14]. Loosely speaking, in a predicate encryption scheme, one can encrypt a message M under a certain attribute $I \in \Sigma$ using a master public key mpk where Σ is the universe of all possible attributes. The encryption algorithm outputs a ciphertext that can be decrypted with a secret key sk_f associated with a predicate $f \in \mathcal{F}$, if and only if I fulfills f, i.e., $f(I) = 1$, where $\mathcal{F}$ is the universe of all predicates.

Next, we explain the security notion of predicate encryption, called *attribute-hiding*, with the following toy example. Consider the scenario where professors, students, and employees are working at a university and by *Prof*, *Emp*, and *Stud* we denote the corresponding attributes. Every member of a group will be equipped with a secret key sk_f such that f is either the predicate mayAccProf, mayAccEmp, or mayAccStud. We use the toy policy that professors may read everything and employees and students may only read encryptions created using *Emp* and *Stud*, respectively. Now, attribute-hiding states that a file *file* which is encrypted using the attribute *Prof*, can not be decrypted by a student equipped with $sk_{\text{mayAccStud}}$ and the student also can not tell with which attribute *file* was encrypted (except for the fact that it was not *Stud*). Furthermore, even a professor does not learn under which attribute *file* was encrypted, she only learns the content of the file and nothing more.

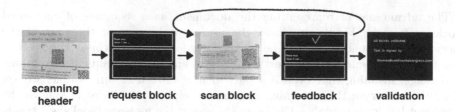

scanning header   **request block**   **scan block**   **feedback**   **validation**

Fig. 9. Interaction cycle with VeriDoc. The user initiates the interaction by scanning the header QR code at the top of the document. After sequential scanning of each content block, the user is informed if the document was verified or not. The black screens are what the user sees on the Google Glass display. They cover the whole screen but only a small part of the users view.

Extending Our Scheme. We extend our scheme to also support fine grained access control by replacing the public-key encryption scheme with a predicate encryption scheme. Thus, the user encrypting the message in addition chooses an attribute $I \in \Sigma$ that specifies which users can decrypt the message. Formally, our encryption algorithm is almost the same as described in Figure 7, but the public-key encryption step is replaced with $c \leftarrow \mathsf{PrEnc}(mpk, I, k)$, where mpk is a master public key that works for all attributes. The only difference in the decryption algorithm is that instead of using the public-key decryption algorithm Dec, we are now running the decryption algorithm of the predicate encryption scheme $\mathsf{PrDec}(sk_f, c)$ and the user can only decrypt if $f(I) = 1$.

Efficient Implementation. Our implementation is based on the predicate encryption scheme due to Katz, Sahai, and Waters [14] (see Section A for a formal description of the scheme). However, for efficiency reasons, we did not implement the scheme in composite order groups, but adapted the transformation to prime order groups as suggested by Freeman [15].

6   The VeriDoc Interface

In the following, we describe our document format VeriDoc. A high-level overview of the document scanning process is shown in Figure 9. Throughout this process we provide visual feedback to make the scanning process transparent to the user. As already described, the user initiates the document verification by scanning the header code of the document. Amongs other information, the header code contains the layout information. This information contains additional information about the document that facilitates the scanning process. In particular, this information contains the used font, the aspect ratio of each message block, and the document language. After scanning the header code, the user is asked to scan the message blocks. We display brackets on the HMD to help the user to position the camera properly over the text block Accurate alignment and content extraction is further facilitated by a computer vision subsystem as described below. After each scanned block, its content is extracted and verified against the

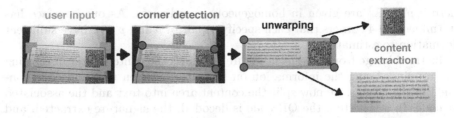

Fig. 10. Vision subsystem to assist the user in working with VeriDoc: The user points the front-facing camera roughly at the VeriDoc document, the system detects the four corners of the first content block and snaps the locations of the brackets to them, and the system unwarps and extracts the content of that block.

signature encoded in the QR code. The user is informed about the validity of each text block and once all blocks of a given document are scanned the system informs the user if the document, as a whole, was successfully verified.

ALIGNMENT AND CONTENT EXTRACTION: To assist the user in scanning Veri-Doc document content we provide a refinement procedure that allows the user to roughly indicate relevant text blocks, but still provide the required accuracy for the computer vision processing pipeline (see Figure 10). On the very left, a typical user interaction is depicted showing a coarse alignment of the brackets with the first text block. We proceed by a corner detection algorithm and snap the locations of the brackets provided by the user to the closest corners. We use the Harris corner measure M to robustly detect corners [16]:

$$A = g(\sigma_I) * \begin{pmatrix} I_x^2(\sigma_D) & I_x I_y(\sigma_D) \\ I_x I_y(\sigma_D) & I_y^2(\sigma_D) \end{pmatrix} \tag{1}$$

$$M = \det(A) - \kappa \operatorname{trace}(A)^2 \tag{2}$$

where I_x and I_y are the spatial image derivatives in x and y direction, σ_D smoothing of the image with the detection scale and σ_I smoothing the response with the integration scale and $\kappa = 0.04$ according to best practice. Intuitively, the pre-smoothing with σ_D eliminates noise and allows detection of corners at a desired scale [17] while the smoothing σ_I suppresses local maxima in the response function. In order to be robust to the choice of these scales, we employ the multi-scale harris detector that finds corners across multiple scales [18].

The second image at the top shows a visualization of the closest corner and the box spanned by them in green. Under the assumption of a pinhole camera model as well as a planar target (documents in our case), we can compute a homography $H \in \mathbb{R}^{3 \times 3}$ in order to undo the perspective transformation under which the content is viewed. The matrix H relates the points under the perspective project p' to the points under an orthogonal viewing angle p by

$$p' = Hp \tag{3}$$

where $p, p' \in \mathbb{R}^3$ are given in homogeneous coordinates. As our interface has determined the 4 corners that each specify a pair of p and p', we have sufficient information to estimate matrix H.

The third image from the left in Figure 10 shows the content after unwarping and cropping. Using the information on the ratio between text and code contained in the header, we now split the content area into text and the associated QR code. In a last step, the QR code is decoded, the signature extracted, and the text area is further processed using OCR in combination with the font and language information from the header code.

7   Prototype Implementation

We provide a prototype implementation, written in Java, of our Ubic framework on the Google Glass device. The device runs Android 4.0.4 as its underlying operating system, features a 640×360 optical head-mounted display as well as an egocentric camera with a resolution of 1280×720 pixels. Our current developer version only features an embedded microcontroller with 1.2 GHz and 1GB of memory.

We used the Bouncy Castle Crypto API 1.50 [19] and the Java Pairing-Based Cryptography Library 2.0.0 (JPBC) [20] to implement all required cryptographic primitives. In particular, we used SHA-1 as our collision-resistant hash function, SHA1+RSA-PSS as our signature, AES-256 in CTR-Mode as our private-key encryption, and RSA-OAEP with 2048 bit long keys as our public-key encryption scheme. For our predicate encryption scheme, we use a MNT curve [21] with a security parameter of 112 according to the NIST recommendations [22]. For the computer vision part of our framework, we used the OpenCV 2.4.8 image processing library [23], and QR codes are being processed with the barcode image processing library zxing 1.7.6 [24]. For optical character recognition, we used the Tesseract OCR engine [25].

8   Related Work

Head-mounted displays, such as Google Glass, have raised strong privacy concerns in the past and recent publications [26,27,28] have tried to address these issues. In [26], the authors suggest that operating systems should provide high-level abstractions for accessing perceptual data. Following this line of work, [27] proposes a system, which makes a first step towards providing privacy guarantees for sensor feeds. There, applications access the camera through a new interface rather than accessing the camera directly. Depending on the application's permissions, the camera is pre-processed with different sets of image filters, which aim to filter sensitive information. In [28], the notion of recognizers is introduced. Rather than passing a filtered sensor feed to the requesting application, they provide a set of recognizers that fulfil the most common tasks, such as face detection or recognition. Applications obtain permissions for certain recognizer and can request the output of certain computations on the sensor feed. In contrast to our work, this line of research regards the device as a threat.

Another line of research concentrates on establishing trust between devices based on the visual channel [29,30,31]. In [31], for instance, the visual channel is used for demonstrative authentication, where two devices authenticate themselves towards each other by basing their trust on the visual channel between them. One possible application for this authentication mechanism is access points with QR codes printed onto them. The user scans the QR code to authenticate the access point.

In [32], a survey of different techniques for scanning and analyzing documents with the help of cameras, cell phones, and wearable computers is provided. The survey shows that even though constant progress is made, current methods are not robust enough for real world deployment. Ubic tackles this problem in a different way by facilitating the task of scanning documents by encoding additional information into them.

9 Conclusion

We presented Ubic, a framework that makes an important step towards a tighter integration of digital cryptography in real-world applications. Using HMDs in combination with established cryptographic primitives and resource friendly computer vision techniques, we provide users with more security and privacy guarantees in a wide range of common real-world applications. We present user-friendly, easy-to-use solutions for authentication, content verification, content hiding, that can seamlessly be integrated into the current infrastructure. We hope that our work will stimulate further research investigating the possibilities of combining ubiquitous computing technologies with cryptographic primitives in a user-friendly fashion.

Acknowledgements. Andreas Bulling and Mario Fritz are supported by a Google Glass Research Award. Work of Dominique Schröder and Mark Simkin was supported by the German Federal Ministry of Education and Research (BMBF) through funding for the Center for IT-Security, Privacy, and Accountability (CISPA; see www.cispa-security.org). Dominique Schröder is also supported by an Intel Early Career Faculty Honor Program Award.

References

1. News, B.: Cash machines raided with infected usb sticks (2013)
2. Bankrate: Skimming the cash out of your account (2002)
3. Times, N.Y.: Target missed signs of a data breach (2014)
4. Telegraph, T.: Mind how you move that chair - it's hot hot-desking is a growing trend, bringing a new culture writes violet johnstone (2002)
5. House, T.W.: Bring your own device (2012)
6. for Visual Data Security, E.A.: Visual Security White Paper (2012)
7. Kumar, M., Garfinkel, T., Boneh, D., Winograd, T.: Reducing shoulder-surfing by using gaze-based password entry. In: Proceedings of the 3rd Symposium on Usable Privacy and Security, SOUPS 2007, pp. 13–19. ACM (2007)

8. International Organization for Standardization: Information technology — automatic identification and data capture techniques — qr code 2005 bar code symbology specification (2006)
9. Wicker, S.B.: Reed-Solomon Codes and Their Applications. IEEE Press, Piscataway (1994)
10. Katz, J., Lindell, Y.: Introduction to Modern Cryptography (Chapman & Hall/Crc Cryptography and Network Security Series). Chapman & Hall/CRC (2007)
11. Marforio, C., Karapanos, N., Soriente, C., Kostiainen, K., Capkun, S.: Smartphones as practical and secure location verification tokens for payments. In: Proceedings of the Network and Distributed System Security Symposium, NDSS 2014 (2014)
12. Van Rijswijk, R.M., Van Dijk, J.: Tiqr: A novel take on two-factor authentication. In: Proceedings of the 25th International Conference on Large Installation System Administration, LISA 2011, p. 7. USENIX Association (2011)
13. Cramer, R., Shoup, V.: Design and analysis of practical public-key encryption schemes secure against adaptive chosen ciphertext attack. SIAM J. Comput. 33(1), 167–226 (2004)
14. Katz, J., Sahai, A., Waters, B.: Predicate encryption supporting disjunctions, polynomial equations, and inner products. In: Smart, N.P. (ed.) EUROCRYPT 2008. LNCS, vol. 4965, pp. 146–162. Springer, Heidelberg (2008)
15. Freeman, D.M.: Converting pairing-based cryptosystems from composite-order groups to prime-order groups. In: Gilbert, H. (ed.) EUROCRYPT 2010. LNCS, vol. 6110, pp. 44–61. Springer, Heidelberg (2010)
16. Harris, C., Stephens, M.: A combined corner and edge detector. In: Proceedings of the 4th Alvey Vision Conference, pp. 147–151 (1988)
17. Lindeberg, T.: Scale-Space Theory in Computer Vision. Kluwer Academic Publishers, Norwell (1994)
18. Mikolajczyk, K., Schmid, C.: A performance evaluation of local descriptors. IEEE Transactions on Pattern Analysis and Machine Intelligence 27(10), 1615–1630 (2005)
19. The Legion of the Bouncy Castle: Lightweight Cryptography API (Release 1.50)
20. De Caro, A., Iovino, V.: jpbc: Java pairing based cryptography. In: Proceedings of the 16th IEEE Symposium on Computers and Communications, ISCC 2011, Kerkyra, Corfu, Greece, June 28-July 1, pp. 850–855 (2011)
21. Miyaji, A., Nakabayashi, M., Takano, S.: New explicit conditions of elliptic curve traces for fr-reduction (2001)
22. Barker, E., Barker, W., Burr, W., Polk, W., Smid, M.: Recommendation for Key Management Part 1: General (Revision 3). Technical report (July 2012)
23. Bradski, G.: Open source computer vision library (opencv) (2000)
24. ZXing: ZXing Multi-format 1D/2D barcode image processing library (2012)
25. Smith, R.: An overview of the tesseract ocr engine. In: Proceedings of the Ninth International Conference on Document Analysis and Recognition, ICDAR 2007, vol. 2, pp. 629–633. IEEE Computer Society, Washington, DC (2007)
26. D'Antoni, L., Dunn, A., Jana, S., Kohno, T., Livshits, B., Molnar, D., Moshchuk, A., Ofek, E., Roesner, F., Saponas, S., Veanes, M., Wang, H.J.: Operating system support for augmented reality applications. In: Proceedings of the 14th USENIX Conference on Hot Topics in Operating Systems, HotOS 2013, p. 21. USENIX Association, Berkeley (2013)
27. Jana, S., Narayanan, A., Shmatikov, V.: A scanner darkly: Protecting user privacy from perceptual applications. In: IEEE Symposium on Security and Privacy, pp. 349–363. IEEE Computer Society (2013)

28. Jana, S., Molnar, D., Moshchuk, A., Dunn, A., Livshits, B., Wang, H.J., Ofek, E.: Enabling Fine-Grained Permissions for Augmented Reality Applications With Recognizers. In: 22nd USENIX Security Symposium (USENIX Security 2013), Washington DC (August 2013)
29. Starnberger, G., Froihofer, L., Goeschka, K.M.: Qr-tan: Secure mobile transaction authentication. In: 2012 Seventh International Conference on Availability, Reliability and Security, pp. 578–583 (2009)
30. Saxena, N., Ekberg, J.E., Kostiainen, K., Asokan, N.: Secure device pairing based on a visual channel. In: 2006 IEEE Symposium on Security and Privacy, pp. 306–313 (2006)
31. Mccune, J.M., Perrig, A., Reiter, M.K.: Seeing-is-believing: Using camera phones for human-verifiable authentication. In: IEEE Symposium on Security and Privacy, pp. 110–124 (2005)
32. Liang, J., Doermann, D., Li, H.: Camera-based analysis of text and documents: a survey. International Journal on Document Analysis and Recognition 7, 84–104–104 (2005)

A   Predicate Encryption

For completeness, we recall the predicate encryption scheme due to Katz, Sahai, and Waters [14].

Definition 1 (Predicate Encryption). *A predicate encryption scheme for the universe of predicates and attributes $\mathcal{F}$ and Σ, respectively, is a tuple of efficient algorithms $\Pi_{\mathsf{PE}} = (\mathsf{PrGen}, \mathsf{PrKGen}, \mathsf{PrEnc}, \mathsf{PrDec})$, where the generation algorithm PrGen takes as input a security parameter 1^λ and returns a master public and a master secret key pair (mpk, psk); the key generation algorithm PrKGen takes as input the master secret key psk and a predicate description $f \in \mathcal{F}$ and returns a secret key sk_f associated with f; the encryption algorithm PrEnc takes as input the master public key mpk, an attribute $I \in \Sigma$, and a message m and it returns a ciphertext c; and the decryption algorithm PrDec takes as input a secret key sk_f associated with a predicate f and a ciphertext c and outputs either a message m or $\perp$.*

A predicate encryption scheme Π_{PE} is *correct* if and only if, for all λ, all key pairs $(mpk, psk) \leftarrow \mathsf{PrGen}(1^\lambda)$, all predicates $f \in \mathcal{F}$, all secret keys $sk_f \leftarrow \mathsf{PrKGen}(psk, f)$, and all attributes $I \in \Sigma$ we have that (i) if $f(I) = 1$ then $\mathsf{PrDec}(sk_f, \mathsf{PrEnc}(mpk, I, m)) = m$ and (ii) if $f(I) = 0$ then $\mathsf{PrDec}(sk_f, \mathsf{PrEnc}(mpk, I, m)) = \perp$ except with negligible probability.

The KSW Predicate Encryption Scheme. The scheme is based on composite order groups with a bilinear map. More precisely, let $N = pqr$ be a composite number where p, q, and r are large prime numbers. Let $\mathbb{G}$ be an order-N cyclic group and $e : \mathbb{G} \times \mathbb{G} \to \mathbb{G}_T$ be a bilinear map. Recall that e is *bilinear*, i.e., $e(g^a, g^b) = e(g, g)^{ab}$, and *non-degenerate*, i.e., if $\langle g \rangle = \mathbb{G}$ then $e(g, g) \neq 1$. Then, by the chinese remainder theorem, $\mathbb{G} = \mathbb{G}_p \times \mathbb{G}_q \times \mathbb{G}_r$ where $\mathbb{G}_s$ with $s \in \{p, q, r\}$ are the s-order subgroups of $\mathbb{G}$. Moreover, given a generator g for $\mathbb{G}$, $\langle g^{pq} \rangle = \mathbb{G}_r$,

$\langle g^{pr} \rangle = \mathbb{G}_q$, and $\langle g^{qr} \rangle = \mathbb{G}_p$. Another insight is the following, given for instance $a \in \mathbb{G}_p$ and $b \in \mathbb{G}_q$, we have $e(a, b) = e((g^{qr})^c, (g^{pr})^d) = e(g^{rc}, g^d)^{pqr} = 1$, i.e., a pairing of elements from different subgroups cancels out. Finally, let $\mathcal{G}$ be an algorithm that takes as input a security parameter 1^λ and outputs a description $(p, q, r, \mathbb{G}, \mathbb{G}_T, e)$. We describe the algorithms PrGen, PrKGen, PrEnc, and PrDec in the sequel.

Algorithm PoGen($1^\lambda, n$) *and* PrGen($1^\lambda, n$). First, the algorithm runs $\mathcal{G}(1^\lambda)$ to obtain $(p, q, r, \mathbb{G}, \mathbb{G}_T, e)$ with $\mathbb{G} = \mathbb{G}_p \times \mathbb{G}_q \times \mathbb{G}_r$. Then, it computes g_p, g_q, and g_r as generators of $\mathbb{G}_p$, $\mathbb{G}_q$, and $\mathbb{G}_r$, respectively. The algorithm selects $R_0 \in \mathbb{G}_r$, $R_{1.i}, R_{2,i} \in \mathbb{G}_r$ and $h_{1,i}, h_{2,i} \in \mathbb{G}_p$ uniformly at random for $1 \leq i \leq n$. ($N = pqr, \mathbb{G}, \mathbb{G}_T, e$) constitutes the public parameters. The public key for the predicate-only encryption scheme is

$$opk = (g_p, g_r, Q = g_q \cdot R_0, \{H_{1,i} = h_{1,i} \cdot R_{1,i}, H_{2,i} = h_{2,i} \cdot R_{2,i}\}_{i=1}^n)$$

and the master secret key is $osk = (p, q, r, g_q, \{h_{1,i}, h_{2,i}\}_{i=1}^n)$. For the predicate encryption with messages, the algorithm additionally chooses $\gamma \in \mathbb{Z}_N$ and $h \in \mathbb{G}_p$ at random. The public key is

$$mpk = (g_p, g_r, Q = g_q \cdot R_0, P = e(g_p, h)^\gamma, \{H_{1,i} = h_{1,i} \cdot R_{1,i}, H_{2,i} = h_{2,i} \cdot R_{2,i}\}_{i=1}^n)$$

and the master secret key is $psk = (p, q, r, g_q, h^{-\gamma}, \{h_{1,i}, h_{2,i}\}_{i=1}^n)$.

Algorithm PoKGen($osk, \vec{v}$) *and* PrKGen($psk, \vec{v}$). Parse $\vec{v}$ as $(v_1, \ldots, v_n)$ where $v_i \in \mathbb{Z}_N$. The algorithm picks random $r_{1,i}, r_{2,i} \in \mathbb{Z}_p$ for $1 \leq i \leq n$, random $R_5 \in \mathbb{G}_r$, random $f_1, f_2 \in \mathbb{Z}_q$, and random $Q_6 \in \mathbb{G}_q$. For the predicate-only encryption scheme, it outputs a secret key

$$osk_{\vec{v}} = \begin{pmatrix} K_0 = R_5 \cdot Q_6 \cdot \prod_{i=1}^n h_{1,i}^{-r_{1,i}} \cdot h_{2,i}^{-r_{2,i}}, \\ \{K_{1,i} = g_p^{r_{1,i}} \cdot g_q^{f_1 \cdot v_i}, K_{2,i} = g_p^{r_{2,i}} \cdot g_q^{f_2 \cdot v_i}\}_{i=1}^n \end{pmatrix}.$$

For the predicate encryption scheme with messages, the secret key $sk_{\vec{v}}$ is the same as $osk_{\vec{v}}$ except for

$$K_0 = R_5 \cdot Q_6 \cdot h^{-\gamma} \cdot \prod_{i=1}^n h_{1,i}^{-r_{1,i}} \cdot h_{2,i}^{-r_{2,i}}.$$

Algorithm PoEnc($opk, \vec{x}$) *and* PrEnc($mpk, \vec{x}, m$). Parse $\vec{x}$ as $(x_1, \ldots, x_n)$ where $x_i \in \mathbb{Z}_N$. The algorithm picks random $s, \alpha, \beta \in \mathbb{Z}_N$ and random $R_{3,i}, R_{4,i} \in \mathbb{G}_r$ for $1 \leq i \leq n$. For the predicate-only encryption scheme, it outputs the ciphertext

$$C = \begin{pmatrix} C_0 = g_p^s, \{C_{1,i} = H_{1,i}^s \cdot Q^{\alpha \cdot x_i} \cdot R_{3,i}, \\ C_{2,i} = H_{2,i}^s \cdot Q^{\beta \cdot x_i} \cdot R_{4,i}\}_{i=0}^n \end{pmatrix}.$$

For the predicate encryption scheme with messages notice that $m \in \mathbb{G}_T$. The ciphertext is

$$
C = \begin{pmatrix} C' = m \cdot P^s, C_0 = g_p^s, \\ \{C_{1,i} = H_{1,i}^s \cdot Q^{\alpha \cdot x_i} \cdot R_{3,i}, \\ C_{2,i} = H_{2,i}^s \cdot Q^{\beta \cdot x_i} \cdot R_{4,i}\}_{i=0}^n \end{pmatrix}.
$$

Algorithm $\mathsf{PoDec}(osk_{\vec{v}}, C)$ *and* $\mathsf{PrDec}(sk_{\vec{v}}, C)$. The predicate-only encryption outputs whether the following equation is equal to 1

$$
e(C_0, K_0) \cdot \prod_{i=1}^n e(C_{1,i}, K_{1,i}) \cdot e(C_{2,i}, K_{2,i}).
$$

The predicate encryption scheme with messages outputs the result of the following equation

$$
C' \cdot e(C_0, K_0) \cdot \prod_{i=1}^n e(C_{1,i}, K_{1,i}) \cdot e(C_{2,i}, K_{2,i}).
$$

Updaticator: Updating Billions of Devices by an Efficient, Scalable and Secure Software Update Distribution over Untrusted Cache-enabled Networks

Moreno Ambrosin[1,*], Christoph Busold[2], Mauro Conti[1,**],
Ahmad-Reza Sadeghi[3], and Matthias Schunter[4]

[1] University of Padua, Italy
{lastname}@math.unipd.it
[2] Intel CRI-SC, TU Darmstadt, Germany
christoph.busold@trust.cased.de
[3] CASED/TU Darmstadt, Germany
ahmad.sadeghi@trust.cased.de
[4] Intel Labs, Darmstadt, Germany
schunter@acm.org

Abstract. Secure and fast distribution of software updates and patches is essential for improving functionality and security of computer systems. Today, each device downloads updates individually from a software provider distribution server. Unfortunately, this approach does not scale to large systems with billions of devices where the network bandwidth of the server and the local Internet gateway become bottlenecks. Cache-enabled Network (CN) services (either proprietary, as Akamai, or open Content-Distribution Networks) can reduce these bottlenecks. However, they do not offer security guarantees against potentially untrusted CN providers that try to threaten the confidentiality of the updates or the privacy of the users. In this paper, we propose Updaticator, the first protocol for software updates over Cache-enabled Networks that is scalable to billions of concurrent device updates while being secure against malicious networks. We evaluate our proposal considering Named-Data Networking, a novel instance of Cache-enabled overlay Networks. Our analysis and experimental evaluation show that Updaticator removes the bottlenecks of individual device-update distribution, by reducing the network load at the distribution server: from linear in the number of devices to a constant, even if billions of devices are requesting updates. Furthermore, when compared to the state-of-the-art individual device-update mechanisms, the download time with Updaticator is negligible, due to local caching.

* Corresponding author.
** Mauro Conti is supported by a Marie Curie Fellowship funded by the European Commission under the agreement n. PCIG11-GA-2012-321980. This work has been partially supported by the TENACE PRIN Project 20103P34XC funded by the Italian MIUR. Part of this work has been performed while Mauro Conti was visiting TU Darmstadt thanks to a German DAAD fellowship.

M. Kutyłowski and J. Vaidya (Eds.): ESORICS 2014, Part I, LNCS 8712, pp. 76–93, 2014.

Keywords: Software Updates, Secure Updates Distribution, Attribute-based Encryption, Internet of Things, Cache-enabled Network.

1 Introduction

The growing diffusion of electronic devices creates new issues and challenges. Consider billions of lighting devices [29], embedded controllers, or mobile and wearable devices. More generally, the so-called Internet of Things is extending the Internet to billions of devices that need to be connected and updated. One of the resulting challenges is efficient and secure distribution of software updates to these devices. According to the 2013 US-CERT Security Alerts [1], most of the new software vulnerabilities can be resolved by applying software updates. Hence, fast and secure delivery of software updates plays a key role in securing software systems. In particular, once a vulnerability is published (e.g., see the case of the recent SSL "Heartbleed" vulnerability [18]), the system becomes exposed to a large base of potential adversaries. Here, a fast update is fundamental.

Most of the existing remote update protocols focus on ensuring integrity and authenticity of the transmitted updates, i.e., they guarantee that only untampered updates from a legitimate source will be installed on the device. However, in many cases software updates are required to be confidential. Examples include protection of embedded software against reverse-engineering or the distribution of valuable map updates in automotive systems and portable devices. A simplistic approach to achieve confidentiality for updates is securing the communication between client and software provider server applying end-to-end encryption (e.g., using SSL [31]). Each client device then requests and downloads the latest available update directly from the software provider, encrypted and signed by the software update source. Although this approach guarantees confidentiality and authenticity of software updates, it is not suitable for large-scale systems, since it would not scale due to the load on the software distribution servers, which is increasing linearly in the number of devices.

To mitigate this efficiency problem, software providers usually rely on third-party distribution infrastructures [5], e.g., Content Delivery Networks (CDNs) such as Akamai [2] or Windows Azure CDN [33]. These infrastructures apply in-network caching and replication strategies in order to speed-up content distribution. However, by using third-party distribution networks, software providers can no longer apply end-to-end encryption. Instead, they must allow point-to-point encryption between client devices and the distribution network, and between the distribution network and the software provider [3]. This poses security and privacy issues, since transferred updates are cached unencrypted by each distribution network server, and the software provider or the distribution nodes know which device (or user) is asking for what.

Our Contribution. In this paper, we propose a new solution for efficient distribution of confidential software updates that is scalable and optimized for untrusted distribution media which support in-network caching. The contributions of this paper are threefold:

i) We present Updaticator, a protocol for efficient distribution of confidential software updates, optimized for untrusted cache-enabled distribution media. The protocol reduces bandwidth consumption and server load, provides end-to-end security, and is scalable to billions of devices. To enable caching, one main goal is to encrypt each given update under a corresponding symmetric key to ensure identical ciphertexts for all devices receiving this update. These keys are then distributed using Attribute-based Encryption (ABE).

ii) We define a system model and security requirements for this class of protocols and analyze the security of the proposed protocol.

iii) We describe a prototype implementation of our protocol on Named-Data Networking [21] as broadcast medium for efficient and secure distribution of updates, and evaluate its performance.

Organization. The remainder of the paper is organized as follows. In Sec. 2 we describe the system model and the security requirements for the design of Updaticator. In Sec. 3 we introduce the primitives used in the description of our protocol. In Sec. 4 we introduce the Updaticator protocol while in Sec. 5 we provide a security analysis, based on the security requirements introduced in Sec. 2. In Sec. 6 we present an experimental evaluation, which demonstrates the benefits of our solution. Finally, in Sec. 7 we analyze current state-of-the-art approaches to updates delivery and differentiate our results. Eventually, we conclude in Sec. 8 and describe possible future work.

2   System Model and Requirements

In this section we introduce the system model, on which we base our work, and derive the security requirements for our software updates distribution protocol.

2.1   System Model

In our model, groups of *clients* request software updates from a specified update source. As shown in Fig. 1, we assume the presence of an *Update Server* (*US*), as introduced in [14]. Each client queries *US* to retrieve information about the latest available update package. Furthermore, we assume the presence of a *Distribution Server* (*DS*), which is responsible for efficient dissemination of updates. For the sake of generality, we also assume the presence of a *Policy Server* (*PS*), that generates keys, imports updates into the system, and defines the update policy, i.e., which update should be provided to which device.

2.2   Security Requirements

We now define the desirable security requirements for Updaticator.

Confidentiality. Our solution for update distribution must be able to guarantee the confidentiality of updates, since we assume the distributed updates to be proprietary data. This means that each client should be able to decrypt a software update if and only if it has been authorized by *PS*.

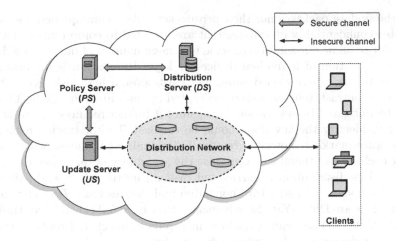

Fig. 1. System model

Authenticity and Integrity. Our solution for update distribution must guarantee the possibility for all the clients to verify the integrity and authenticity of the downloaded software updates, in order to prevent attackers from replacing legitimate software updates with malicious code.

Freshness. Network caches reduce network traffic and server load. However, it is possible that device requests are satisfied by outdated updates still in cache. Furthermore, attackers could intentionally mask the presence of new updates in order to prevent devices from patching security issues. For this reason, our solution should provide clients with the means to verify whether the answer to its update request is fresh, i.e., corresponds to the most recent update released by PS. We achieve this by introducing a freshness interval Δt that defines the maximum age of the latest update information.

2.3 Adversary Model

Informally, we consider the following attack scenarios:

(1) Legitimate devices could try to obtain software updates which are not intended for them.
(2) Network attackers could try to get access to confidential updates or compromise devices by injecting unauthorized or modified updates.

More formally, the adversary model is defined as follows: the policy server PS is an internal server that feeds information to the externally-facing servers US and DS. We assume that the update infrastructure consisting of US and PS is secure (including the internal communication between US and PS) and trusted by all devices that are updated by these servers. For the confidentiality of a given update, we assume that the client devices receiving this update neither reveal the update packages nor their private keys. As a consequence, we cannot guarantee confidentiality of updates that are targeted to compromised devices.

In order to allow our solution to scale to a huge number of devices, we do not consider revocation of individual devices or keys. Revocation is important for broadcast media, where cloned subscriber cards pose a high risk. For software updates, in contrast, rebroadcasts of decrypted updates are more likely. This risk cannot be mitigated by revocation alone, since it further requires traitor tracing in order to identify the key that should be revoked. Traitor tracing techniques such as watermarking, however, require individualized updates, which would prevent caching and thereby compromise the scalability of our scheme.

The update distribution is carried out over an untrusted network, therefore neither the update infrastructure nor individual devices trust *DS*. The considered attackers are Dolev-Yao [13] adversaries that have full control over the communication channel and can eavesdrop, manipulate, inject and replay messages between any device and the update infrastructure.

3   Background

We now provide some background knowledge, introducing Attribute-based Encryption, and Named-Data Networking.

3.1   Attribute-Based Encryption

Attribute-based Encryption (ABE), first proposed by Sahai and Waters in 2005 [30], is a type of public-key encryption that allows fine-grained data access control based on *attributes*. With ABE, the data owner defines an *access policy* w, i.e., a combination of attributes that a legitimate user must own in order to access the data. An access policy can be represented as a Boolean expression, specifying the attributes required to access the data. For example, suppose we define three different attributes, *Student*, *MSc*, and *Professor*. If we want to make some data accessible only to users that are professors or MSc students, a possible access policy can be expressed as $\{\{Student \wedge MSc\} \vee Professor\}$.

In our work, we consider Ciphertext-Policy Attribute-based Encryption (CP-ABE), an Identity-based Encryption scheme first introduced by Bethencourt et al. [6], and then refined and extended in several other works [36], [35]. With CP-ABE, the access policy is bound to the ciphertext, while users' private keys are generated based on the users' attributes. CP-ABE allows the definition of high-level policies, and therefore is particularly useful in scenarios where an entity wants to restrict the access of a piece of information only to a subset of users within the same broadcast domain [15]. Moreover, CP-ABE is resistant against collusion attacks by design [6].

A generic CP-ABE scheme provides the following four basic algorithms:

– SETUP(). This algorithm generates public key pk^{ABE} and master secret mk^{ABE}.

- KEYGEN($mk^{ABE}, Attr^C$). This algorithm takes as input the master key mk^{ABE} and the user attribute list $Attr^C$, and outputs the user's private key $sk^{ABE,C}$.
- ABENC$_{pk^{ABE},w}(m)$. The encryption algorithm takes the public key pk^{ABE}, the specified access policy w, and the message m as input. It outputs a ciphertext that can only be decrypted by a user with an attribute list $Attr^C$ such that $Attr^C$ satisfies the access policy w.
- ABDEC$_{sk^{ABE},C}(c)$. The decryption algorithm takes as input the public key pk^{ABE}, the private key $sk^{ABE,C}$ of user C, and the ciphertext c. It returns the plaintext m if and only if user attribute list $Attr^C$ satisfy the access policy w.

3.2   Named-Data Networking

Named-Data Networking (NDN) [21] is a new Internet architecture optimized for efficient content distribution. NDN is an instantiation of the Content-Centric Networking (CCN) approach [19], in which data is accessed by name instead of location, and the routing is based on content names. In NDN, each content is bound to a unique hierarchically-structured name, formed by different components separated by "/". As an example, a possible name for the opinions webpage of the CNN website is /cnn/politics/opinion, while /cnn/politics/ is a *name prefix* for that name.

Communication in NDN is *consumer-driven*: each consumer requests data by issuing *interest packets*, which are then satisfied by *data packets* provided by content *producers*. When a consumer sends a request for a particular content, the corresponding interest is forwarded to the first-hop router. Each NDN router maintains two lookup tables: Pending Interest Table (PIT) and Forwarding Information Base (FIB). PIT is used to keep track of all the pending requests for a given content name. Each entry of the PIT is in the form $<$ *interest, arrival_interfaces* $>$, where *arrival_interface* is the set of the router's interfaces to which the interest have been already forwarded. FIB is populated by a name-based routing protocol, and used by routers to forward outgoing interests to the right interface(s). When a router receives an interest, it first checks its PIT to determine whether another interest for the same name is currently outstanding. If the same name is already inside the PIT, then the interest arrival interface is searched inside the corresponding *arrival_interfaces* set. If the router finds a match, the interest is discarded, otherwise, the new interface is added to *arrival_interfaces* set, but the interest is not forwarded. If no matching entry was found in the PIT, a new PIT entry is created, and the interest is forwarded based on the FIB table. Once received the interest, the producer of the content injects a matching data packet into the network, thus *satisfying* the interest. The data packet is then forwarded towards the consumer, traversing, in reverse, the path of the corresponding interest.

An important feature of NDN is distributed caching, which is intended to reduce traffic and load of the network. Once a data packet is received by a router, it is stored inside its local cache, named Content Store (CS), according to some cache policies. In this way, all subsequent interests matching the same data packet previously stored inside the CS, will be immediately satisfied with the local copy of the content, thus being no longer forwarded.

Most currently existing implementations of NDN are built as an overlay on top of the TCP/UDP transport protocols, e.g., NDNx [23]. This allows easy integration with the current Internet infrastructure.

4   Updaticator: Our Scalable Update Protocol with End-to-End Security

We now describe Updaticator, our solution for scalable and secure software updates distribution over Cache-enabled networks. Our protocol comprises three different phases:

(1) *Update publication.* In this phase, a new available update is published. The Policy Server (PS) generates and sends the access policy for the update package, and a new random encryption key for this update, to the Update Server (US). Then, PS sends the encrypted package to the Distribution Server (DS), which takes care of its distribution.

(2) *Update selection.* In this phase, a client (C) checks for the presence of new updates, issuing a request to US. The information is used to eventually retrieve a new software update.

(3) *Update retrieval.* In this phase, C downloads the update package, issuing a request to DS.

Without loss of generality, we now provide a detailed description of each phase of our protocol on top of NDN.

Notation. In the remainder of this paper, we assume that both PS and US have a key pair, (sk^{PS}, pk^{PS}) and (sk^{US}, pk^{US}), respectively, that they can use for generating signatures. We refer to pkg_u as the software update package, and to id_u as its identifier, calculated as $\text{HASH}(pkg_u)$, where HASH is a collision-resistant hash function. Moreover, we suppose that each software update package pkg_u has an associated access policy w_u, set by PS. Each client C has an attribute list $Attr^C$, which is represented by his private key $sk^{ABE,C}$. We indicate with k_u the symmetric key used to encrypt pkg_u, and with ENC_{k_u} and DEC_{k_u} symmetric encryption and decryption functions, respectively. We also indicate with SIGN_{sk^X} the computation of a signature using secret key sk^X, and with VERIFY_{pk^X} the verification of a signature.

On Scalability. In typical deployments, devices are connected to the Internet via a gateway with limited bandwidth. Our main goal is to ensure scalability to billions of devices, i.e., to ensure that the network load on the distribution server as well as the network load on the gateway is constant in the number of devices and only depends on the stable number of available updates. This is achieved by ensuring that all the phases of our protocol, involving client devices, are non-interactive and cacheable. Regarding the complexity of CP-ABE policies, each device class can be targeted with one instance of the CP-ABE scheme. Furthermore, each device usually has a limited set of (licensing) options that determine the set of updates (and corresponding keys) this device may receive. Therefore the complexity does not increase with the number of devices.

4.1   Update Publication Phase

The update publication phase of Updaticator is presented in Fig. 2. When a new software update package, pkg_u, is released, PS computes its identifier id_u as the hash value of pkg_u, and generates a new key k_u, for symmetric encryption.

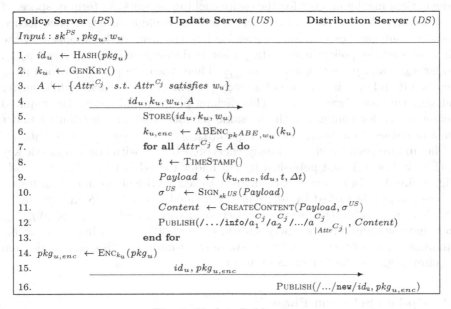

Fig. 2. Update Publication

Then, PS associates an access policy w_u to pkg_u, creates the set A of all the existing attribute combinations that match with w_u, and finally forwards the tuple (id_u, k_u, w_u, A) to US, where it is stored inside a database (Fig. 2, lines 1-5). After that, US proceeds with the publication of the symmetric key k_u. Here, the idea is to allow scalable distribution of the encryption key k_u, at the same time taking advantage from in-network caching provided by the NDN distribution network, and providing fine-grained access control to k_u. We achieve this with the aid of CP-ABE. In our solution, each client has an attribute-specific decryption key $sk^{ABE,C}$ corresponding to its set of attributes $Attr^C$, while US has the public key pk^{ABE} that is used for encryption. US encrypts the key k_u with the public key pk^{ABE}, together with the access policy w_u (Fig. 2, line 6). Then, US records the current timestamp t and determines the time interval Δt within which the update information should be considered *fresh* by clients. This will allow clients to verify the *freshness* of the retrieved information (Fig. 2, lines 8-9). Finally, US produces a signature σ^{US} of id_u, k_u, t and Δt (Fig. 2, line 10), and publishes the NDN content $data = (id_u, k_{u,enc}, t, \Delta t, \sigma^{US})$, according to a specific naming scheme (Fig. 2, line 12). A possible example is the following. Suppose $Attr^C = [a_1^C, a_2^C, ..., a_n^C]$ being the list of attributes of client C. US distributes $data$ under the NDN name $/\ldots/\texttt{info}/a_1^C/a_2^C/\ldots/a_n^C$, for each $Attr^C$ that satisfies the access policy w_u. Let A be the set of all m different possible combinations of client attributes that satisfies the access policy w_u. US will publish the content $data$ under m different names, thus treated by NDN as m different contents. Let $size(data)$ be the size of the packet $data$. In the worst case, the same content will be cached m times by the distribution network, with a theoretical maximum cost for the entire caching network, in term of space, of $m \cdot size(data)$. However, optimized caching policies could reduce the space needed to cache contents. For example, a possible improvement is the adoption of the following caching policy: each data packet is decomposed into payload p_{data}, header h_{data} and packet signature sig_{data}. Then, the data packet payload p_{data} is cached if and only if p_{data} is not already present in router cache, while header and signature are always stored. This caching policy could reduce the required caching space for contents with the same payload that are distributed under different names, to a maximum of $m \cdot [size(h_{data}) + size(sig_{data})] + size(p_{data})$.

The update package pkg_u is finally encrypted by PS with the symmetric key k_u (Fig. 2, line 14), and published by DS under the NDN name $/\ldots/\texttt{new}/id_u$ (Fig. 2, line 16). In this way, each interest issued by the client, for the software update package identified by id_u, will be satisfied either by DS directly or by a NDN router within the distribution network, with a cached copy of $pkg_{u,enc}$. Note that the communication between PS, US and DS does not impose a specific communication protocol to be used. We only assume that this communication is secure (e.g., via the SSL/TLS protocol).

4.2 Update Selection Phase

The update selection phase of Updaticator is presented in Fig. 3. In order to obtain information on the latest available update, a client C sends a request specifying its attributes $Attr^C$, i.e., issuing an interest for $/\ldots/\texttt{info}/a_1^C/a_2^C/\ldots/a_n^C$ (Fig. 3, line 1). The interest is forwarded to the NDN distribution network, which either satisfies it with a matching copy of the required content, or forwards the interest up to US, if no matching contents are available. In the latter case, the information is then stored by the routers on its path back to the client (Fig. 3, lines 2-5).

Upon receiving the response, the client first verifies the freshness of the received content, i.e., if the software update information is outdated (Fig. 3, line 6). This is done checking if the value $t + \Delta t$ is greater than the current time. If the information is fresh, C proceeds by verifying the signature σ^{US} and checking if id_u is already contained in $UpdatesList$, the list of all the updates previously

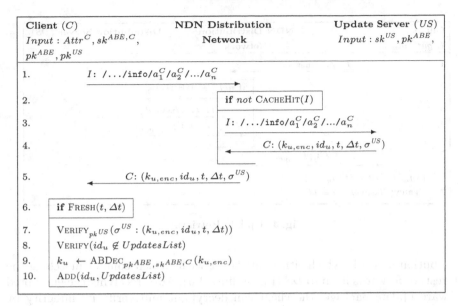

Fig. 3. Update Selection

installed by C (Fig. 3, lines 7-8). If all these tests pass, C decrypts $k_{u,enc}$ with its secret key $sk^{ABE,C}$ and finally adds id_u to *UpdatesList* (Fig. 3, lines 9-10).

In case either the authentication or the freshness verification fails, C will repeat the update selection procedure, this time requesting the update information directly from *US*. In NDN, this can be achieved by setting the AnswerOriginKind parameter of the interest packet to 0 [22]. In this way, NDN routers will never satisfy the interest with cached content, but route it up to *US* instead. It should be noted that in this case, the newly received message is expected to be fresh, since it should originate directly from *US*. Otherwise the client will conclude that it is under a DoS attack. Similarly, if the response is not authentic, the client can detect the presence of a possible DoS attack, which prevents the client from downloading new updates. Finally, only in the case in which the newly received response is authentic and fresh, and $id_u \in UpdatesList$, the client will conclude that there are no available updates. Since any client whose attributes match the access policy w_u, can decrypt the response *data*, the same content can be cached by the network and served to all the clients with the same attributes.

4.3 Update Retrieval Phase

Fig. 4 shows the Updaticator update retrieval phase. After obtaining a valid update identifier id_u and the corresponding symmetric key k_u, the client can download the encrypted update package $pkg_{u,enc}$ from *DS*, specifying only the update identifier id_u, i.e., issuing an interest for /.../new/id_u (Fig. 4, line 1). Similar to the update selection phase, the interest is forwarded to the NDN

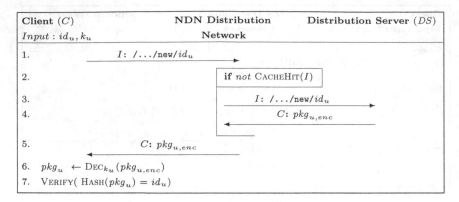

Fig. 4. Update Retrieval

distribution network, which either satisfies it with cached content matching the interest, or forwards it up to DS (Fig. 4, lines 2-5). After receiving the encrypted software update package, the client can decrypt it and verify its integrity by comparing $\mathrm{HASH}(pkg_u)$ with id_u (Fig. 4, lines 6-7).

It should be noted that the probability of the request hitting a cache closer to the client increases with the number of clients downloading the same software update. Finally, for low-memory devices the encryption of the distributed software updates can be performed with the encryption technique proposed by Nilsson et al. in [25]. This technique splits the update in fragments. In reverse order, for each fragment a hash is computed and the hash of each fragment is stored together with the following fragment, i.e., forming a hash chain. Only the fragment containing the information about the update, together with the hash of the first fragment, is signed. In this way, a client can verify the authenticity and integrity of the first fragment, and of all the other fragments verifying the hash chain, thus allowing "load-and-install" of the update.

5 Security Analysis

We now provide a security analysis regarding the requirements from Sec. 2.2.

Confidentiality. Updaticator provides software update confidentiality through the use of symmetric encryption. During the update publication phase of our protocol, PS generates a key k_u and associates it with the new software update package pkg_u. Since each key k_u is randomly chosen, we can assume that it is unique for each pkg_u. Following the assumption that the publication infrastructure is secure, during this phase an attacker can neither extract k_u from PS or US, nor access the unencrypted update package. Furthermore, only the encrypted package $pkg_{u,enc}$ and the hash of pkg_u, i.e., id_u, are transmitted or published during each phase. As a consequence, since the cryptographic primitives are assumed to be secure, both values do not allow the attacker to gain information on the unencrypted update package or key k_u. The confidentiality of the update package can therefore be reduced to the confidentiality of k_u, i.e., an attacker can obtain the update package if and only if she is in possession of k_u, which she only can obtain through the update selection protocol. The update selection phase uses CP-ABE in order to distribute k_u. Each client has a decryption key sk^{ABE}, which matches exactly its set of attributes. Only clients with a matching list of attributes will be able to decrypt it. We can conclude that the confidentiality of each software update is assured.

Authenticity and Integrity. During update publication phase, the update identifier id_u is computed as the hash value of pkg_u. Then, during the update selection phase id_u is provided by *US* in response to each device request inside a signed message. Hence, the client can verify the authenticity of id_u. As the client verifies the hash of the package against id_u during the update retrieval phase of Updaticator, and the hash function is collision-resistant, the authenticity and integrity of the update package depends solely on the authenticity and integrity of id_u. Since *US* is trusted and the signature scheme is assumed to be secure, id_u is authentic and the client can conclude that the package is authentic as well.

Freshness of the Interactive Update Selection Protocol. During update selection phase, the information about the latest software update available is distributed in a cacheable form, i.e., it is intended for offline updates and is identical for a class of clients. Consequently, such a response can also be provided by caches or by offline media. When *US* first publishes a new available update package pkg_u, it also specifies the publication timestamp t and a time interval Δt, that indicates the time interval in which a client should consider the information fresh. A client can verify information freshness by checking its current timestamp against $t+\Delta t$. If the content is not fresh, i.e., not received before $t+\Delta t$, the client, once verified data authenticity, requests the same information directly from *US*. For this reason, we conclude that Updaticator guarantees content freshness.

6   Prototype and Evaluation

We now present an evaluation of the proposed updates distribution scheme. While arbitrary Cache-enabled Networks can be used, we benchmarked our scheme using a distribution network built with Named-Data Networking as an overlay network on top of TCP/IP. In this scenario, NDN nodes can be distributed over the Internet and can be used for cached distribution of arbitrary content including updates.

6.1   Evaluation Setup

In order to provide a large-scale evaluation of the use of Named-Data Networking (NDN) to build a network for efficient software update distribution, we carried out our tests on the ns-3 simulator [24]. We focused on update requests generated by always-on-line devices, which check for updates periodically. We assumed that update requests are generated in bursts, i.e., n devices check for updates and/or download an update within a *time window interval* $tw = [t_u, t_u + \Delta t]$.

We compared content download via the HTTP protocol and a distribution network built with NDN as a TCP/IP overlay. In the former case, we published the content through an `thttpd` Web Server [32], while in the latter case, we published the content on an NDN repository built using the NDNx protocol [23]. The integration of such an application with the ns-3 simulator has been achieved by leveraging the DCE module [12] of ns-3. Our experiments were carried out on a DFN-like topology [11], depicted in Fig. 5.

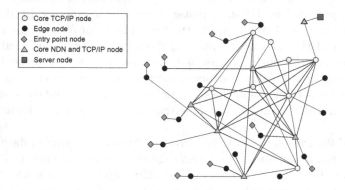

Fig. 5. DFN-like network topology

In our simulated topology, we introduced three different types of nodes. *Core nodes* represent the main part of the topology and are connected through 1 Gbps point-to-point links. We introduced two types of core nodes: NDN-capable core nodes (triangles in Fig. 5), which can communicate via the NDN protocol, and simple TCP/IP core nodes (white circles in Fig. 5). *Edge nodes* (dark circles in Fig. 5) are used to access the network. In our simulation, edge nodes are connected to core nodes through 100 Mpbs links. *Entry nodes* (rhombus in Fig. 5) are nodes to which all clients are connected. Each client can perform both HTTP and NDN requests.

We considered an increasing number of clients, from 100 to 900, connected on the entry point nodes. Each device requested a content of 1 MB, starting the download at a uniformly chosen time t in $tw = [t_u, t_u + 30]$ seconds. We then measured the average Content Retrieval Time (CRT) for the devices and the total amount of traffic at the server side. Moreover, in order to provide a complete vision of the advantages in adopting a Cache-enabled Network, we analyzed the bandwidth utilization.

6.2   Network Load on the Update Server

The first result of our analysis was that our approach indeed reduces the network load on the update server from linear (or worse) to just a constant level (Fig. 6).

This is achieved by the caching of updates over the NDN distribution network so that the server only needs to deliver a small number of original copies of each update to populate the caches. Fig. 6a and Fig. 6b depict average data traffic sent and received by the server. Results are shown for a time window of 30 seconds. The results show that the use of a Cache-enabled Network as NDN highly reduces the load at the server side from linear (please note that graphs in Fig. 6a and Fig. 6b are represented in log-scale) to constant, thus allowing system scalability and preventing DDoS attacks against DS.

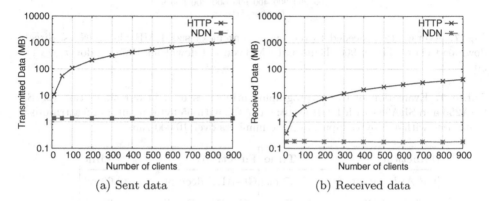

(a) Sent data   (b) Received data

Fig. 6. Sent and received data by the server, NDN vs. direct download (content size 1 MB; time window of 30 s; log-scale transforms linear growth into a log curve)

6.3   Time Required to Retrieve an Update

The introduction of a Cache-enabled Network also reduces the average Content Retrieval Time (CRT) (Fig. 7) to a constant even for large numbers of devices. The traditional scheme without caching only performs for a small number of devices. For larger numbers the performance drops dramatically. Furthermore, under load the individual times vary within in a wide range. This makes the individual update times largely unpredictable.

Crypto Performance. For performance testing purposes, we adopted the `cpabe` library [9], which provides an implementation of the CP-ABE scheme proposed by Walters et al. [6], and the `openssl` library [27]. We selected AES-CBC, with key size of 256 bits for the symmetric encryption of the software update package and the symmetric key k_u, and adopted the RSA algorithm with a 4096 bits key for content signing. Moreover, we considered SHA256 and SHA384 for hashing. Our tests have been conducted on a system equipped with two 2.4 GHz Intel Core[TM] 2 Duo CPUs and 4 GB RAM and a 256 bit key k_u for AES-CBC. Results are reported in Table 1.

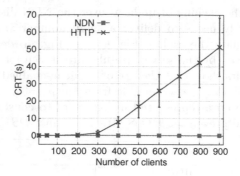

Fig. 7. Average time needed to retrieve a content of size 1 MB via NDN vs. direct download via HTTP for 900 clients and 1 MB content download; time window $t_{MAX} = 30$

Table 1. Evaluation of the cryptographic primitives used in our simulation (AES, SHA256 and SHA384 with 1 MB input; CP-ABE with 65 bytes input and 5 attributes; signatures with 438 bytes input; average numbers over 10,000 runs

Function	Time	Function	Time
CP-ABE encrypt	77.47 ms	CP-ABE decrypt	32.62 ms
AES-256-CBC encrypt	28.77 ms	AES-256-CBC decrypt	26.61 ms
RSA signature create	31.64 ms	RSA signature verify	5.20 ms
SHA256	13.3 ms	SHA384	10.99 ms

6.4 Power Consumption of the Client Devices

Reducing the network load and required computation is essential in order to limit power consumption. This is particularly true for resource-constrained devices. The introduction of the freshness interval "Δt" allows each device to remain off-line most of the time (only checking for updates once in each time interval), and also provides the possibility for software distributors to determine the best tradeoff between client device power consumption and software update freshness.

7   Related Work

In this section we provide an overview of previous work related to secure software update distribution. Bellissimo et al. [5] provide a security analysis of existing update systems, which reveals several weaknesses such as vulnerabilities against man-in-the-middle attacks. This emphasizes the importance of secure software update distribution mechanisms.

We focus on encrypted updates that can be cached. Due to space limitations, we do not survey non-cacheable updates distribution protocols such as the one proposed in [14], or mechanisms that do not provide encryption such as the one in [8]. Instead, we contrast our work to related work on updates using broadcast encryption as the underlying key management mechanism. Adelsbach et al. [4] propose to use broadcast encryption to distribute confidential software updates to embedded controllers inside an automotive system. Therefore their solution provides confidentiality and at the same time enables caching of updates, since the encrypted update is identical for all devices. Misra et al. [20] propose to use broadcast encryption to ensure confidentiality of a Content-Distribution Network built on top of NDN. Unfortunately, in this work the authors do not provide a cacheable "content selection" mechanism.

Similarly to OMA DRM [26], our scheme allows cacheable distribution of content (by separating the encrypted object from the associated decryption key). However, in order to retrieve the decryption key and the associated access policy, OMA DRM requires each client to establish an interactive session with the Policy Server. By using CP-ABE, our protocol does not require this interaction hence allowing a cacheable and scalable distribution of the decryption key.

We believe that broadcast encryption schemes (such as the ones in [7] and [17]) are not suitable for our system model. Indeed, adopting a broadcast encryption scheme, the Policy Server would need to define a cryptographic broadcast system for each group of devices, hence complicating the key management for both the Policy Server and the devices. Moreover, public-key broadcast encryption schemes do not provide constant size encryption keys, and therefore do not scale to billions of devices. Finally, while the broadcast encryption scheme proposed in [10] achieves constant size keys, the group management and the encryption must be carried out by the same entity. This is a limitation in our system model, since the creation and management of the device group (usually done by the device vendor) and the encryption of a targeted update (usually done by software vendor) could no longer be separated. In contrast, CP-ABE provides constant size keys, while allowing encryption using public parameters [16].

8   Conclusions and Future Work

Fast and secure software update distribution is a key issue in modern IT systems, particularly when the updates concern the fix of security vulnerabilities or are essential for business. As shown by our analysis, our approach is the first solution that makes large-scale updates practical for billions of devices. Future work in this area will focus on the optimization of software update distribution for local networks and resource-constrained devices. Specific constraints coming from these environments call for novel solutions for these devices. In particular, those solutions should be able to coordinate different devices to maintain the compatibility among them (e.g., specifying constraints via policies), and being resilient to malicious devices that might hinder the success of the proposal.

Finally, we plan to provide revocation of individual devices. This aspect becomes an essential requirement in a stronger adversary model, where we consider compromised clients as possible attackers. Ostrovsky et al. [28] propose a CP-ABE scheme to specify revoked users directly inside the access policy of the ciphertext. However, the size of their policy grows linearly with the number of revoked clients. Therefore we are also looking into other possible solutions, e.g., hybrid schemes such as [35] and [34]. Furthermore, this requires a way to identify the source of a leaked update (traitor tracing), which is particularly challenging in our system model, since existing solutions prevent the cacheability of updates.

References

1. 2013 US-CERT Techical Security Alerts,
   http://www.us-cert.gov/ncas/alerts/2013
2. Akamai Content Delivery Network, http://www.akamai.com
3. Akamai Secure Content Delivery, http://www.akamai.com/dl/
   feature_sheets/fs_edgesuite_securecontentdelivery.pdf
4. Adelsbach, A., Huber, U., Sadeghi, A.-R.: Secure Software Delivery and Installation in Embedded Systems. In: Deng, R.H., Bao, F., Pang, H., Zhou, J. (eds.) ISPEC 2005. LNCS, vol. 3439, pp. 255–267. Springer, Heidelberg (2005)
5. Bellissimo, A., Burgess, J., Fu, K.: Secure Software Updates: Disappointments and New Challenges. In: 1st USENIX Workshop on Hot Topics in Security, pp. 37–43. USENIX Association, Berkeley (2006)
6. Bethencourt, J., Sahai, A., Waters, B.: Ciphertext-Policy Attribute-Based Encryption. In: 2007 IEEE Symposium on Security and Privacy, pp. 321–334. IEEE Computer Society, Washington (2007)
7. Boneh, D., Gentry, C., Waters, B.: Collusion Resistant Broadcast Encryption with Short Ciphertexts and Private Keys. In: Shoup, V. (ed.) CRYPTO 2005. LNCS, vol. 3621, pp. 258–275. Springer, Heidelberg (2005)
8. Cameron, D., Liu, J.: apt-p2p: A Peer-to-Peer Distribution System for Software Package Releases and Updates. In: 28th IEEE Conference on Computer Communications, pp. 864–872. IEEE, New York (2009)
9. Cpabe toolkit, http://hms.isi.jhu.edu/acsc/cpabe/#documentation
10. Delerablée, C., Paillier, P., Pointcheval, D.: Fully Collusion Secure Dynamic Broadcast Encryption with Constant-Size Ciphertexts or Decryption Keys. In: Takagi, T., Okamoto, T., Okamoto, E., Okamoto, T. (eds.) Pairing 2007. LNCS, vol. 4575, pp. 39–59. Springer, Heidelberg (2007)
11. Deutsches forschungsnetz (DFN), https://www.dfn.de/en/
12. Direct Code Execution (DCE),
    https://www.nsnam.org/overview/projects/direct-code-execution/
13. Dolev, D., Yao, A.C.: On the Security of Public Key Protocols. IEEE Transactions on Information Theory 29(2), 198–208 (1983)
14. Gkantsidis, C., Karagiannis, T., Vojnovic, M.: Planet Scale Software Updates. In: 2006 Conference on Applications, Technologies, Architectures, and Protocols for Computer Communications, pp. 423–434. ACM, New York (2006)
15. Goyal, V., Pandey, O., Sahai, A., Waters, B.: Attribute-based Encryption for Fine-grained Access Control of Encrypted Data. In: 13th ACM Conference on Computer and Communications Security, pp. 89–98. ACM, New York (2006)
16. Guo, F., Mu, Y., Susilo, W., Wong, D.S., Varadharajan, V.: CP-ABE With Constant-Size Keys for Lightweight Devices. IEEE Transactions on Information Forensics and Security 9(5), 763–771 (2014)
17. Halevy, D., Shamir, A.: The LSD Broadcast Encryption Scheme. In: Yung, M. (ed.) CRYPTO 2002. LNCS, vol. 2442, pp. 47–60. Springer, Heidelberg (2002)

18. Heartbleed SSL protocol vulnerability,
    https://www.schneier.com/blog/archives/2014/04/heartbleed.html
19. Jacobson, V., Smetters, D.K., Thornton, J.D., Plass, M.F., Briggs, N.H., Braynard, R.L.: Networking Named Content. In: 5th International Conference on Emerging Networking Experiments and Technologies, pp. 1–12. ACM, New York (2009)
20. Misra, S., Tourani, R., Majd, N.E.: Secure Content Delivery in Information-centric Networks: Design, Implementation, and Analyses. In: 3rd ACM SIGCOMM Workshop on Information-centric Networking, pp. 73–78. ACM, New York (2013)
21. Named-Data Networking Project (NDN), http://named-data.org
22. NDNx Documentation - Interest Message,
    http://named-data.net/doc/0.1/technical/InterestMessage.html
23. NDNx – NDN protocol implementation,
    http://named-data.net/codebase/platform/moving-to-ndnx/
24. NS-3 Simulator, https://www.nsnam.org/
25. Nilsson, D.K., Roosta, T., Lindqvist, U., Valdes, A.: Key Management and Secure Software Updates in Wireless Process Control Environments. In: 1st ACM Conference on Wireless Network Security, pp. 100–108. ACM, New York (2008)
26. Open Mobile Alliance. DRM Specification ver. 2.2, Technical Report (2011)
27. OpneSSL project, https://www.openssl.org/
28. Ostrovsky, R., Sahai, A., Waters, B.: Attribute-based Encryption with Non-monotonic Access Structures. In: 14th ACM Conference on Computer and Communications Security, pp. 195–203. ACM, New York (2007)
29. Philips Hue, http://meethue.com/
30. Sahai, A., Waters, B.: Fuzzy Identity-based Encryption. In: Cramer, R. (ed.) EUROCRYPT 2005. LNCS, vol. 3494, pp. 457–473. Springer, Heidelberg (2005)
31. Samuel, J., Mathewson, N., Cappos, J., Dingledine, R.: Survivable Key Compromise in Software Update Systems. In: 17th ACM Conference on Computer and Communications Security, pp. 61–72. ACM, New York (2010)
32. thttpd web server, http://www.acme.com/software/thttpd
33. Windows Azure, http://www.windowsazure.com/en-us/
34. Yu, S., Wang, C., Ren, K., Lou, W.: Attribute Based Data Sharing with Attribute Revocation. In: 5th ACM Symposium on Information, Computer and Communications Security, pp. 261–270. ACM, New York (2010)
35. Zhiqian, X., Martin, K.M.: Dynamic User Revocation and Key Refreshing for Attribute-Based Encryption in Cloud Storage. In: 11th IEEE International Conference on Trust, Security and Privacy in Computing and Communications, pp. 844–849. IEEE, New York (2012)
36. Zhou, Z., Huang, D., Wang, Z.: Efficient Privacy-Preserving Ciphertext-Policy Attribute Based Encryption and Broadcast Encryption. IEEE Transactions on Computers PP(99) (2013)

Local Password Validation Using Self-Organizing Maps

Diogo Mónica and Carlos Ribeiro

INESC-ID, Instituto Superior Técnico,
Universidade de Lisboa
Rua Alves Redol 9, 1000-029, Lisboa
{diogo.monica,carlos.ribeiro}@ist.utl.pt
http://www.gsd.inesc-id.pt

Abstract. The commonly used heuristics to promote password strength (e.g. minimum length, forceful use of alphanumeric characters, etc) have been found considerably ineffective and, what is worst, often counterproductive. When coupled with the predominancy of dictionary based attacks and leaks of large password data sets, this situation has led, in later years, to the idea that the most useful criterion on which to classify the strength of a candidate password, is the frequency with which it has appeared in the past.

Maintaining an updated and representative record of past password choices does, however, require the processing and storage of high volumes of data, making the schemes thus far proposed centralized. Unfortunately, requiring that users submit their chosen candidate passwords to a central engine for validation may have security implications and does not allow offline password generation. Another major limitation of the currently proposed systems is the lack of generalisation capability: a password similar to a common password is usually considered safe.

In this article, we propose an algorithm which addresses both limitations. It is designed for local operation, avoiding the need to disclose candidate passwords, and is focused on generalisation, recognizing as dangerous not only frequently occurring passwords, but also candidates similar to them. An implementation of this algorithm is released in the form of a Google Chrome browser extension.

Keywords: password validation, dictionary attacks, self-organizing maps.

1 Introduction

The need to promote the use of strong passwords has led to the widespread use of password validation heuristic rules, (e.g. minimum length, forceful use of alphanumeric characters, etc). However, these rules are largely ineffective (e.g. "p@ssw0rd" will typically be considered a sufficiently strong password) and are often counterproductive. Minimum size requirements, for example, will typically favor the choice of plain text phrases or other low entropy sequences [1], since users want to be able to remember the chosen long password strings. Even though possibly strong in terms of brute force attacks, this undesirable side-effect leaves the chosen passwords highly vulnerable to dictionary attacks. Also, these heuristics are inadvertently leading users to the repeated use of very common solutions, which can be easily remembered, while still obeying

M. Kutyłowski and J. Vaidya (Eds.): ESORICS 2014, Part I, LNCS 8712, pp. 94–111, 2014.

the requirements. In fact, users typically circumvent the imposed pseudo-randomness, low-memorability, by using a few common tricks ("p@ssw0rd" being again a typical example), which are then used repeatedly. This leads to the reiterated use of what are, in fact, very weak passwords, highly vulnerable to statistical guessing attacks (a dictionary based attack ordered by decreasing probability of occurrence). When coupled with the predominancy of dictionary based attacks, these password validation rules may therefore be decreasing overall security levels, instead of promoting them.

This situation has led, in later years, to the idea that the most useful criterion on which to classify the strength of a given password, is the frequency with which it has appeared in the past (e.g. [2], [3], [4]). In fact, some organizations, like Twitter, are already prohibiting further use of their most common passwords, to hamper the effectiveness of statistical dictionary based attacks.

Maintaining an Internet-wide updated and representative record of past password choices does, however, require access to the passwords of at least some representative internet-scale systems (with a high number of users) and the processing of high volumes of data. The schemes thus far proposed are, therefore, centralized. When users want to verify the adequacy of a given password, they will typically submit the password to this centralized engine for validation. While such centralized validation may be acceptable when effected within the scope of the organization under which the password is to be used, it creates some security concerns if users want to validate passwords in a generic engine, since it implies the disclosure of the candidate password. Also, it requires connectivity whenever password choices are to be made.

Alternatively, a compressed version of the observed password database may be downloaded, to enable local validation. This shift towards local validation avoids the need to disclose candidate passwords but, due to the huge amount of passwords (tens to hundreds of millions) in any representative snapshot of past history, requires rates of compression which lossless compression cannot achieve. Another fundamental concern with the local validation approach is the need to guarantee that diffusion of the validation database does not compromise existing passwords, by publicly distributing information capable of supporting dictionary based attacks.

A viable (lossy) compression mechanism was proposed in [4], where the authors propose the creation of an oracle to identify undesirably popular passwords. Their scheme is based on an existing data structure known as a *count-min sketch* (CM-sketch), which the authors populate with existing users' passwords and use to efficiently track password popularity within the user base. The solution proposed addresses both the compression and the password compromise concerns but does so in a centralized fashion.

However, independently of the underlying implementation details of such a popularity-based password validation scheme (local or centralized, compression rates, etc), the overall concept has an underlying weakness, which stems from the way humans tend to make their password choices: when faced with the rejection of their chosen password, users will, with high probability, search for minor variations *"close"* to the desired candidate password, by introducing or replacing non-defacing elements (and thereby maintaining its memorability) until an acceptable instance is obtained. This behavior is the reason passwords such as "p@ssword", "ashley123", or "il0veu" have become so common.

Since attackers are well aware of this type of behavior, smarter dictionary attacks already explore the *"neighborhood"* of the historically more frequent passwords before moving to the next one. In fact, many publicly available password recovery tools are already using several different sets of rules to produce variations of the known dictionary entries (e.g. Hashcat's [5] "best64.rules"). For password validation, this means that if, for example, "password1" is historically a very frequent choice, then *"close-by"* variations such as "password2", or "p@ssw0rd1" should also be classified as weak, even if historically their frequency would not classify them as such.

The goal of this paper is therefore to design a popularity based classification scheme, which is not only capable of classifying a password as weak because it is historically a frequent choice, but also because it is *"too close"* to a frequent password and, hence, is likely to be guessed by a modern statistical attack. Another important side effect of this generalisation capability is the fact that it allows local validation without the need for frequent updates of the validation database, since this intrinsic generalisation capability will protect users from the evolutionary changes of the database between updates. The proposed scheme is envisaged for local operation and, as such, addresses all the above discussed issues concerning size, connectivity, and non-disclosure of historical passwords. As a proof-of-concept we released an implementation of this scheme in the form of a Google Chrome browser extension that anyone can obtain for free on the chrome web store.

The rest of this paper is organized as follows: Section 2 describes the proposed approach, and discusses individually its constituting steps. Section 3 evaluates the performance of the proposed scheme. Section 4 details our proof-of-concept implementation. Finally, Section 5 concludes the paper, and discusses directions for future work.

2   Our Approach

There are three conceptual steps in our classification engine: *compression*, *generalisation* and *hashing*. When validating a password, users will execute the fourth and final conceptual step of the overall scheme: *classification*. This last step is the only that the final user is required to do; it is also the only step where algorithm execution speed is critical. The overall proposed algorithm is depicted in Figure 1, and is best addressed by discussing the *compression* step first.

2.1   Compression

Let us discuss the compression step as applied directly to the raw passwords. The possibility of pre-processing prior to compression (e.g. feature extraction) will not be addressed in this paper.

Since the overall algorithm must recognize the concept of *closeness* between passwords, the compression step must preserve the topological proximity of the input passwords. That is: passwords which are close in the input (non-compressed) space should be also close in the output (compressed) space. This precludes the use of algorithms such as the CM-sketch presented in [4]. In this article, we will be using Self-Organizing Maps (SOM) to achieve the intended similarity preserving compression. SOM are a

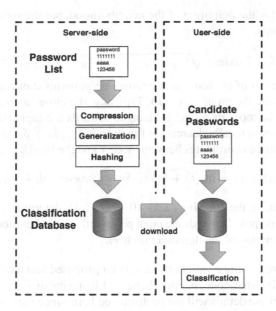

Fig. 1. Overall architecture

simple, well known clustering tool, capable of providing very synthetic summaries of the input data. They are a type of unsupervised neural network, capable of reflecting in the output space the topological proximity relations present in the input space. As will be seen, using a SOM for the compression step of our overall algorithm also provides an easy way to achieve the desired generalisation capability.

Self-Organizing Maps (SOM). A SOM is a lattice of nodes (a 2D rectangular lattice is used in this article). Each node has both a topological position within the lattice (x, y coordinates, in our case), and a vector of weights (the model, m) of the same dimension of the input vectors. Typically, the model vectors are randomly initialized. Training occurs over many iterations; at each iteration, the input vectors (previously used passwords, in our case) are presented to the network, one at a time, in random order (training can also be done in batch, but that is merely an implementation issue). For each input password, the following steps are executed:

- Determine which node has a model *closer* to the input password (according to the similarity measure chosen for the input space). This node is commonly called the BMU (Best Matching Unit);

$$i_{BMU} = \min_i \{\text{similarity}(node_i, password)\}$$

- Find the set $\mathcal{N}$ of all nodes in the lattice neighborhood of the BMU. The radius r of this neighborhood is typically monotonically decreasing; in the first iterations, large radii are used for the definition of the neighborhood, but the radius will decrease for later iterations;

$$\mathcal{N} = \{node_i : \sqrt{(x_i - x_{BMU})^2 + (y_i - y_{BMU})^2} \leq r\}$$

- Update the models of all nodes in the lattice neighborhood of the BMU, to make them approximate the input password. Typically, the closer a node is to the BMU in the lattice, the more its model is changed towards the input password, according to some monotonically decreasing function $h(\delta x_i, \delta y_i)$, δx_i and δy_i being the difference in lattice coordinates between node i and the BMU:

$$m_i(t + 1) = m_i(t) + h(\delta x_i, \delta y_i)\alpha(password_t - m_i(t)).$$

In this equation, α, the *learning factor* $(0 < \alpha < 1)$, determines how heavily the models should be puled towards the input password at each iteration (α is, typically, a decreasing function of the iteration number).

Even though several minor variations have been proposed and analysed in the literature, particularly in what concerns the shape and behavior of r, α and $h(\delta x, \delta y)$ as training proceeds (these details will not be discussed here, since they are essentially not relevant for our results), the intended result of the training step is always the same: to have the nodes of the latticed pulled towards the input vectors, but preserving the desired degree of neighborhood cohesion. Since the number of nodes in the lattice is much smaller than the number of input passwords, the resulting map is a summary replica of the input space, with a much lower number of elements, but maintaining its topological relations. The literature on SOM is abundant. For further details, see, for example, [6] and [7].

Compression Ratio. The compression ratio is $\frac{N}{M}$, N being the number of input passwords, and M the number of nodes in the SOM. As will be shown later, with the proposed implementation, $p_{miss} = 0$, for all compression ratios. That is: for any chosen compression ratio, there will be a null probability of failing to flag as dangerous a password whose historical frequency of appearance is higher than the defined threshold. This means that one may choose any desired rate of compression without fearing that excessive compression may provoke an incorrect password validation. However, if the compression ratio is chosen too high, there will be a loss in the discriminating capability of the network, since too many input passwords will be mapped into each node/neighborhood, resulting in a high false alarm rate when validating prospective candidates. As will be seen in Section 3, good results have been obtained for maps of a few thousand nodes (e.g. 6000 nodes), even when summarising lists with tens of millions of passwords.

Similarity Measures. The concept of similarity is central to SOM operation, since it defines the topological characteristics of the input space to be preserved in the output space. In this particular application, we are therefore faced with the issue of defining an appropriate measure of similarity between passwords. This is, in fact, a two-pronged problem. Firstly, the similarity measure to be used must reflect in some appropriate manner the user perception of "closeness" between passwords, something which is clearly not uniquely defined. Many distances and/or similarity measures for categorical data have been proposed (e.g. [8], [9]), but their resulting notion of similarity is not always compatible with the type of minor variations that a user is likely to use when forced to modify a chosen (and rejected) password. Secondly, the chosen measure of similarity must allow the concept of "fractional approximation". When training the SOM, we will need to change the node models, to make them approximate the input password, and there are no unique solutions to the problem of approximating categorical data; also, we will want to use diminishing degrees of approximation as the distance to the BMU increases, as determined by $h(\delta x, \delta y)$; this implies the use of a similarity measure for which an increase in similarity can be defined in a quasi-continuous way. In this article, we will be using a mixed, non-pure, measure of similarity, capable of addressing both problems. Designating by $d(p_1, p_2)$ the dissimilarity between passwords p_1 and p_2, we define.

$$d('password', 'p@ssw0rd') = \sqrt{(97 - 64)^2 + (111 - 48)^2} \cdot 2^2 = 284.48, \quad (1)$$

$$d(p_1, p_2) = \sqrt{\sum_{j=1}^{n} (p_1(j) - p_2(j))^2 \cdot hamm(p_1, p_2)^\beta}, \quad (2)$$

where n is the maximum number of characters of the input passwords, $p_1(j)$ is the ASCII code of the jth character of p_1 (same for $p_2(j)$), and $hamm(p_1, p_2)$ is the character-wise Hamming distance between the two passwords (that is, the number of characters in which they differ), often referred to as the "overlap measure" (e.g. [8]). For example, for $\beta = 2$, the dissimilarity between "password" and "p@ssw0rd", according to this measure, will be 284.48, as given by the product of 71.12 (euclidean distance between ASCII codes) and 4 (square of the character-wise Hamming distance: 2). Two comments should be made concerning this dissimilarity measure:

- Firstly, we note that the first factor allows for a quasi-continuous solution to the approximation problem: approximating a model from the input password will be made by simply approximating the corresponding ASCII codes. The jth character of the ith model will be updated as:

$$\forall j : m_{i,j}(t + 1) = m_{i,j}(t) + \Delta, \quad (3)$$

where

$$\Delta = round(h(\delta x_i, \delta y_i)\alpha(p_t(j) - m_{i,j}(t))).$$

The approximation of the ASCII codes will also generate, at discrete steps, a decrease in the Hamming distance between the model and the input password and, thus, a decrease in the second factor;

- Secondly, we should note the role of the β parameter. Since the Hamming distance bears a stronger correlation with the human concept of closeness between passwords, an increase in β will pull the overall measure of dissimilarity towards a simple human-related overlap distance, desensitizing the dissimilarity measures relative to the numerical distance between the ASCII codes. In this article, we will use $\beta = 2$.

Procedure. The SOM models are typically initialized with random values between 0 and 128. Training is done with as few as 30/40 iterations, with monotonically decreasing values of the learning factor α and neighborhood radii. The SOM models are updated as presented in Section 2.1. Once training is completed, the full list of passwords is again presented to the network, and nodes are labeled with the (absolute) frequency of appearance of the passwords for which that node is the BMU. If more than one password maps to the same node, the node's label is the frequency of appearance of the most frequent one. The label on each node is, therefore, a measure of the popularity of the most frequent password on the training set for which that node is the BMU.

2.2 Generalisation

Once the compression phase completes, we are left with a map which could be directly used for password classification, as follows: i) a popularity threshold is chosen; ii) each new candidate password is presented to the network, and the corresponding BMU determined; iii) if the popularity level of the resulting BMU is above the chosen threshold, the candidate password is rejected, due to similarity with existing popular passwords; otherwise, it is accepted as a valid password.

Note that, by design, any password in the training set more popular than the chosen threshold will map to a BMU with a popularity label greater or equal to the chosen threshold. Denoting by $L(i)$ the popularity label of the ith node, by $BMU(p)$ the BMU corresponding to password p, and by $f(p)$ its frequency of appearance, we thus have that:

$$\forall \tau : f(p) \geq \tau \Rightarrow L(BMU(p)) \geq \tau. \tag{4}$$

This means that the probability of wrongly classifying a password whose occurrence is higher than the threshold as safe (p_{miss}) is 0, as intended.

At this point, the generalisation capabilities of the scheme may be smaller than desired. At the output of the compression phase, it is possible to have nodes with very low popularity adjacent to nodes of high popularity. However, the topological preservation property of the SOM implies that, with high probability, their models are close to one another. Hence, if one of them is very popular as a BMU within the training data, the desired generalisation capability would dictate that nearby models should also be avoided, even if they were not popular within the password list used to train the SOM.

The generalisation capability of the network may thus be increased by imposing some popularity leakage from local maxima to neighboring nodes. This can be achieved by simple spacial low-pass filtering of the popularity levels across the map. Let us designate by $\phi(x, y)$ the popularity label of the node with lattice coordinates (x, y). The smoothed version of the SOM (and the desired level of generalisation capability) can be obtained as in (5):

$$\phi(x, y) * K(x, y), \tag{5}$$

where the $*$ operator stands for 2D convolution, and $K(x, y)$ is any chosen low pass kernel. Since $\phi(x, y) \geq 0$, to preserve the $p_{miss} = 0$ property, we need to condition the chosen kernel to $K(0, 0) \geq 1$. In this article, no attempt to optimize the choice of the kernel was made. Smoothing was performed with a simple non-linear 2D lowpass mask, designed to preserve local maxima and their popularity levels:

$$K(x, y) = max(k_1(x, y), k_2(x, y)), \tag{6}$$

$k_1(x, y), k_2(x, y)$ being the 2D kernels in Figure 2.

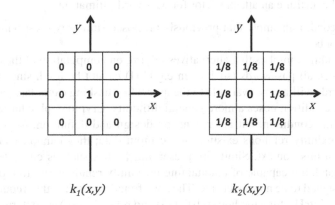

Fig. 2. Smoothing kernel

Decreasing the bandwidth of the used kernel will increase the generalisation capability. However, it will concurrently decrease the resolution of the classification scheme, since the resulting popularity leakage may force bigger subsets of the password space to be flagged as "too popular" and, thus, become unusable.

2.3   Hashing

At the end of the generalisation phase, the SOM map is finalized, and ready to classify candidate passwords as "*acceptable*" or "*not acceptable*", depending on the popularity label of the corresponding BMU. However, at this point, the models in the SOM are a compressed summary of the training passwords. As such, the SOM presents a security risk, since it carries too much information concerning these passwords. In fact, given a strong enough preponderance of the most common training passwords, some models may constitute pure copies of those passwords. This potential security problem becomes even more severe in our case, where a distribution of the SOM is envisaged, to allow client-side offline operation.

To address this problem, the SOM resulting from the generalisation step is hashed, prior to storage and/or disclosure. On the user side, classification will therefore be made on hashed space. As in the compression step, the hash function must not, however, destroy the topological proximity relation between the input and output spaces. If a candidate password is similar to a popular one, their hashes must also be similar. Otherwise, they would not deterministically map to neighboring BMUs, and the intended general-isation capability would be lost.

There is a considerable body of work on similarity preserving hash functions (e.g. [10] to [11]). However, in this particular application, two additional constraints must be met by the hash functions:

- Computing the hash for a single password must not require knowledge of all other passwords. Otherwise, users will not be capable of hashing their candidate passwords;
- The hash function must not be invertible. Otherwise, possession of the hashed SOM would still constitute an attack vector for password estimation.

These two conditions imply that previously proposed similarity preserving hashing methods cannot be used.

The first condition implies that alternatives relying on computation of the adjacency matrices between all passwords (such as in e.g [11]) cannot be used, since the set of known passwords will not be available to the user when hashing candidate passwords.

The second condition poses a more general difficulty. Cryptographic hashes clearly comply with this condition, but are meant, by design and definition, to destroy any topological proximity relations existing in the input data; they cannot, therefore, be directly used in this context. Similarity preserving hashes such as e.g. [10] or [12], on the other hand, are capable of maintaining proximity relations (up to a point), but were never designed to be non-invertible. The hash functions used in the frequently used Locality Preserving Hashing methods ([10], [13] and related work) are deterministically invertible; all methods based on projection on random-spaces such as, for example, the one found in [12], are prone to inversion attacks if the projection matrix and shift vector are known (and they must be known to users, since they must be capable of hashing their candidate passwords). As pointed out in [12], if these quantities are unknown, the method would be secure, from an informational point of view, but that is not the case here. Forcing the non-invertibility of the projection matrix used on these methods does also not provide enough security. Reconstruction can still be attempted and attack vectors obtained algebraically (i.e. by careful use of the Moore-Penrose pseudo inverse, or similar techniques).

In this paper, hashing will still be made by linear vector projection, to maintain prox-imity relations. The possibility of reconstruction is avoided by suppressing some of the information concerning the resulting vectors. More precisely, passwords are projected into the Fourier harmonic space, and the resulting phase information is discarded. That is:

$$hash(p) = |FFT(p)| \tag{7}$$

The classification database to be sent to users is, therefore, not the trained SOM, but a map of the magnitude of the Fourier transform of the nodes' models. The absence of phase information means that the models cannot be reconstructed, and, therefore, the set of training passwords is not compromised by diffusion of the classification database. In fact, the absolute values of the Fourier transform of the models only contain information concerning their second moments (as directly results from the Wiener-Kintchin theo-rem). Passwords cannot thus be inferred from the classification database (even though their autocorrelation function can).

One consequence of the informational loss in the hashing step is that, when classifying a candidate password, users will not be evaluating its direct proximity to the nodes of the trained SOM, but will, instead, be evaluating their spectral similarity. This does not affect the $p_{miss} = 0$ perfect performance (the power spectrum of a password will always be closer to itself than to the power spectrum of a different password), but will introduce a slightly different measure of similarity in the classification phase. Namely, the Hamming distance between the candidate password and the nodes of the SOM cannot be considered at this point, since there simply is not enough information to compute such a distance. This also means that, after the hashing step, the popularity levels of the nodes must be recomputed, since some of the mapping of passwords to nodes in the spectral domain may differ from the corresponding mappings before transformation.

Two further notes must still be made, before addressing the final step of the algorithm. Firstly, we note that, since all models are real valued, their Fourier transforms are symmetric around the origin and, hence, the magnitude of the negative frequency bins can be discarded, thus reducing the size of the classification database by almost a factor of 2. Also, to further restrict the amount of information present in the distributed classification database, the nodes' popularity labels can be recoded at this point with a single bit, to simply label nodes as being "on or above danger threshold" (e.g. "1") or "below danger threshold" (e.g. "0"), since that is all the information needed for the intended binary classification. However, sometimes, the user may want to have some control on the classification threshold being used. A more stringent threshold may be desired in critical contexts (e.g. bank accounts' passwords) than in more relaxed situations (e.g. temporary accounts). Therefore, the popularity levels of the models may be coded with more bits, corresponding to any desired number of discrete levels. The user will then be capable of selecting the desired "password strength" level, with passwords being classified as "dangerous" only if their corresponding BMU has a popularity label higher than the level selected by the user as threshold.

An example of a map of 6000 nodes trained with the Rockyou password set is shown in Figure 3. Forbidden nodes (above threshold) are represented in black and acceptable nodes in white. We also represent the same map after smoothing (with the smoothing kernel of Figure 2) in grey color.

2.4 Classification

The classification step is now trivial. The classifying tool made available to users simply:

1. Computes the power spectrum of the candidate password;
2. Using the local copy of the classification database, determines the BMU (node with the lower Euclidean distance to the power spectrum of the candidate password);
3. Rejects the candidate if the label of the BMU is "1", and validates it as an acceptable password if the BMU's label is "0"

We note that this classification step is very fast. All the computational effort of the overall method lies in the training phase, which is centrally made by the classification database provider, making this method ideal for password validation even in resource constrained devices (e.g. mobile devices).

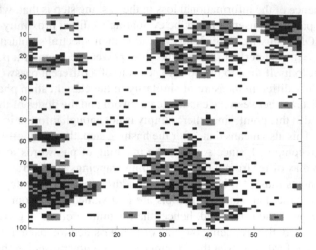

Fig. 3. SOM Map with 6000 nodes

3 Performance

To evaluate the performance of the proposed scheme, we will need to consider its i) *compression rate*, ii) *statistical performance*, and iii) *generalisation capability and consistency*. As expected, these three indicators are highly interdependent (e.g. higher compression rates will typically imply inferior statistical performance). For the first two indicators (compression rate and statistical performance), we will be able to compare the proposed scheme with the CM-sketch [4]. The third parameter must, however, be evaluated without the benefit of comparison since, to our knowledge, there is no other proposed scheme for password validation which, while operating based on the popularity levels of previously seen passwords, is capable of generalizing and flagging as dangerous passwords which, even though not previously seen, are too close to popular choices. A final relevant parameter to be discussed is iv) *classification speed*.

3.1 Compression Rate and Statistical Performance

Since the intended use of the proposed scheme involves a user downloading the classification database, it is important to evaluate the achievable compression rates, and the decrease in performance with increasing compression rate. Let us compare the performance of the SOM approach with CM-sketch[4] by looking at the passwords in the Rockyou set [14] (32602348 passwords of that list were used; the maximum password size is 30 bytes).

Firstly, we must note that both approaches will have $p_{miss} = 0$, for any given compression rate. That is: any password belonging to the training set with a popularity level above the defined threshold will be flagged as dangerous with unit probability, independently of the size of the sketch or the SOM map and, hence, the obtained compression rate. Hence, comparison will be made from the point of view of p_{FA}, the probability of false alarm. The theoretical bounds for the CM-sketch are given in [15]: for a (d, w) CM-sketch, the required number of lines d (each line corresponds to a different hash function) and columns w can be obtained as follows:

$$w = \left\lceil \frac{e}{\epsilon} \right\rceil, \qquad d = \left\lceil ln\frac{1}{\delta} \right\rceil, \tag{8}$$

where e is Napier's constant, and $(1 - \delta)$ is the probability that the estimated number of occurrences of any given password $(\hat{n}_i)$ will be within a semi-interval of ϵN of the real number of occurrences (n_i):

$$\hat{n}_i \leq n_i + \epsilon N, \tag{9}$$

N being the total number of passwords. However, the typical performance of the CM-sketch will typically be well within the theoretical bounds. As such, using these bounds would present the CM-sketch case in an unduly unfavorable light. Furthermore, no equivalent analytic bounds exist for the SOM case. As such, the comparison will be made by Monte Carlo simulation. The SOM models were initialized with random values between 0 and 128. Training was done with a few tens of iterations (typically 30/40 iterations), with monotonically decreasing values of the learning factor α:

$$\alpha = 0.9 \cdot e^{-\frac{(i-1) \cdot ln(9)}{(I-1)}}, \tag{10}$$

where i is the iteration number ($1 \leq i \leq I$). At each iteration, training was done using a batch approach (see e.g. [16], [17]), since sequential training would be computationally prohibitive for the millions of passwords in the training set.

In Figure 4, we can see the False Alarm probability (p_{FA}) given by a (140, 200) SOM, and different sized CM-sketches, when applied to the mentioned list of passwords, with classification thresholds corresponding to the popularity level of each one of the 100000 more popular passwords of the Rockyou set. For each threshold, all 32602348 passwords on the password list were classified as being dangerous (popularity above threshold) or not (popularity below threshold); the presented p_{FA} is the observed ratio of false positives. The x-axis in this figure corresponds to the ordinal position (in decreasing popularity level sort order) of the password whose popularity level is being used as threshold.

Two notes should be made, concerning this Figure. Firstly, we should consider the very different natures of a CM-sketch's false positive, and what we are calling a SOM's false positive. In the CM-sketch case, due to the uniformly distributed randomizing effect of the hash functions, false positives are purely stochastic events, occurring on uniform, flat spaces; in the SOM case, however, a false positive is not a purely stochastic event, since it typically will occur as a (non-stochastic) result of the closeness between the candidate password and an existing popular password. Hence, while a CM-Sketch false positive is a pure statistical classification error, a SOM false positive may not be an error at all, but a manifestation of the desirable generalisation properties that this construct possesses by design. Since any list with real world passwords will, in fact, possess many passwords bearing close proximity relations with popular passwords (e.g. the popular choices "password" or "password1", and the much less popular "password8" or "password9"), a much bigger rate of false positives was expected from the SOM, when compared with the CM-sketch. However, as can be seen in Figure 4, the false alarm rate of the SOM is comparable with the false alarm rate of CM-sketches of an equivalent number of cells. In fact, the SOM even presents mostly lower false positives rates than, for example, the (3, 28000) CM-sketch, which has three times more cells than the SOM.

Secondly, we should point out that, since each output cell of a CM-Sketch is a single scalar, and each node in the SOM is a vector, the number of cells does not directly map the physical size of the compressed password list. For example, the (3, 56000) CM-sketch used in Figure 4 will typically require 672 kbytes, while the (140, 200) SOM, even though with only one sixth of the cells, did require 843.5 kbytes (each node requires 30 bytes for the model, plus one bit for its label).

The most noticeable feature to be appreciated in this comparison is, therefore, the considerably different behavior of the SOM and CM-sketch p_{FA} when the popularity threshold decreases, reflecting the different nature of the classification "errors" in each case. Insofar as compression rates go, both schemes can be considered roughly equivalent (even though with a clear advantage of the CM-sketch in the region of higher popularity thresholds)

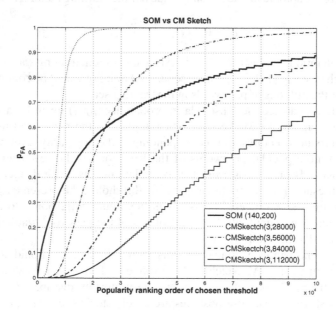

Fig. 4. Size requirements comparison

3.2   Generalisation Capability and Consistency

The fundamental difference between the proposed SOM based scheme and the previously existing CM-Sketch approach is the design objective of having the capability to generalize, and flag as dangerous password choices similar to previously used popular ones. Hence, the evaluation of the achieved generalisation capability of the overall scheme is paramount.

Clearly, generalisation increases with increasing compression rate: smaller SOM will possess fewer nodes and, hence, each node will be chosen as the BMU for an increasing larger number of different entries in the training set. This means that they will become less and less specialized, and its model will, therefore, reflect an increasing larger neighborhood of passwords. On the other hand, a SOM with a large number of nodes, as compared to the size of the training set, will acquire a high degree of specialisation of its models. Each node will therefore be more narrowly tuned to smaller password neighborhoods. To increase specialisation (thus reducing generalisation), one must increase the size of the SOM; to increase generalisation (thus reducing specialisation), one must decrease the SOM size, or apply a smoothing window to the obtained SOM, such as the one presented in Section 2.2. This later alternative (the use of a smoothing window) tends to produce more consistent generalisation behaviour.

As is also clear, evaluating the consistency of the generalisation achieved by the SOM approach, implies answering the following two questions:

- Is the SOM generalising in a useful way? That is: is it flagging as dangerous, not only the previously popular passwords, but also the corresponding mutations of weak passwords that people are prone to use in their defacing attempts?
- Is the SOM generalising too much? That is: is it flagging as dangerous passwords which do not present any real danger and, thus, unduly limiting the space of available choices?

To answer to the first question, one needs to estimate the password mutations that people are prone to use, in their effort to deface their chosen passwords, without losing memorability. Such exercises have previously been done in several fora, though each choice of the set of mutation rules has a high level of subjectivity. A well known set of mutation rules is the one used by John-the-Ripper [18] , a widely known and used password cracking software tool. To evaluate how the proposed scheme deals with the John the Ripper mutations, a (60,100) SOM was trained with the 32 million Rockyou passwords used earlier in this paper; the classification threshold was chosen as 1000 (the popularity level of the 1438th most popular password). The first 500 most popular passwords were then presented to John the Ripper, to produce all possible mutations. Lastly, these 500 passwords and all their mutations were classified by our SOM based scheme. Naturally, one would expect that i) all 500 passwords were flagged as dangerous (since $p_{miss} = 0$), and ii) most of their mutations are also flagged as dangerous (since the John-the-Ripper mutation rules are supposed to reasonably emulate user's password defacing choices). The obtained results can be seen in Table 1.

As can be seen in this table, not only were all previously known popular choices recognised as dangerous, but also the vast majority of their John-the-Ripper mutations were recognised as also being dangerous (not because they were historically popular, but simply by being *similar* to historically popular choices).

To address the second identified question, and determine if the SOM generalising too much, and, thus, unduly limiting the space of available choices, a set of 1 million

Table 1. Passwords flagged as dangerous

Passwords	Flagged as dangerous
500 most probable	100%
All mutations	84%

random passwords was generated. Each password was constituted by a string of random characters (ASCII codes comprised between 32 and 127), and with random lengths between 1 and 21: uniform distributions were used in both cases. Being random, the level of similarity with previously used popular passwords should be small and, hence, on would expect their vast majority to be approved as valid passwords. In fact, only 11.3% were considered dangerous by the (60,100) SOM trained with the Rockyou password list.

The previous results indicate, therefore, that the intended generalisation capability is operating properly: known popular passwords are forbidden; passwords which are similar to known popular passwords are mostly forbidden; random, non-structured passwords are mostly allowed.

As a last example of performance, and still using the same SOM, we classified wordlists of several languages, broadly covering the range from germanic to romanic Indo-European languages, with a total of 1.64 million words, from [19]. Since the SOM was trained with the Rockyou list, where english and spanish derived words are dominant, one would expect a higher percentage of forbidden passwords in the English an Spanish files, not only due to the eventual appearance, in those files, of passwords popular in the training set, but mainly due to syntactic similarities within the languages. The results can be seen in Figure 5. As expected, English and Spanish will provide the higher percentage of words considered dangerous, due to similarities with passwords on the training set. Also, we can see, from this picture, that the classifier seems to be more sensitive to words of romanic structure (right side of the picture), than to languages of germanic origin (left side of the picture). This tendency is not unexpected, since the training set is densely populated with words from english and spanish; what might be unexpected is the capability of the classifier to tune to the syntactic structure of the training set and, thus, display this type of selectivity. As a final note, we may note that, independently of the language, dictionary words tend to be more susceptible to be considered dangerous than random passwords, even if they are new to the classifier. This is, again, an expected result, since dictionary words will possess an underlying similar syntactic structure to dictionary words of similar languages appearing in the training set.

3.3 Classification Speed

Even though training of the classification database (SOM) is a lengthy, computationally heavy process, this step is centralised, and has no stringent timing requisites associated with it. The one step that must be light and fast is the final classification step, since users will locally execute it each time a password is tested. In the proposed scheme, however, the classification of a password as *"allowable"* or *"not allowed"* is extremely fast, and

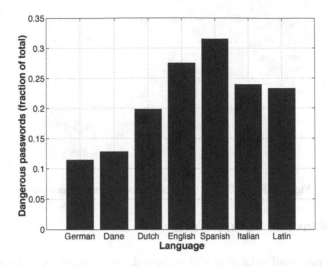

Fig. 5. Flagging in several languages

independent of the size of both the set of previously known passwords. The user sided operations are a simple DFT transform of a very short sequence (whose length is the size of the proposed password), and a search for the BMU in the classification database (whose size is in the order of a few thousand models). As such, classification speed is not an issue in this scheme, which can be used even by devices with very limited computing power or low latency requirements.

4 Proof of Concept Implementation

To empirically test the use of this password validation scheme, we created an independent implementation in the form of a Google Chrome browser extension. This implementation is available on the chrome webstore with the name: SOM Password Validator[1].

There were mainly three things that we wanted to show with this implementation: i) the scheme can be easily implemented; ii) local validation of passwords is fast; iii) and that the final size of the application database distributed to users is small.

The implementation is in javascript, and the final product has less than 500 lines of code. The time taken to validate each individual password is effectively negligible, taking less than one second to validate 1000 different passwords. The database shipped with the application has a total size of 1MB, bringing the total size of the application (with images included) to short of 2MB. A screenshot of the extension can be seen in Figure 6.

---

[1] The extension can be obtained here: http://goo.gl/xjcGW8

Fig. 6. Google Chrome browser extension implementation

5   Conclusions and Future Work

A scheme for password validation was presented. As in previous approaches to the problem, the proposed solution builds on the notion that frequent, common passwords constitute bad choices, and that rarely (or never) seen passwords should be favored, since they are more prone to resist to statistical dictionary attacks. However, our approach differs from existing proposals in that: i) it is envisaged for local, decentralized operation, and ii) it has generalisation capabilities. This generalisation capability not only allows detection of dangerous passwords by proximity to popular ones, but also avoids the need for frequent updates of the validation database, since it protects users from the evolutionary changes of the database between updates.

These goals, even though conceptually simple, imply the recourse to several concepts which are amenable to very different implementations and choices. The base tool used in this article (SOM) can be replaced by other clustering/mapping alternatives; the used similarity measure for non-categorical data is arbitrary in a large degree, and different alternatives could have been pursued; the advantages and implications of a preliminary feature-extraction step prior to SOM training can be discussed and argued; the hashing functions used in the masking step are also nothing else than arbitrary, even though effective; all in all, in almost all steps of the method, many and widely different options could have been made. As such, there is no claim of optimality in this article. In fact, if any claim is made, it is one of almost certainty of non-optimality, and of the need to further pursue potential gains in performance by further work concerning the choices to be made at each individual step. However, the approach has proved feasible. It is possible to build a password classification tool amenable to local operation, and capable of effectively facing the challenges imposed by the "mutation-capable" last generation of statistical dictionary based attacks.

References

1. Clair, L.S., Johansen, L., Enck, W., Pirretti, M., Traynor, P., McDaniel, P., Jaeger, T.: Password exhaustion: Predicting the end of password usefulness. In: Bagchi, A., Atluri, V. (eds.) ICISS 2006. LNCS, vol. 4332, pp. 37–55. Springer, Heidelberg (2006)

2. Castelluccia, C., Durmuth, M., Perito, D.: Adaptive password-strength meters from markov models. In: NDSS. The Internet Society (2012)
3. Spafford, E.H.: Opus: Preventing weak password choices. Computers & Security (1992)
4. Schechter, S., Herley, C., Mitzenmacher, M.: Popularity is everything: A new approach to protecting passwords from statistical-guessing attacks. In: Proceedings of the 5th USENIX Conference on Hot Topics in Security, HotSec 2010. USENIX Association, Berkeley (2010)
5. Hashcat password recovery tool (2013), http://hashcat.net/hashcat/
6. Haykin, S.: Neural Networks: A Comprehensive Foundation, 2nd edn. Prentice Hall PTR, Upper Saddle River (1998)
7. Kohonen, T.: Neurocomputing: Foundations of research. MIT Press, Cambridge (1988)
8. Boriah, S., Chandola, V., Kumar, V.: Similarity measures for categorical data: A comparative evaluation. In: Proceedings of the Eighth SIAM International Conference on Data Mining
9. Huang, Z.: Extensions to the k-means algorithm for clustering large data sets with categorical values (1998)
10. Indyk, P., Motwani, R.: Approximate nearest neighbors: Towards removing the curse of dimensionality. In: Proceedings of the Thirtieth Annual ACM Symposium on Theory of Computing, STOC 1998. ACM, New York (1998)
11. He, K., Wen, F., Sun, J.: K-means hashing: An affinity-preserving quantization method for learning binary compact codes. In: Proceedings of the 2013 IEEE Conference on Computer Vision and Pattern Recognition. IEEE Computer Society, Washington, DC (2013)
12. Boufounos, P., Rane, S.: Secure binary embeddings for privacy preserving nearest neighbors. In: Proceedings of the 2011 IEEE International Workshop on Information Forensics and Security, WIFS 2011. IEEE Computer Society, Washington, DC (2011)
13. Datar, M., Immorlica, N., Indyk, P., Mirrokni, V.S.: Locality-sensitive hashing scheme based on p-stable distributions. In: Proceedings of the Twentieth Annual Symposium on Computational Geometry, SCG 2004. ACM, New York (2004)
14. Rockyou list of leaked passwords (2013), https://wiki.skullsecurity.org/Passwords
15. Cormode, G., Muthukrishnan, S.: An improved data stream summary: The count-min sketch and its applications. J. Algorithms (April 2005)
16. Kohonen, T.: Fast evolutionary learning with batch-type self-organizing maps. Neural Process (April 1999)
17. Fort, J.C., Letremy, P., Cottrell, M.: Advantages and drawbacks of the batch kohonen algorithm. In: Verleysen, M. (ed.) ESANN (2002)
18. John the ripper password cracking tool, http://www.openwall.com/john/
19. Openwall wordlist collection, http://www.openwall.com/wordlists/

Verifiable Delegation of Computations with Storage-Verification Trade-off[*]

Liang Feng Zhang and Reihaneh Safavi-Naini

Institute for Security, Privacy and Information Assurance
Department of Computer Science
University of Calgary, Calgary, Canada

Abstract. Outsourcing computations has attracted much attention in recent years. An important security challenge is ensuring the correctness of the computed results. In the verifiable computation (VC) model of Gennaro, Gentry and Parno (CRYPTO 2010), a client can delegate the computation of its function to a cloud server, and efficiently verify the correctness of any computed results. In the existing VC schemes, the server must store an encoding of the function that doubles the required cloud storage, compared with storing the function itself. In this paper, we introduce a parameter that measures the trade-off between the required cloud storage and the client's verification time. We construct four (privately or publicly) VC schemes for delegating polynomials and matrices. These schemes allow the client to significantly reduce the consumed cloud storage by slightly increasing its verification time.

Keywords: verifiable computation, storage, verification, trade-off.

1   Introduction

Cloud computing allows resource-restricted clients to outsource (delegate) the storage of their data, and/or computations on the data, to cloud servers. The clients can access their data and request for computations on the outsourced data at their will. Outsourcing however, raises many security concerns such as the integrity of the stored data, and the delegated computations on the data. In this paper we are concerned with the latter.

The problem of verifiably outsourcing computation has been extensively studied in recent years, resulting in a number of models motivated by different application scenarios. In the verifiable computation (VC) model of Gennaro, Gentry and Parno [8], the client invests a one-time expensive computational effort to compute and store an encoding of its function with a cloud server, such that any evaluation of the function by the server, can be efficiently verified (using substantially less time than doing the evaluation). The one-time effort spent on encoding can be amortized over many evaluations of the function. Following [8], there has been a long list of papers on verifiable computation, both for generic functions [8,6,1,17,5] and for specific functions [2,7,16].

---

[*] This research is in part supported by Alberta Innovates Technology Futures.

M. Kutyłowski and J. Vaidya (Eds.): ESORICS 2014, Part I, LNCS 8712, pp. 112–129, 2014.
© Springer International Publishing Switzerland 2014

A VC scheme is called *privately verifiable*, if verification of the computed result can only be done by the client who has delegated the function; and *publicly verifiable*, if anyone with access to the computed result and possibly some public information can perform verification. To provide verifiability in a VC scheme, the encoding of the delegated function may include the delegated function itself, as well as some authentication information that will be used by the server to generate proofs. A common drawback of the existing VC schemes [8,6,1,17,5,2,7,16] is that, the encoding requires at least twice more cloud storage, compared with the delegated function. We define the *storage overhead* of a VC scheme as the ratio of the total cloud storage used by the encoding, to the cloud storage required for the delegated function itself. Less overhead is desirable because it means more efficient schemes. Under this definition, the existing VC schemes [8,6,1,17,5,2,7,16] have storage overhead ≥ 2.

1.1 Our Work

The emphasis of all existing VC schemes has been on efficient verification, and little attention has been paid to reducing the storage overhead. In practice a client may be willing to spend a bit more time on verification, if it can substantially reduce the consumed cloud storage. Note that the delegated function can be of tera byte size and so reducing the storage overhead can lead to substantial cost saving. This would be particularly attractive if the client does not need to compute the function very frequently and remains idle in between. In this paper, we investigate the trade-off between the consumed cloud storage and the client's verification time. We focus on the VC schemes of [2,7] for delegating polynomials and matrices (any matrix can define a function that takes a vector as input and outputs the vector-matrix multiplication). Both functions have important applications such as in verifiable keyword search, discrete Fourier transform, and linear transformations.

We introduce a *trade-off parameter s*, that measures the trade-off between the required cloud storage and the client's verification time. We break the delegated computation into s sub-computations, from which the result of the delegated computation can be reconstructed. In our setting, the cloud provides the s sub-computation results, along with *one* proof; the client verifies the correctness of the s results, and then computes the result of the delegated computation. The s subcomputations are the inner products of a common vector, with s vectors which are obtained from the delegated function. We authenticate the s vectors with a single tag vector, and thus obtain a saving of cloud storage (for tags).

We construct two VC schemes for delegating m-variate polynomials of degree $\leq d$ in each variable, a privately verifiable scheme, Π_1, and a publicly verifiable scheme, Π_2; and two VC schemes for delegating $m \times d$ matrices, a privately verifiable scheme, Π_3, and a publicly verifiable scheme, Π_4.

Compared with [2,7], our schemes have storage overhead $1 + 1/s < 2$. To achieve such a smaller storage overhead, the client's verification time in Π_1 and Π_2 is only slightly increased compared with [2] and [7], respectively. The scheme Π_3 is the first private VC scheme for delegating matrices. The scheme Π_4 is more efficient than [7] not only in terms of storage overhead but also in terms of the client's verification time.

1.2   Background and Our Technique

For any finite set X, the notation "$x \leftarrow X$" means choosing an element x from X uniformly at random. Benabbas et al. [2] (Lemma 5.4) proposed a technique that allows a client to securely delegate the inner product computation of a fixed vector $\boldsymbol{f} = (f_i)_{i \in \mathbb{I}} \in \mathbb{Z}_p^N$ with any vector $\boldsymbol{y} = (y_i)_{i \in \mathbb{I}} \in \mathbb{Z}_p^N$, where p is a λ-bit prime and $\mathbb{I}$ is a finite ordered set of cardinality N. The client picks $\alpha \leftarrow \mathbb{Z}_p, \boldsymbol{r} = (r_i)_{i \in \mathbb{I}} \leftarrow \mathbb{Z}_p^N$, and stores f_i and $t_i = \alpha f_i + r_i$ with the server for every $\boldsymbol{i} \in \mathbb{I}$. In order for the client to learn the inner product $\rho = \boldsymbol{f} \cdot \boldsymbol{y}$, the server returns ρ and a proof $\pi = \boldsymbol{t} \cdot \boldsymbol{y}$. The client accepts ρ only if $\pi = \alpha\rho + \boldsymbol{r} \cdot \boldsymbol{y}$. A malicious server may try to deceive the client into accepting $\bar{\rho} \neq \rho$, using a forged proof $\bar{\pi}$ such that $\bar{\pi} = \alpha\bar{\rho} + \boldsymbol{r} \cdot \boldsymbol{y}$. A successful "try" implies (requires) the knowledge of $\alpha = (\bar{\rho} - \rho)^{-1}(\bar{\pi} - \pi)$, which is unknown to the server. Thus, the security is guaranteed. Inner product captures numerous widely used computations. For example, one can take $\mathbb{I} \subseteq \{0, 1, \ldots\}^m$, and consider $\boldsymbol{f}$ as the coefficients of a polynomial $f(\boldsymbol{x}) = \sum_{i \in \mathbb{I}} f_i \cdot \boldsymbol{x^i}$, where $\boldsymbol{x^i} = x_1^{i_1} \cdots x_m^{i_m}$ for $\boldsymbol{x} = (x_1, \ldots, x_m)$, and every $\boldsymbol{i} = (i_1, \ldots, i_m) \in \mathbb{I}$. Let $\boldsymbol{y} = (\boldsymbol{x^i})_{i \in \mathbb{I}}$. Then the inner product $\boldsymbol{f} \cdot \boldsymbol{y}$ exactly represents the polynomial evaluation $f(\boldsymbol{x})$.

The technique however, has two drawbacks: (a1) The client must keep a secret key $(\alpha, \boldsymbol{r})$ which consumes more storage than $\boldsymbol{f}$; (a2) The verification requires the client to compute $\boldsymbol{r} \cdot \boldsymbol{y}$ which is as heavy as the delegated computation (i.e., $\boldsymbol{f} \cdot \boldsymbol{y}$). Benabbas et al. [2] constructed a VC scheme for delegating the polynomial $f(\boldsymbol{x})$, based on an adaption of this technique. Let $\mathbb{G}$ be a cyclic group of prime order $p \approx 2^\lambda$, generated by g. In their scheme, the client picks $\alpha \leftarrow \mathbb{Z}_p$ and a PRF $\mathsf{F}_k : \mathbb{I} \rightarrow \mathbb{G}$; it stores f_i and $t_i = g^{\alpha f_i} \cdot \mathsf{F}_k(i)$ with the server for every $i \in \mathbb{I}$. Given $\boldsymbol{x}$, the server returns $\rho = f(\boldsymbol{x})$ and a proof $\pi = \Pi_{i \in \mathbb{I}}(t_i)^{\boldsymbol{x^i}}$. The client believes that "$\rho = f(\boldsymbol{x})$" only if $\pi = g^{\alpha\rho} \cdot \tau$, where $\tau = \prod_{i \in \mathbb{I}} \mathsf{F}_k(i)^{\boldsymbol{x^i}}$. If we denote $\mathsf{F}_k(i) = g^{r_i}$ for every i, then [2] actually uses their proposed technique, on the exponent of g. The client can keep (α, k) for verification and therefore avoid (a1). On the other hand, a critical observation of [2] is that one can choose F_k (with closed-form efficiency) such that computing τ requires substantially less time than computing ρ. This efficiency property of F_k removes (a2). The scheme of [2] has been extended to construct public VC schemes for delegating polynomials and matrices [7].

Our Technique. We propose a technique for securely delegating the inner product computations of s given vectors, $\boldsymbol{F}_1 = (F_{1,i})_{i \in \mathbb{I}}, \ldots, \boldsymbol{F}_s = (F_{s,i})_{i \in \mathbb{I}} \in \mathbb{Z}_p^N$, with any vector $\boldsymbol{y} = (y_i)_{i \in \mathbb{I}} \in \mathbb{Z}_p^N$, where p is a λ-bit prime and, $\mathbb{I}$ is an ordered set of cardinality N. Note that the technique of [2] can delegate the s given vectors separately but require the server to store a separate vector of N tags for each of the s vectors. Our main observation is that the s inner product computations involve a *common* vector $\boldsymbol{y}$, and we can authenticate the s given vectors with a single vector of N tags such that the server can generate a single proof for the s inner product computations. The details of our technique are as follows. The client picks $\boldsymbol{\alpha} = (\alpha_1, \ldots, \alpha_s) \in \mathbb{Z}_p^s$ and $\boldsymbol{r} = (r_i)_{i \in \mathbb{I}} \leftarrow \mathbb{Z}_p^N$, and computes the tag $t_i = \alpha_1 F_{1,i} + \cdots + \alpha_s F_{s,i} + r_i$ of the data blocks $(F_{1,i}, F_{2,i}, \ldots, F_{s,i})$ for every $i \in \mathbb{I}$. It then stores $\boldsymbol{F}_1, \ldots, \boldsymbol{F}_s$, and a tag vector $\boldsymbol{t} = (t_i)_{i \in \mathbb{I}}$, with the server. In order for the client to learn $\rho_1 = \boldsymbol{y} \cdot \boldsymbol{F}_1, \ldots, \rho_s = \boldsymbol{y} \cdot \boldsymbol{F}_s$, the server returns $\boldsymbol{\rho} = (\rho_1, \ldots, \rho_s)$ and a single proof $\pi = \boldsymbol{t} \cdot \boldsymbol{y}$; the client accepts $\boldsymbol{\rho}$ only if $\pi = \boldsymbol{\alpha} \cdot \boldsymbol{\rho} + \boldsymbol{r} \cdot \boldsymbol{y}$. As expected, the s vectors are authenticated using *one* tag vector $\boldsymbol{t}$ of size N. A malicious server may try to deceive the client into accepting $\bar{\boldsymbol{\rho}} \neq \boldsymbol{\rho}$ with a forged proof $\bar{\pi}$ such that $\bar{\pi} = \boldsymbol{\alpha} \cdot \bar{\boldsymbol{\rho}} + \boldsymbol{r} \cdot \boldsymbol{y}$. A successful "try" implies (requires) the knowledge of a nonzero vector $\boldsymbol{u} = (\pi - \bar{\pi}, \bar{\boldsymbol{\rho}} - \boldsymbol{\rho}) \in \mathbb{Z}_p^{N+1}$ such that $\boldsymbol{u} \cdot \boldsymbol{v} = 0$, where $\boldsymbol{v} = (1, \boldsymbol{\alpha}) \in \mathbb{Z}_p^{N+1}$. As $\boldsymbol{\alpha}$ is hidden from the server, it is intuitively hard for the malicious server to find $\boldsymbol{u}$. Our technical lemma (Lemma 1) in Section 2.2 shows that this intuition is true, even if the malicious server is allowed to make a polynomial (in λ) number of "tries", say $\boldsymbol{u}_1, \ldots, \boldsymbol{u}_q$, and is told whether $\boldsymbol{u}_j \cdot \boldsymbol{v} = 0$ or not for every "try" $\boldsymbol{u}_j$. Our client can choose $\boldsymbol{\alpha}$ in two ways: (b1) pick $\boldsymbol{\alpha} \leftarrow \mathbb{Z}_p^s$; (b2) pick $\alpha \leftarrow \mathbb{Z}_p$, and set $\boldsymbol{\alpha} = (\alpha, \alpha^2, \ldots, \alpha^s)$. In this paper we use our technique, together with the PRFs with closed-form efficiency, to delegate functions whose computations can be captured by the inner product computations of s given vectors, with a common (for all s vectors) vector. The s given vectors represent the delegated function, and the common vector is computed from an input to the delegated function. The functions we consider include polynomials and matrices.

1.3 Verifiable Delegation of Polynomials

Let $f(\boldsymbol{x}) = \sum_{\boldsymbol{i} \in \{0,1,\ldots,d\}^m} f_{\boldsymbol{i}} \cdot \boldsymbol{x}^{\boldsymbol{i}} \in \mathbb{Z}_p[\boldsymbol{x}]$ be an m-variate polynomial of degree $\leq d$ in each variable. Let s be the trade-off parameter, $n = (d+1)/s$ and $\mathbb{I} = \{0, 1, \ldots, n-1\} \times \{0, 1, \ldots, d\}^{m-1}$. Then

$$f(\boldsymbol{x}) = \sum_{\ell=1}^{s} x_1^{(\ell-1)n} \left(\sum_{\boldsymbol{i} \in \mathbb{I}} f_{(\ell-1)n + i_1, i_2, \ldots, i_m} \cdot \boldsymbol{x}^{\boldsymbol{i}} \right). \tag{1}$$

For every $\ell \in [s]$, let $\boldsymbol{F}_\ell = (F_{\ell,i})_{i \in \mathbb{I}} \in \mathbb{Z}_p^{|\mathbb{I}|}$, be a vector such that $F_{\ell,i} = f_{(\ell-1)n + i_1, i_2, \ldots, i_m}$ for every $\boldsymbol{i} = (i_1, \ldots, i_m) \in \mathbb{I}$. Let $\boldsymbol{y} = (\boldsymbol{x}^{\boldsymbol{i}})_{i \in \mathbb{I}}$. The equation (1) reduces the computation $f(\boldsymbol{x})$ to s inner product computations $\rho_1 = \boldsymbol{y} \cdot \boldsymbol{F}_1, \ldots, \rho_s = \boldsymbol{y} \cdot \boldsymbol{F}_s$ since $f(\boldsymbol{x}) = \sum_{\ell=1}^{s} \rho_\ell \cdot x_1^{(\ell-1)n}$. Thus, the verifiable delegation of $f(\boldsymbol{x})$ can be captured by our technique.

In this paper, we construct two schemes Π_1 and Π_2 for verifiably computing the s inner products and thus give two VC schemes for delegating f. In both schemes, the client stores $(F_{1,i}, \ldots, F_{s,i})$ and a corresponding tag t_i with the server for every $i \in \mathbb{I}$. Given $\boldsymbol{x} = (x_1, \ldots, x_m) \in \mathbb{Z}_p^m$, the server returns $\boldsymbol{\rho} = (\rho_1, \ldots, \rho_s)$ and a proof $\pi = \Pi_{i \in \mathbb{I}}(t_i)^{\boldsymbol{x}^{\boldsymbol{i}}}$. Let $\mathbb{G} = \langle g \rangle$ be a group of prime order p, and let $\mathsf{F}_k : \mathbb{I} \to \mathbb{G}$ be a PRF. In Π_1, the client picks $\alpha \leftarrow \mathbb{Z}_p$ and computes $t_i = g^{\alpha F_{1,i} + \cdots + \alpha^s F_{s,i}} \cdot \mathsf{F}_k(i)$, for every $i \in \mathbb{I}$; it accepts $\boldsymbol{\rho}$ only if $\pi = g^{\boldsymbol{\alpha} \cdot \boldsymbol{\rho}} \cdot \tau$, where $\boldsymbol{\alpha} = (\alpha, \ldots, \alpha^s)$ and $\tau = \prod_{i \in \mathbb{I}} \mathsf{F}_k(i)^{\boldsymbol{x}^{\boldsymbol{i}}}$. The scheme Π_2 uses a group $\mathbb{G}$

that admits a bilinear map e (see Section 2.3 for bilinear maps). The client picks $\boldsymbol{\alpha} = (\alpha_1, \ldots, \alpha_s) \leftarrow \mathbb{Z}_p^s$ and computes $t_i = g^{\alpha_1 F_{1,i} + \cdots + \alpha_s F_{s,i}} \cdot \mathsf{F}_k(i)$, for every $i \in \mathbb{I}$. It accepts $\boldsymbol{\rho}$ only if $e(\pi, g) = e(g, g)^{\boldsymbol{\alpha} \cdot \boldsymbol{\rho}} \cdot \tau$, where $\tau = e(\prod_{i \in \mathbb{I}} \mathsf{F}_k(i)^{\boldsymbol{x}^i}, g)$. The scheme is publicly verifiable: $e(g, g)^{\alpha_1}, \ldots, e(g, g)^{\alpha_s}$ and τ are safely made public such that the verification can be done publicly. The F_k in both schemes is chosen such that computing τ requires substantially less time than computing $f(\boldsymbol{x})$. The security of Π_1 is based on the SDDH or DDH assumption for $\mathbb{G}$; the security of Π_2 is based on the DLIN assumption for $\mathbb{G}$.

1.4   Verifiable Delegation of Matrices

Let $\boldsymbol{E} = (E_{i,j})$ be an $m \times d$ matrix over $\mathbb{Z}_p$. Let s be the trade-off parameter, $n = d/s$ and $\mathbb{I} = [m] \times [n]$. We consider $\boldsymbol{E}$ as a block matrix $\boldsymbol{E} = (\boldsymbol{F}_1, \ldots, \boldsymbol{F}_s)$ where the block $\boldsymbol{F}_\ell$ consists of n columns of $\boldsymbol{E}$ numbered from $(\ell - 1)n + 1$ to ℓn for every $\ell \in [s]$. It is easy to see that $\boldsymbol{F}_\ell = (F_{\ell,i})$ is an $m \times n$ matrix such that $F_{\ell,i} = E_{i,(\ell-1)n+j}$ for every $i = (i, j) \in \mathbb{I}$. Let $\boldsymbol{x} = (x_1, \ldots, x_m) \in \mathbb{Z}_p^m$. For every $j \in [n]$, we have s inner product computations of $\boldsymbol{x}$ with the j-th columns of the block matrices $\boldsymbol{F}_1, \ldots, \boldsymbol{F}_s$.

In this paper, we construct two schemes Π_3 and Π_4 for verifiably computing the s inner products for all $j \in [n]$ and thus give two VC schemes for delegating $\boldsymbol{E}$. In both schemes, the client stores $(F_{1,i}, \ldots, F_{s,i})$ and a corresponding tag t_i with the server for every $i = (i, j) \in \mathbb{I}$. Given $\boldsymbol{x} = (x_1, \ldots, x_m) \in \mathbb{Z}_p^m$, the server returns $\boldsymbol{\rho} = (\rho_1, \ldots, \rho_d) = \boldsymbol{x} \cdot \boldsymbol{E}$ and n proofs $\{\pi_j = \Pi_{i=1}^m (t_{i,j})^{x_i}\}_{j=1}^n$, one for each set of s inner products. Let $\mathbb{G} = \langle g \rangle$ be a group of prime order p and let $\mathsf{F}_k : \mathbb{I} \to \mathbb{G}$ be a PRF. In Π_3, the client picks $\alpha \leftarrow \mathbb{Z}_p$ and defines $t_i = g^{\alpha F_{1,i} + \alpha^2 F_{2,i} + \cdots + \alpha^s F_{s,i}} \cdot \mathsf{F}_k(i)$ for every $i = (i, j) \in \mathbb{I}$. The client accepts $\boldsymbol{\rho}$ only if $\pi_j = g^{\sum_{\ell=1}^s \rho_{j+(\ell-1)n} \cdot \alpha^\ell} \cdot \tau_j$ for every $j \in [n]$, where $\tau_j = \prod_{i=1}^m \mathsf{F}_k(i,j)^{x_i}$. The F_k is chosen such that computing $\{\tau_j\}_{j=1}^n$ requires substantially less time than computing $\boldsymbol{x} \cdot \boldsymbol{E}$. The scheme Π_4 is a public version of Π_3 using a group $\mathbb{G}$ that admits bilinear map. The security of Π_3 is based on the DDH assumption for $\mathbb{G}$; the security of Π_4 is based on the DLIN assumption for $\mathbb{G}$.

1.5   Performance Analysis and Extensions

We do performance analysis of the constructed schemes. Our analysis focuses on the trade-off between the required cloud storage, and the client's verification time. The storage overheads of our schemes are all equal to $1 + 1/s$, which is smaller than [2,7]. The clients in Π_1 and the scheme in [2], require around $((m + 2)\lambda + 4s)\lambda^2$ and $(m + 1)\lambda^3$ bit operations for each verification, respectively. Thus, Π_1 achieves significant saving of the cloud storage at the price of slightly increasing the client's verification time. The scheme Π_4 uses a bilinear map instance $(p, \mathbb{G}, \mathbb{G}_T, e, g)$ (see Section 2.3). The client's verification time is dominated by $(m + n)$ exponentiations in $\mathbb{G}$, sn exponentiations in $\mathbb{G}_T$ and $2n$ pairing computations. Compared with Π_4, the client's verification time of [7] is dominated by $(m + sn)$ exponentiations in $\mathbb{G}$, sn exponentiations in $\mathbb{G}_T$, and $2sn$

pairing computations. Thus, our scheme Π_4 is more efficient not only in terms of storage overhead but also in terms of client's verification time. The performance analysis of Π_2 and Π_3 can be done similarly.

Our schemes for delegating $f(\boldsymbol{x})$ reduce $f(\boldsymbol{x})$ to the computations of s shorter polynomials, each taking one of the vectors $\boldsymbol{F}_1, \ldots, \boldsymbol{F}_s$ as coefficients, and having degree $\leq n-1$ in x_1, and degree $\leq d$ in any other variable. We can *repeat this degree reduction* on $x_2, \ldots, x_m$ and thus reduce $f(\boldsymbol{x})$ to the computations of s^m shorter polynomials, each having degree $\leq n-1$, in any variable. Our technique can also be used to delegate multiple distinct functions, resulting in *batch verification*, which is more efficient than delegating the functions separately using the schemes of [2,7]. For example, when $m = 1$ we can treat the vectors $\boldsymbol{F}_1, \ldots, \boldsymbol{F}_s$ in Π_1 as coefficients of s univariate polynomials; Π_1 allows us to efficiently verify the evaluations of the s polynomials at the same point, with a single proof from the server.

1.6   Related Work

The problem of verifiably outsourcing computation has a long history. We refer readers to [8,2] for a more detailed treatment of solutions that use strong assumptions on the adversary, and more theoretical solutions that use interaction. Here we are interested in non-interactive solutions in the standard model.

Verifiable Computation. The verifiable computation (VC) of Gennaro et al. [8] gave a non-interactive solution for verifiably outsourcing computation in the standard model. The VC schemes of [8,6,1] can delegate a function that is represented by a boolean circuit. They stay as mainly theoretical solutions because of using fully homomorphic encryption (FHE). The memory delegation of [5] can delegate computations on an arbitrary portion of the outsourced data. However, the client must be stateful and the solution suffer from the impracticality of PCP techniques. Benabbas et al. [2] initiated the study of practical (private) VC schemes for delegating specific functions such as polynomials. Parno et al. [17] initiated the study of public VC schemes. Fiore et al. [7] extended the constructions of [2] and obtained public VC schemes for delegating polynomials and matrices. Papamanthou et al. [16] constructed a public VC scheme for delegating polynomials that allows efficient update. The storage overhead of all these schemes is ≥ 2.

Homomorphic MACs and Signatures. A homomorphic MAC or signature scheme [10,4] allows one to freely authenticate data and then verify computations on the authenticated data. Such schemes result in VC: the client stores data blocks and their MAC tags (or signatures) with a server; the server computes some admissible functions on an arbitrary subset of the data blocks; the server provides both the result and a MAC tag (or signature) vouching for the correctness of the result. The storage overhead of the resulting VC is ≥ 2.

Non-interactive Proofs. Goldwasser et al. [12] gave a non-interactive scheme for delegating NC computations. However, for any circuit of size n, the server's running time is a high degree polynomial in n, and so not practical. The SNARGs or SNARKs [3,9], gives a non-interactive scheme for delegating computation. However, they rely on non-falsifiable assumptions [11] which are much stronger than the common assumptions (such as DDH), used in this paper.

Proofs of Retrievability. PoR [13,18] allows a client to store a file with a server, and then efficiently check the file's integrity. Homomorphic linear authenticators that are similar to our authenticators, have been used in [18] but not formally proved as an authentication system. We give a formal proof here. Other differences with [18] are as follows: firstly, the α in [18] was chosen using (b1); we can use (b2) and thus have a much shorter secret key; secondly, they cannot use PRFs with closed-form efficiency while we can combine such PRFs with our technique to give VC schemes.

ORGANIZATION. In Section 2 we recall the notions of VC and PRFs with closed-form efficiency; In Section 3 we present the schemes Π_1-Π_4; Section 4 contains some concluding remarks.

2   Preliminaries

Let λ be a security parameter. We denote by "poly(λ)" and "neg(λ)" the classes of polynomial functions and negligible functions in λ, respectively. Let $\mathcal{A}(\cdot)$ be a probabilistic polynomial time (PPT) algorithm. The notation "$y \leftarrow \mathcal{A}(x)$" means that y is the output of $\mathcal{A}$ on input x.

2.1   Verifiable Computation

A verifiable computation (VC) scheme is a tuple $\Pi = (\mathsf{KeyGen}, \mathsf{ProbGen}, \mathsf{Compute}, \mathsf{Verify})$ of four algorithms, where

- $(ek, dk, vk) \leftarrow \mathsf{KeyGen}(1^\lambda, f)$ is a key generation algorithm that takes as input the security parameter λ and a function f and outputs an evaluation key ek, a delegation key dk and a verification key vk;
- $(\sigma, \tau) \leftarrow \mathsf{ProbGen}(dk, x)$ is a problem generation algorithm that takes as input dk and any input x in the domain of f and outputs an encoding σ of x and some auxiliary information τ for verification;
- $(\rho, \pi) \leftarrow \mathsf{Compute}(ek, \sigma)$ is a computation algorithm that takes as input ek and σ and outputs an answer ρ and a proof π; and
- $\{f(x), \bot\} \leftarrow \mathsf{Verify}(vk, \tau, \rho, \pi)$ is a verification algorithm that verifies ρ with (vk, τ, π); it outputs $f(x)$ or $\bot$ (to indicate failure).

Model. The VC model involves a client $\mathcal{C}$ and a server $\mathcal{S}$, where $\mathcal{C}$ has a function f. The client $\mathcal{C}$ picks $(ek, dk, vk) \leftarrow \mathsf{KeyGen}(1^\lambda, f)$ and gives ek to the server. In order to learn $f(x)$, the client computes $(\sigma, \tau) \leftarrow \mathsf{ProbGen}(dk, x)$ and gives σ to the server. Given (ek, σ), the server computes and replies with $(\rho, \pi) \leftarrow \mathsf{Compute}(ek, \sigma)$. At last, the client runs $\mathsf{Verify}(vk, \tau, \rho, \pi)$ to verify ρ and recover $f(x)$. The verification of ρ requires vk, τ and π. The scheme Π is called *privately verifiable* if (vk, τ) must be kept private by $\mathcal{C}$, and *publicly verifiable* if (vk, τ) can be made public (in particular, it can be known to $\mathcal{S}$).

Correctness. This property requires that the client can always learn the correct result of the delegated computation when the server is honest. Formally, the scheme Π is *correct* if for any function f, any $(ek, dk, vk) \leftarrow \mathsf{KeyGen}(1^\lambda, f)$, any x in the domain of f, any $(\sigma, \tau) \leftarrow \mathsf{ProbGen}(dk, x)$ and any $(\rho, \pi) \leftarrow \mathsf{Compute}(ek, \sigma)$, it holds that $\mathsf{Verify}(vk, \tau, \rho, \pi) = f(x)$.

Security. This property requires that no malicious server can cause the client to compute an incorrect result of the delegated computation. Formally, the scheme Π is said to be *secure* if any PPT adversary $\mathcal{A}$ wins with probability $< \mathsf{neg}(\lambda)$ in the security game of **Fig. 1**.

- SETUP. Given f, the challenger picks $(ek, dk, vk) \leftarrow \mathsf{KeyGen}(1^\lambda, f)$. If Π is privately verifiable, it gives ek to $\mathcal{A}$ and keeps (dk, vk); if Π is publicly verifiable, it gives (ek, vk) to $\mathcal{A}$ and keeps dk.
- QUERIES. The adversary $\mathcal{A}$ adaptively makes a polynomial number of queries: for every $j = 1$ to $q = \mathsf{poly}(\lambda)$,
  - $\mathcal{A}$ picks x_j from the domain of f and gives it to the challenger;
  - The challenger computes $(\sigma_j, \tau_j) \leftarrow \mathsf{ProbGen}(dk, x_j)$. If Π is privately verifiable, it gives σ_j to $\mathcal{A}$; if Π is publicly verifiable, it gives (σ_j, τ_j) to $\mathcal{A}$.
  - $\mathcal{A}$ picks a response $(\bar{\rho}_j, \bar{\pi}_j)$ to the challenger;
  - The challenger gives the output of $\mathsf{Verify}(vk, \tau_j, \bar{\rho}_j, \bar{\pi}_j)$ to $\mathcal{A}$.
- FORGERY. $\mathcal{A}$ picks x^* from the domain of f. The challenger computes $(\sigma^*, \tau^*) \leftarrow \mathsf{ProbGen}(dk, x^*)$. If Π is privately verifiable, the challenger gives σ^* to $\mathcal{A}$; if Π is publicly verifiable, the challenger gives (σ^*, τ^*) to $\mathcal{A}$. At last, $\mathcal{A}$ picks $(\bar{\rho}^*, \bar{\pi}^*)$.
- OUTPUT. The adversary *wins* if $\mathsf{Verify}(sk, \tau^*, \bar{\rho}^*, \bar{\pi}^*) \notin \{f(x^*), \bot\}$.

Fig. 1. Security game

Remark. In FORGERY $\mathcal{A}$ behaves just like it has done in any one of the q queries. Without loss of generality, we can suppose $(x^*, \bar{\rho}^*, \bar{\pi}^*) = (x_c, \bar{\rho}_c, \bar{\pi}_c)$ for some $c \in [q]$, i.e., $\mathcal{A}$ picks one of its q queries as forgery.

2.2 A Technical Lemma

In this section we study a problem that underlies the security of our technique in Section 1.1 (and the security proofs of the privately verifiable schemes Π_1 and Π_3). Let λ be a security parameter. Let p be a λ-bit prime and let $\mathbb{F}_p$ be the finite field of p elements. Let $s > 0$. We define an equivalence relation $\sim$ over $\mathbb{F}_p^s \setminus \{0\}$ as below: two vectors $\boldsymbol{u}, \boldsymbol{v} \in \mathbb{F}_p^s \setminus \{0\}$ are *equivalent* if there exists $\xi \in \mathbb{F}_p \setminus \{0\}$ such that $\boldsymbol{u} = \xi \cdot \boldsymbol{v}$. Let $\Omega_{p,s} = (\mathbb{F}_p^s \setminus \{0\})/ \sim$ be the set of all equivalent classes. We represent each equivalent class with a vector in that class. Without loss of generality, we agree that the representative of each class in $\Omega_{p,s}$ is chosen such that its first non-zero element is 1. For example, when $p = 3$ and $s = 2$, we have that $\Omega_{p,s} = \{(0,1), (1,0), (1,1), (1,2)\}$. For any $\boldsymbol{u}, \boldsymbol{v} \in \Omega_{p,s}$, we define $\boldsymbol{u} \odot \boldsymbol{v} = 0$ if the inner product of $\boldsymbol{u}$ and $\boldsymbol{v}$ is 0 and define $\boldsymbol{u} \odot \boldsymbol{v} = 1$ otherwise. For example, when $p = 3$ and $s = 2$, we have that $(1,1) \odot (1,2) = 0$ and $(1,1) \odot (1,1) = 1$. The following problem models the malicious server's attack in our technique.

Problem 1. Let $\mathcal{A}$ be any algorithm. Let $U, V \subseteq \Omega_{p,s+1}$ and let $q = \mathrm{poly}(\lambda)$. In this problem, a vector $\boldsymbol{v}^* \leftarrow V$ is chosen and hidden from $\mathcal{A}$; for $i = 1$ to q, $\mathcal{A}$ adaptively picks a query $\boldsymbol{u}_i \in U$ and learns $b_i = \boldsymbol{u}_i \odot \boldsymbol{v}^* \in \{0, 1\}$; $\mathcal{A}$ *wins* only if there exists an $i^* \in [q]$ such that $b_{i^*} = 0$.

Lemma 1. *Suppose that $0 < \epsilon < 1$. If $|\{\boldsymbol{v} \in V : \boldsymbol{u} \odot \boldsymbol{v} = 0\}| \leq \epsilon \cdot |V|$ for every $\boldsymbol{u} \in U$, then $\mathcal{A}$ wins in Problem 1 with probability $\leq \epsilon q$.*

Proof. For every $i \in [q]$, let $\mathbf{S}_i$ be the event that $b_i = 0$ and let $\neg\mathbf{S}_i$ be the event that $b_i = 1$. We denote $\mathbf{F}_i = \neg\mathbf{S}_i \wedge \cdots \wedge \neg\mathbf{S}_1$ for every $i \in [q]$. Clearly, the probabilities of $\mathbf{S}_i, \neg\mathbf{S}_i$ and $\mathbf{F}_i$ are all taken over the uniform choice of $\boldsymbol{v}^*$ and the adversarial choices of $\boldsymbol{u}_1, \ldots, \boldsymbol{u}_i$ by $\mathcal{A}$. The probability that $\mathcal{A}$ wins in **Problem 1** is bounded by

$$\epsilon^* = \Pr[\mathbf{S}_1] + \sum_{i=2}^{q} \Pr[\mathbf{S}_i \wedge \mathbf{F}_{i-1}]. \tag{2}$$

Note that $|\{\boldsymbol{v} \in V : \boldsymbol{u}_1 \odot \boldsymbol{v} = 0\}| \leq \epsilon|V|$ for any $\boldsymbol{u}_1 \in U$, we must have that $\Pr[\mathbf{S}_1] = \Pr[\boldsymbol{u}_1 \odot \boldsymbol{v}^* = 0] = \frac{|\{\boldsymbol{v} \in V : \boldsymbol{u}_1 \odot \boldsymbol{v}=0\}|}{|V|} \leq \epsilon$. If $\mathbf{F}_1$ occurs, then $\mathcal{A}$ learns that $\boldsymbol{v}^* \notin \{\boldsymbol{v} \in V : \boldsymbol{u}_1 \odot \boldsymbol{v} = 0\}$, which allows $\mathcal{A}$ to rule out at most $\epsilon \cdot |V|$ possibilities of $\boldsymbol{v}^*$. Conditioned on $\mathbf{F}_1$, the $\boldsymbol{v}^*$ will be uniformly distributed over the set $V_1 = \{\boldsymbol{v} \in V : \boldsymbol{u}_1 \odot \boldsymbol{v} = 1\}$. Note that $|\{\boldsymbol{v} \in V_1 : \boldsymbol{u}_2 \odot \boldsymbol{v} = 0\}| \leq |\{\boldsymbol{v} \in V : \boldsymbol{u}_2 \odot \boldsymbol{v} = 0\}| \leq \epsilon|V|$ for any $\boldsymbol{u}_2 \in U$. Thus, $\Pr[\mathbf{S}_2 \wedge \mathbf{F}_1] = \Pr[\boldsymbol{u}_2 \odot \boldsymbol{v}^* = 0|\mathbf{F}_1] \cdot \Pr[\mathbf{F}_1] = \frac{|\{\boldsymbol{v} \in V_1 : \boldsymbol{u}_2 \odot \boldsymbol{v}=0\}|}{|V_1|} \frac{|V_1|}{|V|} \leq \epsilon$, where the second equality follows from the fact that $\boldsymbol{v}^*$ is uniformly distributed over V_1 (conditioned on $\mathbf{F}_1$). In general, for any $i \in [q]$ we can bound the probability $\epsilon_i = \Pr[\mathbf{S}_i \wedge \mathbf{F}_{i-1}]$ that $\boldsymbol{u}_i$ is the first query such that $\boldsymbol{u}_i \odot \boldsymbol{v}^* = 0$. Let $V_{i-1} = \{\boldsymbol{v} \in V : \boldsymbol{u}_1 \odot \boldsymbol{v} = 1, \cdots, \boldsymbol{u}_{i-1} \odot \boldsymbol{v} = 1\}$. Conditioned on $\mathbf{F}_{i-1}$, $\boldsymbol{v}^*$ must be uniformly distributed over V_{i-1}. Note that $|\{\boldsymbol{v} \in V_{i-1} : \boldsymbol{u}_i \odot \boldsymbol{v} = 0\}| \leq \epsilon|V|$ for any $\boldsymbol{u}_i \in U$. We have

$$\epsilon_i = \Pr[\mathbf{S}_i|\mathbf{F}_{i-1}] \Pr[\mathbf{F}_{i-1}] = \Pr[\boldsymbol{u}_i \odot \boldsymbol{v}^* = 0|\mathbf{F}_{i-1}] \prod_{h=2}^{i-1} \Pr[\neg\mathbf{S}_h|\mathbf{F}_{h-1}] \Pr[\mathbf{F}_1]$$

$$= \frac{|\{\boldsymbol{v} \in V_{i-1} : \boldsymbol{u}_i \odot \boldsymbol{v} = 0\}|}{|V_{i-1}|} \frac{|V_{i-1}|}{|V_{i-2}|} \cdots \frac{|V_2|}{|V_1|} \frac{|V_1|}{|V|} \leq \epsilon,$$

where $\Pr[\neg\mathbf{S}_h|\mathbf{F}_{h-1}]$ is the probability that the uniform random variable $\boldsymbol{v}^*$ (over V_{h-1}) falls into $V_h \subseteq V_{h-1}$ for every $h \in [i-1]$. Hence, we have $\epsilon^* \leq \epsilon q$ as each summand on the right hand side of (2) is $\leq \epsilon$. $\qquad\square$

Example 1. Let $V_{\mathrm{lin}} = \{(1, \boldsymbol{w}) : \boldsymbol{w} \in \mathbb{F}_p^s\} \subseteq \Omega_{p,s+1}$ and $U \subseteq \Omega_{p,s+1}$. It is easy to see that $|V_{\mathrm{lin}}| = p^s$. For any $\boldsymbol{u} \in U$, there are $\leq N = (p^s - 1)/(p-1)$ elements $\boldsymbol{v} \in V_{\mathrm{lin}}$ such that $\boldsymbol{u} \odot \boldsymbol{v} = 0$. Thus, $\epsilon \leq N/|V_{\mathrm{lin}}| < 1/(p-1)$.

Example 2. Let $V_{\mathrm{pol}} = \{(1, \alpha, \ldots, \alpha^s) : \alpha \in \mathbb{F}_p\} \subseteq \Omega_{p,s+1}$ and $U \subseteq \Omega_{p,s+1}$. Let $\boldsymbol{u} = (u_0, u_1, \ldots, u_s) \in U$ and $\boldsymbol{v} = (1, \alpha, \ldots, \alpha^s) \in V_{\mathrm{pol}}$. Then $\boldsymbol{u} \odot \boldsymbol{v} = 0$ only if α is a root of $u_0 + u_1 x + \cdots + u_s x^s$. For any $\boldsymbol{u} \in U$, there are $\leq s$ elements $\boldsymbol{v} \in V_{\mathrm{pol}}$

such that $\boldsymbol{u} \odot \boldsymbol{v} = 0$ because a univariate polynomial of degree s has $\leq s$ roots in $\mathbb{F}_p$. Thus, $\epsilon \leq s/p$ in this case.

The two examples provide us with two ways of choosing the $\boldsymbol{\alpha}$ in our technique: (b1) pick $\boldsymbol{\alpha} \leftarrow \mathbb{F}_p^s$; and (b2) pick $\alpha \leftarrow \mathbb{F}_p$ and define $\boldsymbol{\alpha} = (\alpha, \alpha^2, \ldots, \alpha^s)$. We use (b2) in Π_1 and Π_3 such that a short secret key suffices to do verification.

2.3   Cryptographic Assumptions

We assume a *group scheme* $\mathcal{G}(1^\lambda, \ell)$ that takes as input the security parameter λ and an integer $\ell \in \{1, 2\}$ and outputs a *random group instance* Λ. When $\ell = 1$, Λ is a triple $(p, \mathbb{G}, g)$, where $\mathbb{G} = \langle g \rangle$ is a group of prime order $p \approx 2^\lambda$; when $\ell = 2$, Λ is a quintuple $(p, \mathbb{G}, \mathbb{G}_T, e, g)$, where $\mathbb{G} = \langle g \rangle$ and $\mathbb{G}_T$ are groups of prime order $p \approx 2^\lambda$, and $e : \mathbb{G} \times \mathbb{G} \to \mathbb{G}_T$ is an efficiently computable non-degenerated bilinear map. In Section 2.4 we present five PRFs. The security of each PRF is based on one of the following assumptions for $\mathbb{G}$: the *d-strong decision Diffie-Hellman* assumption (*d*-SDDH); the *decision Diffie-Hellman* assumption (DDH); and the *decision linear* assumption (DLIN). We refer the readers to [2,7] for their definitions. There is also a much weaker assumption for $\mathbb{G}$: the hardness of *computational Diffie-Hellman* (CDH) problem. In CDH, one is given (g, g^α, h) and must output h^α, where $\alpha \leftarrow \mathbb{Z}_p$ and $h \leftarrow \mathbb{G}$. The hardness of CDH says that no PPT algorithm can output h^α except with probability $< \mathsf{neg}(\lambda)$.

2.4   PRFs with Closed-Form Efficiency

In this section, we review the notion of PRFs with closed-form efficiency and present several such PRFs for our VC schemes. A PRF is a pair $\Sigma = (\mathsf{Kg}, \mathsf{F})$ of algorithms. The key generation algorithm $\mathsf{Kg}(1^\lambda, \mathsf{params})$ takes as input a security parameter λ and some additional parameters params and outputs a secret key k and a public parameter pp, where pp specifies the domain $\mathbb{I}$ and range $\mathbb{Y}$ of F_k. Given any $i \in \mathbb{I}$, $\mathsf{F}_k(i)$ outputs a value $y \in \mathbb{Y}$. Σ is called *pseudorandom* if for any PPT algorithm $\mathcal{A}$, we have $| \Pr[\mathcal{A}^{\mathsf{F}_k(\cdot)}(1^\lambda, \mathsf{pp}) = 1] - \Pr[\mathcal{A}^{\Phi(\cdot)}(1^\lambda, \mathsf{pp}) = 1]| < \mathsf{neg}(\lambda)$, where the probabilities are taken over $(\mathsf{pp}, k) \leftarrow \mathsf{Kg}(1^\lambda, \mathsf{params})$, the choice of a random function $\Phi : \mathbb{I} \to \mathbb{Y}$ and $\mathcal{A}$'s random coins. Let $C(\boldsymbol{y}, \boldsymbol{x})$ be any computation that takes $\boldsymbol{y} = \{y_i\}_{i \in \mathbb{I}} \in \mathbb{Y}^{|\mathbb{I}|}$ and some $\boldsymbol{x}$ as input. Suppose that computing $C(\boldsymbol{y}, \boldsymbol{x})$ for general $(\boldsymbol{y}, \boldsymbol{x})$ requires time t. We say that Σ has *closed-form efficiency for C* if there is an algorithm $\Sigma.\mathsf{CFE}$ such that $\Sigma.\mathsf{CFE}(k, \mathbb{I}, \boldsymbol{x}) = C(\{\mathsf{F}_k(i)\}_{i \in \mathbb{I}}, \boldsymbol{x})$ but only requires time $o(t)$.

Construction 1. Let $m > 0$ and $d + 1 = sn$. Our first PRF $\Sigma_1 = (\mathsf{Kg}, \mathsf{F})$ is tailored from the $\mathcal{PRF}_{2,d}$ in [2]. The algorithm $\mathsf{Kg}(1^\lambda, (m, s, n))$ picks $\Lambda = (p, \mathbb{G}, g) \leftarrow \mathcal{G}(1^\lambda, 1)$, $k = (k_0, k_1, \ldots, k_m) \leftarrow \mathbb{Z}_p^{m+1}$ and outputs k and $\mathsf{pp} = (\Lambda, m, s, n)$. The domain of F_k is $\mathbb{I} = \{0, 1, \ldots, n - 1\} \times \{0, 1, \ldots, d\}^{m-1}$; the range of F_k is $\mathbb{G}$. For any $\boldsymbol{i} = (i_1, \ldots, i_m) \in \mathbb{I}$, $\mathsf{F}_k(\boldsymbol{i}) = g^{k_0 k_1^{i_1} \cdots k_m^{i_m}}$. In fact, Σ_1 is the restriction of $\mathcal{PRF}_{2,d}$ on $\mathbb{I}$. Theorem 1 of [2] shows that Σ_1 is a PRF under the *d*-SDDH assumption. For $\boldsymbol{x} = (x_1, \ldots, x_m) \in \mathbb{Z}_p^m$ and $\boldsymbol{y} = \{y_i\}_{i \in \mathbb{I}} \in \mathbb{G}^{|\mathbb{I}|}$, let $C'(\boldsymbol{y}, \boldsymbol{x}) = \prod_{i \in \mathbb{I}}(y_i)^{\boldsymbol{x}^i}$. Then we have $C'(\{\mathsf{F}_k(i)\}_{i \in \mathbb{I}}, \boldsymbol{x}) = g^\xi$, where

$\xi = k_0(1 - (k_1x_1)^n)/(1 - k_1x_1) \cdot \prod_{j=2}^m (1 - (k_jx_j)^{d+1})/(1 - k_jx_j)$. Without k, computing $C'(\{F_k(i)\}_{i \in \mathbb{I}}, x)$ requires $O(|\mathbb{I}|)$ operations. Given k, the Σ_1.CFE can compute ξ and then g^ξ using $O(m) = o(|\mathbb{I}|)$ operations. Thus, Σ_1 has closed-form efficiency for C'.

Construction 2. Let $m > 0$ and $d + 1 = 2^a = sn = s \cdot 2^b$. Below is our instantiation $\Sigma_2 = (\mathsf{Kg}, \mathsf{F})$ of the Naor-Reingold PRF (Section 4.1, [15]).

$\mathsf{Kg}(1^\lambda, (m, a, b))$: Picks $\Lambda = (p, \mathbb{G}, g) \leftarrow \mathcal{G}(1^\lambda, 1)$. Picks $k_0 \leftarrow \mathbb{Z}_p$, $k_{1,w} \leftarrow \mathbb{Z}_p$ for every $w \in [b]$ and $k_{u,v} \leftarrow \mathbb{Z}_p$ for every $(u, v) \in \{2, \ldots, m\} \times [a]$. Outputs $k = \{k_0\} \cup \{k_{1,w} : w \in [b]\} \cup \{k_{u,v} : (u, v) \in \{2, \ldots, m\} \times [a]\}$ and $\mathsf{pp} = (\Lambda, m, a, b)$. The domain of F_k is $\mathbb{I} = \{0, 1, \ldots, n-1\} \times \{0, 1, \ldots, d\}^{m-1}$. The range of F_k is $\mathbb{G}$.

$\mathsf{F}_k(\cdot)$: Given $i = (i_1, \ldots, i_m) \in \mathbb{I}$, computes the binary representations of $i_1, \ldots, i_m$, say $i_1 = (i_{1,1}, \ldots, i_{1,b})$ and $i_u = (i_{u,1}, \ldots, i_{u,a})$ for every $2 \le u \le m$. It outputs $\mathsf{F}_k(i) = g^{\xi_i}$, where $\xi_i = k_0 \cdot \prod_{w=1}^b k_{1,w}^{i_{1,w}} \cdot \prod_{u=2}^m \prod_{v=1}^a k_{u,v}^{i_{u,v}}$.

As a Naor-Reingold PRF defined over $\{0, 1\}^{b+(m-1)a}$, Σ_2 is pseudorandom under DDH. Note that $C'(\{F_k(i)\}_{i \in \mathbb{I}}, x) = \prod_{i \in \mathbb{I}} F_k(i)^{x^i} = g^\xi$, where

$$\xi = \sum_{i \in \mathbb{I}} \xi_i \cdot x^i = \sum_{i_1=0}^{2^b-1} \sum_{i_2=0}^{2^a-1} \cdots \sum_{i_m=0}^{2^a-1} k_0 \cdot \prod_{w=1}^b k_{1,w}^{i_{1,w}} x_1^{i_{1,w} \cdot 2^{w-1}} \cdot \prod_{u=2}^m \prod_{v=1}^a k_{u,v}^{i_{u,v}} \cdot x_u^{i_{u,v} \cdot 2^{v-1}}$$

$$= k_0 \cdot \prod_{w=1}^b \left(1 + k_{1,w} x_1^{2^{w-1}}\right) \cdot \prod_{u=2}^m \prod_{v=1}^a \left(1 + k_{u,v} x_u^{2^{v-1}}\right).$$

Computing $C'(\{F_k(i)\}_{i \in \mathbb{I}}, x)$ without k requires $O(|\mathbb{I}|)$ operations. Given k, the Σ_2.CFE can compute ξ and then g^ξ using $O(ma) = o(|\mathbb{I}|)$ operations. Thus, Σ_2 has the closed form efficiency for C'.

Construction 3. Let $m > 0$ and $d + 1 = 2^a = sn = s \cdot 2^b$. Below is an instantiation $\Sigma_3 = (\mathsf{Kg}, \mathsf{F})$ of the Lewko-Waters PRF (Section 3.1, [14]).

$\mathsf{Kg}(1^\lambda, (m, a, b))$: Picks $\Lambda = (p, \mathbb{G}, \mathbb{G}_T, g) \leftarrow \mathcal{G}(1^\lambda, 2)$, $k_0, l_0 \leftarrow \mathbb{Z}_p$, a 2×2 matrix $K_{1,w} \leftarrow \mathbb{Z}_p^{2 \times 2}$ for every $w \in [b]$, and a 2×2 matrix $K_{u,v} \leftarrow \mathbb{Z}_p^{2 \times 2}$ for every $(u, v) \in \{2, \ldots, m\} \times [a]$. Outputs $k = \{k_0, l_0\} \cup \{K_{1,w} : w \in [b]\} \cup \{K_{u,v} : (u, v) \in \{2, \ldots, m\} \times [a]\}$ and $\mathsf{pp} = (\Lambda, m, a, b)$. The domain of F_k is $\mathbb{I} = \{0, 1, \ldots, n-1\} \times \{0, 1, \ldots, d\}^{m-1}$; the range of F_k is $\mathbb{G}$.

$\mathsf{F}_k(\cdot)$: Given $i = (i_1, \ldots, i_m) \in \mathbb{I}$, computes the binary representations of $i_1, \ldots, i_m$, say $i_1 = (i_{1,1}, \ldots, i_{1,b})$ and $i_u = (i_{u,1}, \ldots, i_{u,a})$ for every $2 \le u \le m$. It outputs $\mathsf{F}_k(i) = g^{\xi_i}$, where $(\xi_i, \eta_i) = (k_0, l_0) \prod_{w=1}^b K_{1,w}^{i_{1,w}} \prod_{u=2}^m \prod_{v=1}^a K_{u,v}^{i_{u,v}}$.

As a Lewko-Waters PRF defined over $\{0, 1\}^{b+(m-1)a}$, Σ_3 is pseudorandom under DLIN. Note that $C'(\{F_k(i)\}_{i \in \mathbb{I}}, x) = g^\xi$ with $\xi = \sum_{i \in \mathbb{I}} \xi_i \cdot x^i$. As in construction 2, we can similarly show that Σ_3 has the closed form efficiency for C'.

Construction 4. Let $m, n > 0$. Below is a DDH based PRF $\Sigma_4 = (\mathsf{Kg}, \mathsf{F})$.

$\mathsf{Kg}(1^\lambda, (m, n))$: Picks $\Lambda = (p, \mathbb{G}, g) \leftarrow \mathcal{G}(1^\lambda, 1)$, $u_i \leftarrow \mathbb{G}$ for every $i \in [m]$, $k_j \leftarrow \mathbb{Z}_p$ for every $j \in [n]$; outputs $k = \{u_i\}_{i=1}^m \cup \{k_j\}_{j=1}^n$ and $\mathsf{pp} = (\Lambda, m, n)$. The domain of F_k is $\mathbb{I} = [m] \times [n]$; the range of F_k is $\mathbb{G}$.

$\mathsf{F}_k(\cdot)$: Given $(i, j) \in [m] \times [n]$, it outputs $\mathsf{F}_k(i, j) = u_i^{k_j}$.

In the full version, we show Σ_4 is a DDH-based PRF. Let $\boldsymbol{x} = (x_1, \ldots, x_m) \in \mathbb{Z}_p^m$ and $\boldsymbol{y} = \{y_{i,j}\} \in \mathbb{G}^{m \times n}$. Let $C''(\boldsymbol{y}, \boldsymbol{x}) = \{\prod_{i=1}^m (y_{i,j})^{x_i}\}_{j=1}^n$. Then $\prod_{i=1}^m \mathsf{F}_k(i,j)^{x_i}$ $= \prod_{i=1}^m (u_i^{k_j})^{x_i} = (\prod_{i=1}^m u_i^{x_i})^{k_j}$ for every $j \in [n]$. Computing $C''(\{\mathsf{F}_k(i,j)\}, \boldsymbol{x})$ without k requires $O(mn)$ operations. Given k, the Σ_4.CFE can compute $U = \prod_{i=1}^m u_i^{x_i}$ and then U^{k_j} for all $j \in [n]$ using $O(m+n)$ operations. Thus, Σ_4 has closed-form efficiency for C''.

Construction 5. Fiore et al. (Section 3.1.3, [7]) constructed a PRF $\Sigma_5 = (\mathsf{Kg}, \mathsf{F})$. The $\mathsf{Kg}(1^\lambda, (m,n))$ picks $\Lambda = (p, \mathbb{G}, \mathbb{G}_T, e, g) \leftarrow \mathcal{G}(1^\lambda, 2)$, $u_i, v_i \leftarrow \mathbb{G}$ for every $i \in [m]$, $k_j, l_j \leftarrow \mathbb{Z}_p$ for every $j \in [n]$ and outputs $k = \{(u_i, v_i) : i \in [m]\} \cup \{(k_j, l_j) : j \in [n]\}$ and $\mathsf{pp} = (\Lambda, m, n)$. The domain and range of F_k are $\mathbb{I} = [m] \times [n]$ and $\mathbb{G}$, respectively. For any $(i,j) \in \mathbb{I}$, $\mathsf{F}_k(i,j) = u_i^{k_j} v_i^{l_j}$. They showed that Σ_5 is a DLIN-based PRF and has closed-form efficiency for C''.

3 Our Schemes

3.1 Verifiable Delegation of Polynomials

In this section, we present two VC schemes Π_1 and Π_2 for delegating the polynomial f in Section 1.3. We use all notations from there. Furthermore, we suppose that $d+1 = 2^a = sn = s \cdot 2^b$ for some integers $a, b > 0$. Equation (1) reduces the computation of $f(\boldsymbol{x})$ to the s inner products $\rho_1 = \boldsymbol{y} \cdot \boldsymbol{F}_1, \ldots, \rho_s = \boldsymbol{y} \cdot \boldsymbol{F}_s$. In Π_1 and Π_2 the server must return $\rho_1, \ldots, \rho_s$ and a proof such that the client can verify and then compute $f(\boldsymbol{x})$.

A Privately Verifiable Scheme: Fig. 2 shows our private VC scheme Π_1 for delegating $f(\boldsymbol{x})$. The PRF Σ is Σ_1 or Σ_2. The params is equal to (m, s, n) when $\Sigma = \Sigma_1$ and equal to (m, a, b) when $\Sigma = \Sigma_2$. The τ in Π_1 is computed using Σ.CFE. It is easy to see that Π_1 is correct.

$\mathsf{KeyGen}(1^\lambda, f)$: picks $(\mathsf{pp}, k) \leftarrow \Sigma.\mathsf{Kg}(1^\lambda, \mathsf{params})$, where $\mathsf{pp} = (\Lambda, \mathsf{params})$ and $\Lambda = (p, \mathbb{G}, g)$; picks $\alpha \leftarrow \mathbb{Z}_p$; computes $t_i = g^{\alpha F_{1,i} + \alpha^2 F_{2,i} + \cdots + \alpha^s F_{s,i}} \cdot \mathsf{F}_k(i)$ for every $i \in \mathbb{I}$; then outputs $ek = (f, \{t_i\}_{i \in \mathbb{I}})$, $dk = k$ and $vk = \alpha$.

$\mathsf{ProbGen}(dk, \boldsymbol{x})$: given $\boldsymbol{x} \in \mathbb{Z}_p^m$, outputs $\sigma = \boldsymbol{x}$ and $\tau = \prod_{i \in \mathbb{I}} \mathsf{F}_k(i)^{\boldsymbol{x}^i}$.

$\mathsf{Compute}(ek, \sigma)$: computes $\rho_\ell = \sum_{i \in \mathbb{I}} F_{\ell,i} \cdot \boldsymbol{x}^i$ for every $\ell \in [s]$ and $\pi = \prod_{i \in \mathbb{I}} (t_i)^{\boldsymbol{x}^i}$; then outputs $\boldsymbol{\rho} = (\rho_1, \ldots, \rho_s)$ and π.

$\mathsf{Verify}(vk, \tau, \boldsymbol{\rho}, \pi)$: verifies if $\pi = g^{\rho_1 \cdot \alpha + \rho_2 \cdot \alpha^2 + \cdots + \rho_s \cdot \alpha^s} \cdot \tau$. Outputs $y = \sum_{\ell=1}^s \rho_\ell \cdot x_1^{(\ell-1)n}$ if the equality holds; otherwise, outputs $\bot$.

Fig. 2. The scheme Π_1

Theorem 1. Π_1 *is secure under the d-SDDH assumption for $\mathbb{G}$ when $\Sigma = \Sigma_1$ and secure under the DDH assumption for $\mathbb{G}$ when $\Sigma = \Sigma_2$.*

Proof. Let $\mathbf{G}_0$ be the standard security game for Π_1 (Fig. 1). Let $\mathbf{G}_1$ be a security game which makes no difference with $\mathbf{G}_0$ except that the function F_k is replaced with a random function $\Phi : \mathbb{I} \to \mathbb{G}$. Let $\mathcal{A}$ be any PPT adversary. Let ϵ_i be the probability that $\mathcal{A}$ wins in $\mathbf{G}_i$ for every $i \in \{0, 1\}$. We need to show $\epsilon_0 < \mathsf{neg}(\lambda)$. Firstly, we have $|\epsilon_0 - \epsilon_1| < \mathsf{neg}(\lambda)$ because otherwise one can use $\mathcal{A}$ to break the security of Σ which however is secure under the respective assumptions. Thus, it suffices to show $\epsilon_1 < \mathsf{neg}(\lambda)$. We show $\epsilon_1 < \mathsf{neg}(\lambda)$ even if $\mathcal{A}$ is computationally unbounded.

Consider $\mathbf{G}_1$. We use the notations f, m, d, s, n, a, b and $\mathbb{I}$ from the beginning of this section. Let $ek = (f, \{t_i\}_{i \in \mathbb{I}})$, $dk = k$ and $vk = \alpha$ be the keys generated by $\mathsf{KeyGen}(1^\lambda, f)$. Note that the function F_k is replaced with Φ and therefore $t_i = g^{\alpha F_{1,i} + \alpha^2 F_{2,i} + \cdots + \alpha^s F_{s,i}} \cdot \Phi(i)$ for every $i \in \mathbb{I}$. The adversary $\mathcal{A}$ is given ek. For any choice of $\alpha \in \mathbb{Z}_p$, there is a unique choice of $\Phi(i) \in \mathbb{G}$ for every $i \in \mathbb{I}$ such that t_i is consistent with $\mathcal{A}$'s view. As Φ is truly random, $\mathcal{A}$ learns no information about α from ek even if it is computationally unbounded (such that computing discrete logarithms is easy). Thus, from $\mathcal{A}$'s view, $\boldsymbol{\alpha} = (1, \alpha, \ldots, \alpha^s)$ is uniformly chosen from V_{pol}. Given ek, the adversary $\mathcal{A}$ adaptively makes a polynomial number of queries $\{x_j\}_{j=1}^q$ to $\mathsf{ProbGen}(dk, \cdot)$ and $\{(\bar{\rho}_j, \bar{\pi}_j)\}_{j=1}^q$ to $\mathsf{Verify}(vk, \tau_j, \cdot, \cdot)$:

---

for $j = 1$ to q, the challenger and $\mathcal{A}$ proceeds as below.
 - $\mathcal{A}$ gives an input $x_j = (x_{j,1}, \ldots, x_{j,m}) \in \mathbb{Z}_p^m$ to the challenger;
 - the challenger gives $\sigma_j = x_j$ to $\mathcal{A}$ and keeps $\tau_j = \prod_{i \in \mathbb{I}} \Phi(i)^{x_j^i}$;
 - $\mathcal{A}$ gives $\bar{\rho}_j = (\bar{\rho}_{j,1}, \ldots, \bar{\rho}_{j,s}) \in \mathbb{Z}_p^s$ and $\bar{\pi}_j \in \mathbb{G}$ to the challenger;
 - the challenger gives the output of $\mathsf{Verify}(vk, \tau_j, \bar{\rho}_j, \bar{\pi}_j)$ to $\mathcal{A}$.

After the queries, $\mathcal{A}$ needs to produce a forgery. As remarked in Section 2.1, we can suppose that $\mathcal{A}$'s forgery is $(x_c, \bar{\rho}_c, \bar{\pi}_c)$ for some $c \in [q]$. Let $(\rho_c, \pi_c) \leftarrow \mathsf{Compute}(ek, \sigma_c)$ be the response that could be computed by an honest server, where $\rho_c = (\rho_{c,1}, \ldots, \rho_{c,s}) \in \mathbb{Z}_p^s$ and $\pi_c \in \mathbb{G}$. Due to the correctness of Π_1, we must have that $\pi_c = g^{\sum_{\ell=1}^s \rho_{c,\ell} \cdot \alpha^\ell} \cdot \tau_c$. The adversary $\mathcal{A}$ wins in $\mathbf{G}_1$ only if $\bar{\rho}_c \neq \rho_c$ and $\bar{\pi}_c = g^{\sum_{\ell=1}^s \bar{\rho}_{c,\ell} \cdot \alpha^\ell} \cdot \tau_c$. It follows that $\mathcal{A}$ wins only if $\bar{\rho}_c \neq \rho_c$ and

$$\bar{\pi}_c / \pi_c = g^{\sum_{\ell=1}^s (\bar{\rho}_{c,\ell} - \rho_{c,\ell}) \cdot \alpha^\ell}. \tag{3}$$

Suppose that $\bar{\pi}_c / \pi_c = g^{\beta_c}$. Then (3) holds only if $u_c = (-\beta_c, \bar{\rho}_{c,1} - \rho_{c,1}, \ldots, \bar{\rho}_{c,s} - \rho_{c,s}) \in \mathbb{Z}_p^{s+1}$ is a nonzero vector such that $u_c \cdot \boldsymbol{\alpha} = 0$. Recall that $\boldsymbol{\alpha} \leftarrow V_{\mathrm{pol}}$. Without loss of generality, we can suppose that the first nonzero component of u_c is 1 such that $u_c \in \Omega_{p,s+1}$. This does not matter because if the first nonzero component of u_c is $\gamma \neq 0$ then $\gamma^{-1} \cdot u_c$ will belong to $\Omega_{p,s+1}$ and $\mathcal{A}$ could have made the query $\gamma^{-1} \cdot u_c$ instead of u_c with the same consequence (i.e., success or failure). In general, for every $j \in [q]$ and the j-th queries x_j and $(\bar{\rho}_j, \bar{\pi}_j)$, we can follow the analysis for $j = c$ and learn a vector $u_j \in \Omega_{p,s+1}$. The j-th queries cause $\mathcal{A}$ to win only if $u_j \cdot \boldsymbol{\alpha} = 0$. Thus, the query part of $\mathbf{G}_1$ turns out to be **Problem 1** with $U \subseteq \Omega_{p,s+1}$ and $V = V_{\mathrm{pol}}$. Lemma 1 and Example 2 show that $\mathcal{A}$ wins with probability $\leq sq/p$, which is negligible, i.e., $\epsilon_1 < \mathsf{neg}(\lambda)$. $\square$

A Publicly Verifiable Scheme: Fig. 3 shows our public VC scheme Π_2 for delegating $f(\boldsymbol{x})$. The τ in Π_2 is computed using $\Sigma_3.\mathsf{CFE}$. It is easy to see that Π_2 is correct.

$\mathsf{KeyGen}(1^\lambda, f)$: picks $(\mathsf{pp}, k) \leftarrow \Sigma_3.\mathsf{Kg}(1^\lambda, (m, a, b))$, where $\mathsf{pp} = (\Lambda, m, a, b)$ and $\Lambda = (p, \mathbb{G}, \mathbb{G}_T, e, g)$; picks $\boldsymbol{\alpha} = (\alpha_1, \ldots, \alpha_s) \leftarrow \mathbb{Z}_p^s$; computes $t_i = g^{\alpha_1 F_{1,i} + \cdots + \alpha_s F_{s,i}} \cdot \mathsf{F}_k(i)$ for every $i \in \mathbb{I}$; then outputs $ek = (f, \{t_i\}_{i \in \mathbb{I}})$, $dk = k$ and $vk = (h_1, \ldots, h_s) = (e(g,g)^{\alpha_1}, \ldots, e(g,g)^{\alpha_s})$;

$\mathsf{ProbGen}(dk, \boldsymbol{x})$: given $\boldsymbol{x} \in \mathbb{Z}_p^m$, outputs $\sigma = \boldsymbol{x}$ and $\tau = e\left(\prod_{i \in \mathbb{I}} \mathsf{F}_k(i)^{\boldsymbol{x}^i}, g\right)$.

$\mathsf{Compute}(ek, \sigma)$: computes $\rho_\ell = \sum_{i \in \mathbb{I}} F_{\ell,i} \cdot \boldsymbol{x}^i$ for every $\ell \in [s]$ and $\pi = \prod_{i \in \mathbb{I}}(t_i)^{\boldsymbol{x}^i}$; then outputs $\boldsymbol{\rho} = (\rho_1, \ldots, \rho_s)$ and π.

$\mathsf{Verify}(vk, \tau, \boldsymbol{\rho}, \pi)$: verifies if $e(\pi, g) = \prod_{\ell=1}^s h_\ell^{\rho_\ell} \cdot \tau$. outputs $y = \sum_{\ell=1}^s \rho_\ell \cdot x_1^{(\ell-1)n}$ if the equality holds; otherwise, outputs $\perp$.

Fig. 3. The scheme Π_2

Theorem 2. *Π_2 is secure under the DLIN assumption for $\mathbb{G}$.*

Proof. Let $\mathbf{G}_0$ be the standard security game for Π_2 (see Fig. 1). Let $\mathbf{G}_1$ be a security game which makes no difference with $\mathbf{G}_0$ except that the function F_k is replaced with a random function $\Phi : \mathbb{I} \to \mathbb{G}$. Let $\mathcal{A}$ be any PPT adversary. Let ϵ_i be the probability that $\mathcal{A}$ wins in $\mathbf{G}_i$ for every $i \in \{0, 1\}$. As in Theorem 1, it suffices to show that $\epsilon_1 < \mathsf{neg}(\lambda)$.

Consider $\mathbf{G}_1$. We use the notations f, m, d, s, n, a, b and $\mathbb{I}$ from the beginning of Section 3.1. Suppose that ϵ_1 is non-negligible. We show that there is a challenger $\mathcal{B}$ that can simulate $\mathcal{A}$ to solve the CDH problem, which however should be hard under DLIN. Given a CDH problem (g, g^α, h), $\mathcal{B}$ must output h^α. Fig. 4 shows how $\mathcal{B}$ plays with the adversary $\mathcal{A}$ in $\mathbf{G}_1$. Let $(\boldsymbol{\rho}_c, \pi_c) \leftarrow \mathsf{Compute}(ek, \sigma_c)$ be the response that could be computed by an honest server,

---

SETUP. The challenger $\mathcal{B}$ picks $t_i \leftarrow \mathbb{G}$ for every $i \in \mathbb{I}$; picks $r \leftarrow [s]$ and computes $h_r = e(g^\alpha, h)$; picks $\alpha_\ell \leftarrow \mathbb{Z}_p$ and computes $h_\ell = e(g,g)^{\alpha_\ell}$ for every $\ell \in [s] \setminus \{r\}$; then it defines $ek = (f, \{t_i\}_{i \in \mathbb{I}})$, $dk = \perp$, $vk = (h_1, \ldots, h_s)$; $\mathcal{B}$ gives (ek, vk) to $\mathcal{A}$.

QUERIES. The adversary $\mathcal{A}$ adaptively makes a polynomial number of queries $\{\boldsymbol{x}_j\}_{j=1}^q$ to $\mathsf{ProbGen}(dk, \cdot)$ and $\{(\bar{\rho}_j, \bar{\pi}_j)\}_{j=1}^q$ to $\mathsf{Verify}(vk, \tau_j, \cdot, \cdot)$:

for $j = 1$ to q, $\mathcal{B}$ and $\mathcal{A}$ proceed as below

1. $\mathcal{A}$ picks $\boldsymbol{x}_j = (x_{j,1}, \ldots, x_{j,m}) \in \mathbb{Z}_p^m$ and give it to $\mathcal{B}$;
2. $\mathcal{B}$ gives $\sigma_j = \boldsymbol{x}_j$ and $\tau_j = e\left(\prod_{i \in \mathbb{I}}(t_i)^{\boldsymbol{x}_j^i}, g\right) / \prod_{\ell=1}^s h_\ell^{\sum_{i \in \mathbb{I}} F_{\ell,i} \cdot \boldsymbol{x}_j^i}$ to $\mathcal{A}$;
3. $\mathcal{A}$ picks $\bar{\rho}_j = (\bar{\rho}_{j,1}, \ldots, \bar{\rho}_{j,s}) \in \mathbb{Z}_p^s$ and $\bar{\pi}_j \in \mathbb{G}$ and gives them to $\mathcal{B}$;
4. $\mathcal{B}$ gives the output of $\mathsf{Verify}(vk, \tau_j, \bar{\rho}_j, \bar{\pi}_j)$ to $\mathcal{A}$.

FORGERY. As remarked in Section 2.1, $\mathcal{A}$ outputs $(\boldsymbol{x}_c, \bar{\rho}_c, \bar{\pi}_c)$ as its forgery ($c \in [q]$).

Fig. 4. $\mathcal{B}$'s simulation in the game $\mathbf{G}_1$

where $\rho_c = (\rho_{c,1}, \ldots, \rho_{c,s}) \in \mathbb{Z}_p^s$ and $\pi_c \in \mathbb{G}$. Due to the correctness of Π_2, we have that $e(\pi_c, g) = \prod_{\ell=1}^s h_\ell^{\rho_{c,\ell}} \cdot \tau_c$. The adversary $\mathcal{A}$ wins the game $\mathbf{G}_1$ only if $\bar{\rho}_c \neq \rho_c$ and $e(\bar{\pi}_c, g) = \prod_{\ell=1}^s h_\ell^{\bar{\rho}_{c,\ell}} \cdot \tau_c$. It follows that $\mathcal{A}$ wins only if $\bar{\rho}_c \neq \rho_c$ and

$$e(\bar{\pi}_c/\pi_c, g) = \prod_{\ell=1}^s h_\ell^{\bar{\rho}_{c,\ell} - \rho_{c,\ell}} \tag{4}$$

It is not hard to see that the (ek, vk) and $\{(\sigma_j, \tau_j)\}_{j=1}^q$ generated by $\mathcal{B}$ strictly follow the respective distributions in $\mathbf{G}_1$, although they are not obtained by directly running the algorithms KeyGen and ProbGen. Due to our assumption, $\mathcal{A}$ should win with probability ϵ_1, i.e., the probability that $\bar{\rho}_c \neq \rho_c$ and (4) holds is ϵ_1. As $\bar{\rho}_c \neq \rho_c$, there is a nonempty set $R \subseteq [s]$ such that $\bar{\rho}_{c,r^*} \neq \rho_{c,r^*}$ for any $r^* \in R$. The r in Fig. 4 was uniformly chosen and independent of everything else. Therefore, the probability that r falls into R is $\geq |R|/s \geq 1/s$. The challenger $\mathcal{B}$ as a CDH-solver outputs $\perp$ (to indicate failure) if $r \notin R$. Otherwise, (4) implies that $e(\bar{\pi}_c \cdot \pi_c^{-1}, g) \cdot \prod_{\ell \in [s] \setminus \{r\}} h_\ell^{-(\bar{\rho}_{c,\ell} - \rho_{c,\ell})} = h_r^{\bar{\rho}_{c,r} - \rho_{c,r}} = e(g^\alpha, h)^{\bar{\rho}_{c,r} - \rho_{c,r}} = e(h^{\alpha(\bar{\rho}_{c,r} - \rho_{c,r})}, g)$. It follows that the challenger $\mathcal{B}$ can compute $h^\alpha = (\bar{\pi}_c \cdot \pi_c^{-1} \cdot \prod_{\ell \in [s] \setminus \{r\}} g^{-\alpha_\ell(\bar{\rho}_{c,\ell} - \rho_{c,\ell})})^{\frac{1}{\bar{\rho}_{c,r} - \rho_{c,r}}}$. The probability that $\mathcal{B}$ learns h^α is exactly equal to the probability that $\mathcal{A}$ wins in $\mathbf{G}_1$ and $r \in R$, which is $\geq \epsilon_1/s$ and thus non-negligible. This contradicts the hardness of CDH and thus the DLIN assumption. Hence, ϵ_1 must be negligible.

3.2   Verifiable Delegation of Matrices

In this section, we present two VC schemes Π_3 and Π_4 for delegating the matrix E in Section 1.4. We use all notations from there. Recall that $x \cdot E$ can be reduced to n sets of inner product computations. In Π_3 and Π_4 the server must return $x \cdot E$ and n proofs, one for each set of s inner product computations.

A Privately Verifiable Scheme: Fig. 5 shows our private VC scheme Π_3 for delegating E. The τ in Π_3 is computed using $\Sigma_4.$CFE. It is easy to see that Π_3 is correct. Due to lack of space, we show that Π_3 is secure under the DDH assumption for $\mathbb{G}$ in the full version.

KeyGen$(1^\lambda, E)$: picks $(pp, k) \leftarrow \Sigma_4.Kg(1^\lambda, (m, n))$, where $pp = (\Lambda, m, n)$ and $\Lambda = (p, \mathbb{G}, g)$; picks $\alpha \leftarrow \mathbb{Z}_p$; computes $t_{i,j} = t_i = g^{\alpha F_{1,i} + \alpha^2 F_{2,i} + \cdots + \alpha^s F_{s,i}} \cdot F_k(i)$ for every $i = (i, j) \in [m] \times [n]$; then outputs $ek = (E, \{t_i\})$, $dk = k$ and $vk = \alpha$.

ProbGen(dk, x): given $x \in \mathbb{Z}_p^m$, computes $\tau_j = \prod_{i=1}^m F_k(i, j)^{x_i}$ for every $j \in [n]$; then outputs $\sigma = x$ and $\tau = (\tau_1, \ldots, \tau_n)$.

Compute(ek, σ): computes $\rho = (\rho_1, \ldots, \rho_d) = x \cdot E$ and $\pi_j = \prod_{i=1}^m (t_{i,j})^{x_i}$ for every $j \in [n]$; then outputs ρ and $\pi = (\pi_1, \ldots, \pi_n)$.

Verify(vk, τ, ρ, π): verifies if $\pi_j = g^{\sum_{\ell=1}^s \rho_{j+(\ell-1)n} \cdot \alpha^\ell} \cdot \tau_j$ for every $j \in [n]$; if all equalities hold, outputs ρ; otherwise, outputs $\perp$.

Fig. 5. The scheme Π_3

A Publicly Verifiable Scheme: Fig. 6 shows our public VC scheme Π_4 for delegating E. The τ is in Π_4 is computed using Σ_5.CFE. It is easy to see that Π_4 is correct. Due to lack of space, we show that Π_4 is secure under the DLIN assumption for $\mathbb{G}$ in the full version.

KeyGen$(1^\lambda, E)$: picks $(\mathsf{pp}, k) \leftarrow \Sigma_5.\mathsf{Kg}(1^\lambda, (m,n))$, where $\mathsf{pp} = (\Lambda, m, n)$ and $\Lambda = (p, \mathbb{G}, \mathbb{G}_T, e, g)$; picks $\boldsymbol{\alpha} = (\alpha_1, \ldots, \alpha_s) \leftarrow \mathbb{Z}_p^s$; computes $t_i = t_{i,j} = g^{\alpha_1 F_{1,i} + \cdots + \alpha_s F_{s,i}}$. $\mathsf{F}_k(i)$ for every $i = (i,j) \in [m] \times [n]$; then outputs $ek = (E, \{t_i\})$, $dk = k$ and $vk = (h_1, \ldots, h_s) = (e(g,g)^{\alpha_1}, \ldots, e(g,g)^{\alpha_s})$;

ProbGen$(dk, \boldsymbol{x})$: given $\boldsymbol{x} \in \mathbb{Z}_p^m$, computes $\tau_j = e\left(\prod_{i=1}^m \mathsf{F}_k(i,j)^{x_i}, g\right)$ for every $j \in [n]$; then outputs $\sigma = \boldsymbol{x}$ and $\boldsymbol{\tau} = (\tau_1, \ldots, \tau_n)$.

Compute(ek, σ): computes $\boldsymbol{\rho} = (\rho_1, \ldots, \rho_d) = \boldsymbol{x} \cdot E$ and $\pi_j = \prod_{i=1}^m (t_{i,j})^{x_i}$ for every $j \in [n]$; then outputs $\boldsymbol{\rho}$ and $\boldsymbol{\pi} = (\pi_1, \ldots, \pi_n)$.

Verify$(vk, \boldsymbol{\tau}, \boldsymbol{\rho}, \boldsymbol{\pi})$: verifies if $e(\pi_j, g) = \prod_{\ell=1}^s h_\ell^{\rho_j + (\ell-1)n} \cdot \tau_j$ for every $j \in [n]$; if all equalities hold, outputs $\boldsymbol{\rho}$; otherwise, outputs $\bot$.

Fig. 6. The scheme Π_4

3.3   Performance Analysis and Extensions

In this section we analyze our schemes. We take Π_1 and Π_4 as example. The analysis of Π_2 and Π_3 can be done similarly.

Analysis of Π_1. STORAGE: In Π_1, the client stores $ek = (f, \{t_i\}_{i \in \mathbb{I}})$ with the server, where f can be represented by $(d+1)^m$ elements of $\mathbb{Z}_p$ and t_i belongs to a group $\mathbb{G}$ of order p for every $i \in \mathbb{I}$. The storage overhead of Π_1 is $((d+1)^m + |\mathbb{I}|)/(d+1)^m = 1 + 1/s$. Let $\lambda = 1024, |p| = \lambda, m = 1, d + 1 = 2^{30}, s = \lambda$ and $n = 2^{20}$. Let the $\mathbb{G}$ in Π_1 be an order p subgroup of $\mathbb{Z}_{p'}^*$, where p' is a prime. To delegate f, the client stores $|\mathbb{I}| = 2^{20}$ tags in $\mathbb{G}$ with the server. Thus, to delegate $(d+1)^m \times |p|/2^3\mathsf{B} = 128\mathsf{GB}$ data, Π_1 requires $|\mathbb{I}| \cdot \lambda/2^3\mathsf{B} = 128\mathsf{MB}$ cloud storage for tags. This is only $1/1024$ times the $128\mathsf{GB}$ tags used by [2]. VERIFICATION: Let $\mathsf{E}_p, \mathsf{M}_p$ and A_p be the number of bit operations required by each exponentiation, multiplication, and addition in $\mathbb{Z}_p$, respectively. Let $\mathsf{E}_\mathbb{G}$ and $\mathsf{M}_\mathbb{G}$ be the number of bit operations required by each exponentiation and multiplication in $\mathbb{G}$, respectively. Let $\mathsf{C}_\mathbb{G}$ be the number of bit operations required for comparing two elements of $\mathbb{G}$. In Π_1.ProbGen, the client requires $m\mathsf{E}_p + 3m\mathsf{M}_p + 2m\mathsf{A}_p$ bit operations to compute the τ using Σ_1.CFE. In Π_1.Verify, the client requires $(2s-1)\mathsf{M}_p + (s-1)\mathsf{A}_p$ bit operations to compute $\eta = \rho_1\alpha + \cdots + \rho_s\alpha^s$, $\mathsf{E}_\mathbb{G}$ bit operations to compute g^η, $\mathsf{M}_\mathbb{G}$ bit operations to compute $g^\eta \cdot \tau$ and then $\mathsf{C}_\mathbb{G}$ bit operations to compare π with $g^\eta \cdot \tau$; it also requires E_p bit operations to compute x_1^n, $(s-2)\mathsf{M}_p$ bit operations to compute $x_1^{2n}, \ldots, x_1^{(s-1)n}$, and then $s\mathsf{M}_p + (s-1)\mathsf{A}_p$ bit operations to compute $f(\boldsymbol{x})$. Thus, the client's verification totally requires $(m+1)\mathsf{E}_p + (3m+4s-3)\mathsf{M}_p + (2m+2s-2)\mathsf{A}_p + \mathsf{E}_\mathbb{G} + \mathsf{M}_\mathbb{G} + \mathsf{C}_\mathbb{G}$ bit operations. The scheme of [2] requires $m\mathsf{E}_p + (3m+1)\mathsf{M}_p + 2m\mathsf{A}_p + \mathsf{E}_\mathbb{G} + \mathsf{M}_\mathbb{G} + \mathsf{C}_\mathbb{G}$ bit operations to do verification. Note that $\mathsf{E}_p, \mathsf{E}_\mathbb{G} \approx \lambda^3, \mathsf{M}_p, \mathsf{M}_\mathbb{G} \approx \lambda^2$, and $\mathsf{A}_p, \mathsf{C}_\mathbb{G} \approx \lambda$. The client in Π_1 requires $\approx ((m+2)\lambda + 4s)\lambda^2$ bit operations and the client in [2] requires $\approx (m + 1)\lambda^3$ bit operations. Therefore, our client is roughly $\delta = 1 + \frac{\lambda+4s}{(m+1)\lambda}$ times slower than the client of [2]. When $m = 1$ and $s = \lambda$, we have that $\delta = 3.5$. Our parameter s provides a meaningful trade-off between the size of tags and the client's verification time. The larger the s is, the smaller the storage overhead is and the slower the client of Π_1 is. The δ shows that our client can significantly reduce the consumption of cloud storage by slightly increasing the verification time.

Analysis of Π_4. Our scheme Π_4 uses a random bilinear map instance $(p, \mathbb{G}, \mathbb{G}_T, e, g)$. In Π_4.ProbGen, the client requires $m + n$ exponentiations in $\mathbb{G}$ and n pairing computations to compute $\boldsymbol{\tau} = (\tau_1, \ldots, \tau_n)$ using Σ_5.CFE. In Π_4.Verify, the client requires s exponentiations in $\mathbb{G}_T$, s multiplications in $\mathbb{G}_T$, one pairing computation and one comparision of the elements of $\mathbb{G}_T$ to check the equality $e(\pi_j, g) = \prod_{\ell=1}^{s} h_\ell^{\rho_{j+(\ell-1)n}} \cdot \tau_j$ for every $j \in [n]$. Thus, the client's verification time is dominated by $m + n$ exponentiations in $\mathbb{G}$, sn exponentiations in $\mathbb{G}_T$, and $2n$ pairing computations. The scheme of [7] is a special case of Π_4 with $s = 1$. In their scheme, the client requires $m + sn$ exponentiations in $\mathbb{G}$ and sn pairing computations to compute $d = sn$ elements $\tau_1, \ldots, \tau_d$ for future verification. The client also requires one exponentiation in $\mathbb{G}_T$, one multiplication in $\mathbb{G}_T$, one pairing computation and one comparision of the elements of $\mathbb{G}_T$ to check an equality for each of the sn components of $\boldsymbol{x} \cdot \boldsymbol{E}$. Therefore, the verification time of their client is dominated by $(m+sn)$ exponentiations in $\mathbb{G}$, sn exponentiations in $\mathbb{G}_T$, and $2sn$ pairing computations. Hence, our publicly verifiable scheme Π_4 for delegating matrices is much more efficient than [7] not only in terms of storage overhead $(1 + 1/s$ vs. 2) but also in terms of the client's verification time.

Extensions. The coefficients of f are considered as s vectors in Π_1 and the computation of $f(\boldsymbol{x})$ is reduced to computing inner products with them. Each inner product is an evaluation of an m-variate polynomial of degree $\leq n - 1$ in x_1 and degree $\leq d$ in any other variables. We can *repeatedly apply* our technique on these shorter polynomials to further reduce the degrees of $x_2, \ldots, x_m$ such that the computation of $f(\boldsymbol{x})$ is reduced to evaluating s^m different m-variate polynomials of degree $\leq n - 1$ in each variable. This is particularly useful when $d = O(1)$ but $m = O(\log \lambda)$. Our schemes also provide *batch verifications* of multiple functions. For example, if we set $m = 1$, then Π_1 allows the client to verify the evaluations of s univariate polynomials of degree $\leq n - 1$ using substantially less time ($\approx 7\lambda^3$ bit operations when $s = \lambda$) than delegating the s polynomials separately using [2] (which requires $\approx 2s\lambda^3$ bit operations for verification).

4   Conclusions

In this paper, we construct VC schemes for delegating polynomials and matrices that provide trade-offs between the consumed cloud storage and the client's verification time. As [2,7], our polynomial f must have special form. For example, in Π_1 we require that $d+1 = 2^a = sn = s2^b$. This is necessary to use PRFs with closed-form efficiency. For a general polynomial, one may add redundant terms to meet the requirement. It is interesting to extend our results to more general functions such as the m-variate polynomials of total degree $\leq d$.

References

1. Applebaum, B., Ishai, Y., Kushilevitz, E.: From Secrecy to Soundness: Efficient Verification via Secure Computation. In: Abramsky, S., Gavoille, C., Kirchner, C., Meyer auf der Heide, F., Spirakis, P.G. (eds.) ICALP 2010. LNCS, vol. 6198, pp. 152–163. Springer, Heidelberg (2010)
2. Benabbas, S., Gennaro, R., Vahlis, Y.: Verifiable Delegation of Computation over Large Datasets. In: Rogaway, P. (ed.) CRYPTO 2011. LNCS, vol. 6841, pp. 111–131. Springer, Heidelberg (2011)
3. Bitansky, N., Canetti, R., Chiesa, A., Tromer, E.: From Extractable Collision Resistance to Succinct Non-Interactive Arguments of Knowledge, and Back Again. In: ITCS, pp. 326–349 (2012)
4. Boneh, D., Freeman, D.M.: Homomorphic Signatures for Polynomial Functions. In: Paterson, K.G. (ed.) EUROCRYPT 2011. LNCS, vol. 6632, pp. 149–168. Springer, Heidelberg (2011)
5. Chung, K.-M., Kalai, Y.T., Liu, F.-H., Raz, R.: Memory Delegation. In: Rogaway, P. (ed.) CRYPTO 2011. LNCS, vol. 6841, pp. 151–168. Springer, Heidelberg (2011)
6. Chung, K.-M., Kalai, Y., Vadhan, S.P.: Improved Delegation of Computation Using Fully Homomorphic Encryption. In: Rabin, T. (ed.) CRYPTO 2010. LNCS, vol. 6223, pp. 483–501. Springer, Heidelberg (2010)
7. Fiore, D., Gennaro, R.: Publicly Verifiable Delegation of Large Polynomials and Matrix Computations, with Applications. In: CCS, pp. 501–512 (2012)
8. Gennaro, R., Gentry, C., Parno, B.: Non-Interactive Verifiable Computing: Outsourcing Computation to Untrusted Workers. In: Rabin, T. (ed.) CRYPTO 2010. LNCS, vol. 6223, pp. 465–482. Springer, Heidelberg (2010)
9. Gennaro, R., Gentry, C., Parno, B., Raykova, M.: Quadratic Span Programs and Succinct NIZKs without PCPs. In: Johansson, T., Nguyen, P.Q. (eds.) EUROCRYPT 2013. LNCS, vol. 7881, pp. 626–645. Springer, Heidelberg (2013)
10. Gennaro, R., Wichs, D.: Fully Homomorphic Message Authenticators. In: Sako, K., Sarkar, P. (eds.) ASIACRYPT 2013, Part II. LNCS, vol. 8270, pp. 301–320. Springer, Heidelberg (2013)
11. Gentry, C., Wichs, D.: Separating Succinct Non-Interactive Arguments from All Falsifiable Assumptions. In: STOC, pp. 99–108 (2011)
12. Goldwasser, S., Kalai, Y.T., Rothblum, G.N.: Delegating Computation: Interactive Proofs for Muggles. In: STOC, pp. 113–122 (2008)
13. Juels, A., Kaliski, B.: PORs: Proofs of Retrievability for Large Files. In: CCS, pp. 584–597 (2007)
14. Lewko, A.B., Waters, B.: Efficient Pseudorandom Functions from the Decisional Linear Assumption and Weaker Variants. In: CCS, pp. 112–120 (2009)
15. Naor, M., Reingold, O.: Number-Theoretic Constructions of Efficient Pseudo-Random Functions. J. ACM 51(2), 231–262 (2004)
16. Papamanthou, C., Shi, E., Tamassia, R.: Signatures of Correct Computation. In: Sahai, A. (ed.) TCC 2013. LNCS, vol. 7785, pp. 222–242. Springer, Heidelberg (2013)
17. Parno, B., Raykova, M., Vaikuntanathan, V.: How to Delegate and Verify in Public: Verifiable Computation from Attribute-Based Encryption. In: Cramer, R. (ed.) TCC 2012. LNCS, vol. 7194, pp. 422–439. Springer, Heidelberg (2012)
18. Shacham, H., Waters, B.: Compact Proofs of Retrievability. In: Pieprzyk, J. (ed.) ASIACRYPT 2008. LNCS, vol. 5350, pp. 90–107. Springer, Heidelberg (2008)

Identity-Based Encryption with Post-Challenge Auxiliary Inputs for Secure Cloud Applications and Sensor Networks

Tsz Hon Yuen[1,*], Ye Zhang[3], Siu Ming Yiu[2], and Joseph K. Liu[4]

[1] Huawei, Singapore
yuen.tsz.hon@huawei.com
[2] The University of Hong Kong, Hong Kong
smyiu@cs.hku.hk
[3] Pennsylvania State University, USA
yxz169@cse.psu.edu
[4] Infocomm Security Department, Institute for Infocomm Research, Singapore
ksliu@i2r.a-star.edu.sg

Abstract. Identity-based encryption (IBE) is useful for providing end-to-end access control and data protection in many scenarios such as cloud applications and wireless sensor networks However, there are some practical threats for the data owner or the sensor, who encrypts raw data; and the data user or the control centre, who decrypts the ciphertext and recovers the raw data.

In this paper, we tackle the open problem of proposing a leakage-resilience encryption model that can capture leakage from both the secret key owner (the data user or control centre) and the encryptor (the data owner or sensor), in the auxiliary input model. Existing models only allow the leakage of the secret key and do not allow adversaries to query more leakage information *after* seeing the challenge ciphertext of the security games. We solve this problem by defining the *post-challenge auxiliary input* model in which the family of leakage functions must be defined before the adversary is given the public key. The post-challenge query will return the leakage of the encryption randomness used by the encryptor. This model is able to capture a wider class of real-world attacks.

To realize our model, we propose a generic transformation from the auxiliary input model to our new post-challenge auxiliary input model for both public key encryption (PKE) and IBE. Furthermore, we extend Canetti *et al.*'s technique, that converts CPA-secure IBE to CCA-secure PKE, into the leakage-resilient setting.

Keywords: IBE, leakage-resilient, auxiliary inputs, randomness.

1   Introduction

In autonomic provisioning of applications hosted in cloud server, all customer requirements and constraints must be fulfilled, as specified in Service Level

---

[*] The research was mainly conducted when the first author was affiliated with the University of Hong Kong.

M. Kutyłowski and J. Vaidya (Eds.): ESORICS 2014, Part I, LNCS 8712, pp. 130–147, 2014.

Agreement. Confidentiality, integrity and access control are important issues for security and privacy of such open infrastructure [1]. Access control is classified as one to the top 10 challenges in big data security by the Cloud Security Alliance (CSA) [2]. Sensitive data must be protected by using cryptographically secure algorithm and suitable access control. It is challenging to adapt unpredictable changes of access control policy in autonomic computing.

It was reported that a Google employee monitored some teenagers' communication records in Google Voice, stalked them by recovering their names and phone numbers [3]. Therefore, end-to-end access control is more resilient to attacks from the system administrator of the cloud server. Moreover, the data owner has more control on who is allowed to access by using end-to-end access control. The CSA suggested the use of identity-based encryption (IBE) as one of the possible cryptographic approach to enforce access control in big data applications [2]. In IBE, the data owner (encryptor) can encrypt a message by using the recipient's (decryptor) identity as his public key. The decryptor has to request a third party called Private Key Generator (PKG) to issue an identity-based secret key to him. By using this secret key, the decryptor recovers the original message. Access control is enforced by the data owner since he can choose the identity of the recipient of his choice.

The case of sensor networks is similar. After getting raw data by the sensor, it encrypts these sensitive information by using the identity of the control centre and sends the ciphertext back to it for further analysis. IBE eliminates the costly certificate verification process and thus it is preferred in sensor networks.

1.1   Practical Threats of Using IBE for Access Control

Although IBE can protect the users from malicious cloud server administrator, there are still a number of practical threats for both the encryptor and the decryptor.

Side Channel Attacks to the Decryptor. Real world attackers can obtain partial information about the secret key of the decryptor. Side-channel attacks explore the physical weakness of the implementation of cryptosystems. For example, the hamming weight of the secret key can be leaked by observing the running time of the decryption process, or the power consumption used.

Weak Randomness Used by the Encryptor. The randomness used in the encryption process may be leaked by poor implementation of pseudorandom number generator (PRNG). Argyros and Kiayias [4] outlined the flaws of PRNG in PHP. Lenstra et al. [5] inspected millions of public keys and found that some of the weak keys could be a result of poorly seeded PRNGs. Michaelis et al. [6] uncovered significant weaknesses of PRNG of some java runtime libraries, including Android. The NIST standard for pseudorandom number generation has fallen into dispute after the discovery of back door algorithm in [7] and received great attention through the Snowden disclosures [8]. These practical attacks demonstrate the potential weakness of the encryption randomness when using PRNG in practice. In big data applications, data are usually generated by some devices with limited computational power. It is possible that the data are encrypted using such weak randomness from java runtime libraries. This situation is particular serious in the case of wireless sensors as they are usually exposed in the open air but contain only very limited computation power. Attackers may easily guess the randomness they are using for generating the ciphertext.

1.2   Motivation for Post-Challenge Auxiliary Inputs

We need to provide leakage-resilient protection for users of the cloud applications, including the encryptor and the decryptor. It motivates the new Post-Challenge Auxiliary Inputs model for IBE setting. We first review the background of leakage-resilient cryptography.

Protecting the Decryptor: Leakage-Resilient Cryptography. In modern cryptography, we use a security model to capture the abilities of a potential attacker (the adversary). For example, in the chosen-ciphertext attack (CCA) model for public key encryption (PKE), the adversary is allowed to ask for the decryption of arbitrary ciphertexts, except for the one that he intends to attack. This models the real-world scenario that the adversary may obtain some pairs of messages and ciphertexts from the secret key owner. Under a given model, a cryptographic scheme is said to be *proven secure* if the scheme is capable of withstanding the attacks from adversaries with the abilities captured by the model. But if the adversary has some extra abilities, the security of the scheme is no longer guaranteed. In most traditional security models, it is assumed that the adversary does not have the ability to obtain any information (even one single bit) about the secret key. However, due to the advancement of a large class of *side-channel attacks* on the physical implementation of cryptographic schemes, obtaining partial information of the secret key becomes feasible and relatively easier. Thus, the assumption for absolute secrecy of the secret key may not hold. In recent years, a number of works have been done in *leakage-resilient cryptography* to formalize these attacks in the security model.

Leakage-resilient cryptography models various side-channel attacks by allowing the adversary to specify an arbitrary, efficiently computable function f and to obtain the output of f (representing the information leaked) applied to the secret key sk. Clearly, we must have some restrictions on f such that the adversary should not be able to recover sk completely and to win the security game trivially. One approach is to restrict the output size of f to be at most ℓ bits such that ℓ must be less than $|\text{sk}|$ [9]. Naor and Segev [10] considered the entropy of sk and required that the decrease in entropy of the sk is at most ℓ bits upon observing $f(\text{sk})$. Dodis *et al.* [11] further generalized the leakage functions and proposed the model of *auxiliary input* which only requires the leakage functions to be computationally hard to compute sk given $f(\text{sk})$.

Restriction of the Auxiliary Input Model. The auxiliary input model is general enough to capture a large class of side-channel leakages. However, there are still shortcomings. For example, in the CCA security model for PKE and IBE, the adversary $\mathcal{A}$ is allowed to ask for the decryption of arbitrary ciphertexts *before and after* receiving the challenge ciphertext C^*, in order to maximize the ability of $\mathcal{A}$[1]. But for most leakage-resilient PKE or IBE, the adversary $\mathcal{A}$ can only specify and query the leakage function $f(\mathsf{sk})$ *before* getting C^*. In real situations, this is not true. The adversary should be able to obtain more information even after the attack target is known. The main reason for not being able to have *post-challenge leakage queries* (queries from the adversary after the challenge ciphertext is given) is as follows. If we allow $\mathcal{A}$ to specify the leakage function after getting C^*, he can easily embed the decryption of C^* as the leakage function, which will lead to a trivial break to the security game. So, the issue is to come up with a model with minimal restriction needed to allow post-challenge leakage query after getting the challenge ciphertext, while avoiding the above trivial attack. Comparing with the existing leakage-resilient PKE and IBE, the objective is to increase the ability of the adversary to make the model more realistic and capture a larger class of side-channel attacks.

Protecting the Encryptor: Leakage-Resilient from the Encryptor's Randomness. Another direction for considering post-challenge leakage query is to model the leakage of encryptor (data owner). In the previous section, we showed the practical threats of using weak PRNG as the source of encryption randomness. This random value is critical. If the adversary $\mathcal{A}$ can obtain the entire r, it can encrypt the two challenge messages m_0 and m_1 by itself using r and compare if they are equal to the challenge ciphertext, thus wins the game easily. Therefore, the leakage of this randomness should not be overlooked. We demonstrate the impact of leaking encryption randomness in the following artificial encryption scheme. We use $(\mathsf{Enc}, \mathsf{Dec})$ a leakage-resilient PKE scheme in the auxiliary input model and one-time pad to form a new encryption scheme:

- $\mathsf{Enc'}$: On input a message M and a public key pk, pick a random one-time pad P for M and calculate $C_1 = \mathsf{Enc}(\mathsf{pk}, P), C_2 = P \oplus M$, where $\oplus$ is the bit-wise XOR. Return the ciphertext $C = (C_1, C_2)$.
- $\mathsf{Dec'}$: On input a secret key sk and a ciphertext $C = (C_1, C_2)$, calculate $P' = \mathsf{Dec}(\mathsf{sk}, C_1)$ and output $M = C_2 \oplus P'$.

The randomness used in $\mathsf{Enc'}$ by the encryptor is P and the randomness in Enc. However, leaking the first bit of P will lead to the leakage of the first bit in M. Therefore, leakage from the encryptor helps the adversary to recover the message. Without post-challenge leakage query, the side-channel attacks to the encryption randomness cannot be modeled easily.

In both scenarios, we should avoid the adversary $\mathcal{A}$ submitting a leakage function as the decryption of C^* in the security game (in case of leakage from secret key owner) or to submit a leakage function to reveal the information for the encryption randomness r for a trivial attack (in case of leakage from encryptor). A possible direction is to ask $\mathcal{A}$ to submit a set of functions $\mathcal{F}_0$ before seeing the public key or C^*. After seeing the challenge ciphertext, $\mathcal{A}$ can only ask for the

---

[1] Sometimes this is known as the CCA2 security, in contrast with the CCA1 security, where the adversary is only allowed to ask the decryption oracle before getting the challenge ciphertext.

leakage of arbitrary function $f' \in \mathcal{F}_0$. Therefore, f' cannot be the decryption of C^* and cannot lead to a trivial attack for the case of encryption randomness. This restriction is reasonable in the real world since most side-channel attacks apply to the physical implementation rather than the algorithm used (e.g. the leakage method of the power or timing attacks are the same, no matter RSA or ElGamal encryption are applied; 512-bit or 1024-bit keys are used.). Similar restriction was proposed by Yuen et al. [12] for leakage-resilient signatures in the auxiliary input model[2]. However, directly applying this idea to PKE, by simply allowing both pre-challenge and post-challenge leakages on sk, is not meaningful. Specifically, as the possible choice of leakage function f' is chosen before seeing the challenge ciphertext C^*, the post-challenge leakage $f'(\mathsf{sk})$ can simply be asked before seeing C^*, as a pre-challenge leakage. Therefore this kind of post-challenge leakage can be captured by slightly modifying the original auxiliary input model and does not strengthen our security model for PKE and IBE. Hence, we propose the leakage $f'(r)$ on the encryption randomness of C^* as the post-challenge leakage query. This kind of post-challenge leakage cannot be captured by the existing models. Since we focus on the auxiliary input model in this paper, we call our new model as the *post-challenge auxiliary input* model.

1.3 Our Contributions

In this paper, we propose the post-challenge auxiliary input model for public key and identity-based encryption. The significance of our post-challenge auxiliary input model is twofold. Firstly, it allows the leakage *after* seeing the challenge ciphertext. Secondly, it considers the leakage of two different parties: the secret key owner and the encryptor. In most leakage-resilient PKE and IBE schemes, they only consider the leakage of the secret key. However, the randomness used by the encryptor may also suffer from side-channel attacks. There are some encryption schemes which only consider the leakage on randomness, but not the secret key. Bellare et al. [13] only allows randomness leakage before receiving the public key. Namiki et al. [14] only allows randomness leakage before the challenge phase. Therefore our post-challenge auxiliary input model also improves this line of research on randomness leakage. To the best of the authors' knowledge, no existing leakage-resilient PKE or IBE schemes consider the leakage of secret key and randomness at the same time. Therefore, our post-challenge auxiliary input model is the *first* model to consider the leakage from both the secret key owner and the encryptor. This model captures a wider class of side-channel attacks than the previous models in the literature. We allow for leakage on the values being computed on, which will be a function of both the encryption random r and the public key pk. Specifically, we allows for $g(\mathsf{pk}, f(r))$ where g is any polynomial-time function and f is any computationally hard-to-invert function. We put the restriction on $f(r)$ to avoid trivial attacks on our security model.

To illustrate the feasibility of the model, we propose a generic construction of CPA-secure PKE in our new post-challenge auxiliary input model (pAI-CPA

---

[2] Yuen et al. [12] named their model as the selective auxiliary input model, due to similarity to the selective-ID model in identity-based encryption.

PKE). It is a generic transformation from the CPA-secure PKE in the auxiliary input model (AI-CPA PKE, e.g. [15]) and a new primitive called the *strong extractor with hard-to-invert auxiliary inputs*. The strong extractor is used to ensure that given the partial leakage of the encryption randomness, the ciphertext is indistinguishable from uniform distribution. As an independent technical contribution, we instantiate the strong extractor using the extended Goldreich-Levin theorem. Similar transformation can also be applied to identity-based encryption (IBE). Therefore we are able to construct pAI-ID-CPA IBE from AI-ID-CPA IBE (e.g. [16]).

Furthermore, we extend the generic transformation for CPA-secure IBE to CCA-secure PKE by Canetti *et al.* [17] into the leakage-resilient setting. The original transformation by Canetti *et al.* [17] only requires the use of strong one-time signatures. However, the encryption randomness of the PKE now includes both the encryption randomness used in IBE and the randomness used in the strong one-time signatures. Leaking either one of them will not violate our post-challenge auxiliary input model, but will lead to a trivial attack (details are explained in §5.1). Therefore, we have to link the randomness used in the IBE and the strong one-time signatures. We propose to use strong extractor with hard-to-invert auxiliary inputs as the linkage. It is because the strong extractor allows us to compute the randomness of IBE and the strong one-time signature from the same source, and yet remains indistinguishable from uniform distribution. It helps to simulate the leakage of the randomness in the security proof. Our contributions on encryption can be summarized in Fig. 1.

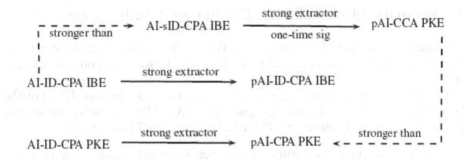

Fig. 1. Our Contributions on Encryption

Related Work. Dodis *et al.* [11] introduced the model of *auxiliary inputs* leakage functions. PKE secure in the auxiliary input model was proposed in [15]. Signature schemes secure in the auxiliary input model were independently proposed by Yuen *et al.* [12] and Faust *et al.* [18], under different restrictions to the security model. All of these works only consider the leakage from the owner of the secret key.

For leakage-resilient PKE, Naor and Segev wrote in [10] that

> "It will be very interesting to find an appropriate framework that allows a certain form of challenge-dependent leakage."

Halevi and Lin [19] proposed the model for *after-the-fact leakage* which also considered leakage that occurs after the challenge ciphertext is generated. In their entropic leakage-resilient PKE, even if the adversary designs its leakage function according to the challenge ciphertext, if it only leaks k bits then it cannot *amplify* them to learn more than k bits about the plaintext. Halevi and Lin [19] mentioned that

> "Our notion only captures leakage at the receiver side (i.e., from the secret key) and not at the sender side (i.e., from the encryption randomness). It is interesting to find ways of simultaneously addressing leakage at both ends."

Recently, Bitansky *et al.* [20] showed that any non-committing encryption scheme is tolerant to leakage on both the secret key sk and encryption randomness r (together), such that leaking L bits on (sk, r) reveals no more than L bits on the underlying encrypted message.

We solve the open problem of allowing simultaneous leakage from sender and encryptor by our *post-challenge auxiliary input model*, which allows hard-to-invert leakage and does not reveals *any bit* on the underlying encrypted message.

2   Security Model of Post-Challenge Auxiliary Inputs

We denote the security parameter by λ. We use the notation $\mathsf{neg}(\lambda)$ to refer to some negligible function of λ, and $\mathsf{poly}(\lambda)$ to refer to some polynomial function of λ.

We give the new post-challenge auxiliary input model for (probabilistic) public key encryption. Denote the message space as $\mathcal{M}$. A public-key encryption scheme Π consists of three Probabilistic Polynomial Time (PPT) algorithms:

- $\mathsf{Gen}(1^\lambda)$: On input the security parameter λ, output a public key pk and a secret key sk.
- $\mathsf{Enc}(\mathsf{pk}, M)$: Denote the message space as $\mathcal{M}$. On input a message $M \in \mathcal{M}$ and pk, output a ciphertext C.
- $\mathsf{Dec}(\mathsf{sk}, C)$: On input sk and C, output the message M or $\perp$ for invalid ciphertext.

For *correctness*, we require $\mathsf{Dec}(\mathsf{sk}, \mathsf{Enc}(\mathsf{pk}, M)) = M$ for all $M \in \mathcal{M}$ and $(\mathsf{pk}, \mathsf{sk}) \leftarrow \mathsf{Gen}(1^\lambda)$.

As introduced in §1.2, the basic setting of our new security model is similar to the classic IND-CCA model and the auxiliary input model for public key encryption. Our improvement is to require the adversary $\mathcal{A}$ to submit a set of possible leakages $\mathcal{F}_0$ that may be asked later in the security game, in order to avoid the trivial attacks mentioned in §1.2. Since $\mathcal{A}$ is a PPT algorithm, we consider that $m := |\mathcal{F}_0|$ is polynomial in the security parameter λ.

During the security game, $\mathcal{A}$ is only allowed to ask for at most q queries $f'_1, \ldots f'_q \in \mathcal{F}_0$ to the post-challenge leakage oracle and obtains $f'_1(r'), \ldots f'_q(r')$, where r' is the encryption randomness of the challenge ciphertext, but $\mathcal{A}$ cannot recover r' with probability better than ϵ_r. $\mathcal{A}$ can make these choices adaptively after seeing the challenge ciphertext. Hence, the post-challenge leakage query is meaningful. Denote the number of pre-challenge leakage oracle queries as q'.

We are now ready to give the formal definition of the model below. Let $\Pi = (\mathsf{Gen}, \mathsf{Enc}, \mathsf{Dec})$ be a public-key encryption scheme. The security against post-challenge auxiliary inputs and adaptive chosen-ciphertext attacks is defined as the following game pAI-CCA, with respect to the security parameter λ.

1. The adversary $\mathcal{A}$ submits a set of leakage functions $\mathcal{F}_0$ to the challenger $\mathcal{C}$ with $m := |\mathcal{F}_0|$ is polynomial in λ.
2. $\mathcal{C}$ runs $(\mathsf{pk}, \mathsf{sk}) \leftarrow \mathsf{Gen}(1^\lambda)$ and outputs pk to $\mathcal{A}$.
3. $\mathcal{A}$ may adaptively query the (pre-challenge) leakage oracle:
   - $\mathcal{LO}_s(f_i)$ with f_i. $\mathcal{LO}_s(f_i)$ returns $f_i(\mathsf{sk}, \mathsf{pk})$ to $\mathcal{A}$.
4. $\mathcal{A}$ submits two messages $m_0, m_1 \in \mathcal{M}$ of the same length to $\mathcal{C}$. $\mathcal{C}$ samples $b \leftarrow \{0, 1\}$ and the randomness of encryption $r' \leftarrow \{0, 1\}^*$. It returns $C^* \leftarrow \mathsf{Enc}(\mathsf{pk}, m_b; r')$ to $\mathcal{A}$.
5. $\mathcal{A}$ may adaptively query the (post-challenge) leakage oracle and the decryption oracle:
   - $\mathcal{LO}_r(f'_i)$ with $f'_i \in \mathcal{F}_0$. It returns $f'_i(r')$ to $\mathcal{A}$.
   - $\mathcal{DEC}(C)$ with $C \neq C^*$. It returns $\mathsf{Dec}(\mathsf{sk}, C)$ to $\mathcal{A}$.
6. $\mathcal{A}$ outputs its guess $b' \in \{0, 1\}$. The advantage of $\mathcal{A}$ is $Adv_{\mathcal{A}}^{\text{pAI−CCA}}(\Pi) = |\Pr[b = b'] - \frac{1}{2}|$.

Note that in the pre-challenge leakage stage, $\mathcal{A}$ may choose $f_i(\mathsf{sk}, \mathsf{pk})$ to encode $\mathsf{Dec}(\mathsf{sk}, \cdot)$ to query the pre-challenge leakage oracle $\mathcal{LO}_s$. Recall that we do not restrict f_i to be in $\mathcal{F}_0$. Therefore to provide an explicit decryption oracle is superfluous.

Furthermore, our model implicitly allows the adversary to obtain some leakage g on intermediate values during the encryption process, in the form of $g(\mathsf{pk}, m_0, f(r^*))$ and $g(\mathsf{pk}, m_1, f(r^*))$, where f is any hard-to-invert function. Since the adversary knows pk, m_0 and m_1, it can compute this kind of leakage for any polynomial time function g given the knowledge of $f(r^*)$.

Denote the set of functions asked in the pre-challenge leakage oracle $\mathcal{LO}_s$ as $\mathcal{F}_s$. We have to define the families $(\mathcal{F}_s, \mathcal{F}_0)$ for the leakage functions asked in the oracles. We can define the family of length-bounded function by restricting the size of the function output as in [11] (Refer to [11] for the definition of such family). In this paper, we consider the families of one-way function for auxiliary input model. We usually consider $\mathcal{F}_0$ as a family of one-way function $\mathcal{H}_{\mathsf{ow}}$, which is extended from the definition in [11]:

- Let $\mathcal{H}_{\mathsf{ow}}(\epsilon_r)$ be the class of all polynomial-time computable functions $h : \{0, 1\}^{|r'|} \rightarrow \{0, 1\}^*$, such that given $h(r')$ (for a randomly generated r'), no PPT algorithm can find r' with probability greater than $\epsilon_r{}^3$. The function $h(r')$ can be viewed as a composition of $q \in \mathbb{N}^+$ functions: $h(r') = (h_1(r'), \ldots, h_q(r'))$. Therefore $\{h_1, \ldots, h_q\} \in \mathcal{H}_{\mathsf{ow}}(\epsilon_r)$.

Also, we consider $\mathcal{F}_s$ as a family of one-way function $\mathcal{H}_{\mathsf{pk-ow}}$:

- Let $\mathcal{H}_{\mathsf{pk-ow}}(\epsilon_s)$ be the class of all polynomial-time computable functions $h : \{0,1\}^{|\mathsf{sk}|+|\mathsf{pk}|} \to \{0,1\}^*$, such that given $(\mathsf{pk}, h(\mathsf{sk}, \mathsf{pk}))$ (for a randomly generated $(\mathsf{sk}, \mathsf{pk})$), no PPT algorithm can find sk with probability greater than $\epsilon_s{}^4$. The function $h(\mathsf{sk}, \mathsf{pk})$ can be viewed as a composition of q' functions: $h(\mathsf{sk}, \mathsf{pk}) = (h_1(\mathsf{sk}, \mathsf{pk}), \ldots, h_{q'}(\mathsf{sk}, \mathsf{pk}))$. Therefore $\{h_1, \ldots, h_{q'}\} \in \mathcal{H}_{\mathsf{pk-ow}}(\epsilon_s)$.

Definition 1. *We say that Π is pAI-CCA secure with respect to the families $(\mathcal{H}_{\mathsf{pk-ow}}(\epsilon_s), \mathcal{H}_{\mathsf{ow}}(\epsilon_r))$ if the advantage of any PPT adversary $\mathcal{A}$ in the above game is negligible.*

We can also define the security for chosen plaintext attack (CPA) similarly. By forbidding the decryption oracle query, we have the security model for pAI-CPA. If we further forbid the leakage of the encryption randomness, we get the original AI-CPA model in [11].

We also define the security model for identity-based encryption in the full version of the paper [21].

3 Strong Extractor with Hard-to-Invert Auxiliary Inputs

Definition 2 ((ϵ, δ)-Strong extractor with auxiliary inputs). *Let* $\mathsf{Ext} : \{0,1\}^{l_1} \times \{0,1\}^{l_2} \to \{0,1\}^{m'}$, *where l_1, l_2 and m' are polynomial in λ. Ext is said to be a (ϵ, δ)-strong extractor with auxiliary inputs, if for every PPT adversary $\mathcal{A}$, and for all pairs (x, f) such that $x \in \{0,1\}^{l_2}$ and $f \in \mathcal{H}_{\mathsf{ow}}(\epsilon)$, we have:*

$$|\Pr[\mathcal{A}(r, f(x), \mathsf{Ext}(r, x)) = 1] - \Pr[\mathcal{A}(r, f(x), u) = 1]| < \delta.$$

where $r \in \{0,1\}^{l_1}$, $u \in \{0,1\}^{m'}$ are chosen uniformly random.

An interesting property of the above definition is that such a strong extractor itself is 2δ-hard-to-invert. This property is useful when we prove pAI-CCA encryption security.

Lemma 1. *Let $r \in \{0,1\}^{l_1}$ be chosen uniformly random. For any pair (x, f) where $x \in \{0,1\}^{l_2}$ and $f \in \mathcal{H}_{\mathsf{ow}}(\epsilon)$, given $(r, f(x))$ and $\mathsf{Ext}(r, x)$, no PPT adversary can find x with probability $\geq 2\delta$, provided that $\mathsf{Ext}(r, x)$ is a (ϵ, δ)-strong extractor with auxiliary inputs.*

---

[3] Otherwise, for example, $\mathcal{A}$ can choose an identity mapping f. Then, $\mathcal{A}$ can learn $r' = f(r')$ and test if $C^* = \mathtt{Enc}(\mathsf{pk}, m_0^*; r')$ to determine b and win the game.

[4] Note that we consider the probability of hard-to-invert function given the public key, the public parameters and other related parameters in the security game. Similar to the weak-AI-CPA model in [11], no PPT algorithm will output sk with ϵ_s probability given f_i, pk, as pk leaks some information about sk. Therefore, we also define that no PPT algorithm will output r' with ϵ_r probability given $f_i', C^*, \mathsf{pk}, m_0^*, m_1^*$. We omit these extra input parameters for simplicity in the rest of the paper.

Proof. Suppose on the contrary, x can be recovered with probability 2δ when knowing $r, f(x)$ and $\text{Ext}(r, x)$. However by the definition of strong extractor, fix any auxiliary-input function $f \in \mathcal{H}_{\text{ow}}(\epsilon)$, $\langle r, f(x), \text{Ext}(r, x) \rangle$ is δ-indistinguishable with $\langle r, f(x), u \rangle$. It leads to a contradiction, since if x can be recovered with probability 2δ, the attacker of Ext can compare that: (1) if $f(x)$ value is correct, then it receives $\text{Ext}(r, x)$; (2) else it receives u instead. It breaks the strong extractor with probability δ, which is a contradiction.   □

Interestingly, we find that a (ϵ, δ)-strong extractor with auxiliary inputs can be constructed from the modified Goldreich-Levin theorem from [15]. Denote $\langle r, x \rangle = \sum_{i=1}^{l} r_i x_i$ as the inner product of $x = (x_1, \ldots x_l)$ and $r = (r_1, \ldots, r_l)$.

Theorem 1 ([15]). *Let q be a prime, and let $\bar{H}$ be an arbitrary subset of $GF(q)$. Let $f : \bar{H}^{\bar{n}} \to \{0, 1\}^*$ be any (possibly randomized) function. s is chosen randomly from $\bar{H}^{\bar{n}}$, r is chosen randomly from $GF(q)^{\bar{n}}$ and u is chosen randomly from $GF(q)$. We also have $y = f(s)$. If there is a distinguisher D that runs in time t such that*

$$|\Pr[D(r, y, \langle r, s \rangle) = 1] - \Pr[D(r, y, u)] = 1| = \delta,$$

then there is an inverter $\mathcal{A}$ that runs in time $t' = t \cdot \text{poly}(\bar{n}, |\bar{H}|, \frac{1}{\delta})$ such that $\Pr[\mathcal{A}(y) = s] \geq \frac{\delta^3}{512\bar{n}q^2}$.

Now we are ready to show that strong extractor with ϵ-hard-to-invert auxiliary inputs can be instantiated using inner product.

Theorem 2. *Let λ be the security parameter. Let x be chosen uniformly random from $\{0, 1\}^{l(\lambda)}$ where $l(\lambda) = \text{poly}(\lambda)$. Similarly, we choose r uniformly random from $GF(q)^{l(\lambda)}$ and u uniformly random from $GF(q)$. Then, given $f \in \mathcal{H}_{\text{ow}}(\epsilon)$, no PPT algorithm $\mathcal{A}'$ can distinguish $(r, f(x), \langle r, x \rangle)$ from $(r, f(x), u)$ with probability $\epsilon' \geq (512l(\lambda)q^2\epsilon)^{1/3}$.*

Proof. Now, we let $\bar{H} = \{0, 1\} \subset GF(q)$, $\bar{n} = l(\lambda)$. Suppose there is an algorithm that can distinguish $(r, f(x), \langle r, x \rangle)$ and $(r, f(x), u)$ in time $t = \text{poly}_1(\lambda)$ with probability ϵ'. Then, there exists an inverter $\mathcal{A}$ that runs in time $t \cdot \text{poly}(l(\lambda), 2, \frac{1}{\epsilon})$ $= \text{poly}'(\lambda)$ such that $\Pr[\mathcal{A}(f(x)) = x] \geq \frac{\epsilon'^3}{512l(\lambda)q^2} \geq \epsilon$ if $\epsilon' \geq (512l(\lambda)q^2\epsilon)^{1/3}$. It contradicts that $f \in \mathcal{H}_{\text{ow}}(\epsilon)$.   □

4   CPA Secure PKE Construction against Post-Challenge Auxiliary Inputs

In this section, we give the construction of a public key encryption which is pAI-CPA secure. We show that it can be constructed from an AI-CPA secure encryption (e.g., [15]) and a *strong extractor with ϵ-hard-to-invert auxiliary inputs leakage*.

4.1   Construction of pAI-CPA Secure PKE

Let $\Pi' = (\mathsf{Gen'}, \mathsf{Enc'}, \mathsf{Dec'})$ be an AI-CPA secure encryption (with respect to family $\mathcal{H}_{\mathsf{pk-ow}}(\epsilon_s)$) where the encryption randomness is in $\{0,1\}^{m'}$, $\mathsf{Ext} : \{0,1\}^{l_1} \times \{0,1\}^{l_2} \to \{0,1\}^{m'}$ is a $(\epsilon_r, \mathsf{neg}(\lambda))$-strong extractor with auxiliary inputs, then a pAI-CPA secure (with respect to families $(\mathcal{H}_{\mathsf{pk-ow}}(\epsilon_s), \mathcal{H}_{\mathsf{ow}}(\epsilon_r)))$ encryption scheme Π can be constructed as follows.

1. $\mathsf{Gen}(1^\lambda)$: It runs $(\mathsf{pk}, \mathsf{sk}) \leftarrow \mathsf{Gen'}(1^\lambda)$ and chooses r uniformly random from $\{0,1\}^{l_1}$. Then, we set the public key $\mathsf{PK} = (\mathsf{pk}, r)$ and the secret key $\mathsf{SK} = \mathsf{sk}$.
2. $\mathsf{Enc}(\mathsf{PK}, M)$: It picks x uniformly random from $\{0,1\}^{l_2}$. Then, it computes $y = \mathsf{Ext}(r, x)$. The ciphertext is $c = \mathsf{Enc'}(\mathsf{pk}, M; y)$.
3. $\mathsf{Dec}(\mathsf{SK}, c)$: It returns $\mathsf{Dec'}(\mathsf{sk}, c)$.

Theorem 3. *If Π' is an AI-CPA secure encryption with respect to family $\mathcal{H}_{\mathsf{pk-ow}}(\epsilon_s)$ and Ext is a $(\epsilon_r, \mathsf{neg}(\lambda))$-strong extractor with auxiliary inputs, then Π is pAI-CPA secure with respect to families $(\mathcal{H}_{\mathsf{pk-ow}}(\epsilon_s), \mathcal{H}_{\mathsf{ow}}(\epsilon_r))$.*

Proof. Denote the randomness used in the challenge ciphertext as x^*. Let Game_0 be the pAI-CPA security game with Π scheme. Game_1 is the same as Game_0 except that when encrypting the challenge ciphertext $c = \mathsf{Enc'}(\mathsf{pk}, m_b; y)$, we replace $y = \mathsf{Ext}(r, x^*)$ with y' which is chosen uniformly at random in $\{0,1\}^{m'}$. The leakage oracle outputs $f_i(x^*)$ for both games.

Let $Adv_{\mathcal{A}}^{\mathsf{Game}_i}(\Pi)$ be the advantage that the adversary $\mathcal{A}$ wins in Game_i with Π scheme. Now, we need to show for any PPT adversary $\mathcal{A}$:

$$|Adv_{\mathcal{A}}^{\mathsf{Game}_0}(\Pi) - Adv_{\mathcal{A}}^{\mathsf{Game}_1}(\Pi)| \leq \mathsf{neg}(\lambda).$$

Assume that there exists an adversary $\mathcal{A}$ such that $|Adv_{\mathcal{A}}^{\mathsf{Game}_0}(\Pi) - Adv_{\mathcal{A}}^{\mathsf{Game}_1}(\Pi)| \geq \epsilon_A$ which is non-negligible.

The simulator $\mathcal{S}$ is given $(r, f_1(x^*), f_2(x^*), \ldots, f_q(x^*), T)$ where T is either $T_0 = \langle r, x^* \rangle$ or $T_1 = u$ which is a random number as in Definition 2. Given $f_1(x^*), \ldots, f_q(x^*)$, no PPT adversary can recover x^* with probability greater than ϵ_r by the definition of $\mathcal{H}_{\mathsf{ow}}(\epsilon_r)$. Then, the simulator generates $(\mathsf{pk}, \mathsf{sk}) \leftarrow \mathsf{Gen'}(1^\lambda)$. It sets $\mathsf{SK} = \mathsf{sk}$ and gives the adversary $\mathsf{PK} = (\mathsf{pk}, r)$. The simulator can answer pre-challenge leakage oracle as it has PK and SK. The adversary submits two message m_0 and m_1 to the simulator where the simulator flips a coin b. It encrypts the challenge ciphertext $C^* = \mathsf{Enc}(\mathsf{pk}, m_b; T)$ and gives it to $\mathcal{A}$. $\mathcal{A}$ can ask $f_i(x)$ as the post-challenge leakage queries. $\mathcal{A}$ outputs its guess bit b' to the simulator. If $b = b'$, the simulator outputs 1; otherwise, it outputs 0.

Since the difference of advantage of $\mathcal{A}$ between Game_0 and Game_1 is ϵ_A, then

$$Adv_{\mathcal{S}} = \left| \frac{1}{2} \Pr[\mathcal{S} \text{ outputs } 1 | T_1] + \frac{1}{2} \Pr[\mathcal{S} \text{ outputs } 0 | T_0] - \frac{1}{2} \right|$$

$$= \left| \frac{1}{2} \Pr[\mathcal{S} \text{ outputs } 1 | T_1] + \frac{1}{2}(1 - \Pr[\mathcal{S} \text{ outputs } 1 | T_0]) - \frac{1}{2} \right|$$

$$= \frac{1}{2}(|\Pr[b = b' | T_1] - \Pr[b = b' | T_0]|) \geq \frac{\epsilon_A}{2}.$$

which is non-negligible if ϵ_A is non-negligible. It contradicts the definition of strong extractor in Definition 2. Therefore, no PPT adversary can distinguish Game_0 from Game_1 with non-negligible probability.

Next, we want to show that

$$Adv_A^{\mathsf{Game}_1}(\Pi) = \mathsf{neg}(\lambda).$$

Note that the challenge ciphertext now is $c = \mathsf{Enc}'(\mathsf{pk}, M; y')$ where y' is chosen uniformly at random in $\{0,1\}^{m'}$. Therefore the output of the leakage oracle $f_i(x^*)$ will not reveal any information related to c. Then Game_1 is the same as the AI-CPA game with Π'. As Π is based on Π' which is AI-CPA secure, we have that $Adv_A^{\mathsf{Game}_1}(\Pi)$ is negligible. $\qquad\square$

Extension to IBE. We can use the same technique to construct pAI-ID-CPA secure IBE. Let $\Sigma' = (\mathsf{Setup}', \mathsf{Extract}', \mathsf{Enc}', \mathsf{Dec}')$ be an AI-ID-CPA secure IBE (e.g. [16]) where the encryption randomness is in $\{0,1\}^{m'}$, $\mathsf{Ext}: \{0,1\}^{l_1} \times \{0,1\}^{l_2} \to \{0,1\}^{m'}$ is a $(\epsilon_r, \mathsf{neg}(\lambda))$-strong extractor with auxiliary inputs, then construct a pAI-ID-CPA secure IBE scheme Σ as follows.

1. $\mathsf{Setup}(1^\lambda)$: It runs $(\mathsf{mpk}, \mathsf{msk}) \leftarrow \mathsf{Setup}'(1^\lambda)$ and chooses r uniformly random from $\{0,1\}^{l_1}$. Then, we set the master public key $\mathsf{MPK} = (\mathsf{mpk}, r)$ and the master secret key $\mathsf{MSK} = \mathsf{msk}$.
2. $\mathsf{Extract}(\mathsf{MSK}, \mathsf{ID})$: It returns $\mathsf{sk}_{\mathsf{ID}} \leftarrow \mathsf{Extract}(\mathsf{MSK}, \mathsf{ID})$.
3. $\mathsf{Enc}(\mathsf{MPK}, \mathsf{ID}, M)$: It chooses x uniformly random from $\{0,1\}^{l_2}$. Then, it computes $y = \mathsf{Ext}(r, x)$. The ciphertext is $c = \mathsf{Enc}'(\mathsf{mpk}, \mathsf{ID}, M; y)$.
4. $\mathsf{Dec}(\mathsf{sk}_{\mathsf{ID}}, c)$: It returns $\mathsf{Dec}'(\mathsf{sk}_{\mathsf{ID}}, c)$.

Theorem 4. *If Σ' is an AI-ID-CPA secure IBE with respect to family $\mathcal{H}_{\mathsf{pk-ow}}(\epsilon_s)$ and Ext is a $(\epsilon_r, \mathsf{neg}(\lambda))$-strong extractor with auxiliary inputs, then Σ is pAI-ID-CPA secure with respect to families $(\mathcal{H}_{\mathsf{pk-ow}}(\epsilon_s), \mathcal{H}_{\mathsf{ow}}(\epsilon_r))$.*

The proof is similar to the proof of Theorem 3 and hence is omitted.

Corollary 1. *Instantiating with the strong extractor construction in §3 and the identity-based encryption scheme in [16], the identity-based encryption construction Σ' is pAI-ID-CPA secure.*

5   CCA Public Key Encryption from CPA Identity-Based Encryption

In this section, we show that auxiliary-inputs (selective-ID) CPA secure IBE and strong one-time signatures imply post-challenge auxiliary-inputs CCA secure PKE. Canetti *et al.* [17] showed that a CCA secure encryption can be constructed from a (selective-ID) CPA secure IBE and a strong one-time signatures. We would like to show that this transformation can also be applied to the auxiliary input model after some modifications. As in [17], we use the strong one-time signature to prevent the PKE adversaries asking for decrypting ciphertexts of ID^* in the post stage as the IBE adversaries are not allowed to ask for $\mathsf{Extract}(\mathsf{ID}^*)$. However, we cannot apply the technique in [17] directly.

5.1   Intuition

Let $(\mathsf{Gen}_s, \mathsf{Sign}, \mathsf{Verify})$ be a strong one-time signature scheme. Let $(\mathsf{Setup}', \mathsf{Extract}', \mathsf{Enc}', \mathsf{Dec}')$ be an auxiliary-inputs CPA secure IBE scheme (refer to the definition in the full version of the paper [21], by dropping the post-challenge query). The construction directly following Canetti $et\ al.$'s transformation [17] is as follows.

1. $\mathsf{Gen}(1^\lambda)$: Run $(\mathsf{mpk}, \mathsf{msk}) \leftarrow \mathsf{Setup}'(1^\lambda)$. Set the public key $\mathsf{pk} = \mathsf{mpk}$ and the secret key $\mathsf{sk} = \mathsf{msk}$.
2. $\mathsf{Enc}(\mathsf{pk}, M)$: Run $(\mathsf{vk}, \mathsf{sk}_s) \leftarrow \mathsf{Gen}_s(1^\lambda)$. Calculate $c \leftarrow \mathsf{Enc}'(\mathsf{pk}, \mathsf{vk}, M)$ and $\sigma \leftarrow \mathsf{Sign}(\mathsf{sk}_s, c)$. Then, the ciphertext is $C = (c, \sigma, \mathsf{vk})$.
3. $\mathsf{Dec}(\mathsf{sk}, C)$: First, test $\mathsf{Verify}(\mathsf{vk}, c, \sigma) \overset{?}{=} 1$. If it is "1", compute $\mathsf{sk}_{\mathsf{vk}} = \mathsf{Extract}'(\mathsf{sk}, \mathsf{vk})$ and return $\mathsf{Dec}'(\mathsf{sk}_{\mathsf{vk}}, c)$. Otherwise, return $\perp$.

Problems in the Post-Challenge Auxiliary Input Model. At first glance it seems that Canetti $et\ al.$'s transformation [17] also works in our pAI-CCA model for PKE, if we simply change the underlying IBE to be secure in the corresponding post-challenge auxiliary input model. However, we find that this is not true. The main challenge of pAI-CCA secure PKE is how to handle the leakage of the randomness used in the challenge ciphertext. It includes the randomness used in Gen_s, Sign and Enc', denoted as r_{sig_1}, r_{sig_2} and r_{enc} respectively. Specifically, we have $(\mathsf{vk}, \mathsf{sk}_s) \leftarrow \mathsf{Gen}_s(1^\lambda; r_{\mathsf{sig}_1})$, $\sigma \leftarrow \mathsf{Sign}(\mathsf{sk}_s, c; r_{\mathsf{sig}_2})$ and $c \leftarrow \mathsf{Enc}'(\mathsf{mpk}, \mathsf{vk}, m_b; r_{\mathsf{enc}})$.

Let $\mathcal{A}$ be a pAI-CCA adversary of the PKE. Let f be (one of) the post-challenge leakage function submitted by $\mathcal{A}$ before seeing the public key. Then, after receiving the challenge ciphertext $C^* = (c^*, \sigma^*, \mathsf{vk}^*)$, $\mathcal{A}$ can ask the leakage $f(r')$ where $r' = (r_{\mathsf{enc}}, r_{\mathsf{sig}_1}, r_{\mathsf{sig}_2})$ is the randomness used to produce C^*. To some extreme, $\mathcal{A}$ may ask:

- $f_1(r') = r_{\mathsf{enc}}$, such that f_1 is still hard-to-invert upon r'. In this case, $\mathcal{A}$ can test $c^* \overset{?}{=} \mathsf{Enc}'(\mathsf{mpk}, \mathsf{vk}, m_0; r_{\mathsf{enc}})$ to win the pAI-CCA game; or
- $f_2(r') = (r_{\mathsf{sig}_1}, r_{\mathsf{sig}_2})$, such that f_2 is still hard-to-invert upon r'. In this case, given r_{sig_1}, $\mathcal{A}$ can generate $(\mathsf{vk}, \mathsf{sk}_s) = \mathsf{Gen}_s(1^\lambda; r_{\mathsf{sig}_1})$ which causes $\Pr[\mathsf{Forge}]$ defined in [17] to be non-negligible ("Forge" is the event that $\mathcal{A}$ wins the game by outputting a forged strong one-time signature).

Therefore, leaking part of the randomness in r' will make the proof of [17] fail in our model.

Our Solution: We set both $r_{\mathsf{sig}_1}, r_{\mathsf{sig}_2}$ and r_{enc} are generated from the same source of randomness $x \in \{0,1\}^{l_2}$. Suppose $r_{\mathsf{sig}_1} \| r_{\mathsf{sig}_2}$ and r_{enc} are bit-strings of length n'. Suppose $\mathsf{Ext} : \{0,1\}^{l_1} \times \{0,1\}^{l_2} \to \{0,1\}^{n'}$ is a strong extractor with ϵ_r-hard-to-invert auxiliary inputs; r_1 and r_2 are independent and uniformly chosen from $\{0,1\}^{l_1}$ which are also included in the public key pk. Then the $randomness$ used in the IBE and the one-time signature can be calculated by

$r_{\mathsf{enc}} = \mathsf{Ext}(r_1, x)$ and $(r_{\mathsf{sig}_1} \| r_{\mathsf{sig}_2}) = \mathsf{Ext}(r_2, x)$ respectively. In the security proof, the pAI-CCA adversary $\mathcal{A}$ can ask for the leakage of $f(x)$, where f is any *hard-to-invert* function.

The main part of the security proof is to use the pAI-CCA adversary $\mathcal{A}$ to break the AI-ID-CPA security of the underlying IBE scheme Π'. The simulator of the pAI-CCA game has to simulate the post-challenge leakage oracle without knowing the encryption randomness x of the challenge ciphertext, which was produced by the challenger of Π'. We solve this problem by proving that it is indistinguishable by replacing $r^*_{\mathsf{enc}} = \mathsf{Ext}(r_1, x^*)$ and $r^*_{\mathsf{sig}_1} \| r^*_{\mathsf{sig}_2} = \mathsf{Ext}(r_2, x^*)$ with random numbers. Therefore, the post-challenge leakages on x^* will be independent with r^*_{enc} and $r^*_{\mathsf{sig}_1} \| r^*_{\mathsf{sig}_2}$ which are used to produce the real challenge ciphertext. Then, the simulator can randomly choose x^* and simulate the post-challenge oracles by it own. However, when we show to replace $r^*_{\mathsf{sig}_1} \| r^*_{\mathsf{sig}_2}$ with a random number, the simulator needs to compute $r_{\mathsf{enc}^*} = \mathsf{Ext}(r_1, x^*)$. One way to solve it is to include $\mathsf{Ext}(r_1, x^*)$ as a post-challenge leakage query in the pAI-CCA game. As we will see later (by Lemma 1), including $\mathsf{Ext}(r_1, x^*)$ in leakage queries is still $\mathsf{neg}(\lambda)$-hard-to-invert.

Following [17], the transformation also works for the weaker selective identity (sID) model. As a result, we only need a AI-sID-CPA secure IBE. To sum up, we need three primitives to construct a pAI-CCA secure PKE: *strong extractor with auxiliary inputs, strong one-time signatures and AI-sID-CPA secure IBE.*

5.2   Post-Challenge Auxiliary Inputs CCA Secure PKE

We are now ready to describe our post-challenge auxiliary inputs CCA secure PKE. Denote a AI-sID-CPA secure IBE scheme $\Pi' = (\mathsf{Setup}', \mathsf{Extract}', \mathsf{Enc}', \mathsf{Dec}')$, a strong one-time signature scheme $\Pi_s = (\mathsf{Gen}_s, \mathsf{Sign}, \mathsf{Verify})$ and a strong extractor with ϵ_r-hard-to-invert auxiliary input $\mathsf{Ext} : \{0,1\}^{l_1} \times \{0,1\}^{l_2} \to \{0,1\}^{n'}$, where the size of r_{enc} and $r_{\mathsf{sig}_1} \| r_{\mathsf{sig}_2}$ are both $\{0,1\}^{n'}$; and the verification key space of Π_s is the same as the identity space of Π'. We construct a PKE scheme $\Pi = (\mathsf{Gen}, \mathsf{Enc}, \mathsf{Dec})$ as follows.

1. $\mathsf{Gen}(1^\lambda)$: Run $(\mathsf{mpk}, \mathsf{msk}) \leftarrow \mathsf{Setup}'(1^\lambda)$. Choose r_1, r_2 uniformly random from $\{0,1\}^{l_1}$. Set the public key $\mathsf{pk} = (\mathsf{mpk}, r_1, r_2)$ and the secret key $\mathsf{sk} = \mathsf{msk}$.

2. $\mathsf{Enc}(\mathsf{pk}, m)$: Randomly sample $x \in \{0,1\}^{l_2}$, calculate $r_{\mathsf{enc}} = \mathsf{Ext}_1(r_1, x)$ and $r_{\mathsf{sig}_1} \| r_{\mathsf{sig}_2} = \mathsf{Ext}_2(r_2, x)$. Run $(\mathsf{vk}, \mathsf{sk}_s) = \mathsf{Gen}_s(1^\lambda; r_{\mathsf{sig}_1})$. Let $c = \mathsf{Enc}'(\mathsf{pk}, \mathsf{vk}, m; r_{\mathsf{enc}})$; $\sigma = \mathsf{Sign}(\mathsf{sk}_s, c; r_{\mathsf{sig}_2})$. Then, the ciphertext is $C = (c, \sigma, \mathsf{vk})$.

3. $\mathsf{Dec}(\mathsf{sk}, C)$: First, test $\mathsf{Verify}(\mathsf{vk}, c, \sigma) \overset{?}{=} 1$. If it is "1", compute $\mathsf{sk}_{\mathsf{vk}} = \mathsf{Extract}(\mathsf{sk}, \mathsf{vk})$ and return $\mathsf{Dec}'(\mathsf{sk}_{\mathsf{vk}}, c)$. Otherwise, return $\perp$.

Theorem 5. *Assuming that Π' is a AI-sID-CPA secure IBE scheme with respect to family $\mathcal{H}_{\mathsf{pk-ow}}(\epsilon_s)$, Π_s is a strong one-time signature, and Ext_1 is $(\epsilon_r, \mathsf{neg}_1)$-strong extractor with auxiliary inputs and Ext_2 is $(2\mathsf{neg}_1, \mathsf{neg}_2)$-strong extractor with auxiliary inputs, then there exists a PKE scheme Π which is pAI-CCA secure with respect to families $(\mathcal{H}_{\mathsf{pk-ow}}(\epsilon_s), \mathcal{H}_{\mathsf{ow}}(\epsilon_r))$.*

Proof. We prove the security by a number of security games. Let Game_0 be the original pAI-CCA game for the PKE scheme Π. Specifically for the challenge ciphertext, the simulator picks a random number x^* to compute $r^*_{\mathsf{enc}} = \mathsf{Ext}_1(r_1, x^*)$ and $r^*_{\mathsf{sig}_1} \| r^*_{\mathsf{sig}_2} = \mathsf{Ext}_2(r_2, x^*)$. Let Game_1 be the same as Game_0, except that $r^*_{\mathsf{sig}_1} \| r^*_{\mathsf{sig}_2}$ is randomly chosen from $\{0,1\}^{n'}$. Let Game_2 be the same as Game_1, except that r^*_{enc} is randomly chosen from $\{0,1\}^{n'}$.

Lemma 2. *For any PPT adversary $\mathcal{A}$, Game_0 is indistinguishable from Game_1 if Ext_1 is $(\epsilon_r, \mathsf{neg}_1)$-strong extractor with auxiliary inputs and Ext_2 is $(2\mathsf{neg}_1, \mathsf{neg}_2)$-strong extractor with auxiliary inputs.*

Lemma 3. *For any PPT adversary $\mathcal{A}$, Game_1 is indistinguishable from Game_2 if Ext_1 is $(\epsilon_r, \mathsf{neg}_1)$-strong extractor with auxiliary inputs.*

Lemma 4. *For any PPT adversary $\mathcal{A}$, the advantage in Game_2 is negligible if Π' is a AI-sID-CPA secure IBE scheme with respect to family $\mathcal{H}_{\mathsf{pk-ow}}(\epsilon_s)$ and Π_s is a strong one-time signature.*

$\square$

Proof (Lemma 2). Let $Adv^{\mathsf{Game}_i}_{\mathcal{A}}(\Pi)$ be the advantage that the adversary $\mathcal{A}$ wins in Game_i with Π scheme. Now, we need to show for any PPT adversary $\mathcal{A}$:

$$|Adv^{\mathsf{Game}_0}_{\mathcal{A}}(\Pi) - Adv^{\mathsf{Game}_1}_{\mathcal{A}}(\Pi)| \leq \mathsf{neg}(\lambda).$$

Assume that there exists an adversary $\mathcal{A}$ such that $|Adv^{\mathsf{Game}_0}_{\mathcal{A}}(\Pi) - Adv^{\mathsf{Game}_1}_{\mathcal{A}}(\Pi)| \geq \epsilon_A$ which is non-negligible.

The simulator $\mathcal{S}$ picks a random $r_1, r_2 \in \{0,1\}^{l_1}$. The simulator is given $(r_2, f_1(x^*), \ldots, f_q(x^*), f_{q+1}(x^*), T)$ where $f_1, \ldots, f_q \in \mathcal{F}_0$, $f_{q+1}(x^*) = \mathsf{Ext}_1(r_1, x^*)$, and T is either $T_0 = \langle r_2, x^* \rangle$ or $T_1 = u$ (a random number as in Definition 2). Given $f_1(x^*), \ldots, f_q(x^*)$, no PPT adversary can recover x^* with probability greater than ϵ_r by the definition of $\mathcal{H}_{\mathsf{ow}}(\epsilon_r)$ (We will later show that including $\mathsf{Ext}(r_1, \cdot)$ is also $2\mathsf{neg}_1$-hard-to-invert).

Then, the simulator generates $(\mathsf{mpk}, \mathsf{msk}) \leftarrow \mathsf{Setup}'(1^\lambda)$. It sets $\mathsf{sk} = \mathsf{msk}$ and gives the adversary $\mathsf{pk} = (\mathsf{mpk}, r_1, r_2)$. The simulator can answer pre-challenge leakage oracle as it has pk and sk. The adversary submits two messages m_0 and m_1 to the simulator where the simulator flips a coin b. It sets $r_{\mathsf{sig}_1} \| r_{\mathsf{sig}_2} = T$, runs $(\mathsf{vk}, \mathsf{sk}_s) \leftarrow \mathsf{Gen}_s(1^\lambda; r_{\mathsf{sig}_1})$, $c = \mathsf{Enc}'(\mathsf{pk}, \mathsf{vk}, m_b; f_{q+1}(x^*))$ and $\sigma = \mathsf{Sign}(\mathsf{sk}_s, c; r_{\mathsf{sig}_2})$. It returns the challenge ciphertext $C^* = (c, \sigma, \mathsf{vk})$ to $\mathcal{A}$. $\mathcal{A}$ can ask $f_i(x^*)$ as the post-challenge leakage queries. $\mathcal{A}$ outputs its guess bit b' to the simulator. If $b = b'$, the simulator outputs 1; otherwise, it outputs 0.

Since the difference of advantage of $\mathcal{A}$ between Game_0 and Game_1 is ϵ_A, then

$$Adv_{\mathcal{S}} = \frac{1}{2}(|\Pr[b = b'|T_1] - \Pr[b = b'|T_0]|) \geq \frac{\epsilon_A}{2}.$$

which is non-negligible if ϵ_A is non-negligible. It contradicts the fact that Ext_2 is $(2\mathsf{neg}_1, \mathsf{neg}_2)$-strong extractor with auxiliary inputs. Therefore, no PPT adversary can distinguish Game_0 from Game_1 with non-negligible probability.

Finally, we need to show that including $\mathsf{Ext}_1(r_1, \cdot)$ is also $2\mathsf{neg}_1(\lambda)$-hard-to-invert, provided that Ext_1 is a $(\epsilon_r, \mathsf{neg}_1)$-strong extractor with auxiliary inputs. This follows directly from Lemma 1 if we set $f = (f_1(x^*), \ldots, f_q(x^*)) \in \mathcal{H}_{ow}(\epsilon_r)$.

□

Proof (Lemma 3). The post-challenge query functions $(f_1, \ldots, f_q) \in \mathcal{F}_0$ are ϵ_r-hard-to-invert by definition. Fix any auxiliary-input function $f_1, \ldots, f_q$, $\langle r_1, f_1(x^*), \ldots, f_q(x^*), \mathsf{Ext}(r_1, x^*) \rangle$ is indistinguishable with $\langle r_1, f_1(x^*), \ldots, f_q(x^*), u \rangle$ where u is randomly chosen from $\{0,1\}^{n'}$, by the definition of strong extractor. Hence Game_1 is indistinguishable from Game_2. The reduction is similar to the previous proof.

□

Proof (Lemma 4). Let $\mathcal{A}$ be an adversary to Π on Game_2 and we construct an AI-sID-CPA adversary $\mathcal{A}'$ to Π' that runs $\mathcal{A}$ as a subroutine. Initially, $\mathcal{A}$ submits a set of leakage functions $\mathcal{F}_0$ that he would like to ask in the Game_2 to $\mathcal{A}'$. $\mathcal{A}'$ picks $r_{\mathsf{sig}_1} \| r_{\mathsf{sig}_2}$ uniformly random from $\{0,1\}^{n'}$ and computes $(\mathsf{vk}^*, \mathsf{sk}_s^*) = \mathsf{Gen}_s(1^\lambda; r_{\mathsf{sig}_1})$. $\mathcal{A}'$ submits the challenge identity vk^* to the AI-sID-CPA challenger $\mathcal{C}$, and $\mathcal{C}$ returns mpk to $\mathcal{A}'$. Then $\mathcal{A}'$ picks r_1 and r_2 which are independent and uniformly chosen from $\{0,1\}^{l_1}$. $\mathcal{A}'$ gives $\mathsf{pk} = (\mathsf{mpk}, r_1, r_2)$ to $\mathcal{A}$.

In the pre-challenge query phase, $\mathcal{A}$ can adaptively query $f_i(\mathsf{pk}, \mathsf{msk})$. $\mathcal{A}'$ records and forwards all the queries to $\mathcal{C}$; and uses the output by $\mathcal{C}$ to answer $\mathcal{A}$.

In the challenge phase, $\mathcal{A}$ submits m_0, m_1 to $\mathcal{A}'$, and $\mathcal{A}'$ forwards m_0, m_1 as the challenge message to $\mathcal{C}$. $\mathcal{C}$ returns $c^* = \mathsf{Enc}'(\mathsf{mpk}, \mathsf{vk}^*, m_b; r_{\mathsf{enc}})$ to $\mathcal{A}'$ for some random bit b and randomness r_{enc}. Then $\mathcal{A}'$ computes $\sigma^* = \mathsf{Sign}(\mathsf{sk}_s^*, c^*; r_{\mathsf{sig}_2})$. $\mathcal{A}'$ sends $C^* = (c^*, \sigma^*, \mathsf{vk}^*)$ to $\mathcal{A}$ as its challenge ciphertext. $\mathcal{A}'$ picks a random $x^* \in \{0,1\}^{l_2}$.

In the post-challenge query phase, $\mathcal{A}'$ can answer the adaptive query f_i' on the randomness x^* asked by $\mathcal{A}$. $\mathcal{A}$ may also adaptively query $\mathcal{DEC}(c, \sigma, \mathsf{vk})$. $\mathcal{A}'$ returns $\perp$ if $\mathsf{Verify}(\mathsf{vk}, c, \sigma) \neq 1$. Otherwise, there are two cases. If $\mathsf{vk} = \mathsf{vk}^*$, it means $(c, \sigma) \neq (c^*, \sigma^*)$. However, it implies that $\mathcal{A}$ forges the one-time signature. This happens with only a negligible probability. Else, $\mathsf{vk} \neq \mathsf{vk}^*$, $\mathcal{A}'$ asks the extraction oracle $\mathcal{EO}(\mathsf{vk})$ to $\mathcal{C}$ and uses $\mathsf{sk}_{\mathsf{vk}}$ to decrypt c.

Finally $\mathcal{A}$ outputs its guess b' and $\mathcal{A}'$ forwards it to $\mathcal{C}$ as its guess bit. Therefore, if $\mathcal{A}$ wins the Game_2 with a non-negligible probability, then $\mathcal{A}'$ will win the AI-sID-CPA game also with a non-negligible probability, which contradicts that Π' is AI-sID-CPA secure.

To show that the probability that $\mathcal{A}$ asks for the decryption of a valid ciphertext with identity vk^* is negligible, let $\mathcal{C}'$ be the challenger of the strong one-time signature scheme. We construct an algorithm $\mathcal{B}$ to break the strong one-time signature scheme by running $\mathcal{A}$ as a subroutine. Initially, $\mathcal{A}$ submits its post-challenge leakage class $\mathcal{F}_0$ to $\mathcal{B}$. $\mathcal{C}'$ gives vk^* to $\mathcal{B}$. $\mathcal{B}$ runs $(\mathsf{mpk}, \mathsf{msk}) \leftarrow \mathsf{Setup}'(1^\lambda)$ and picks r_1 and r_2 which are independent and uniformly chosen from $\{0,1\}^{l_1}$. $\mathcal{B}$ returns $\mathsf{pk} = (\mathsf{mpk}, r_1, r_2)$ to $\mathcal{A}$.

In the pre-challenge query phase, $\mathcal{A}$ can adaptively query $f_i(\mathsf{pk}, \mathsf{msk})$ and $\mathcal{B}$ can answer them by itself.

In the challenge phase, $\mathcal{A}$ submits m_0, m_1 to $\mathcal{B}$. $\mathcal{B}$ picks r_{enc} uniformly random from $\{0,1\}^{n'}$. $\mathcal{B}$ picks a random bit b and calculates $c^* = \mathsf{Enc}'(\mathsf{mpk}, \mathsf{vk}^*, m_b; r_{\mathsf{enc}})$.

Then $\mathcal{B}$ asks $\mathcal{C}'$ to sign on c^* and obtains the signature σ^*. $\mathcal{B}$ gives the challenge ciphertext $C^* = (c^*, \sigma^*, \mathsf{vk}^*)$ to $\mathcal{A}$. $\mathcal{B}$ picks a random $x^* \in \{0, 1\}^{l_2}$.

In the post query phase, $\mathcal{A}$ can adaptively ask the post-challenge leakage $f_i' \in \mathcal{F}_0$ to $\mathcal{B}$ and $\mathcal{B}$ can answer it with x^*. $\mathcal{A}$ may also ask for the decryption oracle. Decryption of ciphertext involving $\mathsf{vk} \neq \mathsf{vk}^*$ can be answered by using msk. However, if $\mathcal{A}$ asks for the decryption of a valid ciphertext $(c, \sigma, \mathsf{vk}^*)$ that is not identical to $(c^*, \sigma^*, \mathsf{vk}^*)$, $\mathcal{B}$ returns (c, σ) to $\mathcal{C}'$. Therefore, the probability that $\mathcal{A}$ can output a forged signature is negligible provided that Π_s is a strong one-time signature, which completes the proof. $\square$

Acknowledgements. We thank anonymous reviewers for their helpful comments. Ye Zhang was supported by NSF award #0747294. Siu Ming Yiu was partially supported by an NSFC/RGC Joint Research Scheme N_HKU 729/13. Joseph K. Liu was supported by A*STAR project SPARK-1224104047.

References

1. Franke, C., Robinson, P.: Autonomic provisioning of hosted applications with level of isolation terms. In: 2010 Seventh IEEE International Conference and Workshops on Engineering of Autonomic and Autonomous Systems, pp. 131–142 (2008)
2. Cloud Security Alliance: Expanded top ten big data security and privacy challenges (2013)
3. Hough, A.: Google engineer fired for privacy breach after "staking and harassing teenagers". The Telegraph (September 15, 2010)
4. Argyros, G., Kiayias, A.: I forgot your password: randomness attacks against php applications. In: USENIX Security 2012, p. 6. USENIX Association (2012)
5. Lenstra, A.K., Hughes, J.P., Augier, M., Bos, J.W., Kleinjung, T., Wachter, C.: Public keys. In: Safavi-Naini, R., Canetti, R. (eds.) CRYPTO 2012. LNCS, vol. 7417, pp. 626–642. Springer, Heidelberg (2012)
6. Michaelis, K., Meyer, C., Schwenk, J.: Randomly failed! the state of randomness in current java implementations. In: Dawson, E. (ed.) CT-RSA 2013. LNCS, vol. 7779, pp. 129–144. Springer, Heidelberg (2013)
7. Shumow, D., Ferguson, N.: On the possiblity of a back door in the NIST SP800-90 dual ec prng, http://rump2007.cr.yp.to/15-shumow.pdf
8. Perlroth, N., Larson, J., Shane, S.: N.S.A. able to foil basic safeguards of privacy on web New York Times (September 5, 2013),
http://www.nytimes.com/2013/09/06/us/
nsa-foils-much-internet-encryption.html
9. Akavia, A., Goldwasser, S., Vaikuntanathan, V.: Simultaneous hardcore bits and cryptography against memory attacks. In: Reingold, O. (ed.) TCC 2009. LNCS, vol. 5444, pp. 474–495. Springer, Heidelberg (2009)
10. Naor, M., Segev, G.: Public-key cryptosystems resilient to key leakage. In: Halevi, S. (ed.) CRYPTO 2009. LNCS, vol. 5677, pp. 18–35. Springer, Heidelberg (2009)
11. Dodis, Y., Kalai, Y.T., Lovett, S.: On cryptography with auxiliary input. In: Mitzenmacher, M. (ed.) STOC 2009, pp. 621–630. ACM (2009)
12. Yuen, T.H., Yiu, S.M., Hui, L.C.K.: Fully leakage-resilient signatures with auxiliary inputs. In: Susilo, W., Mu, Y., Seberry, J. (eds.) ACISP 2012. LNCS, vol. 7372, pp. 294–307. Springer, Heidelberg (2012)

13. Bellare, M., Brakerski, Z., Naor, M., Ristenpart, T., Segev, G., Shacham, H., Yilek, S.: Hedged public-key encryption: How to protect against bad randomness. In: Matsui, M. (ed.) ASIACRYPT 2009. LNCS, vol. 5912, pp. 232–249. Springer, Heidelberg (2009)

14. Namiki, H., Tanaka, K., Yasunaga, K.: Randomness leakage in the kem/dem framework. In: Boyen, X., Chen, X. (eds.) ProvSec 2011. LNCS, vol. 6980, pp. 309–323. Springer, Heidelberg (2011)

15. Dodis, Y., Goldwasser, S., Kalai, Y.T., Peikert, C., Vaikuntanathan, V.: Public-key encryption schemes with auxiliary inputs. In: Micciancio, D. (ed.) TCC 2010. LNCS, vol. 5978, pp. 361–381. Springer, Heidelberg (2010)

16. Yuen, T.H., Chow, S.S.M., Zhang, Y., Yiu, S.M.: Identity-based encryption resilient to continual auxiliary leakage. In: Pointcheval, D., Johansson, T. (eds.) EUROCRYPT 2012. LNCS, vol. 7237, pp. 117–134. Springer, Heidelberg (2012)

17. Canetti, R., Halevi, S., Katz, J.: Chosen-ciphertext security from identity-based encryption. In: Cachin, C., Camenisch, J.L. (eds.) EUROCRYPT 2004. LNCS, vol. 3027, pp. 207–222. Springer, Heidelberg (2004)

18. Faust, S., Hazay, C., Nielsen, J.B., Nordholt, P.S., Zottarel, A.: Signature schemes secure against hard-to-invert leakage. In: Wang, X., Sako, K. (eds.) ASIACRYPT 2012. LNCS, vol. 7658, pp. 98–115. Springer, Heidelberg (2012)

19. Halevi, S., Lin, H.: After-the-fact leakage in public-key encryption. In: Ishai, Y. (ed.) TCC 2011. LNCS, vol. 6597, pp. 107–124. Springer, Heidelberg (2011)

20. Bitansky, N., Canetti, R., Halevi, S.: Leakage-tolerant interactive protocols. In: Cramer, R. (ed.) TCC 2012. LNCS, vol. 7194, pp. 266–284. Springer, Heidelberg (2012)

21. Yuen, T.H., Zhang, Y., Yiu, S.M., Liu, J.K.: Encryption schemes with post-challenge auxiliary inputs. Cryptology ePrint Archive, Report 2013/323 (2013), http://eprint.iacr.org/

Verifiable Computation over Large Database with Incremental Updates

Xiaofeng Chen[1,4], Jin Li[2,4], Jian Weng[3], Jianfeng Ma[1], and Wenjing Lou[4]

[1] State Key Laboratory of Integrated Service Networks (ISN),
Xidian University, Xi'an 710071, P.R. China
xfchen@xidian.edu.cn, jfma@mail.xidian.edu.cn
[2] School of Computer Science and Educational Software,
Guangzhou University, Guangzhou 510006, P.R. China
jinli71@gmail.com
[3] Department of Computer Science,
Jinan University, Guangzhou 510632, P.R. China
cryptjweng@gmail.com
[4] Department of Computer Science,
Virginia Polytechnic Institute and State University, USA
wjlou@vt.edu

Abstract. The notion of verifiable database (VDB) enables a resource-constrained client to securely outsource a very large database to an untrusted server so that it could later retrieve a database record and update a record by assigning a new value. Also, any attempt by the server to tamper with the data will be detected by the client. When the database undergoes frequent while small modifications, the client must re-compute and update the encrypted version (ciphertext) on the server at all times. For very large data, it is extremely expensive for the resources-constrained client to perform both operations from scratch. In this paper, we formalize the notion of verifiable database with incremental updates (Inc-VDB). Besides, we propose a general Inc-VDB framework by incorporating the primitive of vector commitment and the encrypt-then-incremental MAC mode of encryption. We also present a concrete Inc-VDB scheme based on the computational Diffie-Hellman (CDH) assumption. Furthermore, we prove that our construction can achieve the desired security properties.

Keywords: Verifiable Database, Incremental Cryptography, Outsourcing Computations, Vector Commitment.

1 Introduction

With the availability of cloud services, the techniques for securely outsourcing the prohibitively expensive computations are getting widespread attentions in the scientific community [1–3, 18, 19]. That is, the clients with resource-constraint devices can outsource the heavy computation workloads into the untrusted cloud servers and enjoy the unlimited computing resources in a pay-per-use manner.

M. Kutyłowski and J. Vaidya (Eds.): ESORICS 2014, Part I, LNCS 8712, pp. 148–162, 2014.
© Springer International Publishing Switzerland 2014

Since the cloud servers may return an invalid result in some cases (e.g., the servers might contain a software bug that will fail on a constant number of invocation), one crucial requirement of outsourcing computation is that the client has the ability to verify the validity of computation result efficiently.

The primitive of verifiable computation has been well studied by plenty of researchers in the past decades [4, 8, 9, 20, 21, 23–25]. Most of the prior work focused on generic solutions for arbitrary function (encoded as a Boolean circuit). Though in general the problem of verifiable computation has been theoretically solved, the proposed solutions are still much inefficient for real-world applications. Therefore, it is still meaningful to seek for efficient protocols for verifiable computation of specific functions.

Benabbas, Gennaro and Vahlis [12] first proposed the notion of verifiable database (VDB), which is extremely useful to solve the problem in the context of verifiable outsourcing storage. Assume that a resource constrained client would like to store a very large database on a server so that it could later retrieve a database record and update a record by assigning a new value. If the server attempts to tamper with the database, it will be detected by the client with an overwhelming probability. Besides, the computation and storage resources invested by the client must not depend on the size of the database (except for an initial setup phase).

For the case of static database, we can construct VDB based on simple solutions using message authentication codes or digital signatures. That is, the client signs each database record before sending it to the server, and the server is requested to output the record together with its valid signature. The solution does not work if the client performs updates on the database. As noted in [12], the main technical difficulty is that the client must have a mechanism to revoke the signatures given to the server for the previous values. Otherwise, the malicious server can utilize the previous (while valid) database records and corresponding signatures to responde the current query of the client. This is called the Backward Substitution updates (BSU) attack on VDB. In order to solve this issue, the client should keep track of every change locally. However, this totally contradicts the goal of outsourcing, i.e., the client should use much less resources than those needed to store the database locally.

This problem has been addressed by works on accumulators [15, 16, 29] and authentication data structures [27, 28, 30, 31]. However, it seems that the previous solutions based on the two techniques either rely on non-constant size assumptions (such as q-Strong Diffie-Hellman assumption), or require expensive operations such as generation of primes and expensive "re-shuffling" procedures. Benabbas, Gennaro and Vahlis [12] presented the first practical verifiable computation scheme for high degree polynomial functions and used it to design an efficient VDB scheme. The construction relies on a constant size assumption in bilinear groups of composite order, while does not support public verifiability (i.e., only the owner of the database can verify the correctness of the proofs). Very recently, Catalano and Fiore [13] proposed an elegant solution to build

VDB from a primitive named vector commitment. The concrete construction relies on standard constant-size assumption and supports public verifiability.

The data records often contain some sensitive information that should not be exposed to the cloud server. Therefore, the client should encrypt the database and store the encrypted version on the server. In some scenarios, the data (plaintext) of client undergoes frequent while small modifications and the client must *re-compute* and *update* the encrypted version (ciphertext) on the server at all times [5, 6]. For very large data, it is extremely expensive for the resources-constrained client to re-compute and update the ciphertext from scratch each time. Therefore, it is meaningful to seek for efficient constructions for VDB with incremental updates (Inc-VDB, for short). Loosely speaking, Inc-VDB means that re-computing and updating the ciphertext in VDB are both incremental algorithms, i.e., the client can efficiently perform both operations with previous values, rather than from scratch.

Bellare, Goldreich, and Goldwasser [5, 6] introduced the notion of incremental cryptography to design cryptographic algorithms whose output can be updated very efficiently when the underlying input changes. For example, if a single block of the data is modified (we can view the data as a sequence of blocks), the client only needs to re-compute the ciphertext on this certain block and the ciphertext of other blocks remains identical [7, 26]. Nevertheless, we argue that the incremental encryption does not provide a full solution for constructing efficient Inc-VDB schemes. The reasons are two folds: Firstly, previous incremental encryption schemes cannot solve the case of distributed updates on the data. That is, multiple blocks of the plaintext are modified while the modification on each single block is very small. The worst case is that every block of the plaintext is updated while only one bit for each single block is changed. If this case happens, the client must re-compute the whole ciphertext from scratch. Secondly, previous incremental encryption schemes cannot necessarily lead to incremental updates on VDB. That is, the update algorithm of VDB is not incremental and the client still needs to re-compute new updated token from scratch each time. To the best of our knowledge, it seems that there is no research work on constructing efficient Inc-VDB schemes.

1.1 Our Contribution

In this paper, we further study the problem of constructing verifiable database with efficient updates. Our contributions are three folds:

- We first introduce the notion of verifiable database with incremental updates (Inc-VDB). The update algorithm in Inc-VDB is an incremental one, i.e., the client can efficiently compute the new ciphertext and the updated tokens with previous values, rather than from scratch. Thus, Inc-VDB schemes can lead to huge efficiency gain when the database undergoes frequent while small modifications.
- We propose a general Inc-VDB framework by incorporating the primitive of vector commitment [13] and the encrypt-then-incremental MAC mode

of encryption [7]. We also present a concrete Inc-VDB scheme based on the computational Diffie-Hellman (CDH) assumption. Besides, the proposed Inc-VDB scheme supports the public verifiability.

– We first introduce a new property called accountability for VDB schemes. That is, after the client detected the tampering of the server, the client should be able to provide a proof to convince the judge of the facts. All of the existing VDB schemes does not satisfy the property of accountability. We prove that the proposed Inc-VDB scheme satisfies the property of accountability.

1.2 Organization

This paper is organized as follows. Some preliminaries are presented in Section 2. We present the formal definition and security requirements of Inc-VDB in Section 3. We propose a new efficient Inc-VDB framework and a concrete Inc-VDB scheme in Section 4. The security and efficiency analysis of the proposed Inc-VDB scheme are given in Section 5. Finally, concluding remarks will be made in Section 6.

2 Preliminaries

In this section, we first introduce the basic definition and properties of bilinear pairings. We then present the formal definition of VDB.

2.1 Bilinear Pairings

Let $\mathbb{G}_1$ and $\mathbb{G}_2$ be two cyclic multiplicative groups of prime order p. Let g be a generator of $\mathbb{G}_1$. A bilinear pairing is a map $e : \mathbb{G}_1 \times \mathbb{G}_1 \to \mathbb{G}_2$ with the following properties:

1. Bilinear: $e(u^a, v^b) = e(u, v)^{ab}$ for all $u, v \in \mathbb{G}_1$, and $a, b \in \mathbb{Z}_p^*$.
2. Non-degenerate: $e(g, g) \neq 1$.
3. Computable: There is an efficient algorithm to compute $e(u, v)$ for all $u, v \in \mathbb{G}_1$.

The examples of such groups can be found in supersingular elliptic curves or hyperelliptic curves over finite fields, and the bilinear pairings can be derived from the Weil or Tate pairings. In the following, we introduce the Computational Diffie-Hellman (CDH) problem in $\mathbb{G}_1$.

Definition 1. *The Computational Diffie-Hellman (CDH) problem in $\mathbb{G}_1$ is defined as follows: given a triple (g, g^x, g^y) for any $x, y \in_R \mathbb{Z}_p$ as inputs, output g^{xy}. We say that the CDH assumption holds in $\mathbb{G}_1$ if for every probabilistic polynomial time algorithm $\mathcal{A}$, there exists a negligible function $\mathsf{negl}(\cdot)$ such that $\Pr[\mathcal{A}(1^k, g, g^x, g^y) = g^{xy}] \leq \mathsf{negl}(k)$ for all security parameter k.*

A variant of CDH problem is the Square Computational Diffie-Hellman (Squ-CDH) problem. That is, given (g, g^x) for $x \in_R \mathbb{Z}_p$ as inputs, output g^{x^2}. It has been proved that the Squ-CDH assumption is equivalent to the classical CDH assumption.

2.2   Verifiable Database

Informally, a VDB scheme allows a resource-constraint client to outsource the storage of a very large database to a server in such a way that the client can later retrieve and update the data records from the server. Besides, any attempts to tamper with the data by the dishonest server will be detected when the client queries the database. The formal definition for VDB is given as follows [12, 13]:

Definition 2. *A verifiable database scheme VDB =* (Setup, Query, Verify, Update) *consists of four algorithms defined below.*

- Setup($1^k, DB$): *On input the security parameter k, the setup algorithm is run by the client to generate a secret key SK to be secretly stored by the client, and a public key PK that is distributed to all users (including the client itself) for verifying the proofs.*
- Query(PK, x): *On input an index x, the query algorithm is run by the server, and returns a pair $\tau = (v, \pi)$.*
- Verify($PK/SK, x, \tau$): *The public/private verification algorithm outputs a value v if τ is correct with respect to x, and an error $\bot$ otherwise.*
- Update(SK, x, v'): *In the update algorithm, the client firstly generates a token t'_x with the secret key SK and then sends the pair (t'_x, v') to the server. Then, the server uses v' to update the database record in index x, and t'_x to update the public key PK.*

Remark 1. There are two different kinds of verifiability for the outputs of the query algorithm, i.e., $\tau = (v, \pi)$. In the Catalano-Fiore's scheme [13], anyone can verify the validity of τ with the public key PK. Therefore, it satisfies the property of public verifiability. However, in some applications, only the client can verify the proofs generated by the server since the secret key of the client is involved in the verification. This is called the private verifiability [12]. Trivially, a verifiable database scheme should support both verifiability for various applications.

3   Verifiable Database with Incremental Updates

3.1   Formal Definition

Without loss of generality, we consider the database DB as a set of tuples (x, m_x) in some appropriate domain, where x is an index and m_x is the corresponding value which can be arbitrary payload sizes. In order to achieve the confidentiality of the data record m_x, the client can use an arbitrary semantically-secure encryption scheme ENC (the key is implicit in the notaton) to encrypt each m_x. Trivially, given the ciphertext $v_x = \mathsf{ENC}(m_x)$, only the client can compute the record m_x. Therefore, we only consider the case of encrypted database (x, v_x). This is also implicitly assumed in the existing academic research.

Informally, verifiable database with incremental updates (Inc-VDB) can be viewed a special case of VDB in which the updated record m'_x is only slightly different from the previous one m_x (note that the corresponding ciphertexts v_x' and v_x may be totally different). The distinct feature of Inc-VDB is that the update algorithm is an incremental one. That is, the client can efficiently compute a new token t_x' from the previous one, rather than re-computing it from scratch (similarly, the server can efficiently update the public key rather than re-computing it from scratch). Trivially, Inc-VDB can lead to huge efficiency gains, especially in the scenario when the database is subject to frequent, small modification. In the following, we present a formal definition for Inc-VDB.

Definition 3. *A verifiable database scheme with incremental updates* Inc-VDB = (Setup, Query, Verify, Inc-Update) *consists of four algorithms defined below.*

- Setup($1^k, DB$): *On input the security parameter k, the setup algorithm is run by the client to generate a secret key SK to be secretly stored by the client, and a public key PK that is distributed to all users (including the client itself) for verifying the proofs.*
- Query(PK, x): *On input an index x, the query algorithm is run by the server, and returns a pair $\tau = (v, \pi)$.*
- Verify($PK/SK, x, \tau$): *The public/private verification algorithm outputs a value v if τ is correct with respect to x, and an error $\perp$ otherwise.*
- Inc-Update(SK, x, v'): *In the update algorithm, the client utilizes the secret key SK to compute a new token t_x' from the previous one in an incremental manner rather than computing it from scratch. Then, the client sends the pair (t_x', v') to the server. If the token t_x' is valid, the server uses v' to update the database record in index x, and t_x' to incrementally update the public key PK.*

3.2 Security Requirements

In the following, we introduce some security requirements for Inc-VDB. Obviously, Inc-VDB should inherently satisfy three security properties of VDB [12], i.e., security, correctness, and efficiency. Besides, we also introduce a new property named accountability for Inc-VDB.

The first requirement is the **security** of Inc-VDB scheme. Intuitively, an Inc-VDB scheme is secure if a malicious server cannot convince a verifier to accept an invalid output, i.e., $v \neq v_x$ where v_x is the value of database record in the index x. Note that v_x can be either the initial value given by the client in the setup stage or the latest value assigned by the client in the update procedure.

Definition 4. *(Security) An Inc-VDB scheme is secure if for any database $DB \in [q] \times \{0,1\}^*$, where $q = poly(k)$, and for any probabilistic polynomial time (PPT) adversary A, we have*

$$Adv_A(\textit{Inc-VDB}, DB, k) \leq negl(k),$$

where $Adv_A(\textit{Inc-VDB}, DB, k) = Pr[\textbf{Exp}_A^{\textit{Inc-VDB}}(DB, k) = 1]$ is defined as the advantage of A in the experiment as follows:

$$\text{Experiment } Exp_A^{Inc\text{-}VDB}[DB, k]$$

$$(PK, SK) \leftarrow \text{Setup}(DB, k);$$

$$\text{For } i = 1, \ldots, l = poly(k);$$

Verify query :

$$(x_i, \tau_i) \leftarrow A(PK, t'_1, \ldots, t'_{i-1});$$

$$v_i \leftarrow \text{Verify}(PK/SK, x_i, \tau_i);$$

Inc-Update query :

$$(x_i, v_{x_i}^{(i)}) \leftarrow A(PK, t'_1, \ldots, t'_{i-1});$$

$$t'_i \leftarrow \text{Inc-Update}(SK, x_i, v_{x_i}^{(i)});$$

$$(\hat{x}, \hat{\tau}) \leftarrow A(PK, t'_1, \ldots, t'_l);$$

$$\hat{v} \leftarrow \text{Verify}(PK/SK, \hat{x}, \hat{\tau})$$

If $\hat{v} \neq \perp$ and $\hat{v} \neq v_{\hat{x}}^{(l)}$, output 1; else output 0.

In the above experiment, we implicitly assign $PK \leftarrow PK_i$ after every update query.

The second requirement is the **correctness** of Inc-VDB scheme. That is, the value and proof generated by the honest server can be always verified successfully and accepted by the client.

Definition 5. *(Correctness) An Inc-VDB scheme is correct if for any database $DB \in [q] \times \{0, 1\}^*$, where $q = poly(k)$, and for any valid pair $\tau = (v, \pi)$ generated by an honest server, the output of verification algorithm is always the value v.*

The third requirement is the **efficiency** of Inc-VDB scheme. That is, the client in the verifiable database scheme should not be involved in plenty of expensive computation and storage (except for an initial pre-processing phase)[1].

Definition 6. *(Efficiency) An Inc-VDB scheme is efficient if for any database $DB \in [q] \times \{0, 1\}^*$, where $q = poly(k)$, the computation and storage resources invested by the client must be independent of the size of the database DB. Besides, the cryptographic operations performed by the client should be incremental.*

Finally, we introduce a new requirement named **accountability** for Inc-VDB scheme. That is, after the client has detected the tampering of dishonest server, he should provide some evidence to convince a judge of the facts.

Definition 7. *(Accountability) An Inc-VDB scheme is account if for any database $DB \in [q] \times \{0, 1\}^*$, where $q = poly(k)$, the client can provide a proof for this misbehavior if the dishonest server has tampered with the database.*

---

[1] In some scenarios, the client is allowed to invest a one-time expensive computational effort. This is known as the amortized model of outsourcing computations [22].

4   Inc-VDB Framework from Vector Commitment

In this section, we present an efficient Inc-VDB framework from vector commitment and the incremental encrypt-then-MAC mode of encryption. Besides, we propose a concrete Inc-VDB scheme based on the CDH assumption.

4.1   High Description

Catalano and Fiore presented an elegant construction for building a general VDB framework from vector commitment [13]. The main idea is as follows: Let C be the vector commitment on the database. Given a query on index x by the client, the server provide the value v_x and the opening of commitment as a proof that v_x has not been tampered with. During the update phase, the client computes a new ciphertext v'_x and a token t'_x and then sends them to the server. Finally, the server updates the database and the corresponding public key with the pair (t'_x, v'_x). We also use the vector commitment to construct incremental VDB schemes. However, the main difference is that the client in our construction does not compute the updated ciphertext v'_x and the corresponding (updated) commitment C' in the token t'_x. The main trick is that we use a special incremental encryption to generate the ciphertext v'_x. More precisely, we define $v'_x = (v_x, P_x)$, where $P_x = (p_1, p_2, \cdots, p_\omega)$ denotes the bit positions where m'_x and m_x have different values, i.e, $m'_x[p_i] \neq m_x[p_i]$ for $1 \leq i \leq \omega$. Trivially, given $v'_x = (v_x, P_x)$, the client firstly decrypts v_x to obtain m_x, and then perform the bit flipping operation on the positions of P_x to obtain m'_x. Since the bit flipping operation is extremely fast, the computation overhead of decrypting v'_x is almost the same as that of decrypting v_x. Moreover, it requires much less storage since $|P_x| << |v'_x|$ (note that we only consider the case of incremental updates). Besides, we argue that the incremental encryption scheme (ENC, P) is more suitable for discrete and uniform update on the data record (note that previous incremental encryption schemes mainly focus on local updates, e.g., updates on a single block of the data).

Note that the secret key of the client should be involved in the update algorithm. That is, only the client is allowed to update the database. In order to achieve this goal, we utilize the encrypt-then-incremental MAC mode of encryption [7], i.e., an incremental encryption together with an incremental MAC of the ciphertext (the encrypt-then-MAC approach [11]). Trivially, we could use an incremental signature scheme to substitute the incremental MAC. In our concrete construction, we adopt the (incremental) BLS signature scheme [10]. For every update, the client first verify the current BLS signature on the commitment C_R and all the current modifications $(P_x^{(1)}, \cdots, P_x^{(T)})$ of the data record v_x, where $P_x^{(i)}$ denotes the modification in the i-th update for $1 \leq i \leq T$. This ensures that the current database is not tampered with by the server. If the verification holds, the client then sends a new modification $P_x^{(T+1)}$ and the corresponding (incremental) BLS signature to the server.

Since we also use the signature to achieve the integrity of the database, it is essential to invoke the previous signatures given to the server. Our trick is that we introduce a counter T_x to denote the update times of each index x. Also, the server computes a BLS signature σ on all counters T_x for $1 \leq x \leq q$. After an update on the record v_x is accomplished, let $T_x \leftarrow T_x + 1$. Then, the server computes an incremental BLS signature on the updated counters (note that only the value of T_x is slightly modified). Given a previous signature σ on the count T_x, the client can reject it by providing a new signature σ' on the latest counter T_x' since $T_x < T_x'$. Note that the server cannot deny his signature, therefore this is a proof that the server is dishonest when a dispute occurred.

4.2   A Concrete Inc-VDB Scheme

In this section, we propose a concrete Inc-VDB scheme based on the CDH assumption.

- Setup($1^k, DB$): Let k be a security parameter. Let the database be $DB = (x, v_x)$ for $1 \leq x \leq q$. Let $\mathbb{G}_1$ and $\mathbb{G}_2$ be two cyclic multiplicative groups of prime order p equipped with a bilinear pairing $e : \mathbb{G}_1 \times \mathbb{G}_1 \to \mathbb{G}_2$. Let g be a generator of $\mathbb{G}_1$. Let $\mathcal{H} : \mathbb{G}_1 \times \{0,1\}^* \to \mathbb{G}_1$ be a cryptographic hash function. Randomly choose q elements $z_i \in_R \mathbb{Z}_p$ and compute $h_i = g^{z_i}$, $h_{i,j} = g^{z_i z_j}$, where $1 \leq i,j \leq q$ and $i \neq j$. Set PP $= (p, q, \mathbb{G}_1, \mathbb{G}_2, \mathcal{H}, e, g, \{h_i\}_{1 \leq i \leq q}, \{h_{i,j}\}_{1 \leq i,j \leq q, i \neq j})$, and the message space $\mathcal{M} = \mathbb{Z}_p$.

  Let $(\alpha, Y = g^\alpha)$ be the secret/public key pair of the client. Let $(\beta, S = g^\beta)$ be the secret/public key pair of the server. Trivially, the validity of Y and S are ensured by the corresponding certificate of a trusted third party, i.e, certificate authority. Let $C_R = \prod_{i=1}^q h_i^{v_i}$ be the root commitment on the database record vector $(v_1, v_2, \cdots, v_q)$. For $1 \leq x \leq q$, let T_x be a counter for index x with the initial value 0 and $H_x^{(0)} = \mathcal{H}(C_R, x, 0)^\alpha$. The server can use the batch verification technique of BLS signatures [14] to ensure the validity of $H_x^{(0)}$ for $1 \leq x \leq q$, which requires only the workload of two pairings. Then, the server computes a signature $\sigma = \mathcal{H}(C_R, 0, 0, \cdots, 0)^\beta$ on C_R and all initial counters $(0, 0, \cdots, 0)$ (note that all T_x has an initial value 0). Also, set aux $= \{\text{aux}_1, \cdots, \text{aux}_q\}$, where $\text{aux}_x = (H_x^{(0)}, 0)$ for $1 \leq x \leq q$. Define PK $= (\text{PP}, C_R, \text{aux}, DB)$ and SK $= \alpha$.

- Query(PK, x): Assume that the current public key PK $= (\text{PP}, C_R, \text{aux}, DB)$. Given a query index x, the server computes $\pi_x = \prod_{1 \leq j \leq q, j \neq x} h_{x,j}^{v_j}$ and returns the proofs

$$\tau = (v_x, \pi_x, H_x^{(T_x)}, P_x^{(1)}, \cdots, P_x^{(T_x)}, T_x).$$

- Verify(PK, x, τ): Parse the proofs $\tau = (v_x, \pi_x, H_x^{(T_x)}, P_x^{(1)}, \cdots, P_x^{(T_x)}, T_x)$. If the counter T_x in τ is less than the one in σ that the client stored locally, the client rejects the proofs τ. Otherwise, the client can verify the validity of τ by checking whether the following two equations $e(C_R/h_x^{v_x}, h_x) = e(\pi_x, g)$ and $e(H_x^{(T_x)}, g) = e(\mathcal{H}(C_R, x, P_x^{(1)}, \cdots, P_x^{(T_x)}, T_x), Y)$ hold. If the proofs τ

is valid, the verifier accepts it and outputs $v_x^{(T_x)} = (v_x, P_x^{(1)}, \cdots, P_x^{(T_x)})$. Otherwise, outputs an error $\perp$.

- Inc-Update($\mathsf{SK}, x, P_x^{(T_x+1)}$): To update the record of index x, the client firstly retrieves the current record $v_x^{(T_x)}$ from the server. That is, the client obtains $\tau \leftarrow \mathsf{Query}(\mathsf{PK}, \mathsf{S}, x)$ from the server and checks that $\mathsf{Verify}(\mathsf{PK}, x, \tau) = v_x^{(T_x)} \neq \perp$. Then, the client computes the incremental signature

$$t'_x = H_x^{(T_x+1)} = \mathcal{H}(C_R, x, P_x^{(1)}, \cdots, P_x^{(T_x+1)}, T_x + 1)^\alpha$$

and then sends $(t'_x, P_x^{(T_x+1)})$ to the server. If t'_x is valid, then the server adds $P_x^{(T_x+1)}$ to the record of index x, and updates aux_x in PK, i.e., $\mathsf{aux}_x \leftarrow (t'_x, P_x^{(1)}, \cdots, P_x^{(T_x+1)}, T_x + 1)$. Also, the server computes an updated incremental signature $\sigma = \mathcal{H}(C_R, T_1, T_2, \cdots, T_x + 1, \cdots, T_q)^\beta$ and sends it to the client. If σ is valid, the client updates it together with $T_x + 1$ locally. Finally, set $T_x \leftarrow T_x + 1$.

Remark 2. As pointed out in [6], incremental encryption leaks some information that is kept secret when using a traditional encryption scheme. In the resulting incremental encryption scheme (ENC, P) in our construction, an adversary can determine where a modification takes place, but still cannot determine the symbol being modified (i.e., hide details about the data record and its modifications). This is similar to previous incremental encryptions [6, 7, 26]. Actually, we can prove that the incremental encryption (ENC, P) is semantically-secure if and only if the original one ENC is semantically-secure (the formal proof will be given in the full version of this paper). On the other hand, though we only focus on the bit flipping operation in the our construction, it can be extended to other operations such as insert, delete, etc.

Remark 3. The storage overhead of client in our construction is all counters T_x and the latest BLS signature σ. Note that the number of T_x is dependent of q, it is highly undesirable when q becomes very large. Trivially, we can still use the vector commitment to solve this issue. The server computes the signature $\sigma = \mathcal{H}(C_R, C_T)^\beta$, where C_T is the vector commitment on all counters $(T_1, T_2, \cdots, T_q)$. Therefore, the client only requires to store σ and C_T and the storage overhead is independent of q. Trivially, the server should provide a valid opening of C_T as a proof during the verification phase. Due to the property of vector commitment, the update of C_T is still incremental.

5   Analysis of Our Proposed Inc-VDB Scheme

5.1   Security Analysis

Theorem 1. *The proposed Inc-VDB scheme is secure.*

Proof. Similar to [13], we prove the theorem by contradiction. Assume there exists a polynomial-time adversary A that has a non-negligible advantage ϵ in the experiment $\mathbf{Exp}_A^{\mathsf{Inc\text{-}VDB}}[DB, k]$ for some initial database DB, then we can use A to build an efficient algorithm B to break the Squ-CDH assumption. That is, B takes as input a tuple (g, g^a) and outputs g^{a^2}.

Without loss of generality, we assume that the secret/public key pairs of B and A are $(\alpha, Y = g^\alpha)$ and $(\beta, S = g^\beta)$, respectively. First, B randomly chooses an element $x^* \in_R \mathbb{Z}_q$ as a guess for the index x^* on which A succeeds in the experiment $\mathbf{Exp}_A^{\mathsf{Inc\text{-}VDB}}[DB, k]$. Then, B randomly chooses $z_i \in_R \mathbb{Z}_p$ and computes $h_i = g^{z_i}$ all $1 \le i \ne x^* \le q$. Let $h_{x^*} = g^a$. Besides, B computes:

$h_{i,j} = g^{z_i z_j}$ for all $1 \le i \ne j \le q$ and $i, j \ne x^*$;
$h_{i,x^*} = h_{x^*,i} = (g^a)^{z_i}$ for all $1 \le i \le q$ and $i \ne x^*$.

Set $\mathsf{PP} = (p, q, \mathbb{G}_1, \mathbb{G}_2, \mathcal{H}, e, g, \{h_i\}, \{h_{i,j}\})$, where $1 \le i \ne j \le q$. Given a database DB, B computes the commitment $C_R = \prod_{i=1}^q h_i^{v_i}$. Also, B computes $H_x^{(0)} = \mathcal{H}(C_R, x, 0)^\alpha$ for $1 \le x \le q$. Set $\mathsf{aux} = \{\mathsf{aux}_1, \cdots, \mathsf{aux}_q\}$, where $\mathsf{aux}_x = (H_x^{(0)}, 0)$ for $1 \le x \le q$.

Define $\mathsf{PK} = (\mathsf{PP}, C_R, \mathsf{aux}, DB)$ and $\mathsf{SK} = \alpha$. Note that PK is perfectly distributed as the real ones. B sends PK to A and A responds with $\sigma = \mathcal{H}(C_R, 0, 0, \cdots, 0)^\beta$.

To answer the verify and update queries of A in the experiment, B just simply runs the real $\mathsf{Query}(\mathsf{PK}, x)$ and $\mathsf{Inc\text{-}Update}(\mathsf{SK}, x, P_x^{(T_x+1)})$ algorithms and responds with the same value. Note that the $\mathsf{Inc\text{-}Update}(\mathsf{SK}, x, P_x^{(T_x+1)})$ algorithm requires the secret key α of B, and A cannot perform this algorithm without the help of B. After every update query, A responds with $\sigma = \mathcal{H}(C_R, T_1, T_2, \cdots, T_x + 1, \cdots, T_q)^\beta$.

Suppose that $(\hat{x}, \hat{\tau})$ be the tuple returned by A at the end of the experiment, where $\hat{\tau} = (\hat{v}, \hat{\pi}_{\hat{x}}, H_{\hat{x}}^{(T_{\hat{x}})})$ and $\hat{v} = (\hat{v}_{\hat{x}}, \hat{P}_{\hat{x}}^{(1)}, \cdots, \hat{P}_{\hat{x}}^{(T_{\hat{x}})}, T_{\hat{x}})$. Besides, note that if A wins with a non-negligible advantage ϵ in the experiment, then we have $\hat{v} \ne \bot$, $\hat{v} \ne v_{\hat{x}}^{(T_{\hat{x}})}$. Since $H_{\hat{x}}^{(T_{\hat{x}})}$ is a valid BLS signature generated with the secret key α of B, we have $\hat{P}_{\hat{x}}^{(i)} = P_{\hat{x}}^{(i)}$ for all $1 \le i \le T_{\hat{x}}$. Otherwise, A successfully forged a new BLS signature. Therefore, we have $\hat{v}_{\hat{x}} \ne v_{\hat{x}}$.

If $\hat{x} \ne x^*$, B aborts the simulation and fails. Otherwise, note that $h_{\hat{x}} = g^a$ and $e(C_R, h_{\hat{x}}) = e(h_{\hat{x}}^{v_{\hat{x}}}, h_{\hat{x}})e(\pi_{\hat{x}}, g) = e(h_{\hat{x}}^{\hat{v}_{\hat{x}}}, h_{\hat{x}})e(\hat{\pi}_{\hat{x}}, g)$, B can compute

$$g^{a^2} = (\hat{\pi}_{\hat{x}}/\pi_{\hat{x}})^{(v_{\hat{x}} - \hat{v}_{\hat{x}})^{-1}}.$$

The success probability of B is ϵ/q.

Theorem 2. *The proposed Inc-VDB scheme is correct.*

Proof. If the server is assumed to be honest, then the proofs

$$\tau = (v_x, \pi_x, H_x^{(T_x)}, P_x^{(1)}, \cdots, P_x^{(T_x)}, T_x).$$

Firstly, note that $C_R/h_x^{v_x} = \prod_{1 \le j \le q, j \ne x} h_j^{v_j}$ and $\pi_x = \prod_{1 \le j \le q, j \ne x} h_{x,j}^{v_j}$, we have $e(C_R/h_x^{v_x}, h_x) = e(\pi_x, g)$. Secondly, since $H_x^{(T_x)} = \mathcal{H}(C_R, x, P_x^{(1)}, \cdots, P_x^{(T_x)}, T_x)^\alpha$, we have $e(H_x^{(T_x)}, g) = e(\mathcal{H}(C_R, x, P_x^{(1)}, \cdots, P_x^{(T_x)}, T_x), Y)$. Hence, the output of the verification algorithm is always the value $v_x^{(T_x)}$.

Theorem 3. *The proposed Inc-VDB scheme is efficient.*

Proof. It is trivial that the computational and storage resources invested by the client in our scheme is independent of the size of the database (except for a one-time Setup phase). More precisely, in the Verify algorithm, the client requires the workload of four pairings and an exponentiation in $\mathbb{G}_1$ (note that it can be reduced to two pairings and two exponentiations in $\mathbb{G}_1$). Besides, in the Inc-Update algorithm, the client only requires the workload of computing an incremental BLS signature. On the other hand, the storage of client is only two elements in $\mathbb{G}_1$ (please refer to Remark 3 for more discussions).

Theorem 4. *The proposed Inc-VDB scheme is account.*

Proof. Given the proofs τ with the counter T_x for index x, the client firstly compare it with the latest counter T_c for same index x that he stored locally. If $T_x < T_c$, then the client sends the corresponding signature σ on T_c to the judge as a proof. Otherwise, he sends τ to the judge as a proof since the verification of τ will fail if the server has tampered with the database (i.e., either v_x or $P_x^{(i)}$ for $1 \le i \le T_x$).

5.2   Efficiency Analysis

In this section, we present the efficacy analysis of the proposed scheme and give a comparison with schemes [12, 13]. We compare our scheme with Benabbas-Gennaro-Vahlis's scheme and Catalano-Fiore's scheme.

Firstly, all of the three schemes require a one-time expensive computational effort in the Setup phase. Secondly, our proposed scheme simultaneously satisfies the properties of public verifiability and accountability. Besides, our scheme is efficient since the computational resources invested by the client is independent on the size of the database. Finally, the server invests almost all of the storage resources in order to store and update the database. Trivially, as shown in Remark 3, the storage overhead of client is only two elements in $\mathbb{G}_1$.

Table 1 presents the comparison among the three schemes. We denote by M a multiplication in $\mathbb{G}_1$ (or $\mathbb{G}_2$), by E an exponentiation in $\mathbb{G}_1$, by I an inverse in $\mathbb{G}_1$, by P a computation of the pairing[2], by F an operation on a pseudo-random function, by H a regular hashing operation[3], by En a regular encryption operation, and by $\mathcal{H}$ an incremental hashing operation. We omit other operations such as addition in $\mathbb{G}_1$ for all three schemes.

---

[2] We argue that the groups $\mathbb{G}_1$ and $\mathbb{G}_2$ in Benabbas-Gennaro-Vahlis's scheme are different from those in our scheme since their scheme uses bilinear groups of composite order. Thus, the operations in the groups require different computational overload though we use the same notions for both schemes.

[3] Note that *regular* means the output of operation should be computed from scratch.

In the query algorithm of our scheme, the server does not need to compute the proof each time. Betises, in the the verify and update algorithms, the client in our scheme requires less computational overhead since it does not require to perform the operations of encryption and hashing from scratch. Therefore, our scheme is much more efficient than schemes [12, 13] in these three algorithms. On the other hand, the server in update algorithm of our scheme requires a little more computational overhead, i.e., an incremental BLS signature, in order to achieve accountability. If we use the incremental hash-then-sign paradigm, the server only performs the operations of an an exponentiation in $\mathbb{G}_1$ and an incremental hashing.

Table 1. Efficiency Comparison

Scheme	Scheme [12]	Scheme [13]	Our Scheme
Computational Model	Amortized	Amortized	Amortized
ComputationalAssumption	Subgroup Member	CDH	CDH
Public Verifiability	No	Yes	Yes
Accountability	No	No	Yes
Server Computation (Query)	$(q-1)M + 2P$	$(q-1)(M+E)$	/
Verifier Computation (Verify)	$4M + 3E + 2F$ $+1P + 1H$	$1M + 1E + 1I$ $+2P + 1H$	$1M + 1E + 1I$ $+4P + 1\mathcal{H}$
Client Computation (Update)	$2M + 3E + 2F$ $+1P + 1En + 1H$	$1M + 1E$ $+1En + 2H$	$1E + 1\mathcal{H}$
Server Computation (Update)	$1M$	/	$1E + 1\mathcal{H}$

6   Conclusion

The primitive of verifiable database with efficient updates is useful to solve the problem of verifiable outsourcing of storage. However, the existing schemes cannot satisfy the property of incremental update, i.e., the client must re-compute the new ciphertext and the updated tokens from scratch each time. In this paper, we first introduce the notion of verifiable database with incremental updates (Inc-VDB) that can lead to huge efficiency gain when the database undergoes frequent while small modifications. Besides, we propose a general Inc-VDB framework by incorporating the primitive of vector commitment and the encrypt-then-incremental MAC mode of encryption. We also present a concrete Inc-VDB scheme based on the computational Diffie-Hellman (CDH) assumption.

Acknowledgement. This work is supported by the National Natural Science Foundation of China (Nos. 61272455 and 61100224), China 111 Project (No. B08038), Doctoral Fund of Ministry of Education of China (No. 20130203110004), Program for New Century Excellent Talents in University

(No. NCET-13-0946), and the Fundamental Research Funds for the Central Universities (No. BDY151402). Besides, Lou's work is supported by US National Science Foundation under grant (CNS-1217889).

References

1. Atallah, M.J., Frikken, K.B.: Securely outsourcing linear algebra computations. In: Proceedings of the 5th ACM Symposium on Information, Computer and Communications Security (AsiaCCS), pp. 48–59 (2010)

2. Atallah, M.J., Pantazopoulos, K.N., Rice, J.R., Spafford, E.H.: Secure outsourcing of scientific computations. Advances in Computers 54, 216–272 (2001)

3. Backes, M., Fiore, D., Reischuk, R.M.: Verifiable Delegation of Computation on Outsourced Data. In: Proceedings of the ACM conference on Computer and Communications Security (CCS), pp. 863–874 (2013)

4. Ben-Or, M., Goldwasser, S., Kilian, J., Wigderson, A.: Multi-prover interactive proofs: How to remove intractability assumptions. In: Proceedings of the ACM Symposium on Theory of Computing (STOC), pp. 113–131 (1988)

5. Bellare, M., Goldreich, O., Goldwasser, S.: Incremental cryptography: The case of hashing and signing. In: Desmedt, Y.G. (ed.) CRYPTO 1994. LNCS, vol. 839, pp. 216–233. Springer, Heidelberg (1994)

6. Bellare, M., Goldreich, O., Goldwasser, S.: Incremental Cryptography and Application to Virus Protection. In: Proceedings of the 27th ACM Symposium on the Theory of Computing (STOC), pp. 45–56 (1995)

7. Buonanno, E., Katz, J., Yung, M.: Incremental Unforgeable Encryption. In: Matsui, M. (ed.) FSE 2001. LNCS, vol. 2355, pp. 109–124. Springer, Heidelberg (2002)

8. Blum, M., Luby, M., Rubinfeld, R.: Program result checking against adaptive programs and in cryptographic settings. DIMACS Series in Discrete Mathematics and Theoretical Computer Science, pp. 107–118 (1991)

9. Blum, M., Luby, M., Rubinfeld, R.: Self-testing/correcting with applications to numerical problems. Journal of Computer and System Science, 549–595 (1993)

10. Boneh, D., Lynn, B., Shacham, H.: Short signatures from the Weil pairings. In: Boyd, C. (ed.) ASIACRYPT 2001. LNCS, vol. 2248, pp. 514–532. Springer, Heidelberg (2001)

11. Bellare, M., Namprempre, C.: Authenticated Encryption: Relations Among Notions and Analysis of the Generic Composition Paradigm. In: Okamoto, T. (ed.) ASIACRYPT 2000. LNCS, vol. 1976, pp. 531–545. Springer, Heidelberg (2000)

12. Benabbas, S., Gennaro, R., Vahlis, Y.: Verifiable delegation of computation over large datasets. In: Rogaway, P. (ed.) CRYPTO 2011. LNCS, vol. 6841, pp. 111–131. Springer, Heidelberg (2011)

13. Catalano, D., Fiore, D.: Vector commitments and their applications. In: Kurosawa, K., Hanaoka, G. (eds.) PKC 2013. LNCS, vol. 7778, pp. 55–72. Springer, Heidelberg (2013)

14. Camenisch, J., Hohenberger, S., Pedersen, M.: Batch Verification of Short Signatures. In: Naor, M. (ed.) EUROCRYPT 2007. LNCS, vol. 4515, pp. 246–263. Springer, Heidelberg (2007)

15. Camenisch, J., Kohlweiss, M., Soriente, C.: An accumulator based on bilinear maps and efficient revocation for anonymous credentials. In: Jarecki, S., Tsudik, G. (eds.) PKC 2009. LNCS, vol. 5443, pp. 481–500. Springer, Heidelberg (2009)

16. Camenisch, J., Lysyanskaya, A.: Dynamic accumulators and application to efficient revocation of anonymous credentials. In: Yung, M. (ed.) CRYPTO 2002. LNCS, vol. 2442, pp. 61–76. Springer, Heidelberg (2002)
17. Canetti, R., Riva, B., Rothblum, G.: Practical delegation of computation using multiple servers. In: Proceedings of the 18th ACM Conference on Computer and Communications Security (CCS), pp. 445–454 (2011)
18. Chen, X., Li, J., Susilo, W.: Efficient Fair Conditional Payments for Outsourcing Computations. IEEE Transactions on Information Forensics and Security 7(6), 1687–1694 (2012)
19. Chen, X., Li, J., Ma, J., Tang, Q., Lou, W.: New algorithms for secure outsourcing of modular exponentiations. In: Foresti, S., Yung, M., Martinelli, F. (eds.) ESORICS 2012. LNCS, vol. 7459, pp. 541–556. Springer, Heidelberg (2012)
20. Goldwasser, S., Kalai, Y.T., Rothblum, G.N.: Delegating computation: interactive proofs for muggles. In: Proceedings of the ACM Symposium on the Theory of Computing (STOC), pp. 113–122 (2008)
21. Goldwasser, S., Micali, S., Rackoff, C.: The knowledge complexity of interactive proof-systems. SIAM Journal on Computing 18(1), 186–208 (1989)
22. Gennaro, R., Gentry, C., Parno, B.: Non-interactive verifiable computing: Outsourcing computation to untrusted workers. In: Rabin, T. (ed.) CRYPTO 2010. LNCS, vol. 6223, pp. 465–482. Springer, Heidelberg (2010)
23. Kilian, J.: A note on efficient zero-knowledge proofs and arguments. In: Proceedings of the ACM Symposium on Theory of Computing (STOC), pp. 723–732 (1992)
24. Kilian, J.: Improved efficient arguments. In: Coppersmith, D. (ed.) CRYPTO 1995. LNCS, vol. 963, pp. 311–324. Springer, Heidelberg (1995)
25. Micali, S.: CS proofs. In: Proceedings of the 35th Annual Symposium on Foundations of Computer Science (FOCS), pp. 436–453 (1994)
26. Mironov, I., Pandey, O., Reingold, O., Segev, G.: Incremental Deterministic Public-Key Encryption. In: Pointcheval, D., Johansson, T. (eds.) EUROCRYPT 2012. LNCS, vol. 7237, pp. 628–644. Springer, Heidelberg (2012)
27. Martel, C.U., Nuckolls, G., Devanbu, P.T., Gertz, M., Kwong, A., Stubblebine, S.G.: A general model for authenticated data structures. Algorithmica 39(1), 21–41 (2004)
28. Naor, M., Nissim, K.: Certificate revocation and certificate update. In: Proceedings of the 7th conference on USENIX Security Symposium, vol. 7, p. 17 (1998)
29. Nguyen, L.: Accumulators from bilinear pairings and applications. In: Menezes, A. (ed.) CT-RSA 2005. LNCS, vol. 3376, pp. 275–292. Springer, Heidelberg (2005)
30. Papamanthou, C., Tamassia, R.: Time and space efficient algorithms for two-party authenticated data structures. In: Qing, S., Imai, H., Wang, G. (eds.) ICICS 2007. LNCS, vol. 4861, pp. 1–15. Springer, Heidelberg (2007)
31. Tamassia, R., Triandopoulos, N.: Certification and authentication of data structures. In: Alberto Mendelzon Workshop on Foundations of Data Management (2010), http://www.cs.bu.edu/~nikos/papers/cads.pdf

DroidMiner: Automated Mining and Characterization of Fine-grained Malicious Behaviors in Android Applications

Chao Yang[1], Zhaoyan Xu[1], Guofei Gu[1], Vinod Yegneswaran[2], and Phillip Porras[2]

[1] Texas A&M University, College Station, TX, USA
{yangchao,z0x0427,guofei}@cse.tamu.edu
[2] SRI International, Menlo Park, CA, USA
{vinod,porras}@csl.sri.com

Abstract. Most existing malicious Android app detection approaches rely on manually selected detection heuristics, features, and models. In this paper, we describe a new, complementary system, called *DroidMiner*, which uses static analysis to *automatically* mine malicious program logic from known Android malware, abstracts this logic into a sequence of threat modalities, and then seeks out these threat modality patterns in other unknown (or newly published) Android apps. We formalize a two-level behavioral graph representation used to capture Android app program logic, and design new techniques to identify and label elements of the graph that capture malicious behavioral patterns (or malicious modalities). After the automatic learning of these malicious behavioral models, DroidMiner can scan a new Android app to (*i*) determine whether it contains malicious modalities, (*ii*) diagnose the malware family to which it is most closely associated, (*iii*) and provide further evidence as to why the app is considered to be malicious by including a concise description of identified malicious behaviors. We evaluate DroidMiner using 2,466 malicious apps, identified from a corpus of over 67,000 third-party market Android apps, plus an additional set of over 10,000 official market Android apps. Using this set of real-world apps, we demonstrate that DroidMiner achieves a 95.3% detection rate, with only a 0.4% false positive rate. We further evaluate DroidMiner's ability to classify malicious apps under their proper family labels, and measure its label accuracy at 92%.

Keywords: Mobile Security, Android Malware Analysis and Detection.

1 Introduction

Analysis of Android applications (apps) is complicated by the nature of the interaction between the various entities in its component-based framework. Existing static analysis approaches for detecting Android malware rely on either matching against *manually-selected* heuristics and *pre-defined* programming patterns [1,2] or designing detection models that use *coarse-grained* features such as permissions registered in the apps [3]. Some studies [4,5] design detection models by calculating the frequencies of isolated framework API calls, which still miss capturing the important programming logic of Android malware.

In this work, we introduce **DroidMiner**, a new approach to detect and characterize Android malware through robust and automated learning of fine-grained

M. Kutyłowski and J. Vaidya (Eds.): ESORICS 2014, Part I, LNCS 8712, pp. 163–182, 2014.

programming logic and patterns in known malware. Specifically, DroidMiner extends traditional static analysis techniques to map the functionalities of an Android app into a two-tiered behavior graph. This two-tiered behavior graph is specialized for modeling the complex, multi-entity interactions that are typical for Android applications. Within this behavior graph, DroidMiner automatically identifies *modalities*, i.e., programming logic segments in the graph that correspond to known suspicious behavior. The set of identified modalities is then used to define a modality vector. DroidMiner then uses common modality vectors to offer a more robust classification scheme, in which variant applications can be grouped together based on their shared patterns of suspicious logic. While DroidMiner also relies on analyzing Framework API calls, different from existing approaches that merely analyze the isolated usage of Framework APIs, DroidMiner relies on the modalities that robustly capture the semantic relationships across multiple APIs and proposes new techniques to automatically extract them. Rather than simply examining whether or not the target app is malicious (a binary answer), DroidMiner also provides specific app behavior traits (modalities) to support detection decisions.

We present DroidMiner's algorithm for discovering and automatically extracting malware modalities. We evaluate DroidMiner using 2,466 malicious apps, identified from a corpus of over 67,000 third-party market apps, plus an additional set of over 10,000 official market apps from *GooglePlay*. We measure the utility of DroidMiner modalities with respect to three specific use cases: (i) malware detection, (ii) malware family classification, and (iii) malware behavioral characterization. Our results validate that DroidMiner modalities are useful for classification and capable of isolating a wide range of suspicious behavioral traits embedded within parasitic Android applications. Furthermore, the composite of these traits enables a unique means by which Android malware can be identified with a high degree of accuracy. We anticipate that programs identified as sharing common modalities with known malicious apps would then be subject to more in-depth scrutiny through, potentially more expensive, dynamic analysis tools.

The contributions of our paper include the following:

- A description of our new two-tiered behavioral graph model for characterizing Android application behavior, and labeling its logical paths within known malicious apps as malicious modalities.
- The design and implementation of DroidMiner, a novel system for *automated* extraction of robust and fine-grained Android app program behaviors into modalities, as well as *automated* characterization of such behaviors to support detection decisions.
- An in-depth evaluation of DroidMiner including its run-time performance and efficacy in malware detection, family classification, and behavioral characterization.

2   Motivation and System Goals

2.1   Motivations

We motivate our system design by introducing the inner working of a real-world Android malware (MD5: c05c25b 769919fd7f1b12b4800e374b5). It attempts to perform the following malicious behaviors in the background after the phone is booted: stealing users' personal sensitive information (e.g., IMEI and IMSI) and sending them to remote servers, sending and deleting SMS messages, downloading unsolicited apps, and issuing HTTP search requests to increase websites' search rankings on the search engine.

As illustrated in Figure 1, once the phone is booted, the receiver will send out an alarm every two minutes and trigger another receiver (named "MyAlarmReceiver") by using three API calls: AlarmManager(), getServiceSystem(), and getBroadcast(). Then, MyAlarmReceiver starts a background service (named "MyService") by calling startService() in its lifecycle call onReceive(). Once the service is triggered, it will read the device ID (getDeviceId()) and subscriber ID (getSubscriberId()) in the phone, and register an object handler to access the short message database (content://sms/). Meanwhile, the service monitors changes to the SMS Inbox database (content://sms/inbox/) by calling ContentObserver.onChange() and deleting particular messages using delete(), and also attempts to download unsolicited APK files (e.g., "myupdate.apk"). More details can be found in our extended technical report [6].

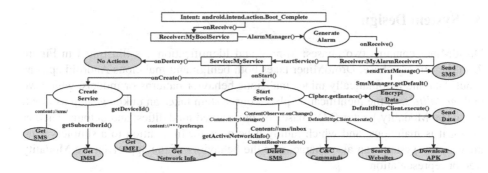

Fig. 1. Capabilities embedded in malware from the ADRD family. The sample achieves its malicious functionalities by mainly invoking a series of framework APIs in order.

The above description motivates an important design premise that when malware authors design malicious apps to achieve specific malicious behaviors, they typically require the use of sets of framework API calls and specific resources (e.g., content providers). More specifically, although attackers may attempt to launch malicious behaviors in a more surreptitious way, they would still have to use those framework APIs or access those important resources.

2.2 Goals and Assumptions

The goal of DroidMiner is to automatically, effectively and efficiently mine Android apps and interrogate them for potentially malicious behaviors. Given an unknown app, DroidMiner should be able to determine whether or not it is malicious. Going beyond just providing a yes or no answer, our system should be able to provide further evidence as to why the app is considered as malicious by including a concise description of identified malicious behaviors. This kind of information is typically considered the hallmark of a good malware detection system. For example, DroidMiner can inform us that a given app is malicious, and that it contains behaviors such as sending SMS messages and blocking certain incoming SMS messages.

Currently, we do not analyze native Android apps implemented using the Android Native Develop Kit (Android NDK). According to our observations, an overwhelming majority of Android apps today are developed using the Android SDK. Furthermore, the vast majority of malicious behaviors in Android apps are achieved by using Android SDK rather than Android NDK. Even for those malicious apps that use the NDK to achieve some malicious behaviors, they typically also use certain Android Framework APIs to obtain some auxiliary information. For example, "rooting" malware (e.g., samples in the family of DroidKungFu), which utilizes native code to achieve privilege escalation, still needs to use specific Framework APIs to obtain auxiliary information (e.g., the version of the operating system) to successfully root the phone. Hence, the presence of such APIs in the Dalvik bytecode could still provide hints for detecting such malware. Extending our system to include complete analysis of native code in Android apps is future work and outside the scope of this paper.

3 System Design

DroidMiner contains two phases: Mining and Identification. As illustrated in Figure 2, in the mining phase, DroidMiner takes both benign and malicious Android apps as input data and automatically mines malicious behavior patterns or models, which we call *modalities*. In the identification phase, our system takes an unknown app as input, extracts a Modality Vector (MV) based on our trained modalities, and outputs whether or not it is malicious, and which family it belongs to. In addition to a simple yes/no answer, our system can also characterize the behaviors of the app given the Modality Vector representation.

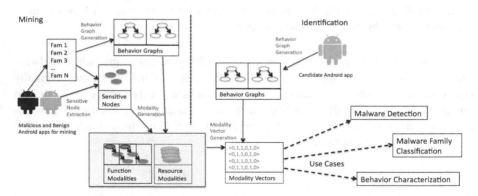

Fig. 2. DroidMiner System Architecture

An important component in our system is the Behavior Graph Generator, which takes an app as input and outputs a behavior graph representation. As illustrated in Figure 1, although Android malware authors have significant flexibility in constructing malicious code, they must obey certain specific rules, pre-defined by the Android platform, to realize malware functionality (e.g., using particular Android/Java framework APIs and accessing particular content providers). These framework APIs and content providers capture the interactions of Android apps with Android framework software or phone hardware, which could be used to model Android apps' behaviors. With this intuition, DroidMiner builds a behavior graph based on the analysis of Android framework APIs and content providers used in apps' bytecode.

In the Mining phase, DroidMiner will attempt to automatically learn the malicious behaviors/patterns from a training set of malicious applications. The basic intuition is that malicious apps in the same family will typically share similar functionalities and behaviors. DroidMiner will examine the similarities from the behavior graphs of these malicious apps and automatically extract common subsets of suspicious behavior specifications, which we call *modalities*. From an intrusion detection perspective, these modalities are essentially micro detection models that characterize various suspicious behaviors found in malicious apps (in Section 3.1).

In the Identification phase, DroidMiner transforms an unknown malicious app into its behavior graph representation (using Behavior Graph Extractor) and extract a Modality Vector (based on all trained modalities), described in Section 3.3. Then, Droid-Miner applies machine-learning techniques to detect whether or not the app is malicious. DroidMiner also has a data-mining module that implements Association Rule Mining to automatically learn the behavior characterization (in Section 3.4).

3.1 Behavior Graph and Modalities

Behavior Graph. DroidMiner detects malware by analyzing the program logic of sensitive Android and Java framework API functions and sensitive Android resources. To represent such logic, we use a two-tiered graphical model. As shown in Figure 3, at upper tier, the behaviors (functionalities) of each Android app could be viewed as the interaction among four types of components (Activities, Services, Broadcast Receivers, and Content Observers). We represent this tier using a **Component Dependency Graph (CDG)**. At the lower tier, each component has its own semantic functionalities and a relatively independent behavior logic during its lifetime. Here, we represent this independent logic using **Component Behavior Graphs (CBG)**.

Component Dependency Graph (CDG) (upper tier of Figure 3) represents the interaction relationships among all components in an app. Each node in the CDG is a component (Activity, Service, or Broadcast Receiver). (Note that multiple nodes could belong to the same type of component.) There is an edge from one node v_i to another node v_j, if the component v_i could activate the start of component v_j's lifecycle.

The **Component Behavior Graphs (CBG)** (lower tier of Figure 3) represents each component's *lifetime*[1] behavior logic (functionalities), i.e., each CBG represents the control-flow logic of those permission-related Android and Java API functions, and actions performed on particular resources of each component. Specifically, as illustrated in Figure 3, a CBG contains four types of node:

---

[1] Lifetime, as defined by Android, is time between the moment when the OS considers a component to be constructed and the moment when the it considers the component to be destroyed.

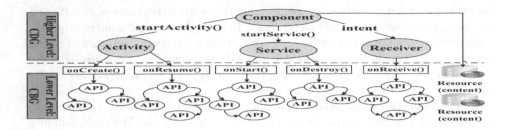

Fig. 3. Two-tier behavior graph

- A *root* note (v_{root}), denoting the component itself (e.g., an Activity).
- *Lifecycle functions* (V_{lcf}), used to achieve the runtime programming logic (e.g., onCreate() in activities, onReceive() in receivers, and onStart() in services).
- *Permission-related API functions* (V_{pf}), representing those permission-related (Android SDK or Java SDK) API functions (e.g., Java API Runtime.execute() or Android API sendTextMessage()). For simplicity, in the rest of paper, we refer both lifecycle functions and API functions as *framework API functions*.
- *Sensitive resource* (V_{res}), i.e., sensitive data (files or databases) that are accessed by the component. In this work, we consider resources as content providers (e.g., content://sms/inbox/), which could be extended to any other type of sensitive data. The usage of framework API functions and sensitive resources in an app essentially captures the interactions of an app with the Android platform hardware and sensitive data. Hence, the control-flow logic of framework API functions and the actions performed on those sensitive resources reflect an application's range of capabilities.

The edges in CBG represent the control-flow logic of framework API functions and sensitive resources. In terms of framework API functions, we consider that there is a direct edge from function node v_i to v_j in the CBG, if (1) when v_i and v_j are in the same control-flow block, v_j is executed just after v_i with no other functions executed between them; or (2) when v_i and v_j are in two continuous control-flow blocks B_i and B_j respectively (i.e., B_j follows B_i), v_i is the last function node in B_i and v_j is the first node in B_j. Then, we call v_j "is a successor of" v_i. For example, in terms of the malware sample illustrated in Figure 1, there is an edge from smsManager.getDefault() to sendTextMessage(). In terms of sensitive resources, since our work mainly focuses on analyzing the control-flow of sensitive functions rather than the data flow of sensitive data, we simply consider that there is an edge from the root to the resource v_r, if the component uses that sensitive resource[2].

Modality. We use the term, *modalities* to refer to malicious behavior patterns that are mined from behavior graphs of Android malware. More specifically, each modality is an ordered sequence (reserving the control-flow order) of framework API functions (function modality) or a set of sensitive resources (resource modality) in commonly

---

[2] We could also choose to build an edge from a framework API function (that uses that resource) to the resource, which relies on the data flow analysis.

shared in malicious apps' behavior graphs[3], which could be used to implement suspicious activities (e.g., sending SMS messages to premium-rate numbers or stealing sensitive information). As an example, the malware sample illustrated in Figure 1 relies on a function modality with an ordered sequence of two framework functions (onChange() $\rightarrow$ ContentResolver.delete()), and a resource modality (content://sms/inbox/) to partially achieve the malicious behavior of deleting messages in the SMS inbox.

3.2 Mining Modalities

Based on previous concepts, DroidMiner's approach to efficient mining of modalities from large malware corpora involves the following three steps: Behavior Graph Generation, Sensitive Node Extraction, and Modality Generation.

Behavior Graph Generation. The generation of the behavior graph of an app contains two phases: generating CDG and generating CBG. Due to the page limitation, we mainly introduce the details of generating CBG (Details of generating CDG can refer [6].) Since Android is component driven, and each component has its own lifetime execution logic, the extraction of control-flow logic of framework API functions is more complex than traditional program analysis. DroidMiner generates the behavior graph by using the following three steps.

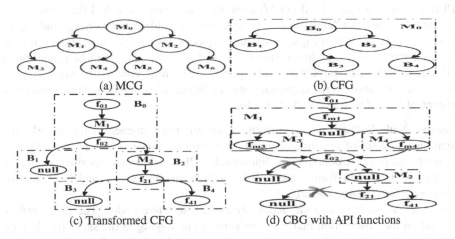

(a) MCG   (b) CFG

(c) Transformed CFG   (d) CBG with API functions

Fig. 4. Illustration of generating a CBG with framework API functions

Step 1: Generate Method Call Graph. For each component, our system generates a method call graph (MCG) containing two types of nodes: Android lifecycle functions and user-defined methods. Since each type of component has fixed lifecycle functions (e.g., onCreate() in an Activity), DroidMiner extracts lifecycle functions by analyzing method names in the component. Those user-defined methods are identified by using a static analysis tool. As illustrated in Figure 4(a), the directed edge from method M_0 to M_1 implies that M_0 calls M_1.

---

[3] Although modalities described in this paper are localized within a CBG, our work could be extended to include cross CBG modalities with the usage of CDG.

Step 2: Generate Control-Flow Graph. To extract the program logic corresponding to the usage of framework APIs, DroidMiner extracts each method's control-flow graph (CFG) by identifying branch-jump instructions in the method's bytecode (e.g., if-nez or packed-switch). Each node is a block of Dalvik bytecode without any jump-branch instructions. For example, M_0 with five blocks is illustrated in Figure 4(b). The directed edge from block B_0 to B_1 implies that B_1 is a successor block of B_0. Then, each block is represented as an ordered sequence of framework API functions and user-defined methods, which are extracted from the Dalvik bytecode with function call instructions (e.g., invoke-direct). We label a block as "null", if it does not contain any function call instructions . For example, in the method M_0, if (1) B_0 contains two API functions and user-defined method M_1, with the execution order of f_{01}, M_1 and f_{02}; (2) B_1 and B_3 do not contain any function calls; (3)B_2 contains method M_2 and one API function f_{21}; (4) B_3 contains one API function f_{41}, then the control-flow graph of M_0 is formed as Figure 4(c).

Step 3: Replace User-Defined Methods. As illustrated in Figure 4(c), since each leaf in the method-call graph does not call any other user-defined method, the leaf either contains a subgraph of framework API functions or is "null". Then, our approach replaces its position in its parents' control-flow graphs with that subgraph. This process is recursively performed, until all user-defined methods are replaced with framework API functions. For example, if (1) M_1 contains three framework API functions (f_{m1}, f_{m3}, and f_{m4}) and one "null" node after replacing its children methods M_3 and M_4 as illustrated in the middle of Figure 4(d), and M_2 does not contain any function nodes, then after replacing its children methods M_5 and M_6, the graph will be transformed to Figure 4(d). Finally, the CBG will be generated by removing those leaves that are "null". After the above three steps, each app's CBG could be generated that represents the control flow of its framework API calls.

Sensitive Node Extraction. A modality is an ordered sequence of framework API functions and a set of sensitive resources that are commonly observed in malware's behavioral graphs. We denote those framework API functions and sensitive resources as sensitive nodes (the former are called *sensitive function nodes*, and the latter are called *sensitive resource nodes*).

We use two strategies to *automatically* extract sensitive nodes. The first strategy is based on the observation that malware samples belonging to the same family tend to share similar malicious logic. Such an observation has been validated by a recent study, which reports that Android malware in the same family tends to hide in multiple categories of fake versions of popular apps [7]. Based on this intuition, we group known malware samples according to their families. Then, for each malware family, we extract function nodes and resource nodes that are commonly shared by at least $\theta\%$ members in this family. Our second strategy is based on the observation that malware samples hosted on third-party market websites tend to be parasitic, i.e., they masquerade as popular benign apps by injecting malicious payloads into original benign apps. Based on this intuition, we automatically extract sensitive nodes by calculating the additional bytecode between the known malicious app and official Android apps sharing similar app names. More details/discussions of the two strategies are in our technical report [6].

Modality Generation. Intuitively, our system generates function modalities by mining an ordered sequence (path) of sensitive function nodes from known malware samples' behavior graphs, as illustrated in Figure 2. In particular, for each path of each known malware's CBG, we denote a subpath of it as a sensitive path, if it starts from one sensitive function node and ends with another sensitive function node. Then, after *removing those non-sensitive nodes* sitting in the middle of the sensitive path, we generate function modalities from the transformed sensitive path by extracting all of its subsequences. Generating function modalities involves the two steps: Extract Sensitive Path and Extract All Subsequences. (Due to the page limit, we leave the detailed algorithm in [6].)

Step 1: Extract Sensitive Path. For each pair of sensitive nodes S_i and S_j, we extract sensitive paths P_{ij} of framework API functions from all known malware samples' CBGs, if P_{ij} starts from S_i and ends with S_j. In particular, for each path in the malware's CBG, we generate modalities from the longest sensitive path, which will cover the results extracted from those shorter sensitive paths. As an illustrative example in Figure 4(d), if f_{01}, f_{m4} and f_{02} are sensitive nodes, the longest sensitive path could be illustrated as Figure 5(a). Then, we could generate a transformed path of function nodes, through removing non-sensitive nodes in the middle. In the previous example, a transformed sensitive path $f_{01} \rightarrow f_{m4} \rightarrow f_{02}$ can be extracted by removing two non-sensitive nodes f_{m1} and "null" in the middle.

Step 2: Extract All Subsequences. We generate function modalities by extracting all *order-preserving*[4] subsequences of the transformed path of sensitive function nodes. Accordingly, we could mine four function modalities from the previous example (see Figure 5(b)). Since DroidMiner utilizes *all subsequences* to generate the modalities instead of using the original single long sequence/path, DroidMiner is resilient to many evasion attempts by malware, e.g., insertion of loop framework API calls in the middle that serve no purpose other than adding noise. Hence, our modalities are a more robust representation of specific malware programming logic than using simple call sequences or frequencies.

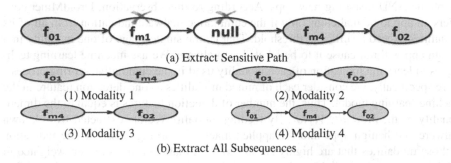

(a) Extract Sensitive Path

(1) Modality 1　　　　　　　　(2) Modality 2

(3) Modality 3　　　　　　　　(4) Modality 4

(b) Extract All Subsequences

Fig. 5. An illustration of function modality generation

---

[4] This implies that the order of two function nodes in the subsequece remains the same as in the original path.

3.3 Identification of Modalities

After mining modalities, the second phase of DroidMiner involves the identification of modalities in unknown apps (i.e., determine which modalities are contained in unknown apps). As illustrated in Figure 2, for each unknown app, DroidMiner identifies its modalities by extracting its behavior graph and generating a Modality Vector, specifying the presence of mined modalities.

More specifically, for each unknown app, DroidMiner generates its behavior graph and extracts sensitive paths from the graph. Then, DroidMiner obtains all potential subpaths by generalizing those sensitive paths. For each sub-path, if it is a modality (belonging to the mined modality set), we consider this app to contain this modality. This process of modality extraction is highly efficient due to the limited number of sensitive nodes present in each app. In this way, once M different modalities are mined from known malware samples, each app could be transformed into a boolean vector $(X_1, X_2, \ldots, X_M)$, denoted as a "Modality Vector": $X_i = 1$, if the app contains the modality M_i; otherwise, $X_i = 0$. In this way, an app's Modality Vector could represent its spectrum of potentially malicious behaviors.

3.4 Modality Use Cases

We introduce how to use an Android app's Modality Vector to address the following three use-case scenarios: Malware Detection, Malware Family Classification, and Malicious Behavior Characterization.

Malware Detection. The first use case involves simply determining whether or not an Android app is malicious. In fact, it is challenging to make a confirmative decision. For example, although some sensitive behaviors (e.g., sending network packets or SMS messages to remote identities) are commonly seen in malware, without a deep analysis about such behaviors (e.g., the analysis of the reputation of those remote identities), we cannot blindly declare all apps with such behaviors to be malware. However, Android malware typically needs to use multiple sensitive functions (or modalities) to achieve its objectives: e.g., (i) sending SMS AND blocking notifications or (ii) rooting the phone AND installing new apps. According to this observation, DroidMiner considers an app to be malicious only if the cumulative malware indication from all of its modalities exceed a sufficient threshold. That is, the single usage of one modality in a benign app will not cause it to be labeled as malware. We use machine learning techniques to learn the indication of each modality used in the cumulative scoring process. More specifically, we consider each of mined modalities as one detection feature in the machine-learning model. Thus, the number of detection features is equal to the dimensionality of the *Modality Vector*. By feeding modality vectors extracted from known malware and benign apps into the applied machine-learning classifier, the indication of those modalities that are highly correlated with malicious apps are up-weighted in judging an app to be malicious; those modalities that are also commonly used in benign apps are down-weighted.

DroidMiner could also be designed to detect malware using pre-defined (strict) detection rules, like policy-based detection systems discussed in Section 5, which may lead to a lower false positive rate. However, such a policy-based design requires considerable domain knowledge and comprehensive manual investigations of malware samples, which can limit overall scalability and thus is more suitable to be applied to detect specific attacks. Our goal of designing a fully automated approach motivated us to use the learning-based approach instead of policy-based ones.

Malware Family Classification. Besides detecting malware from a corpus of apps, another use case is automatically determining the family that an identified malware sample may belong to, given sufficient knowledge from existing known malware families. This problem is also important for understanding and analyzing malware families. In fact, many antivirus vendors still rely on common code extraction techniques, which typically manually extract signatures after gathering a large collection of malware samples belonging to the same malware family.

Different malware samples in the same family tend to share similar malicious behaviors, which could be depicted by *Modality Vectors*. Thus, the degree of similarity between the Modality Vectors of two malware samples provides an indication of whether they belong to the same family. Hence, with the knowledge of Modality Vectors mined from malware samples belonging to existing malware families, we could also build a malware family classifier for unknown malicious apps.

Malicious Behavior Characterization. The final use case involves characterizing the specific malicious functionality embedded within a candidate app. To solve this problem, we essentially need to know which modalities could be used to achieve specific malicious behaviors. Then, if an app contains those modalities, we could claim with high confidence that the app is malicious. To realize this goal, we use a data mining technique, called "Association Rule Mining [8]". Due to the page limit, we only introduce the basic intuition here, and recommend interested readers to read our extended version [6]. Intuitively, we mine relationships (association rules) from modalities to malicious behaviors. More specifically, DroidMiner derives association rules by analyzing the relationship between the modality usage in existing known malware families and their corresponding malicious behaviors. For example, Zsone has two known malicious behaviors: (*i*) sending SMS and (*ii*) blocking SMS. DroidMiner associates modalities generated from this family to these two behaviors.

4   Evaluation

We present our evaluation results by implementing a prototype of DroidMiner and applying it to apps collected from existing third-party Android markets and from the official Android market (*GooglePlay*).

4.1   Prototype Implementation

We implement a prototype of DroidMiner on top of a popular static analysis tool (Androguard [9]). In our experience, comparing with other public Android app decompilers (e.g., Dex2Jar [10] or Smali [11]), Androguard produces more accurate decompilation results, especially in terms of handling exceptions. The prototype decompiles an Android app into Dalvik bytecode, further builds its behavior graph and mines its modalities based on the bytecode.

The method call graph in an app is built by analyzing the caller-callee relationships of all methods used in the app. For each method, DroidMiner extracts its callee methods by analyzing the *invoke-kind* instructions (e.g., *invoke-virtual* and *invoke-direct*) used in the method. Since Android is event-driven, the entrance of an app could also be UI event methods (e.g., onClick). However, such UI event methods could only be executed after the corresponding UI event listeners are registered (e,g., setOnClickListener). Thus, to make the program logic more complete, DroidMiner adds an edge from UI events listeners to corresponding UI event methods, although there is no such caller-callee relationships in the bytecode. We use a similar strategy to address registered event handlers and threads. DroidMiner generate the control-flow graph in each method by analyzing branch jump instructions (e.g., if-eq). In our implementation, all behavior graphs are stored in XGMML [12] format, a highly efficient format for graph representation and matching.

4.2 Data Collection

We crawled four representative marketplaces, including GooglePlay, and three alternative markets (SlideMe [13], AppDH [14], and Anzhi [15]). The collection from the alternative markets occurred during a 13-day period. GooglePlay collection was harvested during a two-months period. As described in Table 1, in total, we collected 67,797 free apps, where 17% of the apps (11,529) were collected from GooglePlay, and the remaining 83% (56,268) were harvested from the alternative markets.

Table 1. Summary of Android App Collection

	Official Market	SlideMe	AppDH	Anzhi
Location	U.S.A	U.S.A	China	China
Number of Apps	11,529	15,129	2,349	38,790
Total Apps	11,529 (17%)	56,268 (83%)		
	67,797			

Next, we isolate the set of malicious apps from our corpus by submitting the set of apps from the alternative markets to "VirusTotal.com", which is a free antivirus (AV) service that scans each uploaded Android app using over 40 different AV products [16]. For each app, if it has been scanned earlier by an AV tool, we can obtain the full Virus-Total report, which includes the first and last time the app was seen, as well as the results from the individual AV scans. For example, BitDefender has a report for a malicious app (*MD5: 7acb7c624d7a19ad4fa92cacfddd9257*) as Droid.Trojan.KungFu.C. Thus, we obtained 1,247 malicious apps identified by at least one AV product. For each malicious app, we extract its associated malware family name, and when AV reports disagree, we derive a consensus label using the label that dominates the responses from the AV tools. In addition, we obtain another set of malware samples from Genome Project [17,18]. This dataset contains the family label for each malware sample. After excluding those already appeared in our crawled malware set, there are 1,219 different malware apps. Thus, in total, our malware dataset consists of *2,466* (1,247+1,219) unique malicious apps that belong to *68* malware families.

We construct a benign dataset using popular apps collected from GooglePlay. To further clean this dataset, we submit our candidate set of 11,529 free GooglePlay apps to VirusTotal, of which 1,126 apps were labeled as malicious by one AV product. We discarded those apps and constructed our benign dataset using the remaining *10,403* free GooglePlay Android apps. Clearly, the benign app dataset may still contain some malicious apps, but this set has at least been vetted by the GooglePlay anti-malware analysis and by more than 40 AV products from VirusTotal. The problem of producing a perfect benign app corpus remains a hard challenge, and we note that a similar approach to construct a benign app dataset has been used in prior related work [3].

4.3 Evaluation Result

Below, we summarize our system evaluation results for malware detection, malware family classification, behavior characterization, and efficiency.

Malware Detection. As introduced in Section 3.4, we utilize machine learning techniques to conduct malicious app detection. To better evaluate the effectiveness of DroidMiner, we utilize four widely used machine learning (ML) classifiers: *Naive-Bayes*, *Support Vector Machine (SVM)*, *DecisionTree* and *Random Forest*.

For each classifier, we conduct a series of experiments using a *ten-fold cross validation* to compute three performance metrics: *False Positive Rate*, *Detection Rate*, and *Accuracy*. Specifically, we divide both malicious and benign datasets randomly into 10 groups, respectively. In each of the 10 rounds, we choose the combination of one group of benign apps and malicious apps as the testing dataset, and the remaining 9 groups as the training dataset. We further compare the performance of DroidMiner with another classifier (used in [3]), which uses registered permissions as major detection features, based on our collected dataset.[5]

Table 2 shows the results of using permission versus DroidMiner based on different classifiers. We see that for all four classifiers, the usage of modalities as the input feature set (DroidMiner) produces a higher detection rate and lower false positive rate than the approach of using permission features [3]. Particularly, using *Random Forest* Droid-Miner achieved a detection rate of 95.3%, roughly 10% higher than the that of using permission. Furthermore, DroidMiner produced a lower false positive rate of (0.4%), or around 1/5th of the compared approach. Also, DroidMiner could maintain the detection rate higher than 86% for all four classifiers. Due to space limit, we leave a more detailed analysis of false positives and negatives in [6].

Table 2. Detection Results (DR denotes detection rate, FP denotes false positive)

Classifier	NaiveBayes		SVM		Decision Tree		Random Forest	
Method	Permission	DroidMiner	Permission[3]	DroidMiner	Permission[3]	DroidMiner	Permission[3]	DroidMiner
DR	75.1%	82.2%	78.8%	86.7%	85.7%	92.4%	87.0%	95.3
FP Rate	7.2%	4.4%	3.5%	1.1%	2.2%	1.0%	2.0%	0.4%

---

[5] We are unable to provide a direct corpus comparative evaluation with other detection systems discussed in related work [1,2], because they are not publicly available and it is generally difficult to completely reproduce similar systems and parameter selections.

Family Classification. The purpose of this experiment is to measure the accuracy of using Modality Vectors to correctly assign apps that are classified as malicious to their correct corresponding malware family. To conduct the malware family classification, we use samples from 12 families, each of which has more than 50 samples. The number of samples of each family is shown in Table 3.

Table 3. Malware samples used for classification

Ind	Family	Num	Ind	Family	Num	Ind	Family	Num	Ind	Family	Num
1	GingerMaster	166	4	AnserverBot	187	7	KMin	52	10	DroidKungFu3	327
2	GoldDream	57	5	DroidKungFu	70	8	BaseBridge	122	11	DroidKungFu4	10
3	Airpush	568	6	Leadbolt	52	9	Geinimi	69	12	Plankton	194

For each family, we use half of the samples as training dataset, and the other half as the testing dataset. In this case, the classification accuracy represents the ratio of the number of correctly classified samples to the total number of samples in the test dataset. Here, we use *Random Forest* for classifying both the training and testing datasets. The classifier produces a relatively high classification accuracy of 92.07%.

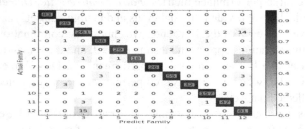

Fig. 6. The confusion matrix of malware classification for multiple malware families

Figure 6 shows the confusion matrix produced from our classification of the dataset into the malware family label set. The value of the cell (i, j) in the matrix shows the number of samples in family i, which are classified as being family j. Thus, the central diagonal in the matrix shows the number of *correctly* predicted samples per malware family. The darker the cell color is, the higher the classification accuracy is. With the exception of *Leadbolt* (index is 6), most of the other families achieve an accuracy higher than 90%. *Leadbolt* is an adware family, and thus its implementation may be influenced by the campaign it is serving, and thus producing a behavior that has a wide variability, leading its samples to appear to match a wider range of potential families.

Behavior Characterization. As described in Section 3.4, to characterize malicious behaviors, we construct a behavior matrix based on malicious behaviors observed within an existing training set of known malware apps. To decrease sampling bias, we produce our *training* dataset using malware samples from families which have a minimum of 5 members. Next, for each family, we manually extract a malicious behavior description for this family using documentation describing the malware family from sites that contain malware analysis reports, such as threat reports from various AV companies (e.g., Symantec.com). There are many detailed public sources of information regarding malicious behavior description for many existing Android malware families. For this experiment, we focus on the following six malicious behaviors commonly observed within many malware families: stealing phone information (GetPho), Sending SMS (SdSMS), blocking SMS (BkSMS), communicating with a C&C (C&C), escalating root privilege (Root) and accessing geographical information (GetGeo). We refer interested readers to [6] for more details.

Table 4. Characterizations on 10 malware samples

MD5	Family	Behavior
917a1aa8fafb97cdb91475709ca15cdb	MobileTX	SdSMS, C&C
49ea90de2336dccee188c3078ea64656	Gappusin	SdSMS, BKSMS, C&C, GetGeo
d6aea5963681cf6415cc3f221e4e403b	Cosha	SdSMS, C&C, GetGeo
8ef081ff9fb2dd866bfc6af6749abdcf	Fakeflash	C&C
a835b82de9e15330893ddf2da67a6a49	HippoSMS	SdSMS, BkSMS
bbb6f9a1aad8cc8c38d4441bac4852c0	DroidDeluxe	Root
9b0d331aa9019bfb550f4753aba45d27	RogueLemon	SdSMS, BKSMS, C&C
cfa9edb8c9648ae2757a85e6066f6515	Spitmo	GetPho, SdSMS, BKSMS, C&C
ee0f74897785eb3f7af84a293263c6c5	Gamex	Root
c00e43c563ecadf1e22097124538c24a	Tapsnake	C&C, GetGeo

Efficiency. We now consider the performance overhead of DroidMiner in identifying modalities. As described in Section 3.3, modality identification involves three steps: 1) decompilation, 2) behavior graph generation and 3) modality vector generation. Table 5 shows the mean and median value of time spent on each step and the overall time required to identify modalities for all collected apps. Table 5 illustrates that DroidMiner expended an average of 19.8 seconds and a median of 5.4 seconds to identify modalities in an app. We provide a fine-grained analysis of the time used for generating behavior graphs in our extended version [6].

Table 5. Time for identifying modalities.

Step	Decompile	Behavior Graph	Modality Vector	Overall
Mean	3.87	15.19	1.10	19.83
Median	1.65	3.08	0.56	5.35

5   Related Work

5.1   Mobile Malware Detection

System Call Monitoring. Systems such as [19,20,21] detect malware by monitoring and analysis of system calls. A fundamental shortcoming of such approaches is the semantic gap between the system calls and specific behaviors. DroidScope [22] is designed to reconstruct both OS-level and Java-level semantics. Their dynamic analysis approach is limited by path exploration challenges.

Android Permission Monitoring. Enck et al. studied the security of Android apps by analyzing the permissions registered in the top official Market apps [23]. Stowaway [24] and COPES [25] are designed to find those apps that request more permissions than they need. PScout [26] analyzes the usage trend of permissions in Android apps. Kirin [27] detected malicious Android apps by finding permissions declared in Android apps that break "pre-defined" security rules. More recent work also detected malicious Android apps by designing several classifiers, whose features were built primarily on the application categories and permissions [3]. A concern with these approaches is false positives stemming from the coarse-grained nature of permissions and the highly common nature of benign apps to over-claim their set of required permissions. Mario et al. [28] presented their studies of permission request patterns of Android and Facebook applications.

Framework API Monitoring. DroidRanger [1] and Pegasus [2] detect malicious Android apps by statically matching against "pre-defined" signatures (permissions and Android Framework API calls) of well-known malware families. Such approaches requires semi-manual analysis of suspicious system calls and manual selection of heuristics (or detection patterns). Thus, they are not systematic and not robust to the evolution of malware. In [4,5], the frequencies of API calls were used as detection features, and more recently in [29], the names and parameters of APIs and packages were used as detection features. Such studies differ fundamentally from DroidMiner in that our modalities capture the connections of multiple sensitive API functions, not just the frequency or names of APIs.

Online Malware Detection Service. We intend to make DroidMiner available as a public webservice for Android malware analysis and detection. Similar public services include AndroTotal [30] which allows users to submit applications and have them simultaneously analyzed by various mobile antivirus systems and CopperDroid [31] which performs system-call centric dynamic analysis.

Due to space limit, we leave more detailed comparisons and discussions in [6].

5.2   Android Platform Security Defense and Analysis

Existing studies have also developed several security extensions to defend against specific types of attacks. TaintDroid [32] detects those apps that may leak users' privacy information. However, it is not designed to detect other types of malicious behaviors such as stealthily sending of SMS. RiskRanker [33] detects malicious apps based on the knowledge of known Android system vulnerabilities, which could be utilized by malicious apps, and several heuristics. Dendroid [34] is a static analysis tool which specializes in text mining of android malware code. Quire [35] prevents confused deputy attacks. Bugiel et al. [36] proposed a security framework to prevent both confused deputy attacks and collusion attacks. AppFence [37] protects sensitive data by either feeding fake data or blocking the leakage path. Apex [38] allows for the selection of granted permissions, and Kirin [27] performs lightweight certification of applications. Paranoid Android [19], L4Android [39] and Cells [40] utilize the virtual environment to secure smartphone OS. SmartDroid [41] automatically finds UI triggers that result in sensitive information leakage.

6 Discussion

DroidMiner against Zero-Day Attacks. Emerging malware generally falls into two classes: fundamentally new strain with entirely novel code bases, and malware that improves (evolves) from an existing code base. The latter form arguably represents the dominant case. We believe DroidMiner is well designed to adapt to evolutionary change in existing code bases, and thus useful in detecting most emerging variant strains. As long as new malware launches malicious behaviors through utilizing modalities observed in known malware families, DroidMiner should detect it. For entirely novel malware strains, an additional strength of DroidMinder is that unlike traditional systems that require human expertise, DroidMiner's features (modalities) can be automatically learned and updated by feeding new malware samples.

DroidMiner against Common Evasion Techniques. We can envision that Android malware may evolve to be more evasive. As observed by DroidChameleon [42], common malware transformation techniques (e.g., repackaging, changing field names, and changing control-flow logic) could evade many existing commercial anti-malware tools. However, DroidMiner is resilient to these common evasion techniques studied in [42]. Specifically, DroidMiner does not rely on specific signing signatures or class/method-/field names to detect malware. The simple program transformation (resigning, repackaging, changing names) will not affect the detection model used in DroidMiner. Another type of evasion technique is to insert noisy code and spurious calls in between malicious sequences, or to change specific control-flow logic. However, DroidMiner is designed to extract *all subsequences* of suspicious control-flow logic commonly seen in malware (instead of relying on the exact matching of one full/long execution path). As long as the malware follows a known programming paradigm to achieve malicious goals (e.g., intercepting short text messages after receiving them, and obtaining the phone number before sending it), DroidMiner could still capture such suspicious logic regardless of the noisy/spurious API injections in the middle of execution paths. Last but not least, malicious apps may include a large number of benign patterns to confuse DroidMiner. As mentioned earlier, our learning procedure typically down-weights modalities commonly used in benign apps and up-weights truly malicious modalities learned before. Thus, DroidMiner still has a good tolerance of such evasion.

Limitations and Future Work. Like any learning-based approach, DroidMiner requires an accurate training dataset to mine its malicious behaviors into modalities. The effectiveness of our approach depends on the quality of the given training data, e.g., labeled malicious Android apps and their families. Fortunately, it was easy for us to obtain such data (thanks to prior research efforts from academia and industry). In fact, one may also recognize DroidMiner's automatic learning approach as a feature rather than a strict liability. Whereas most existing approaches require significant manual labor to generate signature, specifications, and models for detection, DroidMiner offers far more automated model generation.

DroidMiner currently employs static analysis, which is a reasonable choice given that current Android apps are relatively easy to reverse engineer statically, unlike notorious PC-based malware. Like other Java static analysis studies, DroidMiner may fail to identify certain usages of instances/methods, which are encrypted or made by using Java Reflection and native code. This serves as another motivation for us to incorporate dynamic analysis in our future work.

7   Conclusion

DroidMiner is a new static analysis system that automatically mines malicious parasitic code segments from a corpus of malicious mobile applications, and then detects the presence of these code segments within other, previously unlabeled, mobile apps. We present our DroidMiner prototype and an extensive evaluation of this algorithm on a corpus of over 2,400 malicious apps. From these 2,400 malware apps DroidMiner achieves a 95% accuracy rate in processing over 77,000 samples from real-world app stores. Further, we show that DroidMiner achieves a 92% accuracy in assigning malicious labels to blind test suites.

Acknowledgments. This material is based upon work supported in part by the National Science Foundation under Grant CNS-0954096, IIS-0905518 and the Air Force Office of Scientific Research under Grant FA9550-13-1-0077. Any opinions, findings, and conclusions or recommendations expressed in this material are those of the author(s) and do not necessarily reflect the views of NSF and AFOSR.

References

1. Zhou, Y., Wang, Z., Zhou, W., Jiang, X.: Hey, you, get off of my market: Detecting malicious apps in official and alternative android markets. In: Proc. of the 19th NDSS (2012)
2. Chen, K., Johnson, N., Silva, V., Dai, S., MacNamara, K., Magrino, T., Wu, E., Rinard, M., Song, D.: Contextual policy enforcement in android applications with permission event graphs. In: Proc. of the 20th NDSS (2013)
3. Peng, H., Gates, C., Sarm, B., Li, N., Qi, Y., Potharaju, R., Nita-Rotaru, C., Molloy, I.: Using probabilistic generative models for ranking risks of android apps. In: Proc. of the 19th CCS
4. Wu, D., Mao, C., Wei, T., Lee, H., Wu., K.: Droidmat: Android malware detection through manifest and api calls tracing. In: Proc. of the 7th Asia JCIS (2012)
5. Arp, D., Spreitzenbarth, M., Hubner, M., Gascon, H., Rieck, K.: Drebin: Effective and explainable detection of android malware in your pocket. In: Proc. of NDSS (2014)
6. Yang, C., Xu, Z., Gu, G., Yegneswaran, V., Porras, P.: Droidminer: Automated mining and characterization of fine-grained malicious behaviors in android applications. Technical report, Texas A&M University (2014),
http://faculty.cse.tamu.edu/guofei/paper/
DroidMiner_TechReport_2014.pdf
7. 60 percentage of android malware hide in fake versions of popular apps,
http://thenextweb.com/google/2012/10/05/
over-60-percent-of-android-malware-comes-from-one-family-
hides-in-fake-versions-of-popular-apps/

8. Association mining rule,
   http://en.wikipedia.org/wiki/Association_rule_learning
9. Androguard, http://code.google.com/p/androguard/
10. Dex2jar, https://code.google.com/p/dex2jar/
11. Smali, https://code.google.com/p/smali/
12. extensible graph markup and modeling language,
    http://www.cs.rpi.edu/research/groups/pb/punin/public_html/
    XGMML/draft-xgmml-20001006.html
13. Slideme android market, http://slideme.org/
14. App dh android market, http://www.appdh.com/
15. Anzhi android market, http://www.anzhi.com/
16. Virustotal, https://www.virustotal.com/
17. Android malware genome project, http://www.malgenomeproject.org/
18. Zhou, Y., Jiang, X.: Dissecting android malware: Characterization and evolution. In: Proc. of the 33th IEEE Security and Privacy (2012)
19. Portokalidis, G., Homburg, P., Anagnostakis, K., Bos, H.: Paranoid android: versatile protection for smartphones. In: Proc. of the 26th ACSAC (2010)
20. Schmidt, A., Bye, R., Schmidt, H., Clausen, J., Kiraz, O., Yxksel, K., Camtepe, S., Sahin, A.: Static analysis of executables for collaborative malware detection on android. In: ICC Communication and Information Systems Security Symposium (2009)
21. Schmidt, A., Schmidt, H., Clausen, J., Yuksel, K., Kiraz, O., Sahin, A., Camtepe, S.: Enhancing security of linux-based android devices. In: Proc. of 15th International Linux Kongress
22. Yan, L., Yin, H.: Droidscope: Seamlessly reconstructing the os and dalvik semantic views for dynamic android malware analysis. In: Proc. of the 21st USENIX Security (2012)
23. Enck, W., Octeau, D., McDaniel, P., Chaudhuri, S.: A study of android application security. In: Proc. of the 20th USENIX (2011)
24. Felt, A.P., Chin, E., Hanna, S., Song, D., Wagner, D.: Android permissions demystied. In: Proc. of the 18th CCS (2011)
25. Bartel, A., Klein, J., Monperrus, M., Traon, Y.L.: Automatically securing permission-based software by reducing the attack surface: An application to android. In: Proc. of the 27th IEEE/ACM International Conference on Automated Software Engineering (2012)
26. Au, K., Zhou, Y., Huang, Z., Lie, D., Gong, X., Han, X., Zhou, W.: Pscout: Analyzing the android permission specification. In: Proc. of the 19th CCS (2012)
27. Enck, W., Ongtang, M., McDaniel, P.: On lightweight mobile phone application certification. In: Proc. of the 16th CCS (2009)
28. Frank, M., Dong, B., Felt, A.P., Song, D.: Mining permission request patterns from android and facebook applications. In: Proc. of ICDM 2012 (2012)
29. Aafer, Y., Du, W., Yin, H.: DroidAPIMiner: Mining API-level features for robust malware detection in android. In: Zia, T., Zomaya, A., Varadharajan, V., Mao, M. (eds.) SecureComm 2013. LNICST, vol. 127, pp. 86–103. Springer, Heidelberg (2013)
30. Maggi, F., Valdi, A., Zanero, S.: AndroTotal: a flexible, scalable toolbox and service for testing mobile malware detectors. In: Proc. of SPSM 2013 (2013)
31. Reina, A., Fattori, A., Cavallaro, L.: A system call-centric analysis and stimulation technique to automatically reconstruct android malware behaviors. In: Proc. of EUROSEC 2013 (2013)
32. Enck, W., Gilbert, P., Chun, B., Cox, L.P., Jung, J., Mc-Daniel, P., Sheth, A.N.: Taintdroid: An information-flow tracking system for realtime privacy monitoring on smartphones. In: Proc. of the 9th OSDI (2010)
33. Zhou, Y., Zhang, Q., Zou, S., Jiang, X.: Riskranker: scalable and accurate zero-day android malware detection. In: Proc. of the 10th MobiSys (2012)
34. Suarez-Tangil, G., Tapiador, J.E., Peris-Lopez, P., Alis, J.B.: Dendroid: A text mining approach to analyzing and classifying code structures in android malware families (2012)

35. Dietz, M., Shekhar, S., Pisetsky, Y., Shu, A., Wallach, D.S.: Quire: lightweight provenance for smart phone operating systems. In: Proc. of the 20th USENIX Security (2011)
36. Bugiel, S., Davi, L., Dmitrienko, A., Fischer, T., Sadeghi, A.R., Shastry, B.: Towards taming privilege-escalation attacks on android. In: Proc. of the 19th NDSS (2012)
37. Hornyack, P., Han, S., Jung, J., Schechter, S., Wetherall, D.: These aren't the droids you're looking for: Retrofitting android to protect data from imperious applications. In: Proc. of the 18th CCS (2011)
38. Nauman, M., Khan, S., Zhang, X.: Apex: extending android permission model and enforcement with user-defined runtime constraints. In: Proc. of the 5th ICCS (2010)
39. Lange, M., Liebergeld, S., Lackorzynski, A., Warg, A., Peter, M.: L4android: A generic operating system frame- work for secure smartphones. In: Proc. of the 1st Workshop on Security and Privacy in Smartphones and Mobile Devices (2011)
40. Andrus, J., Dall, C., Hof, A.V., Laadan, O., Nieh, J.: Cells: A virtual mobile smartphone architecture. In: Proc. of the 23rd SOSP (2011)
41. Zheng, C., Zhu, S., Dai, S., Gu, G., Gong, X., Han, X., Zhou, W.: Smartdroid: an automatic system for revealing ui-based trigger conditions in android applications. In: Proc. of the 2nd Workshop on Security and Privacy in Smartphones and Mobile Devices (2012)
42. Rastogi, V., Chen, Y., Jiang, X.: Droidchameleon: evaluating android anti-malware against transformation attacks. In: Proc. of the 8th ICCS (2013)

Detecting Targeted Smartphone Malware
with Behavior-Triggering Stochastic Models

Guillermo Suarez-Tangil[1], Mauro Conti[2],
Juan E. Tapiador[1], and Pedro Peris-Lopez[1]

[1] Department of Computer Science, Universidad Carlos III de Madrid, Spain
`guillermo.suarez.tangil@uc3m.es`, {`jestevez,pperis`}`@inf.uc3m.es`
[2] Department of Mathematics, University of Padova, Italy
`conti@math.unipd.it`

Abstract. Malware for current smartphone platforms is becoming increasingly sophisticated. The presence of advanced networking and sensing functions in the device is giving rise to a new generation of targeted malware characterized by a more situational awareness, in which decisions are made on the basis of factors such as the device location, the user profile, or the presence of other apps. This complicates behavioral detection, as the analyst must reproduce very specific activation conditions in order to trigger malicious payloads. In this paper, we propose a system that addresses this problem by relying on stochastic models of usage and context events derived from real user traces. By incorporating the behavioral particularities of a given user, our scheme provides a solution for detecting malware targeting such a specific user. Our results show that the properties of these models follow a power-law distribution: a fact that facilitates an efficient generation of automatic testing patterns tailored for individual users, when done in conjunction with a cloud infrastructure supporting device cloning and parallel testing. We report empirical results with various representative case studies, demonstrating the effectiveness of this approach to detect complex activation patterns.

Keywords: Smartphone security, targeted malware, cloud analysis.

1 Introduction

Malware for smartphones is a problem that has rocketed in the last few years [1]. The presence of increasingly powerful computing, networking, and sensing functions in smartphones has empowered malicious apps with a variety of advanced capabilities [2], including the possibility to determine the physical location of the smartphone, spy on the user's behavioral patterns, or compromise the data and services accessed through the device. These capabilities are rapidly giving rise to a new generation of *targeted* malware that makes decisions on the basis of factors such as the device location, the user's profile, or the presence of other apps (e.g., see [3–6]).

M. Kutyłowski and J. Vaidya (Eds.): ESORICS 2014, Part I, LNCS 8712, pp. 183–201, 2014.
© Springer International Publishing Switzerland 2014

The idea of behaving differently under certain circumstances was also successfully applied in the past. For instance, Stuxnet [7] remained dormant until a particular app was installed and used at certain location, having as a target Iranian nuclear plants. Other malware has targeted governments and private corporations—mostly in the financial and pharmaceutical sectors [8]. Another representative example of targeted malware is Eurograbber [9], a "smart" Trojan targeting online banking users. The situational awareness provided by smartphone platforms makes this type of attacks substantially easier and potentially more dangerous. More recently, other examples of targeted malware include FinSpy Mobile [10], a general surveillance software for mobile devices, and Dendroid Remote Access Toolkit (RAT) [11], which offers capabilities to target specific users.

A similar problem is the emergence of the so-called *grayware* [3], i.e., apps that cannot be completely considered malicious but whose behavior may entail security and/or privacy risks of which the user is not fully aware. For example, many apps using targeted advertisements are particularly aggressive in the amount of personal data they gather, including sensitive contextual information acquired through the device sensors. The purpose of such data gathering activities is in many cases questionable, and many users might well disapprove of it, either entirely or in certain contexts[1].

Both targeted malware and grayware share a common feature that complicates their identification: the behavior and the potential repercussions of executing an app might depend quite strongly on the context where it takes place [12] and the way the user interacts with the app and the device [13]. We stress that this problem is not addressed by current detection mechanisms implemented in app markets, as operators are overwhelmed by the number of apps submitted for revision every day and cannot afford an exhaustive analysis over each one of them [14]. A possible solution to tackle this problem could be to implement detection techniques based on dynamic analysis (e.g., Taintdroid [15]) directly in the device. However, this is simply too demanding for battery-powered platforms. Several recent works [16–19] have proposed to keep a synchronized replica (clone) of the device virtualized in the cloud. This would facilitate offloading resource-intensive security analysis to the cloud, but still does not solve one fundamental problem: grayware and targeted malware instances must be provided with the user's particular context and behavior, so the only option left would be to install the app, use it, and expect that the analysis conducted over the clone—hopefully in real time—detects undesirable behaviors. This is a serious limitation that prevents users from learning in advance what an app would do in certain situations, without the need of actually reproducing such a situation.

Related Work. Recent works such as PyTrigger [20] have approached the problem of detecting targeted malware in Personal Computers (PC). To do so, it

---

[1] Classical examples include two popular games, *Aurora Feint* and *Storm8*, which were removed from the Apple Store for harvesting data and phone numbers from the user's contact list and sending them to unknown destinations [2].

is sought to trigger specific malware behaviors by injecting activities collected from users (e.g., mouse clicks and keyword inputs) and their context. This approach cannot be adopted to platforms such as smartphones because the notion of *sensed* context is radically different here. Other schemes, including the work presented in [13, 21–23], do focus on smartphones but concentrate exclusively on interactions with the Graphical User Interface (GUI) and are vulnerable to context-based targeted attacks. Two works closer to our proposal are Context Virtualizer [24] and Dynodroid [25], where a technique called context fuzzing is introduced in the former and used in the latter. The main aim in [24, 25] is to automatically test apps with real-world conditions, including user-based contexts. These tools, however, are intended for developers who want to learn how their apps will behave when used in a real setting. Contrarily, our focus is on final users who want to find out if they will be targeted by malicious or privacy-compromising behaviors. Finally, other works such as CopperDroid [26] focus on malware detection as we do, but with a static approach based on information extracted from the manifest that, besides, does not consider the user context.

Contribution. In this paper, we address the problem of identifying targeted grayware and malware and propose a more flexible approach compared to other proposals to determining whether the behavior of an app is compliant with a particular set of security and privacy preferences associated with a user. Our solution is based on the idea of obtaining an *actionable* model of user behavior that can be leveraged to test how an app would behave should the user execute it in some context. Such a testing takes place over a clone of the device kept in the cloud. This approach removes the need of actually exposing the device (e.g., we let the device access only to fake data and not real one). More importantly, the analysis is tailored to a given user, either generally or for a particular situation. For example, a user might want to explore the consequences of using an app in the locations visited during working days from 9 to 5, or during a planned trip.

Organization. Section 2 introduces the theoretical framework used to model triggering patterns and app behavior. In Section 3, we describe the architecture of our proposal and a proof-of-concept prototype, and discuss the experimental results obtained in terms of testing coverage and efficiency. In Section 4, we discuss the detection performance with two representative case studies of grayware and targeted malware instances. Finally, Section 5 concludes the paper by summarizing our main contributions and describing future research directions.

2   Behavioral Models

This section introduces the theoretical framework used in our proposal (presented later in Section 4) to trigger particular app behaviors and determining whether they entail security risks to the user. More precisely, we next present models for the user-provided inputs, the resulting app behavior, and the mechanism used to assess potential risks.

2.1 Triggering Patterns

Inputs provided by the user to his device constitute a major source of stimuli for triggering certain app behaviors. We group such inputs into two broad classes of patterns, depending on whether they refer to inputs resulting from the user directly interacting with the app and/or the device (e.g., through the touchscreen), or else indirectly by the context (e.g., location, time, presence of other devices in the surroundings, etc.).

Usage Patterns. Usage patterns model sequences of events resulting from the actions of the user during his interaction with an app. Such events are internal messages passed on to the app by the device, such as starting an activity or clicking a button. We stress that our focus is on the events and not on the actions that generate them, as same event can be triggered through different input interfaces (e.g., touchscreen and voice).

Let the following be a set of all possible events for all apps:

$$\mathcal{E} = \{e_1, e_2, \ldots, e_n\}. \tag{1}$$

Thus, the interaction of a user with an app can be represented as an ordered sequence:

$$\mathbf{u} = \langle \epsilon_1, \epsilon_2, \ldots, \epsilon_k \rangle, \quad \epsilon_i \in \mathcal{E}. \tag{2}$$

We will refer to such sequences as *usage traces*. Interactions with an app at different times and/or with different apps will result in different usage traces.

Context Patterns. Apps may behave differently depending on conditions not directly provided by the user, such as the device location, the time and date, the presence of other apps or devices, etc. We model this using the widely accepted notion of *context* [27]. Assume that $v_1, \ldots, v_m$ are variables representing contextual elements of interest, with $v_i \in \mathcal{V}_i$. Let the following be the set of all possible contexts:

$$\mathcal{C} = \mathcal{V}_1 \times \cdots \times \mathcal{V}_m. \tag{3}$$

As above, monitoring a user during some time interval will result in a sequence:

$$\mathbf{t} = \langle c_1, c_2, \ldots, c_l \rangle, \quad c_i \in \mathcal{C}. \tag{4}$$

We will refer to such sequences as *context traces*.

2.2 Stochastic Triggering Model

Usage and context traces are used to derive a model that captures how the user interacts with an app or a set of apps. For this purpose, we rely on a discrete-time first-order Markov process (i.e., a Markov chain [28]) $\mathbf{M} = (S, A, \Pi)$ where:

- The set of states S is given by:

$$S = \mathcal{E} \times \mathcal{C} = \{s_1, \ldots, s_N\}. \tag{5}$$

We will denote by $q(t) \in S$ the state of the model at time $t = 1, 2, \ldots$, representing one particular input event executed in a given context.

- The transition matrix is given by:

$$A = [a_{ij}] = P[q(t+1) = s_j | q(t) = s_i], \qquad (6)$$

where $a_{ij} \in [0,1]$ and $\sum_{j=1}^{N} a_{ij} = 1$.
- The vector of initial probabilities is given by:

$$\Pi = (\pi_i) = P[q(1) = s_i], \qquad (7)$$

with $\pi_i \in [0,1]$ and $\sum_{i=1}^{N} \pi_i = 1$.

The model above is simple yet powerful enough to model user-dependant behavioral patterns when interacting with an app. The model parameters can be easily estimated from a number of usage and context traces. Assume that $O = \{o_1, o_2, \dots, o_T\}$ is a sequence of observed states (i.e., event-context pairs) obtained by monitoring the user during a representative amount of time. The transition matrix can be estimated as:

$$a_{ij} = \frac{\sum_{t=2}^{T} P[q(t) = s_j | q(t-1) = s_i]}{\sum_{t=2}^{T} P[q(t-1) = s_j]} = \frac{\sum_{t=2}^{T} P[o_t = s_j | o_{t-1} = s_i]}{\sum_{t=2}^{T} P[o_{t-1} = s_j]}, \qquad (8)$$

where both probability terms are obtained by simply counting occurrences from O. The process can be trivially extended when several traces are available.

The model above should be viewed as a general modeling technique that can be applied at different levels. Therefore, if one is interested in modeling input events irrespective of their context, the set of states—and, therefore, the chain—can be reduced to $\mathcal{E}$. The same applies to the context, i.e., states could be composed exclusively of time-location pairs.

Markov chains are often represented as a directed graph where vertices represent states and edges between them are labeled with the associated transition probability. We will call the *degree* of a state, denoted by $\mathbf{deg}(s_i)$, to the number of states reachable from s in just one transition with non-null probability:

$$\mathbf{deg}(s_i) = \#\{p_{ij} | p_{ij} > 0\}. \qquad (9)$$

The degree distribution of a chain is given by

$$\mathbf{P}(k) = P[\mathbf{deg}(s) = k]. \qquad (10)$$

2.3   App Behavior and Risk Assessment

An app interacts with the device by requesting services through a number of available system calls. These define an interface for apps that need to read/write files, send/receive data through the network, make a phone call, etc. Rather than focusing on low-level system calls, in this paper we will describe an app behavior through the sequence of *activities* it executes (see also [29]). Activities represent high-level behaviors, such as for example reading from or writing into a file, opening a network connection, sending/receiving data, etc. In some cases, there will be a one-to-one correspondence between an activity and a system call, while in others an activity may encompass a sequence of system calls executed in a given order. In what follows, we assume that:

$$\mathcal{A} = \{a_1, a_2, \ldots, a_r\} \tag{11}$$

is the set of all relevant activities observable from an app execution.

The execution flow of an app may follow different paths depending on the input events provided by the user and the context. Let $\sigma = \langle \sigma_1, \ldots, \sigma_k \rangle$ be a sequence of states as defined above. We model the behavior of an app when executed with σ as input as the sequence:

$$\beta(\sigma) = \langle \alpha_i, \ldots, \alpha \rangle, \quad \alpha_i \in \mathcal{A}, \tag{12}$$

which we will refer to as the *behavioral signature* induced by σ.

Behavioral signatures constitute dynamic execution traces generated with usage and context patterns specific to one particular user. Analysis of such traces will be instrumental in determining whether there is evidence of security and/or privacy risks for that particular user. The specific mechanism used for that analysis is beyond the scope of our current work. In general, we assume the existence of a *Risk Assessment Function* (RAF) implementing such an analysis. For example, general malware detection tools based on dynamic analysis could be a natural option here. The case of grayware is considerably more challenging, as the user's privacy preferences must be factored in to resolve whether a behavior is safe or not.

3 Targeted Testing in the Cloud

In this section, we first describe the architecture and the prototype implementation of a cloud-based testing system for targeted malware and grayware based on the models discussed in the previous section. We then provide a detailed description of various experimental results obtained in two key tasks in our system: obtaining triggering models and using them to test a cloned device.

3.1 Architecture and Prototype Implementation

A high level architectural view of our system is shown in Fig. 1. There are two differentiated major blocks: (i) the *evidence generation* subsystem, and (ii) the *behavioral modeling and risk assessment* subsystem. The first one extracts usage and context traces from the device and generates the stochastic triggering model. This process is carried out by first cloning the user device in the cloud and then injecting the triggering patterns over the clone. The second block extracts the behavioral signatures from the clone(s) and applies the RAF over the evidences collected. We next provide a detailed description of our current prototype implementation.

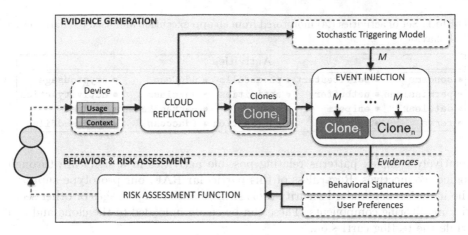

Fig. 1. System architecture and main building blocks

The experiments have been conducted using a smartphone and a virtual mobile device in the cloud, both running Android OS 2.3. In particular, a Google Nexus One is used for the physical device and an Android emulator [30] for the clones. The device is instrumented with various monitoring tools that collect user events, the context, and the device configuration and transmits them to the cloud. For this purpose, we used a combination of `logcat` and `getevent` tools from the Android Debug Bridge (ADB) [30].

Our proof-of-concept implementation builds on a number of previous works for cloud cloning smartphone platforms [16–19] and for performing behavioral analysis [15, 31]. In the cloud end, a middleware implemented in `Python` processes all inputs received, generates the associated models, and runs the simulation. We inject events and contexts into apps with a combination of a testing tool called `Monkeyrunner` [30] and the Android emulator console [30].

As for the behavioral signatures obtained in the virtual device, we have used an open source dynamic analysis tool called `Droidbox` [31] to monitor various activities that can be used to characterize app behavior and tell apart benign from suspicious behavior [2]. `Droidbox` is based on `TaintDroid` [15] and provides a variety of data about how an app is behaving. We chose 20 relevant activities to characterize app behavior (see Table 1), which include information about calls to the crypto API (`cryptousage`), I/O network and file activity (`opennet`, `sendnet`, `accessedfiles`, etc.), phone and SMS activity (`phonecalls`, `sendsms`), data exfiltration through the network (`dataleak`), and dynamic code injection (`dexclass`), among others.

Finally, we implemented a simple yet powerful RAF (*Risk Assessment Function*) for analyzing behavioral signatures. Due to space reasons, we only provide a high-level description of this mechanism. In essence, the scheme is based on a pattern-matching process driven by a user-specified set of rules that identify behaviors of interest according to his security and privacy preferences. Such rules are first-order predicates over the set of activities $\mathcal{A}$, allowing the user to specify

Table 1. Set of activities ($\mathcal{A}$) monitored from an app execution and used to characterize its behavior

Activities				
• sendsms	• servicestart	• phonecalls	• udpConn	• cryptousage
• permissions	• netbuffer	• activities	• dexclass	• activityaction
• dataleak	• enfperm	• opennet	• packageNames	• sendnet
• recvs	• recvnet	• recvsaction	• fdaccess	• accessedfiles

relatively complex patterns relating possible activities in a signature through logical connectives. Regardless of this particular RAF, our prototype supports the inclusion of standard security tools such as antivirus packages or other security monitoring components. These can be easily uploaded to the clone and run while the testing carries on.

3.2   Experiment I: The Structure of a Triggering Model

In this first experiment, we monitored all events triggered by a user executing several apps on his device during a representative amount of time. More precisely, we collected traces from the user while interacting with the OS and several apps such as Facebook, YouTube, and Google Maps. We assumed that the events collected were representative enough, as user behavior is generally very redundant. The resulting event set contained about $|S|$ =8K states, distributed over various observations traces of around $|\mathbf{O}| = 37K$ states. We then used such traces to estimate the transition matrix using Eq. (8). The obtained Markov chain turned out to have various interesting features. For example, its degree distribution follows a power-law of the form $\mathbf{P}(k) = k^{-\alpha}$ (see Fig. 2) with $\alpha = 2.28$ for $k \geq 2$. This suggests that events and contexts follow a scale-free network [32], which is not surprising. Recall that an edge between two nodes (events) indicates that the destination event occurs after the source event.

   A power-law distribution such as the one shown in Fig. 2 reveals that most events have an extremely low number of "neighbors"; i.e., once an event has happened, the most likely ones coming next reduce to about 100 out of the 8K possible. Only a small fraction of all events are highly connected, meaning that almost any other event is possible to occur after them. For instance, in our traces we found that over half of the states were only connected to just one state. In contrast, one state was found to be connected to more than 4K other states.

   These results make sense due to a simple reason: input and context events do depend quite strongly on those issued immediately before. For example, the probability of moving from one place to another nearby is much higher than to a remote place. The same applies to sequences of events, where the probability distribution of the next likely event reflects the way we interact with the app. As we will next see, this structure makes testing extremely efficient.

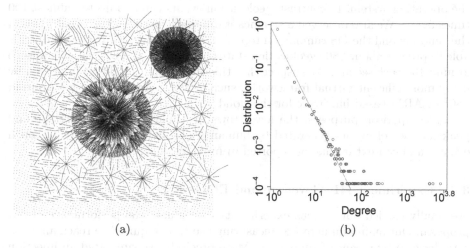

(a)   (b)

Fig. 2. (a) Markov model representing contextual and kernel input events for a user interacting with an Android platform; (b) Degree distribution, in log-log scale, of the model in (a) as defined in Section 2.2

Table 2. Event injection rates for different types of events over a virtualized Android device (top), and rates generated by real users based on profiling 67 apps [33] (bottom)

Automatic Injection		
Injected Event	**Emulator Layer**	**App Layer**
Sensor event	7407.66 events/s	1.26 events/s
Power event	361.77 events/s	19.16 events/s
Geolocation event	2810.15 events/s	111.87 events/s
SMS event	451.27 events/s	0.35 events/s
GSM call/cancel event	1726.91 events/s	0.71 events/s

Human Generated		
Event Type	**Average**	**Peak**
Usage patterns	5 events/s	10 events/s
Context patterns	10 events/s	25 events/s

3.3   Experiment II: Speed of Testing

We performed a number of experiments to measure how fast input events can be injected into an Android application sandbox. Such events include not only input events, but also a variety of context traces comprising phone calls, SMS messages, and GPS locations. We recorded and analyzed the time taken by both the sandbox and the operating system to process each injected event. Our results suggest that the time required to process injected states (input or context events) varies quite strongly depending on the type of state (see Table 2). For instance, it takes around 0.35 seconds, on average, to inject an SMS and process it trough the operating system. In contrast, geolocation events can be injected almost 100 times faster. We also observed a significant difference between the capabilities of the sandbox and the OS running on top of it. For instance, while the sandbox is able to process about 2800 geolocation states per second, the OS can only absorb around 100 each second. We suspect that this throughput might be improved by using more efficient virtual frameworks, such as for example Qemu for Android x86[2] or ARM-based hardware for the cloud[3].

For comparison purposes, the lower rows in Table 2 show the average and peak number of events generated by human users, both for usage (e.g., touch events) and context events, as reported in previous works [33].

3.4 Experiment III: Coverage and Efficiency

We finally carried out various experiments to evaluate the performance of our proposal. Our main aim here was measuring the time required to reach an accurate decision by means of simulation. More precisely, we simulated an injection system configured with randomly generated u and t patterns and with different number of states: $|S| = 100$, 1000, and 4000.

The configuration of each experiment was based on the findings discussed in previous sections, as detailed bellow. First, we generated two types of Markov model chains: (i) one random scale-free network of events using a preferential attachment mechanism as defined by *Barabási-Albert* (BA) [34], and (ii) another random network following the well-known *Erdős-Rényi* (ER) model [35]. Then, we simulated a user providing inputs to a device together with its context at a rate of 10 events per second. We chose this throughput as it is a realistic injection rate (see Table 2).

In each experiment, we generated a number of random Markov chains and calculated the cumulative transition probability covered when traversing from one state to another of the chain for the first time. Formally, let:

$$w = \langle s_{i_1}, s_{i_2}, \ldots, s_{i_n} \rangle, \qquad s_{i_j} \in S, \tag{13}$$

be a random walk over the chain, with $a_{i_j i_{j+1}} > 0 \ \forall i_j$, and let:

$$T(w) = \{(s_{i_j}, s_{i_{j+1}}) \mid s_{i_j} \in S \setminus \{s_{i_n}\}\}, \tag{14}$$

be the set of all transitions made during the random walk. We define the coverage of w as the amount of transitions seen by w, weighted by their respective probabilities and normalized to add up to one, i.e.:

$$\texttt{Coverage}(w) = \frac{1}{N} \sum_{(p,q) \in T(w)} a_{pq}. \tag{15}$$

The coverage is used to evaluate both the efficiency and the accuracy of our system. On the one hand, it can be used to measure the amount of a user's

---
[2] www.android-x86.org/
[3] http://armservers.com/

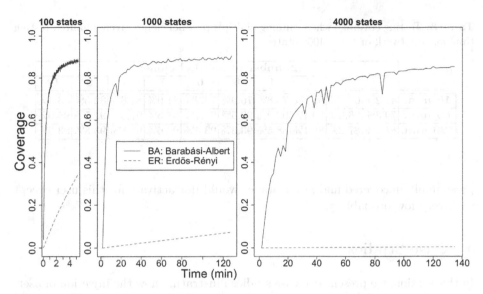

Fig. 3. Efficiency and accuracy of the decision for a Barabási-Albert and Erdős-Rényi network model

common actions triggered given a limited period of testing time. Additionally, it also shows how fast the system tests the most common actions. Results for sets of events of various sizes are shown in Fig. 3, where the curves have been averaged over 10 simulations. The results show that the coverage reached when testing networks of sizes $|S| = 100$, 1000, and 4000 states is very satisfactory. Such a good performance is related to the scale-free distribution of states through time, since this property allows to test the most common actions performed by the user very rapidly. Thus, a coverage above 80% is reached in less than two minutes for 100 states, and in approximately 1 hour for 4000 states.

It is important to emphasize that the coverage reported in Fig. 3 corresponds to one test sequence randomly drawn according to the user behavioral model. If the process is repeated or carried out in parallel over various clones, other test sequences may well explore behaviors not covered by the first one. This is illustrated in Table 3, where we show the total testing coverage as a function of the number of clones tested in parallel, each one provided with a different input sequence. Thus, two hours of testing just one clone results in a coverage slightly above 84%. However, if five clones are independently tested in parallel, the overall result is a coverage of around 93% of the total user behavior. This time-memory trade-off is a nice property, allowing to increase the coverage by just testing multiple clones simultaneously rather than by performing multiple test over the same clone.

Reaching a 100% coverage is, in general, difficult due to the stochastic nature of the models. This is not critical, as those behavioral patterns that are left unexplored correspond to actions extremely unlikely to be executed by the user. In practical terms this is certainly a risk, but one relatively unimportant as the

Table 3. Testing coverage when running multiple parallel clones given a limited testing time for a network of $|S| = 4000$ states

	Number of parallel clones									
	1	2	3	4	5	6	7	8	9	10
10 min.	42.2%	60.6%	68.8%	73.8%	76.9%	79.2%	81.9%	81.8%	82.5%	83.4%
60 min.	79.3%	86.6%	89.1%	90.2%	90.5%	91.1%	91.3%	91.5%	91.7%	95.0%
120 min.	84.3%	87.2%	88.1%	88.5%	93.3%	93.4%	93.6%	93.8%	93.8%	93.9%

presumably uncovered malware instance would not activate for this user except with very low probability.

4   Case Studies

In this section, we present two case studies illustrating how the injection of user-specific behavioral patterns can contribute to revealing malware with targeted activation mechanisms. We cover *dormant* and *anti-analysis* malware, as these scenarios constitute representative cases of targeted behaviors in current smart devices [2]. For each case, we first provide a brief description of the rationale behind the malware activation condition and then discuss the results obtained after applying the injection strategy presented in this paper. In all cases, the evaluation has been conducted by adapting an open source malware called *Androrat* (Android Remote Access Tool, or RAT) [36] and incorporating the specific triggering conditions.

4.1   Case 1: Dormant Malware/Grayware

Piggybacked malware [37] is sometimes programmed to remain dormant until a specific situation of interest presents itself [38]. This type of malware is eventually activated to sense if the user context is relevant for the malware. If so, then some other malicious actions are executed. For instance, a malware aiming at spying a very specific industrial system, such as the case of Stuxnet, will remain dormant until the malware hits the target system. Similarly, in a Bring-Your-Own-Device (BYOD) context, malware targeting a specific office building can remain dormant until the device is near a certain location.

Typically, malicious apps are activated when the BOOT_COMPLETED event is triggered regardless of the context of the infected device. A recent study on Android malware [38] suggests that the tendency is shifting towards more sophisticated activation triggers so as to better align with the malware incentives and the pursued goals. This results in a variety of more complex activation conditions, such as those shown in Table 4.

We instrumented Androrat to activate the RAT component only when the device is in a certain location. We use a mock location near the Bushehr nuclear

Table 4. Typical wake-up conditions for malware activation

Wake-up conditions	
User presence	USB connected, screen-on action, accelerator changed, etc.
Location	Location change event, near an address, leaving an area, etc.
Time	A given day and time, after a certain period of time, etc.
Hardware	Power and LED status, KEY action, LOCK event, etc.
Configuration	Apps installed, a given contact/phone number in the agenda, etc.

plant, simulating a possible behavior for a Stuxnet-like malware. Specifically, the RAT is only activated when the device is near the location: 28.82781 ° (latitude) and 50.89114 ° (longitude). Once the RAT is activated, we send the appropriate commands to exfiltrate ambient and call recordings captured through the microphone, the camera, and the camcorder.

For testing purposes, we built a symbolic model representing the abstract geographic areas of a given user working at the Bushehr plant. Fig. 4 represents the Markov Model chain for the different areas and the transitions between them. For instance, the model represents a user traveling from HOME (c_H) to WORK (c_W) with a probability of $P(c_H|c_W) = 0.7$.

Given the above model, we then injected testing traces drawn from the chain into the sandbox instrumented with Androrat. The sandbox was configured with a generic RAF aiming at identifying when operations involving personal information occur together with network activity. The results show how the malware is not activated until we start injecting mock locations. A few seconds after the first injection, the behavioral signature collected reported, as expected, both data leakage (`dataleak`) and network activity (`sendnet`).

We next defined an alternative scenario in which an app accesses the user location and sends an SMS to one of his contacts whenever he is leaving a certain region, such as for instance WORK (c_W). To this end, we implemented an app and tested it against three users with different contexts and concerns about their privacy. The first user has strict privacy policies and visits very frequently the location c_W. The second user has the same policy as the first one but has never visited such a location. Finally, the last user visits c_W as well but has a more flexible privacy policy. For the sake of simplicity, we used the same triggering model described in the previous example for users one and three (see Fig. 4), while the second user has a different Markov chain. Results show that:

– For the first user, the behavioral signature reported data leakage activity (`dataleak`) as well as SMS activity (`sendsms`). As both are in conflict with this user's privacy preferences, this is marked as undesirable behavior.
– In the case of the second user, the model injects locations other than those triggering the grayware component. Consequently, no significant behavioral signature is produced.

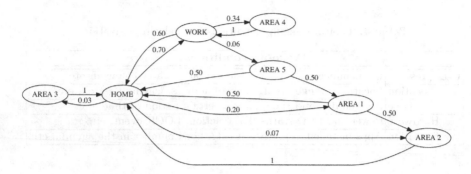

Fig. 4. Markov chain for the location

Table 5. Default hardware configuration for Android emulator

HW feature	Default value
IMEI	000000000000000
IMSI	012345678912345
SIM	012345678912345
Phone Number	1-555-521-PORT (5554)
Model Number	sdk
Network	Android
Battery Status	AC on Charging 50%
IP Address	10.0.2.X

- Finally, the events injected for the third user do trigger the grayware component, resulting in data leakage and SMS activity. However, as these are not in conflict with his privacy preferences, no alert is issued.

This example reinforces the view that not only malware activation can be user specific, but that the consequences of such a malware may also be perceived very differently by each user.

4.2   Case 2: Anti-analysis Malware

Malware analysis is typically performed in a virtual sandbox rather than in a physical device due to economic and efficiency factors [2]. These sandboxes often have a particular hardware configuration that can be leveraged by malware instances to detect that they are being analyzed and deploy evasion countermeasures [11], for example by simply not executing the malicious payload if the environment matches a particular configuration. Sandboxes for smartphone platforms have such artifacts. For instance, the IMEI, the phone number, or the IP address are generally configured by default. Furthermore, other hardware features such as the battery level are typically emulated and kept indefinitely at the same status: e.g., AC on and Charging 50%. Table 5 summarizes some of these features in most Android emulators along with their default value.

Table 6. Different hardware states for power status of the device

status	health	present	AC	capacity
unknown charging discharging not-charging full	unknown good overheat dead overvoltage failure	false true	off on	0 – 100%

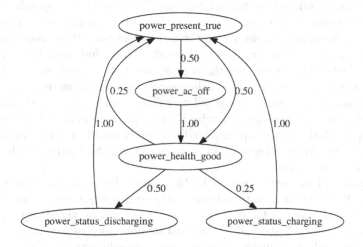

Fig. 5. Markov chain for the battery status

Hardware features such as those described above can be set prior to launching the sandbox. This will prevent basic fingerprinting analysis, for example by setting random values for each execution. However, smarter malware instances might implement more sophisticated approaches, such as waiting for a triggering condition based on a combination of hardware changes. Motivated by this, we modified Androrat to activate the RAT component only after AC is off and the battery status is different from 50%. Once the RAT is activated, we send appropriate commands to exfiltrate some personal information from the device such as SMSs, call history, etc.

In principle, there are as many triggering conditions as combinations of possible hardware events. Although our framework support injection of all possible hardware events via the Android emulator console [30], for simplicity we restricted our experimentation to the subset of power-related events described in Table 6.

Based on the different power states, we built a model of the battery usage extracted from an actual device when used by a real user. The resulting model is shown in Fig. 5. We then tested Androrat against this model generated using the same RAF configuration used in previous cases. The results show that the behavioral signature not only reported `dataleak` and `sendnet`, but also file activity (`accessedfiles`), thus confirming that the malware activated as it failed to recognize its presence in a sandbox.

5   Conclusions

The problem of detecting targeted malware via behavioral analysis requires the ability to reproduce an appropriate set of conditions that will trigger the malicious behavior. Determining those triggering conditions by exhaustively searching through all possible states is a hard problem. In this paper, we have proposed a novel system for mining the behavior of apps in different user-specific contexts and usage scenarios. One of our system's main aims is providing the testing environment (replicas in the cloud) with the same conditions than those the actual device is exposed to. Our experimental results show that modeling such conditions as Markov chains reduces the complexity of the search space while still offering an effective representation of the usage and context patterns. In essence, our system is able to trigger a targeted malware as long as: (i) it also activates in the device; and (ii) the user behavior is appropriately modeled. However, we also anticipate that a more sophisticated adversary could exploit some features of our model to evade detection. This weakness will be further explored and addressed in future work.

Our approach represents a robust building block for thwarting targeted malware, as it allows the analyst to automatically generate patterns of input events to stimulate apps. As the focus of this paper has been on the design of such a component, we have relied on ad hoc replication and risk assessment components to discuss the quality of our proposal. We are currently extending our system to support: (a) a replication system to automatically generate and test clones of the device under inspection; and (b) a general framework to specify risk assessment functions and analyze behavioral signatures obtained in each clone. Finally, in this paper we have not discussed the potential privacy implications associated with obtaining user behavioral models. Even if such profiles are just used for testing purposes, they do contain sensitive information and must be handled with caution. This and other related privacy aspects of targeted testing will be tackled in future work.

Acknowledgment. We are very grateful to the anonymous reviewers for constructive feedback and insightful suggestions that helped to improve the quality of the original manuscript.

The work of G. Suarez-Tangil, J.E. Tapiador, and P. Peris-Lopez was supported by the MINECO grant TIN2013-46469-R (SPINY: Security and Privacy in the Internet of You). Mauro Conti is supported by a Marie Curie Fellowship funded by the European Commission under the agreement No. PCIG11-GA-2012-321980. This work is also partially supported by the TENACE PRIN Project 20103P34XC funded by the Italian MIUR, and by the Project "Tackling Mobile Malware with Innovative Machine Learning Techniques" funded by the University of Padua.

References

1. Juniper: 2013 mobile threats report. Technical report, Juniper Networks (2013)
2. Suarez-Tangil, G., Tapiador, J.E., Peris, P., Ribagorda, A.: Evolution, detection and analysis of malware for smart devices. IEEE Communications Surveys & Tutorials PP(99), 1–27 (2013)
3. Felt, A.P., Finifter, M., Chin, E., Hanna, S., Wagner, D.: A survey of mobile malware in the wild. In: Proceedings of the 1st ACM Workshop on Security and Privacy in Smartphones and Mobile Devices, SPSM 2011, pp. 3–14. ACM, New York (2011)
4. Zawoad, S., Hasan, R., Haque, M.: Poster: Stuxmob: A situational-aware malware for targeted attack on smart mobile devices (2013)
5. Hasan, R., Saxena, N., Haleviz, T., Zawoad, S., Rinehart, D.: Sensing-enabled channels for hard-to-detect command and control of mobile devices. In: Proceedings of the 8th ACM SIGSAC Symposium on Information, Computer and Communications Security, pp. 469–480. ACM (2013)
6. Raiu, C., Emm, D.: Kaspersky security bulletin. Technical report, Kaspersky (2013), http://media.kaspersky.com/pdf/KSB_2013_EN.pdf
7. Langner, R.: Stuxnet: Dissecting a cyberwarfare weapon. IEEE Security & Privacy 9(3), 49–51 (2011)
8. Corporation, S.: Internet security threat report. Technical report, Symantex (2013), http://www.symantec.com/content/en/us/enterprise/other_resources/b-istr_main_report_v18_2012_21291018.en-us.pdf
9. Kalige, E., Burkey, D.: A case study of eurograbber: How 36 million euros was stolen via malware. Technical report, Versafe (December 2012)
10. Marquis-Boire, M., Marczak, B., Guarnieri, C., Scott-Railton, J.: You only click twice: Finfishers global proliferation. Research Brief (March 2013), https://citizenlab.org/wp-content/uploads/2013/07/15-2013-youonlyclicktwice.pdf
11. Rogers, M.: Dendroid malware can take over your camera, record audio, and sneak into google play (March 2014), https://blog.lookout.com/blog/2014/03/06/dendroid/
12. Capilla, R., Ortiz, O., Hinchey, M.: Context variability for context-aware systems. Computer 47(2), 85–87 (2014)
13. Gianazza, A., Maggi, F., Fattori, A., Cavallaro, L., Zanero, S.: Puppetdroid: A user-centric ui exerciser for automatic dynamic analysis of similar android applications. arXiv preprint arXiv:1402.4826 (2014)
14. Chakradeo, S., Reaves, B., Traynor, P., Enck, W.: Mast: Triage for market-scale mobile malware analysis. In: Proceedings of the Sixth ACM Conference on Security and Privacy in Wireless and Mobile Networks, WiSec 2013, pp. 13–24. ACM, New York (2013)
15. Enck, W., Gilbert, P., Chun, B., Cox, L., Jung, J., McDaniel, P., Sheth, A.: Taintdroid: an information-flow tracking system for realtime privacy monitoring on smartphones. In: Proceedings of the 9th USENIX Conference on Operating Systems Design and Implementation, pp. 1–6. USENIX Association (2010)
16. Portokalidis, G., Homburg, P., Anagnostakis, K., Bos, H.: Paranoid android: versatile protection for smartphones. In: Proceedings of the 26th Annual Computer Security Applications Conference, pp. 347–356 (2010)
17. Chun, B.G., Ihm, S., Maniatis, P., Naik, M., Patti, A.: Clonecloud: elastic execution between mobile device and cloud. In: Proceedings of the Sixth Conference on Computer Systems, pp. 301–314 (2011)

18. Kosta, S., Aucinas, A., Hui, P., Mortier, R., Zhang, X.: Thinkair: Dynamic resource allocation and parallel execution in the cloud for mobile code offloading. In: 2012 Proceedings IEEE INFOCOM, pp. 945–953. IEEE (2012)

19. Zonouz, S., Houmansadr, A., Berthier, R., Borisov, N., Sanders, W.: Secloud: A cloud-based comprehensive and lightweight security solution for smartphones. Computers & Security (2013)

20. Fleck, D., Tokhtabayev, A., Alarif, A., Stavrou, A., Nykodym, T.: Pytrigger: A system to trigger & extract user-activated malware behavior. In: 2013 Eighth International Conference on Availability, Reliability and Security (ARES), pp. 92–101. IEEE (2013)

21. Zheng, C., Zhu, S., Dai, S., Gu, G., Gong, X., Han, X., Zou, W.: Smartdroid: an automatic system for revealing UI-based trigger conditions in Android applications. In: Proceedings of the Second ACM Workshop on Security and Privacy in Smartphones and Mobile Devices, SPSM 2012, pp. 93–104. ACM, New York (2012)

22. Rastogi, V., Chen, Y., Enck, W.: Appsplayground: automatic security analysis of smartphone applications. In: Proceedings of the Third ACM Conference on Data and Application Security and Privacy, CODASPY 2013, pp. 209–220. ACM, New York (2013)

23. Jensen, C.S., Prasad, M.R., Møller, A.: Automated testing with targeted event sequence generation. In: Proceedings of the 2013 International Symposium on Software Testing and Analysis, pp. 67–77. ACM (2013)

24. Liang, C.J.M., Lane, N.D., Brouwers, N., Zhang, L., Karlsson, B., Liu, H., Liu, Y., Tang, J., Shan, X., Chandra, R., et al.: Context virtualizer: A cloud service for automated large-scale mobile app testing under real-world conditions

25. Machiry, A., Tahiliani, R., Naik, M.: Dynodroid: An input generation system for android apps. In: Proceedings of the 2013 9th Joint Meeting on Foundations of Software Engineering, ESEC/FSE 2013, pp. 224–234. ACM, New York (2013)

26. Reina, A., Fattori, A., Cavallaro, L.: A system call-centric analysis and stimulation technique to automatically reconstruct android malware behaviors. In: Proceedings of the 6th European Workshop on System Security (EUROSEC), Prague, Czech Republic (April 2013)

27. Conti, M., Crispo, B., Fernandes, E., Zhauniarovich, Y.: Crepe: A system for enforcing fine-grained context-related policies on android. IEEE Transactions on Information Forensics and Security 7(5), 1426–1438 (2012)

28. Norris, J.R.: Markov chains. Number 2008. Cambridge University Press (1998)

29. Suarez-Tangil, G., Lobardi, F., Tapiador, J.E., Pietro, R.D.: Thwarting obfuscated malware via differential fault analysis. IEEE Computer (June 2014)

30. Android: Android developers (visited December 2013), http://developer.android.com/

31. Lantz, P.: Android application sandbox (visited December 2013), https://code.google.com/p/droidbox/

32. Clauset, A., Shalizi, C.R., Newman, M.E.: Power-law distributions in empirical data. SIAM Review 51(4), 661–703 (2009)

33. Wei, X., Gomez, L., Neamtiu, I., Faloutsos, M.: Profiledroid: Multi-layer profiling of android applications. In: Proceedings of the 18th Annual International Conference on Mobile Computing and Networking, Mobicom 2012, pp. 137–148. ACM, New York (2012)

34. Albert, R., Barabási, A.L.: Statistical mechanics of complex networks. Reviews of Modern Physics 74(1), 47 (2002)

35. Erdős, P., Rényi, A.: On the evolution of random graphs. Magyar Tud. Akad. Mat. Kutató Int. Közl 5, 17–61 (1960)
36. Bertrand, A., David, R., Akimov, A., Junk, P.: Remote administration tool for android devices (visited December 2013), https://github.com/DesignativeDave/androrat
37. Zhou, W., Zhou, Y., Grace, M., Jiang, X., Zou, S.: Fast, scalable detection of piggybacked mobile applications. In: Proceedings of the Third ACM Conference on Data and Application Security and Privacy, pp. 185–196. ACM (2013)
38. Zhou, Y., Jiang, X.: Dissecting android malware: Characterization and evolution. In: Proceedings of the 33rd IEEE Symposium on Security and Privacy (Oakland 2012) (May 2012)

TrustDump: Reliable Memory Acquisition on Smartphones

He Sun[1,2,3,4], Kun Sun[4], Yuewu Wang[1,2,*], Jiwu Jing[1,2], and Sushil Jajodia[4]

[1] State Key Laboratory of Information Security, Institute of Information Engineering, CAS, Beijing, P.R. China
[2] Data Assurance and Communication Security Research Center, CAS, Beijing, P.R. China
[3] University of Chinese Academy of Sciences, Beijing, P.R. China
[4] George Mason University, Fairfax, VA, USA

Abstract. With the wide usage of smartphones in our daily life, new malware is emerging to compromise the mobile OS and steal the sensitive data from the mobile applications. Anti-malware tools should be continuously updated via static and dynamic malware analysis to detect and prevent the newest malware. Dynamic malware analysis depends on a reliable memory acquisition of the OS and the applications running on the smartphones. In this paper, we develop a TrustZone-based memory acquisition mechanism called *TrustDump* that is capable of reliably obtaining the RAM memory and CPU registers of the mobile OS even if the OS has crashed or has been compromised. The mobile OS is running in the TrustZone's normal domain, and the memory acquisition tool is running in the TrustZone's secure domain, which has the access privilege to the memory in the normal domain. Instead of using a hypervisor to ensure an isolation between the OS and the memory acquisition tool, we rely on ARM TrustZone to achieve a hardware-assisted isolation with a small trusted computing base (TCB) of about 450 lines of code. We build a TrustDump prototype on Freescale i.MX53 QSB.

Keywords: TrustZone, Non-Maskable Interrupt, Memory Acquisition.

1 Introduction

Smartphones have been widely used to perform both personal and business transactions and process sensitive data with various OEM or third-party mobile applications. However, due to the large code size and complexity of the mobile OS kernel, a malicious code can exploit known and unknown kernel vulnerabilities to compromise the mobile OS and steal sensitive data from the system. It is critical to perform malware analysis on the newest emerging malware and immediately update anti-malware tools on the smartphones

There are two generic types of dynamic malware analysis methods: *in-the-box* approach and *out-of-the-box* approach. For the in-the-box approach, all the anti-malware and debugging tools are installed in the same OS as the malware. This approach is efficient since it can use abundant OS context information and directly call the kernel functions to study malware's behaviors. However, it is vulnerable to armored malware such as rootkits that modify kernel structures and functions to defeat the analysis. For

---

* Corresponding author.

M. Kutyłowski and J. Vaidya (Eds.): ESORICS 2014, Part I, LNCS 8712, pp. 202–218, 2014.

the out-of-the-box approach, the malware analysis tools are installed in an isolated execution environment, which is securely separated from the targeted OS environment. For instance, Virtual Machine Introspection (VMI) [1–6] runs a suspicious OS in one VM and the analysis tools in another VM. This method needs to reconstruct the internal structures of OS kernel to fill the semantic gaps. Recently, Yan et al. [7] extend the out-of-the-box malware analysis approach to Android smartphones using a customized QEMU emulator.

All VMI based malware analysis solutions rely on a trusted hypervisor, which should not easily crash or be compromised. However, due to the large size of the hypervisor, it may contain a number of bugs and vulnerabilities that may be exploited by malware to compromise the hypervisor and then the malware analysis VM. VT-x/SVM [8–10] and System Management Mode (SMM) [11–14] on x86 architecture can be used to create an isolated instruction level execution environment for out-of-the-box malware analysis; however, they are not available on mobile processors. Fortunately, the ARM processors, which have been widely used on smartphones, provide a system level isolation solution with a hardware security support called *TrustZone* [15, 16], which divides the mobile platform into two isolated execution environments, *normal domain* and *secure domain*. The OS running in the normal domain is usually called *Rich OS*, and the one running in the secure domain is called *Secure OS*.

In this paper, we develop a TrustZone-based reliable memory acquisition mechanism called *TrustDump*, which is capable of obtaining the RAM memory and CPU registers of the Rich OS even if the Rich OS has crashed or has been compromised. A memory acquisition module called *TrustDumper* is installed in the secure domain to perform memory dump and malware analysis of the Rich OS. TrustZone can ensure the Trust-Dumper is securely isolated from the Rich OS, so that a compromised Rich OS cannot compromise the memory acquisition module.

When the Rich OS has crashed or some suspicious behaviors have been detected in the Rich OS, TrustDump ensures a reliable system switch from the normal domain to the secure domain by pressing a hardware button on the smartphone to trigger a non-maskable interrupt (NMI) to the ARM processor. The NMI guarantees that a malicious Rich OS cannot launch attacks to block or intercept the switching process. Since the secure domain has the access privilege to the memory and registers in the normal domain, TrustDumper can freely access the physical RAM memory and the CPU states of the Rich OS. When the system switches into the secure domain, the Rich OS is frozen, so the malware has no time to clean its attacking traces. Besides checking the OS kernel integrity and perform online malware analysis, TrustDumper can send the memory dump and CPU states to a remote machine for further analysis. A hash value of the memory dump is also calculated and sent to verify a correct data transmission. The remote machine can use various powerful memory forensics tools to uncover the malicious behaviors recorded in the memory dump.

Instead of using a hypervisor to ensure an isolation between the OS and the memory acquisition tool, we rely on ARM TrustZone to achieve a hardware-assisted isolation with a small trusted computing base (TCB) of about 450 lines of code. Since Trust-Dumper is self-contained, a full-featured OS is not required to be installed in the secure domain. Moreover, TrustDump is OS agnostic and we do not need any changes to the

Rich OS, which satisfies the smartphone forensic principle of extracting the digital evidence without altering the data contents. We build a TrustDump prototype on Freescale i.MX53 QSB.

In summary, we make the following contributions in this paper.

- We design a hardware-assisted memory acquisition mechanism named TrustDump to reliably acquire the RAM memory and CPU registers of the OS on smartphones, even if the OS has crashed or has been compromised.
- The trusted computing base (TCB) of TrustDump is small, only consisting of a small memory acquisition module in the secure domain. We do not need to install a hypervisor or root the OS in the normal domain.
- We implement a TrustDump prototype on Freescale i.MX53 QSB. A non-maskable interrupt (NMI) is constructed for ensuring a reliable switching from the normal domain to the secure domain in 1.7 us.

The remainder of the paper is organized as follows. Section 2 introduces background knowledge. Section 3 describes the threat model and assumptions. We present the framework in Section 4. A prototype implementation is detailed in Section 5. Section 6 discusses the experimental results. We describe related works in Section 7 and conclude the paper in Section 8.

2   Background

2.1   TrustZone Overview

TrustZone [15, 16] is a system-wide approach to provide hardware-level isolation on ARM platforms. It's supported by a wide range of processors including Cortex-A8 [17], Cortex-A9 [18] and Cortex-A15 [19]. It creates two isolated execution domains: *secure domain* and *normal domain*. The secure domain has a higher access privilege than the normal domain, so it can access the resources of the normal domain such as memory, CPU registers and peripherals, but not vice versa. There's an *NS* bit in the CPU processor to control and indicate the state of the CPU - 0 means the secure state and 1 means the normal state. There's an additional CPU mode, *monitor mode*, which only runs in the secure domain regardless of the value of the *NS* bit. The monitor mode serves as a gatekeeper between the normal domain and the secure domain. If the normal domain requests to switch to the secure domain, the CPU must first enter the monitor mode. The system bus also contains a bit to indicate the state of the bus transaction. Thus, normal peripherals can only perform normal transactions, but not the secure transactions.

2.2   TrustZone Aware Interrupt Controller (TZIC)

The TZIC is a TrustZone enabled interrupt controller, which allows complete and independent control over every interrupt connected to the controller. It receives interrupts from peripheral devices and routes them to the ARM processor. The TZIC provides secure and non-secure transaction access to those interrupts, restricting non-secure read-/write transactions to only interrupts configured as non-secure and allowing secure transactions to all interrupts regardless of security configurations. By default, the TZIC uses Fast Interrupt FIQ as secure interrupt and uses Regular Interrupt IRQ as non-secure interrupt. There are three exception vector tables associated with the normal domain, the secure domain, and the monitor mode, respectively.

2.3 General Purpose Input/Output (GPIO)

The GPIO provides general-purpose pins that can be configured as either input or output. It can be connected to the physical buttons, LED lights, and other signals through an I/O multiplexer. The signal can be either 0 or 1, and each pin of GPIO contributes a bit in the GPIO block. The GPIO can be used to trigger interrupts to the TZIC; however, if the source is masked off in the GPIO, the corresponding interrupt request cannot be forwarded.

3 Threat Model and Assumptions

On a TrustZone-enabled ARM platform, when the Rich OS crashes due to system failure, the Rich OS may not be able to send a secure interrupt to switch the system into the secure domain. When the Rich OS has been compromised, an armored malware can intercept the switch request and fake a memory acquisition process with a "Man in the Middle" attack. It is critical to ensure that TrustDump is securely activated to perform reliable memory dump. Since a malicious Rich OS may target at compromising the memory acquisition module to defeat the memory acquisition process, we must protect the integrity of the TrustDump.

We assume the attacker has no physical access to the smartphone. The ROM code is secure and cannot be flashed. The smartphone has the TrustZone hardware support, which is used to protect the memory acquisition module in the secure domain.

4 TrustDump Framework

Figure 1 shows the TrustDump framework using ARM TrustZone hardware security support. The Rich OS running in the normal domain is the target for memory acquisition, while a self-contained software module called TrustDumper in the secure domain is responsible for data acquisition, data analysis, and data transmission of the Rich OS's memory and CPU registers. After a reliable switching from the normal domain to the secure domain, a data acquisition module is responsible for reading the RAM memory and CPU registers of the Rich OS without any support from the Rich OS. TrustDump is capable of performing online analysis such as OS integrity checking and Rootkit detection after filling the semantics gap. Also, the acquired memory and CPU registers can be transmitted to a remote computer for logging and further analysis.

4.1 TrustDumper Deployment

When there is only one OS running on the ARM platform, it is usually running in the secure domain. In our system, since the Rich OS is running in the normal domain, we

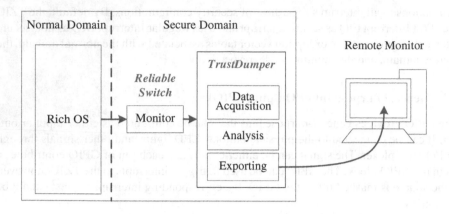

Fig. 1. The System Framework of TrustDump

need to port the Rich OS to the normal domain and then install the TrustDumper in the secure domain. The work of porting Rich OS to the normal domain seems simple, but the source code customized to run in the secure domain cannot be directly executed in the normal domain. Since there is no open source Linux kernel available for running in the normal domain on real platform, we have to port Android OS from the secure domain to the normal domain by ourselves. We allocate a sealed memory region for the secure domain to run the TrustDumper. TrustZone guarantees that the normal domain cannot access the sealed memory. Since TrustDumper is self-contained, we do not need to install a full-featured OS in the secure domain, which dramatically reduces the TCB of the system.

4.2 Reliable Switching

A reliable switching into the secure domain is the prerequisite for a reliable memory acquisition. We must ensure the switching will happen per the user's requests even if the Rich OS is compromised or simply crashes. First, the system can be safely switched into the secure domain when the Rich OS crashes. In other words, we cannot rely on the Rich OS to initiate the switching process even if the Rich OS is secure and trusted. Second, our system should prevent a malicious Rich OS from launching Denial of Service attacks to block or intercept the switching request.

TrustZone provides two ways to enter the secure domain from the normal domain: *SMC* instruction and *Secure Interrupt*. The SMC instruction is a privileged instruction that can only be invoked in the Rich OS's kernel mode. However, when the Rich OS is malicious, it can block or intercept the secure monitor call that uses the SMC instruction. Moreover, when the Rich OS crashes, the SMC instruction may not be called after the crash happens. Alternatively, secure interrupts of TrustZone can be called to switch from the normal domain to the secure domain. TrustZone uses the fast interrupt FIQ as the secure interrupt and uses the normal IRQ interrupt as the normal interrupt.

Non-maskable interrupt (NMI) has been widely used and deployed on mobile platforms [20, 21], which can trigger one NMI by pressing a button or a combination of several buttons. Since the Rich OS cannot block or intercept NMI, we can use one NMI to enforce the system switching. However, for mobile platforms that do not have dedicated NMI (e.g., Freescale i.MX53 QSB [22]), we solve this problem by configuring one secure interrupt as the NMI.

4.3   Data Acquisition and Transmission

The software module in the secure domain has access privileges to the entire physical memory of the normal domain. Moreover, it can access all the banked CPU registers, which are critical to fill the semantic gaps for malware analysis. When the system enters the secure domain, the Rich OS in the normal domain is frozen.

Our system supports both online malware detection and offline malware analysis. For online malware detection, since the analysis module runs outside the Rich OS, it has to fill the semantic gaps. Based on the knowledge of the kernel data structures, the analysis module can reconstruct the context of the Rich OS and then perform malware analysis tasks in the secure domain, such as verifying the integrity of the Rich OS and detecting rootkits. For offline analysis, since we need to transmit a large amount of acquired RAM memory (e.g., 1GB in Freescale i.MX53 QSB) to a remote computer, DMA is used to transfer data from RAM memory to communication peripherals such as a serial port or a network card. A hash value of the acquired memory is also transmitted to verify the data transmission process. Since the DMA and the peripherals may be used by the Rich OS when the switching happens, their states should be saved and restored afterward.

4.4   System Security

With the NMI triggered by a physical button, TrustDump can safely switch the system from the normal domain to the secure domain no matter what state the Rich OS is staying. Thus, a malicious Rich OS cannot launch Denial of Service attacks to block or intercept the switching. After the NMI being triggered, TrustDump will freeze the Rich OS, so the malware in the Rich OS has no chance to clean its traces.

The TrustDumper has the privilege to access all the memory and CPU registers of the Rich OS, so it may check the integrity of the Rich OS and detect various malware such as rootkits in the Rich OS. Since the TrustDumper in the secure domain is securely isolated from the Rich OS by TrustZone, a compromised Rich OS cannot compromise the memory acquisition modules.

5   Implementation

We implement a prototype using Freescale *i.MX53 QSB*, a TrustZone-enabled mobile System on Chip (SoC) [22]. i.MX53 QSB has an ARM Cortex-A8 1 GHz application processor with 1 GB DDR3 RAM memory and a 4GB MicroSD card. We deploy Android 2.3.4 in the normal domain. The development board is connected through the serial port to a Thinkpad-T430 laptop that runs Ubuntu 12.04 LTS. Our TrustDump prototype contains only 450 lines of code.

5.1   Deployment of TrustDump

Since we cannot find any open source OS working in the normal domain, we have to port an Android OS from the secure domain to the normal domain based on the Board Support Package (BSP) published by Adeneo Embedded [23]. Next, we deploy the TrustDumper in the secure domain.

The OS code running in the secure domain cannot execute in the normal domain without proper modification. Since the normal domain has a lower privilege than the secure domain, there are some peripherals that cannot be accessed from the normal domain. For instance, the Deep Sleep Mode Interrupt Holdoff Register (DSMINT) can only be accessed in the secure domain. However, the Rich OS needs DSMINT to hold off the interrupts before entering the low power mode. To run Android in the normal domain, we develop a pair of secure I/O functions, *secure_write* and *secure_read*, to enable the normal domain to access the peripherals in the secure domain.

The function definitions are shown in Listing 1. *secure_write* writes 32-bit data to the physical address pa. Similarly, *secure_read* reads from the physical address pa and returns the result. Each peripheral on the i.MX53 QSB has certain configuration registers, which are usually accessed as physical addresses on the board. A *Whitelist* is maintained in the secure domain to store all the registers that the normal domain can access through these two secure I/O functions.

Listing 1. Definition of *secure_write* and *secure_read*

```
void secure_write(unsigned int data, unsigned int pa);
unsigned int secure_read(unsigned int pa);
```

5.2   Reliable Switching

To ensure the reliable switching, we reserve a secure interrupt (FIQ) of TrustZone to serve as the non-maskable interrupt (NMI). Figure 2 shows the four steps of the switching process, which involves three components, namely, peripheral device, TZIC, and the ARM processor. First, a peripheral device as the source of the interrupt makes the interrupt request. Second, the interrupt request will be sent to the TZIC. Third, based on the type of the interrupt (FIQ or IRQ), the TZIC asserts the corresponding exception to the ARM processor. To trigger a reliable switching, the interrupt request must be an FIQ. Finally, after receiving an FIQ, the ARM processor switches to the secure domain according to the setting of the Secure Configuration Register (SCR) and the Current Program Status Register (CPSR).

Note all the three components are critical to the reliable switching. The compromise of any of the three components will result in an unreliable switching. If the source of the interrupt can be masked by the Rich OS or the Rich OS just blocks all the FIQs to the ARM processor, then the switching to the secure domain will be blocked. To prevent those attacks, we construct an NMI using GPIO-2 interrupt. We first set the GPIO-2 interrupt as a secure interrupt in TZIC. Then we use the peripheral access privilege control in Central Security Unit (CSU) to isolate the peripheral from the normal domain. It guarantees the normal domain cannot configure the peripheral. Moreover, through configuring the registers of ARM processor, we set the FIQ requests to be handled in the secure domain.

To minimize the impacts on the access of the Rich OS to other peripherals that share the same access privilege with GPIO-2, we propose a method to enable *Fine-grained Access Control*. Also, to minimize the impacts on the functionalities of other peripherals, we propose a method to enable *Fine-grained Interrupt Control*. It can differentiate the interrupts that share the same interrupt number and distribute them to dedicated handlers in different domains.

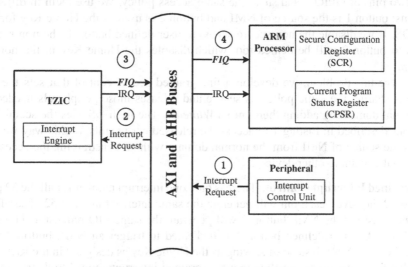

Fig. 2. The Control Flow of Reliable Switching

Non-maskable GPIO-2 Secure Interrupt. In our prototype, we use the user-defined button 1 on the board to trigger reliable switching to the secure domain. There are seven GPIOs from GPIO-1 to GPIO-7 on our board. The user-defined button 1 is attached to the fifteenth pin of the second GPIO: GPIO-2.

First, the interrupt type of GPIO-2 is set as *secure* in Interrupt Security Registers (TZIC_INTSEC). This prevents the normal domain from accessing the GPIO-2 interrupt configuration in the TZIC. Second, we set the F bit in CPSR to 0 to enable FIQ exception. We also set the FW bit in SCR to 0 to ensure the FIQ enable (F) bit in CPSR cannot be modified by the normal domain. After the configuration of these two bits, the normal domain cannot block the FIQ request to the ARM processor. Third, we set the FIQ bit in SCR to 1 to enforce the ARM processor to branch to the monitor mode on an FIQ exception. This step ensures that the FIQ request to secure domain cannot be intercepted or blocked by the normal domain. Finally, we disable the non-secure access to GPIO-2 in CSU so that the interrupt unit of GPIO-2 cannot be configured by the normal domain.

When the ARM processor branches to the monitor mode in the secure domain after the secure interrupt happens, the CPU executes the instruction located in the vector table of the monitor mode at the offset of 0x1C. After the memory acquisition finishes, the CPU executes the instruction: subs pc, lr, #4 to return to the normal domain.

Fine-Grained Access Control. The secure domain and the normal domain have different access control policies over the peripherals. The secure domain can access the peripherals belonging to the normal domain, but not vice versa. CSU determines which domain a peripheral belongs to, so we can set access control policies of peripherals by setting the corresponding registers in CSU. We configure GPIO-2 as secure peripheral to prevent the normal domain from accessing it.

However, this simple access control management forces several peripherals to share the same access control policy. For instance, in our prototype, user-defined button 1 and 2 are two pins of GPIO-2 and share the same access policy. We use them in different domains: button 1 is the source of NMI and button 2 is used as the Home Key for the Rich OS. If we disable the non-secure access to user-defined button 1, the non-secure access to button 2 will be denied too, which disables the Home Key in the normal domain.

To solve this problem, we develop a fine-grained access control that sets the peripherals sharing the same policy as secure and releases those peripherals needed in the normal domain by adding them into a *Whitelist*. The Rich OS uses the secure I/O functions described in Listing 1 to access the released peripherals. In this way we can protect the source of NMI from the normal domain without constraining the access of the normal domain to other devices.

Fine-grained Interrupt Control. There is only one interrupt number for all the 32 pins of GPIO-2; however, each pin will generate the same interrupt number 52. Therefore, after we construct the NMI, button 2 will generate the same FIQ request as button 1 does. When the user-defined button 1 is dedicated to trigger an NMI, button 2 will trigger the same NMI, instead of serving as the Home Key as designed in the Rich OS. We solve this problem by developing a fine-grained interrupt control to distribute the interrupts generated by these two buttons to different handlers.

No matter which button is pressed, CPU goes into the secure domain first. Because the functions of the Rich OS cannot be called in the secure domain, the request of button 2 will be forwarded to the normal domain to call the functions of the Rich OS instead of being processed locally as button 1 does. The FIQ exception handler of the Rich OS receives the request and calls the corresponding operation codes in the Rich OS. The entry of FIQ exception is at a static address 0xFFFF01C. The FIQ mode is not used by the Rich OS, so we can freely use the FIQ exception handlers.

The program flow of hardware interrupts in TrustDump is depicted in Figure 3. The IRQ exception asserted by non-secure interrupt is handled in the Rich OS. The IRQ exception handler gets the number of the pending interrupt from TZIC and gives it to the operation codes.

Upon FIQ request asserted by a secure interrupt, the system will switch to the FIQ exception entry of the secure domain according to the configuration of the TZIC. The FIQ exception handler of the secure domain figures out the source of interrupt through the interrupt control unit of GPIO-2. If the interrupt is an NMI, the handler clears the interrupt status in the TZIC to prevent re-entry. Next, it goes into TrustDumper to perform memory acquisition and analysis. At last, the system returns to the Rich OS.

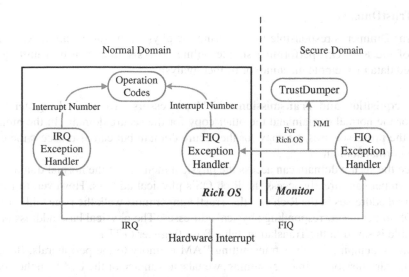

Fig. 3. Program Flow of Interrupt

If the source of the FIQ exception is for the Rich OS, the handler masks the interrupt by setting the interrupt mask register (IMR) in GPIO-2. It stops the interrupt request to TZIC and thus clears the interrupt status in TZIC to prevent re-entry after entering the Rich OS. Besides, masking the interrupt in the handler keeps the interrupt status in the interrupt control unit of GPIO-2, which is used to distinguish different pins of GPIO-2 by the Rich OS. Since the Rich OS can access the interrupt control unit of GPIO-2 to determine which pin generates the interrupt, it can locate the source after receiving an interrupt number 52.

Because the secure domain will not be re-entered, the context of the normal domain stored in the secure domain must be restored before the system jumps to the FIQ handler of the Rich OS. The handler is entered by changing CPU mode to FIQ mode and jumping to the entry of FIQ exception in the normal domain.

In case of return, the FIQ exception handler saves the CPU context first. Then it calls the operation codes in the Rich OS with the interrupt number 52. The operation codes find the source of the interrupt and take the corresponding actions according to the interrupt number. In our prototype, the action function is mx3_gpio_irq_handler, which further checks which pin of GPIO generates the interrupt.

As we have masked off the source bit, the function ignores the interrupt and returns directly without doing anything due to failure to pass the mask status judgment.

We enforce the function to bypass the mask status judgment when button 2 is triggered by or-ing the corresponding bit with 1 in the judgment statement. With the mask status judgment passed, the action of the user-defined button 2 is taken in the normal domain. After the codes finish running, system returns to the handler. The handler then recovers the stored context and starts exception return by executing the instruction: subs pc, lr, #4.

5.3   TrustDumper

The TrustDumper is responsible for acquiring the physical memory and the CPU registers of the Rich OS, performing simple online analysis, and then transmitting the acquired data to a remote machine for further analysis.

Data Acquisition and Transmission. ARM processors have banked registers: one copy for the normal domain and the other copy for the secure domain. In the monitor mode, the processor uses the copy for the secure domain but can also access the copy for the normal domain.

Since the secure domain can access the physical memory of the normal domain, the TrustDumper can directly access the Rich OS's physical address. However, to access the virtual addresses in the Rich OS, the TrustDumper must walk the page tables of the Rich OS to get the corresponding physical addresses. The physical base address of the page table is saved in the Translation Table Base Register (TTBR).

Memory dumping involves transmitting RAM memory to the peripherals. Because this data transmission is time-consuming, we take advantage of the DMA on the board. Since DMA has its own processing core and internal memory, the application processor can continue working on other tasks while the memory is being dumped. The DMA core executes routines that are stored in the internal RAM to perform DMA operations. Before transmitting, the TrustDumper saves the current state of the DMA, exporting the state of the processing core and the routines from the internal RAM to an unused system RAM on the board. Then it downloads the memory dumping code and the corresponding context to the internal RAM. After that, the TrustDumper triggers the DMA and starts to dump memory to the peripherals. When the data transmission is done, an interrupt will be generated for the TrustDumper to restore the core state and DMA internal RAM from the system RAM on the board. In our prototype, we use the serial port as the peripheral to transmit the RAM memory to a remote laptop. In our future work, we will add other peripherals such as network card in our system.

Integrity Checking and Rootkit Detection. In our prototype, the analysis module is capable of checking the integrity of kernel code and detecting rootkits. We provide two implementations, one hardware-based solution and one software-based solution, of SHA-1 algorithm to check the integrity of Android kernel.

We leverage the Symmetric/Asymmetric Hashing and Random Accelerator (SAHARA) of i.MX53 QSB, a security co-processor that implements block encryption algorithms (AES, DES, and 3DES), hashing algorithms (MD5, SHA-1, SHA-224, and SHA-256), a stream cipher algorithm (ARC4) and a hardware random number generator, to perform hardware-based hash. Since not all ARM platforms have a hardware security accelerator, we also provide a software-based SHA-1 implementation by porting the open source project PolarSSL [24] to i.MX53 QSB. The memory operations and output functions of SHA-1 algorithm in PolarSSL are modified to accommodate the bare-metal environment of the secure domain. Since the performance of hardware hash is better than software hash, we use the hardware to check the kernel integrity.

To calculate a hash value, the start address and length of the target code is required. Theres a static offset between the physical address and the virtual address of the continuous kernel code. In our prototype, the virtual start address of kernel is `0x80004000` and the offset is `0x10000000`, so the physical start address is `0x70004000`. The length of the kernel is case-sensitive, varying from different versions of kernel. Yet after the kernel has been compiled, the length is fixed. In Trust-Dump, the length is `9080836` bytes.

Our prototype can also detect rootkits that hide malicious processes. Figure 4 illustrates the list of process in linux kernel 2.6.35. In linux, a process is represented by the struct named `task_struct`, which includes the process number (`pid`) and the memory descriptor of the process (`mm`). All the processes are linked by the struct `list_head`, a doubly linked list in `task_struct`. Becasue `task_struct` is a component of the struct `thread_info`, the address of the `task_struct` corresponding to the current running process can be located through the `thread_info`, which is located at (`stack pointer & (0x1FFF)`). Therefore, through retrieving the doubly linked list, all the information of the processes are listed and can be checked to discover the hidden malicious processes.

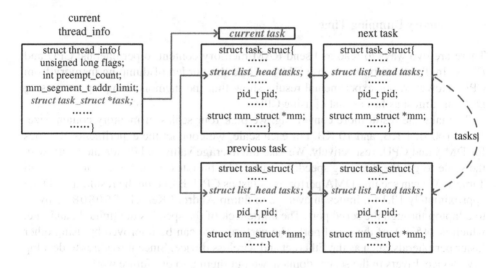

Fig. 4. Process List

6 Performance Evaluation

We evaluate the performance of TrustDump in three aspects: NMI switching time, memory dumping time, and analysis time. We use the performance monitor in the Cortex-A8 core processor to count the CPU cycles and then convert the cycle to time by multiplying $1\ ns\ /\ cycle$. We conduct each experiment 50 times and report the average.

6.1 NMI Switching Time

We measure the time of entering TrustDump with NMI and SMC instruction for comparison. For NMI measurement, since the performance monitor can only be started by software, there is no way to start the performance monitor at the exact time when the button is pressed. It cannot be done to directly measure the time from triggering of the interrupt to handling it in the secure domain. To start the performance monitor right before the NMI is triggered, we assert the NMI in the software-based way. On our board, software can trigger the NMI by writing the NMI interrupt number into the Software Interrupt Trigger Register (TZIC_SWINT) of TZIC. Therefore, we measure the time from writing to the register to receiving the request in the secure domain to evaluate the NMI performance. The result shows that switching time using NMI is 1.7 us, which is neglectable. We also measure the switching time using the SMC instruction by measuring the time from invoking the SMC instruction to receiving the request in the secure domain. The average switching time using SMC instruction is 0.3 us. This is shorter than the time of using NMI because it takes more time for the request of NMI to be transferred to the processor. However, the switching time using NMI is still very small and almost imperceptible. Moreover, using NMI is more reliable than using the SMC instruction to enforce a domain switch.

6.2   Memory Dumping Time

There are two ways to read and send RAM memory content to peripherals: CPU and DMA. In TrustDump, we choose DMA to free the burden of dumping memory from CPU. However, our experimental results show that the memory dumping time using DMA is almost as fast as that of using CPU.

To make the result more convincing, we pick four scales of memory content size: 10 B, 100 B, 1 KB, and 10 KB. For each scale, we conduct the experiments 50 times for DMA and CPU, respectively. We take the average value and divide the result with the scale to get the dumping speed: bit rates. The bit rates of each scale are shown in Table 1. We can see that DMA performs as fast as CPU. Based on the result, it will take approximately 13.14 minutes in average to dump Android Kernel of 9 080 836 bytes to a laptop through the serial port. The bottleneck of the speed is the limited baud rate, which is 115200, of the serial port. The performance can be improved by using other faster peripherals, such as the Ethernet and wireless device. Since it requires to develop new device drivers in the secure domain, we put them into our future work.

Table 1. Memory Dumping Performance

Scale (*Byte*)	Bit Rate (*bit/s*)	
	DMA	CPU
10	92178.12	92178.49
100	92163.38	92165.45
1K	92163.01	92163.43
10K	92163.09	92163.11

6.3   Analysis Performance

We conduct experiments on both the software-based and hardware-based implementations. The result shows that the time to calculate the kernel hash is $1.56\,ms$ by hardware, and $578.6\,ms$ by software. The performance of hardware hash guarantees that Trust-Dumper can be invoked frequently to perform kernel integrity checking when using the hardware-based solution. Though the software-based solution may be too slow for frequent OS integrity checking, it can be used when the Rich OS crashes or is compromised.

Besides kernel integrity checking, TrustDumper can detect hidden processes. We deploy a real rootkit Suterusu [25] that can hide processes in the Rich OS for evaluation. Suterusu performs system call inline hooking on arm platform to hide user-specified processes. Whenever the *ls* or *top* command is called in linux terminal, Suterusu hooks the functions and deletes the information of the hidden malicious processes from the result. TrustDump can successfully detect the rootkit by traversing all the processes of the Rich OS in $2.13\,ms$. According to the implementation in 5.3, TrustDumper running in the monitor mode needs to access the stack pointer of the user mode to obtain the pointer of the current *thread_info* in Rich OS. Because the user mode and the system mode of the CPU share the same stack pointer, and changing between the monitor mode and the system mode can be easily done by modifying the Current Program Status Register (CPSR), we access the stack pointer of the system mode instead. With the stack pointer, we can traverse all the processes listed in Figure 4 as described in 5.3. By comparing the result with what we get using command *ls* or *top*, we can find the processes hidden by the Suterusu.

7   Related Work

Memory acquisition techniques on smartphones can be classified into two categories: the software-based solutions and the hardware-based solutions. A software-based memory acquisition solution typically relies on either an OS running on the bare metal to acquire its own memory or a hypervisor to acquire the memory of one VM. Without /dev/mem support in the Android kernel, Linux Memory Extractor (LiME) has been developed as a loadable kernel module in Android to directly dump the memory to the SD card or over the network [26]. It requires rooted devices to insert the module into the kernel. Based on LiME, another work called DMD [27] can acquire the volatile memory of Android. Moreover, DDMS [28] provided by Android SDK can also be used to get memory information. On smartphones, the Android Recovery Mode [29] can give the user a root privilege and bypass the passcodes to acquire the OS memory; however, it requires a reboot before the memory acquisition.

In recent years, Hypervisors have been developed and enabled on ARM platforms [30, 31] with hardware support. Thus, the virtual machine inspection techniques [1] can also be implemented on the smartphones to protect the memory acquisition module from being tampered by the malicious OS. All above software-based solutions are efficient and easy to use. However, since they rely on the Android OS or a hypervisor to acquire the RAM memory, they cannot ensure a reliable memory acquisition when the OS/hypervisor has been compromised.

Hardware-based techniques usually utilize dedicated hardware components to directly access the memory through physical addresses [32], where the OS has been totally bypassed. JTAG [33] and chip-off technique [34] can be used to achieve memory acquisition; however, it works only if a JTAG debug port is identified on the smartphones. Moreover, most deployed OSes deny the debugging requests from JTAG to protect its own security. The cost of the equipment and the destructive nature of chip-off technique make it difficult to be used widely. Gianluigi Me et al. [35] propose a removable memory card based solution to overcome the heterogeneity of the tools adopted to retrieve smartphone contents. The existing hardware-based solution is more secure and reliable. However, it usually demands certain dedicated extra hardware components that may not be available on all smartphone platforms. Fortunately, the ARM processors, which have been widely used on smartphones, now provide a system level isolation solution with a hardware security support called *TrustZone* [15, 16]. TrustZone can ensure a trusted execution environment to protect the memory acquisition module and provide enough access privileges to access the Rich OS memory. Our work is based on TrustZone.

8 Conclusions

Based on ARM TrustZone technology, we propose a reliable memory acquisition mechanism named TrustDump on Smartphone to perform forensic analysis and facilitate malware analysis. TrustDump installs an Android OS in the normal domain and the memory acquisition module in the secure domain, and it relies on TrustZone to ensure a hardware-assisted isolation between the two domains. TrustDump ensures the reliability of the memory acquisition with a non-maskable interrupt, which prevents user's request from being intercepted or blocked by a malicious Rich OS. We propose fine-grained access control and fine-grained interrupt control techniques to minimize the impacts on the Rich OS. Our prototype on i.MX53 QSB can enter TrustDump and begin memory dumping in 1.7 us and calculate a hash value of the Android kernel in 1.56 ms.

Acknowledgment. This work is partially supported by National 973 Program of China under award No. 2014CB340603. Dr. Kun Sun's work is supported by U.S. Army Research Office under Grant W911NF-12-1-0060.

References

1. Garfinkel, T., Rosenblum, M.: A virtual machine introspection based architecture for intrusion detection. In: NDSS (2003)
2. Jiang, X., Wang, X., Xu, D.: Stealthy malware detection through vmm-based "out-of-the-box" semantic view reconstruction. In: ACM Conference on Computer and Communications Security, pp. 128–138 (2007)
3. Fu, Y., Lin, Z.: Space traveling across vm: Automatically bridging the semantic gap in virtual machine introspection via online kernel data redirection. In: IEEE Symposium on Security and Privacy, pp. 586–600 (2012)

4. Dolan-Gavitt, B., Leek, T., Zhivich, M., Giffin, J.T., Lee, W.: Virtuoso: Narrowing the semantic gap in virtual machine introspection. In: IEEE Symposium on Security and Privacy, pp. 297–312 (2011)
5. Dinaburg, A., Royal, P., Sharif, M.I., Lee, W.: Ether: malware analysis via hardware virtualization extensions. In: ACM Conference on Computer and Communications Security, pp. 51–62 (2008)
6. Deng, Z., Zhang, X., Xu, D.: Spider: stealthy binary program instrumentation and debugging via hardware virtualization. In: ACSAC, pp. 289–298 (2013)
7. Yan, L.K., Yin, H.: Droidscope: Seamlessly reconstructing the os and dalvik semantic views for dynamic android malware analysis. In: Proceedings of the 21st USENIX Conference on Security Symposium, Security 2012, p. 29. USENIX Association (2012)
8. McCune, J.M., Parno, B., Perrig, A., Reiter, M.K., Isozaki, H.: Flicker: an execution infrastructure for tcb minimization. In: EuroSys, pp. 315–328 (2008)
9. McCune, J.M., Li, Y., Qu, N., Zhou, Z., Datta, A., Gligor, V.D., Perrig, A.: Trustvisor: Efficient tcb reduction and attestation. In: IEEE Symposium on Security and Privacy, pp. 143–158 (2010)
10. Martignoni, L., Poosankam, P., Zaharia, M., Han, J., McCamant, S., Song, D., Paxson, V., Perrig, A., Shenker, S., Stoica, I.: Cloud terminal: secure access to sensitive applications from untrusted systems. In: Proceedings of the 2012 USENIX Conference on Annual Technical Conference, p. 14. USENIX Association (2012)
11. Zhang, F., Leach, K., Sun, K., Stavrou, A.: Spectre: A dependable introspection framework via system management mode. In: DSN, pp. 1–12 (2013)
12. Azab, A.M., Ning, P., Wang, Z., Jiang, X., Zhang, X., Skalsky, N.C.: Hypersentry: enabling stealthy in-context measurement of hypervisor integrity. In: ACM Conference on Computer and Communications Security, pp. 38–49 (2010)
13. Wang, J., Stavrou, A., Ghosh, A.: Hypercheck: A hardware-assisted integrity monitor. In: Jha, S., Sommer, R., Kreibich, C. (eds.) RAID 2010. LNCS, vol. 6307, pp. 158–177. Springer, Heidelberg (2010)
14. Azab, A.M., Ning, P., Zhang, X.: Sice: a hardware-level strongly isolated computing environment for x86 multi-core platforms. In: ACM Conference on Computer and Communications Security, pp. 375–388 (2011)
15. ARM: TrustZone Introduction, http://www.arm.com/products/processors/technologies/trustzone/index.php
16. Alves, T., Felton, D.: Trustzone: Integrated hardware and software security. ARM White Paper 3(4) (2004)
17. ARM: Cortex-A8 Technical Reference Manual, http://infocenter.arm.com/help/topic/com.arm.doc.ddi0344k/DDI0344K_cortex_a8_r3p2_trm.pdf
18. ARM: Cortex-A9 Technical Reference Manual, http://infocenter.arm.com/help/topic/com.arm.doc.ddi0388f/DDI0388F_cortex_a9_r2p2_trm.pdf
19. ARM: ARM Cortex-A15 MPCore Processor Technical Reference Manual, http://infocenter.arm.com/help/index.jsp?topic=/com.arm.doc.ddi0438i/index.html
20. ARM: Interrupt Behavior of Cortex-M1, http://infocenter.arm.com/help/index.jsp?topic=/com.arm.doc.dai0211a/index.html
21. ARM: Cortex-M4 Devices Generic User Guide, http://infocenter.arm.com/help/index.jsp?topic=/com.arm.doc.dui0553a/Cihfaaha.html
22. Freescale: Imx53qsb: i.mx53 quick start board, http://www.freescale.com/webapp/sps/site/prod_summary.jsp?code=IMX53QSB&tid=vanIMXQUICKSTART

23. Adeneo Embedded: Reference BSPs for Freescale i.MX53 Quick Start Board, http://www.adeneo-embedded.com/en/Products/Board-Support-Packages/Freescale-i.MX53-QSB
24. Paul Bakker: PolarSSL, https://polarssl.org/
25. Michael Coppola: Suterusu Rootkit: Inline Kernel Function Hooking on x86 and ARM, http://poppopret.org/2013/01/07/suterusu-rootkit-inline-kernel-function-hooking-on-x86-and-arm/
26. Heriyanto, A.P.: Procedures and tools for acquisition and analysis of volatile memory on android smartphones. In: Proceedings of The 11th Australian Digital Forensics Conference. SRI Security Research Institute, Edith Cowan University, Perth, Western Australia (2013)
27. Sylve, J., Case, A., Marziale, L., Richard III, G.G.: Acquisition and analysis of volatile memory from android devices. Digital Investigation 8(3-4), 175–184 (2012)
28. Google: Using ddms for debugging, http://developer.android.com/tools/debugging/ddms.html
29. Stevenson, A.: Boot into Recovery Mode for Rooted and Un-rooted Android devices, http://androidflagship.com/605-enter-recovery-mode-rooted-un-rooted-android
30. Dall, C., Nieh, J.: Kvm for arm. In: Proceedings of the 12th Annual Linux Symposium (2010)
31. Dall, C., Nieh, J.: Kvm/arm: The design and implementation of the linux arm hypervisor. In: Proceedings of the 19th International Conference on Architectural Support for Programming Languages and Operating Systems, ASPLOS 2014 (2014)
32. Carrier, B.D., Grand, J.: A hardware-based memory acquisition procedure for digital investigations. Digital Investigation 1(1), 50–60 (2004)
33. Breeuwsma, I.M.F.: Forensic Imaging of Embedded Systems Using JTAG (Boundary-scan). Digit. Investig. 3(1) (March 2006)
34. Jovanovic, Z., Redd, I.D.D.: Android forensics techniques. International Academy of Design and Technology (2012)
35. Me, G., Rossi, M.: Internal forensic acquisition for mobile equipments. In: IPDPS, pp. 1–7 (2008)

A Framework to Secure Peripherals at Runtime

Fengwei Zhang[1], Haining Wang[2], Kevin Leach[3], and Angelos Stavrou[1]

[1] George Mason University, Fairfax, VA, USA
[2] College of William and Mary, Williamsburg, VA, USA
[3] University of Virginia, Charlottesville, VA, USA

Abstract. Secure hardware forms the foundation of a secure system. However, securing hardware devices remains an open research problem. In this paper, we present IOCheck, a framework to enhance the security of I/O devices at runtime. It leverages System Management Mode (SMM) to quickly check the integrity of I/O configurations and firmware. IOCheck is agnostic to the operating system. We use random-polling and event-driven approaches to switch into SMM. We implement a prototype of IOCheck and conduct extensive experiments on physical machines. Our experimental results show that IOCheck takes 10 milliseconds to check the integrity of a network card and a video card. Also, IOCheck introduces a low overhead on Windows and Linux platforms. We show that IOCheck achieves a faster switching time than the Dynamic Root of Trust Measurement approach.

Keywords: Integrity, Firmware, I/O Configurations, SMM.

1 Introduction

As hardware devices have become more complex, firmware functionality has expanded, exposing new vulnerabilities to attackers. The National Vulnerabilities Database (NVD [1]) shows that 183 firmware vulnerabilities have been found since 2011. The Common Vulnerabilities and Exposures (CVE) list from Mitre shows 537 entries that match the keyword 'firmware,' and 94 new firmware vulnerabilities were found in 2013 [2]. A recent study shows that 40,000 servers are remotely exploitable due to vulnerable management firmware [3]. Attackers can exploit these vulnerabilities in firmware [4] or tools for updating firmware [5].

After compromising the firmware of an I/O device (e.g., NIC card), attackers alter memory via DMA [4, 6, 7] or compromise surrounding I/O devices [8, 9]. Fortunately, the Input Output Memory Management Unit (IOMMU) mechanism can protect the host memory from DMA attacks. It maps each I/O device to a specific area in the host memory so that any invalid access fails. Intel Virtualization Technology for Directed I/O (VT-d) is one example of IOMMU. AMD also has its own I/O virtualization technology called AMD-Vi. However, IOMMU cannot always be trusted as a countermeasure against DMA attacks, as it relies on a flawless configuration to operate correctly [10]. In particular, researchers have demonstrated several attacks against IOMMU [11–13].

M. Kutyłowski and J. Vaidya (Eds.): ESORICS 2014, Part I, LNCS 8712, pp. 219–238, 2014.
© Springer International Publishing Switzerland 2014

Static Root of Trust for Measurement (SRTM) [14] with help from the Trust Platform Module (TPM) [15] can check the integrity of the firmware and I/O configurations while booting. It uses a fixed or immutable piece of trusted code, called the Core Root of Trust for Measurement (CRTM), contained in the BIOS at the start of the entire booting chain, and every piece of code in the chain is measured by the predecessor code before it is executed, including firmware. However, SRTM only secures the booting process and cannot provide runtime integrity checking.

Trust Computing Group introduced Dynamic Root of Trust for Measurement (DRTM) [16]. To implement this technology, Intel developed Trusted eXecution Technology (TXT) [17], providing a trusted way to load and execute system software (e.g., OS or VMM). TXT uses a new CPU instruction, SENTER, to control the secure environment. Intel TXT does not make any assumptions about the system state, and it provides a dynamic root of trust for Late Launch. Thus, TXT can be used to check the runtime integrity of I/O configurations and firmware. AMD has a similar technology called Secure Virtual Machine, and it uses the SKINIT instruction to enter the secure environment. However, both TXT and SVM introduce a significant overhead on the late Launch Operation (e.g., the SKINIT instruction in [18]).

In this paper, we present IOCheck, a framework to enhance the security of I/O devices at runtime. It leverages System Management Mode (SMM), a CPU mode in the x86 architecture, to quickly check the integrity of I/O configurations and firmware. IOCheck identifies the target I/O devices on the motherboard and checks the integrity of their corresponding configurations and firmware. In contrast to existing firmware integrity checking systems [19, 20], our approach is based on SMM instead of Protected Mode (PM). While PM-based approaches assume the booting process is secure and the OS is trusted, our approach only assumes a secure BIOS boot to set up SMM, which is easily achieved via SRTM.

The superiority of SMM over PM is two-fold. First, we can reduce the Trusted Computing Base (TCB) of the analysis platform. Similar to Viper [20] and NAVIS [19], IOCheck is a runtime integrity checking system. Viper and NAVIS assume the OS is trusted and use software in PM to check the integrity, while IOCheck uses SMM without relying on the OS, resulting in a much smaller TCB. IOCheck is also immune to attacks against the OS, facilitating a stronger threat model than the checking systems running in the OS. Second, we achieve a much higher performance compared to the DRTM approaches [18] running in PM. DRTM does not rely on any system code; it can provide a dynamic root of trust for integrity checking. IOCheck can achieve the same security goal because SMM is a trusted and isolated execution environment. However, IOCheck is able to achieve a much higher performance over Intel TXT or AMD SVM approaches. Based upon experimental results, SMM switching time takes microseconds, while the switching operation of the DRTM approach [18] takes milliseconds.

We implement a prototype of our system using different methods to enter SMM. First, we develop a random polling-based integrity checking system that checks the integrity of I/O devices, which can mitigate transient attacks [21, 22].

To further defend against transient attacks, we also implement an event-driven system that checks the integrity of a network card's management firmware.

We conduct extensive experiments to evaluate IOCheck on both Microsoft Windows and Linux systems. The experimental results show that the SMM code takes about 10 milliseconds to check PCI configuration space and firmware of NIC and VGA. Through testing IOCheck with popular benchmarks, IOCheck incurs about a 2% overhead when we set the random polling instruction interval between [1,0xffffffff][1]. We also compare IOCheck with the DRTM approach; our results indicate that our system's switching time is three orders of magnitude faster than DRTM. Furthermore, the switching time of IOCheck is constant while the switching operation in DRTM depends on the size of the loaded secure code.

Contributions. This work makes the following contributions:

- We provide a framework that checks the integrity of I/O devices at runtime.
- IOCheck is OS-agnostic and is implemented in SMM.
- We implement a prototype that uses random-polling and event-driven approaches to mitigate transient attacks.
- We demonstrate the effectiveness of our system by checking the integrity of a popular network card and video card, and we show that our system introduces a low operating overhead on both Windows and Linux platforms.

2   Background

2.1   Computer Hardware Architecture

The Central Processing Unit (CPU) connects to the Northbridge via the Front-Side Bus. The Northbridge contains the Memory Management Unit (MMU) and IOMMU, collectively called the Memory Controller Hub (MCH). The Northbridge also connects to the memory, graphics card, and Southbridge. The Southbridge connects a variety of I/O devices including USB, SATA, and Super I/O, among others. The BIOS is also connected to the Southbridge. Figure 2 in Appendix shows the hardware architecture of a typical computer.

2.2   Firmware Rootkits

A firmware rootkit creates a persistent malware image in hardware devices such as network cards, disks, and the BIOS. The capabilities of firmware rootkits can be summarized thusly. First, firmware rootkits can modify the host memory via DMA if a system does not have an IOMMU or if it is incorrectly configured. Second, a compromised device can access sensitive data that passes through it [23]. For instance, a NIC rootkit can eavesdrop network packets containing passwords. Third, a hardware device with malicious firmware may be able to compromise surrounding devices via peer-to-peer communication. For example, a compromised NIC may access GPU memory [24]. Last but not least, an advanced firmware rootkit can even survive a firmware update [25].

---

[1] It takes about .5s to run 0xffffffff instructions. Table 2 explains this further.

2.3   System Management Mode and Coreboot

System Management Mode (SMM) is a CPU mode in the x86 architecture. It is similar to Real and Protected Modes. It provides an isolated execution environment for implementing system control functions such as power management. SMM is initialized by the BIOS. Before the system boots up, the BIOS loads the SMM code into System Management RAM (SMRAM), a special memory region that is inaccessible from other CPU modes. SMM is triggered by asserting the System Management Interrupt (SMI) pin on the motherboard. Both hardware and software are able to assert this pin, although the specific method depends on the chipset. After assertion, the system automatically saves its CPU states into SMRAM and then executes the SMI handler code. An RSM instruction is executed at the end of the SMI hander to switch back to Protected Mode.

Coreboot [26] aims to replace legacy BIOS in most computers. It performs some hardware initialization and then executes additional boot logic, called a payload. With the separation of hardware initialization and later boot logic, Coreboot provides flexibility to run custom bootloaders or a Unified Extensible Firmware Interface (UEFI). It switches to Protected Mode early in the booting process and is written mostly in C language. Google Chromebooks are manufactured and shipped with Coreboot.

3   Threat Model and Assumptions

3.1   Threat Model

We consider two attack scenarios. First, we consider an attacker who gains control of a host through a software vulnerability and then attempts to remain resident in a stealthy manner. We assume such an attacker installs firmware rootkits (specifically, a backdoor [23]) after infecting the OS so that the malicious code remains even if the user reinstalls the OS.

In the second scenario, we assume the firmware itself can be remotely exploited due to vulnerabilities. For instance, Duflot et al. [4] demonstrate an attack that remotely compromises a Broadcom NIC with crafted UDP packets. Additionally, Bonkoski et al. [3] show a buffer overflow vulnerability in management firmware that affected thousands of servers.

3.2   Assumptions

An attacker is able to tamper with the firmware by exploiting zero-day vulnerabilities. Since IOCheck does not rely on the operating system, we assume the attacker has ring 0 privilege. Thus, attackers are granted more capabilities in our work than those OS-based systems [19, 20]. We assume the system is equipped with SRTM, in which CRTM is trusted so that it can perform a self-measurement of the BIOS. Once the SMM code is securely loaded into the SMRAM, we lock the SMRAM in the BIOS. We assume the SMM is secure after locking SMRAM, and we will discuss attacks against SMM in Section 7. Moreover, we assume the attacker does not have physical access to our system.

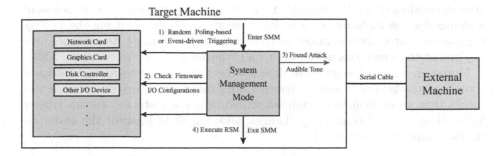

Fig. 1. Architecture of IOCheck

4 System Framework

Figure 1 shows the architecture of IOCheck. The target machine connects to the external machine via a serial cable. In the target machine, the box on the left lists all of the I/O devices on a motherboard; the box on the right represents the System Management Mode code that checks the integrity of I/O configurations and firmware. The framework performs four steps for each check: 1) the target machine switches into SMM; 2) the SMI handler checks the integrity of target I/O devices; 3) if a potential attack has been found, the target machine plays an audible tone and SMM sends a message to the external machine via the serial cable; and 4) the target machine executes the RSM instruction to exit SMM. These steps are further described below.

4.1 Triggering an SMI

In general, there are software- and hardware-based methods to trigger an SMI. In software, we can write to an ACPI port to raise an SMI. For example, Intel chipsets use port 0x2b as specified by the Southbridge datasheet. Our testbed with a VIA VT8237r Southbridge uses 0x52f as the SMI trigger port [27]. In terms of hardware-based methods, there are many hardware devices that can be used to raise an SMI, including keyboards, network cards, and hardware timers.

The algorithm for triggering SMIs plays an important role in the system design. In general, there are polling-based and event-driven approaches used to generate SMIs. The polling-based approach polls the state of a target system at regular intervals. When we use this approach to check the integrity of a target system, it compares the newly retrieved state with a known pristine state to see if any malicious changes have occurred. However, polling at regular intervals in the system is susceptible to transient [21] or evasion attacks [22].

Transient attacks are a class of attacks that do not produce persistent changes within a victim's system. Polling-based systems suffer from transient attacks because they infer intrusions based upon the presence of an inconsistent state. Transient attacks can thus avoid detection by remove any evidence before a polling event and resuming malicious activity between polls. Mitigating these attacks requires either 1) minimizing the polling window so that there is less of a chance for the malware to clean its evidence, or 2) randomizing the polling window so that malware cannot learn a pattern for cleaning its evidence. We implement these methods in IOCheck via performance counters to trigger SMIs.

Moreover, we can use an event-driven triggering method to further mitigate transient attacks. Polling-based systems are likely to miss events between two checks that an event-driven approach would not. For instance, we can trigger SMIs when a region of memory changes, allowing us to monitor the state, including malicious changes.

4.2   Checking I/O Configurations and Firmware

Configurations of I/O Devices. Before the system boots up, the BIOS initializes all of the hardware devices on the motherboard and populates corresponding configuration spaces for each one. These devices rely on the configurations to operate correctly. Here we use the PCI configuration space and IOMMU configuration as examples.

PCI Configuration Space: Each PCI or PCIe controller has a configuration space. Device drivers read these configurations to determine what resources (e.g., memory-mapped location) have been assigned by the BIOS to the devices. Note that the PCI configurations should be static after the BIOS initialization. However, an attacker with ring 0 privilege can modify the PCI configuration space. For example, the attacker can relocate the device memory by changing the Base Address Register in the PCI configuration space. Additionally, PCI/PCIe devices that support Message Signaled Interrupts (MSI) contain registers in the PCI configuration space to configure MSI delivery. Wojtczuk and Rutkowska demonstrate that the attacker in the driver domain of a VM can generate malicious MSIs to compromise a Xen hypervisor [13]. Note that IOCheck assumes the PCI configuration remains the same after the BIOS initialization and does not consider "Plug-and-Play" PCI/PCIe devices.

IOMMU Configurations: IOMMU restricts memory access from I/O devices. For example, it can prevent a DMA attack from a compromised I/O device. IOMMU is comprised of a set of DMA Remapping Hardware Units (DRHU). They are responsible for translating addresses from I/O devices to physical addresses in the host memory. The DRHU first identifies a DMA request by BDF-ID (Bus, Device, Function number). Then, it uses BDF-ID to locate the page tables associated with the requested I/O controller. Finally, it translates the DMA Virtual Address (DVA) to a Host Physical Address (HPA), much like MMU translation. Although IOMMU gives us effective protection from DMA attacks, it relies on proper configurations to operate correctly. Several techniques have been demonstrated to bypass IOMMU [11, 13]. We can mitigate these attacks by checking the integrity of the critical configurations of IOMMU at runtime. Table 4 in Appendix shows the static configuration of IOMMU.

Firmware Integrity. We aim to check the firmware of I/O devices including the network card, graphics card, disk controller, keyboard, and mouse. We describe the process of checking a NIC, VGA, and the BIOS as examples.

Network Interface Controller: Modern network cards continue to increase in complexity. NICs usually include a separate on-chip processor and memory to support various functions. Typically, a NIC loads its firmware from Electric Erasable Programmable Read-Only Memory (EEPROM) to flash memory, and it then executes the code on the on-chip processor. IOCheck stores a hash value of the original firmware image and checks the integrity of the NIC's firmware at runtime. For some network cards [28], we can monitor the instruction pointer of the on-chip CPU through the NIC's debugging registers. This can restrict the instruction pointer to the code section of the memory region. If the instruction pointer points to a memory region that stores heap or stack data, then a code injection or control flow hijacking may have occurred.

Monitoring the integrity of the static code and instruction pointer can prevent an attacker from injecting malicious code into the firmware; however, it cannot detect advanced attacks, such as Return Oriented Programming attacks, since they technically do not inject any code. To detect these attacks, we can implement a shadow stack to protect the control flow integrity of the NIC firmware. Duflot et al. implemented a similar concept in NAVIS [19]. We will study the control flow integrity of the firmware in future work.

Video Graphics Adapter: The Video Graphics Adapter (VGA) normally requires device-specific initialization, and the motherboard BIOS does not have the knowledge of all possible vendor-specific initialization procedures. Fortunately, the PCI expansion ROM (i.e., option ROM) can be executed to initialize the VGA device. The VGA expansion ROM code is stored on the device, and this mechanism allows ROM to contain multiple images that support different processor architectures (e.g, x86, HP RISC). However, the ROM code on the device can be flashed with a customized image [29] or malicious code [30]. IOCheck uses SMM to ensure the integrity of the VGA option ROM at runtime.

Basic Input Output System: As mentioned before, SRTM can check the integrity of the BIOS at the booting time, which helps us to securely load the SMM code from the BIOS to the SMRAM. After the system boots up, attackers with ring 0 privilege might modify the BIOS using various tools (e.g., flashrom [31]). However, they are not able to access locked SMRAM. Thus, we can use the SMM code to check the runtime integrity of the BIOS. Although the modified BIOS with malicious code cannot be executed until the system resets and SRTM will detect this BIOS attack before booting, we can detect this attack earlier than SRTM, which provides runtime detection and serves as a complementary defense. Earlier detection of such attacks can also limit the damage they wreak against the system. Note that we assume CRTM in the BIOS is immutable and trusted, but attackers can modify any other BIOS code (e.g., ACPI tables). Otherwise, we cannot perform SRTM correctly.

4.3 Reporting an Alert and Exiting SMM

The last stage of IOCheck is to report any alerts to a human operator. We accomplish this task by playing an audible tone to notify a user that a potential attack may happen. To distinguish the type of attack, we use different tone frequency for a variety of I/O attacks. In addition, we use a serial cable to connect the target machine to the external machine. IOCheck assumes attackers with ring 0 privilege, which means they are able to modify hardware registers to block SMI assertions and launch a Denial-of-Service (DoS) attack against our system. We use the external machine to detect the DoS attack. For example, the random polling-based triggering in IOCheck must generate SMIs at least every maximum time interval, whereupon the external machine expects a message from SMM via the serial cable. If the external machine does not receive a log message in the interval, we conclude that a DoS attack has occurred. We also use a secret key to authenticate the log messages to avoid fake messages. Specifically, the target machine establishes a shared secret key with the external machine in the BIOS while booting. Since we trust the BIOS at startup, we can store the secret in the trusted SMRAM. Later, only the SMI handler can access it, which prevents attackers from spoofing messages.

Note that the reporting stage executes within SMM. Even if an attack disables the PC speaker or serial console in PM, we can enable it in SMM and guarantee that an audible tone and a serial message is delivered. After the reporting stage, the SMI handler simply executes the RSM instruction to exit from SMM.

5 System Implementation

We implement a prototype of IOCheck system using two physical machines. The target machine uses an ASUS M2V-MX_SE motherboard with an AMD K8 Northbridge and a VIA VT8237r Southbridge. It has a 2.2 GHz AMD LE-1250 CPU and 2GB Kingston DDR2 RAM. We use a PCIe-based Intel 82574L Gigabit Ethernet Controller and a PCI-based Jaton VIDEO-498PCI-DLP Nvidia GeForce 9500GT as the testing devices. To program SMM, we use open-source BIOS, Coreboot. Since IOCheck is OS-agnostic, we install Microsoft Windows 7 and CentOS 5.5 on the target machine. The external machine is a Dell Inspiron 15R laptop with Ubuntu 12.04 LTS. It uses a 2.4GHz Intel Core i5-2430M CPU and 6 GB DDR3 RAM.

5.1 Triggering an SMI

We implement a random polling-based triggering algorithm to check integrity of I/O configurations and firmware by using performance counters to generate SMIs. The performance monitoring registers count hardware events such as instruction retirement, L1 cache miss, or branch misprediction. The x86 machines provide four of these counters from which we can select a specific hardware event to count [32]. To generate an SMI, we first configure one of the performance counters to store its maximum value. Next, we select a desired event (e.g., a retired instruction or cache miss) to count so that the next occurrence of that event will overflow the counter. Finally, we configure the Local Advanced Programmable Interrupt Controller (APIC) to deliver an SMI when an overflow occurs. Thus, we are able to trigger an SMI for the desired event. The performance counting event is configured by the `PerfEvtSel` register, and the performance counter is set by the `PerfCtr` register [32].

To randomly generate SMIs, we first generate a pseudo-random number, r, ranging from 1 to m, where m is a user-configurable maximum value. For example, a user could set m as 0xffff ($2^{16} - 1$), so the random number resides in the set [1,0xffff]. Next, we set the performance counter to its maximum value (0xffffffffffff) minus this random number ($2^{48} - 1 - r$). We also set the desired event in `PerfEvtSel` and start to count the event. Thus, an SMI will be raised after r occurrences of the desired event. We use a linear-congruential algorithm to generate the pseudo-random number, r, in SMM. We use the parameters of the linear-congruential algorithm from Numerical Recipes [33]. We use the TSC value as the initial seed and save the current random number in SMRAM as the next round's seed.

To further mitigate transient attacks, we consider event-driven-based triggering approaches. We implement an event-driven-based version of IOCheck for checking the integrity of a NIC's management firmware, and the detailed implementation is described as follows. When a management packet arrives at the PHY interface of the NIC, the manageability firmware starts to execute. We use Message Signalled Interrupts (MSI) to trigger an SMI when a manageability packet arrives at the network card. First, we configure the network card to deliver an MSI to the I/O APIC with the delivery mode specified as SMI. When the I/O APIC receives this interrupt, it automatically asserts the SMI pin, and an SMI is generated. Next, we use the SMM code to check the integrity of the management firmware. Note that the act of this triggering is generated via a hardware interrupt in the NIC, and the management firmware code is decoupled from this. Thus, we trigger an SMI for every manageability packet before the firmware has an opportunity to process it.

5.2   Checking I/O Configurations and Firmware

Network Interface Controller. We use a popular commercial network card, an Intel 82574L Gigabit PCIe Ethernet Controller, as our target I/O device. First, we check the PCIe configuration space of the network card. The NIC on our testbed is at bus 3, device 0, and function 0. To read the configuration space, we use standard PCI reads to dump the contents. We use a standard hash function MD5 [34] to hash these 256 bytes of the configuration and compare the hash value with the original one generated during booting.

Network management is an increasingly important requirement in today's networked computer environments, especially on servers. It routes manageability network traffic to a Management Controller (MC). One example of MC is the Baseboard Management Controller (BMC) in Intelligent Platform Management Interface (IPMI). The management firmware inevitably contains vulnerabilities that could be easily exploited by attackers. Bonkoski et al. [3] identified more than 400 thousand IPMI-enabled servers running on publicly accessible IP addresses that are remotely exploitable due to textbook vulnerabilities in the management firmware. The 82574L NIC [35] provides two different and mutually exclusive bus interfaces for manageability traffic. One is the Intel proprietary System Management Bus (SMBus) interface, and the other is the Network Controller - Sideband Interface (NC-SI). For each manageability interface, it has its own firmware code that implements the functions. Figure 3 in Appendix shows a high-level architectural block diagram of the 82574L NIC.

The management firmware of these two interfaces is stored in a Non-Volatile Memory (NVM). The NVM is I/O mapped memory in the NIC, and we use the EEPROM Read Register (EERD 0x14) to read it. EERD is a 32-bit register used to cause the NIC to read individual words in the EEPROM. To read a word, we write a 1b to the Start Read field. The NIC reads the word from the EEPROM and places it in the Read Data field and then sets the Read Done field to 1b. We poll the Read Done bit to make sure that the data has been stored in the Read Data field. All of the configuration and status registers of 82574L NIC, including EERD, are memory-mapped when the system boots up. To access EERD, we use normal memory read-and-write operations. The memory address of EERD is INTEL_82574L_BASE plus EERD offset.

Video Graphics Adapter. Jaton VIDEO-498PCI-DLP GeForce 9500GT is a PCI-based video card. It is at bus 7, device 0, and function 0 on our testbed. Similar to the checking approach of NIC, we first check the PCI configuration space of the VGA device. Then, we check the integrity of the VGA expansion ROM. The VGA expansion ROM is memory-mapped, and the four-byte register at offset 0x30 in the PCI configuration space specifies the base address of the expansion ROM. Note that bit 0 in the register enables the accesses to the expansion ROM. PCI expansion ROMs may contain multiple images for different architectures. Each image must contain a ROM header and PCI data structure, which specify image information such as code type and size. Table 5 in Appendix shows the formats of ROM header and PCI data structure. Note that we only check the image for x86 architecture since our testbed is on Intel x86.

We first use the base address of expansion ROM to locate the header of the first image. Next, we read the pointer to PCI data structure at offset 0x18 to 0x19. Then, we identify the code type at offset 0x14 in the PCI data structure. If this image is for Intel x86 architecture, we check the integrity of this image by comparing the hash values. Otherwise, we repeat the steps above for the next image.

5.3   Reporting an Alert and Exiting SMM

To play a tone, we program the Intel 8253 Programmable Interval Timer (PIT) in the SMI handler to generate tones. The 8253 PIT performs timing and counting functions, and it exists in all x86 machines. In modern machines, it is included as part of the motherboard's Southbridge. This timer has three counters (Counters 0, 1, and 2), and we use the third counter (Counter 2) to generate tones via the PC speaker. In addition, we can generate different kinds of tones by adjusting the output frequency. In the prototype of IOCheck, a continuous tone would be played by the PC speaker if a attack against NIC has been found. If an attack against VGA has been found, an intermittent tone would be played.

We use a serial cable to print status messages and debug corresponding I/O devices in SMM. The `printk` function in Coreboot prints the status messages to the serial port on the target machine. When the target machine executes the BIOS code during booting, the external machine sends a 16-byte random number to the target machine through the serial cable. Then, the BIOS will store the random number as a secret in the SMRAM. Later, the status messages are sent with the secret for authentication. We run a `minicom` instance on the external machine and verify if the secret is correct. If a status message is not received in an expected time window or the secret is wrong, we conclude that an attack has occurred.

6 Evaluation and Experimental Results

6.1 Code Size

In total, there are 310 lines of new C code in the SMI handler. The MD5 hash function has 140 lines of C code [34], and the rest of the code implements the firmware and PCI configuration space checking. After compiling the Coreboot, the binary size of the SMI handler is only 1,409 bytes, which introduces a minimal TCB to our system. The 1,409-byte code encompasses all functions and instructions required to check the integrity of the NIC and VGA firmware and their PCI configuration spaces. The code size will increase if we check more I/O devices. Additionally, other static code exists in Coreboot related to enabling SMM to run on a particular chipset. For example, a `printk` function is built into the SMM code to enable raw communication over a serial port.

6.2 Attack Detection

We conduct four attacks against our system on both Windows and Linux platforms. Two of them are I/O configuration attacks, which relocate the device memory by manipulating the PCI configuration space of NIC and VGA. The other two attacks modify the management firmware of the NIC and VGA option ROM. The Base Address Registers (BARs) in the PCI configuration space are used to map the device's register space. They reside from offset `0x10` to `0x27` in the PCI configuration space. For example, the memory location BAR0 specifies the base address of the internal NIC registers. An attacker can relocate these memory-mapped registers for malicious purposes by manipulating the BAR0 register. To conduct the experiments, we first enable IOCheck to check the PCI configuration space. Next, we modify the memory location specified by the BAR0 register on Windows and Linux platforms. We write a kernel module to modify the BAR0 register in Linux and use the RWEverything [36] tool to configure it in Windows. We also modify the management firmware of NIC and the VGA option ROM. The management firmware is stored as a Non-Volatile memory, and it is I/O mapped memory; the VGA option ROM is memory-mapped. These attacks are also conducted on both Windows and Linux platforms.

After we modify NIC's PCIe configuration or the firmware, IOCheck automatically plays a continuous tone to alert users and, the minicom instance on the external machine shows an attack against NIC has been found. After the modification of VGA's PCI configuration or option ROM, an intermittent tone is played by the PC speaker.

6.3   Breakdown of SMI Handler Runtime

To quantify how much time each individual step is required to run, we break down the SMI handler into eight operations. They are 1) switch into the SMM; 2) check the PCIe configuration of NIC; 3) check the firmware of NIC; 4) check the PCI configuration of VGA; 5) check the option ROM of VGA; 6) send a status message; 7) configure the next SMI; and 8) resume Protected Mode. For each operation, we measure the average time taken in SMM. We use the Time Stamp Counter (TSC) register to calculate the time. The TSC register stores the number of CPU cycles elapsed since powering on. First, we record the TSC values at the beginning and end of each operation, respectively. Next, we use the CPU frequency to divide the difference in the TSC register to calculate how much time this operation.

We repeat this experiment 40 times. Table 1 shows the average times taken for each operation. We can see that the SMM switching and resuming take only 4 and 5 microseconds, respectively. Checking 256 bytes of the PCIe/PCI configuration space register takes about 1 millisecond. The 82574L NIC has 70 bytes of SMBus Advanced Pass Through (APT) management firmware and 138 bytes of NC-SI management firmware. The size of x86 expansion ROM image is 1 KB in the testing VGA. Checking NIC's firmware takes about 1 millisecond, while checking VGA's option ROM takes about 5 milliseconds. Naturally, the

Table 1. Breakdown of SMI Handler Runtime (Time: μs)

Operations	Mean	STD	95% CI
SMM switching	3.92	0.08	[3.27,3.32]
Check NIC's PCIe configuration	1169.39	2.01	[1168.81,1169.98]
Check NIC's firmware	1268.12	5.12	[1266.63,1269.60]
Check VGA's PCI configuration	1243.60	2.61	[1242.51,1244.66]
Check VGA's expansion ROM	4609.30	1.30	[4608.92,4609.68]
Send a message	2082.95	3.00	[2082.08,2083.82]
Configure the next SMI	1.22	0.06	[1.20,1.24]
SMM resume	4.58	0.10	[4.55,4,61]
Total	10,383.07		

size of the firmware affects the time of the checking operation. We send a status message (e.g., I/O devices are OK) in each run of the SMI handler, which is about 2 milliseconds. The time is takes to generate a random number and configure performance counters for the next SMI is only 1.22 microseconds. Thus, the total time spent in SMM is about 10 milliseconds. Additionally, we calculate the standard deviation and 95% confidence interval for the runtime of each operation.

6.4 System Overhead

To measure system overhead introduced by this approach, we use the SuperPI [37] program to benchmark our system on Windows and Linux. We first run the benchmark without IOCheck enabled. Then, we run it with different random-polling intervals. Table 2 shows the experimental results. The first column shows the random polling intervals used in the experiment. For example, (0,0xfffff] means a random number, r, is generated in that interval. We use retired instructions as the counting event in the performance counter. Thus, after running r sequential instructions, an SMI will be asserted. The second column also indicates the time elapsed. Since the CPU (AMD K8) on our testbed is 3-way superscalar [38], we assume an average number of instructions-per-cycle (IPC) is 3, and the equation for this transformation is $T = \frac{I}{(C*IPC)}$, where T is the real time, I is the number of instructions, and C is the clock speed on the CPU.

Table 2. Random Polling Overhead Introduced on Microsoft Windows and Linux

	Random Polling Intervals		Benchmark Runtime(s)		System Slowdown	
	Instructions	Time (μs)	Windows	Linux	Windows	Linux
1	[1,0xffffffff]	(0,~650,752]	0.285	0.393	0.014	0.011
2	[1,0xffffffff]	(0,~40,672]	0.297	0.398	0.057	0.023
3	[1,0xffffff]	(0,~2,542]	0.609	0.463	1.167	0.190
4	[1,0xffffff]	(0,~158]	4.359	1.480	14.512	2.805
5	[1,0xffff]	(0,~10]	91.984	18.382	~326	~46

We can see from Table 2 that the overhead will increase if we reduce the random-polling interval, while small intervals have a higher probability of quickly detecting attacks. Intervals in rows 1 and 2 introduce less than 6% overhead, so intervals similar to or between them are suitable for normal users in practice. Other intervals in the table have large overhead making them unsuitable in practice. These results demonstrate the feasibility and scalability of our approach.

6.5 Comparison with the DRTM Approach

IOCheck provides a new framework for checking firmware and I/O devices at runtime. Compared to the well-known DRTM approach (e.g., Flicker [18]), SMM in IOCheck serves a similar role as the trusted execution environment in DRTM. However, IOCheck achieves a better performance in comparison. AMD uses the SKINIT instruction to perform DRTM, and Intel implements DRTM using a CPU

Table 3. Comparison between SMM-based and DRTM-based Approaches

	IOCheck	Flicker [18]
Operation	SMM switching	SKINIT instruction
Size of secure code	Any	4 KB
Time	3.92 μs	12 ms
Trust BIOS boot	Yes	No

instruction called SENTER. The SMM switching operation in IOCheck plays the same role as SKINIT or SENTER instructions in the DRTM approach. As stated in the Table II of Flicker [18], the time required to execute the SKINIT instruction depends on the size of the Secure Loader Block (SLB). It shows a linear growth in runtime as the size of the SLB increases. From Table 3, we can see that the SKINIT instruction takes about 12 milliseconds for 4KB of SLB. However, SMM switching only takes about 4 microseconds, which is about three orders of magnitude faster than the SKINIT instruction. Furthermore, SMM switching time is independent from the size of the SMI handler. This is because IOCheck does not need to measure the secure code every time before executing it, and we lock the secure code in SMRAM.

Note that IOCheck trusts the BIOS boot while Flicker does not. IOCheck requires a secure BIOS boot to ensure the SMM code is securely loaded into SMRAM. However, the DRTM approach (e.g., Intel TXT) also requires that the SMM code is trusted. Wojtczuk and Rutkowska demonstrate several attacks [12, 39, 40] against Intel TXT by using SMM if the SMM-Transfer Monitor is not present. From this point of view, both systems must trust the SMM code.

7   Limitations and Discussions

IOCheck is a runtime firmware and configuration integrity checking framework. We also demonstrate the feasibility of this approach using a commercial network card. However, the current prototype of IOCheck is specific to the target system, which uses an Intel 82574L network card and JATON VIDEO-498PCI-DLP Nvidia video card. Human effort is required to expand the functionality (e.g., checking BMC or Disk Controller).

SMM uses isolated memory (SMRAM) for execution. The initial size of SM-RAM is 64 KB, ranging from SMM_BASE to SMM_BASE + 0xFFFF. The default value of SMM_BASE is 0x30000, and Coreboot relocates it to 0xA0000. As the size of our SMI handler code is only 1,409 bytes, the small capacity of SMRAM may limit the scalability of IOCheck. However, the chipset in our testbed allows for an additional 4MB memory in a region called TSeg within SMRAM. Furthermore, SICE [41] demonstrates that SMM can support up to 4GB of isolated memory that can be used for memory-intensive operations such as virtualization.

Wojtczuk and Rutkowska [42] use cache poisoning to bypass the SMM lock by configuring the Memory Type Range Registers (MTRR) to force the CPU to execute code from the cache (which they injected) instead of SMRAM. Duflot also independently found the same vulnerability [43]. This vulnerability was fixed with Intel's addition of the System Management Range Register (SMRR). More recently, Butterworth et al. [25] used a buffer overflow vulnerability during the BIOS update process in SMM, although this was a bug in the particular BIOS version. Our SMM code in Coreboot does not have the same vulnerable code that facilitates this attack. To the best of our knowledge, there is no general attack that can bypass the SMM lock and compromise SMM.

The implementation of IOCheck contains 310 lines of C code. This part of the code may contain vulnerabilities that could be exploited by attackers. To reduce the possibility of vulnerable code, we sanitize the input of the SMI handler to reduce the attack surface. For instance, we do not accept any data input to the SMI handler except for the target firmware and configurations. We also carefully check the size of the input data to avoid overflow attacks [25].

SMM was not originally designed for security purposes. Researchers may argue that this makes it unsuitable for security operations. Additionally, some researchers feel that SMM is not essential to x86. However, there is no indication that Intel will remove SMM. Moreover, Intel introduced the SMM-Transfer Monitor [44] that virtualizes SMM code in order to defeat attacks [40] against TXT. In our case, SMM can be thought of as a mechanism to provide an isolated computing environment and hardware support to meet the system's requirements.

8   Related Work

To identify malware running in I/O devices, Li et al. propose VIPER [20], a software-based attestation method to verify the integrity of peripherals' firmware. VIPER runs a verifier program on the host machine, and it trusts the operating system. NAVIS [19] is an anomaly-detection system checking the memory accesses performed by the NIC's on-chip processor. It builds a memory layout profile of the NIC and raises an alert if any unexpected memory access is detected. The NAVIS program runs inside of the operating system and assumes the OS is trusted. Compared to VIPER and NAVIS, IOCheck is not running in the normal Protected Mode. It uses SMM to check the integrity of the firmware, which significantly reduces the TCB. In addition, IOCheck checks the configurations of I/O devices, which further protects them.

Compromised firmware normally performs DMA attacks against the main memory, and IOMMU (e.g., Intel VT-d or AMD-Vi) is an efficient defense. However, Sang et al. [11] identify an array of vulnerabilities on Intel VT-d. Wojtczuk et al. [12] use a bug in the SINIT module of the SENTER instruction to misconfigure VT-d, and then attackers are able to compromise the securely loaded hypervisor using a classic DMA attack so it can bypass Intel TXT. Although the main goal of this attack is to circumvent Intel TXT, we can learn that VT-d is easy to misconfigure and then an attacker can launch a DMA attack. Moreover, Stewin [10] explains several reasons that we cannot trust IOMMU as a countermeasure against DMA attacks. However, IOCheck is a generic framework that can check IOMMU configurations and provide further protection for I/O devices.

BARM [10] aims to detect and prevent DMA-based attacks. It is based on modeling the expected memory bus activity and comparing it to the actual activity. BARM relies on the OS and software applications to record all I/O bus activity in the form of I/O statistics, while IOCheck uses SMM without trusting any code in PM. IronHide [45] is a tool to analyze potential I/O attacks against PCs. It can be used either as an offensive or defensive tool. On the offensive side, it can be used to sniff out the I/O buses, spoof the bus address used by other I/O controller, and log/inject keystrokes. On the defensive side, it injects faults over the I/O buses to simulate various I/O attacks and to identify various possible vulnerabilities. However, IronHide requires a specialized PCI-Express device, while IOCheck uses existing technology in chipsets.

Recently, SMM-based systems have been brewing in the security area [46–50]. HyperCheck [46] checks the integrity of hypervisors and uses a network card to transmit the registers and memory contents to a remote server for verification. Therefore, a compromised network card would be problematic in HyperCheck. HyperSentry [47] also uses SMM for hypervisor integrity checking, and it uses Intelligent Platform Management Interface (IPMI) to stealthily trigger an SMI. IPMI relies on BMC and its firmware to operate, while IOCheck can mitigate those attacks against firmware. SPECTRE [49] is a periodically polling-based system that introspects the host memory for malware detection. It uses SMM to periodically check the host memory for heap overflow, heap spray, and rootkit attacks. However, IOCheck aims to enhance the security of I/O devices, and we use random-polling and event-driven approaches to mitigate transient attacks against the periodic polling-based systems. In addition, researchers use SMM to implement stealthy rootkits [51], which requires an unlocked SMRAM to load the rootkit. As explained in [51], all post-2006 machines have locked SMRAM in the BIOS. IOCheck locks the SMM in Coreboot so that SMRAM is inaccessible after booting.

9   Conclusions

In this paper, we present IOCheck, a framework to enhance the security of I/O devices at runtime. It checks the firmware and configurations of I/O devices and does not require the trust on the OS. We implement a prototype of IOCheck using random-polling-based and event-driven approaches, and it is robust against transient attacks. We demonstrate the effectiveness of IOCheck by checking the integrity of Intel 82574L NIC and Jaton VIDEO-498PCI-DLP VGA. The experimental results show that IOCheck is able to successfully detect firmware and I/O configuration attacks. IOCheck only takes about 10 milliseconds to check the firmware and configurations, and it introduces a low overhead on both Microsoft Windows and Linux platforms. Furthermore, we compare IOCheck with the DRTM approach and show that the switching time of IOCheck is three orders of magnitude faster than that of the DRTM approach.

Acknowledgement. The authors would like to thank all of the reviewers for their valuable comments and suggestions. This work is supported by the United States Air Force Research Laboratory (AFRL) through Contract FA8650-10-C-7024, National Science Foundation CRI Equipment Grant No. CNS-1205453, and

ONR Grant N00014-13-1-0088. Opinions, findings, conclusions and recommendations expressed in this material are those of the authors and do not necessarily reflect the views of the U.S. Government, Air Force, or Navy.

References

1. National Institute of Standards, NIST: National Vulnerability Database, http://nvd.nist.gov (access time March 4, 2014)
2. Mitre: Vulnerability list, http://cve.mitre.org/cve/cve.html
3. Bonkoski, A.J., Bielawski, R., Halderman, J.A.: Illuminating the Security Issues Surrounding Lights-out Server Management. In: Proceedings of the 7th USENIX Conference on Offensive Technologies (WOOT 2013) (2013)
4. Duflot, L., Perez, Y.A.: Can You Still Trust Your Network Card? In: Proceedings of the 13th CanSecWest Conference (CanSecWest 2010) (2010)
5. Chen, K.: Reversing and Exploiting an Apple Firmware Update. Black Hat (2009)
6. Stewin, P., Bystrov, I.: Understanding DMA Malware. In: Flegel, U., Markatos, E., Robertson, W. (eds.) DIMVA 2012. LNCS, vol. 7591, pp. 21–41. Springer, Heidelberg (2013)
7. Aumaitre, D., Devine, C.: Subverting Windows 7 x64 Kernel With DMA Attacks. In: HITBSecConf Amsterdam (2010)
8. Triulzi, A.: Project Maux Mk.II. In: CanSecWest (2008)
9. Sang, F., Nicomette, V., Deswarte, Y.: I/O Attacks in Intel PC-based Architectures and Countermeasures. In: SysSec Workshop (SysSec 2011) (2011)
10. Stewin, P.: A Primitive for Revealing Stealthy Peripheral-Based Attacks on the Computing Platform's Main Memory. In: Stolfo, S.J., Stavrou, A., Wright, C.V. (eds.) RAID 2013. LNCS, vol. 8145, pp. 1–20. Springer, Heidelberg (2013)
11. Sang, F., Lacombe, E., Nicomette, V., Deswarte, Y.: Exploiting an I/OMMU vulnerability. In: 5th International Conference on Malicious and Unwanted Software (MALWARE 2010), pp. 7–14 (2010)
12. Wojtczuk, R., Rutkowska, J.: Another Way to Circumvent Intel® Trusted Execution Technology (2009), http://invisiblethingslab.com/resources/misc09/Another
13. Wojtczuk, R., Rutkowska, J.: Following the White Rabbit: Software Attacks against Intel® VT-d (2011)
14. Trusted Computing Group: TCG PC Client Specific Implementation Specification for Conventional BIOS (February 2012), http://www.trustedcomputinggroup.org/files/resource_files/CB0B2BFA-1A4B-B294-D0C3B9075B5AFF17/TCG_PCClientImplementation_1-21_1_00.pdf
15. Trusted Computing Group: TPM Main Specification Level 2 Version 1.2, Revision 116 (2011), http://www.trustedcomputinggroup.org/resources/tpm_main_specification
16. Trusted Computing Group: TCG D-RTM Architecture Document Version 1.0.0 (June 2013), http://www.trustedcomputinggroup.org/resources/drtm_architecture_specification
17. Intel: Trusted Execution Technology, http://www.intel.com/content/www/us/en/trusted-execution-technology/trusted-execution-technology-security-paper.html
18. McCune, J., Parno, B., Perrig, A., Reiter, M., Isozaki, H.: Flicker: An Execution Infrastructure for TCB Minimization. In: Proceedings of the 3rd ACM SIGOPS/EuroSys European Conference on Computer Systems (2008)

19. Duflot, L., Perez, Y.-A., Morin, B.: What If You Can't Trust Your Network Card? In: Sommer, R., Balzarotti, D., Maier, G. (eds.) RAID 2011. LNCS, vol. 6961, pp. 378–397. Springer, Heidelberg (2011)
20. Li, Y., McCune, J., Perrig, A.: VIPER: Verifying the Integrity of PERipherals' Firmware. In: Proceedings of the 18th ACM Conference on Computer and Communications Security (CCS 2011) (2011)
21. Moon, H., Lee, H., Lee, J., Kim, K., Paek, Y., Kang, B.: Vigilare: Toward Snoop-based Kernel Integrity Monitor. In: Proceedings of the 19th ACM Conference on Computer and Communications Security (CCS 2012) (2012)
22. Wang, J., Sun, K., Stavrou, A.: A Dependability Analysis of Hardware-Assisted Polling Integrity Checking Systems. In: Proceedings of the 42nd Annual IEEE/IFIP International Conference on Dependable Systems and Networks (DSN 2012) (2012)
23. Zaddach, J., Kurmus, A., Balzarotti, D., Blass, E.O., Francillon, A., Goodspeed, T., Gupta, M., Koltsidas, I.: Implementation and Implications of a Stealth Hard-Drive Backdoor. In: Proceedings of the 29th Annual Computer Security Applications Conference (ACSAC 2013) (2013)
24. Triulzi, A.: The Jedi Packet Trick Takes Over the Deathstar: Taking NIC Back-doors to the Next Level. In: The 12th Annual CanSecWest Conference (2010)
25. Butterworth, J., Kallenberg, C., Kovah, X.: BIOS Chronomancy: Fixing the Core Root of Trust for Measurement. In: Proceedings of the 20th ACM Conference on Computer and Communications Security (CCS 2013) (2013)
26. Coreboot: Open-Source BIOS, http://www.coreboot.org/
27. VIA: VT8237R Southbridge, http://www.via.com.tw/
28. Broadcom Corporation: Broadcom NetXtreme Gigabit Ethernet Controller, http://www.broadcom.com/products/BCM5751
29. Salihun, D.: BIOS Disassembly Ninjutsu Uncovered, http://bioshacking.blogspot.com/2012/02/bios-disassembly-ninjutsu-uncovered-1st.html
30. Salihun, D.: Malicious Code Execution in PCI Expansion ROM (June 2012), http://resources.infosecinstitute.com/pci-expansion-rom/
31. Flashrom: Firmware flash utility, http://www.flashrom.org/
32. Advanced Micro Devices, Inc.: BIOS and Kernel Developer's Guide for AMD Athlon 64 and AMD Opteron Processors
33. William, H., Teukolsky, S.A., Vetterling, W.T., Flannery, B.P.: Numerical Recipes: The Art of Scientific Computing. Cambridge University Press, New York (2007)
34. MD5 Hash Functions, http://en.wikipedia.org/wiki/MD5
35. Intel: 82574 Gigabit Ethernet Controller Family: Datasheet, http://www.intel.com/content/www/us/en/ethernet-controllers/82574l-gbe-controller-datasheet.html
36. Jeff: RWEverything Tool, http://rweverything.com/
37. SuperPI, http://www.superpi.net/
38. Advanced Micro Devices, Inc.: AMD K8 Architecture, http://commons.wikimedia.org/wiki/File:AMD_K8.PNG
39. Wojtczuk, R., Rutkowska, J.: Attacking Intel Trust Execution Technologies (2009), http://invisiblethingslab.com/resources/bh09dc/Attacking
40. Wojtczuk, R., Rutkowska, J.: Attacking Intel TXT via SINIT Code Execution Hijacking (November 2011), http://www.invisiblethingslab.com/resources/2011/Attacking_Intel_TXT_via_SINIT_hijacking.pdf
41. Azab, A.M., Ning, P., Zhang, X.: SICE: A Hardware-level Strongly Isolated Computing Environment for x86 Multi-core Platforms. In: Proceedings of the 18th ACM Conference on Computer and Communications Security (CCS 2011) (2011)

42. Wojtczuk, R., Rutkowska, J.: Attacking SMM Memory via Intel CPU Cache Poisoning (2009)
43. Duflot, L., Levillain, O., Morin, B., Grumelard, O.: Getting into the SMRAM: SMM Reloaded. In: Proceedings of the 12th CanSecWest Conference (CanSecWest 2009) (2009)
44. Intel: Intel® 64 and IA-32 Architectures Software Developer's Manual
45. Sang, F.L., Nicomette, V., Deswarte, Y.: A Tool to Analyze Potential I/O Attacks Against PCs. IEEE Security & Privacy (2013)
46. Zhang, F., Wang, J., Sun, K., Stavrou, A.: HyperCheck: A Hardware-assisted Integrity Monitor. IEEE Transactions on Dependable and Secure Computing (2013)
47. Azab, A.M., Ning, P., Wang, Z., Jiang, X., Zhang, X., Skalsky, N.C.: HyperSentry: Enabling Stealthy In-Context Measurement of Hypervisor Integrity. In: Proceedings of the 17th ACM Conference on Computer and Communications Security (CCS 2010) (2010)
48. Reina, A., Fattori, A., Pagani, A., Cavallaro, L., Bruschi, D.: When Hardware Meets Software: A Bulletproof Solution to Forensic Memory Acquisition. In: Proceedings of the Annual Computer Security Applications Conference (ACSAC 2012) (2012)
49. Zhang, F., Leach, K., Sun, K., Stavrou, A.: SPECTRE: A Dependable Introspection Framework via System Management Mode. In: Proceedings of the 43rd Annual IEEE/IFIP International Conference on Dependable Systems and Networks (DSN 2013) (2013)
50. Zhang, Y., Pan, W., Wang, Q., Bai, K., Yu, M.: HypeBIOS: Enforcing VM Isolation with Minimized and Decomposed Cloud TCB. Technical report, Virginia Commonwealth University (2012)
51. Embleton, S., Sparks, S., Zou, C.: SMM rootkits: A New Breed of OS Independent Malware. In: Proceedings of the 4th International Conference on Security and Privacy in Communication Networks (SecureComm 2008) (2008)
52. PCI-SIG: PCI Local Bus Specification Revision 3.0, http://www.pcisig.com/specifications/

Appendix

Table 4. IOMMU Configurations

Register/Table Name	Description
Root-entry table address	Defines the base address of the root-entry table (first-level table identified by bus number)
Domain mapping tables	Includes root-entry table and context-entry tables (second-level tables identified by device and function numbers)
Page tables	Defines memory regions and access permissions of I/O controllers (third-level tables)
DMA remapping ACPI table	Defines the number of DRHUs present in the system and I/O controllers associated with each of them

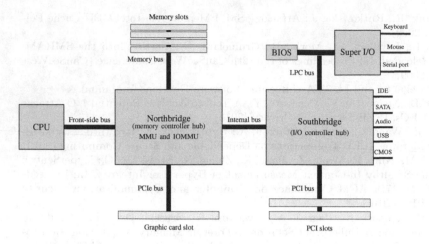

Fig. 2. Typical Hardware Layout of a Computer

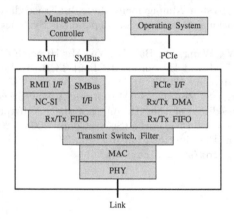

Fig. 3. Architecture Block Diagram of Intel 82574L [35]

Table 5. PCI Expansion ROM Format [52]

(a) PCI Expansion ROM Header Format for x86

Offset	Length	Value	Description
0h	1	55h	ROM signature, byte 1
1h	1	AAH	ROM signature, byte 2
2h	1	xx	Initialization size
3h	3	xx	Entry point for INIT function
6h-17h	12h	xx	Reserved
18h-19h	2	xx	Pointer to PCI data structure

(b) PCI Data Structure Format

Offset	Length	Description
0h	4	Signature, the string "PCIR"
4h	2	Vendor identification
6h	2	Device identification
8h	2	Reserved
Ah	2	PCI data structure length
Ch	1	PCI data structure revision
Dh	3	Class code
10h	2	Image length
12h	2	Revision level of code/data
14h	1	Code type
15h	1	Indicator
16	2	Reserved

StealthGuard: Proofs of Retrievability
with Hidden Watchdogs

Monir Azraoui, Kaoutar Elkhiyaoui, Refik Molva, and Melek Önen

EURECOM, Sophia Antipolis, France
{azraoui,elkhiyao,molva,onen}@eurecom.fr

Abstract. This paper presents **StealthGuard**, an efficient and provably secure proof of retrievabillity (POR) scheme. **StealthGuard** makes use of a privacy-preserving word search (WS) algorithm to search, as part of a POR query, for randomly-valued blocks called watchdogs that are inserted in the file before outsourcing. Thanks to the privacy-preserving features of the WS, neither the cloud provider nor a third party intruder can guess which watchdog is queried in each POR query. Similarly, the responses to POR queries are also obfuscated. Hence to answer correctly to every new set of POR queries, the cloud provider has to retain the file in its entirety. **StealthGuard** stands out from the earlier sentinel-based POR scheme proposed by Juels and Kaliski (JK), due to the use of WS and the support for an unlimited number of queries by **StealthGuard**. The paper also presents a formal security analysis of the protocol.

Keywords: Cloud storage, Proofs of Retrievability, Privacy-preserving word search.

1 Introduction

Nowadays outsourcing, that is, delegating one's computing to external parties, is a well established trend in cloud computing. Along with unprecedented advantages such as lower cost of ownership, adaptivity, and increased capacity, outsourcing also raises new security and privacy concerns in that critical data processing and storage operations are performed remotely by potentially untrusted parties. In this paper we focus on data retrievability, a security requirement akin to outsourced data storage services like Dropbox[1] and Amazon Simple Storage Service[2]. Data retrievability provides the customer of a storage service with the assurance that a data segment is actually present in the remote storage. Data retrievability is a new form of integrity requirement in that the customer of the storage or the data owner does not need to keep or get a copy of the data segment in order to get the assurance of retrievability thereof. A cryptographic building block called Proof of Retrievability (POR) was first developed by Juels and Kaliski [1] (JK) to meet this requirement. In the definition of [1], a successful execution of the POR scheme assures a verifier that it can retrieve F in its entirety. Classical integrity techniques such as transferring F with some integrity check value are not practical since

---

[1] Dropbox - https://www.dropbox.com/

[2] Amazon Simple Storage Service - http://aws.amazon.com/fr/s3/

M. Kutyłowski and J. Vaidya (Eds.): ESORICS 2014, Part I, LNCS 8712, pp. 239–256, 2014.

they incur very high communication or computational costs that are linear with the size of F. POR schemes aim at much lower cost both in terms of communications and processing by avoiding transmission or handling of F in its entirety. To that effect, POR schemes require the prover to perform some operations on some randomly selected parts of F and the verifier is able to check the result returned by the prover with the knowledge of very brief reference about the data like a secret key. Most POR schemes thus are probabilistic and their performance is measured in the trade-off between the bandwidth and processing overhead and the rate of retrievability assurance.

In this paper we develop **StealthGuard**, a new POR scheme that achieves good retrievability assurance with acceptable costs. The main idea behind the new scheme is a combination of a privacy-preserving word search (WS) algorithm suited to large datastores with the insertion in data segments of randomly generated short bit sequences called **watchdogs**. In **StealthGuard**, the user inserts these watchdogs in randomly chosen locations of the file F and stores the resulting file in the cloud. In order to check the retrievability of F the user issues lookup queries for selected values of watchdogs using the WS scheme. The user decrypts the WS replies from the cloud server in order to get the proof of retrievability for each segment targeted by the WS queries. Each positive result is the proof of presence for the corresponding data segment. Thanks to the features of the WS, neither the cloud server nor a third party intruder can guess which watchdogs are targeted by each WS query or response.

Even though there is an analogy between the watchdogs used in **StealthGuard** and the sentinels akin to the JK scheme [1], there is a major difference between the two schemes due to the use of WS by **StealthGuard**: the number of POR queries that can be issued in **StealthGuard** without requiring any update of the watchdogs is unbounded whereas in the JK scheme a given set of sentinels can be used for a finite number of POR queries only. **StealthGuard** only requires the transfer of some additional data that is a small percentage of F in size and a good POR rate can be achieved by only processing a fraction of F. In addition to the description of our proposal, we give a new security model that enhances existing security definitions of POR schemes [1, 2]. We state a generic definition of the soundness property that applies to any POR scheme.

Contributions. To summarize, this paper offers two main contributions:

– We present **StealthGuard**, a new POR scheme based on the insertion of watchdogs that requires a light file preprocessing and on a privacy-preserving WS that allows a user to issue an unbounded number of POR queries. Besides, the user is stateless since it only needs to keep a secret key to be able to run the POR protocol.
– We propose a new security model which improves existing security definitions [1, 2]. We also provide a formal proof of our proposal under this new security model.
The rest of the paper is organized as follows. Section 2 defines the entities and the algorithms involved in a POR scheme. Section 3 describes the adversary models that are considered in this paper. Section 4 provides an overview of **StealthGuard** and Section 5 gives details of the protocol. Section 6 analyses its security properties. Section 7 evaluates its security and its efficiency. We review the state of the art in Section 8.

2 Background

Before presenting the formal definition of PORs and the related security definitions, we introduce the entities that we will refer to in the remainder of this paper.

2.1 Entities

A POR scheme comprises the following entities:

- Client $\mathcal{C}$: It possesses a set of files $\mathcal{F}$ that it outsources to the cloud server $\mathcal{S}$. Without loss of generality, we assume that each file $F \in \mathcal{F}$ is composed of n splits $\{S_1, S_2, ..., S_n\}$ of equal size L bits. In practice, if the size of F is not a multiple of L, then padding bits will be added to F. We also suppose that each split S_i comprises m blocks of l bits $\{b_{i,1}, b_{i,2}, ..., b_{i,m}\}$, i.e., $L = m \cdot l$.
- Cloud Server $\mathcal{S}$ (a potentially malicious prover): For each file $F \in \mathcal{F}$, the cloud server $\mathcal{S}$ stores an "enlarged" verifiable version $\hat{F}$ of that file, that enables it to prove to a verifier $\mathcal{V}$ that the client $\mathcal{C}$ can still retrieve its original file F.
- Verifier $\mathcal{V}$: It is an entity which via an interactive protocol can check whether the cloud server $\mathcal{S}$ (i.e., the prover) is still storing some file $F \in \mathcal{F}$ or not. The verifier can be either the client itself or any other *authorized* entity, such as an auditor.

2.2 POR

A POR scheme consists of five polynomial-time algorithms (cf. [1, 2]):

- KeyGen(1^τ) $\rightarrow$ K: This probabilistic key generation algorithm is executed by client $\mathcal{C}$. It takes as input a security parameter τ, and outputs a *secret key* K for $\mathcal{C}$.
- Encode(K, F) $\rightarrow$ (fid, $\hat{F}$): It takes the key K and the file $F = \{S_1, S_2, ..., S_n\}$ as inputs, and returns the file $\hat{F} = \{\hat{S}_1, \hat{S}_2, ..., \hat{S}_n\}$ and F's *unique* identifier fid. Cloud server $\mathcal{S}$ is required to store $\hat{F}$ together with fid. $\hat{F}$ is obtained by first applying to F an *error-correcting code* (ECC) which allows client $\mathcal{C}$ to recover the file from minor corruptions that may go undetected by the POR scheme, and further by adding some *verifiable redundancy* that enables client $\mathcal{C}$ to check whether cloud server $\mathcal{S}$ still stores a *retrievable* version of F or not.
  Note that the Encode algorithm is invertible. Namely, there exists an algorithm Decode that allows the client $\mathcal{C}$ to recover its original file F from the file $\hat{F}$.
- Challenge(K, fid) $\rightarrow$ chal: The verifier $\mathcal{V}$ calls this *probabilistic* algorithm to generate a challenge chal for an execution of the POR protocol for some file F. This algorithm takes as inputs the secret key K and the file identifier fid, and returns the challenge chal that will be sent to cloud server $\mathcal{S}$.
- ProofGen(fid, chal) $\rightarrow$ $\mathcal{P}$: On receiving the challenge chal and the file identifier fid, cloud server $\mathcal{S}$ executes ProofGen to generate a proof of retrievability $\mathcal{P}$ for the file $\hat{F}$ whose identifier is fid. The proof $\mathcal{P}$ is then transmitted to verifier $\mathcal{V}$.
- ProofVerif(K, fid, chal, $\mathcal{P}$) $\rightarrow$ $b \in \{0, 1\}$: Verifier $\mathcal{V}$ runs this algorithm to check the validity of the proofs of retrievability sent by cloud server $\mathcal{S}$. On input of the key K, the file identifier fid, the challenge chal, and the proof $\mathcal{P}$, the ProofVerif algorithm outputs bit $b = 1$ if the proof $\mathcal{P}$ is a valid proof, and $b = 0$ otherwise.

3   Adversary Models

A POR scheme should ensure that if cloud server S is storing the outsourced files, then the ProofVerif algorithm should always output 1, meaning that ProofVerif does not yield any false negatives. This corresponds to the *completeness* property of the POR scheme. PORs should also guarantee that if S provides a number (to be determined) of valid proofs of retrievability for some file F, then verifier V can deduce that server S is storing a retrievable version of F. This matches the *soundness* property of POR. These two properties are formally defined in the following sections.

3.1   Completeness

If cloud server S and verifier V are both honest, then on input of a challenge chal and some file identifier fid sent by verifier V, the ProofGen algorithm generates a proof of retrievability P that will be accepted by verifier V with probability 1.

Definition 1 (Completeness). *A POR scheme is* complete *if for any honest pair of cloud server S and verifier V, and for any challenge* chal $\leftarrow$ Challenge(K, fid):

$$\Pr(\mathsf{ProofVerif}(K, \text{fid}, \text{chal}, P) \to 1 \mid P \leftarrow \mathsf{ProofGen}(\text{fid}, \text{chal})) = 1$$

3.2   Soundness

A proof of retrievability is deemed sound, if for any malicious cloud server S, the only way to convince verifier V that it is storing a file F is by actually keeping a retrievable version of that file. This implies that any cloud server S that generates (a polynomial number of) valid proofs of retrievability for some file F, must possess a version of that file that can be used later by client C to recover F. To reflect the intuition behind this definition of soundness, Juels and Kaliski [1] suggested the use of a file extractor algorithm $\mathcal{E}$ that is able to retrieve the file F by interacting with cloud server S using the *sound* POR protocol. Along these lines, we present a new and a more generic soundness definition that refines the formalization of Shacham and Waters [2] which in turn builds upon the work of Juels and Kaliski [1]. Although the definition of Shacham and Waters [2] captures the soundness of POR schemes that empower the verifier with unlimited (i.e. exponential) number of "possible" POR challenges [2–4], it does not define properly the soundness of POR schemes with limited number of "possible" POR challenges such as in [1, 5] and in **StealthGuard**[3]. We recall that the formalization in [2] considers a POR to be sound, if a file can be recovered whenever the cloud server generates a valid POR response for that file with a *non-negligible* probability. While this definition is accurate in the case where the verifier is endowed with unlimited number of POR challenges, it cannot be employed to evaluate the soundness of the mechanisms introduced in [1, 5] or the solution we will present in this paper. For example, if we take the POR scheme in [5] and if we consider a scenario where the cloud server corrupts

---

[3] Note that having a bounded number of POR challenges does not negate the fact that the verifier can perform unlimited number of POR queries with these same challenges, cf. [5].

randomly half of the outsourced files, then the cloud server will be able to correctly answer half (which is non-negligible) of the POR challenges that the verifier issues, yet the files are irretrievable. This implies that this POR mechanism is not secure in the model of Shacham and Waters [2], still it is arguably sound.

The discrepancy between the soundness definition in [2] and the work of [1, 5] springs from the fact that in practice to check whether a file is correctly stored at the cloud server, the verifier issues a polynomial number of POR queries to which the server has to respond correctly; otherwise, the verifier detects a corruption attack (the corruption attack could either be malicious or accidental) and flags the server as malicious. This is actually what the PORs of [1, 5] and **StealthGuard** aim to capture. In order to remedy this shortcoming, we propose augmenting the definition of Shacham and Waters [2] (as will be shown in Algorithm 2) with an additional parameter γ that quantifies the number of POR queries that verifier should issue to either be sure that a file is retrievable or to detect a corruption attack on that file.

Now in accordance with [2], we first formalize *soundness* using a game that describes the capabilities of an adversary $\mathcal{A}$ (i.e., malicious cloud server) which can deviate arbitrarily from the POR protocol, and then we define the extractor algorithm $\mathcal{E}$.

To formally capture the capabilities of adversary $\mathcal{A}$, we assume that it has access to the following oracles:

- $\mathcal{O}_{\text{Encode}}$: This oracle takes as inputs a file F and the client's key K, and returns a file identifier fid and a verifiable version $\hat{F}$ of F that will be outsourced to $\mathcal{A}$.
  Note that adversary $\mathcal{A}$ can corrupt the outsourced file $\hat{F}$ either by modifying or deleting $\hat{F}$'s blocks.
- $\mathcal{O}_{\text{Challenge}}$: On input of a file identifier fid and client's key K, the oracle $\mathcal{O}_{\text{Challenge}}$ returns a POR challenge chal to adversary $\mathcal{A}$.
- $\mathcal{O}_{\text{Verify}}$: When queried with client's key K, a file identifier fid, a challenge chal and a proof of retrievability $\mathcal{P}$, the oracle $\mathcal{O}_{\text{Verify}}$ returns bit b such that: $b = 1$ if $\mathcal{P}$ is a valid proof of retrievability, and $b = 0$ otherwise.

Adversary $\mathcal{A}$ accesses the aforementioned oracles in two phases: a learning phase and a challenge phase. In the learning phase, adversary $\mathcal{A}$ can call oracles $\mathcal{O}_{\text{Encode}}$, $\mathcal{O}_{\text{Challenge}}$, and $\mathcal{O}_{\text{Verify}}$ for a polynomial number of times in any interleaved order as depicted in Algorithm 1. Then, at the end of the learning phase, the adversary $\mathcal{A}$ specifies a file identifier fid^* that was already output by oracle $\mathcal{O}_{\text{Encode}}$.

We note that the goal of adversary $\mathcal{A}$ in the challenge phase (cf. Algorithm 2) is to generate γ valid proofs of retrievability $\mathcal{P}_)^*$ for file F^* associated with file identifier fid^*. To this end, adversary $\mathcal{A}$ first calls the oracle $\mathcal{O}_{\text{Challenge}}$ that supplies $\mathcal{A}$ with γ challenges chal_i^*, then it responds to these challenges by outputting γ proofs $\mathcal{P}_i^*$. Now, on input of client's key K, file identifier fid^* challenges chal_i^* and proofs $\mathcal{P}_i^*$, oracle $\mathcal{O}_{\text{Verify}}$ outputs γ bits b_i^*. Adversary $\mathcal{A}$ is said to be successful if $b^* = \bigwedge_{i=1}^{\gamma} b_i^* = 1$. That is, if $\mathcal{A}$ is able to generate γ proofs of retrievability $\mathcal{P}^*$ for file F^* that are accepted by oracle $\mathcal{O}_{\text{Verify}}$.

Given the game described above and in line with [1, 2], we formalize the soundness of POR schemes through the definition of an extractor algorithm $\mathcal{E}$ that uses adversary $\mathcal{A}$ to recover/retrieve the file F^* by processing as follows:

– $\mathcal{E}$ takes as inputs the client's key K and the file identifier fid*;
– $\mathcal{E}$ is allowed to initiate a polynomial number of POR executions with adversary $\mathcal{A}$ for the file F^*;
– $\mathcal{E}$ is also allowed to rewind adversary $\mathcal{A}$. This suggests in particular that extractor $\mathcal{E}$ can execute the challenge phase of the soundness game a polynomial number of times, while the state of adversary $\mathcal{A}$ remains unchanged.

Intuitively, a POR scheme is sound, if for any adversary $\mathcal{A}$ that wins the soundness game with a non-negligible probability δ, there exists an extractor algorithm $\mathcal{E}$ that succeeds in retrieving the challenge file F^* with an overwhelming probability. A probability is overwhelming if it is equal to $1 - \varepsilon$, where ε is negligible.

Algorithm 1. Learning phase of the soundness game	**Algorithm 2.** Challenge phase of the soundness game
// $\mathcal{A}$ executes the following in any interleaved // order for a polynomial number of times $(\text{fid}, \hat{F}) \leftarrow \mathcal{O}_{\text{Encode}}(F, K);$ chal $\leftarrow \mathcal{O}_{\text{Challenge}}(K, \text{fid});$ $\mathcal{P} \leftarrow \mathcal{A};$ $b \leftarrow \mathcal{O}_{\text{Verify}}(K, \text{fid}, \text{chal}, \mathcal{P});$ // $\mathcal{A}$ outputs a file identifier fid* fid* $\leftarrow \mathcal{A};$	**for** $i = 1$ **to** γ **do** $\quad$ chal$_i^* \leftarrow \mathcal{O}_{\text{Challenge}}(K, \text{fid}^*);$ $\quad \mathcal{P}_i^* \leftarrow \mathcal{A};$ $\quad b_i^* \leftarrow$ $\quad \mathcal{O}_{\text{Verify}}(K, \text{fid}_i^*, \text{chal}_i^*, \mathcal{P}_i^*);$ **end** $b^* = \bigwedge\limits_{i=1}^{\gamma} b_i^*$

Definition 2 (Soundness). *A POR scheme is said to be (δ, γ)-sound, if for every adversary $\mathcal{A}$ that provides γ valid proofs of retrievability in a row (i.e., succeeds in the soundness game described above) with a non-negligible probability δ, there exists an extractor algorithm $\mathcal{E}$ such that:*

$$Pr(\mathcal{E}(K, \text{fid}^*) \to F^* \mid \mathcal{E}(K, \text{fid}^*) \overset{\text{interact}}{\longleftrightarrow} \mathcal{A}) \geq 1 - \varepsilon$$

Where ε is a negligible function in the security parameter τ.

The definition above could be interpreted as follows: if verifier $\mathcal{V}$ issues a sufficient number of queries ($\geq \gamma$) to which cloud server $\mathcal{S}$ responds correctly, then $\mathcal{V}$ can ascertain that $\mathcal{S}$ is still storing a retrievable version of file F^* with high probability. It should be noted that while γ characterizes the number of *valid* proofs of retrievability that $\mathcal{E}$ has to receive (successfully or in a row) to assert that file F^* is still retrievable, δ quantifies the number of operations that the extractor $\mathcal{E}$ has to execute and the amount of data that it has to download to first declare F^* as retrievable and then to extract it. Actually, the computation and the communication complexity of extractor $\mathcal{E}$ will be of order $O(\frac{\gamma}{\delta})$.

4 Overview

4.1 Idea

In **StealthGuard**, client $\mathcal{C}$ first injects some pseudo-randomly generated *watchdogs* into random positions in the encrypted data. Once data is outsourced, $\mathcal{C}$ launches lookup queries to check whether the watchdogs are stored as expected by the cloud. By relying on a privacy-preserving word search (WS), we ensure that neither the cloud server S nor eavesdropping intruders can discover which watchdog was targeted by search queries. As a result, C can launch an unbounded number of POR queries (even for the same watchdog) without the need of updating the data with new watchdogs in the future. The responses are also obfuscated thanks to the underlying WS scheme. This ensures that the only case in which S returns a valid set of responses for the POR scheme is when it stores the entire file and executes the WS algorithm correctly (soundness property).

Besides, as in [1], in order to protect the data from small corruptions, **StealthGuard** applies an ECC that enables the recovery of the corrupted data. Substantial damage to the data is detected via the watchdog search.

4.2 StealthGuard Phases

A client C uploads to the cloud server S a file F which consists of n splits $\{S_1, ..., S_n\}$. Thereafter a verifier V checks the retrievability of F using **StealthGuard**.

The protocol is divided into three phases:

- *Setup*: During this phase, client C performs some transformations over the file and inserts a certain number of watchdogs in each split. The resulting file is sent to cloud server S.
- *WDSearch*: This phase consists in searching for some watchdog w in a privacy-preserving manner. Hence, verifier V prepares and sends a lookup query for w; the cloud S in turn processes the relevant split to generate a correct response to the search and returns the output to V.
- *Verification*: Verifier V checks the validity of the received response and makes the decision about the existence of the watchdog in the outsourced file.
  We note that if V receives at least γ (γ is a threshold determined in Section 6.2) correct responses from the cloud, then it can for sure decide that F is retrievable. On the other hand, if V receives one response that is not valid, then it is convinced either the file is corrupted or even lost.

5 StealthGuard

This section details the phases of the protocol. Table 1 sums up the notation used in the description. We also designed a dynamic version of **StealthGuard** that allows efficient POR even when data is updated. Due to space limitations, we only present in Section 5.4 an overview of dynamic **StealthGuard**.

5.1 Setup

This phase prepares a verifiable version $\hat{F}$ of file $F = \{S_1, S_2, ..., S_n\}$. Client C first runs the KeyGen algorithm to generate the master secret key K. It derives $n + 3$ additional keys, used for further operations in the protocol: $K_{enc} = H_{enc}(K)$, $K_{wdog} = H_{wdog}(K)$, $K_{permF} = H_{permF}(K)$ and for $i \in [\![1, n]\!], K_{permS,i} = H_{permS}(K, i)$

Table 1. Notation used in the description of StealthGuard

Index	Description
n	number of splits S_i in F
m	number of blocks in a split S_i
D	number of blocks in an encoded split $\tilde{S}_i$
v	number of watchdogs in one split
C	number of blocks in a split $\hat{S}_i$ with watchdogs
i	index of a split $\in [\![1, n]\!]$
k	index of a block in $\hat{S}_i \in [\![1, C]\!]$
j	index of a watchdog $\in [\![1, v]\!]$
l	size of a block
p	index of a block in $\tilde{F} \in [\![1, n \cdot D]\!]$
q	number of cloud's matrices
κ	index of a cloud's matrix $\in [\![1, q]\!]$
(s, t)	size of cloud's matrices
(x, y)	coordinates in a cloud's matrix $\in [\![1, s]\!] \times [\![1, t]\!]$

with H_{enc}, H_{wdog}, H_{permF} and H_{permS} being four cryptographic hash functions. K is the single information stored at the client.

Once all keying material is generated, $\mathcal{C}$ runs the Encode algorithm which first generates a pseudo-random and unique file identifier fid for file F, and then processes F as depicted in Figure 1.

1. **Error correcting:** The error-correcting code (ECC) assures the protection of the file against small corruptions. This step applies to each split S_i an ECC that operates over l-bit symbols. It uses an efficient $[m+d-1, m, d]$-ECC, such as Reed-Solomon codes [6], that has the ability to correct up to $\frac{d}{2}$ errors[4]. Each split is expanded with $d - 1$ blocks of redundancy. Thus, the new splits are made of $D = m + d - 1$ blocks.

2. **File block permutation:** StealthGuard applies a pseudo-random permutation to permute all the blocks in the file. This operation conceals the dependencies between the original data blocks and the corresponding redundancy blocks within a split. Without this permutation, the corresponding redundancy blocks are just appended to this split. An attacker could for instance delete all the redundancy blocks and a single data block from this split and thus render the file irretrievable. Such an attack would not easily be detected since the malicious server could still be able to respond with valid proofs to a given POR query targeting other splits in the file. The permutation prevents this attack since data blocks and redundancy blocks are mixed up among all splits. Let $\Pi_F : \{0, 1\}^\tau \times [\![1, n \cdot D]\!] \to [\![1, n \cdot D]\!]$ be a pseudo-random permutation: for each $p \in [\![1, n \cdot D]\!]$, the block at current position p will be at position $\Pi_F(K_{permF}, p)$ in the permuted file that we denote $\tilde{F}$. $\tilde{F}$ is then divided into n splits $\{\tilde{S}_1, \tilde{S}_2, ..., \tilde{S}_n\}$ of equal size D.

---

[4] d is even.

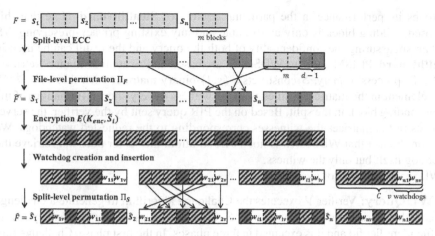

Fig. 1. Setup phase in StealthGuard

3. **Encryption: StealthGuard** uses a semantically secure encryption E that operates over l-bit blocks[5] to encrypt the data. An encryption scheme like AES in counter mode [7] can be used. The encryption E is applied to each block of $\tilde{F}$ using K_{enc}.

4. **Watchdog creation:** For each encrypted split, v l-bit watchdogs are generated using a pseudo-random function $\Phi : \{0,1\}^\tau \times [\![1,n]\!] \times [\![1,v]\!] \times \{0,1\}^* \to \{0,1\}^l$. Hence, for $j \in [\![1,v]\!]$, $w_{i,j} = \Phi(K_{wdog}, i, j, \text{fid})$. The use of fid guarantees that two different files belonging to the same client have different watchdogs. Since the watchdogs are pseudo-randomly generated and the blocks in the split are encrypted, a malicious cloud cannot distinguish watchdogs from data blocks.

5. **Watchdog insertion:** The v watchdogs are appended to each split. Let $C = D + v$ be the size of the new splits. A split-level pseudo-random permutation $\Pi_S : \{0,1\}^\tau \times [\![1,C]\!] \to [\![1,C]\!]$ is then applied to the blocks within the same split in order to randomize the location of the watchdogs: for $i \in [\![1,n]\!]$, the block at current position k will be at position $\Pi_S(K_{permS,i}, k)$ in the permuted split. Note that in practice, the permutation is only applied to the last v blocks: for $k \in [\![D,C]\!]$, this step swaps block at current position k for block at position $\Pi_S(K_{permS,i}, k)$. We denote $\hat{S}_i$, $i \in [\![1,n]\!]$, the permuted split and $\hat{b}_{i,k}$, $k \in [\![1,C]\!]$ its blocks.

These operations yield file $\hat{F}$. The client uploads the splits $\{\hat{S}_i\}_{i=1}^n$ and fid to the cloud.

5.2   WDSearch

Verifier $\mathcal{V}$ wants to check the retrievability of F. Hence, it issues lookup queries for randomly selected watchdog, one watchdog for one split in one query. Cloud server $\mathcal{S}$ processes these queries without knowing what the values of the watchdogs are and where they are located in the splits. We propose WDSearch, a privacy-preserving WS solution derived from PRISM in [8]. Our proposal is a simpler version of PRISM and

---

[5] Practically, l will be 128 or 256 bits.

improves its performance in the particular context of **StealthGuard**. Note that this proposed building block is only an example and any existing privacy-preserving WS mechanism assuring the confidentiality of both the query and the result can be used in **StealthGuard**. PRISM and thus WDSearch are based on Private Information Retrieval (PIR). To process a query, S constructs q (s, t)-binary matrices such that $s \cdot t = C$. Each element in the matrices is filled with the witness (a very short information) of the corresponding block in the split. Based on the PIR query sent by the verifier, the server retrieves in the matrices the witnesses corresponding to the requested watchdogs. We insist on the fact that WDSearch is not a PIR solution: the server does not retrieve the watchdog itself but only the witness.

WDSearch consists of two steps:

- **WDQuery:** Verifier V executes the Challenge algorithm to generate a challenge chal that is transmitted to cloud server S. Challenge takes as input master key K and file identifier fid and it is executed in three phases. In the first phase, Challenge randomly selects a split index i and a watchdog index j ($i \in [\![1, n]\!]$ and $j \in [\![1, v]\!]$), and computes the position pos_j of the watchdog $w_{i,j}$ in the split $\hat{S}_i$ by applying the permutation performed during the watchdog insertion step: $\text{pos}_j = \Pi_S(K_{permS,i}, D + j)$. Then, Challenge maps the position pos_j to a unique position (x_j, y_j) in an (s, t)-matrix:

$$x_j = \lceil \frac{\text{pos}_j}{t} \rceil \qquad\qquad y_j = \text{pos}_j - \lceil \frac{\text{pos}_j}{t} \rceil \times t + t$$

  In the second phase, given (x_j, y_j) and using any efficient PIR algorithm, Challenge computes a PIR query, denoted WitnessQuery, to retrieve the witness (and not the watchdog) at position (x_j, y_j) in the matrix. In the last phase, Challenge generates a random number r (this nonce will be used by the cloud when filling the binary matrices to guarantee freshness), and outputs the challenge chal $=$ (WitnessQuery, r, i). Eventually, verifier V sends the challenge chal and file identifier fid to cloud server S.

- **WDResponse:** Upon receiving the challenge chal $=$ (WitnessQuery, r, i) and file identifier fid, cloud server S runs ProofGen to process the query. The cloud creates q binary matrices of size (s, t). For each block $\hat{b}_{i,k}$ in $\hat{S}_i$, the cloud computes $h_{i,k} = H(\hat{b}_{i,k}, r)$, where $k \in [\![1, C]\!]$. Here, H denotes a cryptographic hash function. The use of r forces the cloud to store the actual data block. Otherwise it could drop the block, only store the hash and respond to the query using that hash. Let $h_{i,k}|_q$ be the first q bits of $h_{i,k}$. For $\kappa \in [\![1, q]\!]$, let $\mathcal{M}_\kappa$ be one of the matrices created by the cloud. It fills the κth matrix with the κth bit of $h_{i,k}|_q$ as Algorithm 3 shows. It should be noted that according to the assignment process described in Algorithm 3, the witness at position (x_j, y_j) in $\mathcal{M}_\kappa$ is associated with watchdog $w_{i,j}$: it is the κth bit of $H(w_{i,j}, r)$.

  Once all the q binary matrices are filled, the cloud processes WitnessQuery by executing a PIR operation that retrieves one bit from each matrix $\mathcal{M}_\kappa$, $\kappa \in [\![1, q]\!]$. We denote WitnessResponse$_\kappa$ the result of the PIR on matrix $\mathcal{M}_\kappa$. The ProofGen algorithm outputs $\mathcal{P}$, i.e. the proof of retrievability that consists in the set $\mathcal{P} = \{\text{WitnessResponse}_1, ..., \text{WitnessResponse}_q\}$. Cloud server S sends the proof $\mathcal{P}$ to verifier V.

Algorithm 3. Filling the cloud matrices

// For a given (s,t)-matrix $\mathcal{M}_\kappa$, a given split $\hat{S}_i$ and a given random number r
// k is the index of a block in split $\hat{S}_i$
$k = 1$;
for $x = 1$ **to** s **do**
    for $y = 1$ **to** t **do**
        $\mathcal{M}_\kappa[x,y] \leftarrow \kappa^{th}$ bit of $H(\hat{b}_{i,k}, r)$;
        $k = k + 1$;
    end
end

5.3 Verification

Verifier $\mathcal{V}$ runs ProofVerif to analyze the received proof $\mathcal{P}$. This algorithm takes as input master key K, proof $\mathcal{P}$, split index i, watchdog index j, and file identifier fid. ProofVerif outputs a bit equal to 1 if the proof is valid or 0 otherwise.

$\mathcal{V}$ processes the q WitnessResponse$_\kappa$ in order to retrieve the q bits ϵ_κ at position (x_j, y_j) in the matrix $\mathcal{M}_\kappa$, for $\kappa \in [\![1, q]\!]$. Let h denote $\epsilon_1\epsilon_2...\epsilon_q$.

We recall that verifier $\mathcal{V}$ queried watchdog $w_{i,j}$ for split $\hat{S}_i$ and that by having access to the master key K, $\mathcal{V}$ can recompute the value of $w_{i,j} = \Phi(K_{wdog}, i, j, \text{fid})$ and its position in the split $\hat{S}_i$, $\text{pos}_j = \Pi_S(K_{permS,i}, D + j)$. Thereafter, $\mathcal{V}$ computes the hash of the watchdog $h_{i,\text{pos}_j} = H(w_{i,j}, r)$, with the same r chosen during the challenge and considers the q first bits of h_{i,pos_j}. Based on the value of $h = \epsilon_1\epsilon_2...\epsilon_q$ and h_{i,pos_j}, $\mathcal{V}$ checks whether $h = h_{i,\text{pos}_j}|_q$. If it is the case, then $\mathcal{V}$ judges the proof valid and returns 1, otherwise it interprets the invalid proof as the occurrence of an attack and outputs 0.

As mentioned in section 4.2, in order to acknowledge the retrievability of F, verifier $\mathcal{V}$ needs to initiate at least γ POR queries[6] from randomly selected splits in order to either ascertain that F is retrievable or detect a corruption attack: if $\mathcal{V}$ receives γ valid POR responses, then it can conclude that cloud server $\mathcal{S}$ stores a retrievable version of F, otherwise it concludes that $\mathcal{S}$ has corrupted part of the file.

5.4 Dynamic StealthGuard

The previously described protocol does not consider update operations that the client can perform over its data. Similarly to the work in [5, 9–17], we propose a scheme that handles these updates. Due to space limitations we present only an idea of how dynamic **StealthGuard** operates. Any update in the data impacts the security of our protocol. For example, if the client modifies the same block several times then the cloud can discover that this particular block is not a watchdog. Therefore, dynamic **StealthGuard** updates the watchdogs in a split each time an update occurs on that split. Besides, the verifier must be ensured that the file stored at the server is actually the latest version. Dynamic **StealthGuard** offers a versioning solution to assure that the cloud always correctly applies the required update operations and that it always stores the latest version of the

---

[6] The value of γ will be determined in Section 6.2.

file. Our proposal uses Counting Bloom Filters [18] and Message Authentication Codes (MAC) [19]. Each time a split is updated, some information regarding the split number and the version number is added into the counting Bloom filter which is authenticated using a MAC that can only be computed by the client and the verifier. Additionally, to guarantee the freshness of the response at each update query, a new MAC key is generated. This protocol does not imply any additional cost at the verifier except of storing an additional MAC symmetric key.

Another challenging issue is that updating a data block requires to update the corresponding redundancy blocks, resulting in the disclosure to the cloud server of the dependencies between the data blocks and the redundancy blocks. Therefore, the file permutation in the *Setup* phase becomes ineffective. Some techniques are available to conceal these dependencies such as batch updates [5] or oblivious RAM [16]. However, these approaches are expensive in terms of computation and communication costs. Hence, we choose to trade off between POR security and update efficiency by omitting the file permutation.

6 Security Analysis

In this section, we state the security theorems of **StealthGuard**.

6.1 Completeness

Theorem 1. *StealthGuard is complete.*

Proof. Without loss of generality, we assume that the honest verifier $\mathcal{V}$ runs a POR for a file F. To this end, verifier $\mathcal{V}$ sends a challenge chal $= (\text{WitnessQuery}, r, i)$ for watchdog $w_{i,j}$, and the file identifier fid of F. Upon receiving challenge chal and file identifier fid, the cloud server generates a proof of retrievability $\mathcal{P}$ for F.

According to **StealthGuard**, the verification of POR consists of first retrieving the first q bits of a hash h_{i,pos_j}, then verifying whether $h_{i,\text{pos}_j}|q$ corresponds to the first q-bits of the hash $H(w_{i,j}, r)$. Since the cloud server $\mathcal{S}$ is honest, then this entails that it stores $w_{i,j}$, and therewith, can always compute $h_{i,\text{pos}_j} = H(w_{i,j}, r)$.

Consequently, $\text{ProofVerif}(K, \text{fid}, \text{chal}, \mathcal{P}) = 1$.

6.2 Soundness

As in Section 5, we assume that each split S_i in a file F is composed of m blocks, and that the Encode algorithm employs a $[D, m, d]$-ECC that corrects up to $\frac{d}{2}$ errors per split (i.e., $D = m + d - 1$). We also assume that at the end of its execution, the Encode algorithm outputs the encoded file $\hat{F}$ which consists of a set of splits $\hat{S}_i$ each comprising $C = (D + v)$ blocks (we recall that v is the number of watchdogs per split).

In the following, we state the main security theorem for **StealthGuard**.

Theorem 2. *Let τ be the security parameter of* **StealthGuard** *and let ρ denote $\frac{d}{2D}$.*

StealthGuard is (δ, γ)-sound in the random oracle model, for any $\delta > \delta_{neg}$ and $\gamma \geq \gamma_{neg}$, where

$$\delta_{neg} = \frac{1}{2^{\tau}}$$

$$\gamma_{neg} = \lceil \frac{\ln(2)\tau}{\rho_{neg}} \rceil$$

$$(1 - \frac{\rho}{\rho_{neg}})^2 \rho_{neg} = \frac{3\ln(2)\tau}{D} \text{ and } \rho_{neg} \leq \rho$$

Actually if $\gamma \geq \gamma_{neg}$, then there exists an extractor $\mathcal{E}$ that recovers a file F with a probability $1 - \frac{n}{2^{\tau}}$, such that n is the number of splits in F, by interacting with an adversary $\mathcal{A}$ against StealthGuard who succeeds in the soundness game with a probability $\delta > \frac{1}{2^{\tau}}$.

Due to space limitations, a proof sketch of this theorem is provided in our long report [20]. We note that the results derived above can be interpreted as follows: if verifier $\mathcal{V}$ issues $\gamma \geq \gamma_{neg}$ POR queries for some file F to which the cloud server $\mathcal{S}$ responds correctly, then $\mathcal{V}$ can declare F as retrievable with probability $1 - \frac{n}{2^{\tau}}$. Also, we recall that a POR execution for a file F in **StealthGuard** consists of fetching (obliviously) a witness of a watchdog from the encoding $\hat{F}$ of that file. Consequently, to ensure a security level of $\frac{1}{2^{\tau}}$, the client $\mathcal{C}$ must insert at least γ_{neg} watchdogs in F. That is, if file F comprises n splits, then $nv \geq \gamma_{neg}$ (v is the number of watchdogs per split).

7 Discussion

StealthGuard requires the client to generate $v > \frac{\gamma_{neg}}{n}$ watchdogs per split where n is the number of splits and γ_{neg} is the threshold of the number of queries that verifier $\mathcal{V}$ should issue to check the retrievability of the outsourced data. As shown in Theorem 2, this threshold does not depend on the size of data (in bytes). Instead, γ_{neg} is defined solely by the security parameter τ, the number $D = m + d - 1$ of data blocks and redundancy block per split and the rate $\rho = \frac{d}{2D}$ of errors that the underlying ECC can correct. Namely, γ_{neg} is inversely proportional to both D and ρ. This means that by increasing the number of blocks D per split or the *correctable* error rate ρ, the number of queries that the client should issue decreases. However, having a large ρ would increase the size of data that client $\mathcal{C}$ has to outsource to cloud server $\mathcal{S}$, which can be inconvenient for the client. Besides, increasing D leads to an increase of the number of blocks $C = s \cdot t$ per split $\hat{S}_i$ which has a direct impact on the communication cost and the computation load *per query* at both the verifier $\mathcal{V}$ and the cloud server $\mathcal{S}$. It follows that when defining the parameters of **StealthGuard**, one should consider the tradeoff between the affordable storage cost and the computation and communication complexity per POR query.

To enhance the computation performances of **StealthGuard**, we suggest to use the **Trapdoor Group Private Information Retrieval** which was proposed in [21] to implement the PIR instance in WDSearch. This PIR enables the verifier in **StealthGuard** to fetch a row from an (s, t) matrix (representing a split) without revealing to the cloud which row the verifier is querying. One important feature of this PIR is that it only involves random number generations, additions and multiplications in $\mathbb{Z}_p$ (where p is a prime of size $|p| = 200$ bits) which are not computationally intensive and could be performed by a lightweight verifier. In addition, we emphasize that PIR in **Stealth-Guard** is not employed to retrieve a watchdog, but rather to retrieve a q-bit hash of the watchdog (typically $q = 80$), and that it is not performed on the entire file, but it is instead executed over a split. Finally, we indicate that when employing **Trapdoor Group Private Information Retrieval**, the communication cost of **StealthGuard** is minimal when $s \simeq \sqrt{Cq}$ and $t \simeq \sqrt{\frac{C}{q}}$. This results in a computation and a communication complexity (per query) at the verifier of $O(\sqrt{Cq})$ and a computation and communication complexity at the server of $O(C)$ and $O(\sqrt{Cq})$ respectively.

Example. A file F of 4GB is divided into $n = 32768$ splits $F = \{S_1, S_2, ..., S_n\}$, and each split S_i is composed of 4096 blocks of size 256 bits. **StealthGuard** inserts 8 watchdogs per split and applies an ECC that corrects up to 228 corrupted blocks (i.e., $\rho = 5\%$). We obtain thus $\hat{F} = \{\hat{S}_1, \hat{S}_2, ..., \hat{S}_n\}$, where $\hat{S}_i$ is composed of 4560 blocks of size 256 bits. This results in a redundancy of $\simeq 11.3\%$, where 11.1% redundancy is due to the use of ECC, and 0.20% redundancy is caused by the use of watchdogs.

If $(s, t) = (570, 8)$, $q = 80$ and **StealthGuard** implements the Trapdoor Group PIR [21] where $|p| = 200$ bits, then the verifier's query will be of size $\simeq 13.9$ KB, whereas the cloud server's response will be of size $\simeq 15.6$KB. In addition, if the cloud server still stores the file $\hat{F}$, then the verifier will declare the file as retrievable with probability $1 - \frac{n}{2^{60}} \simeq 1 - \frac{1}{2^{45}}$ by executing the POR protocol 1719 times. That is, by downloading 26.2MB which corresponds to 0.64% of the size of the original file F.

8   Related Work

The approach that is the closest to **StealthGuard** is the sentinel-based POR introduced by Juels and Kaliski [1]. As in **StealthGuard**, before outsourcing the file to the server, the client applies an ECC and inserts in the encrypted file special blocks, *sentinels*, that are indistinguishable from encrypted blocks. However, during the challenge, the verifier asks the prover for randomly-chosen sentinels, disclosing their positions and values to the prover. Thus, this scheme suggests a limited number of POR queries. Therefore, the client may need to download the file in order to insert new sentinels and upload it again to the cloud. [1] mentions, without giving any further details, a PIR-based POR scheme that would allow an unlimited number of challenges by keeping the positions of sentinels private, at the price of high computational cost equivalent in practice to downloading the entire file. In comparison, **StealthGuard** uses a PIR within the WS technique to retrieve a witness of the watchdog (a certain number of bits instead of the entire watchdog), and does not limit the number of POR verifications.

Ateniese et al. [22] define the concept of Provable Data Possession (PDP), which is weaker than POR in that it assures that the server possesses parts of the file but does not guarantee its full recovery. PDP uses RSA-based homomorphic tags as check-values for each file block. To verify possession, the verifier asks the server for tags for randomly chosen blocks. The server generates a proof based on the selected blocks and their respective tags. This scheme provides public verifiability meaning that any third party can verify the retrievability of a client's file. However, this proposal suffers from an initial expensive tag generation leading to high computational cost at the client. The same authors later propose in [3] a *robust auditing* protocol by incorporating erasure codes in their initial PDP scheme [22] to recover from small data corruption. To prevent an adversary from distinguishing redundancy blocks from original blocks, the latter are further permuted and encrypted. Another permutation and encryption are performed on the redundancy blocks only which are then concatenated to the file. This solution suffers from the fact that a malicious cloud can selectively delete redundant blocks and still generate valid proofs. Even though these proofs are valid, they do not guarantee that the file is retrievable.

Shacham and Waters in [2] introduce the concept of Compact POR. The client applies an erasure code and for each file block, it generates *authenticators* (similar to tags in [22]), with BLS signatures [23], for public verifiability, or with Message Authentication Codes (MAC) [19], for private verifiability. The generation of these values are computationally expensive. Moreover, the number of authenticators stored at the server is linear to the number of data blocks, leading to an important storage overhead. Xu and Chang [4] propose to enhance the scheme in [2] using the technique of polynomial commitment [24] which leads to light communication costs. These two schemes employ erasure codes in conjunction with authentication tags, which induces high costs at the time of retrieving the file. Indeed, erasure coding does not inform the verifier about the position of the corrupted blocks. Thus, the verifier has to check each tag individually to determine whether it is correct or not. When a tag is detected as invalid, meaning that the corresponding block is corrupted, the verifier applies the decoding to recover the original data block.

A recent work of Stefanov et al. [5], Iris, proposes a POR protocol over authenticated file systems subject to frequent changes. Each block of a file is authenticated using a MAC to provide file-block integrity which makes the tag generation very expensive.

Compared to all these schemes, **StealthGuard** performs computationally lightweight operations at the client, since the generation of watchdogs is less expensive than the generation of tags like in [2, 22]. In addition, the storage overhead induced by the storage of watchdogs is less important than in the previous work. At the cost of more bits transmitted during the POR challenge-response, **StealthGuard** ensures a better probability of detecting adversarial corruption.

Table 2 depicts the performance results of **StealthGuard** and compares it with previous work. We analyze our proposal compared to other schemes [1–4] with respect to a file of size 4 GB. The comparison is made on the basis of the POR assurance of $1 - \frac{1}{2^{45}}$ computed in Section 7. We assume that all the compared schemes have three initial operations in the *Setup* phase: the application of an ECC, the encryption and the file-level permutation of data and redundancy blocks. Since these three initial operations have comparable costs for all the schemes, we omit them in the table. Computation costs are represented with exp for exponentiation, mul for multiplication, PRF for pseudo-random function or PRP for pseudo-random permutation. For **StealthGuard**, we compute the different costs according to the values provided in Section 7. For the other schemes, all initial

Table 2. Comparison of relevant related work with **StealthGuard**

Scheme	Parameter	Setup cost	Storage overhead	Server cost	Verifier cost	Communication cost
Robust PDP [3]	block size: 2 KB tag size: 128 B	4.4×10^6 exp 2.2×10^6 mul	tags: 267 MB	764 PRP 764 PRF 765 exp 1528 mul	challenge: 1 exp verif: 766 exp 764 PRP	challenge: 168 B response: 148 B
JK POR [1]	block size: 128 bits number of sentinels: 2×106	2×10^6 PRF	sentinels: 30.6 MB	$\perp$	challenge: 1719 PRP verif: $\perp$	challenge: 6 KB response:26.9 MB
Compact POR [2]	block size: 80 bits number of blocks in one split: 160 tag size: 80 bits	1 enc 5.4×10^6 PRF 1.1×10^9 mul	tags: 51 MB	7245 mul	challenge: 1 enc, 1 MAC verif: 45 PRF, 160 + 205 mul	challenge: 1.9 KB response: 1.6 KB
Efficient POR [4]	block size: 160 bits number of blocks in one split: 160	2.2×10^8 mul 1.4×10^6 PRF	tags: 26 MB	160 exp $2.6 * 10^5$ mul	challenge:$\perp$ verif: 2 exp, 1639 PRF, 1639 mul	challenge: 36 KB response: 60 B
StealthGuard	block size: 256 bits number of blocks in one split: 4096	2.6×10^5 PRF 2.6×10^5 PRP	watchdogs: 8 MB	6.2×10^8 mul	challenge: 2.0×10^6 mul verif: 1.4×10^5 mul	challenge: 23.3 MB response: 26.2 MB

parameters derive from the respective papers. In [2] since the information on the number of blocks in a split is missing, we choose the same one as in [4].

Setup. In our scheme, the client computes $32768 \times 8 \approx 2.6 \times 10^5$ PRF and 2.6×10^5 PRP for the generation and the insertion of watchdogs. One of the advantages of **StealthGuard** is having a more lightweight setup phase when the client preprocesses large files. Indeed, the setup phase in most of previous work [2–5] requires the client to compute an authentication tag for each block of data in the file which is computationally demanding in the case of large files.

Storage Overhead. The insertion of watchdogs in **StealthGuard** induces a smaller storage overhead compared to other schemes that employ authentication tags.

Proof Generation and Verification. For **StealthGuard**, we consider the PIR operations as multiplications of elements in $\mathbb{Z}_p$ where $|p| = 200$ bits. To get the server and verifier computational costs of existing work, based on the parameters and the bounds given in their respective papers, we compute the number of requested blocks in one challenge to obtain a probability of $1 - \frac{1}{2^{45}}$ to declare the file as irretrievable: 764 blocks in [3], 1719 sentinels in [1], 45 blocks in [2] and 1639 blocks in [4]. **StealthGuard** induces high cost compared to existing work but is still acceptable.

Communication. Even if its communication cost is relatively low compared to **Stealth-Guard**, JK POR [1] suffers from the limited number of challenges, that causes the client to download the whole file to regenerate new sentinels. Although we realize that

StealthGuard's communication cost is much higher than [2–4], such schemes would induce additional cost at the file retrieval step, as mentioned earlier.

To summarize, **StealthGuard** trades off between light computation at the client, small storage overhead at the cloud and significant but still acceptable communication cost. Nevertheless, we believe that **StealthGuard**'s advantages pay off when processing large files. The difference between the costs induced by existing schemes and those induced by **StealthGuard** may become negligible if the size of the outsourced file increases.

9 Conclusion

StealthGuard is a new POR scheme which combines the use of randomly generated watchdogs with a lightweight privacy-preserving word search mechanism to achieve high retrievability assurance. As a result, a verifier can generate an unbounded number of queries without decreasing the security of the protocol and thus without the need for updating the watchdogs. **StealthGuard** has been proved to be complete and sound.

As future work, we plan to implement **StealthGuard** in order to not only evaluate its efficiency in a real-world cloud computing environment but also to define optimal values for system parameters.

Acknowledgment. This work was partially funded by the Cloud Accountability project - A4Cloud (grant EC 317550).

References

[1] Juels, A., Kaliski Jr., B.S.: Pors: proofs of retrievability for large files. In: Ning, P., di Vimercati, S.D.C., Syverson, P.F. (eds.) ACM Conference on Computer and Communications Security, pp. 584–597. ACM (2007)

[2] Shacham, H., Waters, B.: Compact proofs of retrievability. In: Pieprzyk, J. (ed.) ASIACRYPT 2008. LNCS, vol. 5350, pp. 90–107. Springer, Heidelberg (2008)

[3] Ateniese, G., Burns, R.C., Curtmola, R., Herring, J., Khan, O., Kissner, L., Peterson, Z.N.J., Song, D.: Remote data checking using provable data possession. ACM Trans. Inf. Syst. Secur. 14(1), 12 (2011)

[4] Xu, J., Chang, E.C.: Towards efficient proofs of retrievability. In: ASIACCS, pp. 79–80 (2012)

[5] Stefanov, E., van Dijk, M., Juels, A., Oprea, A.: Iris: a scalable cloud file system with efficient integrity checks. In: ACSAC, pp. 229–238 (2012)

[6] Reed, I.S., Solomon, G.: Polynomial Codes Over Certain Finite Fields. Journal of the Society of Industrial and Applied Mathematics 8(2), 300–304 (1960)

[7] Dworkin, M.: Recommendation for Block Cipher Modes of Operation: Methods and Techniques. National Institute of Standards and Technology. Special Publication 800-38A (2001)

[8] Blass, E.-O., Di Pietro, R., Molva, R., Önen, M.: PRISM – Privacy-Preserving Search in MapReduce. In: Fischer-Hübner, S., Wright, M. (eds.) PETS 2012. LNCS, vol. 7384, pp. 180–200. Springer, Heidelberg (2012)

[9] Ateniese, G., Pietro, R.D., Mancini, L.V., Tsudik, G.: Scalable and efficient provable data possession. In: Proceedings of the 4th International Conference on Security and Privacy in Communication Networks, SecureComm 2008, pp. 9:1–9:10. ACM, New York (2008)

[10] Erway, C., Küpçü, A., Papamanthou, C., Tamassia, R.: Dynamic provable data possession. In: Proceedings of the 16th ACM Conference on Computer and Communications Security, CCS 2009, pp. 213–222. ACM, New York (2009)

[11] Wang, Q., Wang, C., Li, J., Ren, K., Lou, W.: Enabling public verifiability and data dynamics for storage security in cloud computing. In: Backes, M., Ning, P. (eds.) ESORICS 2009. LNCS, vol. 5789, pp. 355–370. Springer, Heidelberg (2009)

[12] Zheng, Q., Xu, S.: Fair and dynamic proofs of retrievability. In: CODASPY, pp. 237–248 (2011)

[13] Wang, Q., Wang, C., Ren, K., Lou, W., Li, J.: Enabling public auditability and data dynamics for storage security in cloud computing. IEEE Trans. Parallel Distrib. Syst. 22(5), 847–859 (2011)

[14] Mo, Z., Zhou, Y., Chen, S.: A dynamic proof of retrievability (por) scheme with o(logn) complexity. In: ICC, pp. 912–916 (2012)

[15] Chen, B., Curtmola, R.: Robust dynamic provable data possession. In: ICDCS Workshops, pp. 515–525 (2012)

[16] Cash, D., Küpçü, A., Wichs, D.: Dynamic proofs of retrievability via oblivious RAM. In: Johansson, T., Nguyen, P.Q. (eds.) EUROCRYPT 2013. LNCS, vol. 7881, pp. 279–295. Springer, Heidelberg (2013)

[17] Shi, E., Stefanov, E., Papamanthou, C.: Practical dynamic proofs of retrievability. In: ACM Conference on Computer and Communications Security, pp. 325–336 (2013)

[18] Fan, L., Cao, P., Almeida, J., Broder, A.Z.: Summary Cache: a Scalable Wide-Area Web Cache Sharing Protocol. IEEE/ACM Trans. Netw. 8(3), 281–293 (2000)

[19] Bellare, M., Canetti, R., Krawczyk, H.: Keying Hash Functions for Message Authentication. In: Koblitz, N. (ed.) CRYPTO 1996. LNCS, vol. 1109, pp. 1–15. Springer, Heidelberg (1996)

[20] Azraoui, M., Elkhiyaoui, K., Molva, R., Önen, M.: Stealthguard: Proofs of retrievability with hidden watchdogs. Technical report, EURECOM (June 2014)

[21] Trostle, J., Parrish, A.: Efficient Computationally Private Information Retrieval from Anonymity or Trapdoor Groups. In: Burmester, M., Tsudik, G., Magliveras, S., Ilić, I. (eds.) ISC 2010. LNCS, vol. 6531, pp. 114–128. Springer, Heidelberg (2011)

[22] Ateniese, G., Burns, R.C., Curtmola, R., Herring, J., Kissner, L., Peterson, Z.N.J., Song, D.: Provable data possession at untrusted stores. In: Ning, P., di Vimercati, S.D.C., Syverson, P.F. (eds.) ACM Conference on Computer and Communications Security, pp. 598–609. ACM (2007)

[23] Boneh, D., Lynn, B., Shacham, H.: Short Signatures from the Weil Pairing. J. Cryptology 17(4), 297–319 (2004)

[24] Kate, A., Zaverucha, G.M., Goldberg, I.: Constant-size commitments to polynomials and their applications. In: Abe, M. (ed.) ASIACRYPT 2010. LNCS, vol. 6477, pp. 177–194. Springer, Heidelberg (2010)

An Efficient Cloud-Based Revocable Identity-Based Proxy Re-encryption Scheme for Public Clouds Data Sharing

Kaitai Liang[1], Joseph K. Liu[2], Duncan S. Wong[1], and Willy Susilo[3]

[1] Department of Computer Science, City University of Hong Kong
[2] Infocomm Security Department, Institute for Infocomm Research, Singapore
[3] School of Computer Science and Software Engineering, University of Wollongong
kliang4-c@my.cityu.edu.hk, ksliu@i2r.a-star.edu.sg, duncan@cityu.edu.hk,
wsusilo@uow.edu.au

Abstract. Identity-based encryption (IBE) eliminates the necessity of having a costly certificate verification process. However, revocation remains as a daunting task in terms of ciphertext update and key update phases. In this paper, we provide an affirmative solution to solve the efficiency problem incurred by revocation. We propose the first cloud-based revocable identity-based proxy re-encryption (CR-IB-PRE) scheme that supports user revocation but also delegation of decryption rights. No matter a user is revoked or not, at the end of a given time period the cloud acting as a proxy will re-encrypt all ciphertexts of the user under the current time period to the next time period. If the user is revoked in the forthcoming time period, he cannot decrypt the ciphertexts by using the expired private key anymore. Comparing to some naive solutions which require a private key generator (PKG) to interact with non-revoked users in each time period, the new scheme provides definite advantages in terms of communication and computation efficiency.

Keywords: Revocable identity-based encryption, cloud-based revocable identity-based proxy re-encryption, standard model.

1 Introduction

In a traditional public-key infrastructure (PKI), user revocation can be conducted via a certificate mechanism. If a user is revoked, his/her certificate will be added to a certificate revocation list (CRL) by certificate authority. Anyone who wants to encrypt a message for this user has to check the certificate of the user against the CRL. If the certificate is on the list, the sender knows that this user has been revoked and therefore, will not further share any sensitive information with him/her. Different from PKI, there is no certificate in identity-based encryption (IBE) cryptosystem. Therefore user revocation remains an elusive open problem in this paradigm.

To solve this problem, Boneh and Franklin [1] proposed a naive but inefficient solution (the first revocable IBE scheme) such that the computation and

M. Kutyłowski and J. Vaidya (Eds.): ESORICS 2014, Part I, LNCS 8712, pp. 257–272, 2014.
© Springer International Publishing Switzerland 2014

communication complexity of private key generator (PKG) are both linearly in the total number N of non-revocable system users, i.e. $O(N)$. Although their work is further studied by different scholars in the following decade, most of the existing revocable IBE systems (e.g. [2]) have not considered how to relieve the cost spent on key and ciphertext updated processes. Therefore, this motivates our work.

1.1 Motivation

Ciphertexts Update. To date cloud-based technology gives birth to the next generation of computing system. With the assistance of cloud server, many costly computations can be performed with ease. For example, in a revocable IBE system, a data sender can encrypt the data under an identity and a time period for a specified receiver such that the receiver can gain access to the data by using his decryption key corresponding to the time period. When the key is expired and the receiver is not on the revocation list, a PKG will issue a new key/token for the next time period to the receiver and the corresponding ciphertext will be updated to the next period as well. Suppose the ciphertext of the data is stored in a public cloud, then for each ciphertext update process the sender has to deal with the download-decrypt-then-re-encrypt process. Although the ciphertext might be stored locally (without loss of confidentiality), the sender should execute decrypt-then-re-encrypt mode. This may consume a great amount of computational resources while there is a great amount of data to be dealt with. Therefore, the sender might not afford the consumption upon using some resource-limited devices.

To off-load the computational workload to the cloud, we might allow the cloud server to handle ciphertext update process. A naive solution is to enable the cloud to gain access to the data. This, nevertheless, violates the confidentiality of data. A better solution is to enable the cloud to re-encrypt an original ciphertext under an old time period to another ciphertext under a new time period without leaking knowledge of either the decryption key or the underlying plaintext. In CRYPTO 2012 Sahai, Seyalioglu and Waters [3] proposed a non-re-encryption methodology to enable a server, given some public information, to fulfill ciphertext update process in the attribute-based encryption setting. In this paper we leverage the technology of proxy re-encryption (PRE) into ciphertext update process to tackle the same problem in the context of revocable IBE. Later, we will show that our system enjoys better efficiency compared to [3]. Using PRE, a ciphertext stored in the cloud can be re-encrypted to another ciphertext by the cloud server acting as a *semi-trusted* proxy. No information related to the data, however, leaks to the proxy. Accordingly, the update process can be executed effectively and efficiently on the side of cloud server such that the workload of data sender is lessen.

Key Update. Using the technology of identity-based PRE (IB-PRE), ciphertext update for user revocation can be *somehow* offloaded to the cloud as well. If a user is revoked, all ciphertexts stored in the cloud server will be re-encrypted to another "identity". For instance, ciphertexts for a user with identity Alice are re-encrypted to ciphertexts for another "identity" `Alice-1` such that the decryption key associated with `Alice` is not applicable to the decryption of the newly ciphertexts. Nonetheless, there is an undesirable trade-off by simply leveraging IB-PRE. The user needs to update a new identity upon entering to the new time period (corresponding to `Alice-1`). A change in identity (e.g. from `Alice` to `Alice-1`) might bring inconvenience to the user who needs to tell all data senders to use the new identity for the further encryption. That already violates the original idea of using identity-based encryption in which the sender only needs to know some simple information, e.g., name, email address of the user, but not other frequently changeable (or periodical updated) information.

In the ideal case, it is desirable to have a cloud-based encryption scheme with the following features:

1. **Efficient Revocation:** It should support both user and decryption key revocation. User revocation guarantees that if a user has left the organization, he/she will be withdrawn from the right of accessing the information (with respect to his/her identity) in clouds. Decryption key revocation ensures that when the decryption key of a user is stolen or compromised by an adversary, the user may have an opportunity to update the key so as to decrypt updated ciphertexts. With these properties, only a legitimate user is allowed to continually access the data under the encryption (e.g. being issued a new private key by PKG) but not the adversary with a compromised key. More importantly, the complexity of revocation *should not* be linearly in the number of non-revocable system users (i.e. $O(N)$).

2. **Efficient Ciphertext Update:** Ciphertext update process can be off-loaded to cloud server such that a data sender enjoys less computational cost while there is a great deal of ciphertexts to be updated.

3. **Consistency of Identity after Revocation:** If the decryption key of a user is compromised (that is the case of decryption key revocation), the user should retain his/her original identity (i.e. keeping identity consistent). No additional information will be added to the identity or identification string.

1.2   A Naive Solution

Using any existing IB-PRE system (e.g. [4]), a naive solution can be achieved with the above features. We denote by "`Name | Time Period`" the "identity" of a system user. That is, the time period is concatenated to the original identity of the user. For example, the identity of Alice at January 2014 is represented as `Alice | JAN 2014`. Any data sender can use this string as public key to encrypt the data for Alice in January 2014. In the upcoming month, the identity will be changed to `Alice | FEB 2014`. Before the beginning of March, the server will re-encrypt all ciphertexts of Alice stored in the cloud to `Alice | Mar 2014` such that Alice cannot access the data unless she is granted a new key for March 2014. On the other side, if the key (for February 2014) is stolen by adversary, the same action can be taken. However, in this case the user is required to be given the decryption key for the next time period (i.e. March 2014) in advance.

However, this solution leads to an undesirable trade-off where it brings unnecessary workload for PKG. The solution requires the PKG to issue a decryption key to every user at the beginning of each time period. Most of key generation/update algorithms of revocable IBE systems fulfill the issue of updated decryption key (resp. corresponding updated information) by establishing a secure channel from the PKG to a user. The cost brought by building up the secure channel for each user is acceptable for a new user joining the system at the first time. But if the PKG and the user need to repeat this at every time period, it might not be practical. It not only brings inconvenience to (non-revocable) system users, but also incurs undesirable workload for the PKG as the complexity grows linearly with the number of (non-revocable) users at each time period. Thus this naive solution is not scalable and not practical at all.

1.3 Our Contributions

In this paper we present the following contributions.

- We define the notion of cloud-based revocable identity-based proxy re-encryption (CR-IB-PRE) and its corresponding security model.
- We propose an efficient and concrete system achieving the notion we propose above. It is worth mentioning that the present system is the first to support user revocation but also delegation of decryption rights in the identity-based cryptographic setting.
- Our scheme achieving the features mentioned in the previous section only requires the PKG to publish a **constant-size** public string at the beginning of each time period. The PKG does not need to interact with each user by establishing an individual secure channel such that the complexity of the PKG is reduced to $O(1)$. This public string only allows non-revoked users (but not the revoked users) to fulfill the key update phase. Without this key updating process, the revoked users cannot decrypt the ciphertexts stored in the cloud any more as the original ciphertexts are already re-encrypted to the next time period when the users are revoked.
- We prove our new scheme to be secure against chosen-plaintext attack (CPA) and collusion resistant in the standard model.

1.4 System Architecture

We describe the system architecture of a CR-IB-PRE as follows. Like a revocable IBE system, a PKG first issues a private key sk_{Alice} associated with an identity, say Alice, to the user Alice. When a time period, say $T5$, has come, the PKG delivers a token τ_{T5} to Alice such that Alice can update her private key to a new decryption key $sk_{Alice|T5}$ to decrypt any ciphertext encrypted under Alice and time period $T5$. When a new time period is approaching, Alice may construct a re-encryption key $rk_{Alice|T5 \rightarrow T6}$ under her identity from $T5$ to $T6$, and then send the key to a cloud server whom will update a ciphertext under Alice and $T5$ to a new ciphertext under Alice and $T6$. However, Alice here cannot immediately decrypt the new ciphertext as a token τ_{T6} is not issued by PKG yet. After the token is issued, Alice can update her decryption key to $sk_{Alice|T6}$ accordingly so as to recover the underlying plaintext. In the key update phase, the PKG only publishes a public token associated with $T6$ such that any user excluded in the revocation list can leverage this token to update his/her decryption key. This makes key update (for N non-revocable users) reduce to constant cost.

One might doubt that the system cannot be seen as a type of IB-PRE because an IB-PRE scheme usually re-encrypts a ciphertext under an identity to another ciphertext under a new identity. Actually, our system does not contradict the notion of IB-PRE by regarding $(Alice, T5)$ and $(Alice, T6)$ as two different identities. One might further question that ciphertext update process may be suspended by a dishonest user if the user refuses to deliver the corresponding re-encryption key to the server. To address this problem, we propose a solution right after our basic construction in Section 4.2.

1.5   Related Work

The first revocable IBE is proposed by Boneh and Franklin [1], in which a ciphertext is encrypted under an identity id and a time period T, and a non-revoked user is issued a private key $sk_{id,T}$ by a PKG such that the user can access the data in T. However, this does not scale well as the complexity of the PKG is linearly in the number N of non-revocable users. Subsequently, Boldyreva, Goyal and Kumar [2] proposed the security notion for revocable IBE, and constructed an efficient revocable IBE scheme from a fuzzy IBE scheme [5] with binary tree structure. To achieve adaptive security, Libert and Vergnaud [6] proposed a revocable IBE scheme based on the variant of Waters IBE [7] and Gentry IBE [8]. Recently, Seo and Emura [9] formalized a revised notion for revocable IBE, and proposed a concrete scheme based on [6]. Since its introduction, there are many variants of revocable IBE. For example, several revocable IBE schemes [10,11,12] leverage a semi-trusted authority to enable users to fulfill valid decryption. There are also some functional encryption schemes [13,14,15,3] considering the property of revocation. Inspired by [9] we will build the first CR-IB-PRE scheme in the standard model.

Decryption rights delegation is introduced in [16]. Blaze, Bleumer and Strauss [17] formally defined the notion of PRE. PRE can be classified as: unidirectional and bidirectional PRE, and single-hop and multi-hop PRE, where the definitions are given in [18]. This present work deals with the multi-hop unidirectional case. Many PRE systems have been proposed in the literature, such as [18,19,20,21,22].

To employ PRE in the IBE setting, Green and Ateniese [4] defined the notion of identity-based PRE (IB-PRE), and proposed two constructions in the random oracle model. Later on, Tang, Hartel and Jonker [23] proposed a CPA-secure IB-PRE scheme in the random oracle model, in which delegator and delegatee can belong to different domains. Chu and Tzeng [24] proposed an IB-PRE scheme without random oracles against replayable chosen-ciphertext attacks (RCCA) [25]. The aforementioned schemes, however, enable proxy to compromise the entire private key of delegator by colluding with delegatee. To tackle the problem, the following systems are proposed. Two CPA-secure IB-PRE schemes without random oracles were proposed by Matsuo [26]. Wang et al. [27,28] proposed two IB-PRE schemes in the random oracle model. Minzuno and Doi [29] constructed an IB-PRE scheme in the standard model with CPA security. Two CPA-secure IB-PRE schemes without random oracles were proposed in [30]. Shao and Cao [31] proposed a generic construction for CCA-secure IB-PRE in the standard model. Recently, Liang et al. [32] proposed the first CCA-secure unidirectional single-hop IB-PRE in the standard model supporting conditional re-encryption.

2   Definitions

Below we define the notion of CR-IB-PRE. Unless stated otherwise, by a CR-IB-PRE we mean a CR-IB-PRE with unidirectional and multi-hop properties. Note please refer to [18] for more details of these properties.

2.1   Definition of CR-IB-PRE

Definition 1. *A Cloud-Based Revocable Identity-Based Proxy Re-Encry-ption (CR-IB-PRE) scheme consists of the following algorithms. Below we let $\mathcal{I}, \mathcal{T}, \mathcal{M}$ be identity space, time space and message space, respectively.*

1. *Setup: the setup algorithm intakes a security parameter k and a maximal number of users N, and outputs the public parameters mpk, the master secret key msk, the initial state st and an empty revocation list RL. For simplicity, we assume the following algorithms include mpk implicitly.*

2. *KeyGen: the private key generation algorithm intakes msk, and a user's identity $id \in \mathcal{I}$, and outputs a private key sk_{id} for the user id and an updated state st.*

3. *TokenUp: the token update algorithm intakes msk, an identity id, a token update time period $T_i \in \mathcal{T}$, the current revocation list RL and st, and outputs a token τ_i, where $i \in [1, poly(1^k)]$.*

4. *DeKeyGen: the decryption key generation algorithm intakes sk_{id}, τ_i, and outputs a decryption key $sk_{id|i}$ for the user id under the time period T_i or $\perp$ if id has been revoked, where $i \in [1, poly(1^k)]$.*

5. *ReKeyGen: the re-encryption key generation algorithm intakes $sk_{id|i}$, msk, T_i and $T_{i'}$, and generates the re-encryption key as follows, where $1 \leq i < i'$.*

   (a) *ReKeyToken: the re-encryption key token generation algorithm intakes msk, T_i and $T_{i'}$, outputs a re-encryption key token $\varphi_{i \to i'}$.*

   (b) *ReKey: the re-encryption key algorithm intakes $sk_{id|i}$ and $\varphi_{i \to i'}$, outputs a re-encryption key $rk_{id|i \to i'}$ which can be used to transform a ciphertext under (id, T_i) to another ciphertext under $(id, T_{i'})$.*

6. *Enc: the encryption algorithm intakes id, T_i, and a message $m \in \mathcal{M}$, and outputs an original ciphertext C under (id, T_i) which can be further re-encrypted.*

7. *ReEnc: the re-encryption algorithm intakes* $rk_{id|i \to i'}$, *and a ciphertext* C *under* (id, T_i), *and outputs either a re-encrypted ciphertext* C *under* $(id, T_{i'})$ *or a symbol* $\perp$ *indicating* C *is invalid, where* $1 \leq i < i'$.

8. *Dec: the decryption algorithm intakes* $sk_{id|i}$, *and a ciphertext* C *under* (id, T_i), *and outputs either a message* m *or a symbol* $\perp$ *indicating* C *is invalid.*

9. *Revoke: the revocation algorithm intakes an identity to be revoked* id, *a re-vocation time period* T_i, *the current revocation list* RL, *and a state* st, *and outputs an updated* RL.

Remarks. Definition 1 is for our basic construction. In this paper we also present extensions for the basic construction. For the extended system, we reuse the above definition except that $TokenUp$ takes msk, ID, T_i, RL and st as input, and outputs a token τ_i for a set ID of non-revocable users.

Correctness: For any (mpk, msk) output by *Setup*, any time period $T_i \in \mathcal{T}$ (where $i \in [1, poly(1^k)]$), any message $m \in \mathcal{M}$, and all possible states st and revocation list RL, if sk_{id} is output by $KeyGen(msk, id)$, $\tau_i \leftarrow TokenUp(msk, id, T_i, RL, st)$, $sk_{id|i} \leftarrow DeKeyGen(sk_{id}, \tau_i)$, $rk_{id|i \to j} \leftarrow ReKeyGen(sk_{id|i}, msk, T_i, T_j)$ (note for simplicity we set $j = i + 1$ here), we have

if id is not revoked by $T_1 : Dec(sk_{id|1}, Enc(id, T_1, m)) = m$;

if id is not revoked by T_i :

$$Dec(sk_{id|i}, ReEnc(rk_{id|i-1 \to i}, ..., ReEnc(rk_{id|1 \to 2}, Enc(id, T_1, m)))...) = m.$$

2.2 Revocation Procedure

The revocation procedure is described based on different cases as follows.

1. **Decryption Key Compromised.** When the decryption key $sk_{id|i}$ of a user id for time period T_i is compromised by an adversary, the user id reports this issue to a PKG. The PKG then immediately returns a re-encryption key token $\varphi_{i \to j}$ to the user, where $j \neq i$ such that the user can generate a re-encryption key $rk_{id|i \to j}$. The user id further sends the re-encryption key to the proxy, and next requests it to re-encrypt all ciphertexts under (id, T_i) to the ones under (id, T_j). Besides, the PKG issues a token τ_j related to a new time period T_j to the user id. After receiving the token, the user id updates his/her decryption key from $sk_{id|i}$ to $sk_{id|j}$, and then uses the newly key to access the data. Note T_j is the time period satisfying $i < j$ such that the user id will update his key for decryption.

2. **Identity Expired.** When the identity of a user is expired (e.g. the resignation of a registered user) at time period T_i, our system notifies the corresponding identity and time period to a PKG. The PKG then generates a re-encryption key $rk_{id|i \to j}$, and requests the proxy to re-encrypt all ciphertexts under (id, T_i) to the ciphertexts under (id, T_j). Here j must satisfy $i < j$ such that the user id cannot reuse his/her decryption keys $sk_{id|z}$ (where $z \leq i$) to decrypt the re-encrypted ciphertexts. The PKG finally adds this user to the revocation list, that is, a re-encryption token and a token related to a new time period will not be issued to this user (after time period i).

3   A New CPA-Secure CR-IB-PRE

3.1   A Basic Construction

To clearly show the technical roadmap of our scheme, we only propose our basic construction for CR-IB-PRE systems in this section. In this construction, a PKG will suffer from $O(N)$ computational complexity for key update phase. But we will present performance improvements for this basic construction in Section 4 such that the complexity of the PKG will reduce to $O(1)$. Below we assume any identity $id \in \{0,1\}^n$ and any time period $T_i \in \mathbb{Z}_q^*$. Some revocable IBE systems, such as [6], leverage KUNode algorithm [2] for efficient revocation whereby a data structure (e.g. a binary tree) is used to represent revocation list. However, we here try to present a general solution such that we do not focus on which data structure we choose to denote the revocation list. In our construction we let state st be an unspecified data structure DS, and it depends on which structure we use, e.g., st can be a binary tree. By a tuple (RL, st) we mean a revocation list and its corresponding data structure.

1. **Setup**$(1^k, N)$. The setup algorithm runs $(q, g, \mathbb{G}, \mathbb{G}_T, e) \leftarrow \mathcal{G}(1^k)$, where q is the order of group $\mathbb{G}$. It chooses $\alpha, \beta \in_R \mathbb{Z}_q^*$, group elements $g_2, g_3, v_1, v_2 \in_R \mathbb{G}$, a random n-length set $U = \{u_j | 0 \leq j \leq n\}$, and a target collision resistant (TCR) hash function $TCR_1 : \mathbb{G} \to \mathbb{Z}_q^*$, where $u_j \in_R \mathbb{G}$. The public parameter is $mpk = (g, g_1, g_2, g_3, v_1, v_2, U, TCR_1)$, the master secret key is $msk = (g_2^\alpha, g_3^\beta)$, $RL = \emptyset$ and $st = DB$, where $g_1 = g^\alpha$.

2. **KeyGen**(msk, id). PKG chooses $r_{id} \in_R \mathbb{Z}_q^*$, sets the partial private key sk_{id} as $sk_{id_1} = g_3^\beta \cdot (u_0 \prod_{j \in \mathcal{V}_{id}} u_j)^{r_{id}}, sk_{id_2} = g^{r_{id}}$, where $\mathcal{V}_{id}$ is the set of all j for which the j-th bit (of id) is equal to 1.

3. **TokenUp**(msk, id, T_i, RL, st). PKG will check RL first so as to see whether id is revoked or not. If it is revoked, output $\perp$; else proceed. Choose $r_{T_i} \in_R \mathbb{Z}_q^*$, and set the token τ_i as $\tau_{i,1} = (g_2^\alpha / g_3^\beta) \cdot (v_1 \cdot v_2^{T_i})^{r_{T_i}}, \tau_{i,2} = g^{r_{T_i}}$, where i is the index for the time period.

4. **DeKeyGen**(sk_{id}, τ_i). A user id runs the algorithm as follows.
   (a) Choose $\tilde{r} \in_R \mathbb{Z}_q^*$, and randomize the token as $\tau_{i,1} = \tau_{i,1} \cdot (v_1 \cdot v_2^{T_i})^{\tilde{r}}$, $\tau_{i,2} = \tau_{i,2} \cdot g^{\tilde{r}}$.
   (b) Choose $r_1, r_2 \in_R \mathbb{Z}_q^*$, and set the updated secret key $sk_{id|i}$ for identity id and time period T_i as

$$sk_{id|i,1} = sk_{id_1} \cdot \tau_{i,1} \cdot (u_0 \prod_{j \in \mathcal{V}_{id}} u_j)^{r_1} \cdot (v_1 \cdot v_2^{T_i})^{r_2}$$

$$= g_2^\alpha \cdot (u_0 \prod_{j \in \mathcal{V}_{id}} u_j)^{\hat{r}_1} \cdot (v_1 \cdot v_2^{T_i})^{\hat{r}_2},$$

$$sk_{id|i,2} = sk_{id_2} \cdot g^{r_1} = g^{\hat{r}_1}, sk_{id|i,3} = \tau_{i,2} \cdot g^{r_2} = g^{\hat{r}_2},$$

where $\hat{r}_1 = r_{id} + r_1$, $\hat{r}_2 = r_{T_i} + \tilde{r} + r_2$. Note the user will share $r_1, r_2, \tilde{r}$ with the PKG (suppose it is fully trusted) such that the PKG can store $(id|i, \hat{r}_1, \hat{r}_2)$ in a list $List^{sk_{id|i}}$ for further use.

5. **ReKeyGen**$(sk_{id|i}, msk, T_i, T_{i'})$. The re-encryption key $rk_{id|i \to i'}$ is generated as follows.

   (a) $ReKeyToken(msk, T_i, T_{i'})$: If a user id holding $sk_{id|i}$ is allowed to update his key to another time period $T_{i'}$, PKG generates the re-encryption key token $\varphi_{i \to i'}$ as $\varphi^{(1)}_{i \to i'} = (v_1 \cdot v_2^{T_{i'}})^{TCR_1(\xi)}/(v_1 \cdot v_2^{T_i})^{\hat{r}_2}$, $\varphi^{(2)}_{i \to i'} = (\hat{C}_0, \hat{C}_1, \hat{C}_2, \hat{C}_3) \leftarrow Enc(id, T_{i'}, \xi)$, where $\xi \in_R \mathbb{G}_T$, $\hat{r}_2$ is recovered from $(id|i', \hat{r}_1, \hat{r}_2)$ which is stored the $List^{sk_{id|i}}$.

   (b) $ReKey(sk_{id|i}, \varphi_{i \to i'})$: After receiving $\varphi_{i \to i'}$ from PKG, the user id generates the re-encryption key as follows.

      i. Choose $\rho \in_R \mathbb{Z}_q^*$, and set $rk_1 = sk_{id|i,1} \cdot \varphi^{(1)}_{i \to i'} \cdot (u_0 \prod_{j \in \mathcal{V}_{id}} u_j)^\rho$, $rk_2 = sk_{id|i,2} \cdot g^\rho$, and $rk_3 = \varphi^{(2)}_{i \to i'}$.

      ii. Output the re-encryption key $rk_{id|i \to i'} = (rk_1, rk_2, rk_3)$.

6. **Enc**(id, T_i, m). Given an identity id, a time period T_i, and a message $m \in \mathbb{G}_T$, the encryption algorithm chooses $t \in_R \mathbb{Z}_q^*$, and sets the original ciphertext C as $C_0 = m \cdot e(g_1, g_2)^t$, $C_1 = g^t$, $C_2 = (u_0 \prod_{j \in \mathcal{V}_{id}} u_j)^t$, $C_3 = (v_1 \cdot v_2^{T_i})^t$. We assume that the identity id and the time period T_i are implicitly included in the ciphertext.

7. **ReEnc**$(rk_{id|i \to i'}, C)$. Parse the ciphertext C under (id, T_i) as (C_0, C_1, C_2, C_3), and the re-encryption key $rk_{id|i \to i'}$ as (rk_1, rk_2, rk_3). The re-encryption algorithm computes $C_4 = \frac{e(C_1, rk_1)}{e(C_2, rk_2)} = e(g^t, g_2^\alpha \cdot (v_1 \cdot v_2^{T_{i'}})^{TCR_1(\xi)})$, and next sets the re-encrypted ciphertext C under $(id, T_{i'})$ as (C_0, C_1, C_4, rk_3). Note if C under $(id, T_{i'})$ needs to be further re-encrypted to the time period $T_{i''}$, then the proxy parses rk_3 as $(\hat{C}_0, \hat{C}_1, \hat{C}_2, \hat{C}_3)$. Given a re-encryption key $rk_{id|i' \to i''} = (rk_1', rk_2', rk_3')$, the proxy computes $C_4' = \frac{e(\hat{C}_1, rk_1')}{e(\hat{C}_2, rk_2')}$, and sets the ciphertext C under $(id, T_{i''})$ as $(C_0, C_1, C_4, \hat{C}_0, \hat{C}_1, C_4', rk_3')$.

8. **Dec**$(sk_{id|i}, C)$. Given a ciphertext C under (id, T_i), the decryption algorithm works as follows.

   (a) For the original ciphertext $C = (C_0, C_1, C_2, C_3)$, the decryptor computes $\frac{e(C_1, sk_{id|i,1})}{e(C_2, sk_{id|i,2})e(C_3, sk_{id|i,3})} = e(g_1, g_2)^t$, and outputs the message $C_0/e(g_1, g_2)^t = m \cdot e(g_1, g_2)^t/e(g_1, g_2)^t = m$.

   (b) For the re-encrypted ciphertext C:

      i. If the re-encrypted ciphertext is re-encrypted only once, i.e. $C = (C_0, C_1, C_4, rk_3 = (\hat{C}_0, \hat{C}_1, \hat{C}_2, \hat{C}_3))$, then the decryptor computes $\frac{\hat{C}_0 e(\hat{C}_2, sk_{id|i,2})e(\hat{C}_3, sk_{id|i,3})}{e(\hat{C}_1, sk_{id|i,1})} = \xi$. Accordingly, the decryptor can finally computer $C_0 \frac{e(C_1, (v_1 v_2^{T_i})^{TCR_1(\xi)})}{C_4} = m$.

      ii. If the ciphertext under id is re-encrypted l times from time period T_1 to T_{l+1}, we denote the re-encrypted ciphertext as $C^{(l+1)} = (C_0^{(1)}, C_1^{(1)}, C_4^{(1)}, ..., C_0^{(l)}, C_1^{(l)}, C_4^{(l)}, rk_3^{(l+1)})$, where $C_0^{(1)}$ and $C_1^{(1)}$ are the components of original ciphertext under (id, T_1), and $rk_3^{(i+1)} = (C_0^{(i+1)}, C_1^{(i+1)}, C_2^{(i+1)}, C_3^{(i+1)})$ is the ciphertext under (id, T_{i+1}),

$i \in [1, l]$. We recover the message m as follows.

First set: $\dfrac{C_0^{(l+1)} e(C_2^{(l+1)}, sk_{id|l+1,2}) e(C_3^{(l+1)}, sk_{id|l+1,3})}{e(C_1^{(l+1)}, sk_{id|l+1,1})} = \xi^{(l)},$

from $i = l$ to 2 set : $C_0^{(i)} \dfrac{e(C_1^{(i)}, (v_1 v_2^{T_{i+1}}) TCR_1(\xi^{(i)}))}{C_4^{(i)}} = \xi^{(i-1)},$

finally compute : $C_0^{(1)} \dfrac{e(C_1^{(1)}, (v_1 v_2^{T_2}) TCR_1(\xi^{(1)}))}{C_4^{(1)}} = m.$

9. **Revoke**(id, T_i, RL, st). Update the revocation list by $RL \leftarrow RL \cup \{id, T_i\}$ and return the updated revocation list.

3.2 Security Analysis

Theorem 1. *Suppose the underlying Waters IBE scheme is IND-CPA secure, TCR_1 is the TCR hash function, our CR-IB-PRE scheme is IND-CPA secure in the standard model.*

Theorem 2. *Suppose the CDH assumption holds, our CR-IB-PRE scheme is collusion resistant.*

Due to limited space, we provide the proof of Theorem 1 and 2 in the full version of the paper [33].

4 Performance Improvement

4.1 Reduce the Complexity of Key Update

In our basic construction the complexity of the key update phase (in terms of communication and computation) is linearly in the number (say N) of users whom are excluded in the revocation list, i.e. $O(N)$. We here reduce the complexity $O(N)$ to $O(1)$. In the algorithm $TokenUp$, the identity id is not taken into the generation of the token τ_i. This gives us a possibility to broadcast the token for time period T_i to all non-revocable users. Below we employ a broadcast encryption in our basic construction. We choose Phan et al. broadcast encryption system [34] as a building block. Note system implementors may choose an appropriate broadcast encryption for different purposes, e.g., security. We let $SYM = (SYM.Enc, SYM.Dec)$ denote a one-time symmetric encryption system in which encryption algorithm $SYM.Enc$ intakes a message and a symmetric key $K \in \{0,1\}^{poly(1^k)}$ and outputs a ciphertext, and decryption algorithm $SYM.Dec$ intakes a ciphertext and a symmetric key K and outputs a message. We only show the modification for our basic system as follows.

1. **Setup**$(1^k, N)$. The setup algorithm additionally chooses $\gamma, \hat{\alpha} \in_R \mathbb{Z}_q^*$, a TCR hash function $TCR_2 : \mathbb{G}_T \rightarrow \{0,1\}^{poly(1^k)}$, and adds $v_0 = g^\gamma$ and TCR_2 to mpk, and $(\gamma, \hat{\alpha})$ to msk.

2. **KeyGen**(msk, id). PKG generates a new key component $sk_{id_3} = g_z^\gamma$, and sets additional public parameters $g_z = g^{\hat{\alpha}^z}$, $g_{z+1} = g^{\hat{\alpha}^{z+1}}$, $g_{\lambda+1-z} = g^{\hat{\alpha}^{\lambda+1-z}}$, $g_{\lambda+1+z} = g^{\hat{\alpha}^{\lambda+1+z}}$ for user id, where z is the index for identity id, and $\lambda - 1 = N$.

3. **TokenUp**(msk, ID, T_i, RL, st). Note ID now is a set of identities. After constructing $(\tau_{i,1}, \tau_{i,2})$, PKG works as follows.

   (a) Choose $\hat{t} \in_R \mathbb{Z}_q^*$, $K \in_R \mathbb{G}_T$, and set an encryption $E_{\tau_i}^{(1)}$ as $\mathcal{T}_1 = K \cdot e(g_{\lambda+1}, g)^{\hat{t}}$, $\mathcal{T}_2 = g^{\hat{t}}$, $\mathcal{T}_3 = (v_0 \cdot \prod_{w \in ID} g_{\lambda+1-w})^{\hat{t}}$, where ID is implicitly included in the ciphertext.

   (b) Run $E_{\tau_i}^{(2)} \leftarrow SYM.Enc(TCR_2(K), \tau_{i,1}\|\tau_{i,2})$, and next upload the token $\tau_i = (E_{\tau_i}^{(1)}, E_{\tau_i}^{(2)})$ for a set ID of identities to the cloud server.

4. **DeKeyGen**(sk_{id}, τ_i). Before constructing a decryption key as in the algorithm $DeKeyGen$ of our basic scheme, a user id (where $id \in ID$) first recovers $\tau_{i,1}$ and $\tau_{i,2}$ as follows. The user computes

$$K = \mathcal{T}_1/(e(\mathcal{T}_3, g_z)/e(sk_{id_3} \prod_{w \in ID \setminus \{z\}} g_{\lambda+1-w+z}, \mathcal{T}_2))$$

and runs $\sigma_i = \tau_{i,1}\|\tau_{i,2} \leftarrow SYM.Dec(TCR_2(K), E_{\tau_i}^{(2)})$.

Note the rest of the algorithms are the same as that of our basic scheme.

4.2   Reduce Size of Re-encrypted Ciphertext and Decryption Complexity

Our basic construction suffers from a drawback that the size of re-encrypted ciphertext and the complexity of decryption expand linearly in the number of time periods. To reduce the complexity to constant, we leverage the following idea.

We can delegate the generation of re-encryption key to PKG as PKG has knowledge of private keys of all system users and tokens of all time periods. Here users can only focus on decryption key generation, message encryption and decryption, i.e. the common actions of using a revocable IBE system, such that the re-encryption functionality and its corresponding workload are transparent in the view of the users.

Being granted the rights of re-encryption key generation, PKG works as follows. Suppose the decryption keys of a user id associated with time periods T_i and T_j are $sk_{id|i} = (sk_{id|i,1}, sk_{id|i,2}, sk_{id|i,3})$ and $sk_{id|j} = (sk_{id|j,1}, sk_{id|j,2}, sk_{id|j,3})$, and the corresponding tuples stored in the list $List^{sk_{id|z}}$ are $(id|i, \hat{r}_{i,1}, \hat{r}_{i,2})$ and $(id|j, \hat{r}_{j,1}, \hat{r}_{j,2})$, where $i < j$ (for simplicity we may set $j = i + 1$). PKG then constructs the re-encryption key $rk_{id|i \to j}$ as $rk_1 = (v_1 \cdot v_2^{T_j})^{-\hat{r}_{j,2}} \cdot (v_1 \cdot v_2^{T_i})^{\hat{r}_{i,2}} \cdot (v_1 \cdot v_2^{T_i})^\theta$, $rk_2 = sk_{id|j,3}^{-1} \cdot sk_{id|i,3} = g^{\hat{r}_{i,2} - \hat{r}_{j,2}} \cdot g^\theta$, where $\theta \in_R \mathbb{Z}_q^*$.

For simplicity, we suppose a user id has l available time periods (in which T_1 is the first time period, and T_l is the last one). Given $rk_{id|1\to2} = (rk_{1\to2,1}, rk_{1\to2,2})$, the re-encryption algorithm $ReEnc$ computes

$$C_4^{(1)} = \frac{e(C_3, rk_{1\to2,2})}{e(C_1, rk_{1\to2,1})} = \frac{e((v_1 v_2^{T_1})^t, g^{-\hat{r}_{2,2}})}{e(g^t, (v_1 v_2^{T_2})^{-\hat{r}_{2,2}})},$$

and next sets the re-encrypted ciphertext C under (id, T_2) as $(C_0, C_1, C_2, C_3, C_4^{(1)})$, where an original ciphertext C under (id, T_1) is $C_0 = m \cdot e(g_1, g_2)^t$, $C_1 = g^t$, $C_2 = (u_0 \prod_{j \in \mathcal{V}_{id}} u_j)^t$, $C_3 = (v_1 \cdot v_2^{T_1})^t$. At the time period T_l, the re-encrypted ciphertext C under (id, T_l) is $(C_0, C_1, C_2, C_3, C_4^{(l-1)})$, in which $C_4^{(l-1)} = C_4^{(l-2)} \cdot \frac{e(C_3, rk_{l-1\to l,2})}{e(C_1, rk_{l-1\to l,1})} = \frac{e((v_1 \cdot v_2^{T_1})^t, g^{-\hat{r}_{l,2}})}{e(g^t, (v_1 \cdot v_2^{T_l})^{-\hat{r}_{l,2}})}$, and $C_4^{(l-2)}$ is a component of ciphertext C under (id, T_{l-1}).

The decryption algorithm Dec works as follows. Given $sk_{id|i} = (sk_{id|i,1}, sk_{id|i,2}, sk_{id|i,3})$ and a re-encrypted ciphertext $(C_0, C_1, C_2, C_3, C_4^{(i-1)})$ under (id, T_i), set $C_0 \cdot C_4^{(i-1)} \cdot \frac{e(sk_{id|i,3}, C_3) \cdot e(C_2, sk_{id|i,2})}{e(sk_{id|i,1}, C_1)} = \frac{m \cdot e(g_1, g_2)^t}{e(g_2^\alpha, g^t)} = m$.

5   Comparison

In this section we compare our improved version with an ABE system supporting revocability [3] and the most efficient revocable IBE scheme [9] in terms of security, functionality and efficiency. Table 1 illustrates the comparison of security and functionality, Table 2 depicts the comparison of computation cost, and Table 3 shows the comparison of communication complexity. Note we do not compare our scheme with the existing IB-PRE schemes here as we pay more attention in the functionality of revocability.

To define the notations and parameters used in the Tables, we let $|\mathbb{G}|$ denote the bit-length of an element in $\mathbb{G}$, and $|\mathbb{G}_T|$ denote the bit-length of an element in $\mathbb{G}_T$, $|U|$ denote the number of attributes used in the system, $|f|$ denote the size of an access formula, $|S|$ denote the size of an attribute set, n denote the bit-length of an identity, c_p, c_e, c_e^T denote the computation cost of a bilinear pairing, an exponentiation in $\mathbb{G}$ and in $\mathbb{G}_T$, respectively. Suppose [3], [9] and our scheme share the same number (N) of non-revocable system users in each time period. It can be seen that [3] only presents generic constructions for the revocable ABE systems. To bring convenience for the comparison, we use Waters ABE scheme [35] to implement one of the generic constructions of [3]. The implementation yields a revocable CP-ABE system.

From Table 1, we see that our scheme supports not only revocability but also re-encryption functionality with CPA security and collusion resistance under the decisional bilinear Diffie-Hellman (BDH) assumption and computational Diffie-Hellman (CDH) assumption, respectively. [3] is CPA secure under the decisional q-parallel bilinear Diffie-Hellman exponent (BDHE) assumption (suppose it is built on Waters ABE) but only supporting revocability, whereas ours additionally enjoys the delegation of decryption rights. Compared to [9], supporting

Table 1. Security and Functionality Comparison

Schemes	Security	Complexity Assumption	Delegation of Decryption Rights
[3]	CPA	decisional q-parallel-BDHE	✗
[9]	CPA	decisional BDH	✗
Ours	CPA Collusion Resistance	decisional BDH and CDH	✓

revocability with CPA security under the decisional BDH assumption, ours offers additional property without degrading security level. Note [9] and our scheme are secure under simple complexity assumptions, while [3] relies on a complex one. Although our system achieves more flexible functionality, it is only CPA secure. The problem of proposing a CR-IB-PRE scheme with CCA security in the standard model remains open.

Table 2. Computation Cost Comparison

Schemes	Computation Cost			
	Encryption	Decryption	Key Gen.	Update Info. (including key update token and rk)
[3]	$O(\|f\|)c_e + O(1)c_e^T$	$O(\|S\|)(c_p + c_e^T)$	$O(\|S\|)c_e$	$\epsilon_1 = O(N \cdot \|S\|)c_e$
[9]	$O(1)c_e + O(1)c_e^T$	$O(1)c_p$	$O(1)c_e$	$\epsilon_2 = O(N)c_e$
Ours	$O(1)c_e + O(1)c_e^T$	$O(1)c_p$	$O(1)c_e$	$\epsilon_3 = O(1)c_e + O(1)c_e^T$

From Table 2, we see that [3] suffers from the largest complexity in each merit, and the PKG of [9] suffers from $O(N)$ computational complexity in updating key information for each time period. Besides, both [3] and [9] require a secure communication channel from the PKG to each non-revocable user (for issuing key update information), while our system can eliminate this cost. Compared with [3,9], ours enjoys constant complexity in each merit. To achieve re-encryption property, we need $O(1)c_e$ and $O(1)c_p$ in constructing re-encryption key and re-encrypted ciphertext, respectively. However, when comparing with the linear complexity of [3], the above additional cost is acceptable.

Table 3 shows that [9] and our scheme achieve the least complexity, while [3] suffers from linear cost in each merit. Although our scheme requires additional cost $O(1)|\mathbb{G}|$ in delivering re-encryption key, it enjoys constant communication cost in key update information for each time period but [3,9] suffer from $O(N)$ complexity. As N increases, our scheme has better efficiency in communication.

Table 3. Communication Cost Comparison

| Schemes | Communication Cost | | |
	Private Key Size	Ciphertext Size	Update Info. Size (including size of key update token and rk)
[3]	$O(|S|)|\mathbb{G}|$	$O(|f|)|\mathbb{G}| + O(1)|\mathbb{G}_T|$	$O(N \cdot |S|)|\mathbb{G}|$
[9]	$O(1)|\mathbb{G}|$	$O(1)|\mathbb{G}| + O(1)|\mathbb{G}_T|$	$O(N)|\mathbb{G}|$
Ours	$O(1)|\mathbb{G}|$	$O(1)|\mathbb{G}| + O(1)|\mathbb{G}_T|$	$O(1)|\mathbb{G}| + O(1)|\mathbb{G}_T|$

Acknowledgements. This work was supported by a grant from the RGC of the HKSAR, China, under Project CityU 123913, and it was done when Kaitai Liang was an intern with Institute for Infocomm Research. This work is also partially supported by the Australian Research Council Linkage Project (LP120200052). Joseph K. Liu is supported by A*STAR funded project SecDC-112172014.

References

1. Boneh, D., Franklin, M.: Identity-based encryption from the weil pairing. In: Kilian, J. (ed.) CRYPTO 2001. LNCS, vol. 2139, pp. 213–229. Springer, Heidelberg (2001)
2. Boldyreva, A., Goyal, V., Kumar, V.: Identity-based encryption with efficient revocation. In: Ning, P., Syverson, P.F., Jha, S. (eds.) ACM Conference on Computer and Communications Security, pp. 417–426. ACM (2008)
3. Sahai, A., Seyalioglu, H., Waters, B.: Dynamic credentials and ciphertext delegation for attribute-based encryption. In: Safavi-Naini, R., Canetti, R. (eds.) CRYPTO 2012. LNCS, vol. 7417, pp. 199–217. Springer, Heidelberg (2012)
4. Green, M., Ateniese, G.: Identity-based proxy re-encryption. In: Katz, J., Yung, M. (eds.) ACNS 2007. LNCS, vol. 4521, pp. 288–306. Springer, Heidelberg (2007)
5. Sahai, A., Waters, B.: Fuzzy identity-based encryption. In: Cramer, R. (ed.) EUROCRYPT 2005. LNCS, vol. 3494, pp. 457–473. Springer, Heidelberg (2005)
6. Libert, B., Vergnaud, D.: Adaptive-id secure revocable identity-based encryption. In: Fischlin, M. (ed.) CT-RSA 2009. LNCS, vol. 5473, pp. 1–15. Springer, Heidelberg (2009)
7. Waters, B.: Efficient identity-based encryption without random oracles. In: Cramer, R. (ed.) EUROCRYPT 2005. LNCS, vol. 3494, pp. 114–127. Springer, Heidelberg (2005)
8. Gentry, C.: Practical identity-based encryption without random oracles. In: Vaudenay, S. (ed.) EUROCRYPT 2006. LNCS, vol. 4004, pp. 445–464. Springer, Heidelberg (2006)
9. Seo, J.H., Emura, K.: Revocable identity-based encryption revisited: Security model and construction. In: Kurosawa, K., Hanaoka, G. (eds.) PKC 2013. LNCS, vol. 7778, pp. 216–234. Springer, Heidelberg (2013)
10. Baek, J., Zheng, Y.: Identity-based threshold decryption. In: Bao, F., Deng, R., Zhou, J. (eds.) PKC 2004. LNCS, vol. 2947, pp. 262–276. Springer, Heidelberg (2004)
11. Ding, X., Tsudik, G.: Simple identity-based cryptography with mediated rsa. In: Joye, M. (ed.) CT-RSA 2003. LNCS, vol. 2612, pp. 193–210. Springer, Heidelberg (2003)

12. Libert, B., Quisquater, J.J.: Efficient revocation and threshold pairing based cryptosystems. In: Borowsky, E., Rajsbaum, S. (eds.) PODC, pp. 163–171. ACM (2003)
13. Attrapadung, N., Imai, H.: Attribute-based encryption supporting direct/indirect revocation modes. In: Parker, M.G. (ed.) Cryptography and Coding 2009. LNCS, vol. 5921, pp. 278–300. Springer, Heidelberg (2009)
14. Attrapadung, N., Imai, H.: Conjunctive broadcast and attribute-based encryption. In: Shacham, H., Waters, B. (eds.) Pairing 2009. LNCS, vol. 5671, pp. 248–265. Springer, Heidelberg (2009)
15. Nieto, J.M.G., Manulis, M., Sun, D.: Fully private revocable predicate encryption. In: Susilo, W., Mu, Y., Seberry, J. (eds.) ACISP 2012. LNCS, vol. 7372, pp. 350–363. Springer, Heidelberg (2012)
16. Mambo, M., Okamoto, E.: Proxy cryptosystems: Delegation of the power to decrypt ciphertexts. IEICE Transactions E80-A(1), 54–63 (1997)
17. Blaze, M., Bleumer, G., Strauss, M.: Divertible protocols and atomic proxy cryptography. In: Nyberg, K. (ed.) EUROCRYPT 1998. LNCS, vol. 1403, pp. 127–144. Springer, Heidelberg (1998)
18. Ateniese, G., Fu, K., Green, M., Hohenberger, S.: Improved proxy re-encryption schemes with applications to secure distributed storage. ACM Trans. Inf. Syst. Secur. 9(1), 1–30 (2006)
19. Canetti, R., Hohenberger, S.: Chosen-ciphertext secure proxy re-encryption. In: Ning, P., di Vimercati, S.D.C., Syverson, P.F. (eds.) ACM Conference on Computer and Communications Security, pp. 185–194. ACM (2007)
20. Isshiki, T., Nguyen, M.H., Tanaka, K.: Proxy re-encryption in a stronger security model extended from ct-rsa2012. In: Dawson, E. (ed.) CT-RSA 2013. LNCS, vol. 7779, pp. 277–292. Springer, Heidelberg (2013)
21. Libert, B., Vergnaud, D.: Unidirectional chosen-ciphertext secure proxy re-encryption. In: Cramer, R. (ed.) PKC 2008. LNCS, vol. 4939, pp. 360–379. Springer, Heidelberg (2008)
22. Hanaoka, G., Kawai, Y., Kunihiro, N., Matsuda, T., Weng, J., Zhang, R., Zhao, Y.: Generic construction of chosen ciphertext secure proxy re-encryption. In: Dunkelman, O. (ed.) CT-RSA 2012. LNCS, vol. 7178, pp. 349–364. Springer, Heidelberg (2012)
23. Tang, Q., Hartel, P.H., Jonker, W.: Inter-domain identity-based proxy re-encryption. In: Yung, M., Liu, P., Lin, D. (eds.) Inscrypt 2008. LNCS, vol. 5487, pp. 332–347. Springer, Heidelberg (2009)
24. Chu, C.-K., Tzeng, W.-G.: Identity-based proxy re-encryption without random oracles. In: Garay, J.A., Lenstra, A.K., Mambo, M., Peralta, R. (eds.) ISC 2007. LNCS, vol. 4779, pp. 189–202. Springer, Heidelberg (2007)
25. Canetti, R., Krawczyk, H., Nielsen, J.B.: Relaxing chosen-ciphertext security. In: Boneh, D. (ed.) CRYPTO 2003. LNCS, vol. 2729, pp. 565–582. Springer, Heidelberg (2003)
26. Matsuo, T.: Proxy re-encryption systems for identity-based encryption. In: Takagi, T., Okamoto, T., Okamoto, E., Okamoto, T. (eds.) Pairing 2007. LNCS, vol. 4575, pp. 247–267. Springer, Heidelberg (2007)
27. Wang, L., Wang, L., Mambo, M., Okamoto, E.: Identity-based proxy cryptosystems with revocability and hierarchical confidentialities. IEICE Transactions 95-A(1), 70–88 (2012)
28. Wang, L., Wang, L., Mambo, M., Okamoto, E.: New identity-based proxy re-encryption schemes to prevent collusion attacks. In: Joye, M., Miyaji, A., Otsuka, A. (eds.) Pairing 2010. LNCS, vol. 6487, pp. 327–346. Springer, Heidelberg (2010)

29. Mizuno, T., Doi, H.: Secure and efficient IBE-PKE proxy re-encryption. IEICE Transactions E94-A(1), 36–44 (2011)
30. Luo, S., Shen, Q., Chen, Z.: Fully secure unidirectional identity-based proxy re-encryption. In: Kim, H. (ed.) ICISC 2011. LNCS, vol. 7259, pp. 109–126. Springer, Heidelberg (2012)
31. Shao, J., Cao, Z.: Multi-use unidirectional identity-based proxy re-encryption from hierarchical identity-based encryption. Information Sciences 206, 83–95 (2012)
32. Liang, K., Liu, Z., Tan, X., Wong, D.S., Tang, C.: A CCA-secure identity-based conditional proxy re-encryption without random oracles. In: Kwon, T., Lee, M.-K., Kwon, D. (eds.) ICISC 2012. LNCS, vol. 7839, pp. 231–246. Springer, Heidelberg (2013)
33. Liang, K., Liu, J.K., Wong, D.S., Susilo, W.: An efficient cloud-based revocable identity-based proxy re-encryption scheme for public clouds data sharing. Cryptology ePrint Archive, Report 2014/473 (2014), http://eprint.iacr.org/
34. Phan, D.H., Pointcheval, D., Shahandashti, S.F., Strefler, M.: Adaptive CCA broadcast encryption with constant-size secret keys and ciphertexts. Int. J. Inf. Sec. 12(4), 251–265 (2013)
35. Waters, B.: Ciphertext-policy attribute-based encryption: An expressive, efficient, and provably secure realization. In: Catalano, D., Fazio, N., Gennaro, R., Nicolosi, A. (eds.) PKC 2011. LNCS, vol. 6571, pp. 53–70. Springer, Heidelberg (2011)

Verifiable Computation on Outsourced Encrypted Data

Junzuo Lai[1,2], Robert H. Deng[3], Hweehwa Pang[3], and Jian Weng[1],*

[1] Department of Computer Science, Jinan University, China
{laijunzuo,cryptjweng}@gmail.com
[2] The State Key Laboratory of Integrated Services Networks,
Xidian University, China
[3] School of Information Systems,
Singapore Management University, Singapore 178902
{robertdeng,hhpang}@smu.edu.sg

Abstract. On one hand, homomorphic encryption allows a cloud server to perform computation on outsourced encrypted data but provides no verifiability that the computation is correct. On the other hand, homomorphic authenticator, such as homomorphic signature with public verifiability and homomorphic MAC with private verifiability, guarantees authenticity of computation over outsourced data but does not provide data confidentiality. Since cloud servers are usually operated by third-party providers which are almost certain to be outside the trust domain of cloud users, neither homomorphic encryption nor homomorphic authenticator suffices for verifiable computation on outsourced encrypted data in the cloud. In this paper, we propose *verifiable* homomorphic encryption (VHE), which enables *verifiable* computation on outsourced encrypted data.

We first introduce a new cryptographic primitive called homomorphic encrypted authenticator (HEA), which may be of independent interest. Informally, HEA can be viewed as a homomorphic authenticator in which the authenticator itself does not leak any information about the message it authenticates. Next, we show that the *fully* homomorphic MAC scheme, proposed by Gennaro and Wichs recently, is a *fully* HEA with *weak* unforgeability in the sense that an adversary is not allowed to make verification queries. We then propose a *linearly* HEA which can tolerate *any* number of malicious verification queries, i.e., it achieves (*strong*) unforgeability. Finally, we define VHE formally, and give a generic construction of VHE based on homomorphic encryption and HEA. Instantiating the generic construction, we derive a *fully* VHE with *weak* verifiability as well as a *linearly* VHE with (*strong*) verifiability.

Keywords: Cloud Computing, Outsourced Encrypted Data, Verifiable Homomorphic Encryption.

---

* Corresponding author.

M. Kutyłowski and J. Vaidya (Eds.): ESORICS 2014, Part I, LNCS 8712, pp. 273–291, 2014.

1 Introduction

Cloud computing has become increasingly popular because it offers users the illusion of having infinite computing resources, of which they can use as much as they need, without having to worry about how those resources are provided and managed. Since cloud servers are usually operated by third-party providers which are almost certain to be outside the trust domain of cloud users, the cloud computing paradigm raises many security and privacy concerns. One problem is how can users securely outsource their data to the cloud, and later entrust it to perform computation over the data. In a nutshell, this problem can be described in the following scenario. A user Alice has a large collection of data $m_1, \ldots, m_n$ and intends to outsource her data to the cloud. In order to prevent leakage of sensitive information to the cloud service provider, Alice first encrypts the data to produce ciphertexts $c_1, \ldots, c_n$, where c_i is the encryption of m_i. She then uploads the ciphertexts to the cloud, without having to keep a copy of the data due to her limited local storage capacity. At some later point, Alice wishes to derive some information from her data, such as the sum or mean of $m_1, \ldots, m_n$. For this purpose, Alice sends an instruction to the cloud server, specifying a program $\mathcal{P}$ to be executed on her data. The cloud server executes $\mathcal{P}$ over the ciphertexts and returns the result of the execution, c, to Alice. Alice then retrieves $\mathcal{P}(m_1, \ldots, m_n)$ from c. This problem has been addressed by the recent ground-breaking development of *fully homomorphic encryption* [1], which allows a cloud server to perform *any* computation over outsourced encrypted data. Unfortunately, existing fully homomorphic encryption schemes provide no guarantee that the cloud server performed the computation correctly. In the cloud computing setting, there may be incentives for a cloud server to try to cheat and return an incorrect result to the client. This may be related to the nature of the computation being performed, e.g., if the cloud server wants to convince the client of a particular result because it will have beneficial consequences for the server or the server may simply be minimizing the use of its own computational overhead. Errors can also occur due to faulty algorithm implementation or system failure. Thus, the client needs some guarantee that the result returned from the server is correct. In particular, the cloud server needs to convince Alice that c is the correct result of the computation $\mathcal{P}$ over ciphertexts $c_1, \ldots, c_n$, i.e., the ciphertext of $\mathcal{P}(m_1, \ldots, m_n)$.

Consider another scenario in cloud computing. Alice outsources her data $m_1, \ldots, m_n$ in plaintext to a cloud server, and later asks the server to run a program $\mathcal{P}$ over the outsourced data $(m_1, \ldots, m_n)$. The server computes $\mathcal{P}(m_1, \ldots, m_n)$ and sends the result m to Alice. The problem now is that Alice wants to be sure that $m = \mathcal{P}(m_1, \ldots, m_n)$. Homomorphic authenticator, including homomorphic signature [2–12] (for public verification) and homomorphic MAC [13, 14] (for private verification), is the cryptographic primitive that addresses this problem. Roughly speaking, a homomorphic authenticator scheme enables Alice using her secret key to produce an authenticator (called signature in homomorphic signature, or tag in homomorphic MAC) which authenticates a data item so that later, given a set of data $m_1, \ldots, m_n$ and the corresponding authenticators $\sigma_1, \ldots, \sigma_n$, anyone can perform a computation $\mathcal{P}$ over $(\sigma_1, \ldots, \sigma_n)$ to generate an authenticator σ that authenticates $\mathcal{P}(m_1, \ldots, m_n)$. However, homomorphic authenticator does not maintain *confidentiality* of outsourced data. That is, the cloud server has total access to user's data since they are not encrypted.

The above observations motivate us to consider *verifiable* homomorphic encryption (VHE), which enables *verifiable* computation on outsourced encrypted data. Informally, a VHE scheme allows a user using her secret key to encrypt data $m_1, \ldots, m_n$ and obtain independent ciphertexts $c_1, \ldots, c_n$ so that later, given ciphertexts $c_1, \ldots, c_n$, anyone can execute a program $\mathcal{P}$ over $(c_1, \ldots, c_n)$ to generate a ciphertext c. The user using her secret key can then decrypt ciphertext c to obtain plaintext m and check whether $m = \mathcal{P}(m_1, \ldots, m_n)$. There is a trivial solution to construct VHE in which the user authenticates the output of a computation $\mathcal{P}$ over $(c_1, \ldots, c_n)$ by accessing all the ciphertexts, i.e., $c_1, \ldots, c_n$. Thus, VHE is only interesting if authenticity of the output of $\mathcal{P}$ over the ciphertexts $c_1, \ldots, c_n$ can be verified with significantly lower communication cost than that of simply transmitting $c_1, \ldots, c_n$ to the user. This is particularly important where the outsourced data are large in size.

A naive approach to construct VHE is to combine homomorphic encryption and homomorphic authenticator directly. In the above cloud computing scenario, before outsourcing her data $m_1, \ldots, m_n$ to a cloud server, Alice first runs the encryption algorithm of a homomorphic encryption scheme and the authentication algorithm of a homomorphic authenticator scheme on m_i, $i = 1, \ldots, n$, then she uploads the ciphertext of m_i, $c_i = (\tilde{c}_i, \sigma_i)$, to the server, where $\tilde{c}_i$ and σ_i are the outputs of the encryption and authentication algorithms, respectively. Later, when the server is asked to execute a program $\mathcal{P}$ on the ciphertexts, it runs the evaluation algorithms of the homomorphic encryption scheme and homomorphic authenticator scheme on $((\tilde{c}_1, \ldots, \tilde{c}_n), \mathcal{P})$ and $((\sigma_1, \ldots, \sigma_n), \mathcal{P})$, respectively, and returns the result $c = (\tilde{c}, \sigma)$ to Alice, where $\tilde{c}$ and σ are the outputs from the evaluation algorithms of the homomorphic encryption scheme and homomorphic authenticator scheme, respectively. The client decrypts $\tilde{c}$ to obtain message m and checks that the server correctly applied $\mathcal{P}$ to the ciphertexts by verifying that the authenticator σ authenticates the message $m = \mathcal{P}(m_1, \ldots, m_n)$. Unfortunately, homomorphic authenticator schemes provide no guarantee that the authenticator σ_i on m_i does not leak information about m_i. Indeed, with a homomorphic signature scheme, the signature σ_i on message m_i always leaks information about m_i since, given a message m, anyone can check whether σ_i is a valid signature on m. Thus, the above naive construction of VHE does not guarantee that the outsourced data $m_1, \ldots, m_n$ is *semantically secure*.

OUR CONTRIBUTIONS. We first introduce a new cryptographic primitive called homomorphic encrypted authenticator (HEA), which may be of independent interest, and formally define its *semantic security* and *unforgeability*. Informally, a HEA can be viewed as a homomorphic authenticator in which the authenticator does not leak any information about the message that it authenticates. Then, we show that the *fully* homomorphic MAC scheme, proposed by Gennaro and

Wichs [13] recently, is a *fully* HEA scheme with *weak* unforgeability, where the adversary is not allowed to make verification queries. We emphasize that a homomorphic MAC scheme is not necessarily a HEA scheme, since the tag in a homomorphic MAC scheme may leak information about the message it authenticates. For example, the homomorphic MAC schemes tolerating any number of malicious verification queries, proposed by Catalano and Fiore [14] recently, are not HEA schemes because anyone can retrieve the message from its tag in these schemes. While a *fully* HEA scheme with weak unforgeability allows anyone to perform *any* authenticated computation on authenticated data, it is only secure in the setting where the adversary cannot make verification queries to test if a maliciously constructed authenticator verifies correctly. In practice, this means that the user needs to abort and completely stop using the scheme whenever she gets the first authenticator that doesn't verify correctly, and this motivates us to seek HEA schemes with (*strong*) unforgeability which allows an adversary to make arbitrarily many verification queries.

We observe that, in a homomorphic signature scheme, an adversary cannot obtain any additional information by making verification queries since, given a signature, anyone (including the adversary) can check whether it is a valid signature on a message. Thus, we resort to homomorphic signature for constructing HEA schemes with (strong) unforgeability. As mentioned above, a homomorphic signature scheme may not be a HEA scheme; so we have to adopt some techniques to convert the former into the latter. Drawing on a *linearly* homomorphic signature scheme proposed by Freeman [8], we propose a *linearly* HEA which can tolerate *any* number of malicious verification queries, i.e., it achieves (*strong*) unforgeability.

Finally, we formally introduce the notion and security requirements of VHE, and provide a generic construction of VHE from homomorphic encryption and HEA. Instantiating the generic construction, we obtain a *fully* VHE with *weak* verifiability, which allows anyone to perform *any* verifiable computation on outsourced encrypted data but does not tolerate malicious verification queries, as well as a *linearly* VHE with (*strong*) verifiability, which allows anyone to perform *linear* verifiable computations on outsourced encrypted data and can tolerate *any* number of malicious verification queries.

ORGANIZATION. The rest of this paper is organized as follows. Section 2 reviews related work. Section 3 provides some preliminaries. Section 4 introduces the new cryptographic primitive HEA, shows that the fully homomorphic MAC scheme proposed by Gennaro and Wichs [13] is a fully HEA in a weaker security model, and proposes a linearly HEA scheme in a full security model. The formal definition of VHE and the generic construction of VHE from homomorphic encryption and HEA are given in Section 5. Section 6 concludes the paper.

2   Related Work

We review related literature including non-interactive verifiable computation, fully homomorphic encryption, homomorphic signature/MAC, linearly homomorphic structure-preserving signature and homomorphic authenticator-encryption. We refer the reader to [15] for discussions on other related effort, such as succinct non-interactive arguments of knowledge [16].

Non-Interactive Verifiable Computation. The notion of non-interactive verifiable computation was introduced by Gennaro et al. [17]. Non-interactive verifiable computation enables a computationally weak client to outsource the computation of a function to a server, which returns the result of the function evaluation as well as a non-interactive proof that the computation was carried out correctly, with the crucial requirement that verification of the proof needs substantially less *computational* effort than computing the function by the client from scratch. The existing non-interactive verifiable computation schemes [17–22] focus on delegating general functions. In order to achieve higher efficiency, there exist non-interactive verifiable computation schemes which permit only a very limited class of functions, such as polynomials [23–26, 15, 22] and set operations [27]. Non-interactive verifiable computation schemes either do not protect privacy of outsourced data from a malicious server, or the functions to be evaluated must be known at system setup, or the outsourced data must be fixed a-priori (i.e., a client cannot outsource her data incrementally). VHE does not suffer from any of the limitations of non-interactive verifiable computation mentioned above.

Our goals are very different from non-interactive verifiable computation. We seek to save the clients from storing large amount of data as well as to save on *communication* cost. The key requirement that makes our definition of VHE interesting is that the output of the program $\mathcal{P}$ over the ciphertexts $c_1, \ldots, c_n$ be *succinct*; otherwise, there is a trivial solution in which a client can verify the output of a computation $\mathcal{P}$ by simply being provided with the ciphertexts $c_1, \ldots, c_n$. The succinctness requirement ensures that the client can verify the output of a computation $\mathcal{P}$ over encrypted data with much smaller *communication* overhead than that of simply transmitting the encrypted data from the server to the client. VHE is especially useful when verifying computations that require a large amount of encrypted data as input but have a short output (e.g., computing the median in a large database).

Fully Homomorphic Encryption. The notion of fully homomorphic encryption (FHE) was first put forward by Rivest et al. [28]. However, only in the past few years have candidate FHE schemes been proposed. The first such scheme was constructed by Gentry [1]; his work inspired a tremendous amount of research effort on improving the efficiency of his scheme [29–35], realizations of FHE based on different assumptions [36–39], and so on.

Homomorphic Signature and MAC. Homomorphic authenticator in both the asymmetric setting (i.e., homomorphic signature) and the symmetric setting (i.e., homomorphic MAC) has been considered in many prior works. The notion of homomorphic signature was introduced by Johnson et al. [40]. Since then, many homomorphic signature schemes [2–8] for *linear functions* have been proposed, mainly because of the important application to *network coding* [41, 42]. Linearly homomorphic authenticator has also been considered in the context of *proofs of data possession and retrievability* [43–45]. The work of Ahn et al. [10] and Attrapadung et al. [11, 12] considered a new security requirement of homomorphic signature, i.e., *context hiding*, which requires that a derived signature be indistinguishable from a fresh signature on the same message. In a recent breakthrough, Boneh and Freeman [9] showed how to use ideal lattices to construct homomorphic signature for bounded degree polynomials; this scheme is currently the only one that goes beyond linear functions.

Gennaro and Wichs [13] introduced fully homomorphic MAC (i.e., homomorphic MAC for any computation) and gave a concrete construction which is only proven secure in a weaker model where an adversary cannot ask verification queries. We will show later in the paper that the fully homomorphic MAC scheme in [13] is in fact a fully HEA scheme. Catalano and Fiore [14] presented efficient realizations of homomorphic MAC that tolerate verification queries, for a restricted class of computations (i.e., arithmetic circuits with polynomially-bounded degree). The homomorphic MAC schemes proposed in [14] are not HEA schemes, and how to convert these schemes into HEA is an interesting open problem.

Linearly Homomorphic Structure-Preserving Signatures. Structure-preserving signatures (SPS) [46, 47] are signature schemes where public keys, messages and signatures all consist of elements of a group over which a bilinear map is efficiently computable. Recently, Libert et al. [48] introduced and realized the notion of linearly homomorphic structure-preserving signature (LHSPS), which is similar to SPS but equipped with a linearly homomorphic property. Catalano et al. [49] followed their work and proposed some new methodologies. Libert et al. [48] showed that LHSPS enables linear verifiable computations on outsourced encrypted data (i.e., linearly VHE), but their treatment is informal and decryption in their system takes polynomial time in the size of the message space (i.e., their system can only be used to encrypt short messages). In this paper, we present the notion and security models of VHE formally, give a generic construction for VHE, and derive a fully VHE scheme which is proven secure in a weaker security model and a linearly VHE scheme which is proven secure in a full security model.

Homomorphic Authenticator-Encryption. Gennaro and Wichs [13] showed that their proposed homomorphic MAC can be extended to homomorphic authenticator-encryption, also called homomorphic authenticated encryption in [50]. A homomorphic authenticator-encryption scheme is a homomorphic authenticator scheme with an additional **decrypt** algorithm, which allows a user with a secret key to retrieve the authenticated message from an authenticator. Our notion of HEA is different from homomorphic authenticator-encryption. A HEA scheme only requires that an authenticator not leak information about the authenticated message; thus HEA is a weaker cryptographic primitive than homomorphic authenticator-encryption. In fact, homomorphic authenticator-encryption, which also enables verifiable computation on outsourced encrypted data, is similar to our notion of VHE. However, the schemes proposed in [13, 50] cannot tolerate malicious verification queries. Compared with their work, we investigate the relationships among homomorphic encryption, homomorphic signature/MAC and VHE, and provide a general method to construct VHE. We also propose a linearly VHE scheme which can tolerate any number of malicious verification queries.

3 Preliminaries

If S is a set, then $s \xleftarrow{\$} S$ denotes the operation of picking an element s uniformly at random from S. Let $\mathbb{N}$ denote the set of natural numbers. If $n \in \mathbb{N}$ then $[n]$ denotes the set $\{1, \ldots, n\}$. If $\lambda \in \mathbb{N}$ then 1^λ denotes the string of λ ones. Let $z \leftarrow \mathsf{A}(x, y, \ldots)$ denote the operation of running an algorithm A with inputs $(x, y, \ldots)$ and output z. A function $f(\lambda)$ is *negligible* if for every $c > 0$ there exists a λ_c such that $f(\lambda) < 1/\lambda^c$ for all $\lambda > \lambda_c$.

3.1 Bilinear Groups

Let $\mathcal{G}$ be an algorithm that takes as input a security parameter λ and outputs a tuple $(p, \mathbb{G}, \mathbb{G}_T, e)$, where $\mathbb{G}$ and $\mathbb{G}_T$ are multiplicative cyclic groups of prime order p, and $e : \mathbb{G} \times \mathbb{G} \to \mathbb{G}_T$ is a map that possesses the following properties:

1. **Bilinearity:** $e(g^a, h^b) = e(g, h)^{ab}$ for all $g, h \in \mathbb{G}$ and $a, b \in \mathbb{Z}_p^*$.
2. **Non-degeneracy:** $e(g, h) \neq 1$ whenever $g, h \neq 1_{\mathbb{G}}$.
3. **Computable:** efficient computability for any input pair.

We refer to the tuple $(p, \mathbb{G}, \mathbb{G}_T, e)$ as a *bilinear group*. We consider the following problems in bilinear groups.

q-**Strong Diffie-Hellman (q-SDH) Problem.** The q-SDH problem in $\mathbb{G}$ is defined as follows: Given a tuple $(\bar{g}, \bar{g}^\alpha, \ldots, \bar{g}^{\alpha^q})$ as input for randomly chosen $\bar{g} \xleftarrow{\$} \mathbb{G}$ and $\alpha \xleftarrow{\$} \mathbb{Z}_p^*$, output a pair $(\bar{g}^{1/(\alpha+\vartheta)}, \vartheta)$ where $\vartheta \in \mathbb{Z}_p^*$. The advantage of an algorithm $\mathcal{A}$ in solving q-SDH problem is defined as $|\Pr[\mathcal{A}(\bar{g}, \bar{g}^\alpha, \ldots, \bar{g}^{\alpha^q}) = (\bar{g}^{1/(\alpha+\vartheta)}, \vartheta)]|$, where the probability is over the random choices of $\bar{g} \in \mathbb{G}, \alpha \in \mathbb{Z}_p^*$, and the random bits of $\mathcal{A}$.

Definition 1. *We say that the q-SDH assumption holds in $\mathbb{G}$ if all probabilistic polynomial time algorithms have at most a negligible advantage in solving the q-SDH problem in $\mathbb{G}$.*

Decision Linear (DLN) Problem [51]. The DLN problem in $\mathbb{G}$ is defined as follows: Given a tuple $(\bar{g}, \tilde{g}, \hat{g}, \bar{g}^x, \tilde{g}^y, \hat{g}^z)$ as input, output 1 if $x + y = z$ and 0 otherwise. The advantage of an algorithm $\mathcal{A}$ in solving the DLN problem is defined as $|\Pr[\mathcal{A}(\bar{g}, \tilde{g}, \hat{g}, \bar{g}^x, \tilde{g}^y, \hat{g}^z) = 1 : \bar{g}, \tilde{g}, \hat{g} \xleftarrow{\$} \mathbb{G}, x, y, z \xleftarrow{\$} \mathbb{Z}_p^*] - \Pr[\mathcal{A}(\bar{g}, \tilde{g}, \hat{g}, \bar{g}^x, \tilde{g}^y, \hat{g}^{x+y}) = 1 : \bar{g}, \tilde{g}, \hat{g} \xleftarrow{\$} \mathbb{G}, x, y \xleftarrow{\$} \mathbb{Z}_p^*]|$, where the probability is over the random choices of $\bar{g}, \tilde{g}, \hat{g} \in \mathbb{G}$ and $x, y, z \in \mathbb{Z}_p^*$, and the random bits of $\mathcal{A}$.

Definition 2. *We say that the DLN assumption holds in $\mathbb{G}$ if all probabilistic polynomial time algorithms have at most a negligible advantage in solving the DLN problem in $\mathbb{G}$.*

4   Homomorphic Encrypted Authenticator

Informally, a homomorphic encrypted authenticator (HEA) can be viewed as a homomorphic authenticator, where the authenticator on a message does not leak any information about the message. Before presenting the definition of HEA formally, we need to establish some syntax for specifying which data is being authenticated and over which data a program $\mathcal{P}$ should be evaluated. We recall the notion of labeled data and programs introduced by Gennaro and Wichs in [13].

Labeled Data and Programs. Whenever a user wants to authenticate some data item, she chooses a *label* $\tau \in \{0,1\}^*$ for it, and the authentication algorithm authenticates the data with respect to the label τ. A labeled program $\mathcal{P}$ consists of a tuple $(f, \tau_1, \ldots, \tau_k)$ where $f : \mathbb{F}^k \to \mathbb{F}$ is a circuit/function, and $\tau_1, \ldots, \tau_k$ are the *labels* of the input nodes of f. Given some labeled programs $\mathcal{P}_1, \ldots, \mathcal{P}_t$ and a function $g : \mathbb{F}^k \to \mathbb{F}$, the *composed program*, denoted by $\mathcal{P}^* = g(\mathcal{P}_1, \ldots, \mathcal{P}_k)$, corresponds to evaluating g on the outputs of $\mathcal{P}_1, \ldots, \mathcal{P}_k$. The labeled inputs of $\mathcal{P}^*$ are all the distinct labeled inputs of $\mathcal{P}_1, \ldots, \mathcal{P}_k$. We denote by $\mathcal{I}_\tau = (g_{id}, \tau)$ the *identity program* with label τ where g_{id} is the canonical identity function and τ is some label. Notice that any program $\mathcal{P} = (f, \tau_1, \ldots, \tau_k)$ can be expressed as the composition of identity programs $\mathcal{P} = f(\mathcal{I}_{\tau_1}, \ldots, \mathcal{I}_{\tau_k})$.

Homomorphic Encrypted Authenticator. A homomorphic encrypted authenticator scheme consists of the following four algorithms:

Setup(1^λ) takes as input a security parameter λ. It outputs a pair of public key PK and secret key SK. The public key PK defines a message space $\mathcal{M}$ and a set $\mathcal{F}$ of "admissible" functions $f : \mathcal{M}^k \to \mathcal{M}$.

Auth(SK, τ, m) takes as input secret key SK, a label $\tau \in \{0,1\}^*$ and a message $m \in \mathcal{M}$. It outputs an authenticator σ.

Ver(SK, m, $\mathcal{P}$, σ) takes as input secret key SK, a message $m \in \mathcal{M}$, a labeled program $\mathcal{P}$ and an authenticator σ. It outputs either 0 (reject) or 1 (accept).

Eval(PK, f, $\boldsymbol{\sigma}$) takes as input public key PK, a function $f \in \mathcal{F}$ and a vector of authenticators $\boldsymbol{\sigma} = (\sigma_1, \ldots, \sigma_k)$. It outputs a new authenticator σ.

For correctness, we require that for each (PK, SK) output by Setup(1^λ), the following properties hold:

1. For all labels $\tau \in \{0,1\}^*$ and all $m \in \mathcal{M}$, if $\sigma \leftarrow$ Auth(SK, τ, m), then Ver(SK, m, $\mathcal{I}_\tau$, σ) = 1.
2. Given an admissible function $g : \mathcal{M}^k \leftarrow \mathcal{M}$ and any set of message/program/authenticator triples $\{(m_i, \mathcal{P}_i, \sigma_i)\}_{i=1}^k$ such that Ver(SK, m_i, $\mathcal{P}_i$, σ_i) = 1, if $m = g(m_1, \ldots, m_k)$, $\mathcal{P} = g(\mathcal{P}_1, \ldots, \mathcal{P}_k)$ and $\sigma =$ Eval(PK, g, $(\sigma_1, \ldots, \sigma_k)$), then Ver(SK, m, $\mathcal{P}$, σ) = 1.

The above requirements capture the basic correctness of computing over freshly authenticated data, as well as the composability of computing over the authenticated outputs of prior computations. If the set of admissible functions $\mathcal{F}$ of a HEA scheme consists of *linear* functions (resp. *any* functions) from $\mathcal{M}^k$ to $\mathcal{M}$, then we say that the HEA scheme is a *linearly* (resp. *fully*) HEA scheme.

4.1 Security Model for Homomorphic Encrypted Authenticator

We now introduce the security requirements of HEA, including *semantic security* and *unforgeability*. Informally, *semantic security* requires that an authenticator σ of a message m with label τ should not leak any information about m. Let σ_i be an authenticator on message m_i with label τ_i for $i = 1, \ldots, k$. *Unforgeability* requires that given $(\sigma_1, \ldots, \sigma_k)$, it should be impossible to output an authenticator σ and an admissible function f such that σ is a valid authenticator on a message-program pair $(m, \mathcal{P} = (f, \tau_1, \ldots, \tau_k))$ and $m \neq f(m_1, \ldots, m_k)$.

The semantic security of HEA is defined in terms of the following game, played between a challenger and an adversary $\mathcal{A}$:

Setup. The challenger runs $\mathsf{Setup}(1^\lambda)$ to obtain a pair of public key PK and secret key SK. It gives the public key PK to adversary $\mathcal{A}$ and keeps SK to itself. It also initializes a list $T = \emptyset$.

Authentication queries. The adversary $\mathcal{A}$ adaptively queries the challenger for authenticators. $\mathcal{A}$ submits a message $m \in \mathcal{M}$. If there exists a tuple (τ, m) in T, the challenger computes $\sigma \leftarrow \mathsf{Auth}(\mathsf{SK}, \tau, m)$; otherwise, the challenger chooses a fresh label $\tau \in \{0, 1\}^*$, updates the list $T = T \cup (\tau, m)$ and computes $\sigma \leftarrow \mathsf{Auth}(\mathsf{SK}, \tau, m)$. Then, the challenger gives the authenticator σ to $\mathcal{A}$.

Challenge. Adversary $\mathcal{A}$ submits a label $\tau^* \in \{0, 1\}^*$ and two messages $m_0, m_1 \in \mathcal{M}$. The challenger selects a random bit $\beta \in \{0, 1\}$, computes $\sigma^* \leftarrow \mathsf{Auth}(\mathsf{SK}, \tau^*, m_\beta)$ and sends σ^* to the adversary.

Guess. Adversary $\mathcal{A}$ outputs its guess $\beta' \in \{0, 1\}$ for β and wins the game if $\beta = \beta'$.

The advantage of the adversary in this game is defined as $|\Pr[\beta = \beta'] - \frac{1}{2}|$ where the probability is taken over the random bits used by the challenger and the adversary.

Definition 3. *A HEA scheme is* semantically secure *if all probabilistic polynomial time adversaries have at most a negligible advantage in this security game.*

The unforgeability of HEA is defined in terms of the following game, played between a challenger and an adversary $\mathcal{A}$:

Setup. The challenger runs $\mathsf{Setup}(1^\lambda)$ to obtain a pair of public key PK and secret key SK. It gives the public key PK to adversary $\mathcal{A}$ and keeps SK to itself. It also initializes a list $T = \emptyset$.

Queries. Adversary $\mathcal{A}$ adaptively issues the following queries:

- *Authentication queries.* Adversary $\mathcal{A}$ submits a message $m \in \mathcal{M}$. If there exists a tuple (τ, m) in T, the challenger computes $\sigma \leftarrow \mathsf{Auth}(\mathsf{SK}, \tau, m)$; otherwise, the challenger chooses a fresh label $\tau \in \{0, 1\}^*$, updates the list $T = T \cup (\tau, m)$ and computes $\sigma \leftarrow \mathsf{Auth}(\mathsf{SK}, \tau, m)$. Then, the challenger gives the authenticator σ to $\mathcal{A}$.
- *Verification queries.* Adversary $\mathcal{A}$ submits $(m, \mathcal{P}, \sigma)$ and the challenger replies with the output of $\mathsf{Ver}(\mathsf{SK}, m, \mathcal{P}, \sigma)$.

Output. Adversary $\mathcal{A}$ outputs a message m^*, a labeled program $\mathcal{P}^* = (f^*, \tau_1^*, \ldots, \tau_k^*)$ and an authenticator σ^*.

The adversary *wins* if $\mathsf{Ver}(\mathsf{SK}, m^*, \mathcal{P}^*, \sigma^*) = 1$ and one of the following conditions hold:

1. there exists $i \in \{1, \ldots, k\}$ such that $(\tau_i^*, \cdot) \notin T$ (a *Type 1 forgery*),
2. T contains tuples $(\tau_1^*, m_1), \ldots, (\tau_k^*, m_k)$, for some message $m_1, \ldots, m_k$, and $m^* \neq f^*(m_1, \ldots, m_k)$ (a *Type 2 forgery*).

Informally, in a Type 1 forgery the adversary produces a valid authenticator σ on a message-program pair $(m^*, \mathcal{P}^* = (f^*, \tau_1^*, \ldots, \tau_k^*))$ where no message was ever authenticated under the label τ_i^* involved in the forgery, whereas in a Type 2 forgery the adversary produces a valid authenticator σ on a message-program pair $(m^*, \mathcal{P}^* = (f^*, \tau_1^*, \ldots, \tau_k^*))$ where m^* is not the correct output of the labeled program $\mathcal{P}^*$ when executed on previously authenticated message $(m_1, \ldots, m_k)$.

The advantage of the adversary in this game is defined as $|\Pr[\mathcal{A} \ wins]|$ where the probability is taken over the random bits used by the challenger and the adversary.

Definition 4. *A HEA scheme is* (strongly) *unforgeable, or simply unforgeable, if all probabilistic polynomial time adversaries have at most a negligible advantage in this security game.*

We say that a HEA scheme is *weakly* unforgeable (or unforgeable without verification queries) if in the above security game the adversary cannot make verification queries.

4.2 Proposed HEA Constructions

In this subsection, we first show that the fully homomorphic authenticator scheme proposed by Gennaro and Wichs [13] recently, is a secure fully HEA with weak unforgeability. Drawing on the linearly homomorphic signature scheme proposed by Freeman [8], we then present a secure linearly HEA scheme which can tolerate any number of malicious verification queries, i.e., it achieves (strong) unforgeability.

A Secure Fully HEA with Weak Unforgeability. In [13], Gennaro and Wichs proposed a fully homomorphic authenticator scheme and proved that it is *unforgeable without verification queries*. Observe that in an authenticator $\sigma = (c_1, \ldots, c_\lambda, \nu)$ on a message m with label τ, $\nu = F_K(\tau)$ is a value independent of the message m and c_i, $i \in [\lambda]$, is a ciphertext of a homomorphic encryption scheme HE. If the underlying fully homomorphic encryption scheme HE is semantically secure, then for each $i \in [\lambda]$, c_i does not leak any information about m, thus σ will not leak any information about m. That is, the fully homomorphic authenticator proposed in [13] is also *semantically secure*. To sum up, the fully homomorphic authenticator proposed by Gennaro and Wichs [13], is a secure fully HEA with weak unforgeability.

As shown in [13], there is an efficient attack against the scheme in the setting of security *with* verification queries. That is, the fully HEA scheme with weak unforgeability is only secure in the setting where the adversary cannot make verification queries to test if a maliciously constructed authenticator verifies correctly. In practice, this means that the user needs to abort and completely stop using the scheme whenever she gets the first authenticator that doesn't verify correctly. This motivates the need for HEA schemes with (*strong*) unforgeability that allow the adversary to make arbitrarily many verification queries.

A Secure Linearly HEA with (Strong) Unforgeability. Drawing on the linearly homomorphic signature scheme proposed by Freeman [8], which is based on the Boneh-Boyen (BB) signature scheme [52], we now show how to construct a *linearly* HEA scheme which can tolerate any number of malicious verification queries, i.e., it achieves (strong) unforgeability. We emphasize that a linearly homomorphic signature scheme is not necessarily a linearly HEA scheme; so we have to adopt some techniques to convert the former into the latter.

In the proposed linearly HEA construction, we also use the notion of "data set" introduced in [8]. That is, each set of messages is grouped together into a "data set" or "file", and each file is associated with a label τ that serves to bind the messages together in that file. Therefore, in our proposed construction, the algorithm Setup includes an additional input parameter, k, which indicates the maximum data size of a file; and the algorithm Auth includes an additional input parameter, an index i, which indicates that the authenticated message is the ith message in the file. Verifiable homomorphic operations in our scheme only apply to the data associated with the same label. That is, for an admissible labeled program $\mathcal{P} = (f, \tau_1, \ldots, \tau_k)$, we require that $\tau_1 = \cdots = \tau_k$; thus, for simplicity, we denote by (f, τ) a labeled program $\mathcal{P}$. Since the client can group as many related messages as possible into a file (i.e., associated with an identical label), the requirement of the admissible labeled program should not constrain the usability of a general storage service overly.

Concretely, the proposed linearly HEA scheme consists of the following algorithms:

Setup($1^\lambda, k$) Given a security parameter λ and a maximum data size k, the setup algorithm runs $\mathcal{G}(1^\lambda)$ to obtain a bilinear group $(p, \mathbb{G}, \mathbb{G}_T, e)$. Next, it chooses $g, u, v_1, \ldots, v_k, h, h_0 \in \mathbb{G}$ and $\alpha, a, b \in \mathbb{Z}_p^*$ uniformly at random. Then, it sets $g_1 = g^\alpha, h_1 = h_0^{1/a}, h_2 = h_0^{1/b}$ (note that $h_1^a = h_2^b = h_0$), and chooses a collision-resistant hash function $H : \{0, 1\}^* \to \mathbb{Z}_p^*$. The public key is published as $\mathsf{PK} = (g, g_1, u, v_1, \ldots, v_k, h, h_0, h_1, h_2, H)$ and the secret key is $\mathsf{SK} = (\alpha, a, b)$.

The message space of our proposed scheme is $\mathbb{F}_p$ and the set of admissible functions $\mathcal{F}$ is all $\mathbb{F}_p$-linear functions from $\mathbb{F}_p^k$ to $\mathbb{F}_p$. We represent a function $f \in \mathcal{F}$ as the vector $(c_1, \ldots, c_k) \in \mathbb{F}_p^k$, i.e., $f(m_1, \ldots, m_k) = \sum_{i=1}^{k} c_i m_i$.

Auth(SK, τ, m, i) Given secret key SK, a label $\tau \in \{0, 1\}^*$, a message $m \in \mathbb{F}_p$ and an index $i \in \{1, \ldots, k\}$, it chooses $r_1, r_2, s \in \mathbb{Z}_p^*$ uniformly at random. Then, it outputs the authenticator $\sigma = (\tilde{C}, C_0, C_1, C_2, s)$, where

$$\tilde{C} = g^{1/(\alpha + H(\tau))}, \quad C_0 = h_0^{r_1 + r_2}(h^m u^s v_i)^{1/(\alpha + H(\tau))}, \quad C_1 = h_1^{r_1}, \quad C_2 = h_2^{r_2}.$$

Note that the index i indicates that m is the ith message in the file associated with label τ.

Ver(SK, m, $\mathcal{P} = (f, \tau), \sigma$) Given secret key SK, a message $m \in \mathbb{F}_p$, a label τ, a function $f = (c_1, \ldots, c_k) \in \mathbb{F}_p^k$ and an authenticator $\sigma = (\tilde{C}, C_0, C_1, C_2, s)$, it checks whether $e(g_1 g^{H(\tau)}, \tilde{C}) = e(g, g)$ and $e(C_0/(C_1^a C_2^b), g) = e(\tilde{C}, h^m u^s \cdot (\prod_{i=1}^k v_i^{c_i}))$. If so, it outputs 1 (accept); otherwise it outputs 0 (reject).

Eval(PK, f, $\boldsymbol{\sigma}$) Given public key PK, a function $f = (c_1, \ldots, c_k) \in \mathbb{F}_p^k$ and a vector of authenticators $\boldsymbol{\sigma} = (\sigma_1, \ldots, \sigma_k)$ where $\sigma_i = (\tilde{C}^{(i)}, C_0^{(i)}, C_1^{(i)}, C_2^{(i)}, s^{(i)})$ for $i = 1, \ldots, k$, it outputs a new authenticator $\sigma = (\tilde{C}, C_0, C_1, C_2, s)$ where

$$\tilde{C} = \tilde{C}^{(1)}, \quad C_0 = \prod_{i=1}^k (C_0^{(i)})^{c_i}, \quad C_1 = \prod_{i=1}^k (C_1^{(i)})^{c_i}, \quad C_2 = \prod_{i=1}^k (C_2^{(i)})^{c_i}, \quad s = \sum_{i=1}^k c_i s^{(i)}.$$

Correctness. We show that the proposed homomorphic encrypted authenticator scheme satisfies the correctness properties of HEA.

1. Let $\tau \in \{0,1\}^*$ be a label, $m \in \mathbb{F}_p$ be a message and $i \in \{1, \ldots, k\}$ be an index. Suppose $\sigma = (\tilde{C}, C_0, C_1, C_2, s) \leftarrow$ Auth(SK, τ, m, i). We now show that Ver(SK, $m, \mathcal{I}_\tau, \sigma) = 1$. Observe that $\tilde{C} = g^{1/(\alpha + H(\tau))}$, $C_0/(C_1^a C_2^b) = h_0^{r_1 + r_2}(h^m u^s v_i)^{1/(\alpha + H(\tau))}/(h_1^{a r_1} h_2^{b r_2}) = (h^m u^s v_i)^{1/(\alpha + H(\tau))}$.
   Thus, we have $e(g_1 g^{H(\tau)}, \tilde{C}) = e(g_1 g^{H(\tau)}, g^{1/(\alpha + H(\tau))}) = e(g, g)$,

   $$e(C_0/(C_1^a C_2^b), g) = e((h^m u^s v_i)^{1/(\alpha + H(\tau))}, g) = e(h^m u^s v_i, g^{1/(\alpha + H(\tau))})$$
   $$= e(\tilde{C}, h^m u^s v_i).$$

   It follows that Ver(SK, $m, \mathcal{I}_\tau, \sigma) = 1$.

2. Let $\tau \in \{0,1\}^*$ be a label, and $f', f_1, \ldots, f_k$ be linear functions represented as vectors in $\mathbb{F}_p^k$, with $f' = (c_1, \ldots, c_k)$ and $f_i = (d_{i1}, \ldots, d_{ik})$ for $i = 1, \ldots, k$. Suppose $\boldsymbol{\sigma} = (\sigma_1, \ldots, \sigma_k)$ is a vector of authenticators with $\sigma_i = (\tilde{C}^{(i)}, C_0^{(i)}, C_1^{(i)}, C_2^{(i)}, s^{(i)})$ for $i = 1, \ldots, k$, such that Ver(SK, $m_i, \mathcal{P}_i = (f_i, \tau), \sigma_i) = 1$ for some $m_i \in \mathbb{F}_p$. We show that Ver(SK, $f'(m_1, \ldots, m_k), \mathcal{P} = (f' \circ \boldsymbol{f}, \tau), $ Eval(PK, $f', \boldsymbol{\sigma})) = 1$, where $f' \circ \boldsymbol{f}$ denotes the function that sends $\boldsymbol{x} = (x_1, \ldots, x_k)$ to $f'(f_1(\boldsymbol{x}), \ldots, f_k(\boldsymbol{x}))$. Note that $f' \circ \boldsymbol{f}$ can be represented as a vector $(d_1, \ldots, d_k) \in \mathbb{F}_p^k$ where $d_i = \sum_{j=1}^k c_j d_{ji}$ for $i = 1, \ldots, k$.
   Since Ver(SK, $m_i, \mathcal{P}_i = (f_i, \tau), \sigma_i) = 1$ for $i = 1, \ldots, k$, we have

   $$\tilde{C}^{(i)} = g^{1/(\alpha + H(\tau))}, \quad C_0^{(i)} = h_0^{r_{i1} + r_{i2}}(h^{m_i} u^{s^{(i)}} \cdot \prod_{j=1}^k v_j^{d_{ij}})^{1/(\alpha + H(\tau))},$$
   $$C_1^{(i)} = h_1^{r_{i1}}, \quad C_2^{(i)} = h_2^{r_{i2}},$$

   for some random $r_{i1}, r_{i2} \in \mathbb{Z}_p^*$. Let Eval(PK, $f', \boldsymbol{\sigma}) = \sigma = (\tilde{C}, C_0, C_1, C_2, s)$.
   We have $\tilde{C} = g^{1/(\alpha + H(\tau))}$, $C_1 = h_1^{r_1}$, $C_2^{(i)} = h_2^{r_2}$, $C_0 = h_0^{r_1 + r_2}(h^m u^s \cdot \prod_{i=1}^k v_i^{\sum_{j=1}^k c_j d_{ji}})^{1/(\alpha + H(\tau))} = h_0^{r_1 + r_2}(h^m u^s \cdot \prod_{i=1}^k v_i^{d_i})^{1/(\alpha + H(\tau))}$, where $m = \sum_{i=1}^k c_i m_i$, $r_1 = \sum_{i=1}^k c_i r_{i1}$, $r_2 = \sum_{i=1}^k c_i r_{i2}$ and $s = \sum_{i=1}^k c_i s^{(i)}$. Observe that $C_0/(C_1^a C_2^b) = (h^m u^s \cdot \prod_{i=1}^k v_i^{d_i})^{1/(\alpha + H(\tau))}$. Thus,

$e(g_1 g^{H(\tau)}, \tilde{C}) = e(g_1 g^{H(\tau)}, g^{1/(\alpha + H(\tau))}) = e(g, g)$, and $e(C_0/(C_1^a C_2^b), g) = e((h^m u^s \prod_{i=1}^{k} v_i^{d_i})^{1/(\alpha + H(\tau))}, g) = e(\tilde{C}, h^m u^s \prod_{i=1}^{k} v_i^{d_i})$. It follows that $\mathsf{Ver}(\mathsf{SK}, m, \mathcal{P} = (f' \circ \boldsymbol{f}, \tau), \sigma) = 1$, where $m = \sum_{i=1}^{k} c_i m_i = f'(m_1, \ldots, m_k)$ and $\sigma = \mathsf{Eval}(\mathsf{PK}, f', \boldsymbol{\sigma})$.

Security. We state the security theorems of our proposed scheme, including semantic security and unforgeability. The proofs of the security theorems are given in the full version of this paper.

Theorem 1. *If the DLN assumption holds in* $\mathbb{G}$, *then the proposed HEA scheme is semantically secure.*

Theorem 2. *If the q-SDH assumption holds in* $\mathbb{G}$, *the BB signature scheme is strongly unforgeable against a weak chosen message attack and the hash function H is collision-resistant, then the proposed HEA scheme is unforgeable.*

5   Verifiable Homomorphic Encryption

Informally, a verifiable homomorphic encryption (VHE) is a symmetric-key homomorphic encryption which enables *verifiable* computation on outsourced encrypted data. In a VHE scheme, a user with secret key SK can encrypt messages $m_1, \ldots, m_k$ to obtain k independent ciphertexts $c_1, \ldots, c_k$. Given ciphertexts $c_1, \ldots, c_k$ and an admissible function f, anyone can compute a ciphertext c on the value $f(m_1, \ldots, m_k)$. The user can then decrypt ciphertext c to obtain message m with secret key SK, and check whether $m = f(m_1, \ldots, m_k)$.

We also use the syntax of *labeled data and programs* for specifying which data is being encrypted and which data a program $\mathcal{P}$ should be evaluated on. Formally, a VHE scheme consists of the following four algorithms:

$\mathsf{Setup}(1^\lambda)$ takes as input a security parameter λ. It outputs the public parameters PP and a secret key SK. The public parameters PP defines a message space $\mathcal{M}$ and a set $\mathcal{F}$ of "admissible" functions $f : \mathcal{M}^k \to \mathcal{M}$.

$\mathsf{Enc}(\mathsf{SK}, \tau, m)$ takes as input a secret key SK, a label $\tau \in \{0, 1\}^*$ and a message $m \in \mathcal{M}$. It outputs a ciphertext c.

$\mathsf{Dec}(\mathsf{SK}, \mathcal{P}, c)$ takes as input a secret key SK, a labeled program $\mathcal{P}$ and a ciphertext c. It outputs a message $m \in \mathcal{M}$ or an error symbol $\perp$.

$\mathsf{Eval}(\mathsf{PP}, f, \boldsymbol{c})$ takes as input the public parameters PP, a function $f \in \mathcal{F}$ and a vector of ciphertexts $\boldsymbol{c} = (c_1, \ldots, c_k)$. It outputs a new ciphertext c.

For correctness, we require that for each $(\mathsf{PP}, \mathsf{SK})$ output by $\mathsf{Setup}(1^\lambda)$, the following properties hold:

1. For all labels $\tau \in \{0, 1\}^*$ and all $m \in \mathcal{M}$, if $c \leftarrow \mathsf{Enc}(\mathsf{SK}, \tau, m)$ then $\mathsf{Dec}(\mathsf{SK}, \mathcal{I}_\tau, c) = m$.
2. Given an admissible function $g : \mathcal{M}^k \leftarrow \mathcal{M}$ and any set of message/program/ciphertext triples $\{(m_i, \mathcal{P}_i, c_i)\}_{i=1}^{k}$ such that $\mathsf{Dec}(\mathsf{SK}, \mathcal{P}_i, c_i) = m_i$, if $\mathcal{P} = g(\mathcal{P}_1, \ldots, \mathcal{P}_k)$ and $c = \mathsf{Eval}(\mathsf{PP}, g, (c_1, \ldots, c_k))$, then $\mathsf{Dec}(\mathsf{SK}, \mathcal{P}, c) = g(m_1, \ldots, m_k)$.

The above requirements capture the basic correctness of decrypting over freshly encrypted data, as well as the composability of decrypting over the outputs of prior computations. If the set of admissible functions $\mathcal{F}$ of a VHE scheme consists of *linear* functions (resp. *any* functions) from $\mathcal{M}^k$ to $\mathcal{M}$, then we say that the VHE scheme is a *linearly* (resp. *fully*) VHE scheme.

The security requirements of VHE, including *semantic security* and *verifiability*. Informally, *semantic security* requires that a ciphertext c of a message m with label τ should not leak any information about m. Let c_i be a ciphertext on a message m_i with label τ_i for $i = 1, \ldots, k$. *Verifiability* requires that given $(c_1, \ldots, c_k)$, it should be impossible to output a ciphertext c and an admissible function f such that $m' \leftarrow \mathsf{Dec}(\mathsf{SK}, \mathcal{P} = (f, \tau_1, \ldots, \tau_k), c)$ and $m' \neq \{\bot, f(m_1, \ldots, m_k)\}$. The formal definitions of the security requirements of VHE are given in the full version of this paper.

5.1 Generic Construction of VHE from HE and HEA

Given a homomorphic encryption scheme $\mathsf{HE} = (\mathsf{HE.Setup}, \mathsf{HE.Enc}, \mathsf{HE.Dec}, \mathsf{HE.Eval})$ and a homomorphic encrypted authenticator scheme $\mathsf{HEA} = (\mathsf{HEA.Setup}, \mathsf{HEA.Auth}, \mathsf{HEA.Ver}, \mathsf{HEA.Eval})$, we define the 4-tuple algorithms of a VHE scheme $(\mathsf{Setup}, \mathsf{Enc}, \mathsf{Dec}, \mathsf{Eval})$ as follows. (Notice that, both public-key homomorphic encryption and secret-key homomorphic encryption can be used in the following generic construction, although the description uses a public-key homomorphic encryption scheme.)

$\mathsf{Setup}(1^\lambda)$ Given a security parameter λ, the setup algorithm performs $(\mathsf{PK}^{\mathsf{HE}}, \mathsf{SK}^{\mathsf{HE}}) \leftarrow \mathsf{HE.Setup}(1^\lambda)$, $(\mathsf{PK}^{\mathsf{HEA}}, \mathsf{SK}^{\mathsf{HEA}}) \leftarrow \mathsf{HEA.Setup}(1^\lambda)$. Then, it sets the public parameters $\mathsf{PP} = (\mathsf{PK}^{\mathsf{HE}}, \mathsf{PK}^{\mathsf{HEA}})$ and the secret key $\mathsf{SK} = (\mathsf{SK}^{\mathsf{HE}}, \mathsf{SK}^{\mathsf{HEA}})$. We assume that $\mathsf{PK}^{\mathsf{HE}}$ and $\mathsf{PK}^{\mathsf{HEA}}$ are defined over the same message space $\mathcal{M}$ and the same set of admissible functions $\mathcal{F}$.

$\mathsf{Enc}(\mathsf{SK}, \tau, m)$ Given the secret key, a label $\tau \in \{0, 1\}^*$ and a message $m \in \mathcal{M}$, it runs $c^{\mathsf{HE}} \leftarrow \mathsf{HE.Enc}(\mathsf{PK}^{\mathsf{HE}}, m)$, $\sigma^{\mathsf{HEA}} \leftarrow \mathsf{HEA.Auth}(\mathsf{SK}^{\mathsf{HEA}}, \tau, m)$. Then, it outputs the ciphertext $c = (c^{\mathsf{HE}}, \sigma^{\mathsf{HEA}})$.

$\mathsf{Dec}(\mathsf{SK}, \mathcal{P}, c)$ Given the secret key, a labeled program $\mathcal{P}$ and a ciphertext $c = (c^{\mathsf{HE}}, \sigma^{\mathsf{HEA}})$, it runs $m \leftarrow \mathsf{HE.Dec}(\mathsf{SK}^{\mathsf{HE}}, c^{\mathsf{HE}})$. Then, it checks whether $\mathsf{HEA.Ver}(\mathsf{SK}^{\mathsf{HEA}}, m, \mathcal{P}, \sigma^{\mathsf{HEA}}) = 1$. If so, it outputs the message m; otherwise, it outputs $\bot$.

$\mathsf{Eval}(\mathsf{PP}, f, \boldsymbol{c})$ With the public parameters $\mathsf{PP} = (\mathsf{PK}^{\mathsf{HE}}, \mathsf{PK}^{\mathsf{HEA}})$, a function $f \in \mathcal{F}$ and a vector of ciphertexts $\boldsymbol{c} = (c_1, \ldots, c_k)$ where $c_i = (c_i^{\mathsf{HE}}, \sigma_i^{\mathsf{HEA}})$ for $i = 1, \ldots, k$, it runs $c^{\mathsf{HE}} \leftarrow \mathsf{HE.Eval}(\mathsf{PK}^{\mathsf{HE}}, f, \boldsymbol{c}^{\mathsf{HE}})$, $\sigma^{\mathsf{HEA}} \leftarrow \mathsf{HEA.Eval}(\mathsf{PK}^{\mathsf{HEA}}, f, \boldsymbol{\sigma}^{\mathsf{HEA}})$, where $\boldsymbol{c}^{\mathsf{HE}} = (c_1^{\mathsf{HE}}, \ldots, c_k^{\mathsf{HE}})$ and $\boldsymbol{\sigma}^{\mathsf{HEA}} = (\sigma_1^{\mathsf{HEA}}, \ldots, \sigma_k^{\mathsf{HEA}})$. Then, it outputs a ciphertext $c = (c^{\mathsf{HE}}, c^{\mathsf{HEA}})$.

Obviously, the above scheme satisfies the correctness of VHE if the underlying homomorphic encryption scheme and homomorphic encrypted authenticator scheme are correct. Now, we state the security theorems of our proposed VHE scheme.

Theorem 3. *If the homomorphic encryption scheme HE and homomorphic encrypted authenticator scheme HEA are semantically secure, then the proposed VHE scheme is semantically secure.*

Proof. Let $c = (c^{\text{HE}}, \sigma^{\text{HEA}})$ be a ciphertext of message m. Since the underlying homomorphic encryption scheme and homomorphic encrypted authenticator are semantically secure, c^{HE} and σ^{HEA} do not leak any information about m. Thus, the proposed VHE scheme is also semantically secure.

Theorem 4. *If the homomorphic encrypted authenticator scheme HEA is (resp. weakly) unforgeable, then the proposed VHE scheme is (resp. weakly) verifiable.*

Proof. Suppose there exists an adversary $\mathcal{A}$ that breaks the verifiability of the proposed VHE scheme. We can build an algorithm $\mathcal{B}$ that breaks the unforgeability of the underlying homomorphic encrypted authenticator scheme as follows.

Let $\mathcal{C}$ be the challenger corresponding to $\mathcal{B}$ in the unforgeability game of the underlying HEA scheme. $\mathcal{B}$ is given the public key PK^{HEA} of the underlying HEA scheme and runs $\mathcal{A}$ executing the following steps.

Setup. $\mathcal{B}$ first runs $(\text{PK}^{\text{HE}}, \text{SK}^{\text{HE}}) \leftarrow \text{HE.Setup}(1^\lambda)$. Then, it sends the public parameters $\text{PP} = (\text{PK}^{\text{HE}}, \text{PK}^{\text{HEA}})$ to adversary $\mathcal{A}$.

Queries. Since $\mathcal{B}$ knows the secret key SK^{HE}, with the help of the authentication and verification oracles of HEA provided by $\mathcal{C}$, it can answer $\mathcal{A}$'s ciphertext and verification queries.

Output. Finally, $\mathcal{A}$ outputs a labeled program $\mathcal{P}^*$ and a ciphertext $c^* = (c^{*\text{HE}}, \sigma^{*\text{HEA}})$. $\mathcal{B}$ runs $m^* \leftarrow \text{HE.Dec}(\text{SK}^{\text{HE}}, c^{*\text{HE}})$ and outputs $(m^*, \mathcal{P}^*, \sigma^{*\text{HEA}})$.

Obviously, if $\mathcal{A}$ breaks the verifiability of the proposed VHE scheme with non-negligible advantage, $\mathcal{B}$ will win the unforgeable game of the underlying HEA scheme with non-negligible advantage. This completes the proof of Theorem 4.

Instantiating the above generic construction with existing fully homomorphic encryption (resp. linearly homomorphic encryption) and our proposed fully HEA with weak unforgeability (resp. linearly HEA with unforgeability), it is straightforward to derive a fully VHE with weak verifiability (reps. linearly VHE with verifiability); we omit the details of the constructions here in order to keep the paper compact.

6   Conclusion

In this paper, we study verifiable homomorphic encryption (VHE) which enables verifiable computation on outsourced encrypted data. In order to construct VHE schemes, we introduce a new cryptographic primitive called homomorphic encrypted authenticator (HEA), and show that a VHE scheme can be built upon a homomorphic encryption scheme and a HEA scheme. We observe that the fully homomorphic MAC scheme, proposed by Gennaro and Wichs [13] recently, is a fully HEA scheme in a weaker security model. Then, we present a linearly HEA scheme which is proven secure in a full security model. Instantiating the generic construction of VHE, we can derive a fully VHE scheme which is secure in a weaker security model, and a linearly VHE scheme which is secure in a full security model. An open research problem is to find fully VHE constructions which is secure in a full security model, i.e., it allows *any* verifiable computation over outsourced encrypted data and tolerates *any* number of malicious verification queries.

Acknowledgement. We are grateful to the anonymous reviewers for their helpful comments. The work of Junzuo Lai was supported by the National Natural Science Foundation of China (Nos. 61300226, 61272534), the Research Fund for the Doctoral Program of Higher Education of China (No. 20134401120017), the Guangdong Provincial Natural Science Foundation (No. S2013040014826), and the Fundamental Research Funds for the Central Universities. The work of Jian Weng was supported by the National Science Foundation of China (Nos. 61272413, 61133014), the Fok Ying Tung Education Foundation (No. 131066), the Program for New Century Excellent Talents in University (No. NCET-12-0680), the Research Fund for the Doctoral Program of Higher Education of China (No. 20134401110011), and the Foundation for Distinguished Young Talents in Higher Education of Guangdong (No. 2012LYM 0027).

References

1. Gentry, C.: Fully homomorphic encryption using ideal lattices. In: STOC, pp. 169–178 (2009)
2. Boneh, D., Freeman, D.M., Katz, J., Waters, B.: Signing a linear subspace: Signature schemes for network coding. In: Jarecki, S., Tsudik, G. (eds.) PKC 2009. LNCS, vol. 5443, pp. 68–87. Springer, Heidelberg (2009)
3. Gennaro, R., Katz, J., Krawczyk, H., Rabin, T.: Secure network coding over the integers. In: Nguyen, P.Q., Pointcheval, D. (eds.) PKC 2010. LNCS, vol. 6056, pp. 142–160. Springer, Heidelberg (2010)
4. Boneh, D., Freeman, D.M.: Linearly homomorphic signatures over binary fields and new tools for lattice-based signatures. In: Catalano, D., Fazio, N., Gennaro, R., Nicolosi, A. (eds.) PKC 2011. LNCS, vol. 6571, pp. 1–16. Springer, Heidelberg (2011)
5. Attrapadung, N., Libert, B.: Homomorphic network coding signatures in the standard model. In: Catalano, D., Fazio, N., Gennaro, R., Nicolosi, A. (eds.) PKC 2011. LNCS, vol. 6571, pp. 17–34. Springer, Heidelberg (2011)
6. Catalano, D., Fiore, D., Warinschi, B.: Adaptive pseudo-free groups and applications. In: Paterson, K.G. (ed.) EUROCRYPT 2011. LNCS, vol. 6632, pp. 207–223. Springer, Heidelberg (2011)
7. Catalano, D., Fiore, D., Warinschi, B.: Efficient network coding signatures in the standard model. In: Fischlin, M., Buchmann, J., Manulis, M. (eds.) PKC 2012. LNCS, vol. 7293, pp. 680–696. Springer, Heidelberg (2012)
8. Freeman, D.M.: Improved security for linearly homomorphic signatures: A generic framework. In: Fischlin, M., Buchmann, J., Manulis, M. (eds.) PKC 2012. LNCS, vol. 7293, pp. 697–714. Springer, Heidelberg (2012)

9. Boneh, D., Freeman, D.M.: Homomorphic signatures for polynomial functions. In: Paterson, K.G. (ed.) EUROCRYPT 2011. LNCS, vol. 6632, pp. 149–168. Springer, Heidelberg (2011)

10. Ahn, J.H., Boneh, D., Camenisch, J., Hohenberger, S., Shelat, A., Waters, B.: Computing on authenticated data. In: Cramer, R. (ed.) TCC 2012. LNCS, vol. 7194, pp. 1–20. Springer, Heidelberg (2012)

11. Attrapadung, N., Libert, B., Peters, T.: Computing on authenticated data: New privacy definitions and constructions. In: Wang, X., Sako, K. (eds.) ASIACRYPT 2012. LNCS, vol. 7658, pp. 367–385. Springer, Heidelberg (2012)

12. Attrapadung, N., Libert, B., Peters, T.: Efficient completely context-hiding quotable and linearly homomorphic signatures. In: Kurosawa, K., Hanaoka, G. (eds.) PKC 2013. LNCS, vol. 7778, pp. 386–404. Springer, Heidelberg (2013)

13. Gennaro, R., Wichs, D.: Fully homomorphic message authenticators. In: Sako, K., Sarkar, P. (eds.) ASIACRYPT 2013, Part II. LNCS, vol. 8270, pp. 301–320. Springer, Heidelberg (2013)

14. Catalano, D., Fiore, D.: Practical homomorphic MACs for arithmetic circuits. In: Johansson, T., Nguyen, P.Q. (eds.) EUROCRYPT 2013. LNCS, vol. 7881, pp. 336–352. Springer, Heidelberg (2013)

15. Backes, M., Fiore, D., Reischuk, R.M.: Verifiable delegation of computation on outsourced data. In: ACM Conference on Computer and Communications Security, pp. 863–874 (2013)

16. Bitansky, N., Canetti, R., Chiesa, A., Tromer, E.: From extractable collision resistance to succinct non-interactive arguments of knowledge, and back again. In: ITCS, pp. 326–349 (2012)

17. Gennaro, R., Gentry, C., Parno, B.: Non-interactive verifiable computing: Outsourcing computation to untrusted workers. In: Rabin, T. (ed.) CRYPTO 2010. LNCS, vol. 6223, pp. 465–482. Springer, Heidelberg (2010)

18. Chung, K.-M., Kalai, Y., Vadhan, S.: Improved delegation of computation using fully homomorphic encryption. In: Rabin, T. (ed.) CRYPTO 2010. LNCS, vol. 6223, pp. 483–501. Springer, Heidelberg (2010)

19. Barbosa, M., Farshim, P.: Delegatable homomorphic encryption with applications to secure outsourcing of computation. In: Dunkelman, O. (ed.) CT-RSA 2012. LNCS, vol. 7178, pp. 296–312. Springer, Heidelberg (2012)

20. Parno, B., Raykova, M., Vaikuntanathan, V.: How to delegate and verify in public: Verifiable computation from attribute-based encryption. In: Cramer, R. (ed.) TCC 2012. LNCS, vol. 7194, pp. 422–439. Springer, Heidelberg (2012)

21. Goldwasser, S., Kalai, Y.T., Popa, R.A., Vaikuntanathan, V., Zeldovich, N.: Succinct functional encryption and applications: Reusable garbled circuits and beyond. IACR Cryptology ePrint Archive 2012, 733 (2012)

22. Gennaro, R., Pastro, V.: Verifiable computation over encrypted data in the presence of verification queries. Cryptology ePrint Archive, Report 2014/202 (2014), http://eprint.iacr.org/

23. Benabbas, S., Gennaro, R., Vahlis, Y.: Verifiable delegation of computation over large datasets. In: Rogaway, P. (ed.) CRYPTO 2011. LNCS, vol. 6841, pp. 111–131. Springer, Heidelberg (2011)

24. Fiore, D., Gennaro, R.: Publicly verifiable delegation of large polynomials and matrix computations, with applications. In: ACM Conference on Computer and Communications Security, pp. 501–512 (2012)

25. Catalano, D., Fiore, D., Gennaro, R., Vamvourellis, K.: Algebraic (trapdoor) one way functions and their applications. IACR Cryptology ePrint Archive 2012, 434 (2012)

26. Papamanthou, C., Shi, E., Tamassia, R.: Signatures of correct computation. In: Sahai, A. (ed.) TCC 2013. LNCS, vol. 7785, pp. 222–242. Springer, Heidelberg (2013)

27. Papamanthou, C., Tamassia, R., Triandopoulos, N.: Optimal verification of operations on dynamic sets. In: Rogaway, P. (ed.) CRYPTO 2011. LNCS, vol. 6841, pp. 91–110. Springer, Heidelberg (2011)

28. Rivest, R.L., Adleman, L., Dertouzos, M.L.: On data banks and privacy homomorphisms. Foundations of Secure Computation 32(4), 169–178 (1978)

29. Stehlé, D., Steinfeld, R.: Faster fully homomorphic encryption. In: Abe, M. (ed.) ASIACRYPT 2010. LNCS, vol. 6477, pp. 377–394. Springer, Heidelberg (2010)

30. Smart, N.P., Vercauteren, F.: Fully homomorphic encryption with relatively small key and ciphertext sizes. In: Nguyen, P.Q., Pointcheval, D. (eds.) PKC 2010. LNCS, vol. 6056, pp. 420–443. Springer, Heidelberg (2010)

31. Gentry, C., Halevi, S., Smart, N.P.: Fully homomorphic encryption with polylog overhead. In: Pointcheval, D., Johansson, T. (eds.) EUROCRYPT 2012. LNCS, vol. 7237, pp. 465–482. Springer, Heidelberg (2012)

32. Gentry, C., Halevi, S., Smart, N.P.: Better bootstrapping in fully homomorphic encryption. In: Fischlin, M., Buchmann, J., Manulis, M. (eds.) PKC 2012. LNCS, vol. 7293, pp. 1–16. Springer, Heidelberg (2012)

33. Brakerski, Z., Gentry, C., Halevi, S.: Packed ciphertexts in LWE-based homomorphic encryption. In: Kurosawa, K., Hanaoka, G. (eds.) PKC 2013. LNCS, vol. 7778, pp. 1–13. Springer, Heidelberg (2013)

34. Cheon, J.H., Coron, J.-S., Kim, J., Lee, M.S., Lepoint, T., Tibouchi, M., Yun, A.: Batch fully homomorphic encryption over the integers. In: Johansson, T., Nguyen, P.Q. (eds.) EUROCRYPT 2013. LNCS, vol. 7881, pp. 315–335. Springer, Heidelberg (2013)

35. Gentry, C., Sahai, A., Waters, B.: Homomorphic encryption from learning with errors: Conceptually-simpler, asymptotically-faster, attribute-based. In: Canetti, R., Garay, J.A. (eds.) CRYPTO 2013, Part I. LNCS, vol. 8042, pp. 75–92. Springer, Heidelberg (2013)

36. van Dijk, M., Gentry, C., Halevi, S., Vaikuntanathan, V.: Fully homomorphic encryption over the integers. In: Gilbert, H. (ed.) EUROCRYPT 2010. LNCS, vol. 6110, pp. 24–43. Springer, Heidelberg (2010)

37. Brakerski, Z., Vaikuntanathan, V.: Efficient fully homomorphic encryption from (standard) lwe. In: FOCS, pp. 97–106 (2011)

38. Brakerski, Z., Vaikuntanathan, V.: Fully homomorphic encryption from ring-LWE and security for key dependent messages. In: Rogaway, P. (ed.) CRYPTO 2011. LNCS, vol. 6841, pp. 505–524. Springer, Heidelberg (2011)

39. Brakerski, Z., Gentry, C., Vaikuntanathan, V.: (leveled) fully homomorphic encryption without bootstrapping. In: ITCS, pp. 309–325 (2012)

40. Johnson, R., Molnar, D., Song, D., Wagner, D.: Homomorphic signature schemes. In: Preneel, B. (ed.) CT-RSA 2002. LNCS, vol. 2271, pp. 244–262. Springer, Heidelberg (2002)

41. Ahlswede, R., Cai, N., Li, S.Y.R., Yeung, R.W.: Network information flow. IEEE Transactions on Information Theory 46(4), 1204–1216 (2000)

42. Li, S.Y.R., Yeung, R.W., Cai, N.: Linear network coding. IEEE Transactions on Information Theory 49(2), 371–381 (2003)

43. Ateniese, G., Burns, R.C., Curtmola, R., Herring, J., Kissner, L., Peterson, Z.N.J., Song, D.X.: Provable data possession at untrusted stores. In: ACM Conference on Computer and Communications Security, pp. 598–609 (2007)

44. Juels, A., Kaliski Jr., B.S.: Pors: proofs of retrievability for large files. In: ACM Conference on Computer and Communications Security, pp. 584–597 (2007)
45. Shacham, H., Waters, B.: Compact proofs of retrievability. In: Pieprzyk, J. (ed.) ASIACRYPT 2008. LNCS, vol. 5350, pp. 90–107. Springer, Heidelberg (2008)
46. Groth, J.: Simulation-sound NIZK proofs for a practical language and constant size group signatures. In: Lai, X., Chen, K. (eds.) ASIACRYPT 2006. LNCS, vol. 4284, pp. 444–459. Springer, Heidelberg (2006)
47. Abe, M., Fuchsbauer, G., Groth, J., Haralambiev, K., Ohkubo, M.: Structure-preserving signatures and commitments to group elements. In: Rabin, T. (ed.) CRYPTO 2010. LNCS, vol. 6223, pp. 209–236. Springer, Heidelberg (2010)
48. Libert, B., Peters, T., Joye, M., Yung, M.: Linearly homomorphic structure-preserving signatures and their applications. In: Canetti, R., Garay, J.A. (eds.) CRYPTO 2013, Part II. LNCS, vol. 8043, pp. 289–307. Springer, Heidelberg (2013)
49. Catalano, D., Marcedone, A., Puglisi, O.: Linearly homomorphic structure preserving signatures: New methodologies and applications. IACR Cryptology ePrint Archive 2013, 801 (2013)
50. Joo, C., Yun, A.: Homomorphic authenticated encryption secure against chosen-ciphertext attack. IACR Cryptology ePrint Archive 2013, 726 (2013)
51. Boneh, D., Boyen, X., Shacham, H.: Short group signatures. In: Franklin, M. (ed.) CRYPTO 2004. LNCS, vol. 3152, pp. 41–55. Springer, Heidelberg (2004)
52. Boneh, D., Boyen, X.: Short signatures without random oracles and the sdh assumption in bilinear groups. J. Cryptology 21(2), 149–177 (2008)

Verifiable Computation with Reduced Informational Costs and Computational Costs

Gang Xu, George T. Amariucai, and Yong Guan

Iowa State University, Ames, Iowa, USA
{gxu,gamari,guan}@iastate.edu

Abstract. Outsourcing computation is a fundamental principle of the new cloud computing paradigm. Among its various aspects, the correctness of the computation result remains paramount. This motivates the birth of verifiable computation, which aims at efficiently checking the result for general-purpose computation. The common goal of recently sprouted verifiable computation protocols is to reduce the costs associated with verification at both prover and verifier. Unfortunately, the high computation and communication costs of verification still keep general verifiable computation away from practicality. Besides the computational costs, we observe that another type of verification cost has been generally ignored until now –the informational costs, namely, the information required for the verification. In particular, in the context of the third-party verification, this cost implies the information leakage of sensitive information regarding the computational task and its results. In this paper, we introduce the new verifiable-computation protocol RIVER, which reduces the computational costs of the verifier and of the prover, comparing to the most recent alternative protocols, and (for the first time in the context of verifiable computation) addresses and decreases informational costs.

Keywords: verifiable computing, QAPs, PCPs, clouds, informational costs, privacy.

1 Introduction

In the era of cloud computing, outsourcing computation becomes a new trend. Instead of purchasing, maintaining, and updating expensive computing assets for local computation, users can outsource computation and other IT services from relatively weaker devices to a professional service provider (like the Cloud). But while enjoying the appealing benefits of outsourcing computation – such as reduced financial, personnel and computational burdens – a critical security issue arises: Cloud servers may be error-prone or otherwise not trustworthy. This motivates a great body of research on verifiable computation. Many works focus on specific computational tasks, exploiting their special structure to provide efficient verification [1] [2] [3] [4] [5] [6] [7] [8] [9] [10] [11] [12]. However, when it comes to verifying the results of general computation, most efforts seem to be

M. Kutyłowski and J. Vaidya (Eds.): ESORICS 2014, Part I, LNCS 8712, pp. 292–309, 2014.

concentrated around classic proof systems in theoretical computer science. In this framework, the server plays the role of a *prover*, trying to convince the client, who plays the role of a *verifier*, that the result returned from the server is correct. The verification procedure usually consists of the verifier issuing randomly-chosen queries, and the prover providing answers.

Interactive proof (IP) systems [13] have recently been introduced to the context of delegation of computation [14] [15] [16]. They are efficient in terms of asymptotic complexity. As a new encoding scheme for arithmetic circuits, Quadratic Arithmetic Programs (QAPs, [17]) have shown great potential for the design of verifiable computation protocols [17] [18]. The third notable direction in verifiable computation is based on probabilistically checkable proof (PCP) systems [19] [20]. *Argument systems* [21], one variant of the PCP model, seem to be appropriate for practical verifiable computation. Argument systems hold a more practical assumption that, in addition to the verifier being polynomial-time probabilistic, the prover is also computationally bounded. Combining PCP with a homomorphic cryptographic machinery, recent works on argument systems, such as IKO [22], Pepper [23], Ginger [24], XAG [25], and Zaatar [26], have brought PCP-based approaches closer to practicality – they sharply reduced the number of queries, and the overhead required to prevent the falsification of the proof string.

1.1 Motivation

The state-of-the-art Zaatar [26] showed the connection between Linear PCP and QAP. However, unlike other QAP-based designs [17] [18], Zaatar relies only on standard cryptographic assumptions. It applies QAP into the framework of PCP and generates a novel verifiable computation scheme. Moreover, as an appealing verifiable computation scheme, Zaatar makes the prover more efficient than any other PCP-based designs. However, Zaatar does not bring major improvements to the verifier's computational cost. As in the recent PCP-based works [22] [27] [23] [24], once the prover has committed to the proof, the most computationally-intensive part for the verifier in Zaatar is the generation of queries. The high costs of the verifier are hence lowered by reusing some of the queries for multiple instances of the *same* problem – or *batching*. For computational tasks that can tolerate large batch sizes, the costs of verification in Zaatar can be driven down by amortizing. However, for tasks that require low investment on the verification and tolerate only small batch sizes, a new, more efficient protocol is needed.

Besides the computation and communication costs that have been concerned in existing research of verifiable computation, another type of verification cost has been generally ignored until now. We call this the *informational cost* – the cost associated with information required for verification on both sides. The verifier's information required for verification usually consists of verification keys and the full knowledge of the computation task. The prover's informational costs usually consists of the proof vector.

The informational cost generally has a strong impact on the adoption of the verification algorithms. On one hand, the size of the required information directly influences the memory cost for verification, and the speed of verification. For the memory cost, verifiers in existing research keep the required information in a large memory and frequently access it. For the speed, the length of the proof vector determines the cost of generating, and responding to, the queries while verifying. On the other hand, the informational cost implies the privacy/confidentiality issues. One obvious risk is that, storing this information itself introduces potential leakage of sensitive information about the computational task and its results. A more serious risk occurs in the context of the third party verification. (For example, disputes between the server and the client can be solved by an arbitrator who plays the role of the third-party verifier. Similar verifications may be required by government agencies, nonprofit organizations, and consumer organization, for the purpose of quality evaluation, project management, etc.) In such scenarios, information cost implies the computation task and its results being delivered to the third party. However, once delivered, the information is out of the control of the client and the client can never call them back. This security issue, in turn, may limit the outsourcing of verification [25].

As far as informational costs are concerned, all recent PCP-based works [22] [27] [23] [24], [26] require the verifier to have full knowledge of the computation circuit while performing the verification.

1.2   Our Contributions

In this paper, we introduce **RIVER**, a **R**educed-**i**nvestment **ver**ified computation protocol, whose improvement further enhances the practicality of argument systems in verifiable computation. Our contributions are summarized as follows:

- RIVER reduces the verifier's workload that needs to be amortized. Namely, the number of batched instances of the protocol, required for amortization, will largely decrease. Instead of batching over instances of the same circuit as in existing works, RIVER makes more parts of costs amortized over instances of *all different circuits of the same size*. We model the costs and compare the costs using a typical computation such as matrix multiplication, showing that RIVER is 28% better than state-of-the-art Zaatar at the verifier side.
- As a side effect, RIVER reduces the prover's non-amortized cost. As in the typical computation of matrix multiplication, RIVER achieves 55% better than Zaatar at the prover's non-amortized cost. Although RIVER introduces amortized cost to the prover side, this cost can be amortized over instances of *all different circuits of the same size*.
- RIVER reduces the informational cost of the verifier, by removing the requirement that the verifier has to access the circuit description during query generating. Thus, a third-party verifier can help generating the queries without knowing the computation task details.
- RIVER adopts one of our theoretical findings. We show that under certain assumptions, the Single-Commit-Multi-Decommit protocol provides the inherent linearity tests. Thus, a modified Single-Commit-Multi-Decommit protocol will make the linearity tests obsolete and reduce verification costs.

2   System Model

In the context of cloud computing, we propose a computation architecture involving two parties: the client $\mathcal{V}$, who is computationally weak, has computation tasks to be delegated to the cloud; the cloud server $\mathcal{P}$, who is computationally powerful, provides computing services to the client. The computation tasks are formalized into the *arithmetic circuit* – i.e., the computation task is performed over an arithmetic circuit. This is pretty natural, since arithmetic circuits can be easily mapped to real-world computation tasks[1]. Let Ψ be a $|\Psi|$-gate arithmetic circuit. The client $\mathcal{V}$ is providing the prover $\mathcal{P}$ with Ψ and input $X \in \mathbb{F}^n$, and expects $\mathcal{P}$ to return the correct output $Y \in \mathbb{F}^{n'}$. Then $\mathcal{P}$ tries to convince $\mathcal{V}$ that Y is correct. $\mathcal{P}$ will hold a proof Z, which is a *correct assignment* Z –the concatenation of the input X, output Y with all the intermediate results W inside the circuit, $(Z = X||Y||W)$ and has length $|Z| = m$, where W is the intermediate result vector $W \in \mathbb{F}^{m-n-n'}$ of the circuit Ψ.

3   Preliminaries

3.1   PCP and Commitments

Now we briefly review the line of verifiable computation based on argument systems. To make argument systems efficient, current implementations rely on *probabilistically checkable proofs* (PCPs). However, PCP algorithms assume that the proof is computed by the prover, and fixed before the interaction with the verifier begins. The same assumption cannot be made in the context of argument systems. To bridge the gap between arguments and PCPs, an additional protocol is required, in which the prover commits to the proof before starting the PCP protocol with the verifier. Consequently, an argument is generally formed by joining together two protocols: a *PCP* and a *commitment protocol*.

To avoid the need for convoluted short PCP proofs, as well as the uncertain security of practical hashing primitives, [22] takes a new approach to argument systems: maintain a large (exponential-size) proof, and base the commitment on (computationally) provably-secure encryption primitives – public-key primitives.

The protocols of [22] are restricted to linear PCPs ([28], Section 6). It is shown how SAT problems, formulated in the context of a boolean circuit, can be readily addressed by a simple linear PCP [22]. To form the argument system, [22] complemented the linear PCP with the notion of *commitment with linear decommitment*, which is instantiated with a simple public-key-based protocol. Once the proof is committed, $\mathcal{V}$ will check the proof in the linear PCP fashion.

In Ishai et al.'s original commitment design [22], one query is accompanied by an auxiliary query which is associated to a commitment. This requires many commitments, therefore increases the overhead. As in [22], where the PCP proof is represented by the vector d, the prover $\mathcal{P}$ commits to a certain proof, in a

---

[1] Existing compilers can turn high-level programs into arithmetic circuits [24], [26], [18]. For simplicity, we omit these techniques.

Table 1. The Single-Commit-Multi-Decommit Design [24]

$\mathcal{P}$'s Input: a vector $z \in \mathbb{F}^n$, a linear function $\pi : \mathbb{F}^{n^2+n} \mapsto \mathbb{F}$
where $\pi(\cdot) = \langle Z \| z \otimes z, \cdot \rangle$, n is the length of a correct assignment z.

$\mathcal{V}$'s Input: arity n, security parameter k of the encryption.

Commitment

Step 1: $\mathcal{V}$ generates the key pair: $(pk, sk) \leftarrow Gen(1^k)$.
$\mathcal{V}$ randomly generates a vector: $r = (r_1, r_2, \cdots, r_{n^2+n}) \in_R \mathbb{F}^{n^2+n}$.
$r_i \in \mathbb{F}, i = 1, 2, \cdots, n^2 + n$. $\mathcal{V}$ encrypts each entry of the vector r.
He sends $\mathtt{Enc}(pk, r_1), \cdots, \mathtt{Enc}(pk, r_{n^2+n})$ to $\mathcal{P}$.
Step 2: Using the homomorphism, $\mathcal{P}$ gets: $e = \mathtt{Enc}(pk, \langle r, z \rangle)$ $\mathcal{P}$ sends e to $\mathcal{V}$.
Step 3: $\mathcal{V}$ decrypts e. He gets $s = \langle r, z \rangle = Dec(sk, e)$.

Decommitment

Step 1: $\mathcal{V}$ picks μ secrets $\alpha_1, \cdots, \alpha_\mu \in \mathbb{F}$
$\mathcal{V}$ queries $\mathcal{P}$ with $q_1, \cdots, q_\mu$ and $t = r + \alpha_1 q_1 + \cdots + \alpha_\mu q_\mu$.
Step 2: $\mathcal{P}$ returns $(a_1, \cdots, a_\mu, b)$ where $a_i = \pi(q_i)$ for $i = 1, \cdots, \mu$ and $b = \pi(t)$
Step 3: $\mathcal{V}$ checks whether $b = s + \alpha_1 a_1 + \cdots \alpha_\mu a_\mu$ holds.
If so, $\mathcal{V}$ outputs $a_1, \cdots, a_\mu$. Otherwise, he rejects and output $\perp$.

---

manner that assures the verifier $\mathcal{V}$ that the proof he later queries is the original proof, and not some adaptively-modified false proof. Several recent works build upon the ideas developed in [22]. Of these, [23] introduces several contributions, including a *single-commit-multi-decommit* protocol. In [23], one auxiliary query is made, which is a random linear combination of all the PCP queries and the secret information that is associated to the commitment. In this design, one decommitment could guarantee many PCP queries are bound to the committed function. This sharply reduced the computational cost of generating the commitment information (although remaining cost is still very high.). The Single-Commit-Multi-Decommit design is demonstrated in Table 1. For more details regarding Table 1, refer to [22] and [23].

3.2 Quadratic Programs and Zaatar

Recently Gennaro, Gentry, Parno and Raykova introduced a new characterization of the NP complexity class – the *Quadratic Span Programs (QSPs)* (and *Quadratic Arithmetic Programs (QAPs)*) [17] [18]. They showed that NP can be defined as the set of languages with proofs that can be efficiently verified by QSPs (or QAPs). Similar to PCPs – another characterization of NP, which has already been widely used to obtain verifiable computation schemes – QSPs/QAPs are considered to be well-suited for verifiable computation and zero-knowledge schemes. One limitation of QSPs is that they inherently compute boolean circuits. But since arithmetic circuits are more natural and efficient in real-world computation tasks, we focus on QAPs, the counterpart of QSPs dealing with arithmetic circuit evaluation.

Definition 1 (Quadratic Arithmetic Programs)([17]) *A QAP Q over field $\mathbb{F}$ contains three sets of $m + 1$ polynomials: $\{A_i(t)\}$, $\{B_i(t)\}$, $\{C_i(t)\}$, for $i \in$*

$\{0, 1, \cdots, m\}$, and a target polynomial $D(t)$. For function $\Psi : \mathbb{F}^n \mapsto \mathbb{F}^{n'}$, we say Q computes Ψ if the following holds: $(z_1, z_2, \cdots, z_{n+n'}) \in \mathbb{F}^{n+n'}$ is a valid assignment of Ψ's inputs and outputs, if and only if there exist coefficients $z_{n+n'+1}, \cdots, z_m$ such that $D(t)$ divides $P(t)$, where $P(t) = \left(\sum_{i=1}^{m} z_i \cdot A_i(t) + A_0(t) \right) \cdot$ $\left(\sum_{i=1}^{m} z_i \cdot B_i(t) + B_0(t) \right) - \left(\sum_{i=1}^{m} z_i \cdot C_i(t) + C_0(t) \right)$. In other words, there exists a polynomial $H(t)$ such that $D(t) \cdot H(t) = P(t)$.

Given an arithmetic circuit, its QAP can be constructed by polynomial inter-polation. Consider the set of circuit wires corresponding to the input and output of the circuit, and the outputs of all multiplication gates. Each one of these wires is assigned three interpolation polynomials in Lagrange form, encoding whether the wire is a left input, right input, or output of each multiplication gate. The resulting set of polynomials is a complete description of the original circuit.

The very recent work of [26] observes that QAPs can also be viewed as linear PCPs. By re-designing the PCP query generation and replacing the quadratic consistency checks and circuit correctness checks with the divisibility check of a QAP, they successfully fit QAPs into the framework of Ginger [24]. The result is the novel protocol *Zaatar*, which significantly reduces the prover's workload. The key observation of Zaatar is that the evaluation of the polynomial $P(t)$ in (1) at the point $t = \tau$ can be simply written as:

$$P(\tau) = (\langle Z, q \rangle + A_0(\tau)) \cdot (\langle Z, q' \rangle + B_0(\tau)) - (\langle Z, q'' \rangle + C_0(\tau)), \qquad (1)$$

where $Z = (z_1, \cdots, z_m)$, $q = (A_1(\tau), \cdots, A_m(\tau))$, $q' = (B_1(\tau), \cdots, B_m(\tau))$, $q'' = (C_1(\tau), C_2(\tau), \cdots, C_m(\tau))$. Thus, $P(\tau)$ can be evaluated through three standard PCP queries to the oracle $\pi_Z(\cdot) = \langle Z, \cdot \rangle$. If we represent the polynomi-als $H(t)$ explicitly: $H(t) = h_{|C_Z|} t^{|C_Z|} + \cdots + h_1 t + h_0$ (where C_Z is the set of con-straints in Zaatar), similar observations on $H(\tau)$ can be made: $H(\tau) = \langle K_H, q_H \rangle$, where $K_H = (h_0, h_1, \cdots, h_{|C_Z|})$ and $q_H = (1, \tau, \tau^2, \cdots, \tau^{|C_Z|})$. Thus, $H(\tau)$ can also be evaluated through one PCP query to the oracle $\pi_H(\cdot) = \langle K_H, \cdot \rangle$.

If Z consists of the input X with width $|X| = n$, output Y with width $|Y| = n'$ and intermediate results W with width $|W| = m - (n + n')$, then to guarantee that Y is the correct output when the input is X, the verifier needs to compute a part of $\langle Z, q \rangle$, and also a part of $\langle Z, q' \rangle$ and $\langle Z, q'' \rangle$, by himself. Consequently, $\mathcal{V}$ only queries the linear function oracle $\pi_W(\cdot) = \langle W, \cdot \rangle$, instead of $\pi_Z(\cdot)$.

4   A Technique: A Commitment Providing Inherent Linearity Tests

In the line of linear-PCP fashion verifiable computation designs, once the prover is committed to a proof, the verifier has to perform laborious linearity tests to ensure the proof is linear. In fact, the number of queries required to perform linearity tests dominate the number of overall queries of the protocol. Thus, the cost caused by linearity test is still one of the bottlenecks of current protocols.

Up to now, in the context of Single-Commit-Multi-Decommit protocol (refer to Section 3), whether the linearity tests are necessary was still an open question. In this section, we propose our theoretical result, showing that under an assumption, the Single-Commit-Multi-Decommit protocol will provides inherent linearity tests. Thus, if linear PCP is combined with this commitment protocol, the linearity tests are obsolete. We will adopt the following theoretical results in our protocol design and thus achieve cost savings.

Theorem 1. *The Single-Commit-Multi-Decommit protocol ensures that, if the secret commit information is generated by the prover using an affine function (analytically defined), (or equivalent to the cases that is generated by the verifier himself), for all query tuples, unless the sender (or prover) replies to all queries with the same linear function and he knows the analytic description of this linear function, the prover will not pass the decommitment test except with probability $\frac{1}{|\mathbb{F}|} + \epsilon_S$, where the probability is over the randomness of the prover and the verifier in the decommitment phase.*

Proof. Let $\pi()$ denote the proof in the PCP sense. The prover knows that, when the verifier generates the commitment information $\pi(r)$, he uses the linear function $\mathbf{F}_1(\cdot)$, such that $\pi(r) = \mathbf{F}_1(r)$. We claim that in this scenario, the prover has to answer all queries with the same linear function $\mathbf{F}_1$ – otherwise the probability that the prover passes the decommitment test is less than $\frac{1}{|\mathbb{F}|} + \epsilon_S$.

To prove this, we assume that there exists a PPT prover $\mathcal{P}^*$, and queries $q_1, q_2, \cdots, q_\mu$, such that once committed, with these queries, the probability that $\mathcal{P}^*$ answers the μ queries with a function $f(\cdot)$ – such that there exists at least one index k for which $f(q_k) \neq \mathbf{F}_1(q_k)$ – and passes the decommitment test, is more than $\frac{1}{|\mathbb{F}|} + \epsilon_S$, where the probability is over the randomness of the prover and the verifier in the decommitment phase.

We can now modify $\mathcal{P}^*$ and make it into an algorithm $\mathcal{P}^\dagger$ which can solve the problem stated in Lemma 1 with probability more than $\frac{1}{|\mathbb{F}|} + \epsilon_S$:

1. $\mathcal{P}^\dagger$ has inputs: $\mathbf{Enc(r)}, r + \alpha q_k, q_k$
2. $\mathcal{P}^\dagger$ uses $\mathbf{Enc(r)}$ as inputs and runs $\mathcal{P}^*$'s commitment phase.
3. $\mathcal{P}^*$ outputs with $\mathbf{Enc(F}_1(r))$ which $\mathcal{P}^\dagger$ will neglect.
4. $\mathcal{P}^\dagger$ uses the set of queries $\{q_1, \ldots, q_\mu\}$. He produces a set of coefficients $\{\alpha_1, \cdots, \alpha_{k-1}, \alpha_{k+1}, \cdots, \alpha_{\mu-1}, \alpha_\mu\}$, and runs $\mathcal{P}^*$'s decommitment phase with following: $\{q_1, q_2, \ldots, q_{\mu-1}, q_\mu, (r + \alpha q_k) + \sum_{i=1}^{k-1} \alpha_i q_i + \sum_{i=k+1}^{\mu} \alpha_i q_i\}$..
5. $\mathcal{P}^*$ outputs $\{f(q_1), \ldots, f(q_\mu), \mathbf{F}_1(r) + \alpha f(q_k) + \sum_{i=1}^{k-1} \alpha_i f(q_i) + \sum_{i=k+1}^{\mu} \alpha_i f(q_i)\}$. This will pass the decommitment test with probability more than $\frac{1}{|\mathbb{F}|} + \epsilon_S$.
6. Having access to $\{\alpha_1, \cdots, \alpha_{k-1}, \alpha_{k+1}, \cdots, \alpha_{\mu-1}, \alpha_\mu\}$, and $f(q_1), \ldots, f(q_\mu)$, $\mathcal{P}^\dagger$ can now obtain an equation of the form $\mathbf{F}_1(r) + \alpha f(q_k) = b$ (where $b \in \mathbb{F}$ is easily calculated).

Recall that $\mathcal{P}^\dagger$ has knowledge of $r + \alpha q_k$, which yields a group of n linearly-independent linear equations in the form of $r + \alpha q_k = a$. Given that $\mathbf{F}_1(q_k) \neq$

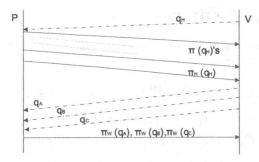

Fig. 1. PCP querying

$f(q_k)$, the equation $\mathbf{F}_1(r) + \alpha f(q_k) = b$ is linearly independent of the former n equations $r + \alpha q_k = a$. Thus, $\mathcal{A}$ can solve for α from these $n+1$ linearly independent equations. This will contradict Lemma 1:

Lemma 1. *(from [22]) For any probabilistic polynomial time algorithm $\mathcal{A}$, any $q \in \mathbb{F}^n$, and any uniformly-randomly picked $r \in \mathbb{F}^n$ we have $Pr[\mathcal{A}(\mathtt{Enc}(\mathbf{r}), r + \alpha q, q) = \alpha] \leq \frac{1}{|\mathbb{F}|} + \epsilon_S$, where ϵ_S is from the semantic security.*

5 A Reduced-Investment Verifiable Computation Protocol: RIVER

In this section, we introduce RIVER(*reduced-investment verifiable computation protocol*), an improvement of Zaatar [26], aimed at reducing the amortized cost of the verifier – or equivalently, the number of instances required before amortization can be considered complete. We accomplishes this by deferring some of the verifier's amortizable computation to the prover. In doing so, two other benefits are achieved as side effects. First, the overall cost for the verifier is decreased when compared to Zaatar (and implicitly also to Ginger). This is despite deferring some of the amortized computation to the prover (the deferred part is almost negligible when compared to the construction of the proof). Second, RIVER enables the verifier to generate queries independently – that is, the query generating stage does not require full knowledge of the circuit. We detail RIVER as follows.

5.1 PCP Querying

Our main observation is that the PCP query generation in Zaatar is somewhat redundant. RIVER removes the redundancy by employing three rounds of PCP querying and one round of decision making. The logical procedure is demonstrated in Figure 1.

5.2 PCP Querying of RIVER

Let $l = |C_R|$. We represent the QAP polynomials $A_i(t)$, $B_i(t)$, $C_i(t)$, with $i = 0, 1, \cdots, m$ explicitly as:

$$A_i(t) = a_l^{(i)} t^l + a_{l-1}^{(i)} t^{l-1} + \cdots + a_1^{(i)} t + a_0^{(i)} \qquad (2)$$

$$B_i(t) = b_l^{(i)} t^l + b_{l-1}^{(i)} t^{l-1} + \cdots + b_1^{(i)} t + b_0^{(i)} \qquad (3)$$

$$C_i(t) = c_l^{(i)} t^l + c_{l-1}^{(i)} t^{l-1} + \cdots + c_1^{(i)} t + c_0^{(i)} \qquad (4)$$

Evaluation of any one of these polynomials at the point $t = \tau$ can be expressed as a linear function: $A_i(\tau) = \pi_A^{(i)}(q_H) = \langle K_A^{(i)}, q_H \rangle$, $B_i(\tau) = \pi_B^{(i)}(q_H) = \langle K_B^{(i)}, q_H \rangle$, $C_i(\tau) = \pi_C^{(i)}(q_H) = \langle K_C^{(i)}, q_H \rangle$, where $q_H = (1, \tau, \tau^2, \cdots, \tau^l)$ and

$$K_A^{(i)} = (a_l^{(i)}, a_{l-1}^{(i)}, \cdots, a_1^{(i)}, a_0^{(i)}) \qquad (5)$$

$$K_B^{(i)} = (b_l^{(i)}, b_{l-1}^{(i)}, \cdots, b_1^{(i)}, b_0^{(i)}) \qquad (6)$$

$$K_C^{(i)} = (c_l^{(i)}, c_{l-1}^{(i)}, \cdots, c_1^{(i)}, c_0^{(i)}). \qquad (7)$$

We can simply express the PCP queries of Zaatar as

$$q_A = (\pi_A^m(q_H), \pi_A^{m-1}(q_H), \ldots, \pi_A^{n+n'+1}(q_H)) \qquad (8)$$

$$q_B = (\pi_B^m(q_H), \pi_B^{m-1}(q_H), \ldots, \pi_B^{n+n'+1}(q_H)) \qquad (9)$$

$$q_C = (\pi_C^m(q_H), \pi_C^{m-1}(q_H), \ldots, \pi_C^{n+n'+1}(q_H)). \qquad (10)$$

In RIVER, the verifier constructs q_A, q_B, q_C by querying linear functions π_A^i, π_B^i, π_C^i ($i = 0, \cdots, m$) by a single query q_H.

Similarly, we can express $H(t)$ and $D(t)$ as:

$$H(t) = h_l t^l + h_{l-1} t^{l-1} + \cdots + h_1 t + h_0 \qquad (11)$$

$$D(t) = d_l t^l + d_{l-1} t^{l-1} + \cdots + d_1 t + d_0, \qquad (12)$$

and define: $\pi_H(\cdot) = \langle K_H, \cdot \rangle$, where $K_H = (h_0, h_1, \cdots, h_l)$, and $\pi_D(\cdot) = \langle K_D, \cdot \rangle$, where $K_D = (d_0, d_1, \cdots, d_l)$. Zaatar points out that the evaluation of $H(\tau)$ can be viewed as querying an oracle $\pi_H(\cdot)$ with q_H. Here, we argue that the same holds for the evaluation of $D(\tau)$ – querying the oracle $\pi_D(\cdot)$ with q_H. The idea is detailed in Table 2. Note that by comparison, Zaatar requires the queries q_A, q_B, q_C, along with $D(\tau)$ to be entirely computed by $\mathcal{V}$. It should be mentioned that computing these queries by querying another set of proofs requires additional commitments and testing. However, the procedure can be simplified by removing all linearity tests for these $3m+4 = 3(m+1)+1$ proofs. The reason this works is that, according to Theorem 1, our decommitment already provides an inherent linearity test. In the second round of our design, $\mathcal{V}$ issues queries q_H as in Table 3. In the third round, $\mathcal{V}$ issues queries q_A, q_B, q_C, q_D as in Table 4. After $\mathcal{V}$ collects all responses, he makes the decision as in Table 5.

Table 2. The First Round of Our QAP-based Linear PCP

For every π in the set of $\pi_A^{(i)}$, $\pi_B^{(i)}$, $\pi_C^{(i)}$, $(i = 0, 1, \cdots m)$ π_D, perform the following:

- Divisibility queries generation. $\mathcal{V}$ randomly selects $\tau \in_R \mathbb{F}$. $\mathcal{V}$ takes $q_H \leftarrow (1, \tau, \tau^2, \cdots, \tau^l)$.
- Querying. $\mathcal{V}$ sends out q_H and gets back $\pi(q_H)$.

If all these proofs pass all linearity tests, $\mathcal{V}$ will have: $\pi_D(q_H)$ and

- $\pi_A^{(m)}(q_H), \pi_A^{(m-1)}(q_H), \cdots, \pi_A^{(0)}(q_H),$
- $\pi_B^{(m)}(q_H), \pi_B^{(m-1)}(q_H), \cdots, \pi_B^{(0)}(q_H),$
- $\pi_C^{(m)}(q_H), \pi_C^{(m-1)}(q_H), \cdots, \pi_C^{(0)}(q_H),$

Table 3. The Second Round of Our QAP-based Linear PCP

$\mathcal{V}$ queries π_H.

- Linearity queries generation. $\mathcal{V}$ selects $q_2, q_3 \in_R \mathbb{F}^l$. Take $q_4 \leftarrow q_3 + q_2$. Perform ρ_{lin} iterations in total.
- QAP queries generation. $\mathcal{V}$ takes $q_H \leftarrow (1, \tau, \tau^2, \cdots, \tau^l)$ and $q_1 \leftarrow (q_H + q_2)$.
- Querying π_H. $\mathcal{V}$ sends out $q_1, q_2, \cdots, q_{1+3\rho}$ and gets back $\pi_H(q_1), \pi_H(q_2), \cdots, \pi_H(q_{1+3\rho})$.
- Linearity tests. Check whether following holds: $\pi_H(q_4) = \pi_H(q_3) + \pi_H(q_2)$ and likewise for all other $\rho - 1$ iterations. If not, reject.

At the end of this phase, if π_H passes all linearity tests, $\mathcal{V}$ will have: $\pi_H(q_H)$.

Table 4. The Second Round of Our QAP-based Linear PCP

$\mathcal{V}$ queries π_W. Remember $\pi_W(\cdot) = \langle W, \cdot \rangle$, where $W = (z_m, z_{m-1}, \cdots, z_{N+1})$

- Linearity queries generation. $\mathcal{V}$ select $q_4, q_5 \in_R \mathbb{F}^{m-N}$. Take $q_6 \leftarrow q_4 + q_5$. Perform ρ_{lin} iterations in total.
- QAP queries generation. $\mathcal{V}$ takes:
  - $q_A \leftarrow (\pi_A^{(m)}(q_H), \pi_A^{(m-1)}(q_H), \cdots, \pi_A^{(n+n'+1)}(q_H))$, and $q_1 \leftarrow (q_A + q_4)$.
  - $q_B \leftarrow (\pi_B^{(m)}(q_H), \pi_B^{(m-1)}(q_H), \cdots, \pi_B^{(n+n'+1)}(q_H))$, and $q_2 \leftarrow (q_B + q_4)$.
  - $q_C \leftarrow (\pi_C^{(m)}(q_H), \pi_C^{(m-1)}(q_H), \cdots, \pi_C^{(n+n'+1)}(q_H))$, and $q_3 \leftarrow (q_C + q_4)$.
- Querying π_W. $\mathcal{V}$ sends out $q_1, q_2, \cdots, q_{3+3\rho}$ and gets back $\pi_W(q_1), \pi_W(q_2), \cdots, \pi_W(q_{3+3\rho})$.
- Linearity tests. Check whether following holds: $\pi_W(q_6) = \pi(q_4) + \pi(q_5)$ and likewise for all other $\rho - 1$ iterations. If not, reject. Otherwise, accept and output $\pi_W(q_A) \leftarrow \pi_W(q_1) - \pi_W(q_4)$, $\pi_W(q_B) \leftarrow \pi_W(q_2) - \pi_W(q_4)$, $\pi_W(q_C) \leftarrow \pi_W(q_3) - \pi_W(q_4)$.

Table 5. The Decision Making Stage of Our QAP-based Linear PCP

Decision Making: (Note: $(z_1, z_2, \cdot, z_{n+n'}) = X\|Y.$)

- $\mathcal{V}$ computes:
  - $p_A \leftarrow \sum_{i=1}^{(n+n')} z_i \cdot \pi_A^{(i)}(q_H) + \pi_A^{(0)}(q_H)$
  - $p_B \leftarrow \sum_{i=1}^{(n+n')} z_i \cdot \pi_B^{(i)}(q_H) + \pi_B^{(0)}(q_H)$
  - $p_C \leftarrow \sum_{i=1}^{(n+n')} z_i \cdot \pi_C^{(i)}(q_H) + \pi_C^{(0)}(q_H)$
- Divisibility Test. $\mathcal{V}$ checks whether the following holds: $\pi_D(q_H) \cdot \pi_H(q_H) = (\pi_Z(q_A) + p_A) \cdot (\pi_Z(q_B) + p_B) - (\pi_Z(q_C) + p_C)$.

5.3 Commit, Decommit and Consistency Verification of RIVER

To ensure the security of the protocol, $\mathcal{P}$ commits to all the linear functions mentioned above. Similarly to Zaatar, our design inherits the single-commit-multiple-decommit protocol from Ginger. For π_H and π_W, $\mathcal{V}$ and $\mathcal{P}$ run the IKO-style single-commit-multi-decommit protocol to generate the commitment. This part is omitted for simplicity.

For $\pi_A^{(i)}$, $\pi_B^{(i)}$, $\pi_C^{(i)}$, $(i = 0, 1, \cdots, m)$ and π_D, the case is a bit more complex. We note that in addition to the commitments and decommitments, $\mathcal{V}$ has to also verify the consistency of the polynomials' coefficient vectors corresponding to $\pi_A^{(i)}$, $\pi_B^{(i)}$, $\pi_C^{(i)}$, for $i = 1, \ldots, m$, and π_D. Namely, $\mathcal{V}$ needs to make sure that $\mathcal{P}$ eventually uses $\pi_A^{(i)}$, $\pi_B^{(i)}$, $\pi_C^{(i)}$, for $i = 1, \ldots, m$, and π_D to answer $\mathcal{V}$'s queries.

To accomplish this, we use the technique in Section 4 and come up with the commitment/decommitment protocol as follows: Before sending $\mathcal{P}$ his computation task, $\mathcal{V}$ secretly generates a random number r and computes by himself the values $A_i(r)$, $B_i(r)$, $C_i(r)$ $(i = 0, 1, \cdots m)$ and $D(r)$, each of which represents, respectively, the commitment for $\pi_A^{(i)}()$, $\pi_B^{(i)}()$, $\pi_C^{(i)}()$, for $i = 0, 1, \ldots, m$, and $\pi_D()$. The algorithm to compute these values is demonstrated in Section 6.1. These values are stored for future decommitment. This setup computation is done only once for different values of τ. In comparison with Zaatar, where the setup requires the verifier to evaluate the queries associated with different values of τ, a single r suffices for all τ's in RIVER, since the verifier outsources extra computation to the prover. As in Table 6, our commitment design guarantees the consistency of the polynomials' coefficient vectors with the linear functions to which $\mathcal{P}$ commits.

Theorem 2. *Let π be any of the linear functions $\pi_A^{(i)}$, $\pi_B^{(i)}$, $\pi_C^{(i)}$ and π_D. By performing our protocol, the commitment to π is guaranteed to be bound to a linear function $\tilde{\pi}$, and the probability that $\pi \neq \tilde{\pi}$ is at most $1/|\mathbb{F}|$. The probability is over all the randomness of the prover.*

Proof. Given that our protocol performs the single-commit-multi-decommit protocol when querying π, the response to the query is guaranteed to be bound to a linear function $\tilde{\pi}$. This feature is provided by the underlying single-commit-multi-decommit protocol. If $\pi \neq \tilde{\pi}$ but $\tilde{\pi}$ still passes the decommitment, $\tilde{\pi}(r) = \pi(r)$

Table 6. Decommit Design for $\pi_A^{(i)}$, $\pi_B^{(i)}$, $\pi_C^{(i)}$, $(i = 0, 1, \cdots, m)$ and π_D

$\mathcal{P}$'s Input: linear functions π_D, $\pi_A^{(i)}$, $\pi_B^{(i)}$, $\pi_C^{(i)}$, for $i = 1, \ldots, m$.

$\mathcal{V}$'s Input: $A_i(r)$, $B_i(r)$, $C_i(r)$, $i = 0, \cdots, m$ and $D(r)$, $t = (1, r, r^2, \cdots, r^l)$. $q_1, \cdots, q_\mu$

Commitment

The verifier generates the commitment information as in Section 6.1.

Decommitment

Step 1: $\mathcal{V}$ picks μ secrets $\alpha_1, \cdots, \alpha_\mu \in \mathbb{F}$

$\mathcal{V}$ queries $\mathcal{P}$ with $q_1, \cdots, q_\mu$ and $T = t + \alpha_1 q_1 + \cdots + \alpha_\mu q_\mu$.

Step 2: $\mathcal{P}$ returns $(\pi_A^{(i)}(q_1), \cdots, \pi_A^{(i)}(q_\mu), \pi_A^{(i)}(T))$, $(\pi_B^{(i)}(q_1), \cdots, \pi_B^{(i)}(q_\mu), \pi_B^{(i)}(T))$, $(\pi_C^{(i)}(q_1), \cdots, \pi_C^{(i)}(q_\mu), \pi_C^{(i)}(T))$, where $i = 0, \cdots, m$ and $(\pi_D(q_1), \cdots, \pi_D(q_\mu), \pi_D(T))$.

Step 3: $\mathcal{V}$ checks whether $\pi_A^{(i)}(T) = A_i(r) + \sum_{j=1}^{\mu} \alpha_j \pi_A^{(i)}(q_j)$ and whether $\pi_B^{(i)}(T) = B_i(r) + \sum_{j=1}^{\mu} \alpha_j \pi_B^{(i)}(q_j)$ and whether $\pi_C^{(i)}(T) = C_i(r) + \sum_{j=1}^{\mu} \alpha_j \pi_C^{(i)}(q_j)$, $i = 0, \cdots, m$ and $\pi_D(T) = D(r) + \sum_{j=1}^{\mu} \alpha_j \pi_D(q_j)$ hold.

If so, $\mathcal{V}$ accepts. Otherwise, he rejects and output $\perp$.

---

must hold. For all possible choices of $\tilde{\pi}$, only $1/|\mathbb{F}|$ of them can satisfy this equation. However, r is unknown by the prover. Thus, the probability that a dishonest prover chooses a $\tilde{\pi} \neq \pi$ that passes the decommitment is at most $1/|\mathbb{F}|$.

6 Performance Analysis

For the informational cost, it is straightforward to see that, once committed, all the queries in the verification are not depending on the circuit description. Namely, during the query generating of the verification stage, the verifier does not need to access the circuit information any more. Our design separates the verification workload that involves only non-sensitive information from the verification workload that involves sensitive information (e.g. the circuit information). In the scenarios with a third-party verifier, the verifier can undertake the workload involving only non-sensitive information (e.g. query generating) without knowing the secrecy of the computation task.

In the following, we derive the computational cost of our RIVER design and compare it with previous work. In the process, we show that, similarly to Ginger and Zaatar, our protocol batches many instances for one *same* circuit to reduce the cost per instance. But RIVER can amortize more parts of amortized cost over *all different circuits of the same size*.

6.1 The Verifier

This section performs an analysis of the verifier's cost. A comparison with the verifier's costs in two other the state-of-the-art designs is given in Table 7.

Setup. The cost that RIVER incurs upon the commitment is $(|W_R| + |C_R|) \cdot (e + c)/\beta$. This is because RIVER needs two commitment query constructions.

Table 7. Comparison of Cost for Verifier in Each Instance

	Ginger	Zaatar	RIVER
Setup: Commit	$|W_G| \cdot e/(\beta \cdot \gamma)$	$(|W_Z|+|C_Z|) \cdot e/(\beta \cdot \gamma)$	$(|W_R| + |C_R|) \cdot e/(\beta \cdot \gamma) + (f_{div} + 5f) \cdot |C_R|/(\beta \cdot \gamma)$
Linearity Query Generation	$\rho \cdot \rho_{lin} \cdot 2 \cdot (|C_G|+|C_G|^2) \cdot c/(\beta \cdot \gamma)$	$\rho \cdot \rho_{lin} \cdot 2 \cdot (|W_Z| + |C_Z|) \cdot c/(\beta \cdot \gamma)$	$\rho \cdot \rho_{lin} \cdot 2 \cdot (|W_R| + |C_R|) \cdot c/(\beta \cdot \gamma)$
Other PCP Query Generation	$\rho \cdot (c \cdot |C_G| + f \cdot K)/\beta$	$\rho \cdot [c + (f_{div} + 5f) \cdot |C_Z| + f \cdot K + 3f \cdot K_2]/\beta$	$\rho \cdot |C_R| \cdot f/(\beta \cdot \gamma)$
Decommitment Query Generation	$\rho \cdot L \cdot f/\beta$	$\rho \cdot (\rho_{lin} \cdot 3 \cdot (|W_Z| + |C_Z|) + (3|W_Z| + |C_Z|)) \cdot f/\beta$	$\rho \cdot (\rho_{lin} \cdot 3 \cdot (|W_R| + |C_R|) + (3|W_R| + |C_R|)) \cdot f/\beta$
Decommitment Test	$d + \rho \cdot L \cdot f$	$d + \rho \cdot (\rho_{lin} \cdot 6 + 4) \cdot f$	$2d + \rho \cdot (\rho_{lin} \cdot 6 + 4) \cdot f + \rho \cdot (3m+4) \cdot f/\beta$
Decision Making	$\rho \cdot (|X| + |Y|) \cdot f$	$\rho \cdot (3|X| + 3|Y|) \cdot f$	$\rho \cdot (2|X| + |Y|) \cdot f$
Total non-amortized cost	$d + \rho \cdot (L + |X| + |Y|) \cdot f$	$2d + \rho \cdot f \cdot (3|X| + 3|Y| + \rho_{lin} \cdot 6 + 4)$	$2d + \rho \cdot f \cdot (2|X| + |Y| + \rho_{lin} \cdot 6 + 4)$
Total amortized cost	$|W_G| \cdot e/(\beta \cdot \gamma) + \rho \cdot \rho_{lin} \cdot 2 \cdot (|C_G| + |C_G|^2) \cdot c/(\beta \cdot \gamma) + \rho \cdot c \cdot |C_G|/\beta + \rho \cdot (L + K) \cdot f/\beta$	$(|W_Z| + |C_Z|) \cdot e/(\beta \cdot \gamma) + \rho \cdot \rho_{lin} \cdot 2 \cdot (|W_Z| + |C_Z|) \cdot c/(\beta \cdot \gamma) + \rho \cdot [c + (f_{div}) \cdot |C_Z|]/\beta + (\rho_{lin} \cdot 3 \cdot (|W_Z| + |C_Z|) + (3|W_Z| + 6|C_Z| + K + 3K_2)) \cdot \rho \cdot f/\beta$	$(|W_R| + |C_R|) \cdot e/(\beta \cdot \gamma) + \rho \cdot \rho_{lin} \cdot 2 \cdot (|W_R| + |C_R|) \cdot c/(\beta \cdot \gamma) + (\rho_{lin} \cdot 3 \cdot (|W_R| + |C_R|) + (3|W_R| + |C_R|) + 3m + 4) \cdot \rho \cdot f/\beta + ((f_{div} + 5f) \cdot |C_R| + \rho \cdot |C_R| \cdot f)/(\beta \cdot \gamma)$

C_G: set of constraints in Ginger

C_Z: set of constraints in Zaatar

C_R: set of constraints in our design

$|X|$: number of input

g: cost of addition over $\mathbb{F}$

β: number of batching

ρ: number of iteration of verification for one instance

f_{div}: cost of division over $\mathbb{F}$

c: cost of pseudorandomly generating an element in $\mathbb{F}$

d: cost of decryption over $\mathbb{F}$

K: number of additive terms in the constraints of Ginger

$|W_G|$: number of variables in the constraints (excluding inputs and outputs) in Ginger

$|W_Z|$: number of variables in the constraints (excluding inputs and outputs) in Zaatar

$|W_R|$: number of variables in the constraints (excluding inputs and outputs) in our design

$|Y|$: number of output

L: number of PCP queries in Ginger

γ: number of circuits of the same size.

ρ_{lin}: number of iterations of linearity tests in one iteration of verification.

f: cost of multiplication over $\mathbb{F}$

e: cost of encryption over $\mathbb{F}$

K_2: number of distinct additive degree-2 terms in the constraints of Ginger

One is for π_H, and incurs a cost of $|C_R| \cdot (e + c)/\beta$, while the other is for π_W, and incurs a cost of $|W_R| \cdot (e + c)/\beta$. This total cost is the same as that of Zaatar.

It is apparent that RIVER introduces additional workload to the setup stage. $\mathcal{V}$ has to evaluate $A_i(r)$, $B_i(r)$, $C_i(r)$ and $D(r)$. However, we have discovered that a large part of the computation cost is independent of the underlying circuits.

Rather, the computation only depends on the size of the circuit. This implies that this part of the computation can be amortized over many different circuits, which only share the same size, rather than over many different instances of the same circuit. To see this, first notice that the target polynomial $D(t) = \prod_{k=1}^{|C_R|}(t - \sigma_k)$ does not depend on the circuit details, but rather $D(t)$ is determined by the circuit size. Hence, we can compute $D(r)$ once for all circuits of the same size, where r is the secret as in Section 5. If given in the form of generalized Newton's interpolation formula ([29], 4.6.4), $D(r)$ can be evaluated in time $|C_R| \cdot f$. Second, we express $A_i(t)$, $B_i(t)$, $C_i(t)$ in the form of Lagrange Polynomial interpolation: $A_i(t) = \sum_{j=1}^{|C_R|} a_{ij} \cdot l_j(t)$, $B_i(t) = \sum_{j=1}^{|C_R|} b_{ij} \cdot l_j(t)$, $C_i(t) = \sum_{j=1}^{|C_R|} c_{ij} \cdot l_j(t)$, where $l_j(t) = \prod_{1 \leq k \leq |C_R|, k \neq j} \frac{(t-\sigma_k)}{(\sigma_j - \sigma_k)}$ are Lagrange basis polynomials. We can represent these Lagrange basis polynomials as follows: $l_j(t) = \frac{D(t)}{(t-\sigma_j) \cdot \frac{1}{v_j}}$, where $v_j = 1/\prod_{0 \leq k \leq |C|, k \neq j}(\sigma_j - \sigma_k)$. If we choose these σ_k ($k = 1, \cdots, |C_R|$) to follow an arithmetic progression [26], $l_j(r)$ ($j = 1, \cdots, |C_R|$) can be evaluated in total time of $(f_{div} + 4f)|C_R|$. (Computing $1/v_{j+1}$ from $1/v_j$ requires only two operations and computing $1/v_0$ uses $|C_R|$ multiplication. Recall that $D(r)$ is computed already. Finally, to get each $l_j(r)$, a multiplication and one division are needed.) Given that both the evaluation of $D(r)$ and $l_j(r)$ are independent of the underlying circuit, we can amortize the cost of the evaluation into all circuits of the same size.

The remaining work is to evaluate $A_i(r)$, $B_i(r)$, $C_i(r)$ from the Lagrange polynomials $l_j(r)$ ($j = 1, \cdots, |C_R|$). But this is reduced to merely several additions of $l_j(r)$ polynomials – note that the coefficients a_{ij}, b_{ij}, c_{ij} are all either 0 or 1. The number of wires in the circuit that can contribute to the multiplication gates is at most $2|C_R|$. The total number of additions to evaluate $A_i(r)$ and $B_i(r)$ is at most the number of wires in the circuit that can contribute to the multiplication gates. Then, the total number of additions to evaluate $A_i(r)$ and $B_i(r)$ is at most $2|C_R|$. The total number of additions to evaluate $C_i(r)$ is $(|W_R| + |Y|)$, since it takes $(|W_R| + |C_R|) \cdot (e + c)$ to generate the commitment queries (where, the whole cost of setup is at most $(|W_R|+|C_R|) \cdot (e+c)/\beta + (f_{div}+5f) \cdot |C_R|/\beta + (2|C_R|+|W_R|+|Y|) \cdot g/\beta)$, where g is the cost of addition over a finite field. Since g is small, we omit addition cost in the tables of cost, as Zaatar [26] does.

Compared to Zaatar, RIVER introduces an extra cost of $(f_{div}+5f) \cdot |C_R|/\beta + (2|C_R|+|W_R|+|Y|) \cdot g/\beta$ to the total cost of setup. However, notice that this part of the computation can be amortized over many different circuits, which only share the same size, rather than over many different instances of the same circuit. Thus, RIVER actually introduces a negligible cost in the setup phase.

Linearity Query Generation. The cost of generating the linearity queries for π_H is $\rho \cdot \rho_{lin} \cdot 2 \cdot |C_R| \cdot c/(\beta \cdot \gamma)$. Another group of linearity queries are for the proof π_W. The cost of generating these linearity queries is $\rho \cdot \rho_{lin} \cdot 2 \cdot |W_R| \cdot c/(\beta \cdot \gamma)$. Thus, the total cost of generating linearity queries amounts to $\rho \cdot \rho_{lin} \cdot 2 \cdot (|C_R| + |W_R|) \cdot c/(\beta \cdot \gamma)$.

Divisibility Query Generation, Decommitment Query Generation and Decommitment Test. These are straight-forward, we omit these for simplicity.

Non-amortized Costs. From the construction above, we draw the following observations:

- For $i = 1, \cdots, n$, we have $C_i(t) = 0$ for any $t \in \mathbb{F}$, since the inputs of the circuit cannot be outputs of multiplication gates.
- For $i = n+1, \cdots, n+n'$, we have $A_i(t) = 0$ for any $t \in \mathbb{F}$, since the outputs of the circuit Ψ' cannot be inputs to multiplication gates.
- For $i = n+1, \cdots, n+n'$, we have $B_i(t) = 0$ for any $t \in \mathbb{F}$, since the outputs of the circuit Ψ' cannot be inputs to multiplication gates.

Thus, the verifier's cost in the decision making stage (computing p_A, p_B, p_C) is merely $\rho \cdot (2|X| + |Y|) \cdot f$.

Comparison with Zaatar. We list the amortized and non-amortized cost of both RIVER and Zaatar in Table 7. At this time, it is useful to take $W_R = W_Z$ and $C_R = C_Z$.

We can see that, both the amortized and non-amortized cost of RIVER are less than Zaatar. For the amortized part, which is known as the *investment*, even for cases when $\beta = 1$ and $\gamma = 1$, the cost of RIVER is less than Zaatar. (To have a clear picture, we look at a real example: computing xA where the input x is a $1 \times M$ vector and A is a fixed $M \times M$ matrix. This is widely used in all kinds of scientific computing such as communications, signal processing, and control systems, and is a basic operation of many computations. We use previously published models ([26]) and instantiate the costs as in Table 7. From the instance, for $M > 5000$, We see the amortized cost in RIVER is at least 28% less than that in Zaatar. For $M < 5000$, the improvement is even greater.) Since the same part of the amortized cost in RIVER and Zaatar is dominated by linearity test queries, if we apply the query compressing technique in Ginger ([30]), RIVER will have a more significant improvement compared to Zaatar.

6.2   The Prover

The method to construct the proof vector is the same as that in Zaatar. The cost is $T + 3f \cdot |C_R| \cdot log^2 |C_R|$. We omit the details here. The remaining cost is from the fact that the prover needs to compute the coefficients of $A_i(t)$, $B_i(t)$, and $C_i(t)$, $(i = 0, 1, \cdots, m)$. However, this could be amortized. First, remember that each of $A_i(t)$, $B_i(t)$ and $C_i(t)$, $(i = 0, 1, \cdots, m)$ are sums of several Lagrange basis polynomials. The cost to get the coefficients of the Lagrange basis polynomials is independent of the underlying circuit and can be amortized into all circuits of the same size and is negligible. Second, similarly to Section 5.2, the number of additions of Lagrange basis polynomials is at most $2|\Psi| + |Y|$. Each Lagrange basis polynomials has degree at most $|C_R|$. Thus, for each instance, the cost of computing the coefficients is at most $(2|\Psi| + |Y|) \cdot |C_R| \cdot g/\beta$, where g is the cost of addition over the field $\mathbb{F}$. As in Zaatar [26], we omit the addition cost.

When the prover issues the PCP responses, he needs to respond to not only queries for π_W and π_H, but also queries for $\pi_A^{(i)}$, $\pi_B^{(i)}$, $\pi_C^{(i)}$, ($i = 0, 1, \cdots, m$) and π_D. The cost for the former is $(h + 1) \cdot (|W_R| + |C_R|) \cdot f + \rho \cdot (3|W_R| + |C_R|) \cdot f + \rho_{lin} \cdot 3 \cdot (|W_R| + |C_R|) \cdot \rho \cdot f$. Given that the length of the latter is $|C_R|$ and these responses do not depend on underlying circuit or the proof vector π_W, the cost to compute the responses for the latter can be amortized into all instances of the same circuit size. This cost is $[h + \rho \cdot (3m + 4) \cdot f] \cdot |C_R|/(\beta \cdot \gamma)$.

The comparison in terms of the prover's cost is in Table 8. We also use the computation example in Section 6.1 to demonstrate the improvement. For any $M > 100$, RIVER's non-amortized cost of the prover is at least 55% better than that of Zaatar. We demonstrate the results using $M = 10000$. Although RIVER introduces amortized cost, this cost becomes negligible since it can be amortized into all instances of the same circuit size.

Table 8. Comparison of Cost for Prover in Each Instance

	Ginger	Zaatar	RIVER
Construct proof	$T + f \cdot |W_G|^2$	$T + 3f \cdot |C_Z| \cdot log^2|C_Z|$	$T + 3f \cdot |C_R| \cdot log^2|C_R|$
	$32s + 3.2 \times 10^9 s$	$32s + 3.2 \times 10^4 s$	$32s + 3.2 \times 10^4 s$
Issue PCP responses	$(h+(\rho \cdot L+1) \cdot f) \cdot (|C_G| + |C_G|^2)$	$(h + (\rho \cdot L' + 1) \cdot f) \cdot (|C_Z| + |W_Z|)$	$(h+1) \cdot (|W_R| + |C_R|) \cdot f + \rho \cdot (3|W_R| + |C_R|) \cdot f + \rho_{lin} \cdot 3 \cdot (|W_R| + |C_R|) \cdot \rho \cdot f + [h + \rho \cdot (3m + 4) \cdot f] \cdot |C_R|/(\beta \cdot \gamma)$
	$2.9 \times 10^{12} s$	$9.0 \times 10^4 s$	$4.0 \times 10^4 s + \frac{7.7 \times 10^{10}}{(\beta \cdot \gamma)} s$

T: cost of computing the task h: cost of ciphertext add plus multiply
$L = 3\rho_{lin} + 2$: number of (high order) PCP queries in Ginger
$L' = 6\rho_{lin} + 4$: number of PCP queries in Zaatar

7   Conclusions

The state-of-the-art designs such as Pepper/Ginger/Zaatar combine a commitment protocol to a linear PCP, achieving breakthroughs in verifiable computation. However, the high computation, communication and storage costs still keep general verifiable computation away from practicality. In this paper, we presented a new verifiable-computation protocol called RIVER. We show that RIVER reduces the amortized computational costs of the verifier and the non-amortized cost of the prover. Namely, the number of batched instances of the protocol, required for amortization, will largely decrease. RIVER introduces only a negligible increase in the prover's costs. However, this increased cost can be amortized over instances of different circuits of the same size. Thus, this part can be done only once, but used for all possible verifications.

In addition, for the first time in the context of verifiable computation, we address the problem of reducing the informational costs. RIVER removes the requirement that the verifier has to access the circuit description during query generating. Furthermore, this feature of RIVER can be viewed as a first step towards applying QAP-based arguments to the secure outsourcing of verification introduced in [25].

References

1. Benabbas, S., Gennaro, R., Vahlis, Y.: Verifiable delegation of computation over large datasets. In: Rogaway, P. (ed.) CRYPTO 2011. LNCS, vol. 6841, pp. 111–131. Springer, Heidelberg (2011)
2. Boneh, D., Freeman, D.M.: Homomorphic signatures for polynomial functions. In: Paterson, K.G. (ed.) EUROCRYPT 2011. LNCS, vol. 6632, pp. 149–168. Springer, Heidelberg (2011)
3. Ergun, F., Kumar, S.R.: Approximate checking of polynomials and functional equations. In: Proceedings of the 37th Annual Symposium on Foundations of Computer Science, pp. 592–607. IEEE Computer Society, Washington, DC (1996)
4. Golle, P., Mironov, I.: Uncheatable distributed computations. In: Naccache, D. (ed.) CT-RSA 2001. LNCS, vol. 2020, pp. 425–440. Springer, Heidelberg (2001)
5. Karame, G.O., Strasser, M., Čapkun, S.: Secure remote execution of sequential computations. In: Qing, S., Mitchell, C.J., Wang, G. (eds.) ICICS 2009. LNCS, vol. 5927, pp. 181–197. Springer, Heidelberg (2009)
6. Sion, R.: Query execution assurance for outsourced databases. In: Proceedings of the 31st International Conference on Very Large Data Bases, VLDB 2005, pp. 601–612. VLDB Endowment (2005)
7. Thompson, B., Haber, S., Horne, W.G., Sander, T., Yao, D.: Privacy-preserving computation and verification of aggregate queries on outsourced databases. In: Goldberg, I., Atallah, M.J. (eds.) PETS 2009. LNCS, vol. 5672, pp. 185–201. Springer, Heidelberg (2009)
8. Wang, C., Ren, K., Wang, J.: Secure and practical outsourcing of linear programming in cloud computing. In: INFOCOM, pp. 820–828. IEEE (2011)
9. Wang, C., Ren, K., Wang, J., Urs, K.M.R.: Harnessing the cloud for securely solving large-scale systems of linear equations. In: Proceedings of the 2011 31st International Conference on Distributed Computing Systems, ICDCS 2011, pp. 549–558. IEEE Computer Society, Washington, DC (2011)
10. Atallah, M.J., Frikken, K.B.: Securely outsourcing linear algebra computations. In: Proceedings of the 5th ACM Symposium on Information, Computer and Communications Security, ASIACCS 2010, pp. 48–59. ACM, New York (2010)
11. Garofalakis, M.: Proof sketches: Verifiable in-network aggregation. In: IEEE Internation Conference on Data Engineering, ICDE (2007)
12. Przydatek, B., Song, D., Perrig, A.: Sia: secure information aggregation in sensor networks. In: Proceedings of the 1st International Conference on Embedded Networked Sensor Systems, SenSys 2003, pp. 255–265. ACM, New York (2003)
13. Goldwasser, S., Micali, S., Rackoff, C.: The knowledge complexity of interactive proof systems. SIAM J. Comput. 18(1), 186–208 (1989)
14. Goldwasser, S., Kalai, Y.T., Rothblum, G.N.: Delegating computation: interactive proofs for muggles. In: Proceedings of the 40th Annual ACM Symposium on Theory of Computing, STOC 2008, pp. 113–122. ACM, New York (2008)
15. Canetti, R., Riva, B., Rothblum, G.N.: Two 1-round protocols for delegation of computation. Cryptology ePrint Archive, Report 2011/518 (2011), http://eprint.iacr.org/

16. Cormode, G., Mitzenmacher, M., Thaler, J.: Practical verified computation with streaming interactive proofs. In: Proceedings of the 3rd Innovations in Theoretical Computer Science Conference, ITCS 2012, pp. 90–112. ACM, New York (2012)

17. Gennaro, R., Gentry, C., Parno, B., Raykova, M.: Quadratic span programs and succinct NIZKs without PCPs. In: Johansson, T., Nguyen, P.Q. (eds.) EURO-CRYPT 2013. LNCS, vol. 7881, pp. 626–645. Springer, Heidelberg (2013)

18. Parno, B., Gentry, C., Howell, J., Raykova, M.: Pinocchio: nearly practical verifiable computation. In: The IEEE Symposium on Security and Privacy, IEEE S&P 2013 (2013)

19. Arora, S., Safra, S.: Probabilistic checking of proofs; a new characterization of np. In: Proceedings of the 33rd Annual Symposium on Foundations of Computer Science, SFCS 1992, pp. 2–13. IEEE Computer Society, Washington, DC (1992)

20. Babai, L., Fortnow, L., Levin, L.A., Szegedy, M.: Checking computations in poly-logarithmic time. In: Proceedings of the Twenty-Third Annual ACM Symposium on Theory of Computing, STOC 1991, pp. 21–32. ACM, New York (1991)

21. Brassard, G., Chaum, D., Crépeau, C.: Minimum disclosure proofs of knowledge. J. Comput. Syst. Sci. 37(2), 156–189 (1988)

22. Ishai, Y., Kushilevitz, E., Ostrovsky, R.: Efficient arguments without short pcps. In: Proceedings of the Twenty-Second Annual IEEE Conference on Computational Complexity, CCC 2007, pp. 278–291. IEEE Computer Society, Washington, DC (2007)

23. Setty, S., McPherson, R., Blumberg, A.J., Walfish, M.: Making argument systems for outsourced computation practical (sometimes). In: NDSS (2012)

24. Setty, S., Vu, V., Panpalia, N., Braun, B., Blumberg, A.J., Walfish, M.: Taking proof-based verified computation a few steps closer to practicality. In: USENIX Security (2012)

25. Xu, G., Amariucai, G., Guan, Y.: Delegation of computation with verification outsourcing: Curious verifiers. In: Proceedings of the ACM Symposium on Principles of Distributed Computing, PODC 2013. ACM (2013)

26. Setty, S., Braun, B., Vu, V., Blumberg, A.J., Parno, B., Walfish, M.: Resolving the conflict between generality and plausibility in verified computation. In: Proceedings of the 8th ACM European Conference on Computer Systems, EuroSys 2013, pp. 71–84. ACM, New York (2013)

27. Setty, S., Blumberg, A.J., Walfish, M.: Toward practical and unconditional verification of remote computations. In: Proceedings of the 13th USENIX Conference on Hot Topics in Operating Systems, HotOS 2013, p. 29. USENIX Association, Berkeley (2011)

28. Arora, S., Lund, C., Motwani, R., Sudan, M., Szegedy, M.: Proof verification and the hardness of approximation problems. J. ACM 45(3), 501–555 (1998)

29. Knuth, D.E.: Seminumerical Algorithms, the art of computer programming, 3rd edn. Addison-Wesley (2007)

30. Setty, S., Vu, V., Panpalia, N., Braun, B., Ali, M., Blumberg, A.J., Walfish, M.: Taking proof-based verified computation a few steps closer to practicality (extended version). Cryptology ePrint Archive, Report 2012/598 (2012), http://eprint.iacr.org/

Detangling Resource Management Functions from the TCB in Privacy-Preserving Virtualization

Min Li[1], Zili Zha[1], Wanyu Zang[1], Meng Yu[1], Peng Liu[2], and Kun Bai[3]

[1] Virginia Commonwealth University
{lim4,zhaz,wzang,myu}@vcu.edu
[2] Pennsylvania State University, University Park
pliu@ist.psu.edu
[3] IBM T.J. Watson Research Center
kunbai@us.ibm.com

Abstract. Recent research has developed virtualization architectures to protect the privacy of guest virtual machines. The key technology is to include an access control matrix in the hypervisor. However, existing approaches have either limited functionalities in the hypervisor or a Trusted Computing Base (TCB) which is too large to secure. In this paper, we propose a new architecture, MyCloud SEP, to separate resource allocation and management from the hypervisor in order to reduce the TCB size while supporting privacy protection. In our design, the hypervisor checks all resource accesses against an access control matrix in the hypervisor. While providing flexibility of plugging-in resource management modules, the size of TCB is significantly reduced compared with commercial hypervisors. Using virtual disk manager as an example, we implement a prototype on x86 architecture. The performance evaluation results also show acceptable overheads.

Keywords: Cloud Computing, Privacy Protection, TCB Minimization, Decomposition, Isolation.

1 Introduction

While more and more companies deploy their service in clouds that provide scalable and effective computing resources, privacy concerns may lead to cloud market loss up to \$35 billion by 2016 [1]. The primary cause of security and privacy concerns is the privilege design in existing cloud platforms. On current cloud platforms, such as Xen [2], KVM [3], and Amazon EC2 [4], the control Virtual Machine (VM) has administrative privileges for resource management. Consequently, both the hypervisor and the control VM are running in the processor's root mode that has the most privileges. Unfortunately, such architecture design gives no chance to the cloud clients to protect their privacy. Furthermore, 1) it enables insider attacks from the cloud administrators; 2) the control domain can evade detection of malicious behaviors; and 3) the Trusted Computing Base (TCB) includes both the control domain and the hypervisor, which is too large to secure.

In order to solve the privacy protection problems, recent research such as Self-Service Cloud (SSC) [5] proposed to divide the privileges of Dom0 (control VM) into

M. Kutyłowski and J. Vaidya (Eds.): ESORICS 2014, Part I, LNCS 8712, pp. 310–325, 2014.

smaller domains including MTSD domains and user domains. The smaller domains are running in the same processor privilege as legacy Dom0. The TCB size of such design is still very large because SSC does not move the third-part drivers and control VM to a non-privileged mode. Our previous work MyCloud [6] achieves a verifiable TCB size with only 6K LOCs by removing the control VM from the processor root mode. We create a user configurable Access Control Matrix (ACM) in the hypervisor to protect the privacy of guest VMs. However, the functionalities of the hypervisor in MyCloud are very limited.

In this paper, we propose an innovative structure, MyCloud SEP (SEP for separation), to solve the separation of functionality and security check. In our design, we put resource allocator and management outside the hypervisor. Security checks are included in the hypervisor. Such design enables the flexibility of resource management. In this paper, we use virtual disk management as an example to explain our technology. The same approach can be applied to other types of resource management in virtualization platforms.

In MyCloud SEP, since the control VM and resource managers are moved to the processor's non-root mode, the new structure reduces the TCB by an order of magnitude (the size is similar to that of MyCloud) compared with commercial hypervisors. Compared with our previous work, the new architecture supports better functionalities without significantly increasing the TCB size. In summary, our new contributions are: 1) To the best of our knowledge, this is the first effort to separate resource allocation from security checks in order to reduce the hypervisor size; 2) The proposed architecture enables privacy protection and full functionality of a hypervisor without significantly increasing the TCB size; and 3) Our performance evaluations show acceptable overheads.

The rest of the paper is organized as follows. Section 2 discusses related work. Section 3 clarifies assumptions and threat model, and describes our proposed architecture. Section 4 describes the detailed implementations. The experimental results are presented in Section 5 . Section 6 discusses how different threats are handled. Finally, Section 7 concludes the paper.

2 Related Work

In traditional cloud platforms, the cloud provider owns full privileges over the VMM and users VMs, providing no way for the cloud users to protect their own privacy. To address the threats from the administrative domain, previous research has been focused on shrinking the TCB either by disaggregation of privileges functionality of the control domain [5,7] or by splitting VMM into smaller components based on nested virtualization[8]. Self-Service Cloud computing (SSC) [5] allows client VMs to execute some management of privileges, which used to be provided in administrative domain. SplitVisor [8] splits VMM into a smaller part as the minimized TCB to enforce isolation and a larger part to provide rich service functionality. Nevertheless, this design is not compatible with current cloud computing schemes because the cloud users are required to upload a specialized guest VMM.

Similar to SplitVisor, some approaches investigate the use of nested virtualization to disaggregate some host VMM components to the guest VMM [9,10,11]. CloudVisor

[9] introduces a small security monitor underneath the VMM to enforce strict isolation among the VMM and the host VMs using nested virtualization. According to our understanding, CloudVisors late launch includes the host operating system of KVM as part of the TCB, though it is not explicitly stated. Hence, the TCB is still too large due to the large code base of the whole operating system. Moreover, to deploy nested virtualization on x86 hardware imposes tremendous performance penalties that increase exponentially with nesting depth [12].

To reduce the size of the TCB even further, NOVA [13,14] constructs a microkernel based VMM with 9K LOCs. Nonetheless, Its TCB is not markedly decreased since the microhypervisor is still in charge of complex management tasks, such as address space allocation, interrupt and exception handling. Therefore, the thin TCB is still difficult to verify dynamically. Compared with this, NoHype [15,16] narrows down the attack surface of the hypervisor by dynamically eliminating VMM layer. However, the number of VMs that can run simultaneously on the physical platform are restricted since it requires one-VM-per-core on multi-core processors and pre-allocated nested page table. Flicker [17] is considered as a privacy protection solution based on the hardware features provided by the hardware vendors, like Intel and AMD. It significantly enhances the security and reliability of the code while at the same time inducing large performance overhead. Other than that, it only offers application level protection and is not a general solution for VMs in cloud.

Besides above architectural improvement attempts, many research efforts focus on protecting the privacy of user application against untrusted operating system using a VMM-based approach [18,19,20,21,22]. The goal of our work is different from that of above research. We aim to protect privacy of guest VMs (including the hosted user applications) against the untrusted cloud administrators, rather than protecting the user applications' privacy against the untrusted OS.

Our previous work, MyCloud, achieves a verifiable TCB size (6K LOCs) by removing the control VM from the processor root mode. It also has a flexible privacy protection mechanism based on a user configured ACM. MyCloud isolates the memory space among guest VMs, physical devices and the hypervisor. However, the functionalities of the hypervisor are limited, e.g., needs device level support of virtualization. To remove the restrictions and better support physical devices, we propose a design that launches resource managers in the non-root mode. The procedure and results of resource management can be monitored by the hypervisor in the root mode. Through this design, MyCloud SEP provides better functionalities without significantly increasing the hypervisor size.

3   MyCloud SEP Architecture

3.1   Threat Model and Assumptions

We take *insider attacks* into consideration but we must distinguish the *cloud administrators* from the *cloud providers*. Generally, the famous cloud providers such as Amazon [4], Microsoft [23] and Hewlett-Packard [24] have strong motivation to protect users' privacy rather than reveal customers' privacy. Protecting users' privacy will increase the reputation of cloud enterprises to a large extent and bring more economic benefits. On the contrary, the cloud administrators employed by the cloud providers may be motivated to disclose cloud tenants' privacy to pursue monetary benefits. Moreover, any mistakes they make by accident may breach users' privacy or help external attackers to compromise guest VMs. Therefore, we consider the cloud administrators malicious.

Due to many vulnerabilities from the device drivers, device emulation and software components in the control VM [25,26,27], the external adversary can compromise the control VM and obtain the administrative privilege of the cloud platform. Afterwards, the external adversary will exploit cloud tenants' private data. Meanwhile, the external adversary can also breach the cloud users' privacy relying on the vulnerabilities found in current virtual machine monitors (VMM) design [28,29,30,31,32]. Furthermore, the console interface provided by the cloud provider is also vulnerable to many *external attacks* [33,34].

In MyCloud SEP design, we take both insider and external attacks into consideration. But the physical attack [35] is out of the scope of this paper. The cloud provider can solve the physical attack by deploying more protection mechanisms on the server side such as secure door control system.

In this paper, we assume that the cloud providers can utilize Intel Trusted Execution Technology (TXT) [36] and chip-based Trusted Platform Module (TPM) [37] to measure the integrity of the hypervisor execution environment before MyCloud SEP is loaded. This is not a strong assumption since now all servers are using the technology or similar ones. Similarly, we assume that the System Management Range Register (SMRR) is properly configured in order to protect the processor System Management Mode (SMM) from attacks [38].

We will not discuss how to make a mutually agreed access control policy between the cloud providers and cloud tenants in this paper. It is up to the cloud providers and cloud users to decide which part of memory can be accessed. MyCloud SEP just provides isolated execution environment and mechanisms to implement the access control policies.

3.2 Virtualization Architecture

The architecture of MyCloud SEP is shown in Figure 1. Using Intel virtualization technology [39], the software stack of MyCloud SEP is divided into *root* mode and *non-root* mode. Each mode in MyCloud SEP has the same ring privilege structure from ring 0 to ring 3. As shown in Figure 1, the hypervisor runs in the root mode, while other components run in non-root mode. When the hypervisor is booted, MyCloud SEP will stay in the root mode. The CPU will enter the non-root mode, when the hypervisor executes VMRESUME/VMLAUNCH instruction. If the guest VMs execute the privileged instructions, CPU will automatically transfer to the root-mode and trigger hypervisor handlers via VMEXITs. After the hypervisor handles the privileged instruction, the guest VM can be resumed.

In Figure 1, the Platform Control VM is moved to non-root mode and a Virtual Disk Manager (VDM) launched in non-root mode will drive physical disks. Different from existing techniques, VDM is not part of the TCB and the access to the physical disks will be examined by the hypervisor against an ACM in the hypervisor. In MyCloud

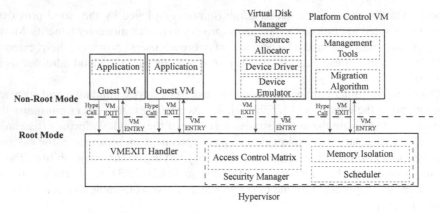

Fig. 1. MyCloud SEP architecture design

SEP design, only the hypervisor and platform hardware are in the TCB. The TCB size is remarkably reduced because there is no operating system, physical device drivers and device emulator running in the privileged mode and the hypervisor will intercept all privileged instruction executed by the components in non-root mode.

Note that our architecture is different from Xen since the control VM is moved out of the processor's root mode. Also, different from other designs, we are not trying to put device management in a separate domain. Instead, our design goal is to put resource management outside the TCB. In the figure, we only show virtual disk management since in cloud environment, we usually need much less device support than a desktop computer does.

Device Management. In this paper, we use virtual disks as an example to explain how to separate resource management from security management in the hypervisor. The virtual disk structure in MyCloud SEP is illustrated in Figure 2. As shown in the figure, each virtual machine, including the Platform Control VM, only has access to limited number of disks in the virtual disk pool. The Virtual Disk Manager manages the disk resources and has access privileges to the physical disks.

Note that all accesses to the physical disks will be checked by the hypervisor against the ACM in it. Although the device drivers and resource allocator work in non-root mode, MyCloud SEP will grant an access if and only if the access is permitted in the ACM. In the initialization process of a VM, the device drivers need a lot of device information such as manufacturer ID, etc.. MyCloud SEP intercepts the guest VM initialization operations and provides a device emulator to guest VMs. The device drivers in guest VMs may be malicious, thus, MyCloud SEP needs to monitor I/O from the device drivers in the guest VMs.

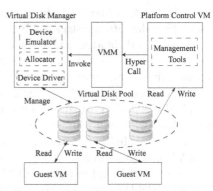

Fig. 2. Virtual disk structure

Since the resource allocator is out of the TCB, MyCloud SEP hypervisor will verify whether the results of resource allocation and allocation procedure (described in Section 4) are secure. For example, allocating the same disk block to multiple VMs is prohibited. The allocation of disks space should have no overlaps either.

The Virtual Disk Manager launched in non-root mode includes device emulators for guest VMs and physical device drivers for disks. In MyCloud SEP implementation, the Virtual Disk Manager is just a piece of codes which provides Intel AHCI [40] emulation and communicates with local SATA disks. The new design reduces the attack surface of Virtual Disk Manager. In order to monitor the activity of disk drivers, the hypervisor will also create a VMCS structure and configure which instructions should be intercepted.

MyCloud SEP Hypervisor. The hypervisor is the only component running in the root mode. Before the hypervisor is initialized, the boot loader of MyCloud SEP will verify the integrity of the hypervisor execution environment using Intel TXT technology. If the environment is secure, the hypervisor will be initialized. The initialization process of hypervisor completes the following tasks.

- Detect E820 map and isolate the physical memory for other component.
- Detect all PCI devices installed in cloud platform.
- Configure IOMMU in order to isolate device memory and guest VM's memory.
- Copy the hypervisor into specific memory address.

After the initialization process is finished, the hypervisor will be able to perform the following tasks

- Create VMCS structure for the control VM, guest VMs and Virtual Disk Manager. Specify what should be trapped in each VMCS structure.
- Create Access Control Matrix.
- Handle interrupts and exceptions happened in the guest VMs and devices while checking those operations against ACM.
- Deliver the device access operations from guest VMs to device emulator.
- Schedule the guest VMs.

The Platform Control VM. The hypervisor creates a VMCS for the Platform Control VM and launches it in non-root mode. In MyCloud SEP, the hypervisor will set VMCS for the control VM so that any memory access not in its EPT will be trapped by CPU. Therefore, even the Platform Control VM cannot access the memory of a guest VM without its explicit permissions. The guest VM can grant access permissions to its own memory space through a hypercall that modifies the ACM in hypervisor.

The Platform Control VM can still allocate resources because the hypervisor will provide resource utilization status through HyperCall API (described in Section 4). Thus, the Platform Control VM can migrate VMs as long as it follows resource allocation procedures and the resource allocation does not violate policies specified in ACM.

Guest VMs. Although guest VMs are running in the non-root mode, they can configure the ACM table via interfaces (HyperCalls) provided by the hypervisor. The guest VMs can also implement some privileged work such as memory introspection. The VM image and configuration file are stored in the local storage. Normally, the guest VMs are running as the same way in physical machine, because all of privileged instructions, interrupt and exceptions will be handled by the hypervisor. When a privileged instruction is executed in guest VMs, CPU will automatically switch to the root mode. Consequently, the hypervisor will receive a VMEXIT containing all information about the privileged instruction. After the hypervisor handles the privilege instruction, it will execute VMRESUME to return to the non-root mode. Guest VMs will receive the results generated by the hypervisor and resume.

4   Implementation

4.1   General Resource Management

There are resources on two types of devices - character devices and block devices. Character devices include keyboard, mouse and serial port etc,. Block devices include disks, network card etc,. In MyCloud SEP, block devices are managed in the unit of a "resource region". A resource region is specified by {start address, end address}. A region is not necessary to be the full address space for a VM. For example, a VM can have a disk block *ResourceRegion_i* {(track #100, head #0, sector #15), (track #500, head #0, sector #15)}.

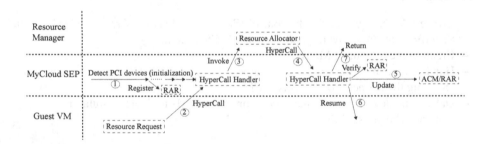

Fig. 3. Workflow of resource allocation

Figure 3 shows the procedure of how guest VMs apply for a block of resource. In step ①, the hypervisor sends I/O commands to port 0xcf8 and 0xcfc in order to obtain each PCI device configurations. The acquired PCI device structure includes base address (BAR), specified command and I/O ports etc,. The hypervisor will then register the allocation information in a data structure – Resource Access Recorder (RAR).

When a guest VM applies a new resource region, it starts with step ②. The guest VM sends a HyperCall to the hypervisor. In order to improve the compatibility for different resource allocators and reduce the TCB size, MyCloud SEP allows multiple resource allocators in the non-root mode. The HyperCall handler invokes the resource allocators in step ③ by VMLAUNCH instruction. The resource allocator will return the allocation

Table 1. Access Control Matrix in MyCloud SEP (VDM-Virtual Disk Manager, CVM-Control Virtual Machine, H-Hyper Calls, R-Read, W-Write, P- Permission Required)

Components	$Hypervisor$	CVM	VDM	$ResourceRegion_i$	$ResourceRegion_j$
$Hypervisor$	Full	Full	Full	Full	Full
CVM	H	Full		P	P
VDM	H		Full		
VM_i	H			Full	
VM_j	H				Full

plan by another HyperCall. Since the resource allocator is not trusted, the hypervisor will verify the allocation plan by checking the RAR table. If the plan is approved, the hypervisor will update the RAR and ACM table. In step ⑥, the hypervisor will resume the guest VM with a new allocated resource region. Finally, the hypervisor returns the responses of the HyperCall sent from resource manager in step ⑦.

The process to free a resource region is similar. First, a guest VM sends the request to the hypervisor. The hypervisor invokes the resource allocator in resource manager to generate a new resource allocation plan. Then, the hypervisor verifies the security of new resource allocation plan by searching the RAR table and checking ACM. Finally, the hypervisor will resume the guest VM after updating the ACM table.

4.2   Access Authorization Based on ACM

In MyCloud SEP, the hypervisor maintains an Access Control Matrix that is configurable by users, as shown in Table 1. The ACM table stores access permissions for each VM and resource regions. In the table, we use VDM as an example of resource managers. The VDM does not have direct access to any allocated resource regions such as disk blocks.

Note that the privilege design in MyCloud SEP is completely different from any of the existing cloud platform because the control VM does not have full privileges over the platform. In MyCloud SEP, the control VM is removed from the root mode and the privileges are specified in the ACM maintained by the hypervisor. The hypervisor relies on Intel Extended Page Table (EPT) technology to intercept CPU memory accesses. We use Intel VT-d technology to isolate IOMMU memory accesses. Besides, the hypervisor will also check ACM table when allocating devices.

As shown in Table 1, only the hypervisor has accesses to all resources in the platform. The control VM has the same privilege level as guest VMs. It can only access resources assigned to the cloud administrator. If the cloud administrator needs to access users resources,

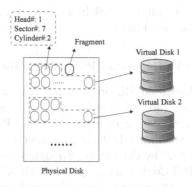

Fig. 4. Physical disk assignment

it needs to be authorized by users through hypercalls of ACM configuration. VDM is responsible to provide device emulator and transfer data between SATA disks and guest VMs. Therefore, VDM has no permissions to access VMs memory. But the hypervisor provides a secure mechanism to verify the activities of VDM. The details will be explained in section 4.4.

4.3   Case Study: Disk Management

Figure 2 shows how to manage virtual disk in MyCloud SEP. The control VM accesses the virtual disks in the same way as guest VMs because it is running in the non-root mode. When the control VM or guest VMs boot, any device initialization in guest VMs or control VM will be trapped into the hypervisor, then handled by a device emulator. In the initialization stage, the guest OS will request device information such as *device ID, mentor ID, Base Address etc,*. The device emulator will offer virtualized device information to enable a guest OS to complete initialization.

In order to protect disk allocation information, the hypervisor in MyCloud SEP will employ a linear mapping from a logical disk space to a physical disk space. Figure 4 shows how the physical disk blocks are mapped to virtual disks. The linear mapping function calculates the address of a physical disk block by three parameters: cylinder number, sector number, and head number. We place the virtual disks in similar size into the same physical disk in order to reduce the number of fragments. If the users try to expand the size of virtual disks, the hypervisor can migrate it into other physical disks or servers. The linear mapping is protected in the hypervisor.

According to Intel AHCI 1.3 specification [40], the AHCI works as an interface between OS and SATA disks. The hypervisor can detect AHCI information throughout PCI configuration space (0xcf8 and 0xcfc). Afterwards, the hypervisor will store device allocation information in RAR table such as base address, AHCI specific I/O port and registers. etc,. When a guest VM applies for new virtual disks, the hypervisor will invoke the resource allocator in VDM. The VDM designs which part of physical disk can be used for virtual disk volume. The hypervisor checks the ACM table and verifies if the physical disk blocks have already been allocated. Finally, the hypervisor updates the ACM table.

4.4   Hypervisor Processing of Disk I/Os

MyCloud SEP implements disk emulator based on Intel ATA AHCI 1.3 Specification [40]. In essential, the Advanced Host Controller Interface (AHCI) encompasses a PCI device, then the AHCI Host Bus Adapter is constructed by a PCI header and PCI Capabilities. In the initialization step, guest VMs will try to access to PCI Configuration Space by I/O port *0xcf8 and 0xcfc*. As shown in Figure 1, when guest VMs try to detect PCI Configuration Space, a VMEXIT will be triggered and the hypervisor will transfer the I/O command to device emulator in VDM.

Figure 5 shows how a guest VM executes a write() function. When an application in the guest VM sends a disk write request to OS kernel, the kernel will process it and issue a series of I/O commands to configure and transfer data with AHCI HBA. The hypervisor can intercept the commands when the guest kernel or driver sends the

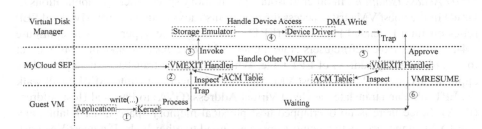

Fig. 5. Workflow of read/write operation

commands to the I/O ports specified in AHCI 1.3. The hypervisor will verify if the trapped I/O commands meet the requirement of AHCI. The hypervisor will also check the ACM table for permissions. After that, the hypervisor will trigger the VDM and deliver the command to the device emulator. The VDM handles the commands and calls physical disk drivers to execute the I/O write operation.

The VDM needs to access guest memory in order to transfer data from memory to disk. If the trapped I/O command indicates the disk is ready to transfer data, the hypervisor will assign the physical disk to the VDM using Intel VT-d technology [41]. To prohibit VDM from visiting memory space assigned to other VMs, MyCloud SEP configures IOMMU DMA remapping hardware and specifies the memory space the VDM can access. If the VDM reads/writes other memory space, the hypervisor will receive a VMEXIT.

To prevent VDM drivers from reconfiguring the device via I/O command, the hypervisor stores the resource region information when users send I/O commands to prepare disk operations. If the access is out of the scope of users-specified resourced region, the hypervisor will block the command. After VDM finishes the write operation, hypervisor resumes the guest VM.

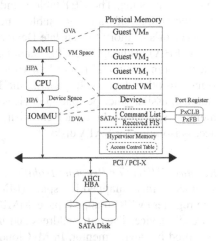

Fig. 6. Device and VM isolation in My-Cloud SEP

4.5 Memory Isolation

Figure 6 shows the isolated memory between VMs, device and hypervisor owned space. The memory isolation is implemented as follows:

MMU Access Isolation. In order to isolate the memory space when the applications or kernel in the guest VMs try to access the data or instructions in memory, MyCloud SEP relies on Intel Extended Page Table (EPT) technology. The hypervisor will configure a 4-layer EPT table before users crate a guest VM. *EPT base pointer* in VMCS is set to record the entry address of EPT table. When a memory translation is requested by applications or kernel in the guest VM, Memory Management Unite (MMU) will walk the EPT table and translate the Guest Virtual Address (GVA) to Physical Host Address (PHA). Since there is no overlapped host physical memory space in EPT table, any guest VM cannot access the memory space assigned to other VMs. If a guest VM wish to share memory with the control VM, it should send the request to the hypervisor via a HyperCall. Next, the hyeprvisor will first verify the request, then revise the ACM table and EPT in order to make the memory space "visible" to the control VM.

IOMMU Access Isolation. Most of device transmit data via DMA access and IOMMU is responsible for translating device virtual memory address to physical memory address. To isolate the DMA access made by physical device, MyCloud SEP implements Intel Virtualization Technology for Directed I/O [41]. Before disks execute DMA access, the hypervisor will set up Context-Entry Table (CET) in IOMMU to implement DMA Remapping. The CET table is indexed by {*PCI bus, device# and function#*} to find the address of translation table. The hypervisor builds Multi-Level Page Table in hypervisor's memory to translate Device Virtual Address (DVA) to Physical Host Address (PHA). Although the CPU cannot control the DMA access, IOMMU can trap the address translation and report DMA remapping faults if disks access the memory assigned to other devices. In general, the DMA Remapping and IOMMU configuration can also assign other peripheral devices (network card) to guest VMs and control the memory space that the device can visit. In our prototype, we implement the IOMMU access isolation for SATA disks.

Resource Allocation Recorder Isolation. MyCloud SEP also protects I/O related space, such as memory mapped I/O space (MMIO), PCI device configuration space and system register (MSR) mapped space. MMIO space is used to store I/O command and data for each device. The entry address and I/O port assigned for each device are basically specified by device mentor. In MyCloud SEP, we protect the MMIO space for AHCI and SATA disks. Based on AHCI specification 1.3, the most data and I/O commands are stored in two structures: Command List and Received FIS. The entry point for Command List and Received FIS is specified at chipset register PXCLB and PxFB. The hypervisor specifies the memory space for those structures by setting up the port register: PxCLB and PxFB. In order to protect PCI configuration space, the hypervisor will detect base address for each PCI devices via I/O port (0xcfc and 0xcf8), then set those space only "visible" to hypervisor. To verify the memory and disk access, the hypervisor should store ACM table and a liner mapping that translates 3-dimension logical disk volume to physical disk volume.

5   Evaluation

Our evaluation test is built on a hardware platform that includes an Intel i7 2600 SEPcessor (with both Vt-x and Vt-d) running at 3.3Ghz, an Intel DQ67SW Motherboard, 4 GB RAM and 1 TB SATA HDD. The guest VM is Ubuntu 10.04 LTS with linux kernel 2.6.32.

5.1   Disk Operation Performance

To evaluate the performance of disk I/O operations in MyCloud SEP, we counted the number of VMEXITs and the time used for creating a 1GB blank file in a guest VM.

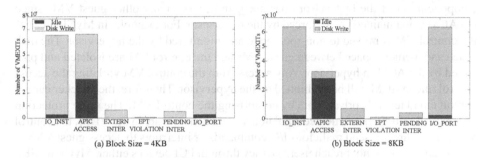

(a) Block Size = 4KB   (b) Block Size = 8KB

Fig. 7. Number of VMEXITs for Disk Operations

Figure 7 shows the types and the corresponding numbers of VMEXITs for creating the file with 4KB and 8KB block size. The figure presents the number of VMEXITs generated when the guest VM is at idle or disk write status. To create a 1GB file, the guest VM will introduce around 2×10^5 VMEXITS with 4KB block, and 1.38×10^5 VMEXITS with 8KB block. Though the number of VMEXITS looks huge, the corresponding extra overhead compared with KVM,

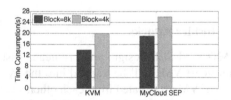

Fig. 8. Time Consumption for Disk Operations

such as time consumption (less than 6s more on 4KB block and 5s more on 8KB block, see Figure 8), is acceptable.

Figure 8 shows the time used for creating the 1GB file on KVM and MyCloud SEP platforms. We set the block size as 4KB and 8KB. In either case, MyCloud SEP takes 20% more time than KVM, because the disk I/O operations will be trapped into hypervisor and examined against ACM in it. According to our evaluation, the bigger the block size is, the less VMEXITs will be generated. The time consumption with 8KB block size is less than that of 4 KB block size.

6 Discussion

In MyCloud SEP design, the ACM is fully protected by the hypervisor. The hypervisor identifies any HyperCall that requests to change to or read from the ACM. A VM is allowed to only read or modify its own element in the ACM table. Any attempt to read or modify the ACM other than its own element will be detected and prohibited by the hypervisor.

6.1 External Attacks

The external attacks come from guest VMs, targeting at the hypervisor, through the hypervisor interfaces. In MyCloud SEP, device drivers, device emulator and the control VM are not part of the TCB. Compromising a guest VM or a malicious software component out of the hypervisor does not gain access to any other guest VMs since the ACM is maintained and enforced by the hypervisor. For example, in MyCloud SEP, the control VM is moved to non-root mode and monitored by the hypervisor. The disk space and memory space between guest VMs and the control VM are isolated and protected by the ACM in hypervisor. Any access from the control VM violating the access control rule in ACM will be prohibited by the hypervisor. Therefore, the attacker cannot exploit cloud tenant's private data by comprising the control VM. The same protection goes with disk drivers and device emulator. The disk drivers are in the VDM, the control VM cannot directly send malicious I/O commands or interrupts to access guest VMs.

The attackers cannot breach users privacy through PCI devices either. MyCloud SEP isolates the device memory from guest memory, therefore, any malicious DMA access will be prohibited by the hypervisor. The hypervisor first identifies all PCI devices at initialization process. Then, the hypervisor records MMIO and PCI Configuration space for each device in order to prevent the attackers from overlapping the device memory to disclose users' private data.

6.2 Insider Attacks

In MyCloud SEP design, any privileged instructions executed in the control VM or other guest VMs will be trapped into the hypervisor for security check. The memory space of VMs is isolated from each other, so a malicious guest VM cannot access other VMs' space. Also, in MyCloud SEP, a malicious cloud administrator cannot access a guest VM space unless the guest VM explicitly grants the access through the ACM configuration. Thus, a malicious cloud administrator cannot gain control over guest VMs either.

6.3 More about the Disk Management

In current design, the virtual disk manager in MyCloud SEP does not utilize popular file systems like Linux extfs for higher level management. The fundamental reason is that the disk access information trapped by the hypervisor are physical disks locations indicated by cylinder number, head number, and track number. The hypervisor level information is different from the file system abstraction like `inode` for a file. There is no simple way using affordable size of codes to map from `inode` to disk blocks in the hypervisor.

Therefore, in MyCloud SEP design, we deploy a resource allocation tool, virtual disk manager, in a Linux VM, rather than using Linux file systems directly. The resource allocation tool maps resource regions to device files. Note that malicious resource allocation does not breach user's privacy. For example, allocating the same disk block to multiple VMs are monitored and prohibited by the hypervisor.

7 Conclusion

In this paper, we described a new architecture, MyCloud SEP, to separate resource allocation and management from the hypervisor. While providing flexibility of plugging-in resource management modules, the TCB size of virtualization platform is significantly reduced compared with commercial hypervisors. In our design, the hypervisor runs security check against an ACM for the resource manager, control VM, and guest VMs in the processor non-root mode. As the results, guest VMs' privacy is protected. Functionality and security check are also separated. Using virtual disk manager as an example, we implement a prototype on x86 architecture. The performance evaluation shows acceptable overheads of MyCloud SEP.

Ackknowledgement. We thank all reviewers for their insightful comments. Meng Yu was supported by NSF CNS-1100221 and NSF IIP-1342664. Peng Liu was supported by ARO W911NF-09-1-0525, NSF CNS-1223710, ARO W911NF-13-1-0421, and AFOSR W911NF1210055.

References

1. Forbes: PRISM Projected To Cost U.S. Cloud Market $35B,
   http://www.forbes.com/sites/louiscolumbus/
   2013/08/08/prism-projected-to-cost-u-s-cloud-computing-
   industry-35b
2. Xen: http://www.xen.org/
3. KVM, http://www.linux-kvm.org/
4. Amazon Inc.: Amazon EC2, http://aws.amazon.com/ec2/
5. Butt, S., Lagar-Cavilla, H.A., Srivastava, A., Ganapathy, V.: Self-service cloud computing. In: Proceedings of the 2012 ACM Conference on Computer and Communications Security, CCS 2012, pp. 253–264. ACM, New York (2012)
6. Li, M., Zang, W., Bai, K., Yu, M., Liu, P.: Mycloud: Supporting user-configured privacy protection in cloud computing. In: Proceedings of the 29th Annual Computer Security Applications Conference, ACSAC 2013, pp. 59–68. ACM, New York (2013)
7. Murray, D., Milos, G., Hand, S.: Improving xen security through disaggregation. In: Proceedings of the Fourth ACM SIGPLAN/SIGOPS International Conference on Virtual Execution Environments, pp. 151–160. ACM (2008)
8. Pan, W., Zhang, Y., Yu, M., Jing, J.: Improving virtualization security by splitting hypervisor into smaller components. In: Cuppens-Boulahia, N., Cuppens, F., Garcia-Alfaro, J. (eds.) DBSec 2012. LNCS, vol. 7371, pp. 298–313. Springer, Heidelberg (2012)

9. Zhang, F., Chen, J., Chen, H., Zang, B.: Cloudvisor: Retrofitting protection of virtual machines in multi-tenant cloud with nested virtualization. In: Proceedings of the Twenty-Third ACM Symposium on Operating Systems Principles, pp. 203–216. ACM (2011)
10. Williams, D., Jamjoom, H., Weatherspoon, H.: The xen-blanket: virtualize once, run everywhere. In: ACM EuroSys (2012)
11. Ben-Yehuda, M., Day, M., Dubitzky, Z., Factor, M., Har'El, N., Gordon, A., Liguori, A., Wasserman, O., Yassour, B.: The turtles project: Design and implementation of nested virtualization. In: Proceedings of the 9th USENIX Conference on Operating Systems Design and Implementation, pp. 1–6. USENIX Association (2010)
12. Kauer, B., Verissimo, P., Bessani, A.: Recursive virtual machines for advanced security mechanisms. In: 2011 IEEE/IFIP 41st International Conference on Dependable Systems and Networks Workshops (DSN-W), pp. 117–122. IEEE (2011)
13. Steinberg, U., Kauer, B.: Nova: a microhypervisor-based secure virtualization architecture. In: Proceedings of the 5th European Conference on Computer Systems, EuroSys 2010, pp. 209–222. ACM, New York (2010)
14. Heiser, G., Uhlig, V., LeVasseur, J.: Are virtual-machine monitors microkernels done right? SIGOPS Oper. Syst. Rev. 40(1), 95–99 (2006)
15. Keller, E., Szefer, J., Rexford, J., Lee, R.: Nohype: virtualized cloud infrastructure without the virtualization. ACM SIGARCH Computer Architecture News 38, 350–361 (2010)
16. Szefer, J., Keller, E., Lee, R., Rexford, J.: Eliminating the hypervisor attack surface for a more secure cloud. In: Proceedings of the 18th ACM Conference on Computer and Communications Security, pp. 401–412. ACM (2011)
17. McCune, J.M., Parno, B.J., Perrig, A., Reiter, M.K., Isozaki, H.: Flicker: an execution infrastructure for tcb minimization. SIGOPS Oper. Syst. Rev. 42(4), 315–328 (2008)
18. Chen, X., Garfinkel, T., Lewis, E.C., Subrahmanyam, P., Waldspurger, C.A., Boneh, D., Dwoskin, J., Ports, D.R.K.: Overshadow: A virtualization-based approach to retrofitting protection in commodity operating systems. In. In: ASPLOS (May 2008)
19. Yang, J., Shin, K.G.: Using hypervisor to provide data secrecy for user applications on a per-page basis. In: Proceedings of the Fourth ACM SIGPLAN/SIGOPS International Conference on Virtual Execution Environments, VEE 2008, pp. 71–80. ACM, New York (2008)
20. Hofmann, O.S., Kim, S., Dunn, A.M., Lee, M.Z., Witchel, E.: Inktag: secure applications on an untrusted operating system. In: Proceedings of the Eighteenth International Conference on Architectural Support for Programming Languages and Operating System, ASPLOS 2013, pp. 265–278. ACM, New York (2013)
21. Ta-Min, R., Litty, L., Lie, D.: Splitting interfaces: making trust between applications and operating system configurable. In: Proceedings of the 7th Symposium on Operating Systems Design and Implementation, OSDI 2006, pp. 279–292. USENIX Association, Berkeley (2006)
22. Cheng, Y., Ding, X., Deng, R.H.: Appshield: Protecting applications against untrusted operating system. In: Singaport Management University Technical Report. smu-sis-13-101 (2013)
23. Cloud, M., http://www.microsoft.com/enterprise/microsoftcloud/
24. Cloud, H.P., http://www.hpcloud.com/
25. CVE-2007-4993: Xen guest root escape to dom0 via pygrub
26. CVE-2010-0431: Qemu-kvm in redhat enterprise virtualization (rhev) 2.2 and kvm 83, does not properly validate guest qxl driver pointers, which allows guest os users to gain privileges via unspecified vectors
27. CVE-2009-1758: The hypervisor callback function in xen, as applied to the linux kernel 2.6.30-rc4 allows guest user applications to cause a denial of service of the guest os by triggering a segmentation fault in certain address ranges
28. Elhage, N.: Virtunoid: Breaking out of kvm (2011)

29. Kortchinsky, K.: Cloudburst: Hacking 3d (and breaking out of vmware). In: Black Hat Conference (2009)
30. Wojtczuk, R., Rutkowska, J.: Xen 0wning trilogy. In: Black Hat Conference (2008)
31. Secunia: Vulnerability report: Vmware esx server 3.x, http://secunia.com/advisories/product/10757/
32. Secunia: Xen multiple vulnerability report, http://secunia.com/advisories/44502/
33. CVE-2009-2277: Cross-site scripting (xss) vulnerability in webaccess in vmware allows attackers to inject arbitrary web script via vectors related to context data
34. CVE-2009-1244: Vulnerability in the virtual machine display function in vmware workstation allows guest os users to execute arbitrary code on host os
35. Anderson, R., Kuhn, M.: Tamper resistance-a cautionary note. In: Proceedings of the Second Usenix Workshop on Electronic Commerce, vol. 2, pp. 1–11 (1996)
36. Intel Coperation: Intel trusted execution technology (2011)
37. Intel Coperation: Intel trusted platform module (2003)
38. Wojtczuk, R., Rutkowska, J.: Attacking smm memory via intel cpu cache poisoning. Invisible Things Lab (2009)
39. Intel Corporation: Intel vprof technology, http://www.intel.com/content/www/us/en/architecture-and-technology/vpro/vpro-technology-general.html
40. Intel Coperation: Serial ATA Advanced Host Controller Interface (2012)
41. Intel Corporation: Intel® Virtualization Technology Specification for Directed I/O Specification, www.intel.com/technology/vt/

Securely Outsourcing Exponentiations with Single Untrusted Program for Cloud Storage

Yujue Wang[1,2,3], Qianhong Wu[3,1], Duncan S. Wong[2], Bo Qin[4],
Sherman S.M. Chow[5], Zhen Liu[2], and Xiao Tan[2]

[1] Key Laboratory of Aerospace Information Security and Trusted Computing
Ministry of Education, School of Computer, Wuhan University, Wuhan, China
[2] Department of Computer Science
City University of Hong Kong, Hong Kong
wyujue2-c@my.cityu.edu.hk, {duncan,zhenliu7}@cityu.edu.hk,
xiaotan4@gapps.cityu.edu.hk
[3] School of Electronic and Information Engineering
Beihang University, Beijing, China
qianhong.wu@buaa.edu.cn
[4] School of Information, Renmin University of China, Beijing, China
bo.qin@ruc.edu.cn
[5] Department of Information Engineering
Chinese University of Hong Kong, Hong Kong
sherman@ie.cuhk.edu.hk

Abstract. Provable Data Possession (PDP) allows a file owner to outsource her files to a storage server such that a verifier can check the integrity of the outsourced file. Public verifiable PDP schemes allow any one other than the file owner to be a verifier. At the client side (file owner or verifier), a substantial number of modular exponentiations is often required. In this paper we make PDP more practical via proposing a protocol to securely outsource the (most generic) variable-exponent variable-base exponentiations in *one* untrusted program model. Our protocol demonstrates advantages in efficiency or privacy over existing protocols coping with only special cases in two or single untrusted program model. We then apply our generic protocol to Shacham-Waters PDP and a variant of Yuan-Yu PDP. The analyses show that our protocol makes PDP much more efficient at the client side.

Keywords: Offloading computation, Verifiable computation, Modular exponentiation, Provable Data Possession, Cloud storage.

1 Introduction

A recent trend to reduce the storage costs is to outsource it to a cloud service provider. It is beneficial to the (cloud service) clients since the outsourced files can be easily shared with others. There are also increasing concerns about the security of their outsourced files. In addition to the many secrecy issues [1–3], there are concerns about whether those outsourced files are still kept intact.

M. Kutyłowski and J. Vaidya (Eds.): ESORICS 2014, Part I, LNCS 8712, pp. 326–343, 2014.
© Springer International Publishing Switzerland 2014

Traditional primitives like signature or signcryption (e.g., [4, 5]) are insufficient for this purpose since it requires the signed message for verification.

Considerable efforts have been devoted to addressing these concerns. A promising one is to verify the outsourced file integrity via *provable data possession* (PDP) [6–11]. In many scenarios, *publicly verifiable* PDP is preferable. However, existing such schemes need many *modular exponentiations*, especially in file processing and integrity verification. Exponentiations are relatively expensive for devices with limited computation capacity such as mobile phones or tablet, albeit outsourcing files is attractive to mobile terminals due to their limited storage space. This motivates us to consider how to make PDP more affordable by securely outsourcing exponentiation to a *computation server*.

1.1   Our Contributions

Secure Exponentiations Outsourcing. We present the first *generic* scheme that allows to securely outsource variable-exponent variable-base multi-exponentiations to just one untrusted computation server. Although a few schemes have been proposed for securely outsourcing *variable-exponent variable-base exponentiations*, they treat the special cases of our setting and are not satisfactory enough for outsourcing multi-exponentiations in practice. Both Hohenberger-Lysyanskaya scheme [12] and Chen *et al.*'s scheme [13] are presented in *two untrusted program model*. This seems a strong assumption hard to be met as the client needs to outsource her exponentiations to two computation servers who will not collude. Our scheme is implemented in *single* untrusted program model, and is also superior since less interactions are needed between the client and the computation server. Although Dijk *et al.*'s scheme [14] is presented in a *single untrusted program model*, it cannot ensure the privacy of the queried input since the base of the outsourced exponentiation is known to the untrusted server. In contrast, our scheme is computationally more efficient and ensures higher privacy level.

Before showing our algorithm of outsourcing exponentiations, we provide two preprocessing subroutines which generate random pairs. The first one, called BPV$^+$, generates statistically indistinguishable random pairs and is suitable to implement outsourcing schemes over cyclic groups of large prime order. The other one, standard multiplicative base list (SMBL), is more efficient especially for applications over finite groups on elliptic curves.

Secure Offloading Provable Data Possession. Built on our scheme of outsourcing generic exponentiations, we investigate how to efficiently and securely offload PDP schemes. As we know, most existing publicly verifiable PDP schemes take many expensive exponentiations. Specifically, those exponentiations intensively occur in two stages. One is the file processing algorithm ProFile, which is carried out by the file owner to generate the verifiable metadata for a given file before uploading it to the storage server. The other one is the verification algorithm Vrfy, which is executed by a verifier to check whether the outsourced file is kept intact. Thus, to speed-up PDP schemes at the client side, we let the file owner and the verifier securely outsource exponentiations to an untrusted computation server. To showcase the effectiveness of our protocol, we show how to securely offload Shacham-Waters PDP [8] and a variant of Yuan-Yu PDP [11]. Analyses show that for both offloaded PDP schemes, the computational efficiency at the client side is greatly improved compared with the plain ones. Furthermore, the saving computation cost increases with the number of elements involved in a multi-exponentiation.

1.2 Related Work

Provable Data Possession. The concept of PDP was first introduced by Ateniese *et al.* [6], which allows the clients to check the integrity of an outsourced file without retrieving its entire version from the cloud storage server. For responding to integrity queries, the cloud server does not need to access the entire file. There are some attempts in outsourcing operations in PDP. Wang *et al.* [15] considered PDP in identity-based setting to relieve the users from complicated certificate management. In Wang *et al.*'s privacy-preserving publicly-verifiable PDP scheme [10], a third party auditor (TPA) is introduced to securely carry out verification algorithm on behalf of file owners. Here the privacy of the file is preserved from the view of the TPA. In another work with privacy concern, Wang *et al.* [9] considered a scenario such that the members of an organization can perform the file processing for PDP with the help of a security-mediator (SEM). As a side effect, part of the computation workloads is also outsourced. The privacy is preserved from the view of the SEM.

Proofs of Retrievability (PoR) is a closely related notion to PDP. PoR was first introduced by Juels and Kaliski [7], which enables the storage server to convince its clients that the outsourced files can be entirely retrieved. In their scheme [7], the clients can only submit a limited number of integrity queries, because the corresponding responses are produced by checking whether the special sentinels have been modified. Shacham and Waters [8] presented (both privately and publicly) verifiable PoR schemes, which are the first ones that being proved in the strongest model. Based on polynomial commitments [16], Yuan and Yu [11] proposed a public verifiable PoR scheme with constant communication costs for integrity verification. Benabbas, Gennaro and Vahlis [17] investigated verifiable delegation of computations for high degree polynomial functions to an untrusted server, and based on which a PoR scheme is discussed where the file blocks are represented as the coefficients in a polynomial. For reducing the computation costs at the client sides, Li *et al.* [18] introduced a semi-honest cloud audit server into PoR framework. Specifically, the audit server takes charge of preprocessing the data for generating metadata as well as auditing the data integrity on behalf of data owners.

Securely Outsourcing Exponentiations. Dijk *et al.* [14] considered outsourcing algorithms of *variable-exponent fixed-base* and *fixed-exponent variable-base exponentiations* in one untrusted server model. Specifically, the computations are outsourced to one powerful but untrusted server, where the variable parts are blinded before sending to the server. Ma, Li and Zhang [19] also proposed secure algorithms of outsourcing these two types of exponentiations by using two non-collusion untrusted servers. An algorithm of outsourcing variable-exponent variable-base exponentiations was also presented in [14], where the outsourced base is known to the server. Both the schemes of Hohenberger and Lysyan-skaya [12] and Chen *et al.* [13] considered outsource-secure algorithms of variable-exponent variable-base exponentiations in one-malicious version of two untrusted program model, that is, the computations are securely outsourced to two servers one of which is trusted and will not collude with the other dishonest one. Chen *et al.* [13] also studied how to securely and efficiently outsource *simultaneous exponentiations* in this security model.

Other Secure Outsourcing Schemes. Tsang, Chow and Smith [20] proposed the concept of batch pairing delegations for securely outsourcing expensive pairing operations in batch. Canard, Devigne and Sanders [21] also showed delegating a pairing can be both secure and efficient. The main operation required by the client is exponentiation. With our new protocol, it provides a "complete solution" of outsourcing many pairing-based schemes, in particular, the PDP schemes we concerned in this work. Xu, Amariucai and Guan [22] considered a scenario in which the burdensome computations are delegated to a server P, and the verification on the outputs of P is also outsourced to another server V. Gennaro, Gentry and Parno [23] first considered verifiable computation by combining Yao's Garbled Circuits with a fully-homomorphic encryption scheme, such that the evaluation of a function can be securely outsourced to a remote untrusted server. Carter *et al.* [24] also considered securely outsourcing function evaluation by using an efficient outsourced oblivious transfer protocol. Zhang and Safavi-Naini [25] considered special cases of securely outsourcing function evaluation, i.e., univariate polynomial evaluation and matrix multiplication, without fully-homomorphic encryption, yet with multilinear maps. Recently, Wang *et al.* [26, 27] showed how to compute over data encrypted under multiple keys in the two-server model. Two-server model is also used in other work such as efficient privacy-preserving queries over distributed databases [28].

2   Definitions and Security Requirements

In this section, we review the definitions of outsource-secure algorithms as well as the corresponding security requirements [12, 13].

An algorithm *Alg* to be outsourced is divided into two parts, namely, a trusted part T which should be efficient compared with *Alg* and is carried out by the outsourcer, and an untrusted part U which is invoked by T. Following the works [12, 13], we use the same notations in the upcoming sections. Specifically, T^U denotes the works that carried out by T by invoking U. The adversary A is modelled by a pair of algorithms $A = (E, U')$, where E represents the adversarial environment, and generates adversarial inputs for *Alg*; we denote U' an adversarial software. It is invoked in the same way as U and thus it is used to mirror the view of U during the execution of T^U.

Definition 1 (Algorithm with Outsource-IO). *An outsourcing algorithm Alg takes five inputs and produces three outputs, i.e., $Alg(x_{hs}, x_{hp}, x_{hu}, x_{ap}, x_{au}) \rightarrow (y_s, y_p, y_u)$.*

Inputs: *All the inputs are classified by how they are generated and how much the adversary $A = (E, U')$ knows about them. The first three inputs are generated by an honest party, while the last two are generated by the adversarial environment E. Specifically, the* honest, secret *input x_{hs} is unknown to both E and U; the* honest, protected *input x_{hp} may be known to E, but is protected from U; the* honest, unprotected *input x_{hu} may be known by both E and U; the* adversarial, protected *input x_{ap} is known by E, but protected from U; and the* adversarial, unprotected *input x_{au} may be known by both E and U.*

Outputs: *Similarly, all the outputs are classified by how much the adversary $A = (E, U')$ knows about them. The first one y_s is called the* secret *output and unknown to both parties of A; the* protected *output y_p may be known by E, but unknown to U; and y_u is the* unprotected *output known by both E and U.*

It is assumed that the adversary A consists of two parties E and U'. Both can only make direct communications before the execution of T^U. In any other cases if necessary, they should be communicated via T. An outsource-secure algorithm (T, U) requires that neither party of A can learn anything interesting during the execution of T^U. This requirement is captured by the *simulatability* of (T, U). In other words, for any probabilistic polynomial-time (PPT) adversary $A = (E, U')$, the view of E on the execution of T^U can be simulated in a computationally indistinguishable way given the protected and unprotected inputs, and similarly, the view of U' can also be simulated but only given the unprotected inputs.

Definition 2 (Correctness). *Let Alg be an algorithm with outsource-IO. A pair of algorithms (T, U) is said to be a* correct *implementation of Alg, if $Alg = T^U$ for any honest, secret, or honest, protected, or adversarial, protected inputs.*

Definition 3 (λ-security). *Let Alg be an algorithm with outsource-IO. A pair of algorithms (T, U) is said to be a λ-outsource-secure implementation of Alg if: for any PPT adversary $A = (E, U')$, both the views of E and U' can be simulated on the execution of T^U, i.e., there exist PPT algorithms (S_1, S_2) such that the following two pairs of random variables are computationally indistinguishable under the security parameter λ,*

$$\Pr[EView_{real} \sim EView_{ideal}] \geq 1 - 2^{-\lambda},$$

and

$$\Pr[UView_{real} \sim UView_{ideal}] \geq 1 - 2^{-\lambda}.$$

Pair One: *$EView_{real} \sim EView_{ideal}$, which means that E learns nothing during the execution of T^U. They are defined by the following processes that proceed in rounds, where the notation "$\leftarrow$" denotes the outputs of the procedure in the right hand side.*

- *The i-th round of* real *process consists of the following steps, in which I is an honest, stateful process that the environment E cannot access:*
  - $(istate^i, x_{hs}^i, x_{hp}^i, x_{hu}^i) \leftarrow I(1^\kappa, istate^{i-1})$;
  - $(estate^i, j^i, x_{ap}^i, x_{au}^i, stop^i) \leftarrow E(1^\kappa, EView_{real}^{i-1}, x_{hp}^i, x_{hu}^i)$;
  - $(tstate^i, ustate^i, y_s^i, y_p^i, y_u^i)$
    $$\leftarrow T^{U'(ustate^{i-1})}(tstate^{i-1}, x_{hs}^{j^i}, x_{hp}^{j^i}, x_{hu}^{j^i}, x_{ap}^i, x_{au}^i).$$

  Thus, the view of E in the i-th round of the real process is $EView_{real}^i = (estate^i, y_p^i, y_u^i)$ *and the overall view is just its view in the last round, i.e.,* $EView_{real} = EView_{real}^i$ *for some i such that* $stop^i = True$.

- *The i-th round of* ideal *process consists of the following steps. In which, the stateful algorithm* S_1 *is given all the non-secret outputs which Alg generates in i-th round, but knows nothing about the secret input* x_{hs}^i. *Finally,* S_1 *outputs* (y_p^i, y_u^i) *or some other values* (Y_p^i, Y_u^i), *which is captured by using a boolean indicator* ind^i.
  - $(istate^i, x_{hs}^i, x_{hp}^i, x_{hu}^i) \leftarrow I(1^\kappa, istate^{i-1})$;
  - $(estate^i, j^i, x_{ap}^i, x_{au}^i, stop^i) \leftarrow E(1^\kappa, EView_{real}^{i-1}, x_{hp}^i, x_{hu}^i)$;
  - $(astate^i, y_s^i, y_p^i, y_u^i) \leftarrow Alg(astate^{i-1}, x_{hs}^{j^i}, x_{hp}^{j^i}, x_{hu}^{j^i}, x_{ap}^i, x_{au}^i)$;
  - $(sstate^i, ustate^i, Y_p^i, Y_u^i, ind^i)$
    $$\leftarrow S_1^{U'(ustate^{i-1})}(sstate^{i-1}, x_{hp}^{j^i}, x_{hu}^{j^i}, x_{ap}^i, x_{au}^i, y_p^i, y_u^i);$$
  - $(z_p^i, z_u^i) = ind^i(Y_p^i, Y_u^i) + (1 - ind^i)(y_p^i, y_u^i)$.

  Thus, the view of E in the i-th round of the ideal process is $EView_{ideal}^i = (estate^i, z_p^i, z_u^i)$ *and the overall view is just its view in the last round, i.e.,* $EView_{ideal} = EView_{ideal}^i$ *for some i such that* $stop^i = True$.

Pair Two: $UView_{real} \sim UView_{ideal}$, *which means that the untrusted software* U' *learns nothing during the execution of* $T^{U'}$.

- *By the definition of Pair One,* U'*'s view in the real process is* $UView_{real} = ustate^i$ *for some i such that* $stop^i = True$.
- *The i-th round of* ideal *process consists of the following steps, in which the stateful algorithm* S_2 *is just given the unprotected outputs which Alg generates in i-th round:*
  - $(istate^i, x_{hs}^i, x_{hp}^i, x_{hu}^i) \leftarrow I(1^\kappa, istate^{i-1})$;
  - $(estate^i, j^i, x_{ap}^i, x_{au}^i, stop^i) \leftarrow E(1^\kappa, EView_{real}^{i-1}, x_{hp}^i, x_{hu}^i)$;
  - $(astate^i, y_s^i, y_p^i, y_u^i) \leftarrow Alg(astate^{i-1}, x_{hs}^{j^i}, x_{hp}^{j^i}, x_{hu}^{j^i}, x_{ap}^i, x_{au}^i)$;
  - $(sstate^i, ustate^i) \leftarrow S_2^{U'(ustate^{i-1})}(sstate^{i-1}, x_{hu}^{j^i}, x_{au}^i)$.

  Thus, U'*'s view in i-th round of ideal process is* $UView_{ideal}^i = (ustate^i)$, *and the overall view is just its view in the last round, i.e.,* $UView_{ideal} = UView_{ideal}^i$ *for some i such that* $stop^i = True$.

As we discussed, by employing the outsource-secure techniques, the clients can relieve from carrying out resource-intensive computations locally. Thus, it is reasonable to measure the efficiency of an outsource-secure algorithm (T, U) by comparing the works that T undertakes to those for the state-of-the-art execution of Alg.

Definition 4 (α-efficient, λ-secure outsourcing). *For a pair of λ-outsource-secure algorithms (T, U) which implement an algorithm Alg, they are α-efficient if for any inputs x, the running time of T is less than an α-multiplicative factor of that of $Alg(x)$.*

Definition 5 (β-checkable, λ-secure outsourcing). *For a pair (T, U) of λ-outsource-secure algorithms which implement an algorithm Alg, they are β-checkable if for any inputs x, T can detect any deviations of U' from its advertised functionality during the execution of $T^{U'(x)}$ with probability at least β.*

In practice, the cloud server can only misbehave with very small probability. Otherwise, it will be caught after outsourcing invocations.

Definition 6 ((α, β, λ)-outsource-security). *A pair of algorithms (T, U) are an (α, β, λ)-outsource-secure implementation of an algorithm Alg if they are both α-efficient and β-checkable, λ-secure outsourcing.*

3 Secure Modular Exponentiation Outsourcing

3.1 Preprocessing

In [13, 12], a subroutine *Rand* is used to generate random pairs. On each invocation, *Rand* takes a prime p, a base $g \in \mathbb{Z}_p^*$ and possibly some other values as inputs, and outputs a random, independent pair $(a, g^a \bmod p)$ for some $a \in_R \mathbb{Z}_p^*$. For security, the distribution of *Rand* outputs should be computationally indistinguishable from truly random ones. There are two ways to realize this subroutine. One is to use a trusted server to generate a number of random and independent pairs for T, and the other is let T generate those random pairs by using EBPV generator [29].

In this paper, we provide two preprocessing subroutines for generating random pairs. Both of them take a cyclic group $\mathbb{G} = \langle g \rangle$ of prime order p and possibly some other values as inputs, and output a random, independent pair (a, g^a) for some $a \in_R \mathbb{Z}_p^*$. Besides, those subroutines maintain two tables, i.e., a *static table ST* and a *dynamic table DT*.

BPV$^+$: The first one is called BPV$^+$ which is derived from the BPV generator [30], i.e., by running BPV or EBPV generator totally offline. In detail, BPV$^+$ is described as follows.

- **ST**: T chooses n random numbers $\beta_1, \cdots, \beta_n \in \mathbb{Z}_p^*$, and computes $\nu_i = g^{\beta_i}$ for each $i \in [1, n]$. T stores these n pairs (β_i, ν_i) in the *static* table ST.
- **DT**: T maintains a dynamic table DT, of which each element (α_j, μ_j) can be produced as follows. T chooses a random subset $\mathbb{S} \subseteq \{1, \cdots, n\}$ such that $|\mathbb{S}| = k$ and computes $\alpha_j = \sum_{i \in \mathbb{S}} \beta_i \bmod p$. If $\alpha_j \neq 0 \bmod p$, then compute $\mu_j = \prod_{i \in \mathbb{S}} \nu_i$; otherwise, discard α_j and repeat this procedure. On each invocation of BPV$^+$, T just picks a pair (α, μ) and removes it from DT, and then replenishes some fresh random pairs in its idle time.

SMBL: Another preprocessing algorithm is called *standard multiplication base list* (SMBL), which produces truly random pairs.

- **ST**: T computes $\nu_i = g^{2^i}$ for every $i \in \{0, \cdots, \lceil \log p \rceil\}$ and stores these pairs (i, ν_i) in the *static* table ST. In fact, $\nu_i = \nu_{i-1} \cdot \nu_{i-1}$ for every $i \in \{1, \cdots, \lceil \log p \rceil\}$.
- **DT**: T maintains a dynamic table DT, of which each element (α_j, μ_j) can be produced as follows. T chooses a random value $\alpha_j \in \mathbb{Z}_p^*$ and denotes its i-th bit by $\alpha_{i,j}$. Let $\mathbb{A} \subseteq \{0, \cdots, \lceil \log p \rceil\}$ be the set of i such that $\alpha_{i,j} = 1$. Computes $\mu_j = \prod_{i \in \mathbb{A}} \nu_i$. On each invocation of SMBL, T just picks a pair (α, μ) and removes it from DT, and then replenishes some fresh random pairs afterwards.

Note that, the preprocessing algorithms, i.e., *Rand*, BPV$^+$ and SMBL just deal with exponentiations with some fixed-base g. The comparison between the proposed subroutines is shown in Table 1 in terms of computation and storage costs and randomness of the generated pairs. Here, $|DT|$ and $ES_{\mathbb{G}}$ denote the cardinality of table DT and the element size of group $\mathbb{G}$, respectively. It is easy to see that BPV$^+$ produces statistically indistinguishable random pairs, while SMBL generates truly random ones. Both the computations and the storage of BPV$^+$ with regard to ST are more costly than its counterpart in SMBL. However, if p is large, then the computations of DT in BPV$^+$ are more efficient than that in SMBL, since the parameter k is relatively small compared with p. Thus, BPV$^+$ will be more effective when used in preprocessing or outsourcing schemes that are designed over cyclic groups of large prime orders, such as DSA scheme, El Gamal scheme as well as RSA-type schemes, etc. While SMBL is well-suited for other cases, e.g., in the applications over ECC such as that discussed in Section 4, where a relatively small p is secure enough.

Table 1. Comparison of preprocessing subroutines BPV$^+$ and SMBL

Subroutines		Computation costs	Storage costs	Randomness
BPV$^+$	ST	$n\mathbf{E}$	$n \log p + nES_{\mathbb{G}}$	-
	DT	$|DT|(k-1)\mathbf{A} + |DT|(k-1)\mathbf{M}$	$|DT| \log p + |DT|ES_{\mathbb{G}}$	Statistically indistinguishable
SMBL	ST	$\lceil \log p \rceil \mathbf{M}$	$(\lceil \log p \rceil + 1) \log \log p$ $+(\lceil \log p \rceil + 1)ES_{\mathbb{G}}$	-
	DT	$|DT|\lceil \log p \rceil / 2\mathbf{M}$	$|DT| \log p + |DT|ES_{\mathbb{G}}$	Truly random

(**A**, **M**, and **E** denote addition, multiplication, and exponentiation, respectively.)

3.2 Generic Algorithm for Outsourcing Exponentiations

Let $\mathbb{G}$ be a cyclic group of prime order p and g be a generator. Takes $a_{i,j} \in_R \mathbb{Z}_p$ and $u_{i,j} \in_R \mathbb{G}$ $(1 \leq i \leq r, 1 \leq j \leq s)$ as inputs, the algorithm $GExp$ outputs $(\prod_{j=1}^s u_{1,j}^{a_{1,j}}, \cdots, \prod_{j=1}^s u_{r,j}^{a_{r,j}})$, i.e.,

$$GExp((a_{1,1}, \cdots, a_{1,s}; u_{1,1}, \cdots, u_{1,s}), \cdots, (a_{r,1}, \cdots, a_{r,s}; u_{r,1}, \cdots, u_{r,s}))$$

$$\rightarrow (\prod_{j=1}^{s} u_{1,j}^{a_{1,j}}, \cdots, \prod_{j=1}^{s} u_{r,j}^{a_{r,j}}),$$

where $\{a_{i,j} : 1 \leq i \leq r, 1 \leq j \leq s\}$ may be secret or (honest/adversarial) protected, $\{u_{i,j} : 1 \leq i \leq r, 1 \leq j \leq s\}$ are distinct and may be (honest/adversarial) protected, and $\{\prod_{j=1}^{s} u_{1,j}^{a_{1,j}} : 1 \leq i \leq r\}$ may be secret or protected.

Step 1: T invokes the algorithm BPV$^+$ or SMBL to generate four pairs $(\alpha_1, \mu_1), \cdots, (\alpha_4, \mu_4)$ where $\mu_i = g^{\alpha_i}$. Pick a random value χ such that $\chi \geq 2^\lambda$ where λ is a security parameter, e.g. $\lambda = 64$. For every pair (i, j) such that $1 \leq i \leq r$ and $1 \leq j \leq s$, pick a random number $b_{i,j} \in_R \mathbb{Z}_p^*$ and compute the following values

- $c_{i,j} = a_{i,j} - b_{i,j}\chi \mod p$;
- $w_{i,j} = u_{i,j}/\mu_1$;
- $h_{i,j} = u_{i,j}/\mu_3$;
- $\theta_i = \left(\alpha_1 \sum_{j=1}^{s} b_{i,j} - \alpha_2\right) \chi + \left(\alpha_3 \sum_{j=1}^{s} c_{i,j} - \alpha_4\right) \mod p$.

Step 2: T invokes BPV$^+$ or SMBL to obtain $(t_1, g^{t_1}), \cdots, (t_{r+2}, g^{t_{r+2}})$ and queries the server U in random order as:

$U(\theta_i/t_i, g^{t_i}) \rightarrow B_i$, for every i $(1 \leq i \leq r)$;
$U(\theta/t_{r+1}, g^{t_{r+1}}) \rightarrow A$, where $\theta = t_{r+2} - \sum_{i=1}^{r} \theta_i \mod p$;
$U(b_{i,j}, w_{i,j}) \rightarrow C_{i,j}$, for every i, j $(1 \leq i \leq r, 1 \leq j \leq s)$;
$U(c_{i,j}, h_{i,j}) \rightarrow D_{i,j}$, for every i, j $(1 \leq i \leq r, 1 \leq j \leq s)$.

Step 3: T checks whether $A \cdot \prod_{i=1}^{r} B_i \overset{?}{=} g^{t_{r+2}}$. If it holds, then compute the results as follows, for $1 \leq i \leq r$,

$$\prod_{j=1}^{s} u_{i,j}^{a_{i,j}} = \left(\mu_2 \prod_{j=1}^{s} C_{i,j}\right)^\chi B_i \mu_4 \prod_{j=1}^{s} D_{i,j};$$

otherwise it indicates that U has produced wrong responses, and thus T outputs "error".

3.3   Security Analysis

Lemma 1 (Correctness). *In single untrusted program model, the above algorithms (T, U) are a correct implementation of GExp, where the inputs $\{(a_{i,1}, \cdots, a_{i,s}; u_{i,1}, \cdots, u_{i,s}) : 1 \leq i \leq r\}$ may be honest, secret; or honest, protected; or adversarial, protected.*

Proof. If U performs honestly, we have

$$A \cdot \prod_{i=1}^{r} B_i = g^\theta \cdot \prod_{i=1}^{r} g^{\theta_i} = g^{t_{r+2} - \sum_{i=1}^{r} \theta_i} \cdot \prod_{i=1}^{r} g^{\theta_i} = g^{t_{r+2}},$$

and for every $1 \leq i \leq r$, we have

$$\left(\mu_2 \prod_{j=1}^{s} C_{i,j}\right)^{\chi} B_i \mu_4 \prod_{j=1}^{s} D_{i,j}$$

$$= \left(g^{\alpha_2} \prod_{j=1}^{s} w_{i,j}^{b_{i,j}}\right)^{\chi} g^{\left(\alpha_1 \sum_{j=1}^{s} b_{i,j} - \alpha_2\right)\chi + \left(\alpha_3 \sum_{j=1}^{s} c_{i,j} - \alpha_4\right)} g^{\alpha_4} \prod_{j=1}^{s} h_{i,j}^{c_{i,j}}$$

$$= \left(\prod_{j=1}^{s} w_{i,j}^{b_{i,j}} g^{\alpha_1 \sum_{j=1}^{s} b_{i,j}}\right)^{\chi} g^{\alpha_3 \sum_{j=1}^{s} c_{i,j}} \prod_{j=1}^{s} h_{i,j}^{c_{i,j}}$$

$$= \left(\prod_{j=1}^{s} w_{i,j}^{b_{i,j}} \prod_{j=1}^{s} \mu_1^{b_{i,j}}\right)^{\chi} \prod_{j=1}^{s} \mu_3^{c_{i,j}} \prod_{j=1}^{s} h_{i,j}^{c_{i,j}}$$

$$= \left(\prod_{j=1}^{s} (\mu_1 w_{i,j})^{b_{i,j}}\right)^{\chi} \prod_{j=1}^{s} (\mu_3 h_{i,j})^{c_{i,j}}$$

$$= \left(\prod_{j=1}^{s} u_{i,j}^{b_{i,j}}\right)^{\chi} \prod_{j=1}^{s} u_{i,j}^{c_{i,j}} = \prod_{j=1}^{s} u_{i,j}^{b_{i,j}\chi + c_{i,j}} = \prod_{j=1}^{s} u_{i,j}^{a_{i,j}}.$$

Thus, the correctness follows.   □

Theorem 1 (λ-security). *In single untrusted program model, the above algorithms (T, U) are a λ-outsource-secure implementation of $GExp$, where the inputs $\{(a_{i,1}, \cdots, a_{i,s}; u_{i,1}, \cdots, u_{i,s}) : 1 \leq i \leq r\}$ may be honest, secret; or honest, protected; or adversarial, protected, and all the bases are distinct.*

The proof of Theorem 1 is given in the full version of this paper.

Theorem 2. *In single untrusted program model, the above algorithms (T, U) are an $\left(O\left(\frac{rs + r\log\chi + r}{rs\ell}\right), \frac{r+1}{2rs+r+1}, \lambda\right)$-outsource-secure implementation of $GExp$.*

Proof. On one hand, the well-known square-and-multiply method to calculate one exponentiation u^a takes roughly 1.5ℓ multiplications, where ℓ denotes the bit-length of a. Accordingly, by using this method, it requires roughly $1.5rs\ell$ multiplications for calculating r multi-exponentiations $(\prod_{j=1}^{s} u_{1,j}^{a_{1,j}}, \cdots, \prod_{j=1}^{s} u_{r,j}^{a_{r,j}})$. On the other hand, $GExp$ makes $(r+3)$ inversions and $(5rs + 6r + 1.5r\log\chi + 1)$ multiplications for calculating the same exponentiations. Thus, the algorithms (T, U) are an $O\left(\frac{rs + r\log\chi + r}{rs\ell}\right)$-efficient implementation of $GExp$.

Since U cannot distinguish the test queries from the other real queries that T makes, if it deviates the execution of $GExp$, the deviations of U will be detected with probability $\frac{r+1}{2rs+r+1}$.   □

3.4 Comparisons

We conduct thorough comparisons between our scheme $GExp$ and the up-to-date schemes [13, 14, 12] on outsourcing variable-exponent variable-base exponentiations, in terms of computation and communication costs at the client side, and security properties.

The schemes with regard to computing just one exponentiation are summarized in Table 2, in which $ES_{\mathbb{G}}$ denotes the element size of $\mathbb{G}$. All of those schemes enjoy results checkability of certain levels. Both schemes [12, 13] implemented in two untrusted program model make several invocations to subroutine $Rand$. For each invocation of $Rand$, the online phase will take roughly $(2k + h - 4)$ multiplications by using their suggested EBPV generator, where k is the same parameter as that in BPV$^+$ and $h \geq 1$. Dijk $et\ al.$'s scheme [14] takes about $(3(3 \log s + 2 \log w_s)/2 + 5)$ multiplications where w_s is determined by the security parameter s. In their scheme, one may note that T makes two rounds of interactions with just one untrusted server U for querying 4 powers. Although Dijk $et\ al.$'s scheme [14] is presented in single untrusted program model, the base g is known to the server U.

Table 2. Comparison of securely outsourcing single exponentiation u^a

	Scheme [12]	Scheme [13]	Scheme [14]	Ours
Multiplications	$6O(Rand) + 9$	$5O(Rand) + 7$	$4.5 \log s$ $+3 \log w_s + 5$	$12 + 1.5 \log \chi$
Inversions	5	3	1	4
Queries to U	8	6	4	4
Communications	$8 \log p + 16ES_{\mathbb{G}}$	$6 \log p + 12ES_{\mathbb{G}}$	$2 \log n + 7ES_{\mathbb{G}}$	$4 \log p + 8ES_{\mathbb{G}}$
Privacy	✓	✓	✕	✓
Checkability	1/2	2/3	1	1/2
Security Model	Two UP	Two UP	Single UP	Single UP

("Two/Single UP" denotes Two / Single Untrusted Program Model respectively)

Chen $et\ al.$ [13] also presented an algorithm for outsourcing simultaneous exponentiations in two untrusted program model. A comparison between their scheme [13] and ours is shown in Table 3.

Table 3. Comparison of securely outsourcing simultaneous exponentiation $u_1^{a_1} u_2^{a_2}$

	Scheme [13]	Ours
Multiplications	$5O(Rand) + 10$	$17 + 1.5 \log \chi$
Inversions	3	4
Queries to U	8	6
Communications	$8 \log p + 16ES_{\mathbb{G}}$	$6 \log p + 12ES_{\mathbb{G}}$
Privacy	✓	✓
Checkability	1/2	1/3
Security Model	Two UP	Single UP

4   Securely Offloading PDP

We first review the definition of PDP (e.g., [6, 8]).

Definition 7 (PDP). *A Provable Data Possession scheme consists of five polynomial time computable algorithms, i.e.,* KeyGen, ProFile, Chall, PrfGen *and* Vrfy.

- KeyGen(1^κ) → (pk, sk): *on input 1^κ where $\kappa \in \mathbb{N}$ is a security parameter, the (randomized) key generation algorithm, which is carried out by the cloud clients, generates a pair of public and secret key* (pk, sk).
- ProFile(sk, M) → (t, M^*): *on input a file M and the secret key* sk, *the processing file algorithm, which is carried out by the file owner, generates a file tag t and a processed file M^* for M.*
- Chall(pk, t) → Q: *on input the public key* pk *and a file tag t, the challenge generation algorithm, which is carried out by the verifier, produces a challenge Q.*
- PrfGen(pk, t, M^*, Q) → R: *on input the public key* pk, *a file tag t, a processed file M^* and a challenge Q, the proof generation algorithm, which is carried out by the cloud storage server, produces a response R.*
- Vrfy(pk, sk, t, Q, R) → $\{0, 1\}$: *on the public key* pk, *the secret key* sk, *a file tag t and a challenge-response pair (Q, R), the deterministic verification algorithm outputs "1" if R is a valid response for Q, or "0" otherwise.*

Our schemes are built from bilinear pairings reviewed below. Suppose $\mathbb{G} = \langle g \rangle$ be a cyclic group of prime order p. The group $\mathbb{G}$ is said to be bilinear if there exists a cyclic group $\mathbb{G}_T$ and a bilinear map $\hat{e} : \mathbb{G} \times \mathbb{G} \to \mathbb{G}_T$ such that: (1) Bilinearity: $\forall \mu, \nu \in \mathbb{G}$, and $\forall a, b \in \mathbb{Z}_p$, $\hat{e}(\mu^a, \nu^b) = \hat{e}(\mu, \nu)^{ab}$; (2) Non-degeneracy: $\hat{e}(g, g) \neq 1$ is a generator of $\mathbb{G}_T$.

4.1   Securely Offloading Shacham-Waters PDP

Let $H : \{0, 1\}^* \to \mathbb{G}$ be the collusion-resistant map-to-point hash function (to be modelled as a random oracle) and $\Sigma = (\mathsf{SKG}, \mathsf{SSig}, \mathsf{SVer})$ be the Boneh-Lynn-Shacham signature scheme [31]. We are ready to describe how to securely offload the Shacham-Waters PDP scheme.

KenGen(1^κ) → (pk, sk): First generate a random signing key pair $(spk, ssk) \leftarrow \Sigma.\mathsf{SKG}(1^\kappa)$. Then random pick $\alpha \leftarrow_R \mathbb{Z}_p^*$ and compute $v = g^\alpha$. Thus, the public key and secret key are pk = (v, spk) and sk = (α, ssk), respectively.

ProFile(sk, M) → (t, M^*): Given a file M, split it into blocks such that each block has s sectors, i.e., $M = \{M_i = (m_{i,1}, \cdots, m_{i,s}) : 1 \leq i \leq n\}$. Parse sk to get (α, ssk). Then, choose a random file name $name \in_R \mathbb{Z}_p^*$ and s random elements $u_1, \cdots, u_s \in_R \mathbb{G}$. Let $t_0 = name \parallel n \parallel u_1 \parallel \cdots \parallel u_s$. Compute the file tag as $t \leftarrow t_0 \parallel \Sigma.\mathsf{SSig}_{ssk}(t_0) = t_0 \parallel GExp(ssk; H(t_0))$. For each file block M_i ($1 \leq i \leq n$), compute $h_i = H(name \parallel i)$ and invoke $GExp$ to generate metadata σ_i as

$$\sigma_i \leftarrow GExp(\alpha, \alpha m_{i,1}, \cdots, \alpha m_{i,s}; h_i, u_1, \cdots, u_s).$$

Then, send the processed file $M^* = \{m_{i,j}\}_{1 \leq i \leq n, 1 \leq j \leq s} \cup \{\sigma_i\}_{1 \leq i \leq n}$ to the cloud storage server.

Chall(pk, t) $\rightarrow$ Q: Parse pk as (v, spk) and use spk to validate t. If it is invalid, output 0 and terminate; otherwise, parse t to obtain $(name, n, u_1, \cdots, u_s)$. Pick a random subset $I \subseteq [1, n]$ and a random value $v_i \in_R \mathbb{Z}_p^*$ for each $i \in I$. Send $Q = \{(i, v_i) : i \in I\}$ to the cloud storage server.

PrfGen(pk, t, M^*, Q) $\rightarrow$ R: Parse the processed file M^* as $\{m_{i,j}\}_{1 \leq i \leq n, 1 \leq j \leq s} \cup \{\sigma_i\}_{1 \leq i \leq n}$, and the challenge Q to obtain $\{(i, v_i) : i \in I\}$. Compute

$$\mu_j = \sum_{(i,v_i) \in Q} v_i m_{i,j} \in \mathbb{Z}_p, \text{ and } \sigma = \prod_{(i,v_i) \in Q} \sigma_i^{v_i} \in \mathbb{G}.$$

Then send $R = (\mu_1, \cdots, \mu_s, \sigma)$ to the verifier.

Vrfy(pk, sk, t, Q, R) $\rightarrow$ $\{0, 1\}$: Parse R to obtain $(\mu_1, \cdots, \mu_s) \in (\mathbb{Z}_p)^s$ and $\sigma \in \mathbb{G}$. If parsing fails, output 0 and terminate. Otherwise, compute $h_i = H(name \parallel i)$ for each $i \in I$ and

$$\rho = GExp\Big((v_i)_{(i,v_i) \in Q}, \mu_1, \cdots, \mu_s; (h_i)_{(i,v_i) \in Q}, u_1, \cdots, u_s\Big).$$

Check whether $\hat{e}(\sigma, g) \stackrel{?}{=} \hat{e}(\rho, v)$ holds; if so, output 1; otherwise, output 0.

Correctness. If the computation server performs honestly, we have

$$\sigma_i = GExp(\alpha, \alpha m_{i,1}, \cdots, \alpha m_{i,s}; h_i, u_1, \cdots, u_s)$$

$$= h_i^\alpha \cdot \prod_{j=1}^s u_j^{\alpha m_{i,j}} = \left(H(name \parallel i) \cdot \prod_{j=1}^s u_j^{m_{i,j}} \right)^\alpha.$$

$$\rho = GExp\Big((v_i)_{(i,v_i) \in Q}, \mu_1, \cdots, \mu_s; (h_i)_{(i,v_i) \in Q}, u_1, \cdots, u_s\Big)$$

$$= \prod_{(i,v_i) \in Q} h_i^{v_i} \cdot \prod_{j=1}^s u_j^{\mu_j} = \prod_{(i,v_i) \in Q} H(name \parallel i)^{v_i} \cdot \prod_{j=1}^s u_j^{\mu_j}.$$

The correctness of the file tag generation is straightforward.

4.2 Securely Offloading a Variant of Yuan-Yu PDP

In the following, for a given vector $c = (c_0, \cdots, c_{s-1})$ for $c_i \in \mathbb{Z}_p$, we use $f_c(x)$ to denote the polynomial defined as $f_c(x) = \sum_{i=0}^{s-1} c_i x^i$ over $\mathbb{Z}_p$.

KenGen(1^κ) $\rightarrow$ (pk, sk): First generate a random signing key pair $(spk, ssk) \leftarrow \Sigma.\mathsf{SKG}(1^\kappa)$. Then pick two random values $\alpha, \beta \leftarrow_R \mathbb{Z}_p^*$, and compute $\gamma = g^\beta$, $\lambda = g^{\alpha\beta}$ and $\{g^{\alpha^j} : j \in [0, s-1]\}$. Thus, the public key and secret key are $pk = (\gamma, \lambda, spk, g, g^\alpha, \cdots, g^{\alpha^{s-1}})$ and $sk = (\alpha, \beta, ssk)$, respectively.

ProFile(sk, M) $\rightarrow$ (t, M^*): Given a file M, split it into blocks such that each block has s sectors, i.e., $M = \{M_i = (m_{i,0}, \cdots, m_{i,s-1}) : 1 \leq i \leq n\}$. Choose a random file name $name \in_R \mathbb{Z}_p^*$ and set $t_0 = name \parallel n$. Compute the file tag as $t \leftarrow t_0 \parallel \Sigma.\mathsf{SSig}_{ssk}(t_0) = t_0 \parallel GExp(ssk; H(t_0))$. For each file block M_i $(1 \leq i \leq n)$:

- compute $h_i = H(name \parallel i)$ and $f_i = \beta \cdot f_{\pi_i}(\alpha) = \beta \sum_{j=0}^{s-1} m_{i,j} \alpha^j \mod p$;
- invoke $GExp$ to generate metadata, i.e., $\sigma_i \leftarrow GExp(\beta, f_i; h_i, g)$.

Then, send the processed file $M^* = \{m_{i,j}\}_{1 \leq i \leq n, 0 \leq j \leq s-1} \cup \{\sigma_i\}_{1 \leq i \leq n}$ to the cloud storage server.

Chall$(\mathsf{pk}, t) \to Q$: Parse pk to obtain spk and use it to validate the signature on t. If it is invalid, output 0 and terminate; otherwise, parse t to obtain $(name, n)$. Pick a random subset $I \subseteq [1, n]$ and a random value $v_i \in_R \mathbb{Z}_p^*$ for each $i \in I$. Choose another random value $r \in_R \mathbb{Z}_p^*$ and send $Q = \{r, (i, v_i) : i \in I\}$ to the cloud storage server.

PrfGen$(\mathsf{pk}, t, M^*, Q) \to R$: Parse the processed file M^* as $\{m_{i,j}\}_{1 \leq i \leq n, 1 \leq j \leq s} \cup \{\sigma_i\}_{1 \leq i \leq n}$, and the challenge Q to obtain $\{r, (i, v_i) : i \in I\}$. Compute

$$\mu_j = \sum_{(i,v_i) \in Q} v_i m_{i,j} \in \mathbb{Z}_p, \text{ and } \sigma = \prod_{(i,v_i) \in Q} \sigma_i^{v_i} \in \mathbb{G}.$$

Define a polynomial $f_\mu(x) = \sum_{j=0}^{s-1} \mu_j x^j \mod p$ and calculate $y = f_\mu(r)$. Then compute the polynomial $f_\omega(x) = \frac{f_\mu(x) - f_\mu(r)}{x - r}$ using polynomial long division, and denote its coefficient vector as $\omega = (\omega_0, \cdots, \omega_{s-2})$. Compute $\psi = g^{f_\omega(\alpha)} = \prod_{j=0}^{s-2} (g^{\alpha^j})^{\omega_j}$ and send $R = (\psi, y, \sigma)$ to the verifier.

Vrfy$(\mathsf{pk}, \mathsf{sk}, t, Q, R) \to \{0, 1\}$: After receiving the proof response R, the verifier parses it to obtain (ψ, y, σ) and parses t to obtain $(name, n)$. If parsing fails, output 0 and halting. Otherwise, compute $h_i = H(name \parallel i)$ for each $i \in I$, and invoke $GExp$ to compute

$$\rho = GExp\Big(y, -r, (v_i)_{(i,v_i) \in Q}; g, \psi, (h_i)_{(i,v_i) \in Q}\Big).$$

If $\hat{e}(\sigma, g) = \hat{e}(\psi, \lambda)\hat{e}(\rho, \gamma)$ holds, then output 1; otherwise, output 0.

Correctness. It is easy to see that, if both the computation server and the storage server perform honestly, we have

$$\sigma_i = GExp(\beta, f_i; h_i, g) = h_i^\beta \cdot g^{\beta f_{\pi_i}(\alpha)} = H(name \parallel i)^\beta \cdot g^{\beta \sum_{j=0}^{s-1} m_{i,j} \alpha^j}$$

$$= \Big(H(name \parallel i) \cdot g^{\sum_{j=0}^{s-1} m_{i,j} \alpha^j}\Big)^\beta = \Big(H(name \parallel i) \cdot \prod_{j=0}^{s-1} g^{m_{i,j} \alpha^j}\Big)^\beta.$$

$$\rho = GExp\Big(y, -r, (v_i)_{(i,v_i) \in Q}; g, \psi, (h_i)_{(i,v_i) \in Q}\Big)$$

$$= g^y \psi^{-r} \prod_{(i,v_i) \in Q} h_i^{v_i} = g^y \psi^{-r} \prod_{(i,v_i) \in Q} H(name \parallel i)^{v_i}.$$

The correctness of file tag generation is straightforward. Specifically,

$$
\hat{e}(\sigma, g) = \hat{e}\Big(\prod_{(i,v_i)\in Q} \sigma_i^{v_i}, g \Big)
$$

$$
= \hat{e}\Big(\prod_{(i,v_i)\in Q} \big(H(name \parallel i) \cdot g^{f_{\pi_i}(\alpha)} \big)^{v_i \beta}, g \Big)
$$

$$
= \hat{e}\Big(\prod_{(i,v_i)\in Q} H(name \parallel i)^{v_i}, g^\beta \Big) \hat{e}\Big(g^{\beta \sum_{(i,v_i)\in Q} v_i f_{\pi_i}(\alpha)}, g \Big)
$$

$$
= \hat{e}\Big(\prod_{(i,v_i)\in Q} H(name \parallel i)^{v_i}, g^\beta \Big) \hat{e}\big(g^{f_\mu(\alpha)}, g^\beta \big).
$$

$$
\hat{e}(\psi, \lambda)\hat{e}(\rho, \gamma) = \hat{e}\Big(g^{f_\omega(\alpha)}, g^{\alpha\beta} \Big) \hat{e}\Big(g^y \psi^{-r} \prod_{(i,v_i)\in Q} H(name \parallel i)^{v_i}, g^\beta \Big)
$$

$$
= \hat{e}\Big(g^{\alpha f_\omega(\alpha)}, g^\beta \Big) \hat{e}\Big(g^{f_\mu(r)} g^{-r f_\omega(\alpha)} \prod_{(i,v_i)\in Q} H(name \parallel i)^{v_i}, g^\beta \Big)
$$

$$
= \hat{e}\Big(g^{(\alpha-r)f_\omega(\alpha)+f_\mu(r)}, g^\beta \Big) \hat{e}\Big(\prod_{(i,v_i)\in Q} H(name \parallel i)^{v_i}, g^\beta \Big)
$$

$$
= \hat{e}\big(g^{f_\mu(\alpha)-f_\mu(r)+f_\mu(r)}, g^\beta \big) \hat{e}\Big(\prod_{(i,v_i)\in Q} H(name \parallel i)^{v_i}, g^\beta \Big)
$$

$$
= \hat{e}\big(g^{f_\mu(\alpha)}, g^\beta \big) \hat{e}\Big(\prod_{(i,v_i)\in Q} H(name \parallel i)^{v_i}, g^\beta \Big).
$$

4.3   Efficiency Analysis

The original Shacham-Waters PDP [8] takes many exponentiations in algorithm ProFile and algorithm Vrfy. For processing a file $M = \{M_i = (m_{i,0}, \cdots, m_{i,s-1}) : 1 \le i \le n\}$, the file owner takes 1 exponentiation and $(s + 1)$ exponentiations for producing the file tag and one metadata, respectively. While the verifier takes $(|I| + s)$ exponentiations during the verification phase. In our variant of the Yuan-Yu PDP [11], since α is a secret key, we assume $\alpha^2, \cdots, \alpha^{s-1}$ have been pre-calculated by the file owner. Thus, the algorithm ProFile and algorithm Vrfy take $(2n + 1)$ and $(|I| + 2)$ exponentiations, respectively. We compare the computation costs as well as the communication overheads between the client and the untrusted computation server of the schemes with/without outsourcing exponentiations in Table 4. It can be seen that offloading makes both schemes much more efficient.

Table 4. Comparison of Two PDP Schemes with and without Outsourcing

	Original scheme	Outsourced scheme	
		Computation costs	Communication costs
		Shacham-Waters PDP	
File tag generation	1h + 1E	1h + (12 + 1.5 log χ)M + 4I	4 log p + 8ES_G
Each metadata generation	1h + sM + (s + 1)E	1h + 4I +(6s + 1.5 log χ + 12)M	(2s + 4) log p +(4s + 8)ES_G
Verification	$\lvert I\rvert$h + ($\lvert I\rvert$ + s − 1)M +($\lvert I\rvert$ + s)E + 2P	(5$\lvert I\rvert$ + 5s + 1.5 log χ + 7)M +$\lvert I\rvert$h + 4I + 2P	(2$\lvert I\rvert$ + 2s + 2) log p +(4$\lvert I\rvert$ + 4s + 4)ES_G
		Our Variant of Yuan-Yu PDP	
File tag generation	1h + 1E	1h + (12 + 1.5 log χ)M + 4I	4 log p + 8ES_G
Each metadata generation	1h + sM + 2E	1h + 4I +(s + 1.5 log χ + 17)M	6 log p + 12ES_G
Verification	$\lvert I\rvert$h + ($\lvert I\rvert$ + 2)M +($\lvert I\rvert$ + 2)E + 3P	$\lvert I\rvert$h + 4I + 3P +(5$\lvert I\rvert$ + 1.5 log χ + 18)M	(2$\lvert I\rvert$ + 6) log p +(4$\lvert I\rvert$ + 12)ES_G

Notations: h denotes hash evaluation; M, I and E denote one multiplication, one inversion and one exponentiation, respectively; P denotes one bilinear pairing evaluation.

5   Concluding Remark

Outsourcing storage can save the cost of a client in maintaining the storage locally. Cryptographic approaches like provable data possession ensures the integrity of the outsourced file can still be verified, yet these often require modular exponentiations expensive to computationally bounded devices. We filled this gap with offloaded PDP by securely and efficiently outsourcing the most generic variable-exponent variable-base exponentiations to one untrusted computation server. Compared with the known schemes, our scheme is not only superior in its security model, but also its efficiency, interactions and privacy. Our protocol may find applications in many other cryptographic solutions which use number-theoretic cryptographic techniques.

Acknowledgements and Disclaimer. We appreciate the anonymous reviewers for their valuable suggestions. Qianhong Wu is the corresponding author. This work is supported by the National Key Basic Research Program (973 program) through project 2012CB315905, by the National Nature Science Foundation of China through projects 61272501, 61173154, 61370190 and 61003214, by a grant from the RGC of the HKSAR, China, under Project CityU 123913, by the Beijing Natural Science Foundation through project 4132056, by the Fundamental Research Funds for the Central Universities, and the Research Funds (No. 14XNLF02) of Renmin University of China and by the Open Research Fund of Beijing Key Laboratory of Trusted Computing. Sherman Chow is supported by the Early Career Scheme and the Early Career Award of the Research Grants

Council, Hong Kong SAR (CUHK 439713), and grants (4055018, 4930034) from Chinese University of Hong Kong.

References

1. Deng, H., Wu, Q., Qin, B., Chow, S.S.M., Domingo-Ferrer, J., Shi, W.: Tracing and Revoking Leaked Credentials: Accountability in Leaking Sensitive Outsourced Data. In: 9th ACM Symposium on Information, Computer and Communications Security (ASIACCS), pp. 425–443. ACM, New York (2014)
2. Deng, H., Wu, Q., Qin, B., Domingo-Ferrer, J., Zhang, L., Liu, J., Shi, W.: Ciphertext-Policy Hierarchical Attribute-Based Encryption with Short Ciphertexts. Information Sciences 275, 370–384 (2014)
3. Deng, H., Wu, Q., Qin, B., Mao, J., Liu, X., Zhang, L., Shi, W.: Who is touching my cloud. In: Kutylowski, M., Vaidya, J. (eds.) ESORICS 2014. LNCS, vol. 8712, pp. 362–379. Springer, Heidelberg (2014)
4. Chow, S.S.M., Yiu, S.M., Hui, L.C.K., Chow, K.P.: Efficient Forward and Provably Secure ID-Based Signcryption Scheme with Public Verifiability and Public Ciphertext Authenticity. In: Lim, J.-I., Lee, D.-H. (eds.) ICISC 2003. LNCS, vol. 2971, pp. 352–369. Springer, Heidelberg (2004)
5. Qin, B., Wang, H., Wu, Q., Liu, J., Domingo-Ferrer, J.: Simultaneous Authentication and Secrecy in Identity-Based Data Upload to Cloud. Cluster Computing 16, 845–859 (2013)
6. Ateniese, G., Burns, R., Curtmola, R., Herring, J., Kissner, L., Peterson, Z., Song, D.: Provable Data Possession at Untrusted Stores. In: 14th ACM Conference on Computer and Communications Security (CCS), pp. 598–609. ACM, New York (2007)
7. Juels, A., Kaliski Jr., B.S.: PoRs: Proofs of Retrievability for Large Files. In: 14th ACM Conference on Computer and Communications Security (CCS), pp. 584–597. ACM, New York (2007)
8. Shacham, H., Waters, B.: Compact Proofs of Retrievability. In: Pieprzyk, J. (ed.) ASIACRYPT 2008. LNCS, vol. 5350, pp. 90–107. Springer, Heidelberg (2008)
9. Wang, B., Chow, S.S.M., Li, M., Li, H.: Storing Shared Data on the Cloud via Security-Mediator. In: 33rd IEEE International Conference on Distributed Computing Systems (ICDCS), pp. 124–133 (2013)
10. Wang, C., Chow, S.S.M., Wang, Q., Ren, K., Lou, W.: Privacy-Preserving Public Auditing for Secure Cloud Storage. IEEE Transactions on Computers 62(2), 362–375 (2013)
11. Yuan, J., Yu, S.: Proofs of Retrievability with Public Verifiability and Constant Communication Cost in Cloud. In: International Workshop on Security in Cloud Computing, pp. 19–26. ACM, New York (2013)
12. Hohenberger, S., Lysyanskaya, A.: How to Securely Outsource Cryptographic Computations. In: Kilian, J. (ed.) TCC 2005. LNCS, vol. 3378, pp. 264–282. Springer, Heidelberg (2005)
13. Chen, X., Li, J., Ma, J., Tang, Q., Lou, W.: New Algorithms for Secure Outsourcing of Modular Exponentiations. In: Foresti, S., Yung, M., Martinelli, F. (eds.) ESORICS 2012. LNCS, vol. 7459, pp. 541–556. Springer, Heidelberg (2012)
14. Dijk, M., Clarke, D., Gassend, B., Suh, G., Devadas, S.: Speeding up Exponentiation using an Untrusted Computational Resource. Designs, Codes and Cryptography 39(2), 253–273 (2006)

15. Wang, H., Wu, Q., Qin, B., Domingo-Ferrer, J.: Identity-Based Remote Data Possession Checking in Public Clouds. Information Security, IET 8(2), 114–121 (2014)
16. Kate, A., Zaverucha, G.M., Goldberg, I.: Constant-Size Commitments to Polynomials and Their Applications. In: Abe, M. (ed.) ASIACRYPT 2010. LNCS, vol. 6477, pp. 177–194. Springer, Heidelberg (2010)
17. Benabbas, S., Gennaro, R., Vahlis, Y.: Verifiable Delegation of Computation over Large Datasets. In: Rogaway, P. (ed.) CRYPTO 2011. LNCS, vol. 6841, pp. 111–131. Springer, Heidelberg (2011)
18. Li, J., Tan, X., Chen, X., Wong, D.S.: An Efficient Proof of Retrievability with Public Auditing in Cloud Computing. In: 5th International Conference on Intelligent Networking and Collaborative Systems (INCoS), pp. 93–98 (2013)
19. Ma, X., Li, J., Zhang, F.: Outsourcing Computation of Modular Exponentiations in Cloud Computing. Cluster Computing 16(4), 787–796 (2013)
20. Tsang, P.P., Chow, S.S.M., Smith, S.W.: Batch Pairing Delegation. In: Miyaji, A., Kikuchi, H., Rannenberg, K. (eds.) IWSEC 2007. LNCS, vol. 4752, pp. 74–90. Springer, Heidelberg (2007)
21. Canard, S., Devigne, J., Sanders, O.: Delegating a Pairing Can Be Both Secure and Efficient. In: Boureanu, I., Owesarski, P., Vaudenay, S. (eds.) ACNS 2014. LNCS, vol. 8479, pp. 549–565. Springer, Heidelberg (2014)
22. Xu, G., Amariucai, G., Guan, Y.: Delegation of Computation with Verification Outsourcing: Curious Verifiers. In: ACM Symposium on Principles of Distributed Computing (PODC), pp. 393–402. ACM, New York (2013)
23. Gennaro, R., Gentry, C., Parno, B.: Non-interactive Verifiable Computing: Outsourcing Computation to Untrusted Workers. In: Rabin, T. (ed.) CRYPTO 2010. LNCS, vol. 6223, pp. 465–482. Springer, Heidelberg (2010)
24. Carter, H., Mood, B., Traynor, P., Butler, K.: Secure Outsourced Garbled Circuit Evaluation for Mobile Devices. In: 22nd USENIX Conference on Security, pp. 289–304. USENIX Association, Berkeley (2013)
25. Zhang, L.F., Safavi-Naini, R.: Private Outsourcing of Polynomial Evaluation and Matrix Multiplication Using Multilinear Maps. In: Abdalla, M., Nita-Rotaru, C., Dahab, R. (eds.) CANS 2013. LNCS, vol. 8257, pp. 329–348. Springer, Heidelberg (2013)
26. Wang, B., Li, M., Chow, S.S.M., Li, H.: Computing Encrypted Cloud Data Efficiently Under Multiple Keys. In: 4th IEEE Security and Privacy in Cloud Computing, co-located with IEEE Conference on Communications and Network Security (CNS), pp. 504–513 (2013)
27. Wang, B., Li, M., Chow, S.S.M., Li, H.: A Tale of Two Servers: Efficient Privacy-Preserving Computation over Cloud Data under Multiple Keys. In: 2nd IEEE Conference on Communications and Network Security, CNS (2014)
28. Chow, S.S.M., Lee, J.H., Subramanian, L.: Two-Party Computation Model for Privacy-Preserving Queries over Distributed Databases. In: Network and Distributed System Security Symposium, NDSS (2009)
29. Nguyen, P., Shparlinski, I.E., Stern, J.: Distribution of Modular Sums and the Security of the Server Aided Exponentiation. In: Cryptography and Computational Number Theory. Progress in Computer Science and Applied Logic, vol. 20, pp. 331–342. Birkhäuser, Basel (2001)
30. Boyko, V., Peinado, M., Venkatesan, R.: Speeding up Discrete Log and Factoring Based Schemes via Precomputations. In: Nyberg, K. (ed.) EUROCRYPT 1998. LNCS, vol. 1403, pp. 221–235. Springer, Heidelberg (1998)
31. Boneh, D., Lynn, B., Shacham, H.: Short Signatures from the Weil Pairing. Journal of Cryptology 17(4), 297–319 (2004)

Quantitative Workflow Resiliency

John C. Mace, Charles Morisset, and Aad van Moorsel

Centre for Cybercrime & Computer Security,
Newcastle University, Newcastle upon Tyne,
NE1 7RU, United Kingdom
{j.c.mace,charles.morisset,aad.vanmoorsel}@ncl.ac.uk

Abstract. A workflow is resilient when the unavailability of some users does not force to choose between a violation of the security policy or an early termination of the workflow. Although checking for the resiliency of a workflow is a well-studied problem, solutions usually only provide a binary answer to the problem, leaving a workflow designer with little help when the workflow is not resilient. We propose in this paper to provide instead a measure of *quantitative resiliency*, indicating how much a workflow is likely to terminate for a given security policy and a given user availability model. We define this notion by encoding the resiliency problem as a decision problem, reducing the finding of an optimal user-task assignment to that of solving a Markov Decision Process. We illustrate the flexibility of our encoding by considering different measures of resiliency, and we empirically analyse them, showing the existence of a trade-off between multiple aspects such as success rate, expected termination step and computation time, thus providing a toolbox that could help a workflow designer to improve or fix a workflow.

Keywords: Workflow Satisfiability Problem, Markov Decision Process, Quantitative Analysis.

1 Introduction

A workflow is the automation of a business process comprising tasks and predicate conditions defining their partial order [1]. Ensuring all workflow instances complete means assigning each task to a user in accordance with business rules specifying when and by whom workflow data may be accessed and modified. From a security perspective, access management ensures users with the correct clearance and capabilities are matched with appropriate tasks while reducing the threat of collusion and fraud. Each user-task assignment may have to satisfy many different kind of security constraints [2, 3, 4], the three most common being: *i*) the user must be authorised to perform the task; *ii*) if the task is related to another task through a *binding of duty*, then the same user should perform both tasks; *iii*) if the task is related to another task through a *separation of duty*, then the same user cannot perform both tasks.

The Workflow Satisfiability Problem (WSP) [5, 6] therefore consists in finding a user-task assignment ensuring both the termination of all instances and the

M. Kutyłowski and J. Vaidya (Eds.): ESORICS 2014, Part I, LNCS 8712, pp. 344–361, 2014.

non-violation of the security constraints, especially in highly dynamic environments, subject to unpredictable events such as user unavailability. This can be an issue for dynamic workflow management systems whose choices made for early tasks can constrict later assignments [7]. In extreme cases, bad assignments will remove all assignment options for an upcoming task and block a workflow from completing [8, 9]. It is therefore important these workflows can be appraised before enactment via suitable tools and useable metrics that aid workflow configuration and formulation of contingency plans, such as *resiliency* [6], which checks whether the unavailability of some users has an impact on satisfiability.

Most existing approaches, e.g. [10, 11, 12, 13, 6], address the WSP from a computational point-of-view, by finding the most efficient algorithm to compute a suitable assignment, which either return a correct assignment if it exists, or nothing. In practice finding such an assignment can be demanding and often unmanageable, especially when facing unforeseen and emergency situations. For example, despite the provision of guidelines stipulating many public service staffing levels (e.g. [14]), high sickness rates, budget cuts, staff shortage, increased workloads and unpredictability all contribute to critical workflows often being attempted without enough available users.

Taking a binary approach therefore fails to address a number of real-life issues where the ideal case is not always reachable. Indeed, declaring a workflow to be either resilient or not may be of little practical use to a workflow designer. Of course, a satisfiable workflow is always better than an unsatisfiable one but a workflow where all but one instance can be correctly assigned provides on average, a better service than one where no instance can be assigned. In addition, if both workflows terminate early instead of violating the policy, they are both better than a workflow violating the policy.

In this paper we take the stance to provide a workflow designer with quantitative measures, indicating a degree of satisfaction and/or resiliency for a given workflow, instead of simply returning an assignment if one exists. In order to do so, we propose to model the WSP as a decision problem, in order to benefit from the extensive collections of tools related to the discipline. More precisely, the contributions of this paper are as follows:

- We first encode the workflow satisfaction problem as finding the optimal solution of a Markov Decision Process (MDP);
- We then encode the *decremental resiliency* problem [6] as an extension of the above one, by modelling user availability in the state of the MDP;
- We illustrate the flexibility of our model by showing how a simple change of the reward function can move the focus from the normal termination rate of the workflow to the expected termination step, and we show on a simple use case that both approaches are in general incomparable, and that in general, finding the optimal assignment requires addressing a trade-off between multiple aspects, including computation time.

Is is important to note that the focus of this paper is not to provide a particularly efficient solution to the WSP, but to propose a novel approach of this problem.

We however believe our approach paves the way to defining an efficient solution by using the extensive literature dedicated to the efficient solving of an MDP.

The rest of this paper is as follows. Section 2 gives a brief overview of related work while Section 3 revisits the workflow satisfiability problem and defines it as an MDP. In Section 4 we define quantitative measures for workflow satisfaction and resiliency. An assessment of our approach is given in Section 5 and concluding remarks in Section 6.

2   Related Work

A number of previous studies on workflow resiliency appear in the literature. Wang et al. took a first step in [6] to quantify resiliency by addressing the problem of whether a workflow can still complete in the absence of users and defined a workflow as k resilient to all failures of up to k users across an entire workflow. Lowalekar et al. show in [15] multiple assignments may provide the same level of k resiliency and give a technique for selecting the most favourable using security attributes that minimize the diffusion of business knowledge across all users.

Basin et al. in [8, 16] allow the reallocation of roles to users thus overcoming workflow blocks created by user failure. This is feasible in certain business domains but may have limited application in public service workflows where roles are more specialised; a nurse cannot step in for a doctor for example. Wainer et al. consider in [17] the explicit overriding of security constraints in workflows, by defining a notion of privilege. Similarly, Bakkali [18] suggests introducing resiliency through delegation and the placement of criticality values over workflows. Delegates are chosen on their suitability but may lack competence; this is considered the 'price to pay' for resiliency. As delegation takes place at a task level it is not currently clear whether a workflow can still complete while meeting security constraints.

A more practical approach is presented by Mace et al. [19] and more formally by Watson [20] who discuss the practicalities of assigning workflows, or parts of workflow across multiple cloud-based platforms while ensuring security constraints are met. Discussion is given on the various trade-offs that must be considered including performance and security risks. Current literature does not address the issue of workflows that must execute but may not be satisfiable nor resilient in every instance. Neither does it provide quantitative measures to analyse and optimise workflows in such cases, which is the focus of this paper.

3   The Workflow Satisfiability Problem

In a nutshell, the Workflow Satisfiability Problem (WSP) [6] consists in assigning each user to a task for a given workflow such that all security constraints are met. Whereas existing work mostly considers WSP as a constraint solving problem (for instance as the graph k-colouring problem when the workflow contains separation of duties constraints [6, 16]), we propose to consider it as a

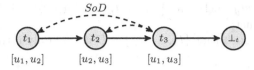

Fig. 1. Running example

Table 1. Workflow assignments

	a_1	a_2	a_3	a_4
t_1	u_1	u_2	u_2	u_2
t_2	u_2	u_2	u_2	u_3
t_3	u_3	u_1	u_3	u_1

decision problem[1], thus modelling the decision made to assign a user to a task in a given context. Hence, we define below an encoding of the WSP as solving a Markov Decision Process (MDP) [21]. We first propose a definition of workflow, which, although driven by the MDP encoding, is general enough to consider complex workflows. After briefly recalling the notion of MDP, we then present the corresponding MDP encoding and the definition of the WSP.

3.1   Workflow

As described in Section 2, there exist several definitions of workflow in the literature. They commonly define a set of users $\mathcal{U}$ and a set of tasks $\mathcal{T}$, structured to indicate which sequences of tasks can be executed, for instance with a partial ordering over tasks. For the sake of generality, we consider a *task manager*, which is a function $\tau : \mathcal{T} \times \mathcal{U} \to \mathcal{P}(\mathcal{T})^2$. In other words, given a task t and a user u, $\tau(t, u)$ is a probability function over tasks indicating the probability of each task to be the next one.

The set of tasks contains an initial task $t_0 \in \mathcal{T}$, and in order to model the fact that a workflow can finish we consider a special task $\perp_t \in \mathcal{T}$, such that, given any user u, $\tau(\perp_t, u) = \perp_t$[3]

Running Example. *As a running example to illustrate the different concepts presented here, we consider the workflow shown in Figure 1 where $\mathcal{T} = \{t_1, t_2, t_3\}$ and where the only possible sequence is $t_1; t_2; t_3$. Hence, the initial task is t_1, and the task manager is defined as, for any user u, $\tau(t_1, u) = t_2$, $\tau(t_2, u) = t_3$, and $\tau(t_3, u) = \perp_t$.*

The second common aspect of workflows across existing definitions is to define a set of users $\mathcal{U}$ coming with a security policy over the set of tasks $\mathcal{T}$, including basic user permissions, separations and bindings of duties, expressed as sets of constraints. Hence, we consider security policies of the form $p = (P, S, B)$ where

- $P \subseteq U \times T$ are *user-task permissions*, such that $(u, t) \in P$ if, and only if u is allowed to perform t;

---

[1] It is worth noting that in the end, both perspectives can join, for instance by solving the decision problem using Linear Programming.

[2] Given a set X, we write $\mathcal{P}(X)$ for the set of functions $f : X \to [0, 1]$, such that $\sum_{x \in X} f(x) = 1$.

[3] For the sake of simplicity, we write $f(x) = y$ whenever $f(x, y) = 1$, where $f(x) \in \mathcal{P}(Y)$, for some Y. In this case, we say that $f(x)$ is *deterministic*.

- $S \subseteq \wp(T)^4$ are *separations of duty*, such that $\{t_1, \ldots, t_n\} \in S$ if, and only if each user assigned to t_i is distinct;
- $B \subseteq \wp(T)$ are *bindings of duty*, such that $\{t_1, \ldots, t_n\} \in B$ if, and only if the same user is assigned to all t_i;

Running Example. *We now consider a set of users* $U = \{u_1, u_2, u_3, u_4\}$ *and a security policy* $p_1 = (P_1, S_1, B_1)$ *that states:*

- $P_1 = \{(u_1, t_1), (u_2, t_1), (u_2, t_2), (u_3, t_2), (u_1, t_3), (u_3, t_3)\}$
- $S_1 = \{\{t_1, t_3\}, \{t_2, t_3\}\}$
- $B_1 = \emptyset$

Figure 1 illustrates this security policy, where a dotted arrow signifies a constraint given in p between the tasks t and t'. A label $[u_m, \ldots, u_n]$ *states the users that are authorised by P to execute t.*

A workflow therefore consists of both a set of tasks, with a task manager and a set of users, with a security policy.

Definition 1 (Workflow). *A workflow is a tuple* $W = (\mathcal{U}, \mathcal{T}, \tau, t_0, p)$*, where* $\mathcal{U}$ *is a set of users,* $\mathcal{T}$ *is a set of tasks,* τ *is a task manager,* t_0 *is the initial task and p is a security policy.*

3.2   Workflow Assignment

A *user-task assignment* is a relation $UA \subseteq \mathcal{U} \times \mathcal{T}$, associating each t_i with some u_i. Given a policy $p = (P, S, B)$, UA satisfies p, and in this case, we write $UA \vdash p$, if, and only if the three following conditions are met:

$$UA \subseteq P \tag{1}$$

$$\forall s \in S \, \forall u \in \mathcal{U} \quad |\{t \in s \mid (u, t) \in UA\}| \leq 1 \tag{2}$$

$$\forall b \in B \quad |\{u \in \mathcal{U} \mid \exists t \in b \, (u, t) \in UA\}| \leq 1 \tag{3}$$

In our running example, Table 1 provides all workflow assignments satisfying p_1, such that each a_i is represented as a function from task to users. For instance, a_2 assigns t_1 and t_2 to u_2 and t_3 to u_1. An *instance* of a workflow is a sequence of tasks $(t_1, \ldots, t_n)$ such that $\tau(t_i, u, t_{i+1}) \neq 0$, for any i and any user u. Informally, the WSP consists of defining a relation UA such that, for any instance of a workflow, the restriction of UA to tasks in this instance satisfies the policy of the workflow.

In some cases, solving the WSP can be relatively simple. For instance, consider a policy where $S = B = \emptyset$, i.e., where there are no separations or bindings of duty. In this case, it is enough to assign each task t with a user u such that $(u, t) \in P$, and if there is no such user, then the workflow is unsatisfiable. However, the enforcement of separations and bindings of duty might require to keep track of the previous assignments. For instance, in our running example, u_1 can only be assigned to t_3 if it has not been assigned neither to t_2 nor to t_1.

---

[4] We use $\wp(X)$ to denote the set of finite subsets of X.

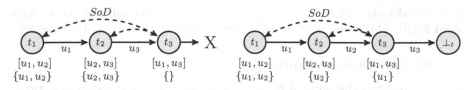

Fig. 2. The task t_3 cannot be executed   **Fig. 3.** The workflow terminates correctly

3.3 Contextual Assignment

As illustrated above, in order to ensure that the security constraints are met, the user-task assignment needs to take into account at least the previous assignments. We call *context* any dynamic information relevant to user-task assignments, such as the security policy, the history of execution, or the user failures. Here again, we aim for generality, and given a workflow $W = (\mathcal{U}, \mathcal{T}, \tau, t_0, p)$, we consider a set $\mathcal{C}$ of contexts, with a *context manager* $\gamma : \mathcal{C} \times \mathcal{T} \times \mathcal{U} \to \mathcal{P}(\mathcal{C})$, such that given a context c, a task t and a user u, $\gamma(c, t, u)$ represents the probability space of the next context. We write $D = (C, \gamma, c_0)$ for a context description, which includes a set of contexts, a context manager and initial context $c_0 \in \mathcal{C}$.

For instance, in order to define the WSP, the context needs to contain all previous assignments, in order to check the validity of separations and bindings of duty at each step. Hence we define $\mathcal{C}_h = \wp(\mathcal{U} \times \mathcal{T})$, such that for any $c \in \mathcal{C}_h$, all $(u, t) \in c$ correspond to previous assignments. We then define the context manager γ_h as, for any context $c \in \mathcal{C}_h$, any task t and any user u, $\gamma_h(c, t, u) = c \cup \{(u, t)\}$. The assignment (u, t) is permitted if it satisfies p when combined with the previous assignments contained in c. Thus, for any context $c \in \mathcal{C}_h$ we write $c, u, t \vdash p$ if, and only if, $c \cup \{(u, t)\} \vdash p$. We write $D_h = (\mathcal{C}_h, \gamma_h, \emptyset)$ for the context description corresponding to previous assignments. In the following, we assume the sets $\mathcal{U}$ and $\mathcal{T}$ to be clear from context when using D_h, unless stated otherwise.

Definition 2 (Assignment). *Given a workflow $W = (\mathcal{U}, \mathcal{T}, \tau, t_0, p)$ and a context description $D = (\mathcal{C}, \gamma, c_0)$, a contextual assignment is a function $\delta : \mathcal{C} \times \mathcal{T} \to \mathcal{U}$, such that $\delta(c, t)$ represents the user assigned to t in the context c.*

For instance, with the context description D_h, a simple contextual assignment is to return any user that can execute the task, taking previous assignments into account. We define the set of all permitted users $PU_{c,t} = \{u \mid c, u, t \vdash p\}$. The on-the-fly assignment is then the function $\delta_o(c, t)$ returning any user from $PU_{c,t}$, if it is not empty, and any user otherwise (meaning that no user can execute t in the context c without violating the workflow policy).

As illustrated on Figure 2, where $\{u_m, ..., u_n\}$ denotes $PU_{c,t}$, δ_o might not select the best possible assignment. For instance if u_1 is assigned to t_1 and u_3 is assigned to t_2, which are both correct assignments in their respective context, then the separation of duty constraints make it impossible to assign t_3 to any user. However, as shown on Figure 3, if u_2 is assigned to t_2 instead, then u_3 can be assigned to t_3. We present in the next section the encoding of the workflow as an MDP, which aims at defining an assignment avoiding the above pitfall.

3.4 Markov Decision Process

In order to define the optimal contextual assignment, we encode the notion of assignment into a Markov Decision Process (MDP) [21], which is a stochastic process where the transition from one state to another is governed both probabilistically and by a decision made by a policy. Each transition is associated with a reward, and solving an MDP consists in defining a policy maximising the expected reward collected by the process. More precisely, an MDP is a tuple $(\mathcal{S}, \mathcal{A}, \mathbf{p}, \mathbf{r})$ where:

- $\mathcal{S}$ is a set of states, describing the possible configurations of the system;
- $\mathcal{A}$ is a set of actions, describing how to go from one state to another;
- $\mathbf{p} : \mathcal{S} \times \mathcal{A} \times \mathcal{S} \to [0,1]$ is a transition function, such that $\mathbf{p}^a_{ss'}$ describes[5] the probability of reaching s' from s when executing the action a;
- $\mathbf{r} : \mathcal{S} \times \mathcal{A} \times \mathcal{S} \to \mathbb{R}$ is a reward function, such that $\mathbf{r}^a_{ss'}$ describes the reward associated with execution a from the state s and reaching s'.

A *policy* for an MDP (which should not be confused with the security policy of a workflow) is a function $\delta : \mathcal{S} \to \mathcal{A}$, i.e., associating each state with an action, and the *value* of a policy for an MDP is given as:

$$V^\delta(s) = \sum_{s' \in \mathcal{S}} \mathbf{p}^{\delta(s)}_{ss'} \mathbf{r}^{\delta(s)}_{ss'} + \beta \sum_{s' \in \mathcal{S}} \mathbf{p}^{\delta(s)}_{ss'} V^\delta(s')$$

where $0 \le \beta < 1$ is a discount factor, giving more or less weight to "future" values. The *optimal* policy is then defined as:

$$\delta^*(s) = arg \max_{a \in \mathcal{A}} \left[\sum_{s' \in \mathcal{S}} \mathbf{p}^a_{ss'} \mathbf{r}^a_{ss'} + \beta \sum_{s' \in \mathcal{S}} \mathbf{p}^a_{ss'} V^*(s') \right] \qquad (4)$$

where V^* is the value function of δ^*. Note that since $\beta < 1$, the optimal policy is always defined, even when $s = s'$. It is possible to show that $V^*(s) \ge V^{\delta'}(s)$, for any other policy δ' and any state s, and we refer to [21] for further details about the proof of this property and further details on the notion of MDP.

In order to reduce the WSP to solving an MDP, we combine three different elements: a workflow, a context and a reward function, the latter expressing the metric we are interested in measuring. Note that this encoding is loosely inspired by the MDP encoding of access control mechanisms proposed in [22].

Definition 3 (MDP Encoding). *Given a workflow* $W = (\mathcal{T}, \mathcal{U}, \tau, t_0, p)$, *a context description* $D = (\mathcal{C}, \gamma, c_0)$ *and a reward function* $\mathbf{r} : (\mathcal{C} \times \mathcal{T}) \times \mathcal{U} \times (\mathcal{C} \times \mathcal{T}) \to \mathbb{R}$, *we write* $\mathsf{MDP}[W, D, \mathbf{r}]$ *for the MDP defined by the tuple* $(\mathcal{C} \times \mathcal{T}, \mathcal{U}, \mathbf{p}_{\gamma, \tau}, \mathbf{r})$, *where given any pairs* $(c, t), (c', t') \in \mathcal{C} \times \mathcal{T}$ *and any user* $u \in \mathcal{U}$:

$$\mathbf{p}_{\gamma, \tau}((c, t), u, (c', t')) = \gamma(c, t, u, c') \cdot \tau(t, u, t')$$

---

[5] For the sake of conciseness, we write $\mathbf{p}^a_{ss'}$ for $\mathbf{p}(s, a, s')$ when no confusion can arise.

A policy for MDP$[W, D, \mathbf{r}]$ is then a function $\delta : \mathcal{C} \times \mathcal{T} \to \mathcal{U}$, that is, a contextual assignment. In other words, the optimal policy δ^* is the optimal contextual assignment for the workflow, the context description and the reward function. Since we focus on the non-violation of the security policy, we define the reward function associating each violation with $-\infty$ for the context description D_h:

$$\mathbf{r}_p((c, t), u, (c', t')) = \begin{cases} -\infty & \text{if } t \neq \bot_t \text{ and } c, u, t \not\vdash p \\ 0 & \text{otherwise.} \end{cases}$$

where we assume that $-\infty * 0 = 0$, meaning that an $-\infty$ reward on a transition that cannot happen has no effect on the overall value function. Note that by construction, we know that transitions starting from $\bot_t$ can only finish at $\bot_t$, so we do not need to measure such transitions.

Definition 4 (WSP). *Given a workflow $W = (\mathcal{U}, \mathcal{T}, \tau, t_0, p)$, we write V_h^* for the optimal value function of MDP$[W, D_h, \mathbf{r}_p]$, and we say that W is satisfiable if, and only if, $V_h^*(\emptyset, t_0) = 0$.*

In the following, we usually write δ_c for the optimal policy of MDP$[W, D_h, \mathbf{r}_p]$, and Table 1 actually presents all possible instance for δ_c in the running example. It is easy to see that this definition of the WSP matches the informal one given above: the optimal policy δ^* avoids any transition reachable from $(\emptyset, t_0)$ with a reward of $-\infty$, i.e., any transition that would violate the policy. So, as long as there is a possible assignment that allows the workflow to reach the task $\bot_t$ without violating the policy, the optimal policy will select it. It is also worth observing that this definition is binary: either $V^*(\emptyset, t_0) = 0$ or $V^*(\emptyset, t_0) = -\infty$. We generalise it in Section 4, since the objective of this model is to go beyond binary satisfaction and resiliency.

3.5 Implementation of the Optimal Policy

Solving an MDP is in general an intractable problem [21, 23], because the optimal value function must be calculated on every possible state (and the WSP is shown to be NP-complete [6]). Hence, we do not aim here to present an *efficient* solution to solve this problem, and we refer to e.g. [24] for recent work on the complexity of solving WSP.

Calculating all possible future states is equivalent to traversing a tree of all possible assignment paths outgoing from the current state. To help visualise this concept Figure 4 depicts an *assignment tree* where each complete path is equivalent to a valid workflow assignment given in Table 1. A node c in the tree represents a context such that c_i at level j represents a state (c_i, t_j). A leaf node is the workflow finish point $\bot_t$. All outgoing edges from c_i at level j define the set of users PU_{c_i, t_j} from which one is selected. Essentially, δ_c ensures all assignments are made within the bounds of an assignment tree composed of *assignment paths* which all finish with $\bot_t$. It follows that in any state, any user selected from $PU_{c,t}$ will allow the workflow to complete. We present in Section 5 an implementation of the optimal policy using Value Iteration under simplifying assumptions.

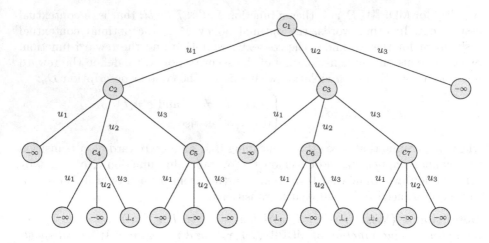

Fig. 4. Workflow assignment tree

4 Quantitative Analyses

4.1 Quantitative Satisfaction

In general, the fact alone that a workflow is unsatisfiable is, as such, of little help for a system designer. Consider for instance a workflow where all but one instance can be correctly assigned, and another where no instance can be correctly assigned. Both workflows are unsatisfiable, however, on average, the first one provides a better service than the second one. In addition, if both workflows terminate early instead of violating the policy, they are both better than a workflow violating the policy. Of course, a satisfiable workflow is always better than an unsatisfiable one, but as said in the Introduction, we aim at providing tools and quantitative measures for concrete situations, where the ideal case is not always reachable.

In order to model the early termination of a workflow, given a workflow $W = (\mathcal{U}, \mathcal{T}, \tau, t_0, p)$ with the context D_h, we introduce a special user $\perp_u \in \mathcal{U}$, such that $\tau(t, \perp_u) = \perp_t$, for any task t. In order to reward successful termination we provide a positive reward for such successful completion, and we associate a null reward for the early termination:

$$\mathbf{r}_s((c,t), u, (c', t')) = \begin{cases} -\infty & \text{if } t \neq \perp_t, \ u \neq \perp_u \text{ and } c, u, t \not\vdash p \\ 1 & \text{if } t \neq \perp_t, \ u \neq \perp_u \text{ and } t' = \perp_t \\ 0 & \text{otherwise.} \end{cases}$$

We are then able to provide a probabilistic statement about satisfiability.

Definition 5. *Given a workflow* $W = (\mathcal{U}, \mathcal{T}, \tau, t_0, p)$ *we define the quantitative satisfaction of* W *by* $V_s^*(\emptyset, t_0)$, *where* V_s^* *is the optimal value function of* $\mathsf{MDP}[W, D_h, \mathbf{r}_s]$.

The quantitative satisfaction of a workflow is either $-\infty$, if the workflow is not satisfiable, or a number between 0 and 1, indicating the probability of the workflow to finish, based on the probabilistic task manager. In particular, it is easy to prove the following proposition, following a similar reasoning to that matching Definition 4 with the informal description of the WSP.

Proposition 1. *Given a workflow W, W is satisfiable if, and only if its quantitative satisfaction is equivalent to 1.*

Note that we cannot define the quantitative satisfaction to be *equal* to 1, which is only possible if $\beta = 1$, which is forbidden, by definition. In practice, if there is no infinite loop in the MDP (as it is the case in Section 5), this factor can be equal to 1. The proof of Proposition 1 is quite straight-forward: in order to obtain $V_s^*(\emptyset, t_0) = 1$, the optimal policy must be able to assign each task to a user without violating the policy nor terminating early.

4.2   Quantitative Resiliency

Wang and Li define in [6] resiliency as a "property of those system configurations that can satisfy the workflow even with absence of some users". As described in the Introduction, there are indeed multiple scenarios where users can fail at some point, thus not being able to execute an assigned task. Hence, a user-task assignment might need to take into account such failures.

Several levels of resiliency are introduced in [6]: static resiliency, where users can only fail before the start of the workflow; decremental resiliency, where users can fail during the workflow, and cannot become available again; and dynamic resiliency, where users can fail and later become available during the workflow.

Let us first observe that the notion of static resiliency does not require any special encoding, since checking for it can be done by directly checking the WSP for the workflow without the failing users. We now focus on the decremental and dynamic resiliency. We consider the set of contexts $C_{f,N} = \{f \subseteq \mathcal{U} \mid |f| \leq N\}$, where each context $c \in C_{f,N}$ corresponds to a set of at most N users not available. For any user u and task t, an assignment (u,t) satisfies p if u is available, hence for any context $c \in C_{f,N}$, we write $c, u, t \vdash p$ if, and only if, $u \notin c.f$. For the sake of simplicity, we assume that each user has the same probability of failing (although this could clearly be easily generalised), and given a context c, the set of all possible next contexts is defined as:

$$nf_N(c) = \{c \cup f \mid f \subseteq (\mathcal{U} \setminus c) \wedge |c \cup f| \leq N\}$$

In particular, when the size of c is already equal to N, then $nf_N(c) = \{c\}$. We can then define the probability of reaching a new context c' from a context c from the user failure perspective:

$$\gamma_{f,N}(c, t, u, c') = \begin{cases} |nf_N(c)|^{-1} & \text{if } c' \in nf_N(c), \\ 0 & \text{otherwise.} \end{cases}$$

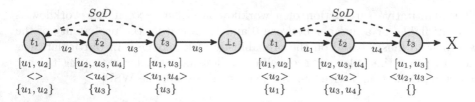

Fig. 5. δ_s - optimal resiliency   **Fig. 6.** δ_s - sub-optimal distance

We write $D_{f,N} = (\mathcal{C}_{f,N}, \gamma_{f,N}, \emptyset)$ for the context description corresponding to the decremental and equiprobable failure of up to N users, and we write $D_{h,f,N} = D_h \times D_{f,N}$ for the cartesian product of this context description and the one modelling previous assignments, where the context manager is defined in a point-wise way, and reward functions applies to the relevant components of a tuple[6]. For any context $c \in \mathcal{C}_{h,f,N}$, user u and task t, an assignment (u,t) satisfies p, and we write $c, u, t \vdash p$, if, and only if, $c \cup \{(u,t)\} \vdash p \wedge u \notin c.f$.

Proposition 2. *A workflow is decrementally resilient up to N users if and only if $\sum_{c \in \mathcal{C}_{f,N}} V_{f,N}^*((\emptyset, c), t_0) \simeq 1$, where $V_{f,N}^*$ is the optimal value function of* $\mathsf{MDP}[W, D_{h,f,N}, \mathbf{r}_s]$.

In the following, we usually write δ_s for the optimal policy of $\mathsf{MDP}[W, D_{h,f,N}, \mathbf{r}_s]$. Note that we sum over all possible contexts, because the notion of decremental resiliency also considers that users can fail before the start of the execution of the workflow. In addition, dynamic resiliency can be encoded similarly by defining $nf_N(c) = \mathcal{C}_{f,N}$, and we therefore focus only in the rest of the paper on decremental resiliency, unless specified otherwise.

Running Example. *Consider now a different security policy $p_2 = (P_2, S_2, B_2)$, where $P_2 = \{(u_1, t_1), (u_2, t_1), (u_2, t_2), (u_3, t_2), (u_4, t_2), (u_1, t_3), (u_3, t_3)\}$, $B_2 = \emptyset$ and $S_2 = \{\{t_1, t_2\}, \{t_1, t_3\}\}$. A label $<u_i>$ denotes u_i has failed. Figure 5 illustrates how δ_s can maximise the quantitative resiliency of the running example for two failed users. Assigning t_1 to u_2 generates two assignment options for t_2. In turn, selecting u_3 for the assignment of t_2 ensures two assignment options for t_3. Despite the failure of u_4 at t_2 and u_1 at t_3, the workflow can terminate.*

Figure 6 illustrates how the workflow can still fail under δ_s due to an unavoidable block caused by two failed users. User u_1 must be assigned t_1 following the failure of u_2. Two assignment options are available at t_2 from which either can be chosen but due to the failure of u_3 at t_3, the workflow is blocked.

4.3   Expected Distance

The quantitative satisfaction of a workflow denotes the probability of a workflow to terminate, taking the context into account. This metric therefore does not

---

[6] In this paper, the only examples of reward functions we consider are defined either on the violation of the policy or the (early) termination. However, in general, we could have more complex reward functions, depending for instance on user availability.

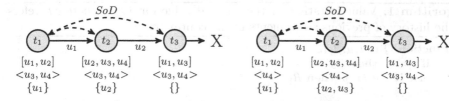

Fig. 7. δ_d - optimal distance   Fig. 8. δ_d - sub-optimal resiliency

differentiate between an instance terminating at the first task and an instance terminating at the penultimate task. In order to illustrate the flexibility of our model, we define the expected distance of the workflow, i.e., the number of tasks performed before terminating, using the following reward function, defined over the context description D_h:

$$\mathbf{r}_d((c,t), u, (c',t')) = \begin{cases} -\infty & \text{if } t \neq \bot_t, u \neq \bot_u \text{ and } c, u, t \not\vdash p \\ 1 & \text{if } t \neq \bot_t \text{ and } u \neq \bot_u, \\ 0 & \text{otherwise.} \end{cases}$$

The expected distance of the workflow can therefore be calculated with $V_d^*(\emptyset, t_0)$, where V_d^* is the optimal value function of $\mathsf{MDP}[W, D_h, \mathbf{r}_d]$. We can also redefine the notion of resiliency to measure the expected distance instead of the success rate with the optimal value function of $\mathsf{MDP}[W, D_{h,f,N}, \mathbf{r}_d]$, and we usually write δ_d for the optimal policy of this model. Interestingly, an assignment optimal for the notion of resiliency as defined in Section 4.2 is not necessarily optimal for this notion of resiliency, as illustrated in Section 5. This reinforces our motivation for building the model presented here, which can provide several metrics and thus help a system designer to improve or fix a workflow, rather than a simple boolean indicating whether the workflow is satisfiable or not.

Running Example. *Figure 7 illustrates how δ_d can optimize the expected distance of our running example for two failed users. Following the failure of u_3 and u_4 at t_1, u_1 is assigned t_1 to generate the assignment option u_2 at t_2. Task t_2 can be assigned before the workflow blocks at t_3. In contrast, δ_s would always finish at t_1 while δ_o and δ_c would assign either u_1 or u_2 at t_1 resulting in the workflow finishing at either t_2 or t_3. Figure 8 illustrates how δ_d can lower the expected distance for two failed users. The failure of u_4 means t_1 must be assigned to u_1 to optimise the distance-resiliency at that point. The failure of u_3 at t_3 means the workflow is now blocked. However, under δ_s, t_1 would be assigned to t_2 which reduces the assignment options for t_2 to just u_3 but increases the options for the final task t_3 to u_1 and u_3. It follows that the workflow would complete with this particular failure under δ_s.*

5   Assessment

In this section, we give an empirical assessment of the different policies introduced in Sections 3 and 4. More precisely, given a uniform distribution of user

Algorithm 1. Value Iteration for the optimal value function, where $c.h$ refers to the history of previous assignments in the context c.

1: **function** $Q^*(c, t, u, \beta, \overline{R})$
2:     **if** $t = \perp_t$ **then** R_S
3:     **else if** $c, u, t \nvdash p$ **then** R_V
4:     **else**
5:         $t' \leftarrow \tau(t, u)$
6:         **if** $u = \perp_u$ **then** 0
7:         **else** $R_T + \beta * \max\limits_{u \in \mathcal{U}} \left[|nf_N(c)|^{-1} * \sum_{i=1}^{|nf_N(c)|} \{ Q^*(c_i, t', u, \beta, \overline{R}) \mid c_i \in nf_N(c) \} \right]$
8:         **end if**
9:     **end if**
10: **end function**

---

failure, we are able to generate resiliency metrics for a workflow and show the average success rate appears higher using the resiliency assignments δ_s and δ_d.

Implementation. We solve the MDP defined in Section 3 using value iteration [21] and implement a simplified version of the optimal policy function δ^* under the assumption that user failures are equiprobable and workflow behaviour is linear, i.e., no loops or branches exist. Given a context c, a task t, a discount factor β and a reward vector $\overline{R} = (R_S, R_T, R_V)$, corresponding to the atomic rewards for successfully terminating, doing one step and violating the policy, respectively, the optimal policy is given as:

$$\delta^*(c, t, \beta, \overline{R}) = \arg\max_{u \in \mathcal{U}} Q^*(c, t, u, \beta, \overline{R})$$

where Q^* is defined in Algorithm 1. We are now in position to define the policies introduced in Section 3 and Section 4. Given $c \in \mathcal{C}_h$, $c' \in \mathcal{C}_{h,f,N}$ and $t \in \mathcal{T}$

$$\delta_o(c, t) = \delta^*(c, t, 0, 1, 0, -\infty) \qquad \delta_c(c, t) = \delta^*(c, t, 1, 1, 0, -\infty)$$
$$\delta_s(c', t) = \delta^*(c', t, 1, 1, 0, -\infty) \qquad \delta_d(c', t) = \delta^*(c', t, 1, 0, 1, -\infty)$$

Note that since we assume the workflow is linear, we can safely assign 1 to β. As δ_c and δ_s concern themselves with optimising workflow satisfaction it is possible to carry out a degree of pre-processing before runtime. Assignments with reward $-\infty$ can be removed offline as they clearly do not contribute to the satisfiability of a workflow. All correct assignments are therefore cached in a tree data structure. Any unavailable users are removed before selecting a user for the current assignment. If multiple users are found to be optimal by any of the four policies, one is simply selected at random.

To model user failure, all possible user failures are generated up to N as a set of failure vectors. The test program takes as input parameters a sequence of tasks, a security policy, a set of users, a single failure vector and an assignment policy. Before assigning each task, the failure vector is checked and users removed as appropriate. A call is made to the given assignment policy for each task in

Table 2. Test results for Example 1

	δ_o	δ_c	δ_s	δ_d
Success rate	0.136	0.769	0.803	0.793
Expected distance (tasks)	5.20	8.83	8.67	9.29
Computation time (μs)	579.06	139.20	1.35×10^5	2.94×10^6

turn and the result logged in an assignment history. The program terminates if the end of the workflow is reached or no assignment can be made and outputs the assignment history and assignment time which is the aggregation of computation time captured through a benchmarking library. For instance, we define Example 1 to contain 10 tasks, 6 users and a security policy consisting 10 separation and 2 binding of duty constraints. We consider 1 user failure per run giving 61 failure vectors in all, each run 10 times. The testing was done on a computing platform incorporating a 2.40Ghz i5 Intel processor and 4GB RAM.

Results. A total of 610 runs were recorded per policy. It should be noted that 150 correct assignments exist for the workflow instance in Example 1. The recorded test data has been analysed and the primary results presented in Table 2. To aid understanding, the sample data is also presented in graphical form. Figure 9 shows the probability of assignment for each task in Example 1. For example, the probability of the workflow to execute until at least t_3 using δ_o is 0.49 while under δ_c the probability is 0.95. The workflow success rate is equivalent to the probability of reaching t_{10}. Figure 10 gives average computation time (excluding pre-computed data, such as the assignment tree). For example, the average time to compute assignments up to and including t_4 under δ_o is 111μs while under δ_c the time is 17.2μs.

Discussion. Table 3 summarises the different characteristics of the different policies. As expected, δ_s generates assignments providing the highest success rate, and δ_d generates assignments giving the highest expected distance. Intuitively δ_s reserves users for the final task assignments and δ_d reserves users to ensure every task has the highest possibility of being assigned. Our results indicate choosing δ_s to optimise success rate does not mean optimal expected distance will follow: since δ_s is only concerned with reaching the finish point, it terminates once it knows failure is guaranteed, thus lowering expected distance achieved by other strategies. This phenomenon is seen in Figure 9 which gives the appearance of δ_s striving straight to the finish point while δ_c and δ_d prioritise assigning tasks along the way.

It is noticeable that average task assignment probabilities are raised when made within the bounds of an assignment tree used in δ_c and δ_s. However an observed side-effect of removing known bad assignments (with reward $-\infty$) is to lower initial task assignment probabilities below that achieved by δ_o and δ_d. Figure 9 shows the probability to assign t_2 under δ_s is 0.9 and δ_c as 0.98, yet

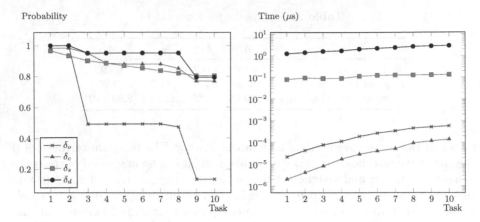

Fig. 9. Example 1 - expected distance   **Fig. 10.** Example 1 - computation time

equals 1 under δ_o and δ_d. It follows that basing decisions solely on initial task assignments would indicate δ_o, δ_c and δ_d are better then δ_s, yet δ_s is more likely to finish. Caution should be taken of this somewhat false impression, especially with δ_o as performance can clearly drop suddenly. The behaviour of δ_o can be attributed to bad assignments made with or without user failure, and a greedy nature of using up critical users for early tasks leaving more and more bad assignment options for later ones. If no bad assignments or user failures exist, δ_o can expect to match the performance of δ_c.

The fastest computation time is achieved by δ_c which is expected due to the least amount of runtime processing it must perform. Note that δ_c uses the assignment tree data structure so does not need to calculate correct task assignments at runtime, nor does it calculate any aspect of resiliency; only the current failed users must be removed. This runtime performance does come with the cost of calculating all correct assignments offline and generating the data tree structure (17.39s for Example 1); the time for this grows exponentially with the number of tasks and users. It follows that timings for each strategy increase with the amount of runtime processing performed. As expected, the slowest strategy δ_d has the heaviest runtime workload, i.e. calculating correct assignments and calculating a resiliency value for each potential task assignment.

To summarise, none of the four policies we have introduced guarantee a full success rate and we do not suggest one is the outright best in terms of optimising workflow satisfaction and resiliency. Optimising success can lower distance while optimising time can lower resiliency for example. These tensions are heavily dependent on the nature of the workflow, the security policy and which users fail and at what point they fail. The results we have presented give a first step in the generation of useable metrics indicating the success rate, expected distance, computation time and task-assignment probabilities of workflow assignments. These values give a more meaningful measure than previous work and make it easier to compare workflow assignments in terms of how much satisfiability and resiliency they can give.

Table 3. Assignment strategy comparison

Characteristic	δ_o	δ_c	δ_s	δ_d
User selection from $PU_{c,t}$	random	random	optimal	optimal
Caches assignment options	$\times$	$\checkmark$	$\checkmark$	$\times$
Calculates resiliency	$\times$	$\times$	$\checkmark$	$\checkmark$
Optimal success rate	random	random	$\checkmark$	random
Optimal expected distance	random	random	random	$\checkmark$
Computation	2nd	1st	3rd	4th

Clearly the establishment of an acceptable workflow is a case of security and business trade-offs. Favouring one measure over another will depend on workflow priorities, i.e., whether the only concern is to finish or instead be confident that a certain point will be reached, or does computation time outweigh the need for resiliency? This decision can become crucial due to tension we have shown existing between these aspects. Providing suitable metrics and tools for workflow designers would facilitate more informed decisions regarding these concerns.

Running Example. In addition, two sets of results for the running example used throughout this paper are given in Table 4. The first, Example 2 are generated using policy p_1 defined in Section 3.1, and second, Example 3 using policy p_2 defined in Section 4.2. A maximum of 2 user failures is considered totalling 67 equiprobable failures, each run 10 times per assignment policy. The testing for Example 2 was carried out on a computing platform incorporating a 2.40Ghz i5 Intel processor, and for Example 3, a 2.3GHz Intel duo-core processor, both with 4GB RAM.

Table 4. Test results

	Example 2				Example 3			
	δ_o	δ_c	δ_s	δ_d	δ_o	δ_c	δ_s	δ_d
Success rate (%)	20.27	26.49	43.24	43.24	62.99	63.43	74.62	73.13
Expected distance (tasks)	2.04	1.93	1.81	2.27	2.57	2.59	2.52	2.67
Computation time (μs)	4.56	0.77	123.27	299.62	12.03	5.10	379.35	678.91

6 Conclusion

We have presented in this paper a Markov Decision Process (MDP) encoding of the workflow satisfaction and resiliency problem. We have therefore reduced the problem of finding optimal user-task assignment to that of solving an MDP, which is a well studied problem. One of the main strengths of our approach is to provide a very flexible approach, where a simple modification of the context or the reward function provides a new metric to analyse a workflow. We believe that by addressing the workflow satisfaction and resiliency problem from a quantitative viewpoint rather than from a binary one, we provide tools and metrics that can be helpful for a workflow designer to analyse all those cases that are neither satisfiable nor resilient ideally, but need to work nevertheless.

We have illustrated that the analysis of a workflow is multi-dimensional, and that there is a trade-off to be established, among others, between computation time, success rate and expected distance. Clearly, other dimensions can be taken into account, such that the possibility to dynamically modify the security policy [16], or perhaps the possibility to override the security constraints [17].

For future work, an interesting point is to develop the tools to help the system designer *fix* a given workflow, using different metrics. For instance, a set of workflow modifications proven to be monotonic with the quantitative satisfaction or with the decremental resiliency could be a very helpful tool, especially in the context of structured workflow design, e.g., with business processes. Another lead is the study of sub-optimal policies. Indeed, calculating a sub-optimal solution might be more tractable [23], at the cost of a loss of accuracy. In this case, it could be worth understanding the impact on the WSP of using a sub-optimal solution.

References

1. Workflow handbook, pp. 243–293. John Wiley & Sons, Inc., New York (1997)
2. Bertino, E., Ferrari, E., Atluri, V.: The specification and enforcement of authorization constraints in workflow management systems. ACM Trans. Inf. Syst. Secur. 2(1), 65–104 (1999)
3. Botha, R., Eloff, J.H.P.: Separation of duties for access control enforcement in workflow environments. IBM Systems Journal 40(3), 666–682 (2001)
4. Kohler, M., Liesegang, C., Schaad, A.: Classification model for access control constraints. In: IEEE International Performance, Computing, and Communications Conference, IPCCC 2007, pp. 410–417 (April 2007)
5. Crampton, J.: A reference monitor for workflow systems with constrained task execution. In: Proceedings of the Tenth ACM Symposium on Access Control Models and Technologies, SACMAT 2005, pp. 38–47. ACM, New York (2005)
6. Wang, Q., Li, N.: Satisfiability and resiliency in workflow authorization systems. ACM Trans. Inf. Syst. Secur. 13(4), 40:1–40:35 (2010)
7. Kumar, A., van der Aalst, W.M.P., Verbeek, E.M.W.: Dynamic work distribution in workflow management systems: How to balance quality and performance. J. Manage. Inf. Syst. 18(3), 157–193 (2002)
8. Basin, D., Burri, S.J., Karjoth, G.: Obstruction-free authorization enforcement: Aligning security with business objectives. In: Proceedings of the 2011 IEEE 24th Computer Security Foundations Symposium, CSF 2011, pp. 99–113. IEEE Computer Society, Washington, DC (2011)
9. Kohler, M., Schaad, A.: Avoiding policy-based deadlocks in business processes. In: Third International Conference on Availability, Reliability and Security, ARES 2008, pp. 709–716 (2008)

10. Crampton, J., Gutin, G., Yeo, A.: On the parameterized complexity of the workflow satisfiability problem. In: Proceedings of the 2012 ACM Conference on Computer and Communications Security, CCS 2012, pp. 857–868. ACM, New York (2012)
11. Crampton, J., Gutin, G.: Constraint expressions and workflow satisfiability. In: Proceedings of the 18th ACM Symposium on Access Control Models and Technologies, SACMAT 2013, pp. 73–84. ACM, New York (2013)
12. Khan, A.A., Fong, P.W.L.: Satisfiability and feasibility in a relationship-based workflow authorization model. In: Foresti, S., Yung, M., Martinelli, F. (eds.) ESORICS 2012. LNCS, vol. 7459, pp. 109–126. Springer, Heidelberg (2012)
13. Tan, K., Crampton, J., Gunter, C.: The consistency of task-based authorization constraints in workflow. In: Proceedings of the 17th IEEE Computer Security Foundations Workshop, pp. 155–169 (June 2004)
14. National Quality Board: How to ensure the right people, with the right skills, are in the right place at the right time @ONLINE (2013)
15. Lowalekar, M., Tiwari, R.K., Karlapalem, K.: Security policy satisfiability and failure resilience in workflows. In: Matyáš, V., Fischer-Hübner, S., Cvrček, D., Švenda, P. (eds.) The Future of Identity. IFIP AICT, vol. 298, pp. 197–210. Springer, Heidelberg (2009)
16. Basin, D., Burri, S.J., Karjoth, G.: Optimal workflow-aware authorizations. In: Proceedings of the 17th ACM Symposium on Access Control Models and Technologies, SACMAT 2012, pp. 93–102. ACM, New York (2012)
17. Wainer, J., Barthelmess, P., Kumar, A.: W-rbac - a workflow security model incorporating controlled overriding of constraints. International Journal of Cooperative Information Systems 12, 2003 (2003)
18. Bakkali, H.E.: Enhancing workflow systems resiliency by using delegation and priority concepts. Journal of Digital Information Management 11(4), 267–276 (2013)
19. Mace, J., van Moorsel, A., Watson, P.: The case for dynamic security solutions in public cloud workflow deployments. In: 2011 IEEE/IFIP 41st International Conference on Dependable Systems and Networks Workshops (DSN-W), pp. 111–116 (June 2011)
20. Watson, P.: A multi-level security model for partitioning workflows over federated clouds. Journal of Cloud Computing 1(1), 1–15 (2012)
21. Bellman, R.: A markovian decision process. Indiana Univ. Math. J. 6, 679–684 (1957)
22. Martinelli, F., Morisset, C.: Quantitative access control with partially-observable markov decision processes. In: Proceedings of the Second ACM Conference on Data and Application Security and Privacy, CODASPY 2012, pp. 169–180. ACM, New York (2012)
23. Cassandra, A.R.: Optimal policies for partially observable markov decision processes. Technical report, Brown University, Providence, RI, USA (1994)
24. Crampton, J., Gutin, G., Yeo, A.: On the parameterized complexity and kernelization of the workflow satisfiability problem. ACM Trans. Inf. Syst. Secur. 16(1), 4 (2013)

Who Is Touching My Cloud

Hua Deng[1,2,3], Qianhong Wu[2,5], Bo Qin[3], Jian Mao[2],
Xiao Liu[2], Lei Zhang[4], and Wenchang Shi[3]

[1] School of Computer, Wuhan University, Wuhan, China
denghua@whu.edu.cn
[2] School of Electronic and Information Engineering, Beihang University, Beijing, China
{qianhong.wu,maojian}@buaa.edu.cn
[3] School of Information, Renmin University of China, Beijing, China
{bo.qin,wenchang}@ruc.edu.cn
[4] Software Engineering Institute, East China Normal University, Shanghai, China
leizhang@sei.ecnu.edu.cn
[5] The Academy of Satellite Application, Beijing

Abstract. Advanced access controls have been proposed to secure sensitive data maintained by a third party. A subtle issue in such systems is that some access credentials may be leaked due to various reasons, which could severely damage data security. In this paper, we investigate leakage tracing enabled access control over outsourced data, so that one can revoke the suspected leaked credentials or prepare judicial evidences for legal procedure if necessary. Specifically, we propose a leaked access credential tracing (LACT) framework to secure data outsourced to clouds and formalize its security model. Following the framework, we construct a concrete LACT scheme that is provably secure. The proposed scheme offers fine-grained access control over outsourced data, by which the data owner can specify an access policy to ensure that the data is only accessible to the users meeting the policy. In case of suspectable illegal access to outsourced data with leaked credentials, a tracing procedure can be invoked to tracing in a black-box manner at least one of the users who leaked their access credentials. The tracing procedure can run without the cloud service provider being disturbed. Analysis shows that the introduction of tracing access credential leakage incurs little additional cost to either data outsourcing or access procedure.

Keywords: Data privacy, Access control, Cloud storage, Access credential leakage, Digital forensics.

1 Introduction

Cloud computing services provide an efficient and cost-effective mechanism for individuals and organizations to enforce highly scalable and technology-enabled management on their data. This new and exciting paradigm has generated significant interests in both industrial and academic world, resulting a number of notable theoretical and practical cloud computing models, such as Amazon EC2, Apple iCloud, Microsoft Azure and some more complex models designed for multi-cloud [21]. In the context of cloud storage [20, 23], users can outsource their data to a cloud storage server (maintained by

M. Kutyłowski and J. Vaidya (Eds.): ESORICS 2014, Part I, LNCS 8712, pp. 362–379, 2014.

a cloud service provider, CSP), so that themselves and other authorized users can access the outsorced data anytime and anywhere. In this way, users are able to share their data with others without worrying about their local hardware and software limitations.

Although cloud storage brings about many benefits, the concerns on data security are believed the major obstacles for the wide usage of cloud services. When users outsource their data to clouds, they may worry about unauthorized data access due to the loss of physical control of their data. Encryption is a standard approach to protect data security but traditional cryptosystems, including symmetric and asymmetric cryptosystems, can not support complicated access policy or suffer from complicated key management in securing outsourced data with flexible access policies. Nevertheless, in cloud storage scenario, users usually do not know who will request to access their data in the future, so a flexible access control over data is desired; besides, it is not practical to issue an access key for each authorized requestor. Attribute-based encryption (ABE, [9, 24]) is a recently proposed promising approach to enable flexible access control on the data outsourced to clouds. In an ABE system, data owners can specify access policies over attributes that the potential authorized users should possess. Then the authorized users with the attributes satisfying the specified access policy can access the outsourced data.

The attribute-based cryptosystem provides a reliable method to protect the data in clouds, while at the same time enabling fine-grained access control over the data. This is realized by assigning access credentials to authorized users so that the encrypted data are only accessible to them. In practice, these access credentials may be leaked due to various reasons, e.g., intentionally leaked by authorized users for their own benefits or compromised by hackers. For instance, a company employs a cloud storage system to store its data and assigns access credentials to its employees. It is possible that some employees unsatisfied with the company disclose their access credentials to the company's competitors who are interested in the sensitive data stored on the clouds. Once this happens, some countermeasures should be taken to find the leaked credentials in order to prevent illegal access in future.

There are some solutions for the purpose of tracing leaked access credentials. Boneh et al. [4, 5] provided a traitor tracing mechanism in broadcast encryption system, while only achieving a gross-grained access control over data. Based on the works [4, 5], the schemes [16–18] resolved the problem of tracing leaked access credentials in attribute-based encryption. Although these schemes achieve fine-grained access control, they either only possess a weak tracing capability or suffer from large-size ciphertexts. A desired solution in the cloud-based scenario is what on the one hand provides fine-grained access control over outsourced data, on the other hand fulfills a strong tracing mechanism to find leaked access credentials, and at the same time achieves short ciphertexts for outsourced data.

1.1 Our Contributions

In this paper, we investigate security-enhanced access control over the data stored in the cloud server, so that an access credential leakage tracing mechanism can be incorporated to find leaked access credentials used for illegal access. We propose a feasible solution to find leaked access credentials with strong tracing capability and achieve short ciphertexts for outsourced data in a cloud-based scenario. Our contributions include the following aspects.

We present a leaked access credential tracing (LACT) framework to secure outsourced data in cloud storage. It allows a user to define an access policy for each file or its any content to be outsourced. Authorized cloud clients will be given a secret access credential for access to outsourced data. In case of illegal access with leaked access credentials, in a black-box way, a tracing procedure can find at least one of the leaked credentials, even if the illegal access credentials were produced with multiple leaked credentials in an unknown way. This implies that the trusted third party does not need to know how the illegal access credentials were forged, which captures powerful collusion attacks in practice.

Following the generic framework, we propose a concrete LACT scheme that is provably secure. When an access credential is assigned to an authorized user associated with his/her attributes, an unique fingerprint code is embedded into each user's access credential. During outsourcing a file, the file owner encrypts the file with a policy, so that only the users having access credentials of the matching attributes can decrypt the outsourced file, without fully trusting the cloud storage provider. When some access credentials are leaked and used to forge illegal credentials for unauthorized access, a trusted third party is employed to find at least one of the leaked credentials involved in the illegal access. Surprisingly, the tracing procedure does not disturb the CSP. The security properties are formally defined and proved by assuming the security of the underlying ABE scheme and the fingerprint codes scheme.

We analyze our LACT scheme and compare it with some up-to-date similar works. The analysis shows that the introduction of a black-box leakage tracing countermeasure does not incur any significant cost to the access control. The comparison demonstrates that the proposed scheme achieves a strong traceability with barely expanding the ciphertexts. Indeed, the most critical data outsourcing and access sub-protocols, which determine the practicality of the system, are almost as efficient as the underlying attribute-based access control model which does not provide any leakage tracing mechanism. Our scheme also supports any access structure admitting a linear secret sharing and enables fine-gained access control over outsourced data. These features make our scheme a practical solution to secure sensitive data outsourced to untrusted clouds.

1.2 Related Work

There is an increasing demand to secure data maintained by a third party in distributed computing systems. Asokan et al. [1] proposed a framework to safely share sensitive data among mobile devices, with the focus on the data privacy and user privacy. Huang et al. [10] exploited the attribute-based encryption (ABE) to protect user's privacy in mobile systems. Considering that in the ABE applied into mobile systems a single authority is too easy to be broken, Li et al. [13] proposed a multi-authority solution to reduce the power of single authority and alleviate overheads of mobile users.

In cloud computing environments, the protection of data security is pressing because of the scalability and easy accessibility requirements. Due to the fine-grained access control feature, ABE has been extensively employed in cloud computing to protect data security. Liu et al. proposed an elegant ABE scheme [15] with arbitrary attributes and security against adaptively chosen ciphertext attacks in the standard. They achieved this goal with a novel application of Chameleon hash functions. Yu et al. [29] used the ABE to protect the security of data stored in clouds, then flexible access control over outsourced data is achieved. Lai et al. [11] presented an ABE scheme with partially hidden access structure to protect the access policies' privacy. To adapt for multi-authority scenario, where each authority may manage the attributes in its domain, Yang and Jia [27] proposed a multi-authority access control scheme for cloud storage to reduce the dependance on a single authority. Recently, Deng et al. [7] presented a novel ABE system allowing hierarchical key delegation and efficient data sharing among large organizations.

A challenging task in access control of sensitive data is to trace access credential leakage. Boneh and Naor presented a paradigm [3] to equip the public key cryptosystems with tracing mechanism by using fingerprint codes. To find the users who leaked their access credentials in broadcasting cryptosystems, Boneh et al. ([5, 4]) constructed two tracing schemes built from the composite-order bilinear groups, which are less efficient than in prime-order bilinear groups. Garg et al. [8] transmitted Boneh et al.'s tracing schemes to being constructed in prime-order bilinear groups to achieve better system performance in terms of encryption and decryption time. Wu and Deng [26] enhanced Boneh et al.'s schemes by considering the denial of tracing and farming attacks and proposed a countermeasure on the framing attack.

A few recent efforts have been made to trace access credential leakage since the employment of ABE for access control in clouds. Wang et al. [25] proposed the attribute-based traitor tracing system while the allowed access policy is not expressive. The systems in [28, 14, 12] support expressive policy, although the traceability is not collusion-resistant, that is, the attacker is not allowed to have more than one credential when building the illegal access devices. Liu et al. [16] proposed traceable ABE schemes allowing more than one access credentials used in forging an illegal access device, while the tracing capability is weak, i.e., white-box tracing. The white-box model can only capture weak attacks in which the dishonest user directly discloses his access credential. Liu et al. [17] suggested a method to construct the black-box traceable CP-ABE from the Boneh et al.'s schemes ([5, 4]). Their schemes require inefficient operations in composite-order bilinear groups and have ciphertexts sub-linear with the number of total users. Liu et al. [18] also proposed a black-box traceable CP-ABE with full security, although it still requires that the size of ciphertext grows sub-linearly with the number of users in the system. Recently, Deng et al. [6] achieved a very efficient trace-and-then-revoke mechanism of illegal access credentials distribution in cloud storage systems. The encryption procedure of their scheme requires to explicitly knows the identities of the ones who may later access the encrypted data.

Data sharing calls for efficient and reliable mechanisms to protect the data security. All the aforementioned works protect data security for different application scenarios and most of them achieve fine-grained access control due to the employment of ABE. In the face of access credentials leakage issue in ABE-based systems, the above countermeasures either allow less expressive access policy, or only withstand weak attacks, or incur heavy burdens. Our LACT scheme overcome these drawbacks in that it supports any access structure admitting a linear secret sharing and provides traceability in a black-box manner which is a stronger security notion than white-box manner. Besides, it is built on prime-order bilinear groups and the computation operations thus are more efficient than in composite-order bilinear groups. Particularly, the LACT scheme incurs almost no extra costs for the most frequent procedures of data outsourcing and access. These advantages make the LACT scheme a very practical and secure solution to enforce a fine-grained access control over outsourced data and a trace mechanism to find out leaked access credentials in cloud storage systems.

1.3   Paper Organization

The rest of this paper is organized as follows. Section 2 presents the LACT framework and a threat model. We present the LACT scheme in Section 3. In Section 4, the security of the proposal is formally analyzed. We conduct detailed performance analysis of the LACT system in Section 5. Section 6 concludes the paper.

2   System Model and Security

2.1   System Architecture

We consider a LACT framework for cloud storage, as depicted in Fig.1. There are four types of entities in the system: the cloud service provider, the trusted authority (TA), the data owner and the data consumer. The cloud service provider (CSP) stores the outsourced data from the data owner and responds to the data access requests from the data consumer. The trusted authority is the key party trusted by other entities to generate system parameters and issue access credentials (i.e., decryption keys) for data consumers. Receiving a data owner's forensics request, the TA executes the digital forensics procedure and returns the forensic results to the data owner. The data owners define access policies and encrypt their data with the access policies before outsourcing them to the clouds. The data consumers are the cloud users who download the data owners' data from the cloud server and then decrypt them.

In our system, neither data owners nor data consumers are required to always keep online. The CSP and the TA are always online. We assume that the TA always correctly responds to the digital forensics requests and honestly returns the results.

2.2   Security Model

Unauthorized users and intruders may try to get the users' data that are outside their access privileges. We assume that the CSP is honest-but-curious in the sense that it is curious about the content of the encrypted data but still honestly execute the tasks assigned by data owners. To protect the security of the data stored in the clouds from unauthorized access, cloud users need to encrypt their data before outsourcing them to the clouds. Therefore, an encryption mechanism is preferable to make the stored data unreadable to any unauthorized users and curious CSP.

A single encryption mechanism is not sufficient to protect data privacy. In practice, there is an unavoidable problem that some access credentials may be leaked to unauthorized users, e.g., some access devices containing access credentials may be stolen

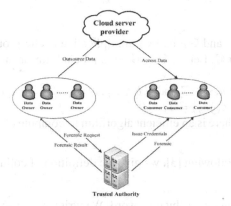

Fig. 1. System architecture

by the unauthorized users, or some users deliberately disclose their access credentials to others for some benefits. For instance, some employees of a company could sell their access rights to the sensitive data stored in clouds to the company's competitors due to economic interests. To avoid being traced, they could probably forge an illegal access credential and sell it in a black market. The misbehavior competitors then can buy the illegal access credential for unauthorized access to the company's sensitive data. In this case, we make a minimum assumption that the data owner (i.e., the sacrifice company) can find that its sensitive data were abnormally accessed, e.g., receiving alarms from the clouds that its data were accessed by some requestors with IP addresses out of the domain of the company's IP addresses, or the company find a decryption device able to access its stored data appearing at some public network market (e.g., eBay). To fulfill this assumption, we can enforce in the clouds an independent regulatory mechanism which monitors the access of the stored data and alarms the data owners in case of abnormal access.

To simplify the discussion about unauthorized access, we suppose that there exists a *pirate decoder* PD, which works in a black-box manner and enables unauthorized users to access to the stored data. The notion of black-box here means that one can access the stored data by using PD without knowing the internal construction of PD. This captures the realistic situation that the attacker may exploit technologies to conceal which access credentials are involved in creating the pirate decoder. To find out the users who leaked their access credentials, a tracing procedure is required. The tracing procedure should be allowed to access the PD and executed in a passive way, which means that it only needs to record and analyze the outputs of the PD on indistinguishable inputs. The formal definition for the security of LACT will be described in Section 4.

3   Our Solution

In this section, we propose our LACT scheme in cloud storage systems. Before presenting our scheme, we first review some basic concepts and technologies underlying our construction.

3.1 Preliminaries

Bilinear Maps. Let $\mathbb{G}$ and $\mathbb{G}_T$ be two multiplicative cyclic groups of prime order p and g be a generator of $\mathbb{G}$. Let $e : \mathbb{G} \times \mathbb{G} \to \mathbb{G}_T$ be a bilinear map with the following properties:

i) Bilinearity: for all $u, v \in \mathbb{G}$ and $a, b \in \mathbb{Z}_p$, $e(u^a, v^b) = e(u, v)^{ab}$;

ii) Non-degeneracy: $e(g, g) \neq 1$;

iii) Computability: there is an efficient algorithm to compute $e(u, v)$ for all $u, v \in \mathbb{G}$.

Fingerprint Codes. Following [3], we give the definition of collusion-resistant fingerprint codes.

- Let $\omega \in \{0, 1\}^L$ denote a L-bit codeword. We write $\omega = \omega_1 \omega_2 \cdots \omega_L$ and ω_i is the i-th bit of ω.
- Let $\mathbb{W} = \{\omega^{(1)}, \omega^{(2)}, ..., \omega^{(t)}\}$ be a set of codewords in $\{0, 1\}^L$. We say that a codeword $\omega^* \in \{0, 1\}^L$ is *feasible* for $\mathbb{W}$ if for all $i = 1, 2, ..., L$ there exists a $j \in \{1, 2, ..., t\}$ such that $\omega_i^* = \omega_i^{(j)}$.
- Let $F(\mathbb{W})$ be a feasible set of $\mathbb{W}$, if it includes all the codewords that are feasible for $\mathbb{W}$.

A t-collusion resistant fingerprint codes scheme is composed of generation algorithm **Gen**$_{FC}$ and tracing algorithm **Tra**$_{FC}$. The algorithm **Gen**$_{FC}$ generates a set Γ of N L-bit codewords. Then each user will be assigned to a unique codeword. The t-collusion traceability guarantees that if the number of colluders is no greater than t, i.e., $|\mathbb{W}| \leq t$, the algorithm **Tra**$_{FC}$ which takes in a feasible codeword $\omega^* \in F(\mathbb{W})$ can output at least one codeword in $\mathbb{W}$, provided that $\mathbb{W} \subseteq \Gamma$.

We will exploit the fingerprint codes scheme of [19] which is an improvement of the well-studied Tardos fingerprint codes [22]. To provide ϵ-security against t colluders in N users, the length L of this fingerprint codes is required to be no less than $-\frac{1}{\log T(t)} \left(\log \frac{N}{\epsilon} + \log \frac{c}{c-1} + \log \log \frac{c}{\epsilon} \right)$, where $T(t) < 1$ is parameterized by t, a fixed $c > 1$ and ϵ denotes the probability that one innocent has been accused.

Access Structure and LSSS [2]. In the following, we review the formal definitions for access structures and LSSS, which are extensively used in ABE schemes [9, 24, 16–18] and will still be adopted in our proposal.

Definition 1. *Let $\{P_1, P_2, \cdots, P_n\}$ be a set of parties. A collection $\mathbb{A} \subseteq 2^{\{P_1, P_2, \cdots, P_n\}}$ is monotone if for $\forall B, C$, we have that $C \in \mathbb{A}$ holds if $B \in \mathbb{A}$ and $B \subseteq C$. An access structure (respectively, monotone access structure) is a collection (respectively, monotone collection) $\mathbb{A}$ of non-empty subsets of $\{P_1, P_2, ..., P_n\}$, i.e., $\mathbb{A} \subseteq 2^{\{P_1, P_2, \cdots, P_n\}} \setminus \{\emptyset\}$. The sets in $\mathbb{A}$ are called the authorized sets, and the sets not in $\mathbb{A}$ are called the unauthorized sets.*

In our LACT scheme, the role of the parties is played by the attributes. Then an access structure is a collection of sets of attributes. The monotone access states that, if a user's attribute set S satisfies an access structure $\mathbb{A}$, i.e., $S \in \mathbb{A}$, then another user associated a larger attribute set $S' \supseteq S$ also satisfies the access structure, i.e., $S' \in \mathbb{A}$. Note that in most applications, the access policy has this monotone feature. Hence, we will only consider the monotone access structures in this paper.

Definition 2. *A secret-sharing scheme Π over a set of parties $\mathcal{P}$ is called linear (over $\mathbb{Z}_p$) if*

1. *The shares for each party form a vector over $\mathbb{Z}_p$.*
2. *There exists a matrix $\mathbf{A}$ called the share-generating matrix for Π, where $\mathbf{A}$ has l rows and n columns. For all $i = 1, \cdots, l$, the i-th row of $\mathbf{A}$ is labeled by a party $\rho(i)$, where ρ is a function from $\{1, \cdots, l\}$ to $\mathcal{P}$. We consider the column vector $s = (s, s_2, \cdots, s_n)$, where $s \in \mathbb{Z}_p$ is the secret to be shared, and $s_2, \cdots, s_n \in \mathbb{Z}_p$ are randomly chosen. Then $\lambda_i = A_i s$ is the share belonging to party $\rho(i)$, where A_i is the i-th row of $\mathbf{A}$.*

In practice, an LSSS scheme is employed to realize an access structure in an ABE scheme. For an access structure $\mathbb{A}$, it generates a share-generating matrix $\mathbf{A}$ with l rows and n columns and define a function that map each row of the matrix to an attribute involved in $\mathbb{A}$. Then for a secret s to be shared, the LSSS scheme forms an n-dimension vector with the first entry equal to s and rests randomly picked. It then computes the inner product of this vector and each row of the matrix, and takes the product as the share for the attribute associated with that row. The following linear reconstruction property guarantees that an LSSS scheme for an access structure $\mathbb{A}$ can recover the secret s if there exists a set S composed by some attribute associated with the rows of $\mathbf{A}$, satisfying that $S \in \mathbb{A}$.

Linear Reconstruction. It has been shown in [2] that every LSSS Π enjoys the linear reconstruction property. Suppose Π is the LSSS for access structure $\mathbb{A}$ and S is an authorized set in $\mathbb{A}$, i.e., $\mathbb{A}$ contains S. There exist constants $\{w_i \in \mathbb{Z}_p\}$ which can be found in time polynomial in the size of the share-generating matrix $\mathbf{A}$ such that if $\{\lambda_i\}$ are valid shares of s, then $\sum_{i \in I} w_i \lambda_i = s$, where $I = \{i : \rho(i) \in S\} \subseteq \{1, \cdots, l\}$.

3.2 The LACT Scheme

We first provide a high-level view of our LACT construction. To fulfill fine-grained access control over the data stored in cloud, we apply the Ciphertext-Policy Attribute-based Encryption (CP-ABE) in [24]. The data owners encrypt their files with some access policies they specified and upload the encrypted files to the CSP. Authorized data consumers will obtain access credentials, serving as decryption keys, issued by the trusted authority. A data consumer can access a file stored in clouds only if his/her associated attribute set satisfies the access policy specified in the file. In practice, some users' access credentials may be stolen or leaked. These leaked credentials might be used to forge an illegal functional access credential. To address this problem, by exploiting the tracing technology of [3], we label each user with a distinct fingerprint such that each functional access credential corresponds to a feasible codeword. The tracing procedure first finds the feasible codeword associated with the illegal access credential used by PD and then takes this feasible codeword as the input of the tracing algorithm of the underlying fingerprint codes scheme. Then the tracing algorithm will output at least one of the codewords of the access credentials used in forging the illegal functional access credential.

The LACT scheme works as follows. First, the system is set up by the TA to generate and publish public parameters. For any user qualified to join the system, the TA generates a user credential (i.e., decryption key) with the set of attributes describing the user and embeds a fingerprint codeword into the credential. Before outsourcing data to the clouds, the data owner encrypts the data with an access structure so that only the users with attribute sets meeting this access structure can access the data. At some point, some user credentials are leaked and used to create a pirate decoder PD. This PD then can be sold on network market such as eBay for anyone interested in the sensitive data that can be decrypted by PD. Once this pirate decoder is found and reported to the data owner, the TA can be called to execute the digital forensics procedure to find out at least one of the user credentials in creating PD. Specifically, our LACT scheme consists of the following procedures.

System Setup: In this procedure, the TA setups the system. It runs the following algorithm to generate system public parameter PP, a set of fingerprint codewords Γ and system master secret key MSK. It keeps MSK secret while publishes PP for other entities.

$(PP, MSK) \leftarrow$ Setup: This algorithm selects a bilinear group $\mathbb{G}$ of prime order p. It chooses a random generator $g \in \mathbb{G}$ and two random elements $\alpha, \gamma \in \mathbb{Z}_p$. It chooses a hash function $H : \{0,1\}^* \rightarrow \mathbb{G}$ that will be modeled as a random oracle in the security proof. By calling the generation algorithm $\mathbf{Gen}_{FC}$ on inputs N and L, this algorithm also generates a set of codewords $\Gamma = \{\omega^{(1)}, ..., \omega^{(N)}\}$, where N denotes the maximum number of cloud users in this system and L denotes the length of each codeword. The public parameter and master secret key are set as

$$PP = (g, g^\gamma, e(g,g)^\alpha, H), \quad MSK = g^\alpha.$$

User Admission: In this procedure, a user requests to join the system. The TA checks whether the requestor is qualified, if so, it works as follows. First, the TA randomly selects a codeword $\omega \in \Gamma$ and specifies an attribute set S which describes the requestor. Then the TA generates a user credential UC, serving as a decryption key, for the requesting user by calling the following credential generation algorithm.

$UC \leftarrow$ CreGen(MSK, S, ω): This algorithm takes as inputs MSK, an attribute set S and a codeword ω. Recall that $\omega = \omega_1 \cdots \omega_L$. First, for each attribute $x \in S$, this algorithm uses the hash function H to compute $H(x||j||\omega_j)$, where $j = 1, 2, ..., L$ and the symbol "$||$" represents the operation of concatenation. Next, the algorithm picks a random exponent $r \in \mathbb{Z}_p$ and computes:

$$K_0 = g^\alpha g^{\gamma \cdot r}, \quad K_1 = g^r,$$

$$\{D_{x,j} = H(x||j||\omega_j)^r\}_{\forall x \in S, j=1,...,L}.$$

The access credential of this user associated with S and ω is set as (including S)

$$UC = (K_0, K_1, \{D_{x,j}\}_{\forall x \in S, j=1,...,L}).$$

Here, the codeword ω is embedded in the user credential and distinctly associated with the user. Then in the tracing procedure, tracing a user is identical to tracing the user's codeword.

File Creation: Before outsourcing data to the CSP, the data owner encrypts his/her data as follows. First, the data owner encrypts the data using a symmetric session key $M \xleftarrow{R} \mathbb{G}_T$ of a symmetric encryption, e.g., AES. The encrypted data under the symmetric encryption forms the body of the file stored in clouds. Second, the data owner specifies an access structure $\mathbb{A}$ over a group of attributes which indicate what attributes the potential decryptors should possess. Then the data owner encapsulates the key M with the $\mathbb{A}$ (that is represented by an LSSS $(\mathbf{A}, \rho)$) by calling the following algorithm. The ciphertexts Hdr output by this algorithm is the header of the file stored in clouds.

$Hdr \leftarrow$ Encapsulate$(PP, M, (\mathbf{A}, \rho))$: This algorithm takes as inputs PP, an LSSS $(\mathbf{A}, \rho)$ and an element $M \in \mathbb{G}_T$, where M is the symmetric session key used in the symmetric encryption. To enable traceability in the system, the algorithm picks a random $j \in \{1, 2, ..., L\}$ and runs the following algorithm twice on input $b = 0$ and $b = 1$, respectively.

$Hdr_{j,b} \leftarrow$ Enc$'(PP, M, (\mathbf{A}, \rho), (j, b))$: In the LSSS $(\mathbf{A}, \rho)$, ρ is a function mapping each row of the matrix $\mathbf{A}$ to an attribute. In this construction, we limit ρ to be an injection function, that is, an attribute is associated with at most one row of $\mathbf{A}$ (note that this requirement can be relaxed to allow multiple use of one attribute by taking multiple copies of each attribute in the system, similar with the work [24]). Let $\mathbf{A}$ be an $l \times n$ matrix. This algorithm first chooses a random vector

$$v = (s, v_2, ..., v_n) \in \mathbb{Z}_p^n$$

where s is the secret exponent needed to be shared by all involved attributes. For each i from 1 to l, the algorithm computes the hash value $H(\rho(i)||j||b)$ for attribute $\rho(i)$ and calculates the share $\lambda_i = A_i \cdot v$, where A_i is the vector corresponding to the i-th row of $\mathbf{A}$. It then computes

$$C = Me(g, g)^{\alpha s}, \quad C_0 = g^s$$

and

$$C_i = g^{\gamma \cdot \lambda_i} H(\rho(i)||j||b)^{-s}$$

for each $i = 1, ..., l$. The algorithm outputs

$$Hdr_{j,b} = \left(C, C_0, \{C_i\}_{i=1}^l\right).$$

After running twice Enc$'$ respectively on input $(j, 0)$ and $(j, 1)$, the algorithm Encapsulate obtains $Hdr_{j,0}$ and $Hdr_{j,1}$. It finally outputs

$$Hdr = (j, Hdr_{j,0}, Hdr_{j,1}).$$

File Access: In this procedure, a data consumer requests a file stored in CSP. CSP gives the requested file to the data consumer. Then, the data consumer decapsulates the file's header to recover the symmetric session key by calling the following algorithm and then uses this key to decrypt the file's body.

$M/\bot \leftarrow$ Decapsulate(Hdr, UC): This algorithm takes as inputs the file's header $Hdr = (j, Hdr_{j,0}, Hdr_{j,1})$ associated with LSSS $(\mathbf{A}, \rho)$ and the data consumer's credential UC associated with attribute set S. If S does not satisfy the access structure, this algorithm returns a false symbol $\bot$. If S satisfies the access structure, i.e., $S \in \mathbb{A}$, due to the the linear reconstruction property of LSSS, the algorithm can find constants $w_i \in \mathbb{Z}_p$ such that

$$\sum_{i \in I} w_i \lambda_i = s,$$

where $I = \{i : \rho(i) \in S\} \subseteq \{1, 2, ..., l\}$. This algorithm only needs to know $\mathbf{A}$ and I to determine these constants.

Recall that ω is associated with the credential UC. If the j-bit $\omega_j = 0$, the algorithm picks $Hdr_{j,0}$ (otherwise, chooses $Hdr_{j,1}$) and computes

$$M' = \frac{e(C_0, K_0)}{\prod_{\rho(i) \in S} \left(e(C_i, K_1) \cdot e(C_0, D_{\rho(i),j})\right)^{w_i}}$$

$$= \frac{e(g^s, g^\alpha)e(g^s, g^{\gamma r})}{e(g^\gamma, g^r)^{\sum_{\rho(i) \in S} w_i \lambda_i}} = e(g, g)^{\alpha s}.$$

It recovers M as $M = C/M'$.

In the above decapsulation algorithm, if the user's codeword has the value 0 at the j-th position, then he can only decapsulate the header $Hdr_{j,0}$ since his credential only has the component $H(\rho(i)||j||0)$ which is required to cancel out the same blind factor in $Hdr_{j,0}$; otherwise, he can only decapsulate $Hdr_{j,1}$ in the same way. This is the key point in the execution of the tracing procedure.

Digital Forensics: In this procedure, when a data owner finds that his/her file stored in clouds can be accessed by a pirate decoder PD, he can request the TA to find out the misbehavior users who have leaked their access credentials in forging the PD. Recall that in the file creation procedure all files stored in clouds are encrypted by symmetric keys which were encapsulated with specific access policies, thus the data owner can identify the access policy associated with his file that was illegally accessed. Note that a PD could possess accessability to different stored files, which means it holds the attribute sets that satisfy different access policies of these files. However, as for this data owner, he/she may only care about the access policy he/she specified for the file accessed by PD. Given this access policy, denoted by $\mathbb{A}_{PD}$, as well as PD, the data owner then can ask the TA to proceed a forensics procedure.

When we consider the pirate decoder PD, it is possible that it correctly decrypts a file with a probability less than 1. This issue has been extensively studied in [3]. In this paper, to simplify the discussion about the tracing procedure, we assume that PD can correctly decrypt a file with probability 1.

Upon a request for digital forensics, the TA responds by calling the following algorithm.

$\mathbb{C} \leftarrow$ Find($PP, PD, \mathbb{A}_{PD}$): This algorithm takes as inputs PP, the pirate decoder PD and the access structure $\mathbb{A}_{PD}$ satisfied by an attribute set involved in PD. It generates an LSSS $(\mathbf{A}, \rho)_{PD}$ for $\mathbb{A}_{PD}$ and works in two steps to find out the users who leaked their access credentials in forging PD.

The first step is to find the feasible codeword ω^* associated with the illegal access credential used by PD to access the data owner's file. This algorithm chooses each j from 1 to L and conducts the following experiment:

1. Choose two distinct random symmetric keys $M_j \neq M_j' \in \mathbb{G}_T$.
2. Compute the header

$$Hdr_{j,0} \leftarrow \text{Enc}'(PP, M_j, (\mathbf{A}, \rho)_{PD}, (j, 0)),$$

$$Hdr_{j,1}' \leftarrow \text{Enc}'(PP, M_j', (\mathbf{A}, \rho)_{PD}, (j, 1)).$$

3. Take the header $Hdr' = (j, Hdr_{j,0}, Hdr_{j,1}')$ as the input of PD and define PD's output as M_j^*. If $M_j^* = M_j$, set $\omega_j^* = 0$; otherwise, set $\omega_j^* = 1$.

Finally, the algorithm defines $\omega^* = \omega_1^* \omega_2^* \cdots \omega_L^*$.

The second step is to find out the users involved in leaking their access credentials. This algorithm runs the tracing algorithm Gen_{FC} of the underlying fingerprint codes scheme on input ω^* to obtain a set $\mathbb{C} \subseteq \{1, ..., N\}$.

The TA returns the set $\mathbb{C}$, as the set of the users who are accused of leaking their access credentials, to the data owner.

4 Security Analysis

In this section, we formally analyze the security of our LACT scheme. At a high level, we show that the LACT scheme is secure against any number of unauthorized accesses colluding with CSP. We also demonstrates that when some users leaked their access credentials to forge an illegal access credential, which was then used to access the files stored in clouds, our LACT scheme can find out at least one of these users with a high probability. Formally, the security of the LACT scheme is defined by the following SS-Game and T-Game.

the security of LACT is composed of semantical security and traceability. The semantic security states that without the access credential, no one can get any useful information about the file outsourced by the data owner. The traceability demonstrates that if one uses an unauthorized access credential to access the file stored in clouds, TA can find out at least one of the access credentials involved in forging the unauthorized one.

SS-Game: To capture the unauthorized access to a file, we define an adversary which can query for any access credential except the authorized one that is able to access that file. We also define a challenger responsible for simulating the system procedures to interact with the adversary. In this game, the adversary is able to choose an access structure $\mathbb{A}^*$ to be challenged and ask for any user's credential for a set S of attributes on the condition that S does not satisfy $\mathbb{A}^*$. This game is formally defined as follows.

Init: The adversary $\mathcal{A}$ outputs the access structure $\mathbb{A}^*$ to be challenged.

Setup: The challenger runs the setup algorithm and gives the system public parameter, PP to the adversary $\mathcal{A}$.

Phase 1: The adversary $\mathcal{A}$ queries the challenger for user credentials corresponding to attribute sets $S_1, S_2, ..., S_{q_1}$,

Challenge: The adversary $\mathcal{A}$ outputs two equal-length messages M_0 and M_1 and an access structure $\mathbb{A}^*$. The restriction is that $\mathbb{A}^*$ can not be satisfied by any of the queried attribute sets in phase 1. The challenger flips a coin $\beta \in \{0, 1\}$, and encapsulates M_β with $\mathbb{A}^*$, producing header Hdr^*. It then returns Hdr^* to $\mathcal{A}$.

Phase 2: The adversary $\mathcal{A}$ queries the challenger for user credentials corresponding to attribute sets $S_{q_1+1}, ..., S_q$, with the added restriction that none of these sets satisfies $\mathbb{A}^*$.

Guess: The attacker outputs a guess $\beta' \in \{0, 1\}$.

The advantage of the adversary $\mathcal{A}$ in this game is defined as $Adv_{\mathcal{A}}^{SS} = |\Pr[\beta = \beta'] - 1/2|$.

Definition 3. *Our LACT scheme is semantically secure if all polynomial-time adversaries have at most negligible advantages in the above game.*

In this semantic security, the adversary is able to query for users' access credentials, which means it can collude with any user, as well as the CSP. When it is challenged, there is a requirement that it cannot trivially win the challenge. The semantic security states that given any user's credential, there is no polynomial time adversary which can distinguish the encapsulations of two symmetric keys, provided that it does not have the access credential able to decapsulate any of these encapsulations.

T-Game: In this game, we define an adversary which can collude with users by querying their access credentials. The adversary can use some or all of the queried access credentials to forge a pirate decoder PD. The adversary outputs the PD as a challenge and terminates the credential queries. This game is formally defined as follows.

Setup: The challenger runs the setup algorithm and gives the system public parameter PP to the adversary $\mathcal{A}$.

Query: The adversary adaptively makes credential queries for attribute sets. In response, the challenger runs the credential generation algorithm and gives the queried credentials to $\mathcal{A}$.

Challenge: The adversary $\mathcal{A}$ stops the credential queries and gives the challenger a pirate decoder PD able to access the file associated with access structure $\mathbb{A}_{PD}$.

Trace: The challenger runs the tracing algorithm on inputs PD and $\mathbb{A}_{PD}$ to obtain the set $\mathbb{C} \subseteq \{1, ..., N\}$. Let $\mathbb{S}$ denote the set of users whose access credentials have been queried by $\mathcal{A}$. We say that the adversary $\mathcal{A}$ wins in this game if:

1. The set $\mathbb{C}$ is empty, or not a subset of $\mathbb{S}$.
2. The pirate decoder can decapsulate any valid header with probability 1.
3. There are at most t credential queries for the attribute sets which can satisfy the access structure $\mathbb{A}_{PD}$.

We briefly explain the correctness of the three conditions above. The first condition is straightforward and the second condition is required by the assumption about

PD discussed in the digital forensics procedure. The third condition is implied by the underlying fingerprint codes scheme. The pirate decoder was created by various credentials for attribute sets, some of which satisfy the access structure $\mathbb{A}_{PD}$. The underlying fingerprint codes scheme that is secure against t-collusion attack restricts that there are at most t queried credentials that can be used to directly decapsulate the header associated with $\mathbb{A}_{PD}$. Then in the traceability definition above, it is also required that at most t credentials associated with the attribute sets satisfying $\mathbb{A}_{PD}$ can be queried by the adversary. Specially, when $t = N$, our scheme is fully resistant.

We define the advantage of the adversary $\mathcal{A}$ in winning in this game as $Adv_{\mathcal{A}}^T = |\Pr[\mathcal{A} \text{ wins}]|$.

Definition 4. *A LACT scheme is t-collusion resistant if all polynomial-time adversaries have at most negligible advantages in both* SS-Game *and* T-Game.

The following theorem claims the semantic security and traceability of the LACT scheme. The proof of this theorem is given in the full version.

Theorem 1. *Our LACT scheme is semantically secure if the underlying CP-ABE scheme [24] is secure. It is also t-collusion resistant with the additional condition that the underlying fingerprint codes scheme [19] is t-collusion resistant, where t is the maximum number of colluders. In particular, let $\mathcal{M}$ denote the message space, L denote the length of fingerprint codes and ϵ denote the probability that one innocent has been accused, then any polynomial-time adversary breaks the LACT system with the advantage at most*

$$Adv_{\mathcal{A}}^T \leq L \cdot Adv_{\mathcal{A}}^{SS} + \epsilon + \frac{L}{|\mathcal{M}|}.$$

The LACT scheme is semantically secure if the underlying CP-ABE scheme is secure. Hence, the advantage $Adv_{\mathcal{A}}^{SS}$ is negligible. In the t-collusion resistant fingerprint codes scheme, the error probability ϵ is negligible too. Moreover, since the size of message space $\mathcal{M}$ is much larger than the codes length L, then $L/|\mathcal{M}|$ is very close to 0. Hence, the advantage $Adv_{\mathcal{A}}^T$ of the adversary in breaking the traceability of our LACT scheme is negligible, which means that the LACT scheme is t-collusion resistant.

5 Performance Analysis

In this section, we analyze the computation cost of each procedure of the LACT scheme. We view the underlying fingerprint codes scheme as a black-box. We use $O(\textbf{Gen})_{FC}$ and $O(\textbf{Tra})_{FC}$ to denote the computation complexity of the generation algorithm and tracing algorithm of the fingerprint codes respectively. Tardos proposed a fingerprint codes scheme which is a milestone in this area and has been well studied, while the codes length is a bit long. Nuida et.al's fingerprint codes [19] achieves a shorter length, about 1/20 of Tardos codes for the same security level. Thus we suggest Nuida et.al's codes to be used. Their fingerprint codes scheme has the length

$$L \geq -\frac{1}{\log T(t)} \left(\log \frac{N}{\epsilon} + \log \frac{c}{c-1} + \log \log \frac{c}{\epsilon} \right) \tag{1}$$

where $T(t)$ is a function of t and valued in $(0, 1)$, c an auxiliary variable larger than 1, N the number of users and ϵ is the error probability of tracing an innocent user.

Our LACT scheme is built on the bilinear groups $\mathbb{G}$ and $\mathbb{G}_T$. We evaluate the time consumed by the basic groups operations, i.e., exponentiation and bilinear pairing map. Although the multiplication operation is also involved, its cost time is negligible compared to the former two operations. We use τ_e and τ_p to denote the time consumed by exponentiation and bilinear pairing map, respectively, without discriminating exponentiation operations in $\mathbb{G}$ and $\mathbb{G}_T$.

Table 1 gives the computation cost of each procedure in our LACT scheme. In this table, L denotes the length of the fingerprint codes, $|S|$ the number of attributes of the set associated with a credential, l the number of attributes involved in the access structure associate with a file and $|S^*|$ the number of attributes of the set S^* which satisfies the access structure. From Table 1, we can see that only the user admission procedure and the digital forensics procedure are affected by the introduction of tracing access credential leakage. Specially, adding the traceability functionality does not affect the file creation and file access procedures. This is a desirable property in practice because the most frequent operations in cloud environments are uploading and downloading files while the user admission operation is only carried out once by the TA.

Table 2 compares our LACT scheme with other similar works in terms of public and secret key size, ciphertext size, the number of pairings required in decryption, fine-grained access control (supported or not), tracing capability (black-box tracing or not) and the type of based bilinear groups (composite order or prime order). In this table, the schemes of [4] and [5] are proposed for the broadcast encryption systems, where the number of total users is denoted by N. The two schemes are built from composite order groups, thus the efficiency of cryptographic operations is much lower (about one-order) than in prime order groups. The scheme of [6] is devised for the identity-based broadcast encryption which assumes the maximal size of the set with each member as a decryptor to be m. This scheme achieves a constant-size ciphertext at the expense of secret key size linear with the length L of codes. The schemes [4–6] all provides black-box tracing, but due to the property of broadcast encryption, they do not support the fine-grained access control. The rest schemes in the table are proposed in the attribute-based encryption systems and support fine-grained access control. The schemes of [16–18], as well as ours, require that the number of pairings in a decryption is linear with the cardinality of the set S^* satisfying the access policy of a ciphertext, which is inevitable in almost all ABE schemes. In the scheme of [16], the size of public key is linear with the size of attribute universe $\mathcal{U}$ and the size of secret key is linear with the size of the attribute set S, while this scheme only provides the weak white-box tracing. The schemes in [17] and [18] achieve black-box tracing, while the size of public key grows linearly with the attribute universe size $|\mathcal{U}|$ and the quadratic root of the number of total users. Besides, the ciphertexts of these two schemes are sub-linear with the number of the users, which results larger amount of data to be uploaded/stored and more bandwidth consumption for the communication between the cloud server and cloud clients.

Table 2 also reveals the better practicality for the LACT scheme to be employed in cloud storage systems. Compared to the schemes [4–6], our scheme achieve the fine-grained access control but still retains the black-box tracing capability. Compared to

Table 1. Computation

Operation	Computation Cost
System Setup	$1\tau_p + 2\tau_e + O(\mathbf{Gen}_{FC})$
User Admission	$(L \cdot |S| + 2)\tau_e$
File Creation	$4(l + 1)\tau_e$
File Access	$(2|S^*| + 1)\tau_p + |S^*|\tau_e$
Digital Forensics	$4L(l + 1)\tau_e + O(\mathbf{Tra}_{FC})$

Table 2. Comparison with related works

	Public key size	Private key size	Ciphertext size	$e(\cdot,\cdot)$ in decryption	Fine-grained control	Black-box tracing	Prime-order groups
[4]	$3 + 4\sqrt{N}$	1	$6\sqrt{N}$	3	×	√	×
[5]	$5 + 9\sqrt{N}$	$1 + \sqrt{N}$	$7\sqrt{N}$	4	×	√	×
[6]	$3 + m$	L	6	2	×	√	√
[16]	$|\mathcal{U}| + 4$	$|S| + 4$	$2l + 3$	$2|S^*| + 1$	√	×	×
[17]	$|\mathcal{U}| + 7 + 8\sqrt{N}$	$|S| + 3$	$2l + 8\sqrt{N}$	$2|S^*| + 5$	√	√	×
[18]	$|\mathcal{U}| + 3 + 4\sqrt{N}$	$|S| + 4$	$2l + 9\sqrt{N}$	$2|S^*| + 6$	√	√	×
Ours	3	$|S|L + 2$	$2l + 4$	$2|S^*| + 1$	√	√	√

the similar works [17, 18], the ciphertext of the LACT scheme is independent of the number of total users in the system. In addition, the LACT scheme achieves constant-size public key. Moreover, the LACT scheme is based on prime order groups, thus the cryptographic operations are much more efficient than those of schemes [17, 18] that are built from composite order bilinear groups. Although the secret keys are linear with the product of the size $|S|$ of the attribute set and the length L of codes, this will not severely impact the system practicality since the key generation operation is run by the TA in offline phase. All these advantages render our scheme as an efficient solution to enable leaked access credentials finding mechanism in cloud storage systems.

6 Conclusion

In this paper, we investigated the access credentials leakage problem in cloud storage systems. The proposed LACT scheme not only offers fine-grained access control over outsourced data, but also provides a tracing mechanism to find the leaked access credentials. Formal proofs show the security and traceability of the LACT scheme. We also conducted detailed performance analysis on the LACT scheme and compared it with similar works. The analysis and comparisons show that our LACT scheme has enjoyable performance and provides an efficient solution to find leaked access credentials in data outsourced environments.

Acknowledgments and Disclaimer. We appreciate the anonymous reviewers for their valuable suggestions. Dr. Bo Qin is the corresponding author. This paper was supported by the National Key Basic Research Program (973 program) under project 2012CB315905, the Natural Science Foundation of China through projects 61370190, 61173154, 61003214, 60970116, 61272501, 61321064 and 61202465, the Beijing Natural Science Foundation under projects 4132056 and 4122041, the Shanghai NSF under Grant No. 12ZR1443500, the Shanghai Chen Guang Program (12CG24), the Science and Technology Commission of Shanghai Municipality under grant 13JC1403500, the Fundamental Research Funds for the Central Universities, and the Research Funds(No. 14XNLF02) of Renmin University of China, the Open Research Fund of The Academy of Satellite Application and the Open Research Fund of Beijing Key Laboratory of Trusted Computing.

References

1. Asokan, N., Dmitrienko, A., Nagy, M., Reshetova, E., Sadeghi, A.-R., Schneider, T., Stelle, S.: CrowdShare: Secure mobile resource sharing. In: Jacobson, M., Locasto, M., Mohassel, P., Safavi-Naini, R. (eds.) ACNS 2013. LNCS, vol. 7954, pp. 432–440. Springer, Heidelberg (2013)
2. Beimel, A.: Secure schemes for secret sharing and key distribution. PhD thesis, Israel Institute of Technology, Technion, Haifa, Israel (1996)
3. Boneh, D., Naor, M.: Traitor tracing with constant size ciphertext. In: ACM CCS 2008, pp. 501–510. ACM Press, New York (2008)
4. Boneh, D., Sahai, A., Waters, B.: Fully collusion resistant traitor tracing with short ciphertexts and private keys. In: Vaudenay, S. (ed.) EUROCRYPT 2006. LNCS, vol. 4004, pp. 573–592. Springer, Heidelberg (2006)
5. Boneh, D., Waters, B.: A fully collusion resistant broadcast, trace, and revoke system. In: ACM CCS 2006, pp. 211–220. ACM Press, New York (2006)
6. Deng, H., Wu, Q., Qin, B., Chow, S.S.M., Domingo-Ferrer, J., Shi, W.: Tracing and revoking leaked credentials: accountability in leaking sensitive outsourced data. In: ASIACCS 2014, pp. 425–434. ACM Press, New York (2014)
7. Deng, H., Wu, Q., Qin, B., Domingo-Ferrer, J., Zhang, L., Liu, J., Shi, W.: Ciphertext-policy hierarchical attribute-based encryption with short ciphertexts. Information Sciences 275, 370–384 (2014)
8. Garg, S., Kumarasubramanian, A., Sahai, A., Waters, B.: Building efficient fully collusion-resilient traitor tracing and revocation schemes. In: ACM CCS 2010, pp. 121–130. ACM Press, New York (2010)
9. Goyal, V., Pandey, O., Sahai, A., Waters, B.: Attribute-based encryption for fine-grained access control of encrypted Data. In: ACM CCS 2006, pp. 89–98. ACM Press, New York (2006)
10. Huang, D., Zhou, Z., Xu, L., Xing, T., Zhong, Y.: Secure data processing framework for mobile cloud computing. In: IEEE Conferenc on Computer Communications Workshops, pp. 614–618. IEEE (2011)
11. Lai, J., Deng, R.H., Li, Y.: Expressive cp-abe with partially hidden access structures. In: ASIACCS 2012, pp. 18–19. ACM Press, New York (2012)
12. Li, J., Huang, Q., Chen, X., Chow, S.S.M., Wong, D.S., Xie, D.: Multi-authority ciphertext-policy attribute-based encryption with accountability. In: ASIACCS 2011, pp. 386–390. ACM Press, New York (2011)

13. Li, F., Rahulamathavan, Y., Rajarajan, M., Phan, R.C.W.: Low complexity multi-authority attribute based encryption scheme for mobile cloud computing. In: IEEE 7th International Symposium on Service Oriented System Engineering, pp. 573–577. IEEE (2013)

14. Li, J., Ren, K., Kim, K.: A2BE: accountable attribute-based encryption for abuse free access control. IACR Cryptology ePrint Archive, Report 2009/118 (2009), http://eprint.iacr.org/

15. Liu, W., Liu, J., Wu, Q., Qin, B., Zhou, Y.: Practical direct chosen ciphertext secure key-policy attribute-based encryption with public ciphertext test. In: Kutylowski, M., Vaidya, J. (eds.) ESORICS 2014. LNCS, vol. 8713, pp. 91–108. Springer, Heidelberg (2014)

16. Liu, Z., Cao, Z.F., Wong, D.S.: White-box traceable ciphertext-policy attribute-based encryption supporting any monotone access structures. IEEE Transaction on Informaction Forensics and Security 8(1), 76–88 (2013)

17. Liu, Z., Cao, Z.F., Wong, D.S.: Expressive black-box traceable ciphertext-policy attribute-based encryption. IACR Cryptology ePrint Archive, Report 2012/669 (2012), http://eprint.iacr.org/

18. Liu, Z., Cao, Z.F., Wong, D.S.: Blackbox traceable cp-abe: how to catch people leaking their keys by selling decryption devices on eBay. In: ACM CCS 2013, pp. 475–486. ACM Press, New York (2013)

19. Nuida, K., Fujitsu, S., Hagiwara, M., Kitagawa, T., Watanabe, H., Ogawa, K., Imai, H.: An improvement of discrete tardos fingerprinting codes. Designs, Codes and Cryptography 52(3), 339–362 (2009)

20. Qin, B., Wang, H., Wu, Q., Liu, J., Domingo-Ferrer, D.: Simultaneous authentication and secrecy in identity-based data upload to cloud. Cluster Computing 16(4), 845–859 (2013)

21. Singhal, M., Chandrasekhar, S., Ge, T., Sandhu, R., Krishnan, R., Ahn, G.J., Bertino, E.: Collaboration in multicloud computing environments: framework and security issues. IEEE Computer 46(2), 76–84 (2013)

22. Tardos, G.: Optimal Probabilistic Fingerprint Codes. In: STOC 2003, pp. 116–125. ACM Press, New York (2003)

23. Wang, Y., Wu, Q., Wong, D.S., Qin, B., Chow, S.S.M., Liu, Z., Tan, X.: Securely outsourcing exponentiations with single untrusted program for cloud storage. In: Kutylowski, M., Vaidya, J. (eds.) ESORICS 2014. LNCS, vol. 8712, pp. 323–340. Springer, Heidelberg (2014)

24. Waters, B.: Ciphertext-policy attribute-based encryption: an expressive, efficient, and provably secure realization. In: Catalano, D., Fazio, N., Gennaro, R., Nicolosi, A. (eds.) PKC 2011. LNCS, vol. 6571, pp. 53–70. Springer, Heidelberg (2011)

25. Wang, Y.T., Chen, K.F., Chen, J.H.: Attribute-based traitor tracing. J. Inf. Sci. Eng. 27(1), 181–195 (2011)

26. Wu, Y., Deng, R.H.: On the security of fully collusion resistant taitor tracing schemes. IACR Cryptology ePrint Archive, Report 2008/450 (2008), http://eprint.iacr.org/

27. Yang, Y., Jia, X.: Attributed-based access control for multi-authority systems in cloud storage. In: IEEE 32nd International Conference on Distributed Computing Systems, pp. 536–545. IEEE (2012)

28. Yu, S., Ren, K., Lou, W., Li, J.: Defending against key abuse attacks in KP-ABE enabled broadcast systems. In: Chen, Y., Dimitriou, T.D., Zhou, J. (eds.) SecureComm 2009. LNICST, vol. 19, pp. 311–329. Springer, Heidelberg (2009)

29. Yu, S., Wang, C., Ren, K., Lou, W.: Achieving secure, scalable, and fine-grained data access control in cloud computing. In: 2010 Proceedings of IEEE INFOCOM, pp. 1–9. IEEE (2010)

A Fast Single Server Private Information Retrieval Protocol with Low Communication Cost

Changyu Dong[1] and Liqun Chen[2]

[1] Department of Computer and Information Sciences, University of Strathclyde, Glasgow, UK
changyu.dong@strath.ac.uk
[2] Hewlett-Packard Laboratories, Bristol, UK
liqun.chen@hp.com

Abstract. Existing single server Private Information Retrieval (PIR) protocols are far from practical. To be practical, a single server PIR protocol has to be both communicationally and computationally efficient. In this paper, we present a single server PIR protocol that has low communication cost and is much faster than existing protocols. A major building block of the PIR protocol in this paper is a tree-based compression scheme, which we call folding/unfolding. This compression scheme enables us to lower the communication complexity to $O(\log \log n)$. The other major building block is the BGV fully homomorphic encryption scheme. We show how we design the protocol to exploit the internal parallelism of the BGV scheme. This significantly reduces the server side computational overhead and makes our protocol much faster than the existing protocols. Our protocol can be further accelerated by utilising hardware parallelism. We have built a prototype of the protocol. We report on the performance of our protocol based on the prototype and compare it with the current most efficient protocols.

Keywords: Private Information Retrieval, Fully Homomorphic Encryption, Privacy.

1 Introduction

Private Information Retrieval (PIR) is an important primitive with many applications. A PIR protocol allows a client to retrieve information from a database without revealing what has been retrieved. We have seen PIR being applied in areas such as location-based services [1] and e-commerce [2]. There are two types of PIR protocols: multi-server PIR [3] and single server PIR [4]. In a multi-server PIR protocol, the database is replicated to multiple servers and the queries will be answered jointly by the servers. In a single server PIR protocol, only one server hosts and serves the database. In this paper, we consider single server PIR. It is well-known that designing a non-trivial yet practical single server PIR protocol is a challenging task. For single server PIR, there exists a trivial protocol such that the server simply sends the whole database to the client. Therefore the first design criteria for non-trivial single server PIR protocols is to have sub-linear communication complexity. Traditionally, research in single server PIR focused almost entirely on how to minimise the communication cost [4–12]. However, low communication cost does not mean the protocols are practical. As pointed out by Sion et al [13],

M. Kutyłowski and J. Vaidya (Eds.): ESORICS 2014, Part I, LNCS 8712, pp. 380–399, 2014.
© Springer International Publishing Switzerland 2014

due to costly server side computation, single server PIR protocols are often slower than the trivial solution despite that they transmit less bits. The most computationally efficient PIR protocol to date [4] requires n big integer modular multiplications, where n is the size of the database. The computation time of each operation is often much more significant than simply transmitting a bit. Therefore, all single server PIR protocols can be easily beaten by the trivial solution even when the network bandwidth is only a few hundred Kbps (300 in Sion's experiment). How to make the server side computation faster has become another important consideration.

There has been some work in reducing server side computation time. One approach is to use trusted hardware [14, 15]. Another approach is to base privacy on anonymity by mixing queries from different users [16]. Lipmaa proposed a BDD-based protocol [17] that is very efficient when the database is sparse, but in general case it requires $O(n/\log n)$ modular exponentiations, which is more expensive than n modular multiplications. Those approaches can improve performance but rely on extra assumptions. To the best of our knowledge, the only work that can significantly reduce server side computation time and without extra assumptions is [18]. Unfortunately as we will discuss in section 2, this protocol is not secure.

Contributions. In this paper, we present a fast single server PIR protocol with low communication cost. Our protocol belongs to the homomorphic encryption based PIR family [19]. Namely, we utilise the ring homomorphism provided by the BGV fully homomorphic encryption (FHE) scheme [20] to privately retrieve the bit. Communication wise, the protocol has low communication complexity $O(\log\log n)$. To achieve low communication, we designed a tree-based compression scheme called folding/unfolding. Computation wise, the protocol is much faster than all previous ones. We show how we design the PIR protocol to take advantage of the internal parallelism provided by the BGV FHE scheme, which allows us to amortise the server side computation. Most operations on the server side will be applied to $10^3 - 10^4$ bits in the database simultaneously. The amortised cost per bit is quite low: only around twelve 64-bit modular multiplications at 128-bit security. In contrast, per bit computational cost in previous protocols is one or more big integer modular multiplications (e.g. 3072-bit integers at 128-bit security). So overall, the server side computational overhead in our protocol is much lower. The security of our protocol is based on the security of the BGV FHE scheme, which is based on the well studied Ring Learning with Errors assumption [21].

We have implemented a prototype. We report performance measurements based on this prototype and make comparison with existing protocols. The performance test shows that our protocol consumes only a few hundreds KB bandwidth and is much faster than the previous fastest protocol by Kushilevitz et al [4]. For example, when the database is 4MB, our protocol consumes only 372 KB bandwidth and is 12 times faster than Kushilevitz's protocol; when the database is 4 GB, our protocol consumes only 423 KB bandwidth and is 90 times faster than Kushilevitz's protocol. With some hardware parallelism, our protocol can beat the trivial solution in 100 Mbps LAN.

2 Related Work

There has been abundant research in multi-server PIR, e.g. [3, 22–25]. We will not elaborate them here since our focus is single server PIR. In the single server case, Kushilevitz et al [4] proposed a protocol based on the Goldwasser-Micali homomorphic encrytion with communication complexity $O(n^\epsilon)$ for $\epsilon > 0$. This homomorphic approach is then generalised by Stern [5], Chang [8] and Lipmaa [10, 17] . Stern and Chang uses the Pallier's scheme [26] and the communication complexity is superpoly-logarithmic. Lipmaa uses the Damgård-Jurik scheme [27]. The protocol can achieve $O(log^2n)$ communication complexity. Our protocol follows this line and uses the BGV FHE scheme. Cachin et al proposed a PIR protocol that has polylogarithmic communication complexity ($O(\log^8 n)$) based on the ϕ-hiding assumption. Gentry et al [9] generalised Cachin et al's approach and proposed a very communication efficient PIR protocol. The total communication cost of the protocol is 3 messages, each of the size of $\Omega(log^{3-o(1)}n)$ bits. Kushilevitz et al [7] showed a single server PIR protocol can also be based on one-way trapdoor permutations (TDPs). The communication complexity is $n - \frac{cn}{k} + O(k^2)$ bits, where c is a constant and k is the security parameter of the one-way trapdoor permutation. Sion et al [13] showed that the trivial single server PIR protocol often out-performed non-trivial ones. To improve computational efficiency, a few approaches have been taken. Williams et al [14] proposed a PIR protocol that has $O(log^2n)$ server side computational complexity. However it requires trusted temper-resistant hardware. Similarly with trusted hardware, Ding et al [15] developed a protocol that requires $O(n)$ offline computation and constant online computation. Ishai et al [16] showed that anonymous communication could be used as a building block to implement more efficient single serve PIR protocols when there are multiple users. Melchor et al [18] proposed a lattice-based PIR protocol. However a practical attack by Bi et al [28] can be applied to break the security of this protocol. Namely the server can obtain the secret matrixes used to generate the request by constructing a reduced-dimension lattice and then recovers the index being queried.

Our protocol is based on FHE. It has been shown that PIR protocols with low communication can be easily obtained by using FHE. In [11], Brakerski et al proposed a generic PIR protocol that uses an FHE scheme with a symmetric encryption scheme. In the protocol, the client encrypts the index bit-by-bit using a symmetric key and encrypts the key using the FHE scheme. Then with the encrypted index and encrypted key, the server evaluates a circuit homomorphically to retrieve from its database the requested bit. The communication cost is $O(\log n)$ but the computational cost can be quite high because of the deep circuit. Gentry [29] proposed a PIR protocol. In the protocol, the client encrypts the index i bit-by-bit using FHE, then sends the ciphertexts to the server. The server homomorphically evaluates $\sum_{t=1}^n x_t \cdot \prod_{j=1}^{\lfloor \log n+1 \rfloor}(t_j - i_j + 1)$, where t_j, i_j are the jth bit of indexes t and i. This approach is also used by Yi et al [12], instantiated using the DGHV FHE scheme [30]. The communication complexity is $O(\log n)$ and the computational complexity is $O(n \log n)$. Our approach is different from previous FHE based PIR protocols, and better both in terms of computation and communication. Yi's paper showed better performance results than ours in their experiments. But in their experiments, γ was set to 2205, which should be at the level of 10^6 to prevent lattice based attack at the targeted security level. If the parameters were set correctly, then the performance of the protocol would be worse than ours.

3 Preliminaries

3.1 Notation

We use bit string and bit vector interchangeably. We use lower case bold face letters to denote vectors, e.g. $\mathbf{q}$. The vector indexes always start at 1. Depending on context, we use bit vectors as plain bit vectors or to represent binary polynomials or vectors of binary polynomials. In the folding/unfolding algorithms, bit vectors are plain bit vectors. On the server side, a query string is viewed as a vector of constant polynomials, i.e. $0 \cdot x^0$ or $1 \cdot x^0$. When encoding server's database, we view a bit vector as a binary polynomial in its coefficient form. Namely, a bit vector $\mathbf{a}$ of size d represents a binary polynomial $\sum_{i=1}^{d} \mathbf{a}_i x^{i-1}$, whose degree is at most $d - 1$. We use capital letters to denote matrices, We denote the ith row of a matrix M by M_i, its jth column by M^j, and a single element at the ith row and the jth column by M_{ij}. Naturally, each row or column in a matrix can be viewed as a vector (not necessarily binary). The base of log is 2 throughout the paper.

3.2 Security Definition for Single Server PIR

A single server PIR protocol is between two parties: a server that has an n-bit database $\mathbf{x} = \mathbf{x}_1\mathbf{x}_2...\mathbf{x}_n$, a client that has some index $i \in [1, n]$. The client wants to obtain the ith bit $\mathbf{x}_i$ without revealing i. Any database can be represented in this string form by concatenating all records into a single bit string. The protocol consists of four algorithms:

1. **Init**: Takes as input a security parameter λ and the size n of the database, outputs a set of private parameters $\mathcal{S}$ and a set of public parameters $\mathcal{P}$, denoted as $(\mathcal{S}, \mathcal{P}) = \text{Init}(\lambda, n)$.
2. **QGen**: Takes as input $\mathcal{S}, \mathcal{P}$, the size n of the database, and the index i of the bit to retrieve, outputs a query $\mathcal{Q} = \text{QGen}(\mathcal{S}, \mathcal{P}, n, i)$.
3. **RGen**: Takes as input $\mathcal{Q}, \mathcal{P}$ and $\mathbf{x}$, outputs a response $\mathcal{R} = \text{RGen}(\mathcal{Q}, \mathcal{P}, \mathbf{x})$.
4. **RExt**: Takes as input $\mathcal{R}, \mathcal{S}, \mathcal{P}$, the index i and the size of the database n, extracts a bit $b = RExt(\mathcal{R}, \mathcal{S}, \mathcal{P}, i, n)$ such that $b = \mathbf{x}_i$.

In this paper, we consider a PIR protocol to be secure in the sense that it is computationally infeasible for an adversary to distinguish two queries. We say a function $\mu(\cdot)$ is *negligible in* n, or just *negligible*, if for every positive polynomial $p(\cdot)$ and any sufficiently large n it holds that $\mu(n) \leq 1/p(n)$. Formally the security of a single server PIR protocol is defined as follows:

Definition 1. *We say a single server PIR protocol is secure if for any PPT adversary $\mathcal{A}$, the advantage of distinguishing two queries is negligible:*

$$Pr \left[b' = b \left| \begin{array}{l} (\mathcal{S}, \mathcal{P}) = Init(\lambda, n), \\ i_0, i_1 \leftarrow \mathcal{A}^{QGen(\mathcal{S}, \mathcal{P}, \cdot, \cdot)}(\mathcal{P}, \mathbf{x}), \\ b \xleftarrow{R} \{0, 1\}, \\ \mathcal{Q} = QGen(\mathcal{S}, \mathcal{P}, n, i_b), \\ b' \leftarrow \mathcal{A}^{QGen(\mathcal{S}, \mathcal{P}, \cdot, \cdot)}(\mathcal{P}, \mathbf{x}, \mathcal{Q}) \end{array} \right. \right] - \tfrac{1}{2} < negl(\lambda)$$

3.3   The BGV Fully Homomorphic Encryption

A homomorphic encryption scheme allows certain operations to be performed on ciphertexts without decrypting the ciphertexts first. In 2009, Gentry [31] developed the first FHE scheme. Following the breakthrough, several FHE schemes based on different hardness assumptions have been proposed, e.g. [30, 20, 32]. In this paper, we use the BGV FHE scheme [20]. We describe it here with improvements introduced in [33, 20, 34]. The security of this scheme is based on the ring-LWE (RLWE) [21] problem.

Let $\Phi_m(x)$ be the m-th cyclotomic polynomial with degree $\phi(m)$, then we have a polynomial ring $\mathbb{A} = \mathbb{Z}[x]/\Phi_m(x)$, i.e. the set of integer polynomials of degree up to $\phi(m) - 1$. Here $\phi(\cdot)$ is the Euler's totient function. The ciphertext space of the BGV encryption scheme consists of polynomials over $\mathbb{A}_q = \mathbb{A}/q\mathbb{A}$, i.e. elements in $\mathbb{A}$ reduced modulo q where q is an odd integer[1]. The plaintext space is usually the ring $\mathbb{A}_2 = \mathbb{A}/2\mathbb{A}$, i.e. binary polynomials of degree up to $\phi(m) - 1$. We also have the following distributions that we will use later in the key generation and encryption algorithms:

- $\mathcal{U}_q$: The uniform distribution over $\mathbb{A}_q$.
- $\mathcal{DG}_q(\sigma^2)$: The discrete Gaussian distribution over $\mathbb{A}_q$ with mean and variance $(0, \sigma^2)$.
- $\mathcal{ZO}(p)$: For a probability p, $\mathcal{ZO}(p)$ draws a polynomial in $\mathbb{A}_q$ such that each coefficient is 0 with a probability of $1 - p$, and is ± 1 with a probability of $p/2$ each.
- $\mathcal{HWT}(h)$: Uniformly draws a polynomial in $\mathbb{A}_q$ with exactly h nonzero coefficient and each nonzero coefficient is either 1 or -1.

The BGV encryption scheme has 3 basic algorithms (G, E, D):

- $G(\lambda, L)$: Given λ and L such that λ is the security parameter and L is the depth of the arithmetic circuit to be evaluated, the key generation algorithm chooses $\Phi_m(x), q, \sigma, h$, generates a secret key, the corresponding public key and a set of public parameters. Namely, we sample

$$s \leftarrow \mathcal{HWT}(h), a \leftarrow \mathcal{U}_q, e \leftarrow \mathcal{DG}_q(\sigma^2)$$

Then the secret key is $sk = s$ and the public key is $pk = (a, b) \in \mathbb{A}_q^2$ where $b = a \cdot s + 2e$. The public parameter set $param = \{m, \phi(m), q, \sigma, L, l\}$, where $m, \phi(m), q$ defines $\mathbb{A}_q$ and l is the number of plaintext slots (will explain later).

- $E_{pk}(m)$: Given $pk = (a, b)$, to encrypt an element $m \in \mathcal{A}_2$, we choose one small polynomial and two Gaussian polynomials:

$$v \leftarrow \mathcal{ZO}(0.5), e_0, e_1 \leftarrow \mathcal{DG}_q(\sigma^2)$$

Then we set $d_0 = b \cdot v + 2e_0 + m, d_1 = a \cdot v + 2 \cdot e_1$, the ciphertext is $c = (d_0, d_1)$.

- $D_{sk}(c)$: Given $sk = s$, to decrypt a ciphertext $c = (d_0, d_1)$, we compute $m = (d_0 - s \cdot d_1 \bmod q) \bmod 2$.

---

[1] In the BGV encryption scheme, there are actually a chain of moduli $q_0 < q_1 < \cdots < q_L$ defined for modulus switching. But for simplicity we just use q throughout the paper.

We denote homomorphic addition by $\boxplus$ and homomorphic multiplication by $\boxtimes$. At a high level, we can express the homomorphic operations as the following:

- Homomorphic Addition: Given two ciphertexts $c = E_{pk}(m)$ and $c' = E_{pk}(m')$ for $m, m' \in \mathbb{A}_2$, then $c_{add} = c \boxplus c' = E_{pk}(m + m')$.
- Homomorphic Multiplication: Given two ciphertexts $c = E_{pk}(m)$ and $c' = E_{pk}(m')$ for $m, m' \in \mathbb{A}_2$, then $c_{mult} = c \boxtimes c' = E_{pk}(m \cdot m')$.
- Homomorphic Addition (with a plaintext): Given a ciphertext $c = E_{pk}(m)$ and a plaintext m' for $m, m' \in \mathbb{A}_2$, then $c_{add} = c \boxplus m' = E_{pk}(m + m')$.
- Homomorphic Multiplication (with a plaintext): Given a ciphertext $c = E_{pk}(m)$ and a plaintext m' for $m, m' \in \mathbb{A}_2$, then $c_{mult} = c \boxtimes m' = E_{pk}(m \cdot m')$.

Apart from the above operations, the BGV scheme also has two maintenance operations: modulus switching and key switching. These two operations are used to control noise in cihpertexts and to keep ciphertext size down. We do not go into the details of them because they do not change the plaintext encrypted in a ciphertext. They can be viewed as background routines that are invoked automatically when necessary.

Another important feature of the BGV scheme is that it allows packing plaintexts and batching homomorphic computation. It was first observed in [33] that the native plaintext space $\mathbb{A}_2$ can be partitioned into a vector of plaintext slots. The idea is that although the ring polynomial $\Phi_m(x)$ is irreducible modulo q, it can be factorised into distinct factors modulo 2. More specifically, we can factor $\Phi_m(x)$ modulo 2 into l irreducible factors $\Phi_m(x) = F_1(x) \cdot F_2(x) \cdots F_l(x) \mod 2$, each factor is of degree $d = \phi(m)/l$. So by the Chinese Remainder Theorem, a single element a in $\mathbb{A}_2$ can represent an l-vector $(a \mod F_1(x), a \mod F_2(x), ..., a \mod F_l(x))$. In other words, we have a mapping $\pi : \mathbb{F}_{2^d}^l \to \mathbb{A}_2$ that packs l elements in field $\mathbb{F}_{2^d}$ into a single element in $\mathbb{A}_2$. Then we can encrypt this packed plaintext as usual. The packed plaintext can be unpacked by the inverse mapping $\pi^{-1} : \mathbb{A}_2 \to \mathbb{F}_{2^d}^l$. For convenience, we use c in normal font to denote a ciphertext that encrypts a native element in $\mathbb{A}_2$, and use $\mathfrak{c}$ in Fraktur font to denote a packed ciphertext that encrypts an l-vector.

A homomorphic operation on packed ciphertexts adds or multiplies componentwise the entire plaintext vectors in an **SIMD** (single instruction multiple data) fashion. Namely, if we have two ciphertexts $\mathfrak{c} = E_{pk}(\pi(\mathbf{p}))$ and $\mathfrak{c}' = E_{pk}(\pi(\mathbf{p}'))$, where $\mathbf{p}$ and $\mathbf{p}'$ are plaintext vectors of size l. Then $\mathfrak{c}_{add} = \mathfrak{c} \boxplus \mathfrak{c}'$ encrypts $\pi(\mathbf{p}^+)$ such that $\mathbf{p}_i^+ = \mathbf{p}_i + \mathbf{p}_i'$, $\mathfrak{c}_{mult} = \mathfrak{c} \boxtimes \mathfrak{c}'$ encrypts $\pi(\mathbf{p}^\times)$ such that $\mathbf{p}_i^\times = \mathbf{p}_i \cdot \mathbf{p}_i'$. Similarly in the multiplication with a plaintext vector case, $\mathfrak{c}_{mult} = \mathfrak{c} \boxtimes \pi(\mathbf{p}')$ encrypts $\pi(\mathbf{p}^\times)$ such that $\mathbf{p}_i^\times = \mathbf{p}_i \cdot \mathbf{p}_i'$.

We can also homomorphically rotate, i.e. circularly shift, a plaintext vector encrypted in a ciphertext. At a high level, we have:

- Homomorphic rotation: Given an integer i such that $1 \le i < l$ and a ciphertext $\mathfrak{c}$ that encrypts $\pi(\mathbf{p})$ where $\mathbf{p}$ is an l-vector, , the ciphertext $\mathfrak{c}_{rot} = \mathfrak{c} \lhd i$ encrypts $\pi(\mathbf{p}^\lhd)$ such that $\mathbf{p}^\lhd = \mathbf{p} \ll i = (\mathbf{p}_{i+1} \cdots \mathbf{p}_l \mathbf{p}_1 \cdots \mathbf{p}_i)$

4 The Single Server PIR Protocol

4.1 Some Intuitions

We start from a non-private protocol. The server has an n-bit database $\mathbf{x}$, and the client wants to retrieve the ith bit $\mathbf{x}_i$. Firstly, the server picks an integer $t < n$ and arranges its database into an $n' \times t$ matrix X, where $n' = \lceil \frac{n}{t} \rceil$. Now $\mathbf{x}_i$ becomes X_{jk} for some j and k in the matrix. To retrieve the bit, it is sufficient that the client retrieves the jth row. Each row in X is a bit vector and can be viewed as a binary polynomial of degree at most $t - 1$. To retrieve a row, the client creates an n'-bit query string $\mathbf{q} = \mathbf{q}_1 \mathbf{q}_2 \ldots \mathbf{q}_{n'}$ such that all bits are 0 except $\mathbf{q}_j$. This query string can be viewed as a vector of constant binary polynomials. The client sends the query string to the server. The server computes the inner product of $\mathbf{q}$ and X (viewed as an n'-vector of binary polynomials) $\mathbf{q}_1 \cdot X_1 + \mathbf{q}_2 \cdot X_2 + \ldots + \mathbf{q}_{n'} \cdot X_{n'}$. Here $\cdot$ and $+$ are polynomial multiplication and addition operations. The server sends the inner product to the client. Clearly, since only $\mathbf{q}_j$ is 1, the inner product equals X_j. Given X_j which is the jth row in the server's matrix, the client checks the kth bit. This is the bit it wants to retrieve. If we use an FHE scheme, we can make the above protocol private. However, the communication complexity is too high. To deal with this problem, we use a tree-based compression scheme described in the next section to compress the query string.

4.2 Folding and Unfolding

In this section we show the folding/unfolding compression scheme we designed to compress query strings in the protocol[2]. Without loss of generality, in the following we always assume the parameter $n' = 2^\zeta$ for some ζ that is a positive integer.

Given a query string $\mathbf{q}$, which is n'-bit long and with only one bit at index j set to 1. To fold it, we create a $d_1 \times d_2$ matrix M. Then we fill the query string into the matrix, starting from the top leftmost cell and wrapping at the end of each row. In the matrix, only one bit $M_{\alpha\beta}$ is 1, and all other bits are 0. We then obtain two strings $\mathbf{u}, \mathbf{v}$ such that $\mathbf{u}$ is d_1-bit and $\mathbf{v}$ is d_2-bit. Both $\mathbf{u}$ and $\mathbf{v}$ have only a single bit set to 1. A toy example is shown in Fig. 1. In this example, $\mathbf{q}$ is 16-bit and $d_1 = d_2 = \sqrt{n'} = 4$. We obtain $\mathbf{u}$ and $\mathbf{v}$ such that in $\mathbf{u}$ the αth ($\alpha = 3$ in the example) bit is 1 and in $\mathbf{v}$ the βth ($\beta = 2$ in the example) bit is 1. To unfold, we create a two-dimensional matrix M', then fill it using $\mathbf{u}$ and $\mathbf{v}$ such that for each $1 \leq a \leq d_1, 1 \leq b \leq d_2$, $M'_{ab} = \mathbf{u}_a \cdot \mathbf{v}_b$. Then we concatenate the rows and get back the original query string q.

Note that since $\mathbf{u}$ and $\mathbf{v}$ are also two strings with only a single bit set to 1, what we have done to $\mathbf{q}$ can be done to $\mathbf{u}$ and $\mathbf{v}$ in the same way. For each of them, we can fold it into two shorter strings. In the example, both strings can be represented as a 2×2 matrix and folded into two 2-bit strings. The four 2-bit strings can be unfolded and allows us to get back to $\mathbf{u}$ and $\mathbf{v}$. In general, for any bit string of size n' with only one bit set to 1, we can always fold it into $\log n'$ strings that each one is only 2-bit long.

Folding a string can be done in different ways if we choose different dimensions for the matrix in each step. In the example in Fig. 1, we can also use a 2×8 matrix to

---

[2] As pointed out by a reviewer, functionally the algorithms are equivalent to the encoder and decoder circuits as described in chapter 2 of [35].

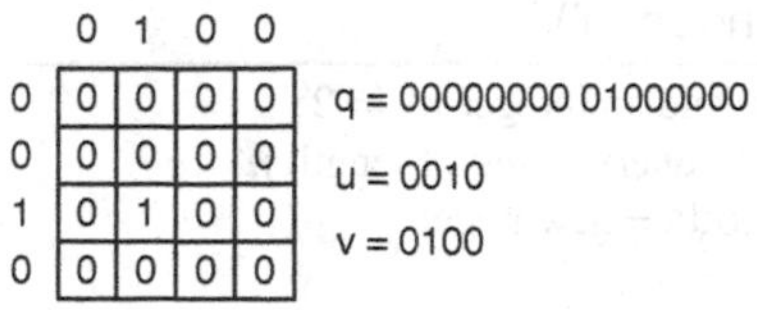

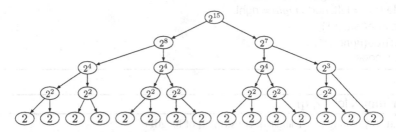

Fig. 1. Fold and unfold a query string

Fig. 2. A folding tree for a 2^{15}-bit query string. The number in each node is the length of the string to be folded/unfolded at the node.

fold q. To be deterministic, we define a tree structure and associated algorithms. The tree is an auxiliary structure that directs how to fold and unfold a string recursively. To build such a tree, the only information we need is the length of the query string. More formally, we define a *folding tree* to be a binary tree, such that each non-leaf node has exactly two children (referred to as the left child and the right child). Each node in the folding tree stores a number that is the length of the string to be folded or unfolded at this node. The algorithm to build a folding tree is given in Algorithm 1 and a folding tree built from the algorithm is shown in Fig. 2. It is easy to prove that a folding tree built from the algorithm has height $\log \log n'$ and has $\log n'$ leaf nodes.

What Algorithm 1 does is to build a tree structure. At each node, it checks the input number n' which is always a power of 2, if $n' > 2$ then n' can always be factored into $n' = 2^{\zeta_1} \cdot 2^{\zeta_2}$. To make it deterministic, we choose ζ_1 such that ζ_1 is an integer and $2^{\zeta_1} < n' \le 2^{2\zeta_1}$. After we find ζ_1, we set $\zeta_2 = \log n' - \zeta_1$. That means we can write the n'-bit string into an $2^{\zeta_1} \times 2^{\zeta_2}$ matrix, thus the string can be folded into two strings of 2^{ζ_1}-bit and 2^{ζ_2}-bit long. Then we invoke the next level recursions with 2^{ζ_1} and 2^{ζ_2}. The recursions will end when the input number is 2.

After we have built the folding tree, we can use it to fold and unfold the query string. Each folding tree is built with an input n' and can only fold/unfold query strings of length n'. The algorithm to fold a query string is shown in Algorithm 2. In the algorithm, we do not really need to fill the string into a matrix. As we can see in line 2, the dimensions of the matrix are stored in the folding tree: the number stored in the left child node is the number of rows and the number stored in the right child node is the number of columns. With this information, then in line 3, given the index j of the 1 bit in the input string, we can convert the index into a row index α and a column index β in

---

Algorithm 1. buldTree(node, n')

---

    input : A tree node node and an integer $n' = 2^\varsigma$
    output: A folding tree for a query string of length n'
1 **if** *node* == *NULL* **then** node = new node;   // a new tree
2 node.$strLen = n'$;
3 **if** n' == 2 **then** return;   // end condition of the recursion
4 $\zeta_1 = \lceil \log n'/2 \rceil, \zeta_2 = \log n' - \zeta_1$;   // determine the dimensions
5 left = new node, right = new node;
6 node.*left* = left, node.*right* = right;
7 buldTree(left, 2^{ζ_1});   // recursion
8 buldTree(right, 2^{ζ_2});
9 return node;

Algorithm 2. fold(T, q)

---

    input : A folding tree T and a query string **q** of length $n' = 2^\varsigma$
    output: A folded representation of **q**, which is a string of $2 \log n'$ bits
1 **if** *T is a leaf node* **then** return **q**;
2 d_1=T.*left.strLen*, d_2= T.*right.strLen*;
3 j = the index of the 1 bit in **q**, $\alpha = \lfloor (j-1)/d_2 \rfloor + 1, \beta = ((j-1) \bmod d_2) + 1$;
4 l = new bit string of length d_1, all bits are initialized to 0;
5 **r** = new bit string of length d_2, all bits are initialized to 0;
6 set the αth bit in l to 1;
7 set the βth bit in **r** to 1;
8 a = fold(T.*left*, l);
9 b = fold(T.*right*, **r**);
10 return a$\|$b;

---

the matrix. Then we can generate two strings, one with the αth bit set to 1 and one with the βth bit set to 1. The strings will be passed to the next recursions. At a leaf node, the recursion ends. At the end of the algorithm, the 2-bit strings at all leaf nodes are concatenated and returned. Since we have $\log n'$ leaf nodes, the query string is folded into a string of $2 \log n'$ bits. Unfolding is essentially the inverse process. The folded query string is broken into $\log n'$ strings each of 2 bits long and assigned to the leaf nodes. Then starting from the leaf nodes, the strings held by sibling nodes are unfolded into a longer string by multiplying the bits. Eventually at the root the original query string is fully unfolded.

The unfolding algorithm can work perfectly with an FHE scheme. Now all strings in the algorithm are replaced by vectors of ciphertexts that encrypt the strings bit-by-bit. The input ciphertext vector is of size $2 \log n'$ and the output ciphertext vector is of size n'. The process is almost identical to the plaintext case. The only difference is that in line 10 of Algorithm 3, the multiplication operation will be the homomorphic multiplication operation.

Algorithm 3. unfold(T, s)

---

    input : A folding tree T and a folded query string s
    output: A query string q of n' bit, unfolded from s
1 **if** T *is a leaf node* **then** return s;
2 d_1=T.$left.strLen$, d_2= T.$right.strLen$, $\zeta_1 = 2 \log d_1$, $\zeta_2 = 2 \log d_2$;
3 Split s into two strings such that s = sl$||$sr, sl is ζ_1-bit and sr is ζ_2-bit;
4 l = unfold(T.$left$, sl);
5 r = unfold(T.$right$, sr);
6 q = new bit string of length $d_1 \times d_2$;
7 **for** $a = 1$ *to* d_1 **do**
8   **for** $b = 1$ *to* d_2 **do**
9         $i = (a - 1) \cdot d_2 + b$;
10        $q_i = l_a \cdot r_b$;
11   **end**
12 **end**
13 return q;

4.3 The PIR Protocol

Now we are ready to describe our PIR protocol. The protocol is the parallelised version of the protocol described in Section 4.1. Recall that in BGV, we can pack an l-vector of elements in $\mathbb{F}_{2^d}$ in a single ciphertext and process the elements in an SIMD fashion. We will use this feature in our protocol to run l instances of the protocol in section 4.1 simultaneously. On the server side, the server represents its database as an $n' \times l$ matrix, each element in the matrix is a d-bit binary vector that can be viewed as an element in $\mathbb{F}_{2^d}$. Later, homomorphic operations will be applied to all elements in the l-vector simultaneously. That is, we can process $l \cdot d = \phi(m)$ bits each time. In this way, we can amortise server side computation. On the client side, the client needs to send the query string q to the server. It uses the folding algorithm to fold q into s. The folded query string s is short, only $2 \log n'$ bits. We can always find BGV parameters such that $2 \log n' \leq l$. Therefore the client can pack s into one single ciphertext and sends it to the server. The protocol is as follows and we will explain why this is correct after the description:

1. **Init:** Given a security parameter λ and the size of the database n, the client chooses the maximum depth of circuit L, and invokes $G(\lambda, L)$ to generate a BGV key pair (pk, sk) and public parameters $param$. The private parameter set $S = \{sk\}$, the public parameter set $S = \{pk, param\}$. Given $\phi(m)$ and the number of plaintext slots l, the server arranges its database into an $n' \times l$ matrix X, where $n' = \lceil \frac{n}{\phi(m)} \rceil$. Each element in the matrix is a bit vector of length d, where $d = \phi(m)/l$.

2. **QGen:** The client does the following to generate a query:
   (a) The client converts i into (α, β, γ), i.e. the bit $\mathbf{x}_i$ is the γth bit of the element at $X_{\alpha\beta}$. Then the client creates a query string q of length n', which contains all 0 bits except the αth bit set to 1. The client creates a folding tree with n' as the input. Then the client folds q into s using the folding algorithm.

(b) The client pads s with 0 to l bits. Then the client circularly right shifts s to get a new string $s' = s \gg (\beta - 1)$ so that in s' the βth bit is the first bit in s. Here s' can be viewed as an l-vector of constant binary polynomials. Then the client uses the packing feature: maps s' to an element in $\mathbb{A}_2$ and encrypts it. The result $\mathfrak{s} = E_{pk}(\pi(s'))$ is the query $\mathcal{Q}$ and is sent to the server.

3. **RGen:** Given $\mathcal{Q} = \mathfrak{s}$, the server generates a response as follows:

(a) The server generates a vector of ciphertext c that contains $2 \log n'$ ciphertexts after receiving $\mathcal{Q}$, such that $c_1 = \mathfrak{s}$ and for each $2 \leq k \leq 2 \log n'$, $c_k = \mathfrak{s} \lhd (k - 1)$. The server generates a folding tree with n' as input. Then the server runs the unfolding algorithm homomorphically with the folding tree and c as input. The result c' is a vector of n' ciphertexts.

(b) The server then computes a single ciphertext $\mathfrak{r} = (c'_1 \boxtimes \pi(X_1)) \boxplus (c'_2 \boxtimes \pi(X_2)) \ldots \boxplus (c'_{n'} \boxtimes \pi(X_{n'}))$. Then the server returns the resoponse $\mathcal{R} = \mathfrak{r}$ to the client.

4. **RExt:** Given $\mathcal{R} = \mathfrak{r}$, the client decrypts $\mathfrak{r}$ and obtains an l-vector. The γth bit in the βth element in the vector is the bit x_i it wants to retrieve.

As we said earlier, in this protocol we work with packed ciphertexts. Homomorphic operations involving packed ciphertexts are component-wise. So one major change in this protocol compared to the protocol described in Section 4.1 is that instead of just one single binary polynomial in a row of the matrix X, now in each row we have a vector of l binary polynomials. The client's goal is to retrieve the βth polynomial in the αth row that contains the bit. In step 2a, the client generates a query string q that can be used to retrieve the αth row in the server's matrix and folds it into s. In step 2b, the client circularly right shifts the string s by $\beta - 1$ positions. The reason is that s contains only information about the row index of the element the client wants to retrieve, by shifting it the result s' contains information about both the row index and the column index. This becomes clearer in step 3a. The server generates a vector of ciphertext c by rotating the ciphertext from the client. The first ciphertext c_1 encrypts s', and the βth bit in s' is s_1, the second ciphertext encrypts $s' \ll 1$, and the βth bit in $s' \ll 1$ is s_2, and so on and so forth. In fact we can view c as encrypting a bit matrix S of size $2 \log n' \times l$. The βth column S^β is the folded query string s generated in step 2a by the client. The server can unfold s back to q by running the unfolding algorithm. This is because the batched homomorphic operations are component-wise. Therefore by running the algorithm with packed ciphertexts, the server actually runs l instances of unfolding simultaneously, each with the same folding tree and a distinct column from S as input. The input string to the βth instance is s and thus q can be unfolded. For the other unfolding instances, it does not matter what the unfolding results are because the client is only interested in the αth element in the βth column of the server's database matrix. So as long as the βth instance is correct then it is fine. The result c' obtained from running the unfolding algorithm can also be viewed as encrypting an $n' \times l$ matrix such that the βth column is q and the other columns contain useless bits. Then in step 3b, the server again uses batched homomorphic operations to run l instances of inner product evaluation. The input to each instance is a column in the unfolding result matrix and the corresponding column in X. The βth instance computes the inner product of q and X^β. The result is $X_{\alpha\beta}$ which is the element the client wants to retrieve. The element is encrypted in the βth slot in $\mathfrak{r}$ and by decrypting the ciphertext, the client can obtain the element. Then by examining the γth bit in the element, the client knows the bit it wants to retrieve. Fig. 3 shows a toy example. In the example $n = 32, l = 4, d = 2$ and $n' = 4$, so the server's database is organised as a 4×4 matrix. The bit the client wants to retrieve is the first bit in $X_{3,2}$.

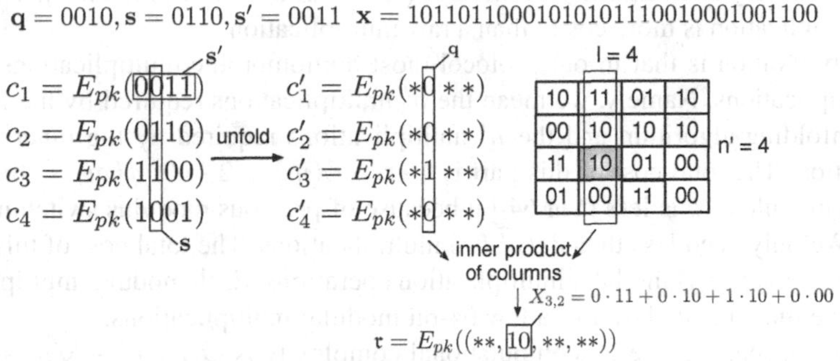

$$\mathbf{q} = 0010, \mathbf{s} = 0110, \mathbf{s}' = 0011 \quad \mathbf{x} = 1011011000101010111001000100100$$

$$
\begin{aligned}
c_1 &= E_{pk}(0011) & c_1' &= E_{pk}(*0**) \\
c_2 &= E_{pk}(0110) \xrightarrow{\text{unfold}} & c_2' &= E_{pk}(*0**) \\
c_3 &= E_{pk}(1100) & c_3' &= E_{pk}(*1**) \\
c_4 &= E_{pk}(1001) & c_4' &= E_{pk}(*0**)
\end{aligned}
$$

inner product of columns

$$X_{3,2} = 0 \cdot 11 + 0 \cdot 10 + 1 \cdot 10 + 0 \cdot 00$$

$$\mathfrak{r} = E_{pk}((**, 10, **, **))$$

Fig. 3. An Example of the PIR Protocol (* means a bit we do not care)

Extensions. With some modifications, we can extend the PIR protocol into a PBR protocol [3] or a symmetric PIR protocol [4]. In a PBR protocol, the client retrieves a block rather than a single bit. In a symmetric PIR protocol, the client retrieves just one bit and learns nothing about the other bits in the server's database. Due to limited space, we do not discuss them here. They will be presented in the full version of the paper.

4.4 Efficiency Analysis

Communication. In the protocol, the client sends a request that is a single ciphertext and the server returns a single ciphertext. The size of the ciphertexts depends on $\mathbb{A}_q$. For each element in $\mathbb{A}_q$, it is a polynomial of degree at most $\phi(m) - 1$. Therefore the size of a ring element is at most $\phi(m) \cdot \log q$ bits. The parameters $\phi(m)$ and q are interdependent. For simplicity, in our protocol we choose a large enough and fixed $\phi(m)$ and therefore q becomes a variable independent of $\phi(m)$. Then we have $\log q = a + b \cdot L$ where a, b are small constants and L is the depth of circuit to be evaluated. Since $L = \log \log n'$, the bit length of q is $O(\log \log n')$. Then overall, the communication cost is $O(\log \log n') = O(\log \log \frac{n}{\phi(m)}) = O(\log \log n)$.

Server Side Computation. The server side computation consists of three parts: homomorphic rotations, unfolding and homomorphic inner product computation. The complexity of the rotation operation is $O(\phi(m) log \phi(m))$ multiplications modulo q. We need in total $2 \log n' - 1$ rotations. To unfold the query string, the server needs $\sum_{i=0}^{\log \log n'} 2^i \sqrt[2^i]{n'} < n' + 3\sqrt{n'}$ homomorphic multiplications. The computational cost of the inner product part is dominated by the n' homomorphic multiplications. To understand the cost of the protocol, we need to understand the cost of homomorphic multiplication operations. We have two different homomorphic multiplication operations:

raw multiplications and full multiplications. A raw multiplication simply computes the tensor product of the parts in the ciphertexts, so the cost is 4 (2 if one operand is a plaintext) multiplications over $\mathbb{A}_q$. A full multiplication is a raw multiplication followed by a modulus switching and a key switching on the product. The maintenance operations are necessary to ensure correctness and maintain the size of the ciphertext. The cost of a multiplication over $\mathbb{A}_q$ is $\phi(m)$ multiplications modulo q. The complexity of modulus switching and key switching is $O(\phi(m)log\phi(m))$ multiplications modulo q. Therefore a full multiplication is more costly than a raw multiplication.

Our observation is that in our protocol most homomorphic multiplications can be raw multiplications. Namely, we mean the n' multiplications required by the last step of the unfolding algorithm and the n' multiplications required by the inner product computation. The total cost of this part is $4 \cdot n' \cdot \phi(m) + 2 \cdot n' \cdot \phi(m) = 6n$ multiplication modulo q (q is less than 64-bit because of previous modulus switching operations). We only need less than $3\sqrt{n'}$ full multiplications. The total cost of this part is $O(\sqrt{n'}\phi(m)log\phi(m))$ modular multiplication operations. Each modular multiplication here can be implemented by 1 or a few 64-bit modular multiplications.

As we can see, the overall computational complexity is $O(\log n' + \sqrt{n'} + n') = O(n)$. For sufficiently large n, the computational cost of the homomorphic rotation part is insignificant compared to the the the other two parts. Moreover, when n is sufficiently large, $\sqrt{n'}$ will be much smaller than n'. That means the number of total operations required by full multiplication part is smaller than the raw multiplication part. Then in this case, the server side computation is bounded by $12n$ 64-bit modular multiplication operations.

Client Side Computation. The client side computation in our protocol is very light. The client needs to do 1 encryption and 1 decryption. The cost of encryption or decryption is $O(\phi(m))$ multiplications modulo q. In practice, each encryption/decryption needs only a couple of milliseconds.

4.5   Security Analysis

In this section, we analyse the security of our PIR protocol. We have the following theorem:

Theorem 1. *If the BGV FHE is semantically secure, then our PIR protocol is a secure single server PIR protocol.*

Proof. We show that if a PPT adversary $\mathcal{A}$ can distinguish two queries with a non-negligible advantage, then an adversary $\mathcal{A}'$ can use $\mathcal{A}$ as a subroutine to win the BGV CPA game with a non-negligible advantage. The BGV CPA game is a standard public key encryption CPA game, in which $\mathcal{A}'$ needs to distinguish two ciphertexts encrypted under a BGV public key. The game is in the appendix. $\mathcal{A}'$ does the following:

- $\mathcal{A}'$ chooses n and generates a database $\mathbf{x}$, chooses λ and L, then receives the BGV public key and parameters $(pk, param)$. It then invokes $\mathcal{A}$ with $\mathbf{x}, pk, param$.
- For any index i, $\mathcal{A}$ can generate the query by itself using the public key. At some point of time, $\mathcal{A}$ outputs two indexes i_0, i_1 and sends them to $\mathcal{A}'$.

- $\mathcal{A}'$ generates m_0 using i_0. $\mathcal{A}'$ first generates a query string $\mathbf{q}$ from i_0, folds $\mathbf{q}$ into $\mathbf{s}$ and then pads and shifts to get $\mathbf{s}'$ from $\mathbf{s}$. The message $m_0 = \pi(\mathbf{s}')$.
- $\mathcal{A}'$ generates m_1 in the same way as above but using i_1 as input.
- $\mathcal{A}'$ sends m_0 and m_1 to the challenger in the BGV CPA game, then receives c_b.
- $\mathcal{A}'$ sends c_b to $\mathcal{A}$, and outputs whatever $\mathcal{A}$ outputs.

It is clear that the probability of $\mathcal{A}'$ winning the BGV game is the same as the probability of $\mathcal{A}$ outputting $b' = b$. Since the BGV encryption is semantically secure, the probability of $\mathcal{A}'$ winning the game is $\frac{1}{2} + \eta$, where η is negligible. Then the advantage of $\mathcal{A}$ is also negligible.

5   Implementation and Performance

5.1   Implementation

We have implemented a prototype in C++. The implementation is based on HElib [36], an open source implementation of the BGV FHE scheme. Currently in the prototype the client and the server run in the same process. This does not affect the evaluation result. To measure network communication, we output the ciphertexts to files and measure the file size. We have done a few optimisations:

Delayed Unfolding. We delay the last unfolding step. Instead of fully unfolding the query string, we combine this step with the inner product computation step. The main reason is that if we fully unfold the query string, we need to store n' ciphertexts. Because n' can be large, we need enormous memory to store the ciphertexts. If we stop at the two children of the root, then we only need to store two vectors of approximate $\sqrt{n'}$ ciphertexts. When we compute the inner product, we can unfold the bit we need on the fly using the two vectors.

Tree Pruning. We can also prune the folding tree to lower the communication cost. The idea is that if we do not fully fold the query string, we will end up with a longer folded string, but we might still be able to pack it into one ciphertext. For space reason, we do not formally present the tree pruning algorithm but use an example to explain the idea. Consider without pruning, the client and the server use the folding tree in Fig. 2, so the client fully folds its query string into a 30-bit string and the server can unfold the query string. If we prune the tree to have only 3 nodes: the root node and the two children of it, then with this tree, the client can fold the the query string into a $2^8 + 2^7 = 384$-bit string. As long as the number of plaintext slot $l \geq 384$, the client can pack the string into one ciphertext. With this packed ciphertext, the server can obtain $\mathbf{c}$ by 383 rotations, and then breaks $\mathbf{c}$ into two vectors, the first one with 2^8 ciphertexts and second one with 2^7 ciphertexts. The encrypted query string can be unfolded from these two vectors, and the server can then compute the inner product. The tree pruning algorithm takes a folding tree and l as input, scans from the root, once it finds a level such that the sum of $strLen$ of all nodes at this level is smaller than l, it prunes all nodes below this level. Tree pruning requires only a minor modification to the unfolding algorithm. Tree pruning can reduce communication cost because lower tree height means lower circuit depth, and then smaller q.

Multithreading. Conceptually, the server side computation in our protocol can be easily parallelised. Each step in unfolding requires $d_1 \cdot d_2$ independent homomorphic multiplications, and the inner product computation step requires n' independent homomorphic multiplications. We can parallelise those multiplications without much effort. However, multithreading is not easy with HElib because it depends on the NTL library that is not thread safe. After analysing the source code of HElib, we managed to make the raw multiplication and addition operations independent of the NTL library and make the prototype partially multithreaded. This enables our implementation to take advantage of multicore hardware.

5.2 Performance

In this section, we report the performance based on our prototype implementation. All experiments were conducted on a MacBook Pro laptop, with an Intel 2720QM quad-core 2.2 GHz CPU and 16 GB RAM. The choice of the BGV parameters is based on the formula given in [37]: $\phi(m) \geq \frac{\log(q/\sigma)(\lambda+110)}{7.2}$, where σ is the noise variance of the discrete Gaussian distribution and λ is the security parameter. The variance $\sigma = 3.2$ in HElib. We chose $m = 8191$ thus $\phi(m) = 8190$ and the number of plaintext slot $l = 630$. The modulus q is an odd integer of $40 + 20L$ bits, where L is the height of the folding tree. When $\lambda = 128$, the largest L supported by the chosen m is 7. In other words, the parameters ensure 128-bit security as long as the database is less than $2^{2^7} = 2^{128}$-bit, which is more than enough in any practical settings.

We first show the communication cost (Table 1). One thing to be noticed is that HElib outputs ciphertexts as textual strings of decimal numbers, so the measured size is bigger than the raw bit size. We used database of size 2^{25} bits (4 MB), 2^{30} bits (128 MB), and 2^{35} bits (4 GB) in our experiments. As we can see, the communication cost is low, only a few hundred KB. The response is only one ciphertext and the size is fixed across all cases. Most time the request is larger than the response despite that it is also just a single ciphertext. The reason is that q is not fixed in the BGV FHE scheme. We use modulus switching to switch to smaller q during the homomorphic operations. So the ciphertext in the response uses a smaller q and in consequence the size of the ciphertext is smaller. Another fact about the response is that has 3 ring elements[3] because we omitted the key switching operations in the last unfolding step. This explains why in the first experiment with pruning (database size $= 2^{25}$), the request is smaller than the response. We can also see that tree pruning does help reduce the request size.

We then show the server side computation time (Fig. 4). In Fig. 4a, we show the computation time for each step as well as the total time. The columns show the time for rotation, full multiplications (unfolding except the last step) and raw multiplications and additions (the last unfolding step plus inner product computation). The line shows the total computation time. As we can see, the rotation step is always fast. When the size

---

[3] The 3-part ciphertext can still be decrypted correctly, so this does not affect the correctness of our protocols.

Table 1. Communication cost with different database size

		Without Pruning			With Pruning	
	L	Request	Response	L	Request	Response
2^{25}	5	336 KB	192 KB	2	180 KB	192 KB
2^{30}	6	389 KB	192 KB	3	231 KB	192 KB
2^{35}	6	389 KB	192 KB	3	231 KB	192 KB

of the database is small, the computation is dominated by the full multiplications. But when the size of the database increases, the raw multiplication and addition step starts to become dominant. From the total time, we can estimate the minimal bandwidth needed to make the trivial solution faster. When the database is 4 MB, 128 MB and 4 GB, the minimal bandwidth is 1.25 Mbps, 5.65 Mbps and 10.44 Mbps. With a more powerful CPU (our experiments were done on a laptop), the minimal bandwidth would be higher. We can make our protocol more practical by utilising hardware parallelism. In Fig. 4b, we show the performance of our multithreaded implementation versus single threaded one. The time compared in the diagram is the raw multiplication and addition step, which is the only step we can currently implement in parallel. The experiments were done with a quad-core CPU, and the performance improvement was about 2.7 - 3 times. If with a fully thread safe BGV implementation and 2 or 3 more CPUs, the performance of our protocol can compete with the trivial solution in 100 Mbps LAN.

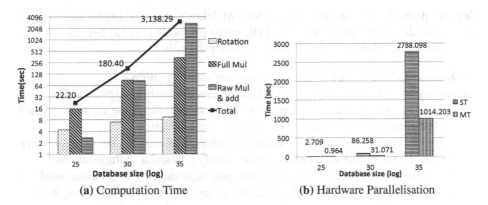

(a) Computation Time   (b) Hardware Parallelisation

Fig. 4. Server Side Computation Time of Our PIR Protocol

5.3 Performance Comparison

Communication. We compare the communication cost with the current most efficient protocols: Lipmaa's protocol [10] and Gentry's protocol [9]. The result is plotted in Fig. 5. Note we use size of ciphertext in the raw bit representation to draw the line for each protocols, so the numbers for our protocol are different from the numbers in Table 1. Lipmaa's protocol assumes that the n-bit database has n' entries each is t

bits. The smallest modulus size is $2k$-bit. When $t = k$, the total cost is $\alpha \cdot ((s + \alpha + 1)\zeta/2)(n'^{1/\alpha} - 1) \cdot k$ bit. In the figure, we set $k = 3072$ for 128-bit security and let $\alpha = \log n', s = 1, \zeta = 1$. Then as we can see, our protocol (without pruning) incurs more communication when the database is small, but would be better when the database is sufficiently large. This is due to the large ciphertext size in the BGV scheme. Gentry's protocol is very communication efficient. The communication cost is $3 \log^{3-o(1)} n$-bit integers. With any practical database size, it would be always more efficient than our protocol in terms of communication. However, the difference is less than 200 KB, which is not significant.

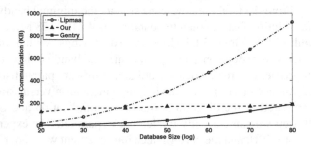

Fig. 5. Communication Cost Comparison

Computation. Here we do not compare with Melchor's protocol [18] because it is not secure. We do not compare with other FHE based protocols [11, 12] because they are obviously less efficient. Among all other existing protocols:

- Kushilevitz's protocol [4] requires n modular multiplications.
- Kushilevitz's TDP-based protocol [7] uses interactive hashing to protect the client's privacy against the server. It requires n TDP evaluations on the server side. Each TDP evaluation requires at least one modular multiplication.
- Gentry's protocol [9] requires only one modular exponentiation but the exponent is $2n$-bit. The computational cost is approximately n modular multiplications.
- Cachin's protocol [6] requires n modular exponentiations. The computational cost is approximately $l_e n/2$ modular multiplications, where l_e is the bit length of the exponent.
- Lipmaa's protocol [10] requires for each $2 \leq j \leq \log n'$, $2^{\log n' - j}$ exponentiations. The computational cost is at least $c \cdot n$ modular multiplications for some c depending on $\log n'$.
- Lipmaa's BDD based protocol [17] requires $O(n/(\log n))$ modular exponentiations. The computational cost is approximately $l_e n/(2 \log n)$ modular multiplications. Because the exponent size l_e is larger than $2 \log n$, the total cost is larger than n modular multiplications.
- Chang's protocol [8] requires n modular multiplications and $2 \log n$ modular exponentiations.

The most efficient protocol of all above ones is Kushilevitz's protocol [4] that requires n modular multiplications. Although the number of operations in Gentry's protocol is similar to Kushilevitz's protocol, in practice it would be less efficient due to the large exponent which is twice as big as the database. Another factor that makes Kushilevitz's protocol the most efficient one is the modulus size. Some protocols, e.g. Cachin's, Lipmaa's (and the BDD-based), and Chang's, require larger moduli. So the modular multiplication operation is slower in those protocols than in Kushilevitz's protocol.

We then compare our protocol with Kushilevitz's protocol. For 128-bit security, the modulus size needs to be at least 3072-bit. We measured time for a 3072-bit modular multiplication using the GMP library [38]. This is done by averaging the time for 1 million operations. The time for a single operation is 8.269×10^{-6} second. Thus, when the database size is 2^{25}, 2^{30} and 2^{35} bits, Kushilevitz's protocol would need 277.46, 8878.72 and 284119.04 seconds respectively. That is 12.5, 49.2 and 90.5 times slower than our protocol in single threaded mode.

6   Conclusion

In this paper, we presented a single server PIR protocol based on the BGV FHE scheme. The protocol is efficient both in terms of communication and computation. We have analysed its efficiency and security. We validated its practicality by a prototype implementation. The test results show that the total communication cost is as low as a few hundreds KB and the server side computation is much faster than existing single server PIR protocols.

In future work, we will test and improve performance over large data. We will extend the protocol to multi-query PIR [39]. Namely to further amortise the server-side computation complexity of PIR over multiple queries performed by a single client.

References

1. Khoshgozaran, A., Shahabi, C.: Private information retrieval techniques for enabling location privacy in location-based services. In: Bettini, C., Jajodia, S., Samarati, P., Wang, X.S. (eds.) Privacy in Location-Based Applications. LNCS, vol. 5599, pp. 59–83. Springer, Heidelberg (2009)
2. Henry, R., Olumofin, F.G., Goldberg, I.: Practical PIR for electronic commerce. In: ACM Conference on Computer and Communications Security, pp. 677–690 (2011)
3. Chor, B., Goldreich, O., Kushilevitz, E., Sudan, M.: Private information retrieval. In: FOCS, pp. 41–50 (1995)
4. Kushilevitz, E., Ostrovsky, R.: Replication is not needed: Single database, computationally-private information retrieval. In: FOCS, pp. 364–373 (1997)
5. Stern, J.P.: A new and efficient all-or-nothing disclosure of secrets protocol. In: Ohta, K., Pei, D. (eds.) ASIACRYPT 1998. LNCS, vol. 1514, pp. 357–371. Springer, Heidelberg (1998)
6. Cachin, C., Micali, S., Stadler, M.: Computationally private information retrieval with poly-logarithmic communication. In: Stern, J. (ed.) EUROCRYPT 1999. LNCS, vol. 1592, pp. 402–414. Springer, Heidelberg (1999)
7. Kushilevitz, E., Ostrovsky, R.: One-way trapdoor permutations are sufficient for non-trivial single-server private information retrieval. In: Preneel, B. (ed.) EUROCRYPT 2000. LNCS, vol. 1807, pp. 104–121. Springer, Heidelberg (2000)

8. Chang, Y.-C.: Single database private information retrieval with logarithmic communication. In: Wang, H., Pieprzyk, J., Varadharajan, V. (eds.) ACISP 2004. LNCS, vol. 3108, pp. 50–61. Springer, Heidelberg (2004)

9. Gentry, C., Ramzan, Z.: Single-database private information retrieval with constant communication rate. In: Caires, L., Italiano, G.F., Monteiro, L., Palamidessi, C., Yung, M. (eds.) ICALP 2005. LNCS, vol. 3580, pp. 803–815. Springer, Heidelberg (2005)

10. Lipmaa, H.: An oblivious transfer protocol with log-squared communication. In: Zhou, J., López, J., Deng, R.H., Bao, F. (eds.) ISC 2005. LNCS, vol. 3650, pp. 314–328. Springer, Heidelberg (2005)

11. Brakerski, Z., Vaikuntanathan, V.: Efficient fully homomorphic encryption from (standard) LWE. In: FOCS, pp. 97–106 (2011)

12. Yi, X., Kaosar, M.G., Paulet, R., Bertino, E.: Single-database private information retrieval from fully homomorphic encryption. IEEE Trans. Knowl. Data Eng. 25(5), 1125–1134 (2013)

13. Sion, R., Carbunar, B.: On the practicality of private information retrieval. In: NDSS (2007)

14. Williams, P., Sion, R.: Usable PIR. In: NDSS (2008)

15. Ding, X., Yang, Y., Deng, R.H., Wang, S.: A new hardware-assisted PIR with $o(n)$ shuffle cost. Int. J. Inf. Sec. 9(4), 237–252 (2010)

16. Ishai, Y., Kushilevitz, E., Ostrovsky, R., Sahai, A.: Cryptography from anonymity. In: FOCS, pp. 239–248 (2006)

17. Lipmaa, H.: First CPIR protocol with data-dependent computation. In: Lee, D., Hong, S. (eds.) ICISC 2009. LNCS, vol. 5984, pp. 193–210. Springer, Heidelberg (2010)

18. Melchor, C.A., Gaborit, P.: A fast private information retrieval protocol. In: ISIT, pp. 1848–1852 (2008)

19. Ostrovsky, R., Skeith III, W.E.: A survey of single-database private information retrieval: Techniques and applications. In: Okamoto, T., Wang, X. (eds.) PKC 2007. LNCS, vol. 4450, pp. 393–411. Springer, Heidelberg (2007)

20. Brakerski, Z., Gentry, C., Vaikuntanathan, V.: (leveled) fully homomorphic encryption without bootstrapping. In: ITCS, pp. 309–325 (2012)

21. Lyubashevsky, V., Peikert, C., Regev, O.: On ideal lattices and learning with errors over rings. In: Gilbert, H. (ed.) EUROCRYPT 2010. LNCS, vol. 6110, pp. 1–23. Springer, Heidelberg (2010)

22. Chor, B., Gilboa, N.: Computationally private information retrieval (extended abstract). In: STOC, pp. 304–313 (1997)

23. Ishai, Y., Kushilevitz, E.: Improved upper bounds on information-theoretic private information retrieval (extended abstract). In: STOC, pp. 79–88 (1999)

24. Beimel, A., Ishai, Y., Kushilevitz, E., Raymond, J.-F.: Breaking the O(n1/(2k-1)) barrier for information-theoretic private information retrieval. In: FOCS, pp. 261–270 (2002)

25. Goldberg, I.: Improving the robustness of private information retrieval. In: IEEE Symposium on Security and Privacy, pp. 131–148 (2007)

26. Paillier, P.: Public-key cryptosystems based on composite degree residuosity classes. In: Stern, J. (ed.) EUROCRYPT 1999. LNCS, vol. 1592, pp. 223–238. Springer, Heidelberg (1999)

27. Damgård, I., Jurik, M.: A generalisation, a simplification and some applications of Paillier's probabilistic public-key system. In: Kim, K.-C. (ed.) PKC 2001. LNCS, vol. 1992, pp. 119–136. Springer, Heidelberg (2001)

28. Bi, J., Liu, M., Wang, X.: Cryptanalysis of a homomorphic encryption scheme from ISIT 2008. In: ISIT, pp. 2152–2156 (2012)

29. Gentry, C.: A fully homomorphic encryption scheme. PhD thesis, Stanford University (2009)

30. van Dijk, M., Gentry, C., Halevi, S., Vaikuntanathan, V.: Fully homomorphic encryption over the integers. In: Gilbert, H. (ed.) EUROCRYPT 2010. LNCS, vol. 6110, pp. 24–43. Springer, Heidelberg (2010)
31. Gentry, C.: Fully homomorphic encryption using ideal lattices. In: STOC, pp. 169–178 (2009)
32. Gentry, C., Sahai, A., Waters, B.: Homomorphic encryption from learning with errors: Conceptually-simpler, asymptotically-faster, attribute-based. In: Canetti, R., Garay, J.A. (eds.) CRYPTO 2013, Part I. LNCS, vol. 8042, pp. 75–92. Springer, Heidelberg (2013)
33. Smart, N.P., Vercauteren, F.: Fully homomorphic SIMD operations. IACR Cryptology ePrint Archive 2011, 133 (2011)
34. Gentry, C., Halevi, S., Smart, N.P.: Fully homomorphic encryption with polylog overhead. In: Pointcheval, D., Johansson, T. (eds.) EUROCRYPT 2012. LNCS, vol. 7237, pp. 465–482. Springer, Heidelberg (2012)
35. Savage, J.E.: Models of Computation: Exploring the Power of Computing, 1st edn. Addison-Wesley Longman Publishing Co., Inc., Boston (1997)
36. Halevi, S., Shoup, V.: Algorithms in HElib. IACR Cryptology ePrint Archive 2014 (2014)
37. Gentry, C., Halevi, S., Smart, N.P.: Homomorphic evaluation of the AES circuit. In: Safavi-Naini, R., Canetti, R. (eds.) CRYPTO 2012. LNCS, vol. 7417, pp. 850–867. Springer, Heidelberg (2012)
38. Granlund, T.: The GMP development team: GNU MP: The GNU Multiple Precision Arithmetic Library. 5.1.3 edn. (2013), http://gmplib.org/
39. Ishai, Y., Kushilevitz, E., Ostrovsky, R., Sahai, A.: Batch codes and their applications. In: STOC, pp. 262–271 (2004)

A   The CPA Game

The security of the BGV scheme is captured by the following CPA game between an adversary and a challenger:

1. The adversary chooses L, then given a security parameter λ, the challenger runs $G(\lambda, L)$ to generate the secret key sk, the public key pk and the public parameters $param$. The challenger retains sk and gives the adversary pk and $param$.
2. The adversary may choose a polynomially bounded number of plaintexts and encrypts them using the public key.
3. Eventually, the adversary submits two chosen plaintexts m_0, m_1 to the challenger.
4. The challenger selects a bit $b \in \{0, 1\}$ uniformly at random, and sends the challenge ciphertext $c = E_{pk}(m_b)$ back to the adversary.
5. The adversary is free to perform a polynomially bounded number of additional computations or encryptions. Finally, it outputs a guess b'.

The adversary wins the game if $b' = b$. Under the RLWE assumption, the BGV scheme is secure which means the probability of any PPT adversary winning this game is $\frac{1}{2} + \eta$ for some negligible η.

Privacy-Preserving Complex Query Evaluation over Semantically Secure Encrypted Data

Bharath Kumar Samanthula[1], Wei Jiang[2], and Elisa Bertino[1]

[1] Department of Computer Science, Purdue University
305 N. University Street, West Lafayette, IN 47907
{bsamanth,bertino}@purdue.edu
[2] Department of Computer Science, Missouri S&T
500 W. 15th Street, Rolla, MO 65409
wjiang@mst.edu

Abstract. In the last decade, several techniques have been proposed to evaluate different types of queries (e.g., range and aggregate queries) over encrypted data in a privacy-preserving manner. However, solutions supporting the privacy-preserving evaluation of complex queries over encrypted data have been developed only recently. Such recent techniques, however, are either insecure or not feasible for practical applications. In this paper, we propose a novel privacy-preserving query processing framework that supports complex queries over encrypted data in the cloud computing environment and addresses the shortcomings of previous approaches. At a high level, our framework utilizes both homomorphic encryption and garbled circuit techniques at different stages in query processing to achieve the best performance, while at the same time protecting the confidentiality of data, privacy of the user's input query and hiding data access patterns. Also, as a part of query processing, we provide an efficient approach to systematically combine the predicate results (in encrypted form) of a query to derive the corresponding query evaluation result in a privacy-preserving manner. We theoretically and empirically analyze the performance of this approach and demonstrate its practical value over the current state-of-the-art techniques. Our proposed framework is very efficient from the user's perspective, thus allowing a user to issue queries even using a resource constrained device (e.g., PDAs and cell phones).

Keywords: Privacy, Complex Query, Encryption, Cloud Computing.

1 Introduction

In the past few years, there has been a significant growth in user's interest to outsource their data as well as operational services to the cloud. Along this direction, many small and medium size businesses have already outsourced their daily business processes to prominent cloud service providers such as Amazon, Google, and IBM. As privacy is a crucial requirement for many users, applications and organizations, data are usually encrypted before being uploaded to the cloud. By doing so, data confidentiality is still guaranteed even when a cloud server is compromised due to a hacking attack. However, the management of encrypted data poses several challenges, the most important

M. Kutyłowski and J. Vaidya (Eds.): ESORICS 2014, Part I, LNCS 8712, pp. 400–418, 2014.

of which is query processing. During query processing, we need to not only keep the data private from the cloud, but also the users' input queries. The question to ask is "how can the cloud perform searches over encrypted data without ever decrypting them or compromising the user's privacy". In the past decade, such question has resulted in a specific research area, known as *privacy-preserving query processing over encrypted data (PPQED)*.

As mentioned in [1], there are three different approaches to perform PPQED: (i) the query issuer downloads the entire encrypted database and performs a local search on the decrypted database, (ii) the cloud employs custom-designed cryptographic protocols to operate over encrypted data directly or indirectly, and (iii) the cloud deploys the tamper-proof trusted hardware (which is either trusted or certified by the clients) on the cloud-side that facilitates the cloud when operating over encrypted data inside a secure environment. The first approach, however, is not practical as it incurs heavy cost (both computation and communication) on the end-user (i.e., the query issuer). Techniques based on trusted hardware (e.g., [1]), such as the IBM 4764 or 4765 cryptographic co-processor, have gained significant attention in recent years. However, secure (or trusted) hardware is still very expensive and may not be suitable for cloud computing which is intended to use cheap commodity machines. Also, services based on secure hardware may not be affordable for some small businesses. Apart from those approaches, another widely investigated approach is based on the deployment of custom-designed crypto-graphic techniques by the cloud to operate over encrypted data.

Along this direction, researchers from both academia and industry have proposed several approaches (e.g., [2–8]). However, most of such approaches focus on privacy-preserving protocols for evaluating specific queries (e.g., range and aggregate) over encrypted data. That is, they are not directly useful to execute complex queries over en-crypted data. As a result, privacy-preserving evaluation of complex and arbitrary queries over encrypted data is still an open and challenging problem for data outsourcing. Some recent approaches have addressed this problem to an extent. However, such approaches are either insecure or not feasible for practical applications (see Section 2 for more de-tails). In particular, as highlighted in [9–11], data access pattern information can leak much valuable information (e.g., correspondence between plaintexts and ciphertexts) to the cloud. We believe that the data access patterns should be protected from the cloud which would otherwise compromise the semantic security [12] of encrypted data stored in the cloud. Unfortunately, most of the existing PPQED methods do not address access pattern issue (see Section 2.2 for more details).

Hence, the primary focus of this paper is to develop a secure cloud computing frame-work that can support the evaluation of complex queries and is also efficient from an end-user's perspective. To obtain the best performance, our framework switches be-tween homomorphic encryption and garbled circuit techniques based on the underlying parametric values and the sub-task (part of query processing) at hand.

1.1 Problem Statement

In our problem setting, we consider three different parties: the data owner (also referred to as Alice), the cloud, and the data consumer (also referred to as Bob). Let T denote Alice's database with n records, denoted by $t_1, \ldots, t_n$, and m attributes. We assume that Alice initially encrypts T attribute-wise using her public key and outsources the encrypted database to a cloud. In this paper, we explicitly assume that Alice's secret key is generated using a semantically secure[1] and additive homomorphic encryption scheme (such as the Paillier cryptosystem [13]). First, it is worth pointing out that semantic security is necessary to ensure that the cloud cannot distinguish the encrypted data in the first place (i.e., ciphertexts should be computationally indistinguishable from the cloud's perspective). Second, by encrypting the data using an additive homomorphic encryption scheme, Alice makes it possible for the cloud to perform certain operations directly over encrypted data, such as operations that might also be useful for other data analytics tasks (e.g., secure clustering and classification). More details regarding the properties of the additive homomorphic encryption scheme used in our approach are provided in Section 3.2.

Let T' denote the encrypted database of Alice. Now consider an authorized user Bob (which would typically be authorized by Alice) who wants to securely retrieve data from T' in the cloud using his private (complex) query Q. In this paper, a complex query is defined as a query with arbitrary number of sub-queries where each sub-query can consist of conjunctions and/or disjunctions of arbitrary number of relational predicates. An example could be $Q = ((Age \geq 40) \vee ((Sex = M) \wedge (Marital\ Status = Married))) \wedge (Disease = Diabetes)$. We assume that Q is represented as a boolean function expressed in disjunctive normal form[2] (DNF) as follows.

$$Q : G_1 \vee G_2 \vee \ldots \vee G_{l-1} \vee G_l \to 0, 1$$

where the input to Q is a data record t_i. Here G_j denotes the jth clause which is a conjunction of b_j predicates, for $1 \leq j \leq l$, and l denotes the number of clauses in Q. More specifically, $G_j = P_{j,1} \wedge P_{j,2} \wedge \ldots \wedge P_{j,b_j-1} \wedge P_{j,b_j}$ and each predicate $P_{j,k}$ is also a boolean function that returns either 0 or 1 depending on the underlying condition. In general, a predicate applies a relational operator (i.e., $>, \geq, <, \leq, =$) on specific attribute values and search input. For example, consider the predicate $P_{1,1} : AGE > 20$, where AGE is an attribute in T, and a record t_i from T. Then, $P_{1,1}(t_i) = 1$ iff the AGE attribute value in data record t_i is greater than 20. Otherwise, $P_{1,1}(t_i) = 0$.

Under the above system model, the goal of our approach is to facilitate Bob in efficiently retrieving the data records from T' (stored in the cloud) that satisfy Q in a privacy-preserving manner. We refer to such a process as privacy-preserving query processing over encrypted data (PPQED). More formally, we define a PPQED protocol as follows:

$$PPQED(T', Q) \to S$$

where $S \subseteq T$ denotes the output set of records that satisfy Q. That is, $\forall\ t' \in S, Q(t') = 1$. In general, a PPQED protocol should meet the following privacy requirements:

- **Data Confidentiality** - during the query processing phase, neither the contents of T nor of any intermediate results are disclosed to the cloud.

---

[1] Precisely, if the encryption scheme is semantically secure, then the ciphertexts are random numbers from the cloud's perspective.

[2] Note that any given boolean function can be represented in both DNF and conjunctive normal form (CNF). In this paper, we simply choose DNF to represent Q. However, our proposed protocol can be easily adopted to the later case upon simple modifications.

- **End-user's Privacy** - At any point of time, Bob's query Q should not be disclosed to the cloud and Alice.
- At the end of the PPQED protocol, S should be revealed only to Bob.
- $T - S$ (i.e., information other than the output) should never be disclosed to Bob.
- Data access patterns should never be disclosed to the cloud (as well as to Alice). That is, for any two queries Q_1 and Q_2, the corresponding output sets S_1 and S_2 should be computationally indistinguishable from the cloud's perspective.

In our proposed PPQED protocol, once Alice outsources her encrypted data to the cloud, she does not participate in the query processing task; therefore, no information is revealed to Alice. However, it may be required that in certain applications, Alice is able to validate Bob's query before forwarding it to the cloud. We claim that such extensions can be easily incorporated into the proposed PPQED protocol upon straightforward modifications. For simplicity, we do not consider such natural extensions to PPQED in the rest of this paper. Also, due to space limitations, we do not discuss how our solution can be extended to protect access pattern information in this paper. However, we refer the reader to our technical report [14] for a detailed discussion on extending our proposed solution to hide the data access pattern information.

1.2 Main Contributions

In this paper, we propose a new two-stage PPQED protocol under the cloud computing environment. At a high level, the main contributions of this paper are as follows.

(a). **Security:** The proposed PPQED protocol protects the confidentiality of data, privacy of the user's input query and also hides the data access patterns under the standard semi-honest model [15].
(b). **Efficiency:** Our proposed protocol incurs negligible computation cost on the end-user. Also, we propose an efficient mechanism that systematically combines the individual predicate results to compute the corresponding query evaluation result. Our theoretical analysis shows that the proposed solution improves the upper bound compared to the naive solution constructed from the existing techniques.
(c). **Flexibility:** Since the proposed PPQED protocol is a hybrid approach, in that it utilizes both homomorphic encryption and garbled circuits, it allows the developers to switch between the two depending on the application requirements, and thus enhancing flexibility. Specifically, our protocol can be used as a building block in larger privacy-preserving applications. E.g., the cloud can perform data analytics on different query results either using homomorphic encryption or garbled circuit techniques. More details on how to convert homomorphic values to garbled values and vice versa are presented in Section 4.

The rest of the paper is organized as follows. In Section 2, we review upon the existing work related to our problem domain. Section 3 introduces relevant background information on the threat model assumed in this paper and on additive homomorphic encryption scheme used in our approach. A set of security primitives that are utilized in the proposed PPQED protocol and their possible implementations are provided in Section 4. Also, the proposed PPQED protocol is explained in detail along with the security and complexity analysis in this section. Finally, we conclude the paper and highlight possible directions for future research in Section 5.

2   Related Work

2.1   Query Processing over Encrypted Data

In general, the computations involved in query processing depend on the query under consideration. Along this direction, several methods have been proposed to securely process range (e.g., [2, 4, 6–8, 16]) and aggregate (e.g., [3, 5, 17]) queries over encrypted data. It is worth noting that such methods are suitable for evaluating only specific queries; thus, they are not directly applicable to solve the PPQED problem (i.e., combination of multiple and different sub-queries) over encrypted data. Also, they leak different kinds of information for efficiency reasons. Due to space limitations, we refer the reader to our technical report [14] for more details regarding their disadvantages.

2.2   Existing PPQED Methods

Unfortunately, only a very few approaches have been proposed to address the PPQED problem. In what follows, we discuss the main differences of our work with approaches proposed along those directions. Table 1 highlights some of the key differences between the existing work and our solution.

Golle et al. [18] were the first to propose a protocol that can evaluate conjunctive equality queries on encrypted documents. However, their protocol supports neither disjunctive queries nor predicates with inequality conditions. As an improvement, Boneh and Waters [16] proposed a new searchable public-key system (referred to as hidden vector encryption) that supports comparison and general subset queries over encrypted data. We emphasize that their technique is very expensive and complex to implement. Also, their method is suitable for conjunctive queries, but not applicable to either disjunctive queries or combination of both. As an alternative approach, Popa et al. [19] proposed CryptDB, a system that executes SQL queries over encrypted data using a set of SQL-aware encryption schemes. At a high level, their system encrypts each data item using an onion of encryption schemes with the outermost layer providing maximum security, whereas the innermost layer provides more functionality and weak security. During the query processing stage, the cloud is given secret keys to decrypt the outer layers and perform the necessary operations over encrypted data at inner layers. However, CryptDB has some major drawbacks: (i) it uses a proxy which is a trusted third-party and thus makes it hard to use the system in practical applications, (ii) it reveals different types of information to the cloud server at different layers, and (iii) multiple onions may have to be generated for each data item which makes the approach very expensive. The actual security offered by an onion in CryptDB is the protection offered by its inner most layer. For example, consider an onion in CryptDB for comparison operations, it reveals the relative ordering among the attribute values to the cloud. Thus, CryptDB does not ensure data confidentiality in all cases. Also, none of the above PPQED methods addressed the access pattern issue which is a crucial privacy requirement [9–11].

In the past few years, researchers have also investigated secure query processing frameworks based on the use of tamper-proof trusted hardware on the cloud side. Along this direction, Bajaj and Sion [1] proposed TrustedDB, an outsourced database framework that allows a client to execute SQL queries by leveraging cloud-hosted tamper-proof trusted hardware in critical query processing stages. However, as mentioned in

Table 1. Comparison with the existing work

Method	Low Cost on Bob	Data Confidentiality	Query Privacy	Hide Data Access Patterns	CNF and DNF Query Support
Golle et al. [18]	✘	✔	✔	✘	✘
Boneh and Waters [16]	✘	✔	✔	✘	✘
Popa et al. [19]	✔	✘	✘	✘	✔
This paper	✔	✔	✔	✔	✔

Section 1, secure hardware is very expensive and may not be suitable for cloud computing which is intended to use cheap commodity machines. Also, services based on secure hardware may not be affordable for some small businesses. Another area of research is based on the use of Oblivious RAM (ORAM) techniques (e.g., [20]) to solve the PPQED problem. However, under ORAM techniques, the query issuer need to know the index structure before hand (which may not always be possible). In particular to the PPQED problem, each authorized user has to efficiently maintain multiple indexes to support complex queries. We believe that more research is needed to investigate the side effects of using secure processors and ORAM techniques to solve the PPQED problem and we leave this interesting open problem for future work.

We may ask whether fully homomorphic cryptosystems such as [21], which can perform arbitrary computations over encrypted data without ever decrypting them, are suitable to solve the PPQED problem. It is a known fact that fully homomorphic encryption schemes can compute any function over encrypted data [22]. However, such schemes are very expensive and their usage in practical applications has yet to be explored. For example, it was shown in [23] that even for weak security parameters one "bootstrapping" operation of the homomorphic operation would take at least 30 seconds on a high performance machine.

Based on the above discussions, it is clear that there is a strong need to develop an efficient PPQED protocol that can protect data confidentiality, privacy of the user's input query and data access patterns at all times.

3 Background

3.1 Adversarial Model

In this paper, privacy/security is closely related to the amount of information disclosed during the execution of a protocol. To maximize security guarantee, we adopt the commonly accepted security definitions and proof techniques in the literature of secure multi-party computation (SMC) to analyze the security of our proposed protocol. SMC was first introduced by the Yao's Millionaire problem [24, 25] under the two-party setting, and it was extended to multi-party computations by Goldreich et al. [26].

There are two common adversarial models under SMC: semi-honest and malicious. Due to space limitations, we refer the reader to [15] for more details regarding their security definitions and proof techniques. In this paper, to develop secure and efficient protocols, we assume that the participating parties are semi-honest. This implicitly assumes that there is no collusion between the parties. We emphasize that this assumption is not new and the existing PPQED methods discussed in Section 2.2 were also proposed under the semi-honest model. Indeed, it is worth noting that such an assumption makes sense especially under the cloud environment. This is because, since the current known cloud service providers are well established IT companies, it is hard to see the possibility for two companies, e.g., Google and Amazon, to collude to damage their reputations and consequently place negative impact on their revenues. Thus, in our problem domain, assuming that the participating parties are semi-honest is realistic. Note that, even under the malicious two-party setting, one has to assume that there is no collusion between the participating parties due to the theoretical limitation [27].

3.2 Paillier Cryptosystem

The Paillier cryptosystem is an additive homomorphic and probabilistic asymmetric encryption scheme [13]. Let E_{pk} be the encryption function with public key pk given by (N, g), where N is a product of two large primes and g is a generator in $\mathbb{Z}_{N^2}^*$. Also, let D_{sk} be the decryption function with secret key sk. Given two plaintexts $x, y \in \mathbb{Z}_N$, the Paillier encryption scheme exhibits the following properties.

a. **Homomorphic Addition:** $E_{pk}(x + y) \leftarrow E_{pk}(x) * E_{pk}(y) \bmod N^2$;
b. **Homomorphic Multiplication:** $E_{pk}(x * y) \leftarrow E_{pk}(x)^y \bmod N^2$;
c. **Semantic Security:** The encryption scheme is semantically secure [12]. Briefly, given a set of ciphertexts, an adversary cannot deduce any additional information about the plaintexts.

We emphasize that any other additive homomorphic encryption scheme (e.g., [28]) that satisfies the above properties can be utilized to implement our proposed framework. However, to be concrete and for efficiency reasons, this paper assumes that Alice encrypts her data using the Paillier cryptosystem before outsourcing them to a cloud.

4 The Proposed Framework

In this section, we first discuss a set of privacy-preserving primitives that will be later used in the proposed PPQED protocol as building blocks. Then, we demonstrate how to securely evaluate a predicate using homomorphic encryption and garbled circuits. Finally, we present our novel PPQED scheme that facilitates Bob in retrieving the data (that satisfy his query Q) from the cloud in a privacy-preserving manner.

In the proposed framework, we assume the existence of two non-colluding semi-honest cloud service providers, denoted by C_1 and C_2, which together form a federated cloud. We emphasize that such a setting is not new and has been commonly used in the recent related works (e.g., [29, 30]). Initially, as part of the key setup stage, the data owner Alice generates a pair of public/secret key pair (pk, sk) based on Paillier's scheme [13]. Suppose Alice outsources her encrypted database T' to C_1 and the secret key sk to C_2. That is, C_1 has $T'_{i,j} = E_{pk}(t_{i,j})$, for $1 \leq i \leq n$ and $1 \leq j \leq m$. In this paper, we explicitly assume that there exist secure communication channels (e.g.,

SSL) between each pair of participating parties. Note that other basic mechanisms, such as authentication and data replication, are well-studied problems under the cloud computing model; therefore, they are outside the scope of this paper.

Though we propose the PPQED protocol under the federated cloud model, we stress that it can also be implemented under the single cloud model with the same security guarantees. More specifically, under the single cloud setting, the role of the second cloud (i.e., C_2) can be played by Alice with her own private server holding the key sk. However, with limited computing resource and technical expertise, it is in the best interest of Alice to completely outsource its data management and operational tasks to a cloud. In general, whether Alice uses a private server or cloud service provider C_2 actually depends on her resources. In particular to our solution, after outsourcing encrypted data to C_1 and C_2, Alice does not participate in any future computations.

4.1 Basic Security Primitives

In this sub-section, we discuss three basic security primitives that will be later used in constructing our proposed PPQED protocol.

- Secure Multiplication (SMP): In this protocol, we assume that C_1 holds the private input $(E_{pk}(a), E_{pk}(b))$ and C_2 holds the secret key sk, where a and b are unknown to C_1 and C_2. The output of SMP is $E_{pk}(a * b)$ and revealed only to C_1. During this process, no information regarding a and b should be revealed to C_1 and C_2.
- Secure Bit-OR (SBOR): In this protocol, C_1 holds private input $(E_{pk}(o_1), E_{pk}(o_2))$ and C_2 holds sk. The goal of SBOR is to securely compute $E_{pk}(o_1 \lor o_2)$, where o_1 and o_2 are two bits. The output $E_{pk}(o_1 \lor o_2)$ should be known only to C_1.
- Secure Comparison (SC): In this protocol, C_1 holds private input $(E_{pk}(a), E_{pk}(b))$ and C_2 holds sk such that a and b are unknown to both parties, where $0 \leq a, b < 2^w$. Here w denotes the domain size (in bits) of a and b. The goal of the secure comparison (SC) protocol is to evaluate the condition $a > b$. At the end of the protocol, the output $E_{pk}(c)$ should be revealed only to C_1, where c denotes the comparison result. More specifically, $c = 1$ if $a > b$, and $c = 0$ otherwise. During this process, no information regarding a, b, and c is revealed to C_1 and C_2.

The efficient implementations of SMP and SBOR are given in [14]. On the other hand, though many SC protocols (under the two-party setting) have been proposed, we observe that they reveal the comparison result c to at least one of the participating parties. In this paper, we extend the SC protocol proposed in [31] to address our problem requirements. More details are given in the next sub-section.

4.2 Secure Evaluation of Individual Predicates (SEIP)

In this sub-section, we consider the scenario of evaluating a given predicate over T' stored in C_1. Without loss of generality, let $P : (k, \alpha, op)$ be a predicate, where α denotes the search input and k denotes the attribute index upon which the relational operator op has to be evaluated. More specifically, t_i satisfies the predicate P (i.e., $P(t_i) = 1$) iff the relational operation op on $t_{i,k}$ and α holds. In general, the possible set for op is $\{>, \geq, <, \geq, =\}$. It is important to note that the value of α should not be revealed to Alice, C_1, and C_2 for privacy reasons (note that Alice does not participate in query processing, so no information is revealed to her). To evaluate P, Bob first needs to send $E_{pk}(P) = (k, E_{pk}(\alpha), op)$ to C_1. However, if the number of predicates is large, Bob's computation cost for encryption can be high. E.g., if Q has 100 predicates, denoted by $P_1, \ldots, P_{100}$, then Bob has to compute $E_{pk}(P_1), \ldots, E_{pk}(P_{100})$.

We adopt the following simple strategy that incurs negligible computation cost on Bob and at the same time preserves the privacy of his predicate. Bob generates two random shares of α such that $\alpha_1 + \alpha_2 \mod N = \alpha$. A simple way to generate these shares is to set $\alpha_1 = N - r$ and $\alpha_2 = \alpha + r \mod N$, where r is a random number in $\mathbb{Z}_N$ known only to Bob. It is clear that $\alpha = \alpha_1 + \alpha_2 \mod N$. After this, he sends $P^{\langle 1 \rangle}$ and $P^{\langle 2 \rangle}$ to C_1 and C_2, respectively, where $P^{\langle 1 \rangle} = (k, \alpha_1, op)$ and $P^{\langle 2 \rangle} = (\alpha_2, op)$. Here Bob needs to send the relational operator op to both C_1 and C_2 in order to evaluate P. Then, C_1 with input $\langle T'_i, P^{\langle 1 \rangle} \rangle$ and C_2 with input $P^{\langle 2 \rangle}$ need to securely verify whether the relational operation op holds between $t_{i,k}$ and α without revealing any information to C_1 and C_2, for $1 \leq i \leq n$. We refer to such a process as secure evaluation of individual predicates (SEIP).

For simplicity, let op be the greater than relational comparison operator (however, similar steps can be derived for other relational operators). Under this case, the goal is for C_1 with private input $\langle T'_i, (k, \alpha_1, >) \rangle$ and C_2 with $(\alpha_2, >)$ to securely determine whether $t_{i,k} > \alpha$, for $1 \leq i \leq n$. Let the evaluation result be c_i. Then the output should be $E_{pk}(c_i)$ such that $c_i = 1$ if $t_{i,k} > \alpha$, and $c_i = 0$ otherwise. At the end, the output $E_{pk}(c_i)$ should be revealed only to C_1. Also, the values of c_i and α should not be revealed to C_1 and C_2. In addition, during this process, no information regarding the contents of T should be revealed to C_1 and C_2.

At first sight, it is clear that the existing secure comparison (SC) protocols can be used to solve the SEIP problem (assuming greater than relational operator). Current SC protocols, under the two-party setting, are based on two techniques: (i) homomorphic encryption and (ii) garbled circuits. We now discuss how to solve the SEIP problem using SC with each of these two techniques.

SEIP Using Homomorphic Encryption. Given that C_1 holds $\langle T'_i, (k, \alpha_1, >) \rangle$ and C_2 holds $(\alpha_2, >)$, we aim to solve the SEIP problem using the homomorphic encryption based SC protocols (denoted by SEIP$_h$) as follows. To start with, C_2 initially sends $E_{pk}(\alpha_2)$ to C_1. Upon receiving, C_1 locally computes $E_{pk}(\alpha) = E_{pk}(\alpha_1) * E_{pk}(\alpha_2)$. Now, the goal is for C_1 and C_2 to securely evaluate the functionality $t_{i,k} > \alpha$ with $(E_{pk}(t_{i,k}), E_{pk}(\alpha))$ as input using the existing SC protocols. Remember that $(E_{pk}(t_{i,k}), E_{pk}(\alpha))$ is known only to C_1.

The existing SC protocols under homomorphic encryption strongly rely on encryptions of individual bits rather than on simple encrypted integers [31]. However, existing secure bit-decomposition (SBD) techniques can be utilized for converting an encrypted integer into encryptions of the corresponding individual bits. For example, consider two integers x and y such that $0 \leq x, y < 2^w$, where w denotes the domain size (in bits) of x and y. Let x_1 (resp., y_1) and x_w (resp., y_w) denote the most and least significant bits of x (resp., y), respectively. Given $E_{pk}(x)$ and $E_{pk}(y)$, C_1 and C_2 can securely convert them into $\langle E_{pk}(x_1), \ldots, E_{pk}(x_w) \rangle$ and $\langle E_{pk}(y_1), \ldots, E_{pk}(y_w) \rangle$ using the existing SBD techniques [32, 33]. Note that the outputs are revealed only to C_1. Next, we detail the main steps involved in the SC protocol, proposed by Blake et al. [31], that takes the encrypted bit-wise vectors of x and y as input and outputs $c = 1$ if $x > y$, and 0 otherwise. To start with, for $1 \le i \le w$, C_1 performs the following operations:

- Compute an encryption of the difference between the ith bits of x and y as $E_{pk}(d_i)$ $= E_{pk}(x_i - y_i)$.
- Compute an encryption of the XOR between the ith bits as $E_{pk}(z_i) = E_{pk}(x_i \oplus y_i)$. Note that $x_i \oplus y_i = x_i + y_i - 2x_i * y_i$. Therefore, this step requires an implicit secure multiplication (SMP) protocol as the building block to compute $E_{pk}(x_i * y_i)$.
- Generate an encrypted vector γ such that $\gamma_0 = 0$ and $\gamma_i = 2\gamma_{i-1} + z_i$.
- Generate an encrypted vector δ such that $\delta_i = d_i + r_i * (\gamma_i - 1)$, where r_i is a random number in $\mathbb{Z}_N$. The observation here is, if $\gamma_k = 1$ (denoting the first position at which the corresponding bits of x and y differ), then $\delta_k = d_k$. For all other indexes (i.e., $i \ne k$), δ_i is a random number in $\mathbb{Z}_N$.
- Let $\delta' = \langle E_{pk}(\delta_1), \ldots, E_{pk}(\delta_w) \rangle$. C_1 permutes δ' using a random permutation function π (known only to C_1) to get $\tau = \pi(\delta')$ and sends it to C_2.

Upon receiving, C_2 decrypts τ component-wise and checks for index k. If $D_{sk}(\tau_k) = 1$, then $x > y$. Similarly, if $D_{sk}(\tau_k) = -1$, then $y > x$. Note that $D_{sk}(\tau_j)$ always yields a random value in $\mathbb{Z}_N$, for $j \ne k$ and $1 \le j \le w$.

It is worth pointing out that we cannot directly use the SC protocol of [31] in SEIP$_h$ as it leaks the comparison result to C_2. Therefore, in order to use the method in [31], we need to somehow prevent this information leakage. Along this direction, with the goal of providing better security, we now provide a mechanism, as an extension to [31], that obliviously hides the comparison result from both C_1 and C_2. We denote the extended version of the SC protocol in [31] by SC$_{obv}$.

The main idea of SC$_{obv}$ is as follows. Instead of evaluating the greater than functionality directly, C_1 can randomly choose a functionality F (by flipping a coin), where F is either $x > y$ or $y \ge x$, and obliviously execute F with C_2. Since F is randomly chosen and known only to C_1, the comparison result is oblivious to C_2. Also, unlike [31], the output of SC$_{obv}$ is the encryption of comparison result (i.e., $E_{pk}(c)$) which will be known only to C_1. Note that the comparison result (i.e., c) should not be revealed to C_1 and C_2. The main steps involved in the SC$_{obv}$ protocol are as given below:

- Initially, C_1 chooses F randomly and proceeds as follows. If $F : x > y$, compute $E_{pk}(d_i) = E_{pk}(x_i - y_i)$. Else, compute $E_{pk}(d_i) = E_{pk}(y_i - x_i)$, for $1 \le i \le w$.
- C_1 computes the encrypted vector δ' using the similar steps (as discussed above) in the SC protocol of [31]. After this, C_1 sends $\tau = \pi(\delta')$ to C_2.
- Upon receiving, C_2 decrypts it component-wise and finds the index k. If $D_{sk}(\tau_k) = 1$, then compute $U = E_{pk}(1)$. Else, i.e., when $D_{sk}(\tau_k) = -1$, compute $U = E_{pk}(0)$. Then, C_2 sends U to C_1.
- Finally, C_1 computes the output $E_{pk}(c)$ as follows. If $F : x > y$, then $E_{pk}(c) = U$. Else, $E_{pk}(c) = E_{pk}(1) * U^{N-1}$.

It is important to note that, since U is in encrypted form, C_1 cannot deduce any information regarding the output c. In addition, as F is randomly chosen and known only to C_1, the output is oblivious to C_2. Hence, we claim that the comparison result c is protected from both C_1 and C_2. Note that $E_{pk}(c)$ is known only to C_1.

SEIP Using Garbled Circuits. In this sub-section, we discuss how to solve the SEIP problem using the garbled circuit technique (denoted by $SEIP_g$) [34]. For this purpose, we first need to convert the homomorphic value $E_{pk}(t_{i,k})$ into a garbled value. Also, a garbled value for α should be generated. To achieve this, we propose a simple solution which is as follows. Initially, C_1 generates random shares for $t_{i,k}$ using $E_{pk}(t_{i,k})$. That is, C_1 computes $E_{pk}(t_{i,k} + r)$, where r is a random value in $\mathbb{Z}_N$, and sends it to C_2. Upon receiving, C_2 decrypts it to get the random share $t_{i,k} + r \mod N$. Also, C_1 sets his/her random share as $N - r$. Apart from this, remember that C_1 and C_2 have α_1 and α_2 (random shares of α), respectively. Also, C_1 picks a random number r' from $\mathbb{Z}_N$. Now, C_1 constructs a garbled circuit by extending the circuit corresponding to the SC protocol of [35] based on the following steps (assuming that C_2 is the circuit evaluator):

– Add the random shares of C_1 and C_2 (with an explicit modulo operation) to get $t_{i,k}$ and α as part of the circuit.
– Compare $t_{i,k}$ with α. It is important to note that the comparison result c is part of the circuit; therefore, not known to C_1 and C_2.
– Add r' to c (within the circuit followed by a modulo operation). The masked comparison result (i.e., $c + r' \mod N$) is the final output of the circuit. Note that the circuit output should be known only to C_2 (i.e., the circuit evaluator).

After this, C_2 sends $E_{pk}(c + r')$ to C_1. Finally, C_1 removes the extra random factor using homomorphic operations to get $E_{pk}(c)$ locally.

In summary, given any predicate (where search input is randomly shared between C_1 and C_2) with relational operators $\{>, \geq, <, \leq\}$; C_1 and C_2 can securely compute the encryption of the predicate result on record t_i using either $SEIP_h$ or $SEIP_g$, for $1 \leq i \leq n$. In general, which technique to use actually depends on the domain size of the attribute under consideration (more details are given in Sections 4.3 and 4.5). Similarly, C_1 and C_2 can securely evaluate the predicate with an equality operator. Once we know how to securely evaluate a given predicate, the next step is to securely combine the results of all predicates in Q and decide whether t_i satisfies Q. Along this direction, we next present a new two-stage protocol to solve the privacy-preserving complex query evaluation over encrypted data (PPQED) problem.

4.3   The Proposed PPQED Protocol

As mentioned in Section 1, this paper explicitly assumes that Bob's input query Q is represented in disjunctive normal form given by $G_1 \vee G_2 \vee \ldots \vee G_{l-1} \vee G_l$. Here G_j is a conjunction of b_j predicates given by $G_j = P_{j,1} \wedge P_{j,2} \wedge \ldots \wedge P_{j,b_j-1} \wedge P_{j,b_j}$.

We now propose a novel solution to the PPQED problem using Q as Bob's input query over encrypted data T' stored in C_1. At a high level, the proposed PPQED protocol consists of the following two stages:

– Stage 1 - Secure Evaluation of Predicates (SEP): In this stage, Bob initially sends his private query Q (using random shares) to C_1 and C_2. Then, C_1 and C_2 jointly

---

Algorithm 1. PPQED$(T', Q) \to S$

Require: C_1 has T', C_2 has sk, and Bob has Q

1: Bob, **for** $1 \leq j \leq l$ **do:**

   (a). Send $P_j^{\langle 1 \rangle} = \{P_{j,1}^{\langle 1 \rangle}, \ldots, P_{j,b_j}^{\langle 1 \rangle}\}$ to C_1 and $P_j^{\langle 2 \rangle} = \{P_{j,1}^{\langle 2 \rangle}, \ldots, P_{j,b_j}^{\langle 2 \rangle}\}$ to C_2

2: **for** $1 \leq i \leq n$ **do:**

   (a). C_1 and C_2, **for** $1 \leq j \leq l$ **do:**

       – $L_{i,j}[h] \leftarrow \text{SEIP}\left(\langle T_i', P_{j,h}^{\langle 1 \rangle}\rangle, P_{j,h}^{\langle 2 \rangle}\right)$, where $\langle T_i', P_{j,h}^{\langle 1 \rangle}\rangle$ is the private input of C_1

       and $P_{j,h}^{\langle 2 \rangle}$ is the private input of C_2, for $1 \leq h \leq b_j$

   (b). $\text{SROD}_s(L_{i,1}, \ldots, L_{i,l})$, where $L_{i,j} = \langle L_{i,j}[1], \ldots, L_{i,j}[b_j]\rangle$ and $1 \leq j \leq l$

---

evaluate the predicates of each clause in Q using SEIP as a sub-routine. At the end of this stage, only C_1 knows the encryptions of the evaluation results of $P_{j,h}$'s on each data record t_i, i.e., $E_{pk}(P_{j,h}(t_i))$, for $1 \leq j \leq l$ and $1 \leq h \leq b_j$.

– Stage 2 - Secure Retrieval of Output Data (SROD): C_1 and C_2 compute $E_{pk}(Q(t_i))$ using the evaluation results on the individual predicates resulted from Stage 1. Then, Bob securely retrieves the output set S with the help of C_1 and C_2.

The main steps involved in the proposed PPQED protocol are given in Algorithm 1. Next, we discuss each stage of PPQED in detail.

Stage 1 - Secure Evaluation of Predicates (SEP). The key steps involved in Stage 1 are shown as steps 1 to 2(a) in Algorithm 1. To start with, as explained in the previous sub-section, Bob initially generates the random shares for each predicate in Q and sends them to C_1 and C_2. More specifically, given a predicate $P_{j,h}$, Bob sends $P_{j,h}^{\langle 1 \rangle} = (k_{j,h}, \alpha_{j,h}^{\langle 1 \rangle}, op_{j,h})$ and $P_{j,h}^{\langle 2 \rangle} = (\alpha_{j,h}^{\langle 2 \rangle}, op_{j,h})$ to C_1 and C_2, respectively, for $1 \leq j \leq l$ and $1 \leq h \leq b_j$. Here $\alpha_{j,h} = \alpha_{j,h}^{\langle 1 \rangle} + \alpha_{j,h}^{\langle 2 \rangle} \bmod N$ is the search input, $k_{j,h}$ is the attribute index to be searched, and $op_{j,h}$ is the relational operator of predicate $P_{j,h}$. Upon receiving the values, C_1 and C_2 jointly evaluate each predicate $P_{j,h}$ on T_i' using the SEIP solution discussed in the previous sub-section. Let the output be denoted by $L_{i,j}[h]$ which will be known only to C_1. Note that $L_{i,j}[h] = E_{pk}(P_{j,h}(t_i))$, where $P_{j,h}(t_i) = 1$ iff t_i satisfies $P_{j,h}$, and $P_{j,h}(t_i) = 0$ otherwise.

We emphasize that, depending on the domain size of the attribute in consideration, either SEIP_h or SEIP_g can be utilized in this step. As it will be clear in Section 4.5, for attributes with smaller domain size (e.g., Age attribute), SEIP_h gives better performance than SEIP_g. On the other hand, for attributes with larger domain sizes (e.g., Bank account numbers), SEIP_g is more efficient than SEIP_h. Hence, by conveniently choosing between homomorphic encryption (SEIP_h) and garbled circuit (SEIP_g) based solution depending on the underlying attribute domain size, our PPQED protocol takes advantage of both techniques and significantly improves the overall performance.

Stage 2 - Secure Retrieval of Output Data (SROD). Following from Stage 1, C_1 has the evaluation results (in encrypted form) for all the predicates in Q on each data record t_i. The goal of Stage 2 is to utilize these predicate results and compute the query evaluation result on t_i. Since $E_{pk}(P_{j,h}(t_i))$ is an encryption of either 0 or 1 and as Q is assumed to be in disjunctive normal form, a naive solution to compute $E_{pk}(Q(t_i))$ is by using secure multiplication (SMP) and secure bit-or (SBOR) protocols as sub-routines. More specifically, C_1 and C_2 can securely compute $E_{pk}(G_j(t_i))$ by applying the SMP protocol on $E_{pk}(P_{j,h}(t_i))$ as inputs, for $1 \leq j \leq l$ and $1 \leq h \leq b_j$. For example, consider the case of computing $E_{pk}(G_1(t_i))$. In this case, C_1 and C_2 initially compute $E_{pk}(P_{1,1}(t_i) \wedge P_{1,2}(t_i))$ by feeding $E_{pk}(P_{1,1}(t_i))$ and $E_{pk}(P_{1,2}(t_i))$ as inputs to the SMP protocol. The above result is fed as an input along with the next predicate result of G_1 to SMP and so on. At the end, C_1 has $E_{pk}(G_1(t_i)) = E_{pk}(P_{1,1}(t_i) \wedge \ldots \wedge P_{1,b_1}(t_i))$. After that, in a similar fashion, they compute $E_{pk}(Q(t_i))$ by applying the SBOR protocol on $E_{pk}(G_j(t_i))$ as inputs, for $1 \leq j \leq l$. We refer to the above basic solution as SROD$_b$. However, since its complexity grows linearly with the number of predicates in Q, we claim that SROD$_b$ is not that efficient. More details regarding the complexities of SROD$_b$ are given in Section 4.5.

To overcome this issue, we next propose an efficient approach to systematically aggregate predicate results (in encrypted form) to compute the corresponding query result on each data record t_i, where $1 \leq i \leq n$. We denote our approach by SROD$_s$ (where the subscript 's' stands for summation). The main steps involved in SROD$_s$ are shown in Algorithm 2. To start with, for each record T_i', C_1 locally aggregates (in encrypted form) the evaluation results of predicates in each clause by computing $L_{i,j}' = \prod_{h=1}^{b_j} L_{i,j}[h] = E_{pk}\left(\sum_{h=1}^{b_j} P_{j,h}(t_i)\right)$, for $1 \leq j \leq l$.

Observation 1. *Since clause G_j is a conjunction of b_j predicates, a record t_i satisfies G_j, i.e., $G_j(t_i) = 1$, only if $P_{j,h}(t_i) = 1$, for $1 \leq h \leq b_j$. This further implies that $G_j(t_i) = 1$ only if $\sum_{h=1}^{b_j} P_{j,h}(t_i) = b_j$. In addition, if $\exists h$ such that $P_{j,h}(t_i) = 0$, then $G_j(t_i) = 0$ and $\sum_{h=1}^{b_j} P_{j,h}(t_i) < b_j$.*

Following from the above observation, in order to evaluate G_j, we need to securely check whether $\sum_{h=1}^{b_j} P_{j,h}(t_i)$ is equal to b_j or not. For this purpose, C_1 with input $L_{i,j}'$ and C_2 jointly involve in the SC$_{obv}$ protocol (i.e., the extended version of the secure comparison protocol in [31] as discussed in Section 4.2). That is, C_1 and C_2 jointly check whether $\sum_{h=1}^{b_j} P_{j,h}(t_i)$ is greater than $b_j - 1$. If the comparison result is 1 (in encrypted form), then $\sum_{h=1}^{b_j} P_{j,h}(t_i) = b_j$. At the end of this step, the output $M_{i,j} = \text{SC}_{obv}(L_{i,j}', b_j)$ will be known only to C_1. Remember that $M_{i,j} = E_{pk}(1)$ iff t_i satisfies G_j, and $E_{pk}(0)$ otherwise, for $1 \leq i \leq n$ and $1 \leq j \leq l$.

Once C_1 knows $E_{pk}(G_j(t_i))$, for $1 \leq i \leq n$ and $1 \leq j \leq l$, the goal is to compute the final evaluation result of Q on t_i (in encrypted form), i.e., $E_{pk}(Q(t_i))$. For this purpose, we use the following observation.

Observation 2. *Given any query Q which is a disjunction of l clauses, $Q(t_i) = 1$ only if $\exists j$ such that $G_j(t_i) = 1$. That is, if t_i satisfies at least one of the clauses in Q, then it also satisfies Q. This further implies that $Q(t_i) = 1$ only if $\sum_{j=1}^{l} G_j(t_i) > 0$. Furthermore, when $\sum_{j=1}^{l} G_j(t_i) = 0$, we have $Q(t_i) = 0$ (i.e., t_i does not satisfy Q).*

Algorithm 2. $\text{SROD}_s(L_{i,1}, \ldots, L_{i,l})$

Require: C_1 has $(L_{i,1}, \ldots, L_{i,l})$
1: **for** $1 \leq j \leq l$ **do:**

    (a). C_1 compute $L'_{i,j} \leftarrow \prod_{h=1}^{b_j} L_{i,j}[h]$
    (b). C_1 and C_2: $M_{i,j} \leftarrow \text{SC}_{\text{obv}}(L'_{i,j}, b_j)$

2: C_1 compute $M'_i \leftarrow \prod_{j=1}^{l} M_{i,j}$
3: C_1 and C_2: $O_i \leftarrow \text{SC}_{\text{obv}}(M'_i, l)$
4: C_1 send O_i to C_2
5: C_2 compute $x_i \leftarrow D_{sk}(O_i)$ and send x_i to C_1
6: C_1: **if** $x_i = 1$ **then:**

    (a). $V_{i,j} \leftarrow T'_{i,j} * E_{pk}(r'_{i,j})$, for $1 \leq j \leq m$, where $r'_{i,j}$ is a random number in $\mathbb{Z}_N$
    (b). Send $r'_{i,j}$ to Bob and $V_{i,j}$ to C_2

7: C_2, **foreach** V_i received **do:** $z_{i,j} \leftarrow D_{sk}(V_{i,j})$ and send $z_{i,j}$ to Bob
8: Bob, **foreach** received entry pair (z_i, r'_i) **do:**

    (a). $t'_j \leftarrow z_{i,j} - r'_{i,j} \mod N$, for $1 \leq j \leq m$, and $S \leftarrow S \cup t'$

Based on the above observation, C_1 locally computes the encryption of sum of the evaluation results on l clauses in Q. That is, he/she computes $M'_i = \prod_{j=1}^{l} M_{i,j}$, for $1 \leq i \leq n$. It is important to observe that $M'_i = E_{pk}\left(\sum_{j=1}^{l} G_j(t_i)\right)$. After this, C_1 and C_2 securely verify whether the value of $\sum_{j=1}^{l} G_j(t_i)$ is greater than 0. For this purpose, they jointly involve in the SC_{obv} protocol. Specifically, they together compute $O_i = \text{SC}_{\text{obv}}(M'_i, l) = E_{pk}(Q(t_i))$, for $1 \leq i \leq n$. Note that the output of SC_{obv}, i.e., O_i will be known only to C_1. Once C_1 computes the evaluation result of Q on a data record t_i (in encrypted form), the next step is for Bob to securely retrieve only those records that satisfy Q with the help of C_1 and C_2. We emphasize that there are many ways through which Bob can obliviously retrieve the output set of records from C_1. In this paper, we present a simple approach that is very efficient from the Bob's perspective.

For $1 \leq i \leq n$, C_1 sends O_i to C_2. Upon receiving, C_2 computes $x_i = D_{sk}(O'_i)$ and sends the result to C_1. After this, C_1 proceeds as follows:

- If $x_i = 1$, then $Q(t_i) = 1$. In this case, C_1 randomizes T'_i attribute-wise and sends $V_{i,j} = T'_{i,j} * E_{pk}(r'_{i,j})$ to C_2, where $r'_{i,j}$ is a random number in $\mathbb{Z}_N$, for $1 \leq j \leq m$. Here m denotes the number of attributes in T'. Also, C_1 sends $r'_{i,j}$ to Bob.

- Else, ignore the data record corresponding to the entry x_i.

Upon receiving the entry V_i, C_2 computes $z_{i,j} = D_{sk}(V_{i,j})$, for $1 \leq j \leq m$, and sends the result to Bob. Then, for each received entry pair (z_i, r'_i), Bob removes the extra random factors attribute-wise to get $t'_j = z_{i,j} - r'_{i,j} \mod N$, for $1 \leq j \leq m$. Based on the above discussions, it is clear that t' will be a data record in T that satisfies the input query Q. Finally, Bob adds the data record t' to the output set: $S = S \cup t'$.

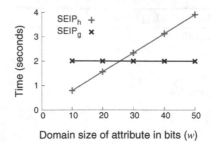

Fig. 1. Computation costs of SEIP$_h$ and SEIP$_g$ for encryption key size 1024 bits

4.4   Security Analysis of PPQED

First of all, since Bob's input query Q is randomly shared between C_1 and C_2, search input values in each predicate are never disclosed to C_1 and C_2. However, the PPQED protocol reveals the attribute index to be searched in each predicate to C_1 (but not C_2) for efficiency reasons. Nevertheless, we stress that such information will not be useful for C_1 to deduce any meaningful information about the attribute values.

We emphasize that the SC$_{obv}$ protocol which is used as a building block in PPQED is secure under the semi-honest model (security proof follows directly from [31]). As a result, the secure evaluation of individual predicates (SEIP) task at step 2(a) of Algorithm 1 do not reveal any information to C_1 and C_2. Thus, Stage 1 of PPQED is secure under the semi-honest model. During Stage 2, all the intermediate results revealed to C_2 are either random or pseudo-random. On the other hand, the intermediate results seen by C_1 are always in encrypted form (except at step 5 of Algorithm 2). Thus, whatever messages C_1 and C_2 receive in Stage 2 are computationally indistinguishable (assuming large key size, say 1024 bits) from random numbers in $\mathbb{Z}_N$. Therefore, Stage 2 is secure under the semi-honest model. Also, the outputs of Stage 1 which are passed as input to Stage 2 are also in encrypted format. According to the Composition Theorem [15], we claim that the sequential composition of Stages 1 and 2 leads to our PPQED protocol that is also secure under the semi-honest model. In short, the proposed PPQED protocol protects the confidentiality of the data as well as privacy of the user's input query. At the same time, it supports evaluation of complex queries over encrypted data.

In the proposed PPQED protocol, C_1 and C_2 know the value of x_i (at step 5 of Algorithm 2) that can reveal the data access pattern information (i.e., whether the data record t_i satisfies the input query) to C_1 and C_2. Nevertheless, our protocol can be easily extended to hide the data access patterns from both C_1 and C_2 at an additional cost. Due to space limitations, we do not go into any details regarding this extension. However, we refer the reader to our technical report [14] for more details on how to hide the access pattern information in the proposed protocol.

4.5   Complexity Analysis of PPQED

During Stage 1 of PPQED, the computation cost of the federated cloud (i.e., the combined cost of C_1 and C_2) is bounded by $O(n * l * s)$ instantiations of SEIP, where s

denotes the upper bound on the number of predicates in each clause. As mentioned earlier, one can use either $SEIP_h$ (i.e., SEIP under homomorphic encryption) or $SEIP_g$ (i.e., SEIP under garbled circuits) in Stage 1. To get more insights, we implemented both $SEIP_h$ and $SEIP_g$, and ran experiments on a Linux machine with an Intel® Xeon® Six-Core™ CPU 3.07 GHz processor and 12GB RAM running Ubuntu 10.04 LTS. We use the Paillier cryptosystem [13] and fix the encryption key size K to 1024 bits. In particular to $SEIP_g$, we constructed and evaluated the circuit under the FastGC [34] framework (the fastest known implementation for garbled circuits). We considered attributes of different domain sizes (in bits), denoted by w, and executed predicates at random using both $SEIP_h$ and $SEIP_g$. The results are shown in Figure 1. Note that, in PPQED, we consider predicates with relation operators $\{>, \geq, <, \leq\}$. Since the underlying operations are almost the same for all these four relational operations, the computation costs reported for $SEIP_h$ and $SEIP_g$ remain the same for any of these relational operators.

Following from Figure 1, the computation cost of $SEIP_h$ increases from 0.79 to 3.93 seconds when w varies from 10 to 50. On the other hand, the computation cost of $SEIP_g$ almost remains constant at 2.01 seconds. This is because the computation cost of $SEIP_g$ mainly depends on the addition circuits (operating over 1024 bits) whose costs remain the same for any fixed encryption key size. From the above results, we conclude that $SEIP_h$ is more efficient than $SEIP_g$ for attributes with domain size 2^{25} (i.e., $w = 25$). Note that the attribute domain size $[0, 2^{25})$ is realistic for most practical applications, e.g., the attribute domain size for Age, Annual Salary, and Temperature is less than 25 bits. Also, the categorical attributes usually take few values. However, if the domain size of an attribute is $\geq 2^{25}$, we would use $SEIP_g$ in PPQED for efficiency reasons. Our experimental results given in Figure 1 are based on one record and it is important to note that these results are independent of the record. Thus the reported costs remain the same for any given data record. As a result, the cloud providers can evaluate a predicate on multiple data records in parallel.

Next, for Stage 2, we analyze the costs associated with the query evaluation step (using the individual predicate results) in $SROD_s$ and compare its performance with the basic solution $SROD_b$. For any given data record t_i, the complexities of $SROD_b$ and $SROD_s$ are shown in Table 2. From Table 2, it is clear that our approach in $SROD_s$ outperforms (in terms of both computations and communications) $SROD_b$ if s is large. Also, the round complexity of both approaches is bounded by $O(\log_2 l + \log_2 s)$. However, if the round complexity is crucial in an application, one can replace SC_{obv} in $SROD_s$ with the SC protocol based on garbled circuits [35] (which takes one round of communication to perform the secure comparison). However, for practical values of l and s, SC_{obv} is more efficient than [35], thus providing a trade-off between efficiency and round complexity. Due to space limitations, we refer the reader to our technical report [14] for a more elaborated theoretical and empirical analysis of PPQED.

Nevertheless, the main advantage of the proposed PPQED protocol is that the computation cost on Bob is negligible. This is especially beneficial if Bob issues queries using a resource-constrained device (e.g., PDAs and cell phones).

Table 2. SROD$_b$ vs. SROD$_s$ for any given record t_i

Method	Computations	Communications
SROD$_b$	$O(l * s)$ encryptions	$O(K * l * s)$ bits
SROD$_s$	$O(l * \log_2 s)$ encryptions	$O(K * l * \log_2 s)$ bits

5   Conclusion and Future Work

In this paper, we proposed a novel protocol to securely evaluate complex queries over encrypted data in the cloud. The core of our protocol is based on a hybrid approach to evaluate the predicates in the user's query using both homomorphic encryption and garbled circuit techniques. Also, we developed an efficient approach to systematically combine the evaluation results of individual predicates to compute the corresponding query evaluation result. Our protocol protects data confidentiality, privacy of the user's input query and access patterns. Our empirical results show that techniques based on homomorphic encryption are efficient for attributes of smaller domain sizes. Also, we theoretically demonstrated the efficiency of our systematic approach to combine the predicate results.

As future work, we will implement and evaluate our framework using the MapReduce technique in a real federated cloud computing environment. We also plan to develop a sequence diagram for the proposed protocol in our future work. Another interesting direction is to extend our protocol to other adversary models, such as the malicious model, and evaluate the trade-offs between security and efficiency. Though our protocol concentrates on the relational operators, we believe that it can also support other SQL operations, such as JOIN and GROUP BY, as they are essentially based on the relational operations. We plan to investigate this problem in our future work.

Acknowledgements. The authors would like to thank the anonymous reviewers for their helpful comments. The work reported in this paper has been partially supported by the Purdue Cyber Center and by the National Science Foundation under grants CNS-1111512, CNS-1016722, and CNS-1011984.

References

1. Bajaj, S., Sion, R.: Trusteddb: a trusted hardware based database with privacy and data confidentiality. In: ACM SIGMOD, pp. 205–216 (2011)
2. Agrawal, R., Kiernan, J., Srikant, R., Xu, Y.: Order preserving encryption for numeric data. In: ACM SIGMOD, pp. 563–574 (2004)
3. Mykletun, E., Tsudik, G.: Aggregation queries in the database-as-a-service model. In: Damiani, E., Liu, P. (eds.) Data and Applications Security 2006. LNCS, vol. 4127, pp. 89–103. Springer, Heidelberg (2006)
4. Shi, E., Bethencourt, J., Chan, T.H.H., Song, D., Perrig, A.: Multi-dimensional range query over encrypted data. In: IEEE Security & Privacy, pp. 350–364. IEEE Computer Society (2007)

5. Chung, S., Ozsoyoglu, S., Anti-tamper, G.: Anti-tamper databases: Processing aggregate queries over encrypted databases. In: ICDE Workshops, p. 98 (2006)
6. Boldyreva, A., Chenette, N., Lee, Y., O'Neill, A.: Order-preserving symmetric encryption. In: Joux, A. (ed.) EUROCRYPT 2009. LNCS, vol. 5479, pp. 224–241. Springer, Heidelberg (2009)
7. Hore, B., Mehrotra, S., Canim, M., Kantarcioglu, M.: Secure multidimensional range queries over outsourced data. The VLDB Journal 21(3), 333–358 (2012)
8. Samanthula, B.K., Jiang, W.: Efficient privacy-preserving range queries over encrypted data in cloud computing. In: IEEE CLOUD, pp. 51–58 (2013)
9. Williams, P., Sion, R., Carbunar, B.: Building castles out of mud: practical access pattern privacy and correctness on untrusted storage. In: CCS, pp. 139–148. ACM (2008)
10. De Capitani di Vimercati, S., Foresti, S., Samarati, P.: Managing and accessing data in the cloud: Privacy risks and approaches. In: 7th International Conference on Risk and Security of Internet and Systems, pp. 1–9 (2012)
11. Islam, M., Kuzu, M., Kantarcioglu, M.: Access pattern disclosure on searchable encryption: Ramification, attack and mitigation. In: NDSS (2012)
12. Goldreich, O.: Encryption Schemes. In: The Foundations of Cryptography, vol. 2, pp. 373–470. Cambridge University Press, Cambridge (2004)
13. Paillier, P.: Public-key cryptosystems based on composite degree residuosity classes. In: Stern, J. (ed.) EUROCRYPT 1999. LNCS, vol. 1592, p. 223. Springer, Heidelberg (1999)
14. Samanthula, B.K., Jiang, W., Bertino, E.: Privacy-preserving complex query evaluation over semantically secure encrypted data. Technical Report TR 2014-05, Dept. of Computer Science, Missouri S&T, Rolla (2014), http://web.mst.edu/~wjiang/PPQED.pdf
15. Goldreich, O.: General Cryptographic Protocols. In: The Foundations of Cryptography, vol. 2, pp. 599–746. Cambridge University Press, Cambridge (2004)
16. Boneh, D., Waters, B.: Conjunctive, subset, and range queries on encrypted data. In: Vadhan, S.P. (ed.) TCC 2007. LNCS, vol. 4392, pp. 535–554. Springer, Heidelberg (2007)
17. Hacıgümüş, H., Iyer, B., Mehrotra, S.: Efficient execution of aggregation queries over encrypted relational databases. In: Lee, Y., Li, J., Whang, K.-Y., Lee, D. (eds.) DASFAA 2004. LNCS, vol. 2973, pp. 125–136. Springer, Heidelberg (2004)
18. Golle, P., Staddon, J., Waters, B.: Secure conjunctive keyword search over encrypted data. In: Jakobsson, M., Yung, M., Zhou, J. (eds.) ACNS 2004. LNCS, vol. 3089, pp. 31–45. Springer, Heidelberg (2004)
19. Popa, R.A., Redfield, C.M.S., Zeldovich, N., Balakrishnan, H.: Cryptdb: Protecting confidentiality with encrypted query processing. In: SOSP, pp. 85–100. ACM (2011)
20. Shi, E., Chan, T.-H.H., Stefanov, E., Li, M.: Oblivious RAM with $o((\log n)^3)$ worst-case cost. In: Lee, D.H., Wang, X. (eds.) ASIACRYPT 2011. LNCS, vol. 7073, pp. 197–214. Springer, Heidelberg (2011)
21. Gentry, C.: Fully homomorphic encryption using ideal lattices. In: STOC, pp. 169–178. ACM (2009)
22. Naehrig, M., Lauter, K., Vaikuntanathan, V.: Can homomorphic encryption be practical? In: The ACM Workshop on Cloud Computing Security, pp. 113–124. ACM (2011)
23. Gentry, C., Halevi, S.: Implementing gentry's fully-homomorphic encryption scheme. In: Paterson, K.G. (ed.) EUROCRYPT 2011. LNCS, vol. 6632, pp. 129–148. Springer, Heidelberg (2011)
24. Yao, A.C.: Protocols for secure computations. In: SFCS, pp. 160–164. IEEE Computer Society (1982)
25. Yao, A.C.: How to generate and exchange secrets. In: SFCS, pp. 162–167. IEEE Computer Society (1986)
26. Goldreich, O., Micali, S., Wigderson, A.: How to play any mental game - a completeness theorem for protocols with honest majority. In: STOC, pp. 218–229. ACM (1987)

27. Chaum, D., Crépeau, C., Damgard, I.: Multiparty unconditionally secure protocols. In: STOC, pp. 11–19. ACM (1988)
28. Damgard, I., Geisler, M., Kroigard, M.: Homomorphic encryption and secure comparison. International Journal of Applied Cryptography 1(1), 22–31 (2008)
29. Bugiel, S., Nürnberger, S., Sadeghi, A.R., Schneider, T.: Twin clouds: An architecture for secure cloud computing (extended abstract). In: Workshop on Cryptography and Security in Clouds (March 2011)
30. Wang, J., Ma, H., Tang, Q., Li, J., Zhu, H., Ma, S., Chen, X.: Efficient verifiable fuzzy keyword search over encrypted data in cloud computing. Computer Science and Information Systems 10(2), 667–684 (2013)
31. Blake, I.F., Kolesnikov, V.: One-round secure comparison of integers. Journal of Mathematical Cryptology 3(1), 37–68 (2009)
32. Schoenmakers, B., Tuyls, P.: Efficient binary conversion for paillier encrypted values. In: Vaudenay, S. (ed.) EUROCRYPT 2006. LNCS, vol. 4004, pp. 522–537. Springer, Heidelberg (2006)
33. Samanthula, B.K., Jiang, W.: An efficient and probabilistic secure bit-decomposition. In: ACM ASIACCS, pp. 541–546 (2013)
34. Huang, Y., Evans, D., Katz, J., Malka, L.: Faster secure two-party computation using garbled circuits. In: Proceedings of the 20th USENIX Conference on Security, pp. 35–35 (2011)
35. Kolesnikov, V., Sadeghi, A.-R., Schneider, T.: Improved garbled circuit building blocks and applications to auctions and computing minima. In: Garay, J.A., Miyaji, A., Otsuka, A. (eds.) CANS 2009. LNCS, vol. 5888, pp. 1–20. Springer, Heidelberg (2009)

Authorized Keyword Search on Encrypted Data

Jie Shi[1,2], Junzuo Lai[2,*], Yingjiu Li[1], Robert H. Deng[1], and Jian Weng[2]

[1] Singapore Management University, Singapore
{jieshi,yjli,robertdeng}@smu.edu.sg
[2] Jinan University, China
{laijunzuo,cryptjweng}@gmail.com

Abstract. Cloud computing has drawn much attention from research and industry in recent years. Plenty of enterprises and individuals are outsourcing their data to cloud servers. As those data may contain sensitive information, it should be encrypted before outsourced to cloud servers. In order to ensure that only authorized users can search and further access the encrypted data, two important capabilities must be supported: *keyword search* and *access control*. Recently, rigorous efforts have been made on either keyword search or access control over encrypted data. However, to the best of our knowledge, there is no encryption scheme supporting both capabilities in a public-key scenario so far. In this paper, we propose an authorized searchable public-key encryption scheme supporting expressive search capability and prove it fully secure in the standard model.

Keywords: Authorized Searchable Public-Key Encryption, Attribute-Based Encryption, Public-Key Encryption with Keyword Search ,Public-Key Encryption.

1 Introduction

Recently, as a new commercial model, cloud computing has attracted much attention from both academia and industry. A major advantage of cloud computing is that it supplies virtually unlimited storage capabilities and elastic resource provisioning [1]. In order to reduce the capital and operational expenditures for hardware and software, plenty of IT enterprises and individuals are outsourcing their data to cloud servers instead of building and maintaining their own data centers [2].

Despite clear benefits provided by cloud computing, there are many impediments to its widespread adoption. Data security and privacy concerns are probably the biggest challenges. As outsourced data may contain much sensitive/private information, such as Personal Health Records (PHRs), personal photos and business documents, some cloud servers or unauthorized users are motivated to access and derive such sensitive/private information. Without addressing such concerns, users may hesitate to outsource their data to cloud servers. As it is shown in many

---

* Corresponding author.

M. Kutyłowski and J. Vaidya (Eds.): ESORICS 2014, Part I, LNCS 8712, pp. 419–435, 2014.

recent works [3,2,4], data encryption is applied on users' data before outsourcing so as to address the security and privacy concerns.

While documents are encrypted and outsourced to cloud servers, two important capabilities should be supported: *keyword search* and *access control*. The keyword search capability facilitates data users to access encrypted data as it enables quick location of required data based on keywords. The access control capability allows data owners to share their information with restricted users according to the access control policies associated with their encrypted data. In the literature, much work has been done on either keyword search or access control over encrypted data. However, no rigorous effort has been dedicated on supporting both keyword search and access control at the same time, which means that only authorized users are allowed to process keyword search and further access encrypted data. We call it *authorized searchable encryption* if an encryption scheme enables authorized users only to perform keyword search. Many real-world applications demand such authorized searchable encryption. One example is the cloud storage system in healthcare as it is shown in Figure 1. In this system, any patient (i.e. data owner) outsources his/her medical records to a cloud server so as to share with authorized users such as hospital doctors. Assuming that the medical records are sensitive, they are encrypted before outsourced to the cloud. The encrypted data should support both keyword search and access control in this scenario. In particular, data owner 1 *John* outsources an encrypted medical record to the cloud with both *keywords* and an *access policy*. The *keywords* specify the features about the encrypted data which can be used in any authorized users' queries, while the *access policy* specifies who are the authorized users (i.e., a cardiologist in Hospital A or a patient with social security number 110-222-1234). Since both *keywords* and *access policy* associated with a medical record contain sensitive/private information, they should be hidden from the cloud service provider or any unauthorized users, just as the medical record itself. Every user in this system is associated with a set of attributes; for example, the attributes of user 1 in Figure 1 include her name, her social security number, her affiliation, and her occupation. When a user intends to obtain certain information from the cloud server, the user submits an authorized token constructed by an authority according to the user's keywords query and the user's attributes. The query token enables the cloud server to locate all medical records such that the *keywords* of the medical records satisfy the user's query and the attributes of the user meet the *access policy* of the medical records.

In this paper, we focus on constructing an *authorized searchable encryption* scheme in a public-key scenario, which we call *authorized searchable public-key encryption (AS-PKE)*. It is challenging to design an AS-PKE scheme supporting both expressive search capability and being fully secure in the standard model. In the literature, there exist two kinds of encryption schemes close to AS-PKE, which are the attribute-based encryption and the public-key encryption with keyword search. First, the attribute-based encryption (ABE) was introduced by Sahai and Waters [5] and further developed into two complimentary forms: KP-ABE [6,7] and CP-ABE [8,9]. There also exist many solutions in ABE with hidden access structures, including predicate encryption [10] and CP-ABE

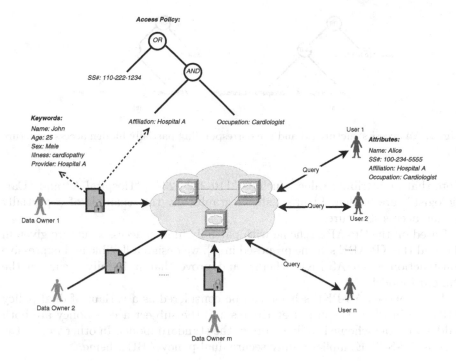

Fig. 1. An example of cloud storage system architecture

with hidden access structures [11]. Second, the public-key encryption with keyword search (PEKS) was proposed by Boneh et al. [12], which supports equality queries only. Later, Park et al. proposed the notion of public key encryption with conjunctive keyword search [13] and Katz et al. proposed the notion of inner-product predicate encryption [10], which can be extended to construct public key encryption with disjunctive keyword search. Neither ABE nor PEKS satisfies the requirements of AS-PKE; in other words, they do not support keyword search and access control at the same time. Simply combining ABE and PEKS schemes cannot achieve AS-PKE too, as in AS-PKE both keywords and access control policies are required to be hidden and expressive search on encrypted data is required to be supported.

1.1   Our Contribution

In [11], Lai et al. proposed a new model of CP-ABE with partially hidden access structures. In this model, each attribute consists of two parts: attribute name and its value. In the access policy associated with a ciphertext, all attribute values are hidden, while the other information, such as attribute names, about the access structure is public. Taking the access policy in Figure 1 as an example, the policy is published in the following format in Lai et al.'s model:

$$SS\# : \star \text{ OR (Affiliation: } \star \text{ AND Occupation:} \star)$$

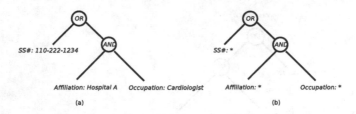

Fig. 2. An access structure (a) and the corresponding partially hidden access structure (b)

Note that all attribute values, such as "110-222-1234", "Hospital A" and "Cardiologist", are hidden. Figure 2 shows graphically this example of a partially hidden access structure.

Based on the CP-ABE scheme with partially hidden access structure given in [11] and the KP-ABE scheme proposed in [7], we design a flexible and expressive construction as an AS-PKE scheme, and prove that it is fully secure in the standard model.

The proposed AS-PKE scheme can be considered as a variant of dual-policy ABE [14] in which the object attributes and the subject access policy are both hidden and the scheme is fully secure in the standard model. In other words, the proposed AS-PKE implies a fully secure dual-policy ABE scheme.

1.2   Related Work

In this section, we briefly review the related works in the areas of ABE, KP-ABE, CP-ABE, PEKS, and PE (Predicate Encryption).

Attribute-Based Encryption (ABE). The concept of ABE was first proposed by Sahai and Waters as an application of *fuzzy identity-based encryption (IBE)* scheme [5], where both ciphertext and secret key are labeled with sets of descriptive attributes. The decryption of a ciphertext is enabled if and only if the cardinality of the intersection of these labeled attributes exceeds a certain threshold.

Key Policy Attribute-Based Encryption (KP-ABE). Two complimentary forms of ABE — KP-ABE and CP-ABE — were formulated by Goyal et al. [6]. In a CP-ABE scheme, each ciphertext is associated with an access structure while each decryption key is associated with a set of attributes. Reversely, in a KP-ABE scheme, each decryption key is associated with an access structure while each ciphertext is associated with a set of attributes. Generally, a KP-ABE scheme can be transformed into a CP-ABE using the method proposed in [15]. While the KP-ABE scheme proposed by Goyal et al. [6] supports monotonic access structures only, Ostrovsky et al. [16] presented a KP-ABE system supporting more flexible access control policies — non-monotone access structures.

Ciphertext Policy Attribute-Based Encryption (CP-ABE). Bethencourt et al. proposed the first CP-ABE scheme [8], which was proven to be secure under the generic group mode. Later, Cheung and Newport presented a CP-ABE scheme that is secure under the standard model [17]. However, the access structures in this scheme are restricted to conjunctions of different attributes. Recently, secure and expressive CP-ABE schemes were proposed in [9,7]. In order to hide access structures, Nishide et al. introduced the concept of CP-ABE with partially hidden access structures [18]. Recently, Lai et al. proposed a fully secure (cf. selectively secure) CP-ABE scheme with partially hidden access structures [19]; however, the scheme only supports restricted access structure as in [18]. Later, Lai et al. proposed a fully secure CP-ABE scheme with partially hidden access structures [11] that can be expressed as an LSSS which is more flexible and expressive than the previous work [18].

Predicate Encryption (PE). Predicate encryption can be considered as attribute-based encryption supporting attribute-hiding. Katz et al. introduced the concept of PE and designed the first inner-product PE [10]. Shi and Waters presented a delegation mechanism for a class of PE [20]; later, Okamota and Takashima presented a (hierarchical) delegation mechanism for an inner-product PE scheme [21]. Shen et al. introduced a new security notion of PE called predicate privacy and also proposed a symmetric-key inner-product PE, which achieves both plaintext privacy and predicate privacy [22]. However, these schemes were proven to be selectively secure only. The first fully secure inner-product PE was proposed by Lweko et al. [7]. Okamota and Takashima presented a fully secure PE for a wide class of admissible predicates, which are specified using non-monotone access structures combined with inner-product predicates [23].

Public-key Encryption with Keyword Search (PEKS). Boneh et al. initiated the research on PEKS and provided a specific scheme, which supports equality query only [12]. Park et al. proposed the notion of public key encryption with conjunctive keyword search [13]; Hwan and Lee made an improvement on the sizes of ciphertext and private key, and extended the scheme in a multi-user setting [24]. Boneh and Waters presented a general framework for analyzing and constructing several schemes that support arbitrary conjunctions [25]. Katz et al. proposed the notion of inner-product predicate encryption (IPE), which can be extended to construct public key encryption with disjunctive keyword search [10]. However, as shown in [10], the resulting solution suffers from a super polynomial blowup in ciphertext size and search-token key size.

Others. Recently, Li et al. [2] presented a framework for authorized private keyword search (APKS) over encrypted cloud data and proposed two schemes for APKS. In their proposed framework, every data owner's trust is delegated to a trusted authority and/or several local trusted authorities who are in charge of determining users' search privileges. Based on this framework, they employed the hierarchical predicate encryption to construct APKS. However, there exists a significant difference between the APKS and our AS-PKE: the access control policies are defined and maintained by trusted authorities in APKS scheme; however, in our AS-PKE scheme, the access control policies are defined by data owners themselves. Therefore, our AS-PKE scheme is more general and can be used in many applications which require access control policies to be defined by data owners. In [26], Sun et al. proposed an attribute-based keyword search with fine-grained owner-enforced search authorization scheme, which supports limited authorization policies with "AND" gates and limited keyword queries with conjunctive keywords only. Our AS-PKE scheme supports more expressive authorization policies and keyword queries supporting arbitrary Boolean formulas. In [27], Narayan et al. combined PEKS and ABE to create a secure electronic health record system providing both keyword search and access control functionalities; however, it does not address the privacy of access control policies as in our work.

1.3 Organization

The rest of the paper is organized as follows. In Section 2, we review necessary standard notations and cryptographic definitions. In Section 3, we define the security model of AS-PKE, and propose a concrete construction of AS-PKE. In Section 4, we conclude our paper.

2 Preliminaries

In this paper, we use $s \xleftarrow{\$} S$ to denote the operation of picking an element s uniformly at random from a set S. Let $\mathbb{N}$ be the set of natural numbers, and 1^λ denote the string of λ ones if $\lambda \in \mathbb{N}$. Let $z \leftarrow A(x, y, \ldots)$ denote the operation of running an algorithm A with inputs $(x, y, \ldots)$ and output z. A function $f(\lambda)$ is *negligible* if for every $c > 0$ there exists a λ_c such that $f(\lambda) < 1/\lambda^c$ for all $\lambda > \lambda_c$.

2.1 Access Structures

Definition 1 (Access Structure [28]). *Let $\{P_1, \ldots, P_n\}$ be a set of parties. A collection $\mathbb{A} \subseteq 2^{\{P_1, \ldots, P_n\}}$ is monotone if $\forall B, C :$ if $B \in \mathbb{A}$ and $B \subseteq C$, then $C \in \mathbb{A}$. An access structure (respectively, monotone access structure) is a collection (respectively, monotone collection) $\mathbb{A}$ of non-empty subsets of $\{P_1, \ldots, P_n\}$, i.e., $\mathbb{A} \subseteq 2^{\{P_1, \ldots, P_n\}} \setminus \{\emptyset\}$. The sets in $\mathbb{A}$ are called authorized sets, and the sets not in $\mathbb{A}$ are called unauthorized sets.*

In our context, attributes play the role of parties. We focus on the monotone access structures in this paper. However, it is possible to (inefficiently) realize general access structures using the proposed technique by taking the negation of an attribute as a separate attribute. In what follows, unless stated otherwise, the access structures are monotone access structures.

2.2 Linear Secret Sharing Schemes

We will make use of linear secret sharing schemes in our design of AS-PKE. The following definition is adapted from those given in [28].

Definition 2. *[Linear Secret-Sharing Schemes (LSSS)] A secret sharing scheme* Π *over a set of parties* $\mathcal{P}$ *is called linear (over* $\mathbb{Z}_p$*) if*

1. *The shares for each party form a vector over* $\mathbb{Z}_p$.
2. *There exists a matrix* $\mathbf{A}$ *with* ℓ *rows and* n *columns called the share-generating matrix for* Π. *For all* $i = 1, \ldots, \ell$, *the* i^{th} *row of* $\mathbf{A}$ *is labeled by a party* $\rho(i)$ *(ρ is a function from* $\{1, \ldots, \ell\}$ *to* $\mathcal{P}$*). When we consider the column vector* $v = (s, r_2, \ldots, r_n)$, *where* $s \in \mathbb{Z}_p$ *is the secret to be shared, and* $r_2, \ldots, r_n \in \mathbb{Z}_p$ *are randomly chosen, then* $\mathbf{A}v$ *is the vector of* ℓ *shares of the secret* s *according to* Π. *The share* $(\mathbf{A}v)_i$ *belongs to party* $\rho(i)$.

It is shown in [28] that every linear secret-sharing scheme according to the above definition enjoys the linear reconstruction property, defined as follows. Suppose that Π is an LSSS for an access structure $\mathbb{A}$. Let $S \in \mathbb{A}$ be any authorized set, and $I \subset \{1, \ldots, \ell\}$ be defined as $I = \{i | \rho(i) \in S\}$. Then there exist constants $\{\omega_i \in \mathbb{Z}_p\}_{i \in I}$ such that, if $\{\lambda_i\}$ are valid shares of any secret s according to Π, then $\sum_{i \in I} \omega_i \lambda_i = s$. Let A_i denote the ith row of $\mathbf{A}$, we have $\sum_{i \in I} \omega_i A_i = (1, 0, \ldots, 0)$. These constants $\{\omega_i\}$ can be found in time polynomial in the size of the share-generation matrix $\mathbf{A}$ [28]. Note that, for unauthorized sets, no such constants $\{\omega_i\}$ exist.

Boolean Formulas. Access structures might also be described in terms of monotonic boolean formulas. Using standard techniques [28] one can convert any monotonic boolean formula into an LSSS representation. When a boolean formula is represented as an access tree with ℓ leaf nodes, it will result in an LSSS matrix of ℓ rows. Details on how to perform this conversion refer to the appendix of [29].

2.3 Composite Order Bilinear Groups

We construct our scheme in composite order bilinear groups whose order is the product of four distinct primes. Composite order bilinear groups were first introduced in [30].

Let $\mathcal{G}$ be a group generator, an algorithm taking a security parameter 1^λ as input and outputting a tuple $(p_1, p_2, p_3, p_4, \mathbb{G}, \mathbb{G}_T, e)$, where p_1, p_2, p_3, p_4 are distinct primes, $\mathbb{G}$ and $\mathbb{G}_T$ are cyclic groups of order $N = p_1 p_2 p_3 p_4$, and $e : \mathbb{G} \times \mathbb{G} \to \mathbb{G}_T$ is a map such that

1. Bilinear: For all $g, h \in \mathbb{G}$, and $a, b \in \mathbb{Z}_N$, we have $e(g^a, h^b) = e(g, h)^{ab}$;
2. Non-degeneracy: $\exists g \in \mathbb{G}$ such that $e(g, g)$ has order N in $\mathbb{G}_T$.

It further requires that the group operation in $\mathbb{G}$ and $\mathbb{G}_T$ and the bilinear map e are both efficiently computable in time polynomial in λ. Let $\mathbb{G}_{p_1}, \mathbb{G}_{p_2}, \mathbb{G}_{p_3}$, and $\mathbb{G}_{p_4}$ be the subgroups of $\mathbb{G}$ having order p_1, p_2, p_3, and p_4 respectively. Thus, $\mathbb{G} = \mathbb{G}_{p_1} \times \mathbb{G}_{p_2} \times \mathbb{G}_{p_3} \times \mathbb{G}_{p_4}$. Note that if $g_1 \in \mathbb{G}_{p_1}$ and $g_2 \in \mathbb{G}_{p_2}$, then $e(g_1, g_2) = 1$. Similar rules hold whenever e is applied to elements in distinct subgroups.

We adopt the following four complexity assumptions in this paper, which were also used in [11,31].

Assumption 1. *Given a group generator $\mathcal{G}$, we define the following distribution:*

$$(p_1, p_2, p_3, p_4, \mathbb{G}, \mathbb{G}_T, e) \leftarrow \mathcal{G}(1^\lambda), \quad N = p_1 p_2 p_3 p_4,$$

$$g \xleftarrow{\$} \mathbb{G}_{p_1}, \quad X_3 \xleftarrow{\$} \mathbb{G}_{p_3}, \quad X_4 \xleftarrow{\$} \mathbb{G}_{p_4},$$

$$D = (\mathbb{G}, \mathbb{G}_T, N, e, g, X_3, X_4),$$

$$T_1 \xleftarrow{\$} \mathbb{G}_{p_1} \times \mathbb{G}_{p_2}, \quad T_2 \xleftarrow{\$} \mathbb{G}_{p_1}.$$

The advantage of an algorithm $\mathcal{A}$ in breaking Assumption 1 is defined as

$$Adv_{\mathcal{A}}^1 = |\Pr[\mathcal{A}(D, T_1) = 1] - \Pr[\mathcal{A}(D, T_2) = 1]|.$$

Definition 3. *we say $\mathcal{G}$ satisfies Assumption 1 if for any polynomial time algorithm $\mathcal{A}$, $Adv_{\mathcal{A}}^1$ is negligible.*

Assumption 2. *Given a group generator $\mathcal{G}$, we define the following distribution:*

$$(p_1, p_2, p_3, p_4, \mathbb{G}, \mathbb{G}_T, e) \leftarrow \mathcal{G}(1^\lambda), \quad N = p_1 p_2 p_3 p_4,$$

$$g, X_1 \xleftarrow{\$} \mathbb{G}_{p_1}, \quad X_2, Y_2 \xleftarrow{\$} \mathbb{G}_{p_2}, \quad X_3, Y_3 \xleftarrow{\$} \mathbb{G}_{p_3}, \quad X_4 \xleftarrow{\$} \mathbb{G}_{p_4},$$

$$D = (\mathbb{G}, \mathbb{G}_T, N, e, g, X_1 X_2, Y_2 Y_3, X_3, X_4),$$

$$T_1 \xleftarrow{\$} \mathbb{G}_{p_1} \times \mathbb{G}_{p_2} \times \mathbb{G}_{p_3}, \quad T_2 \xleftarrow{\$} \mathbb{G}_{p_1} \times \mathbb{G}_{p_3}.$$

The advantage of an algorithm $\mathcal{A}$ in breaking Assumption 2 is defined as

$$Adv_{\mathcal{A}}^2 = |\Pr[\mathcal{A}(D, T_1) = 1] - \Pr[\mathcal{A}(D, T_2) = 1]|.$$

Definition 4. *we say $\mathcal{G}$ satisfies Assumption 2 if for any polynomial time algorithm $\mathcal{A}$, $Adv_{\mathcal{A}}^2$ is negligible.*

Assumption 3. *Given a group generator $\mathcal{G}$, we define the following distribution:*

$$(p_1, p_2, p_3, p_4, \mathbb{G}, \mathbb{G}_T, e) \xleftarrow{\$} \mathcal{G}(1^\lambda), \quad N = p_1 p_2 p_3 p_4,$$

$$s \xleftarrow{\$} \mathbb{Z}_N, \quad g, h \xleftarrow{\$} \mathbb{G}_{p_1}, \quad g_2, X_2, B_2, D_2 \xleftarrow{\$} \mathbb{G}_{p_2},$$

$$X_3 \xleftarrow{\$} \mathbb{G}_{p_3}, \quad B_4, D_4, X_4, Z' \xleftarrow{\$} \mathbb{G}_{p_4},$$

$$D = (\mathbb{G}, \mathbb{G}_T, N, e, g, g_2, hX_2, hZ', g^s B_2 B_4, X_3, X_4),$$

$$T_1 = h^s D_2 D_4, T_2 \xleftarrow{\$} \mathbb{G}_{p_1} \times \mathbb{G}_{p_2} \times \mathbb{G}_{p_4}.$$

The advantage of an algorithm $\mathcal{A}$ in breaking Assumption 3 is defined as

$$Adv_{\mathcal{A}}^3 = |\Pr[\mathcal{A}(D, T_1) = 1] - \Pr[\mathcal{A}(D, T_2) = 1]|.$$

Definition 5. *we say $\mathcal{G}$ satisfies Assumption 3 if for any polynomial time algorithm $\mathcal{A}$, $Adv_{\mathcal{A}}^3$ is negligible.*

Assumption 4. *Given a group generator $\mathcal{G}$, we define the following distribution:*

$$(p_1, p_2, p_3, p_4, \mathbb{G}, \mathbb{G}_T, e) \leftarrow \mathcal{G}(1^\lambda), \quad N = p_1 p_2 p_3 p_4,$$

$$a, s \xleftarrow{\$} \mathbb{Z}_N, \quad g \xleftarrow{\$} \mathbb{G}_{P_1}, \quad g_2, X_2, Y_2, D_2 \xleftarrow{\$} \mathbb{G}_{p_2}$$

$$X_3 \xleftarrow{\$} \mathbb{G}_{p_3}, \quad X_4, Z', Y_4, D_4 \xleftarrow{\$} \mathbb{G}_{p_4}$$

$$D = (\mathbb{G}, \mathbb{G}_T, N, e, g, g_2, g^a X_2, g^a Z', g^s Y_2 Y_4, X_3, X_4),$$

$$T_1 = g^{as} D_2 D_4, \quad T_2 \xleftarrow{\$} \mathbb{G}_{p_1} \times \mathbb{G}_{p_2} \times \mathbb{G}_{p_4}.$$

The advantage of an algorithm $\mathcal{A}$ in breaking Assumption 4 is defined as

$$Adv_{\mathcal{A}}^4 = |\Pr[\mathcal{A}(D, T_1) = 1] - \Pr[\mathcal{A}(D, T_2) = 1]|.$$

Definition 6. *we say $\mathcal{G}$ satisfies Assumption 4 if for any polynomial time algorithm $\mathcal{A}$, $Adv_{\mathcal{A}}^4$ is negligible.*

3 Authorized Searchable Public Key Encryption

In authorized searchable public key encryption (AS-PKE), a document is identified by a vector of m keywords $(o_1, \ldots, o_m)$, where o_x is the keyword of the document in the x-th keyword field. For notational purpose, let x be the x-th keyword field. Similarly, a user has n attributes $(s_1, \ldots, s_n)$ with each attribute belonging to a different category. Let i be the attribute name of the i-th category attribute. Our AS-PKE scheme supports arbitrary monotone boolean predicate for both access policy and user query. We express an access policy by an LSSS $(A, \rho, \mathcal{T})$ over user attributes, where A is an $l_s \times n$ matrix, ρ is a map from each row of A to an attribute field (i.e., ρ is a function from $\{1, \ldots, l_s\}$ to $\{1, \ldots, n\}$), $\mathcal{T}$ can be parsed into $(t_{\rho(1)}, \ldots, t_{\rho(l_s)})$ and $t_{\rho(i)}$ is the value of attribute field $\rho(i)$. Similarly, we express a user query by an LSSS $(\hat{A}, \hat{\rho}, \hat{\mathcal{T}})$ over document keywords, where $\hat{A}$ is an $l_o \times m$ matrix, $\hat{\rho}$ is a map from each row of $\hat{A}$ to a keyword field (i.e., $\hat{\rho}$ is a function from $\{1, \ldots, l_o\}$ to $\{1, \ldots, m\}$), $\hat{\mathcal{T}}$ can be parsed into $(\hat{t}_{\hat{\rho}(1)}, \ldots, \hat{t}_{\hat{\rho}(l_o)})$ and $\hat{t}_{\hat{\rho}(x)}$ is the value of keyword field $\hat{\rho}(x)$.

Before presenting our AS-PKE scheme, we give some intuitions of our construction. Suppose that a document is encrypted with a set of keywords $\mathbb{O} = (o_1, \ldots, o_m)$ and an access policy $(A, \rho, \mathcal{T})$, a query token key $TK_{\mathcal{P}, \mathbb{S}}$ is embedded with a set of user attributes $\mathbb{S} = (s_1, \ldots, s_n)$ and a user query $\mathcal{P} = (\hat{A}, \hat{\rho}, \hat{\mathcal{T}})$. The encrypted document D will be returned if and only if there exist $\mathcal{I} \subseteq \{1, \ldots, l_s\}$, $\hat{\mathcal{I}} \subseteq \{1, \ldots, l_o\}$ and constants $\{w_i\}_{i \in \mathcal{I}}$, $\{\hat{w}_x\}_{x \in \hat{\mathcal{I}}}$ such that

$$\sum_{i \in \mathcal{I}} w_i A_i = (1, 0, \ldots, 0) \text{ and } s_{\rho(i)} = t_{\rho(i)} \text{ for } \forall i \in \mathcal{I},$$

$$\sum_{x \in \hat{\mathcal{I}}} \hat{w}_x \hat{A}_x = (1, 0, \ldots, 0) \text{ and } o_{\hat{\rho}(x)} = \hat{t}_{\hat{\rho}(x)} \text{ for } \forall x \in \hat{\mathcal{I}},$$

where A_i and $\hat{A}_x$ denote the i-th row of A and the x-th row of $\hat{A}$, respectively. We also say that $\mathcal{I} \subseteq \{1, \ldots, l_s\}$ satisfies $(A, \rho, \mathcal{T})$ if there exist constants $\{w_i\}_{i \in \mathcal{I}}$ such that $\sum_{i \in \mathcal{I}} w_i A_i = (1, 0, \ldots, 0)$. This can be applied to $\hat{\mathcal{I}} \subseteq \{1, \ldots, l_o\}$ and $(\hat{A}, \hat{\rho}, \hat{\mathcal{T}})$.

We define $I_{A,\rho}$ and $\hat{I}_{\hat{A}, \hat{\rho}}$ as the set of minimum subsets of $\{1, \ldots, l_s\}$ and $\{1, \ldots, l_o\}$ that satisfy $(A, \rho, \mathcal{T})$ and $(\hat{A}, \hat{\rho}, \hat{\mathcal{T}})$, respectively.

3.1 Authorized Searchable Public Key Encryption

In AS-PKE scheme, keywords $\mathbb{O} = (o_1, o_2, \ldots, o_n)$ of a document are encrypted under an access policy $\mathbb{A}$ and can be searched by an authorized query token. An authorized query token is generated by authority according to a query and user attributes set. An authorized searchable public key encryption (AS-PKE) scheme consists of the following four algorithms:

Setup(1^λ).   This setup algorithm takes in the security parameter λ with output of the public parameters PK and a secret key SK.

Encrypt(PK, $\mathbb{O} = (o_1, \ldots, o_m), \mathbb{A} = (A, \rho, \mathcal{T})$).   This encryption algorithm takes in the public parameter PK, keywords $\mathbb{O} = (o_1, \ldots, o_m)$, and an access policy $\mathbb{A} = (A, \rho, \mathcal{T})$. It outputs a ciphertext $C_{\mathbb{O},\mathbb{A}}$.

GenToken(PK, SK, $\mathbb{P}, \mathbb{S} = (s_1, \ldots, s_n)$).   This algorithm takes in the public key PK, the secret key SK, a user attributes set $\mathbb{S} = (s_1, \ldots, s_n)$ and a query predicate $\mathbb{P}$. It outputs an authorized query token key $\mathsf{TK}_{\mathbb{P},\mathbb{S}}$.

Test(PK, $\mathsf{TK}_{\mathbb{P},\mathbb{S}}, C_{\mathbb{O},\mathbb{A}}$).   This test algorithm takes in the public key PK, an authorized query token $\mathsf{TK}_{\mathbb{P},\mathbb{S}} = $ GenToken(PK, SK, $\mathbb{P}, \mathbb{S}$) and a ciphertext $C_{\mathbb{O},\mathbb{A}} = $ Encrypt(PK, $\mathbb{O}, \mathbb{A}$). It outputs "Yes" if the keywords in $\mathbb{O}$ satisfy the predicate $\mathbb{P}$ (i.e., $\mathbb{P}(\mathbb{O}) = 1$) and the user attributes in set $\mathbb{S}$ satisfy the access policy $\mathbb{A}$ (i.e. $\mathbb{A}(\mathbb{S}) = 1$); and outputs "No" otherwise.

Correctness. The system must satisfy the following **correctness property**:

– Let (PK, SK) $\leftarrow$ Setup(1^λ), $C_{\mathbb{O},\mathbb{A}} \leftarrow$ Encrypt(PK, $\mathbb{O}, \mathbb{A}$), $\mathsf{TK}_{\mathbb{P},\mathbb{S}} \leftarrow$ GenToke(PK, SK, $\mathbb{P}, \mathbb{S}$). If $\mathbb{P}(\mathbb{O}) = 1$ and $\mathbb{A}(\mathbb{S}) = 1$, then Test(PK, $\mathsf{TK}_{\mathbb{P},\mathbb{S}}, C_{\mathbb{O},\mathbb{A}}$) = "Yes"; Otherwise, $\Pr[$Test(PK, $\mathsf{TK}_{\mathbb{P},\mathbb{S}}, C_{\mathbb{O},\mathbb{A}}) = $ "No" $] > 1 - \epsilon(\lambda)$ where $\epsilon(\lambda)$ is a negligible function.

3.2 Security Model for AS-PKE

We define a security model for AS-PKE in the sense of semantic-security using the following game between a challenger and an attacker.

Setup.   The challenger runs Setup(1^λ) to obtain a public PK and a secret key SK. It gives the public key PK to the adversary and keeps SK by itself.

Query phase 1.   The adversary $\mathcal{A}$ adaptively queries the challenger for token keys for pairs of user attributes set and predicate $(\mathbb{S}, \mathbb{P})$. In response, the challenger runs $\mathsf{TK}_{\mathbb{P}_i,\mathbb{S}_i} \leftarrow$ GenToken(PK, SK, $\mathbb{P}_i, \mathbb{S}_i$) and gives the authorized query token $\mathsf{TK}_{\mathbb{P}_i,\mathbb{S}_i}$ to $\mathcal{A}$, for $1 \leq i \leq q$.

Challenge.   The adversary $\mathcal{A}$ submits two pairs of keywords and access policy $(\mathbb{O}_0, \mathbb{A}_0 = (A, \rho, \mathcal{T}_0)), (\mathbb{O}_1, \mathbb{A}_1 = (A, \rho, \mathcal{T}_1))$ subject to the restriction that, for any previous query $(\mathbb{P}_i, \mathbb{S}_i)$ in phase 1, either $\mathbb{O}_j$ does not satisfy $\mathbb{P}_i$ or $\mathbb{S}_i$ does not satisfy $\mathbb{A}_j$ for all $j \in [0, 1]$. The challenger selects a random bit $\beta \in \{0, 1\}$, sets $C_{\mathbb{O}_\beta, \mathbb{A}_\beta} = \mathsf{Encrypt}(\mathsf{PK}, \mathbb{O}_\beta, \mathbb{A}_\beta)$, and sends $C_{\mathbb{O}_\beta, \mathbb{A}_\beta}$ to the adversary as its challenge ciphertext.

Note that, the LSSS matrix A and ρ are the same in the two access structures provided by the adversary. In an AS-PKE scheme, one can distinguish the ciphertexts if the associated access structures have different (A, ρ), since (A, ρ) is sent along with the encrypted document explicitly.

Query phase 2.   The adversary continues to adaptively query the challenger for token keys corresponding to predicates and user attribute sets with the same restriction in **Challenge** phrase.

Guess.   The adversary $\mathcal{A}$ outputs its guess $\beta' \in \{0, 1\}$ for β and wins the game if $\beta' = \beta$.

The advantage of the adversary in this game is defined as $|\mathsf{Pr}[\beta = \beta'] - \frac{1}{2}|$ where the probability is taken over the random bits used by the challenger and the adversary.

Definition 7. *An AS-PKE scheme is secure if all polynomial time adversaries have at most a negligible advantage in this security game.*

3.3   Constructions

Our construction of a secure AS-PKE scheme is shown as follows.

  Setup(1^λ).   The setup algorithm first runs $\mathcal{G}(1^\lambda)$ to obtain $(p_1, p_2, p_3, p_4, \mathbb{G}, \mathbb{G}_T, e)$ with $\mathbb{G} = \mathbb{G}_{p_1} \times \mathbb{G}_{p_2} \times \mathbb{G}_{p_3} \times \mathbb{G}_{p_4}$, where $\mathbb{G}$ and $\mathbb{G}_T$ are cyclic groups of order $N = p_1 p_2 p_3 p_4$. Then, it chooses random elements $g, u, h_1, \ldots, h_n, \hat{h}_1, \ldots, \hat{h}_m \in \mathbb{G}_{p_1}$, $X_3 \in \mathbb{G}_{p_3}$, $X_4, Z, Z', Z_0, Z_1, \ldots, Z_n, \hat{Z}_1, \ldots, \hat{Z}_m \in \mathbb{G}_{p_4}$ and random number $a \in \mathbb{Z}_N$. The public key is published as $\mathsf{PK} = (N, gZ, g^a Z', U = uZ_0, \{H_i = h_i \cdot Z_i\}_{1 \le i \le n}, \{\hat{H}_i = \hat{h}_i \cdot \hat{Z}_i\}_{1 \le i \le m}, X_4)$. The secret key is $\mathsf{SK} = (g, u, h_1, \ldots, h_n, \hat{h}_1, \ldots, \hat{h}_m, X_3, a)$.

  Encrypt($\mathsf{PK}, \mathbb{O} = (o_1, \ldots, o_m) \in \mathbb{Z}_N^m, \mathbb{A} = (A, \rho, \mathcal{T})$). A is an $l_s \times n$ matrix, ρ is a map from each row A_i of A to a user attribute $\rho(i)$, and $\mathcal{T} = (t_{\rho(1)}, \ldots, t_{\rho(l_s)})$. The encryption algorithm chooses a random vector $v = (s, v_2, \ldots, v_n) \in \mathbb{Z}_N^n$. For each row A_i of A, it chooses a random $r_i \in \mathbb{Z}_N$. It also chooses random elements $\tilde{Z}_{1,0}, \{\tilde{Z}_{1,i}\}_{1 \le i \le n}, \{\tilde{Z}'_{1,i}\}_{1 \le i \le n} \in \mathbb{G}_{p_4}, \{Z_{2,x}\}_{1 \le x \le m} \in \mathbb{G}_{p_4}$. The ciphertext $\mathsf{CT} = ((A, \rho), C, C_i, D_i, \hat{C}_x)$ is computed as:

$$C = (gZ)^s \cdot \tilde{Z}_{1,0} = g^s \cdot Z_{1,0},$$

$$C_i = (g^a Z')^{A_i \cdot v} (U^{t_{\rho(i)}} H_{\rho(i)})^{r_i} \cdot \tilde{Z}_{1,i} = g^{a A_i \cdot v} (U^{t_{\rho(i)}} H_{\rho(i)})^{r_i} \cdot Z_{1,i},$$

$$D_i = (gZ)^{-r_i} \cdot \tilde{Z}'_{1,i} = g^{-r_i} \cdot Z'_{1,i}, \quad \hat{C}_x = (U^{o_x} \cdot \hat{H}_x)^s \cdot Z_{2,x} \; \forall x,$$

where $Z_{1,0} = Z^s \cdot \tilde{Z}_{1,0}, Z_{1,i} = Z'^{A_i \cdot v} \cdot \tilde{Z}_{1,i}, Z'_{1,i} = Z^{-r_i} \cdot \tilde{Z}'_{1,i}$.

GenToken(PK, SK, $\hat{\mathcal{P}} = (\hat{A}, \hat{\rho}, \hat{\mathcal{T}}), \mathbb{S} = (s_1, \ldots, s_n))$. $\hat{A}$ is an $l_o \times m$ matrix, $\hat{\rho}$ is a map from each row $\hat{A}_x$ of $\hat{A}$ to a keyword field $\hat{\rho}(x)$, and $\hat{\mathcal{T}} = (\hat{t}_{\hat{\rho}(1)}, \ldots, \hat{t}_{\hat{\rho}(l_o)})$. The algorithm first chooses two random numbers $t_1, t_2 \in \mathbb{Z}_N$ and a random vector $\hat{v} = (t_2, \hat{v}_2, \ldots, \hat{v}_m) \in \mathbb{Z}_N^m$. It also chooses random elements $R_0, R_0', R_x', R_i, \hat{R}_x \in G_{p_3}$. The authorized query token key $\mathsf{TK}_{\hat{\mathcal{P}}, \mathbb{S}} = ((\hat{A}, \hat{\rho}), K, L, K_i, \hat{K}_x, K_x')$ is computed as:

$$K = g^{a(t_1+t_2)}R_0, \quad L = g^{t_1}R_0', \quad K_i = (u^{s_i}h_i)^{t_1}R_i$$

$$\hat{K}_x = g^{a\hat{A}_x \cdot \hat{v}}(u^{\hat{t}_{\hat{\rho}(x)}}\hat{h}_{\hat{\rho}(x)})^{t_x}\hat{R}_x \ \forall x, \quad K_x' = g^{-t_x}R_x' \ \forall x$$

Test(PK, $\mathsf{TK}_{\hat{\mathcal{P}}, \mathbb{S}}$, CT). Let $\mathsf{CT} = ((A, \rho), C, C_i, D_i, \hat{C}_x)$ and $\mathsf{TK}_{\hat{\mathcal{P}}, \mathbb{S}} = ((\hat{A}, \hat{\rho}), K, L, K_i, \hat{K}_x, K_x')$. The test algorithm first calculates $I_{A,\rho}$ from (A, ρ), where $I_{A,\rho}$ denotes the set of minimum subsets of $(1, \ldots, l_s)$ that satisfies $I_{A,\rho}$. It similarly calculates $\hat{I}_{\hat{A}, \hat{\rho}}$ from $(\hat{A}, \hat{\rho})$. Then, it checks if there exist an $I \in I_{A,\rho}$ and an $\hat{I} \in \hat{I}_{\hat{A}, \hat{\rho}}$ that satisfies

$$e(C, K) = \prod_{i \in I}(e(C_i, L)e(K_i, D_i))^{\omega_i} \cdot \prod_{x \in \hat{I}}(e(\hat{K}_x, C)e(\hat{C}_x, K_x'))^{\hat{\omega}_x} \tag{1}$$

where $\sum_{i \in I} \omega_i A_i = (1, 0, \ldots, 0)$ and $\sum_{x \in \hat{I}} \hat{\omega}_x \hat{A}_x = (1, 0, \ldots, 0)$. If no elements in $I_{A,\rho}$ and $\hat{I}_{\hat{A}, \hat{\rho}}$ satisfy the above equation, it outputs "No"; otherwise, it outputs "Yes".

The **correctness** is shown as follows. Suppose $\mathbb{P}(\mathbb{O}) = 1$ and $\mathbb{A}(\mathbb{S}) = 1$, i.e. there exist $\mathcal{I} \subseteq \{1, \ldots, l_s\}$, $\hat{\mathcal{I}} \subseteq \{1, \ldots, l_o\}$ and constants $\{w_i\}_{i \in \mathcal{I}}$, $\{\hat{w}_x\}_{x \in \hat{\mathcal{I}}}$ such that $\sum_{i \in \mathcal{I}} w_i A_i = (1, 0, \ldots, 0)$ and $s_{\rho(i)} = t_{\rho(i)}$ for $\forall i \in \mathcal{I}$, $\sum_{x \in \hat{\mathcal{I}}} \hat{w}_x \hat{A}_x = (1, 0, \ldots, 0)$ and $o_{\hat{\rho}(x)} = \hat{t}_{\hat{\rho}(x)}$ for $\forall x \in \hat{\mathcal{I}}$. Then, the left side of Equation (1) is equal to

$$e(C, K) = e(g^s \cdot Z_{1,0}, g^{a(t_1+t_2)}R_0) = e(g, g)^{as(t_1+t_2)}$$

and the right side of Equation (1) is equal to

$$\prod_{i \in I}(e(C_i, L)e(K_i, D_i))^{\omega_i} \cdot \prod_{x \in \hat{I}}(e(\hat{K}_x, C)e(\hat{C}_x, K_x'))^{\hat{\omega}_x}$$

$$= \prod_{i \in I}(e(g^{aA_i \cdot v(U^{t_{\rho(i)}}H_{\rho(i)})^{r_i}} \cdot Z_{1,i}, g^{t_1}R_0') \cdot e((u^{s_i}h_i)^{t_i}R_i, g^{-r_i}Z_{1,i}'))^{w_i}$$

$$\cdot \prod_{x \in \hat{I}}(e(g^{a\hat{A}_x \cdot \hat{v}}(u^{\hat{(t)}_{\hat{\rho}(x)}}\hat{h}_{\hat{\rho}(x)})^{t_x}\hat{R}_x, g^s Z_{1,0}) \cdot e((U^{o_x}\hat{H}_x)^s \cdot Z_{2,x}, g^{-t_x}R_x'))^{\hat{\omega}_x}$$

$$= \prod_{i \in I}(e(g^{aA_i \cdot v(u^{t_{\rho i}} \cdot h_i)^{r_i}}, g^{t_1}) \cdot e((u^{s_i}h_i)^{t_1}, g^{-r_i}))^{w_i}$$

$$\cdot \prod_{x \in \hat{I}}(e(g^{a\hat{A}_x \cdot \hat{v}}(u^{\hat{t}_{\hat{\rho}(x)}}\hat{h}_{\hat{\rho}(x)})^{t_x}, g^s) \cdot e((u^{o_x}, \hat{h}_x)^s, g^{-t_x}))^{\hat{\omega}_x}$$

$$= e(g, g)^{at_1 s} \cdot e(g, g)^{at_2 s} = e(g, g)^{as(t_1+t_2)}$$

which is equal to the left side of Equation (1).

3.4 Security

Theorem 1. *If assumptions 1, 2, 3 and 4 hold, then the proposed AS-PKE scheme is secure.*

Proof. Following the approach by Lewko and Waters [7], we define two additional structures: *semi-functional* ciphertexts and *semi-functional* keys. They are not used in the real system, only in our proof.

Semi-functional Ciphertext. Let g_2 denote a generator of the subgroup $\mathbb{G}_{p_2}$. A semi-functional ciphertext is created as follows. We first use the encryption algorithm to form a normal ciphertext $\mathsf{CT}' = ((A, \rho), C', C'_i, D'_i, \hat{C}'_i)$. Then, we choose random exponent $c, b' \in \mathbb{Z}_N$ and random values $z_i \in \mathbb{Z}_N$ associated to user attributes, random values $\gamma_i \in \mathbb{Z}_N$ associated to rows i of matrix A, random values $z'_x \in \mathbb{Z}_N$ associated to keywords and a random vector $w \in \mathbb{Z}_N^n$. Then, the semi-functional ciphertext is set to be:

$$(A, \rho), \quad C = C' \cdot g_2^c, \quad C_i = C'_i \cdot g_2^{A_i \cdot w + \gamma_i z_{\rho(i)}},$$

$$D_i = D'_i \cdot g_2^{-\gamma_i} \ \forall i \in [1, n], \quad \hat{C}_x = \hat{C}'_x \cdot g_2^{b' z'_x} \ \forall x \in [1, m]$$

It should be noted that the values z_i and z'_x are chosen randomly once and then fixed — the same values are also involved in semi-functional keys as defined below.

Semi-functional Key. A semi-functional key will take on one of the following two forms. In order to create a semi-functional key, we first use the key generation algorithm to form a normal key $\mathsf{TK}'_{\hat{\mathcal{P}}, \mathcal{S}} = ((\hat{A}, \hat{\rho}), K', L', K'_i, \hat{K}'_x, \tilde{K}'_x)$. Then, we choose random exponents $d, b \in \mathbb{Z}_N$, random values $\gamma'_x \in \mathbb{Z}_N$ associated to row x of matrix $\hat{A}$ and a random vector $\hat{w} \in \mathbb{Z}_N^n$. The semi-functional key of type 1 is set as:

$$(\hat{A}, \hat{\rho}), \quad K = K' \cdot g_2^d \quad L = L' \cdot g_2^b, \quad K_i = K'_i \cdot g_2^{b z_i} \ \forall i \in [1, n]$$

$$\hat{K}_x = \hat{K}'_x \cdot g_2^{\hat{A}_x \cdot \hat{w} + \gamma'_x z'_{\hat{\rho}(x)}} \ \forall x \in [1, m], \quad K'_x = \tilde{K}'_x \cdot g_2^{\gamma'_x} \ \forall x \in [1, m]$$

The semi-functional key of type 2 is set as:

$$(\hat{A}, \hat{\rho}), \quad K = K' \cdot g_2^d \quad L = L', \quad K_i = K'_i \ \forall i \in [1, n]$$

$$\hat{K}_x = \hat{K}'_x \cdot g_2^{\hat{A}_x \cdot \hat{w}} \ \forall x \in [1, m], \quad K'_x = \tilde{K}'_x \ \forall x \in [1, m]$$

We will prove the security of the proposed scheme based on the Assumptions 1, 2, 3 and 4 using a hybrid argument over a sequence of games. The first game, Game_{real}, is the real security game where the ciphertext and all token keys are normal. In the next game, Game_0, all of token keys are normal, but the challenge ciphertext is semi-functional. Let q denote the number of token key queries made by the attacker. For k from 1 to q and l from 1 to m, we define:

Game$_{k,1}$. In this game, the challenge ciphertext is semi-functional, the first $k-1$ token keys are semi-functional of type 2, the kth token key is semi-functional of type 1, and the remaining token keys are normal.

Game$_{k,2}$. In this game, the challenge ciphertext is semi-functional, the first k token keys are semi-functional of type 2, the remaining keys are normal.

Game$_{keyword_l}$. In this game, all token keys are semi-functional of type 2, and the challenge ciphertext $CT = (C, C_i, D_i, \hat{C}_x)$ is a semi-functional ciphertext with $\hat{C}_1, \ldots, \hat{C}_l$ randomly chosen from $\mathbb{G}_{p_1} \times \mathbb{G}_{p_2} \times \mathbb{G}_{p_4}$.

Game$_{Final_0}$. This game is the same as Game$_{keyword_m}$.

Game$_{Final_1}$. This game is the same as Game$_{Final_0}$, except that in the challenge ciphertext C_i are chosen from $\mathbb{G}_{p_1} \times \mathbb{G}_{p_2} \times \mathbb{G}_{G_4}$ at random.

We prove that these games are indistinguishable in five lemmas, which are given in the Appendix. Therefore, we conclude that the advantage of the adversary in Game$_{real}$, i.e. the real security game, is negligible. This completes the proof of Theorem 1.

3.5 Efficiency

Let $|\mathbb{G}|$ be the length of the bit-representation of a group in $\mathbb{G}$. The size of the public key, a token key, and a ciphertext are $(n + m + 4)|\mathbb{G}|$, $(n + 2m + 2)|\mathbb{G}|$, and $(2n + m + 1)|\mathbb{G}|$, respectively. For a predicate $(A, \rho, \mathcal{T})$, let $l_1 = |I_{A,\rho}|, I_{A,\rho} = \{I_1, \ldots, I_{l_1}\}$ and $l_2 = |I_1| + \ldots + |I_{l_1}|$; for a predicate $(\hat{A}, \hat{\rho}, \hat{\mathcal{T}})$, let $\hat{l}_1 = |\hat{I}_{\hat{A},\hat{\rho}}|, \hat{I}_{\hat{A},\hat{\rho}} = \{\hat{I}_1, \ldots, \hat{I}_{\hat{l}_1}\}$ and $\hat{l}_2 = |\hat{I}_1| + \ldots + |\hat{I}_{\hat{l}_1}|$. Then, the computational costs of an encryption and a test are $(4n + 2m + 1)t_e + (4n + 2m + 1)t_m$ and $(2l_1\hat{l}_2 + 2l_2\hat{l}_1 + 1)t_b + (l_1\hat{l}_2 + 2l_2\hat{l}_1)t_{T\_m} + (l_1\hat{l}_2 + l_2\hat{l}_1)t_{T\_e}$, respectively, where t_b, t_e, t_m, t_{T_e}, and t_{T_m} denote the computational costs of bilinear map, exponentiation in $\mathbb{G}$, multiplication in $\mathbb{G}$, exponentiation in $\mathbb{G}_T$, and multiplication in $\mathbb{G}_T$, respectively. We note that the proposed AS-PKE scheme may not be highly practical due to the use of composite order bilinear groups. The major contribution of this paper is more on the theoretical aspects, including the concept and the security model of AS-PKE, and the first AS-PKE scheme and its security proof. In the future, we will investigate how to construct more efficient AS-PKE schemes.

3.6 Discussion

The proposed AS-PKE scheme is based on the KP-ABE scheme proposed by Lewko et al. and the CP-ABE with hidden access structures proposed by Lai et al. [7,11]. Different from the KP-ABE scheme [7] which works in a small universe of attributes, the keywords in the proposed AS-PKE scheme have a large universe (i.e. $\mathbb{Z}_N$). The proposed AS-PKE scheme can be easily extended to obtain an anonymous dual-policy ABE scheme which implies a fully secure dual-policy ABE scheme [14].

Similar to the KP-ABE scheme in [7], the proposed AS-PKE scheme has a restriction that each keyword field can only be used once in a predicate, which is called one-use AS-PKE. We can construct a secure AS-PKE scheme where the keyword fields can be used multiple times (up to a constant number of uses fixed at setup) from a one-use AS-PKE scheme by applying the generic transformation given in Lewko et al. [7].

4 Conclusion

This paper presented AS-PKE, a public-key encryption scheme supporting both keyword search and access control capabilities. The AS-PKE scheme is constructed based on the KP-ABE scheme proposed by Lewko et al. [7] and the CP-ABE with hidden access structure proposed by Lai et al. [11]. The scheme supports monotone boolean predicates and is proven to be fully secure in the standard model.

Acknowledgments. The work of Jie Shi was supported by the National Natural Science Foundation of China (No. 61300227), and the Guangdong Provincial Natural Science Foundation (No. S2013040015711). The work of Junzuo Lai was supported by the National Natural Science Foundation of China (Nos. 61300226, 61272534), the Research Fund for the Doctoral Program of Higher Education of China (No. 20134401120017), the Guangdong Provincial Natural Science Foundation (No. S2013040014826), and the Fundamental Research Funds for the Central Universities. The work of Jian Weng was supported by the National Science Foundation of China (Nos. 61272413, 61133014), the Fok Ying Tung Education Foundation (No. 131066), the Program for New Century Excellent Talents in University (No. NCET-12-0680), the Research Fund for the Doctoral Program of Higher Education of China (No. 20134401110011), and the Foundation for Distinguished Young Talents in Higher Education of Guangdong (No. 2012LYM 0027).

References

1. Armbrust, M., Fox, A., Griffith, R., Joseph, A.D., Katz, R.H., Konwinski, A., Lee, G., Patterson, D.A., Rabkin, A., Stoica, I., Zaharia, M.: A view of cloud computing. Commun. ACM 53(4), 50–58 (2010)
2. Li, M., Yu, S., Cao, N., Lou, W.: Authorized private keyword search over encrypted data in cloud computing. In: ICDCS, pp. 383–392 (2011)
3. Benaloh, J., Chase, M., Horvitz, E., Lauter, K.: Patient controlled encryption: ensuring privacy of electronic medical records. In: CCSW, pp. 103–114 (2009)
4. Li, M., Yu, S., Ren, K., Lou, W.: Securing personal health records in cloud computing: Patient-centric and fine-grained data access control in multi-owner settings. In: Jajodia, S., Zhou, J. (eds.) SecureComm 2010. LNICST, vol. 50, pp. 89–106. Springer, Heidelberg (2010)
5. Sahai, A., Waters, B.: Fuzzy identity-based encryption. In: Cramer, R. (ed.) EUROCRYPT 2005. LNCS, vol. 3494, pp. 457–473. Springer, Heidelberg (2005)

6. Goyal, V., Pandey, O., Sahai, A., Waters, B.: Attribute-based encryption for fine-grained access control of encrypted data. In: ACM Conference on Computer and Communications Security, pp. 89–98 (2006)
7. Lewko, A.B., Okamoto, T., Sahai, A., Takashima, K., Waters, B.: Fully secure functional encryption: Attribute-based encryption and (hierarchical) inner product encryption. In: Gilbert, H. (ed.) EUROCRYPT 2010. LNCS, vol. 6110, pp. 62–91. Springer, Heidelberg (2010)
8. Bethencourt, J., Sahai, A., Waters, B.: Ciphertext-policy attribute-based encryption. In: IEEE Symposium on Security and Privacy, pp. 321–334 (2007)
9. Waters, B.: Ciphertext-policy attribute-based encryption: An expressive, efficient, and provably secure realization. In: Catalano, D., Fazio, N., Gennaro, R., Nicolosi, A. (eds.) PKC 2011. LNCS, vol. 6571, pp. 53–70. Springer, Heidelberg (2011)
10. Katz, J., Sahai, A., Waters, B.: Predicate encryption supporting disjunctions, polynomial equations, and inner products. In: Smart, N.P. (ed.) EUROCRYPT 2008. LNCS, vol. 4965, pp. 146–162. Springer, Heidelberg (2008)
11. Lai, J., Deng, R.H., Li, Y.: Expressive CP-ABE with partially hidden access structures. In: ASIACCS, pp. 18–19 (2012)
12. Boneh, D., Di Crescenzo, G., Ostrovsky, R., Persiano, G.: Public key encryption with keyword search. In: Cachin, C., Camenisch, J.L. (eds.) EUROCRYPT 2004. LNCS, vol. 3027, pp. 506–522. Springer, Heidelberg (2004)
13. Park, D.J., Kim, K., Lee, P.J.: Public key encryption with conjunctive field keyword search. In: Lim, C.H., Yung, M. (eds.) WISA 2004. LNCS, vol. 3325, pp. 73–86. Springer, Heidelberg (2005)
14. Attrapadung, N., Imai, H.: Dual-policy attribute based encryption. In: Abdalla, M., Pointcheval, D., Fouque, P.-A., Vergnaud, D. (eds.) ACNS 2009. LNCS, vol. 5536, pp. 168–185. Springer, Heidelberg (2009)
15. Goyal, V., Jain, A., Pandey, O., Sahai, A.: Bounded ciphertext policy attribute based encryption. In: Aceto, L., Damgård, I., Goldberg, L.A., Halldórsson, M.M., Ingólfsdóttir, A., Walukiewicz, I. (eds.) ICALP 2008, Part II. LNCS, vol. 5126, pp. 579–591. Springer, Heidelberg (2008)
16. Ostrovsky, R., Sahai, A., Waters, B.: Attribute-based encryption with non-monotonic access structures. In: Proceedings of the 14th ACM Conference on Computer and Communications Security, pp. 195–203. ACM (2007)
17. Cheung, L., Newport, C.C.: Provably secure ciphertext policy ABE. In: ACM Conference on Computer and Communications Security, pp. 456–465 (2007)
18. Nishide, T., Yoneyama, K., Ohta, K.: Attribute-based encryption with partially hidden encryptor-specified access structures. In: Bellovin, S.M., Gennaro, R., Keromytis, A.D., Yung, M. (eds.) ACNS 2008. LNCS, vol. 5037, pp. 111–129. Springer, Heidelberg (2008)
19. Lai, J., Deng, R.H., Li, Y.: Fully secure cipertext-policy hiding CP-ABE. In: Bao, F., Weng, J. (eds.) ISPEC 2011. LNCS, vol. 6672, pp. 24–39. Springer, Heidelberg (2011)
20. Shi, E., Waters, B.: Delegating capabilities in predicate encryption systems. In: Aceto, L., Damgård, I., Goldberg, L.A., Halldórsson, M.M., Ingólfsdóttir, A., Walukiewicz, I. (eds.) ICALP 2008, Part II. LNCS, vol. 5126, pp. 560–578. Springer, Heidelberg (2008)
21. Okamoto, T., Takashima, K.: Hierarchical predicate encryption for inner-products. In: Matsui, M. (ed.) ASIACRYPT 2009. LNCS, vol. 5912, pp. 214–231. Springer, Heidelberg (2009)
22. Shen, E., Shi, E., Waters, B.: Predicate privacy in encryption systems. In: Reingold, O. (ed.) TCC 2009. LNCS, vol. 5444, pp. 457–473. Springer, Heidelberg (2009)

23. Okamoto, T., Takashima, K.: Fully secure functional encryption with general relations from the decisional linear assumption. In: Rabin, T. (ed.) CRYPTO 2010. LNCS, vol. 6223, pp. 191–208. Springer, Heidelberg (2010)
24. Hwang, Y.H., Lee, P.J.: Public key encryption with conjunctive keyword search and its extension to a multi-user system. In: Takagi, T., Okamoto, T., Okamoto, E., Okamoto, T. (eds.) Pairing 2007. LNCS, vol. 4575, pp. 2–22. Springer, Heidelberg (2007)
25. Boneh, D., Waters, B.: Conjunctive, subset, and range queries on encrypted data. In: Vadhan, S.P. (ed.) TCC 2007. LNCS, vol. 4392, pp. 535–554. Springer, Heidelberg (2007)
26. Sun, W., Yu, S., Lou, W., Hou, Y.T., Li, H.: Protecting your right: Attribute-based keyword search with fine-grained owner-enforced search authorization in the cloud. In: INFOCOM (2014)
27. Narayan, S., Gagné, M., Safavi-Naini, R.: Privacy preserving EHR system using attribute-based infrastructure. In: CCSW, pp. 47–52 (2010)
28. Beimel, A.: Secure schemes for secret sharing and key distribution. PhD thesis, Israel Institute of Technology, Technion, Haifa, Israel (1996)
29. Lewko, A.B., Waters, B.: Decentralizing attribute-based encryption. In: Paterson, K.G. (ed.) EUROCRYPT 2011. LNCS, vol. 6632, pp. 568–588. Springer, Heidelberg (2011)
30. Boneh, D., Goh, E.-J., Nissim, K.: Evaluating 2-DNF formulas on ciphertexts. In: Kilian, J. (ed.) TCC 2005. LNCS, vol. 3378, pp. 325–341. Springer, Heidelberg (2005)
31. Lai, J., Zhou, X., Deng, R.H., Li, Y., Chen, K.: Expressive search on encrypted data. In: Proceedings of the 8th ACM SIGSAC Symposium on Information, Computer and Communications Security, ASIA CCS 2013, pp. 243–252. ACM, New York (2013)

A   Lemmas

The following five lemmas are used in the proof of Theorem 1. The proof of the lemmas is detailed in (the appendix of) the full version of this paper, which is accessible at http://www.mysmu.edu/faculty/yjli/ASPKE-full.pdf.

Lemma 1. *Suppose that $\mathcal{G}$ satisfies Assumption 1. Then Game_{real} and Game_0 are computationally indistinguishable.*

Lemma 2. *Suppose that $\mathcal{G}$ satisfies Assumption 2. Then $\mathsf{Game}_{k-1,2}$ and $\mathsf{Game}_{k,1}$ are computationally indistinguishable.*

Lemma 3. *Suppose that $\mathcal{G}$ satisfies Assumption 2. Then $\mathsf{Game}_{k,1}$ and $\mathsf{Game}_{k,2}$ are computationally indistinguishable.*

Lemma 4. *Suppose that $\mathcal{G}$ satisfies Assumption 3. Then $\mathsf{Game}_{keyword_{l-1}}$ and $\mathsf{Game}_{keyword_l}$ are computationally indistinguishable.*

Lemma 5. *Suppose that $\mathcal{G}$ satisfies Assumption 4. Then Game_{final_0} and Game_{final_1} are computationally indistinguishable.*

Double-Authentication-Preventing Signatures*

Bertram Poettering[1] and Douglas Stebila[2]

[1] Royal Holloway, University of London, United Kingdom
bertram.poettering@rhul.ac.uk
[2] Queensland University of Technology, Brisbane, Australia
stebila@qut.edu.au

Abstract. Digital signatures are often used by trusted authorities to make unique bindings between a subject and a digital object; for example, certificate authorities certify a public key belongs to a domain name, and time-stamping authorities certify that a certain piece of information existed at a certain time. Traditional digital signature schemes however impose no uniqueness conditions, so a trusted authority could make multiple certifications for the same subject but different objects, be it intentionally, by accident, or following a (legal or illegal) coercion. We propose the notion of a *double-authentication-preventing signature*, in which a value to be signed is split into two parts: a *subject* and a *message*. If a signer ever signs two different messages for the same subject, enough information is revealed to allow anyone to compute valid signatures on behalf of the signer. This double-signature forgeability property discourages signers from misbehaving—a form of *self-enforcement*—and would give binding authorities like CAs some cryptographic arguments to resist legal coercion. We give a generic construction using a new type of trapdoor functions with extractability properties, which we show can be instantiated using the group of sign-agnostic quadratic residues modulo a Blum integer.

Keywords: digital signatures, double signatures, dishonest signer, coercion, compelled certificate creation attack, self-enforcement, two-to-one trapdoor functions.

1 Introduction

Digital signatures are used in several contexts by authorities who are trusted to behave appropriately. For instance, certificate authorities (CAs) in public key infrastructures, who assert that a certain public key belongs to a party with a certain identifier, are trusted to not issue fraudulent certificates for a domain name; time-stamping services, who assert that certain information existed at a

---

* Parts of this work were funded by EPSRC Leadership Fellowship EP/H005455/1 and by European Commission ICT Programme Contract ICT-2007-216676 ECRYPT II (for BP), and by the Australian Technology Network and German Academic Exchange Service (ATN-DAAD) Joint Research Co-operation Scheme and Australian Research Council (ARC) Discovery Project DP130104304 (for DS).

M. Kutyłowski and J. Vaidya (Eds.): ESORICS 2014, Part I, LNCS 8712, pp. 436–453, 2014.
© Springer International Publishing Switzerland 2014

certain point in time, are trusted to not retroactively certify information (they should not "change the past"). In both of these cases, the authority is trusted to make a *unique* binding between a subject—a domain name or time—and a digital object—a public key or piece of information. However, traditional digital signatures provide no assurance of the uniqueness of this binding. As a result, an authority could make multiple bindings per subject.

Multiple bindings per subject can happen due to several reasons: poor management practices, a security breach, or coercion by external parties. Although there have been a few highly publicized certificate authority failures due to either poor management practices or security breaches, the vast majority of certificate authorities seem to successfully apply technological measures—including audited key generation ceremonies, secret sharing of signing keys, and use of hardware security modules—to securely and correctly carry out their role.

However, CAs have few tools to resist coercion, especially in the form of legal demands from governments. This was identified by Soghoian and Stamm [1] as the *compelled certificate creation attack*. For example, a certificate authority may receive a national security letter compelling it to assist in an investigation by issuing a second certificate for a specified domain name but containing the public key of the government agency, allowing the agency to impersonate Internet services to the target of the investigation. Regardless of one's opinions on the merits of these legal actions, they are a violation of the trust promised by certificate authorities: to never issue a certificate to anyone but the correct party. The extent to which legal coercion of CAs occurs is unknown, however there are indications that the technique is of interest to governments. A networking device company named Packet Forensics sells a device for eavesdropping on encrypted web traffic in which, reportedly, "users have the ability to import a copy of any legitimate key they obtain (potentially by court order)".[1] Various documents released by NSA contractor Edward Snowden in June–September 2013 indicate government interest in executing man-in-the-middle attacks on SSL users.[2]

Two certificates for the same domain signed by a single CA indeed constitute a cryptographic proof of fraud. However, in practice, it is currently up to the "market" to decide how to respond: the nature of the response depends on the scope and nature of the infraction and the CA's handling of the issue. The consequences that have been observed from real-world CA incidents range from minimal, such as the CA revoking the extra certificates amid a period of bad publicity (as in the 2011 Comodo incident[3]), up to the ultimate punishment for a CA on the web: removal of its root certificate from web browsers' lists of trusted CAs (as in the 2011 DigiNotar incident [2], which was found to have issued fraudulent certificates that were used against Iranian Internet users [3], and which lead to the bankruptcy of DigiNotar).

For a CA making business decisions on management and security practices, such consequences may be enough to convince it to invest in better systems.

---

[1] http://www.wired.com/threatlevel/2010/03/packet-forensics/

[2] https://www.schneier.com/blog/archives/2013/09/new_nsa_leak_sh.html

[3] https://www.comodo.com/Comodo-Fraud-Incident-2011-03-23.html

For a CA trying to resist a lawful order compelling it to issue a fraudulent certificate, such consequences may not be enough to convince a judge that it should not be compelled to violate the fundamental duty with which it was entrusted.

1.1   Contributions

We propose a new type of digital signature scheme for which the consequences of certain signer behaviours are unambiguous: any double signing, for any reason, leads to an immediate, irreversible, incontrovertible loss of confidence in the signature system. This "fragility" provides no room for mistakes, thereby encouraging "self-enforcement" of correct behaviour and allows a signer to make a more compelling argument resisting lawful coercion. If a CA fulfills a request to issue a double signature even to a lawful agency, the agency, by using the certificate, enables the attacked party to issue arbitrary certificates as well.

In a *double-authentication-preventing signature (DAPS)*, the data that is to be signed is split into two parts: a *subject* and a *message*. If a signer ever signs two messages for the same subject, then enough information is revealed for anyone to be able to forge signatures on arbitrary messages, rendering the signer immediately and irrevocably untrustworthy. More precisely, in addition to unforgeability we require a new security property for DAPS, *double-signature extractability*: from any two signatures on the same subject the signing key can be fully recovered. Depending on the nature of the subjects, an honest signer may need to track the list of subjects signed to avoid signing the same subject twice.

We give a generic construction for DAPS based on a new primitive called *extractable two-to-one trapdoor function* which allows anyone, given two preimages of the same value, to recover the trapdoor required for inverting the function. We show how to construct these functions using the group of sign-agnostic quadratic residues modulo a Blum integer (RSA modulus), an algebraic reformulation of a mathematical construction that has been used in several cryptographic primitives. The resulting DAPS scheme is efficient; with 1024-bit signing and verification keys, the signature size is about 20 KiB, and the runtime of our implementation using libgcrypt is about 0.3 s for signing and 0.1 s for verifying.

1.2   Related Work

Certificate auditing and other techniques. Mechanisms such as Certificate Transparency[4] and others aim to identify malicious or incorrect CA behaviour by collecting and auditing public certificates. Incorrect behaviour, such as a CA issuing two certificates for the same domain name, can be identified and then presented as evidence possibly leading to a loss of trust. DAPS differs in that it provides an immediate and irrevocable loss of confidence and, importantly, provides a completely non-interactive solution.

Self-enforcement and traitor tracing. Dwork *et al.* [4] introduced the notion of *self-enforcement* in cryptography, in which the cryptosystem is designed to force

---

[4] http://www.certificate-transparency.org/

the user to keep the functionality private, that is, to not delegate or transfer the functionality to another user. There are a variety of techniques for ensuring self-enforcement: tradeoffs in efficiency [4] or by allowing recovering of some associated secret value with any delegated version of the secret information [5–7]. Broadcast encryption schemes often aim for a related notion, traitor tracing [8], in which the broadcaster aims to detect which of several receivers have used their private key to construct and distribute a pirate device; typically the broadcaster can identify which private key was leaked. DAPS differs from this line of research in that it does not aim to deter delegation or transferring of keys, rather it aims to deter a single party from performing a certain local operation (double signing).

Accountable IBE. Goyal [9] aimed to reduce trust in the key generation centre (KGC) in identity-based encryption.In accountable IBE, the key generation protocol between the user and the KGC results in one of a large number of possible keys being generated, and which one is generated is unknown to the KGC. Thus if the KGC issues a second key, it will with high probability be different, and the two different keys for the same identity serve as a proof that the KGC misbehaved. This effectively allows IBE to achieve the same level of detection as normal public key infrastructures: two certificates for the same subject serve as a proof that the CA misbehaved. However, neither approach has the stronger level of deterrence of DAPS: double signing leads to an immediate loss of confidence, rather than just proof of misbehaving for consideration of prosecution.

Digital cash. Digital cash schemes [10] often aim to detect double spending: a party who uses a token once maintains anonymity, but a party who uses a token twice reveals enough information for her identity to be recovered and traced. DAPS has some conceptual similarities, in that a party who signs two messages with the same subject reveals enough information for her secret key to be recovered. In both settings, double operations leak information, but double spending in digital cash typically leaks only an identity, whereas double signing in DAPS leaks the signer's private key. It is interesting to note that the number-theoretic structures our DAPS scheme builds on are similar to those used in early digital cash to provide double spending traceability [10]: both schemes use RSA moduli that can be factored if signers/spenders misbehave. However, there does not seem to be a direct connection between the primitives.

One-time signatures. One-time signatures, first proposed by Lamport using a construction based on hash functions [11], allow at most one message to be signed. Many instances can be combined using Merkle trees [12] to allow multiple signatures with just a single verification key, but key generation time becomes a function of the total number of signatures allowed. DAPS differs in that the number of messages to be signed need not be fixed a priori, and our construction relies on number-theoretic trapdoor functions, rather than solely hash functions.

Fail-stop signatures. Fail-stop signatures [13–17] allow a signer to prove to a judge that a forgery has occurred; a signer is protected against cryptanalytic attacks by even an unbounded adversary. Verifiers too are protected against computationally bounded signers who try to claim a signature is a forgery when it is not. When a forgery is detected, generally the security of the scheme collapses, because some secret information can be recovered, and so the security of previous signatures is left in doubt. Forgery-resilient signatures [18] aim to have similar properties to fail-stop signatures—the ability for a signer to prove a cryptanalytic forgery—but discovery of a forgery does not immediately render previous signatures insecure. Both focus on an *honest* signer proving someone else has constructed a forgery, whereas DAPS is about what happens when a *dishonest* or *coerced* signer signs two messages for the same subject.

Chameleon hash functions. Chameleon hash functions [19] are trapdoor-based and randomized. Hashing is collision-resistant as long as only the public parameters are known. However, given the trapdoor and the message-randomness pair used to create a specific hash value, a collision for that value can be efficiently found. Some constructions allow the extraction of the trapdoor from any collision [20, 21]. However, it remains open how DAPS could be constructed from Chameleon hash functions.

2   Definitions

We now present our main definitions: a *double-authentication-preventing signature* and its security requirements: the standard (though slightly adapted) notion of *existential unforgeability*, as well as the new property of *signing key extractability* given two signatures on the same subject.

Notation. If S is a finite set, let $U(S)$ denote the uniform distribution on S and $x \leftarrow_R S$ denote sampling x uniformly from S. If A and B are two probability distributions, then notation $A \approx B$ denotes that the statistical distance between A and B is negligible. If $\mathcal{A}$ is a (probabilistic) algorithm, then $x \leftarrow_R \mathcal{A}^{\mathcal{O}}(y)$ denotes running $\mathcal{A}$ with input y on uniformly random coins with oracle access to $\mathcal{O}$, and setting x to be the output. We use $\mathcal{A}(y; r)$ to explicitly identify the random coins r on which the otherwise deterministic algorithm $\mathcal{A}$ is run.

Definition 1 (Double-authentication-preventing signature). *A double-authentication-preventing signature (DAPS) is a tuple of efficient algorithms* (KGen, Sign, Ver) *as follows:*

- KGen(1^λ): *On input security parameter* 1^λ, *this algorithm outputs a signing key* sk *and a verification key* vk.
- Sign(sk, subj, msg): *On input signing key* sk *and subject/message pair* subj, msg $\in \{0,1\}^*$, *this algorithm outputs a signature* σ.
- Ver(vk, subj, msg, σ): *On input verification key* vk, *subject/message pair* subj, msg $\in \{0,1\}^*$, *and candidate signature* σ, *this algorithm outputs* 0 *or* 1.

Definition 2 (Correctness). *A DAPS scheme is* correct *if, for all* $\lambda \in \mathbb{N}$, *for all key pairs* (sk, vk) $\leftarrow_R$ KGen(1^λ), *for all* subj, msg $\in \{0,1\}^*$, *and for all signatures* $\sigma \leftarrow_R$ Sign(sk, subj, msg), *we have that* Ver(vk, subj, msg, σ) = 1.

Our unforgeability notion largely coincides with the standard unforgeability notion for digital signature schemes [22]; the main difference is that, for DAPS,

$\mathbf{Exp}_{\mathsf{DAPS},\mathcal{A}}^{\mathrm{EUF}}(\lambda)$:
1. SignedList $\leftarrow \emptyset$
2. $(\mathsf{sk},\mathsf{vk}) \leftarrow_R \mathsf{KGen}(1^\lambda)$
3. $(\mathsf{subj}^*,\mathsf{msg}^*,\sigma^*) \leftarrow_R \mathcal{A}^{\mathcal{O}_{\mathsf{Sign}}}(\mathsf{vk})$
   If $\mathcal{A}$ queries $\mathcal{O}_{\mathsf{Sign}}(\mathsf{subj},\mathsf{msg})$:
   (a) Append $(\mathsf{subj},\mathsf{msg})$ to SignedList
   (b) $\sigma \leftarrow_R \mathsf{Sign}(\mathsf{sk},\mathsf{subj},\mathsf{msg})$
   (c) Return σ to $\mathcal{A}$
4. Return 1 iff all the following hold:
   - $\mathsf{Ver}(\mathsf{vk},\mathsf{subj}^*,\mathsf{msg}^*,\sigma^*) = 1$
   - $(\mathsf{subj}^*,\mathsf{msg}^*) \notin$ SignedList
   - $\forall\, \mathsf{subj},\mathsf{msg}_0,\mathsf{msg}_1$:
     if $(\mathsf{subj},\mathsf{msg}_0),(\mathsf{subj},\mathsf{msg}_1) \in$ SignedList
     then $\mathsf{msg}_0 = \mathsf{msg}_1$

$\mathbf{Exp}_{\mathsf{DAPS},\mathcal{A}}^{\mathrm{DSE}}(\lambda)$:
1. $(\mathsf{vk},(S_1,S_2)) \leftarrow_R \mathcal{A}(1^\lambda)$
2. $\mathsf{sk}' \leftarrow_R \mathsf{Extract}(\mathsf{vk},(S_1,S_2))$
3. Return 1 iff all the following hold:
   - (S_1,S_2) is compromising
   - sk' is not the signing key corresponding to vk

$\mathbf{Exp}_{\mathsf{DAPS},\mathcal{A}}^{\mathrm{DSE}^*}(\lambda)$:
1. $(\mathsf{sk},\mathsf{vk}) \leftarrow_R \mathsf{KGen}(1^\lambda)$
2. $(S_1,S_2) \leftarrow_R \mathcal{A}(\mathsf{sk},\mathsf{vk})$
3. $\mathsf{sk}' \leftarrow_R \mathsf{Extract}(\mathsf{vk},(S_1,S_2))$
4. Return 1 iff all the following hold:
   - (S_1,S_2) is compromising
   - $\mathsf{sk}' \neq \mathsf{sk}$

Fig. 1. Security experiments for DAPS: unforgeability and double signature extractability (without and with trusted setup)

forgeries crafted by the adversary are not considered valid if the adversary has requested forgeries on different messages for the same subject.

Definition 3 (Existential unforgeability). *A DAPS scheme is* existentially unforgeable under adaptive chosen message attacks *if, for all efficient adversaries $\mathcal{A}$, the success probability* $\mathbf{Succ}_{\mathsf{DAPS},\mathcal{A}}^{\mathrm{EUF}}(\lambda) := \Pr[\mathbf{Exp}_{\mathsf{DAPS},\mathcal{A}}^{\mathrm{EUF}}(\lambda) = 1]$ *in the EUF experiment of Figure 1 is a negligible function.*

Although Definition 3 ensures that signatures of DAPS are generally unforgeable, we do want signatures to be forgeable in certain circumstances. In fact we aim at an even higher goal: when two different messages have been signed for the same subject, the signing key should leak from the two signatures. The notion of *compromising pairs of signatures* makes this condition precise.

Definition 4 (Compromising pair of signatures). *For a fixed verification key* vk*, a pair* (S_1,S_2) *of subject/message/signature triples* $S_1 = (\mathsf{subj}_1,\mathsf{msg}_1,\sigma_1)$ *and* $S_2 = (\mathsf{subj}_2,\mathsf{msg}_2,\sigma_2)$ *is* compromising *if* σ_1,σ_2 *are valid signatures on different messages for the same subject; that is, if* $\mathsf{Ver}(\mathsf{vk},\mathsf{subj}_1,\mathsf{msg}_1,\sigma_1) = 1$*,* $\mathsf{Ver}(\mathsf{vk},\mathsf{subj}_2,\mathsf{msg}_2,\sigma_2) = 1$*,* $\mathsf{subj}_1 = \mathsf{subj}_2$*, and* $\mathsf{msg}_1 \neq \mathsf{msg}_2$*.*

We now define the double-signature extractability requirement. Here, the adversary takes the role of a malicious signer that aims to generate compromising pairs of signatures that do not lead to successful signing key extraction. We consider two scenarios: the *trusted setup model*, where key generation is assumed to proceed honestly, and the *untrusted setup model*, where the adversary has full control over key generation as well.

Definition 5 (Double-signature extractability). *A double-authentication-preventing signature* DAPS *is* double-signature extractable *(resp. with trusted setup) if an efficient algorithm*

– Extract(vk, (S_1, S_2)): *On input verification key* vk *and compromising pair* (S_1, S_2), *this algorithm outputs a signing key* sk′.

is known such that, for all efficient adversaries $\mathcal{A}$, *the probability* $\mathbf{Succ}_{\mathsf{DAPS},\mathcal{A}}^{\mathrm{DSE}^{(*)}}(\lambda)$ $:= \Pr[\mathbf{Exp}_{\mathsf{DAPS},\mathcal{A}}^{\mathrm{DSE}^{(*)}}(\lambda) = 1]$ *of success in the DSE (resp. DSE*) experiment of Figure 1 is a negligible function in* λ.

The DSE experiment assumes existence of an efficient predicate that verifies that a candidate sk′ is *the* signing key corresponding to a verification key. In some schemes, there may be several signing keys that correspond to a verification key or it may be inefficient to check. However, for the scheme presented in Section 5, when instantiated with the factoring-based primitive of Section 4, it is easy to check that a signing key (p, q) corresponds to a verification key n; note that there is a canonical representation of such signing keys (take $p < q$).

3   2:1 Trapdoor Functions and Extractability

We introduce the concept of 2:1 trapdoor functions (2:1-TDF). At a high level, such functions are *trapdoor one-way functions*, meaning that they should be hard to invert except with knowledge of a trapdoor. They are *two-to-one*, meaning that the domain is exactly twice the size of the range, and every element of the range has precisely two preimages. We also describe an additional property, *extractability*, which means that given two distinct preimages of an element of the range, the trapdoor can be computed.

Consider two finite sets, A and B, such that A is twice the size of B. Let $f : A \to B$ be a surjective function such that, for any element $b \in B$, there are exactly two preimages in A; f is not injective, so the inverse function does not exist. Define instead $f^{-1} : B \times \{0, 1\} \to A$ such that for each $b \in B$ the two preimages under f are given by $f^{-1}(b, 0)$ and $f^{-1}(b, 1)$. This partitions set A into two subsets $A_0 = f^{-1}(B, 0)$ and $A_1 = f^{-1}(B, 1)$ of the same size.

Function f is a 2:1-TDF if the following additional properties hold: sets A_0, A_1, and B are efficiently samplable, function f is efficiently computable, and inverse function f^{-1} is hard to compute unless some specific trapdoor information is known. We finally require an extraction capability: there should be an efficient way to recover the trapdoor for the computation of f^{-1} from any two elements $a_0 \neq a_1$ with $f(a_0) = f(a_1)$ (we will also write $a_0 \stackrel{\curlywedge}{\sim} a_1$ for such configurations). The setting of 2:1-TDFs is illustrated in Figure 2. We will formalize the functionality and security properties below.

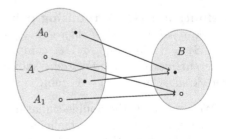

Fig. 2. Illustration of a 2:1 trapdoor function $f : A \to B$. Each element of B has exactly two preimages, one in A_0 and one in A_1

3.1   Definition

We give a formal definition of 2:1-TDF and its correctness, and establish afterwards that it implements the intuition developed above.

Definition 6 (2:1 trapdoor function). *A 2:1 trapdoor function (2:1-TDF) is a tuple of efficient algorithms* (TdGen, Apply, Reverse, Decide) *as follows:*
- TdGen(1^λ): *On input security parameter* 1^λ, *this randomized algorithm outputs a pair* (td, pub), *where* td *is a trapdoor and* pub *is some associated public information. Each possible outcome* pub *implicitly defines finite sets* $A = A(\mathsf{pub})$ *and* $B = B(\mathsf{pub})$.
- Apply(pub, a): *On input public information* pub *and element* $a \in A(\mathsf{pub})$, *this deterministic algorithm outputs an element* $b \in B(\mathsf{pub})$.
- Reverse(td, b, d): *On input trapdoor* td, *element* $b \in B(\mathsf{pub})$, *and bit* $d \in \{0, 1\}$, *this deterministic algorithm outputs an element* $a \in A(\mathsf{pub})$.
- Decide(pub, a): *On input public information* pub *and element* $a \in A(\mathsf{pub})$, *this deterministic algorithm outputs a bit* $d \in \{0, 1\}$.

Definition 7 (Correctness of 2:1-TDF). *A 2:1-TDF is* correct *if, for all* (td, pub) $\leftarrow_R$ TdGen, *all* $d \in \{0, 1\}$, *all* $a \in A(\mathsf{pub})$, *and all* $b \in B(\mathsf{pub})$, *we have that (1)* $a \in$ Reverse(td, Apply(pub, a), $\{0, 1\}$), *(2)* Apply(pub, Reverse(td, b, d)) $= b$, *and (3)* Decide(pub, Reverse(td, b, d)) $= d$.

Let (td, pub) be output by TdGen. Consider partition $A(\mathsf{pub}) = A_0(\mathsf{pub}) \cup A_1(\mathsf{pub})$ obtained by setting $A_d(\mathsf{pub}) = \{a \in A(\mathsf{pub}) : \mathsf{Decide}(\mathsf{pub}, a) = d\}$, for $d \in \{0, 1\}$. It follows from correctness requirement (3) that function $\psi_d :=$ Reverse(td, $\cdot$, d) is a mapping $B(\mathsf{pub}) \to A_d(\mathsf{pub})$. Note that ψ_d is surjective by condition (1), and injective by condition (2). Hence, we have bijections $\psi_0 : B(\mathsf{pub}) \to A_0(\mathsf{pub})$ and $\psi_1 : B(\mathsf{pub}) \to A_1(\mathsf{pub})$. Thus, $|A_0(\mathsf{pub})| = |A_1(\mathsf{pub})| = |B(\mathsf{pub})| = |A(\mathsf{pub})|/2$.

Define now relation $\overset{\times}{\sim} \subseteq A(\mathsf{pub}) \times A(\mathsf{pub})$ such that

$$a \overset{\times}{\sim} a' \iff \mathsf{Apply}(\mathsf{pub}, a) = \mathsf{Apply}(\mathsf{pub}, a') \land \mathsf{Decide}(\mathsf{pub}, a) \neq \mathsf{Decide}(\mathsf{pub}, a').$$

Note that for each $a \in A(\mathsf{pub})$ there exists exactly one $a' \in A(\mathsf{pub})$ such that $a \overset{\times}{\sim} a'$; indeed, if $a \in A_d(\mathsf{pub})$, then $a' = \psi_{1-d}(\psi_d^{-1}(a)) \in A_{1-d}(\mathsf{pub})$. Observe how algorithms Apply and Reverse correspond to functions $f : A \to B$ and $f^{-1} : B \times \{0, 1\} \to A$ discussed at the beginning of Section 3.

We next extend the functionality of 2:1-TDFs to include extraction of the trapdoor: knowledge of any two elements $a_0, a_1 \in A$ with $a_0 \neq a_1 \land f(a_0) = f(a_1)$ shall immediately reveal the system's inversion trapdoor.

Definition 8 (Extractable 2:1-TDF). *A 2:1-TDF is* extractable *if an efficient algorithm*
- Extract(pub, a, a'): *On input public information* pub *and* $a, a' \in A(\mathsf{pub})$, *this algorithm outputs a trapdoor* td*.

is known such that, for all (td, pub) *output by* TdGen *and all* $a, a' \in A(\mathsf{pub})$ *with* $a \overset{\times}{\sim} a'$, *we have* Extract(pub, a, a') = td.

$$\mathbf{Exp}_{X,\mathcal{A}}^{\text{INV-1}}(\lambda):$$
1. $(\text{td}, \text{pub}) \leftarrow_R \text{TdGen}(1^\lambda)$
2. $b \leftarrow_R B(\text{pub})$
3. $a \leftarrow_R \mathcal{A}(\text{pub}, b)$
4. Return 1 iff $\text{Apply}(\text{pub}, a) = b$

$$\mathbf{Exp}_{X,\mathcal{B}}^{\text{INV-2}}(\lambda):$$
1. $(\text{td}, \text{pub}) \leftarrow_R \text{TdGen}(1^\lambda)$
2. $a \leftarrow_R A(\text{pub})$
3. $a' \leftarrow_R \mathcal{B}(\text{pub}, a)$
4. Return 1 iff $a \overset{\sim}{\approx} a'$

Fig. 3. Security experiments for (second) preimage resistance of 2:1-TDF X

3.2 Security Notions

We proceed with the specification of the principal security property of 2:1-TDFs: one-wayness. Intuitively, it should be infeasible to find preimages and second preimages of the Apply algorithm without knowing the corresponding trapdoor.

Definition 9 (Preimage resistance of 2:1-TDF). *A 2:1-TDF X is* preimage resistant *if* $\mathbf{Succ}_{X,\mathcal{A}}^{\text{INV-1}}(\lambda) := \Pr[\mathbf{Exp}_{X,\mathcal{A}}^{\text{INV-1}}(\lambda) = 1]$ *and* second preimage resistant *if* $\mathbf{Succ}_{X,\mathcal{B}}^{\text{INV-2}}(\lambda) := \Pr[\mathbf{Exp}_{X,\mathcal{B}}^{\text{INV-2}}(\lambda) = 1]$ *are respectively negligible functions in λ, for all efficient adversaries $\mathcal{A}$ and $\mathcal{B}$, where $\mathbf{Exp}_{X,\mathcal{A}}^{\text{INV-1}}$ and $\mathbf{Exp}_{X,\mathcal{B}}^{\text{INV-2}}$ are as in Figure 3.*

As expected, second preimage resistance implies preimage resistance. Perhaps more surprising is that notions INV-1 and INV-2 are equivalent for extractable 2:1-TDFs. The proofs of the following lemmas appear in the full version [23].

Lemma 1 (INV-2 $\Rightarrow$ INV-1). *Let X be a 2:1-TDF and let $\mathcal{A}$ be an efficient algorithm for the INV-1 experiment. Then there exist an efficient algorithm $\mathcal{B}$ for the INV-2 experiment such that $\mathbf{Succ}_{X,\mathcal{A}}^{\text{INV-1}}(\lambda) \leq 2 \cdot \mathbf{Succ}_{X,\mathcal{B}}^{\text{INV-2}}(\lambda)$.*

Lemma 2 (INV-1 $\Rightarrow$ INV-2 for extractable 2:1-TDF). *Let X be an extractable 2:1-TDF and let $\mathcal{B}$ be an efficient algorithm for the INV-2 experiment. Then there exists an efficient algorithm $\mathcal{A}$ for the INV-1 experiment such that $\mathbf{Succ}_{X,\mathcal{B}}^{\text{INV-2}}(\lambda) = \mathbf{Succ}_{X,\mathcal{A}}^{\text{INV-1}}(\lambda)$.*

4 Constructing Extractable 2:1 Trapdoor Functions

Having introduced 2:1-TDFs and extractable 2:1-TDFs, we now show how to construct these primitives: we propose an efficient extractable 2:1-TDF and prove it secure, assuming hardness of the integer factorization problem.

Our construction builds on a specific structure from number theory, the *group of sign-agnostic quadratic residues*. This group was introduced to cryptography by Goldwasser, Micali, and Rivest in [22], and rediscovered 20 years later by Hofheinz and Kiltz [24]. We first reproduce the results of [22,24] and then extend them towards our requirements.[5]

---

[5] Goldwasser *et al.* gave no name to this group; Hofheinz and Kiltz called it the group of *signed quadratic residues*, but this seems to be a misnomer as the whole point is to *ignore the sign*, taking absolute values and forcing the elements to be between 0 and $(n-1)/2$; hence our use of the term *sign-agnostic*.

In our exposition, we assume that the reader is familiar with properties of $\mathbb{Z}_n^\times$ (the mutiplicative group of integers modulo n), J_n (the subgroup of $\mathbb{Z}_n^\times$ with Jacobi symbol equal to 1), and QR_n (quadratic residues modulo n), for Blum integers n. If we additionally define $\overline{J}_n = \mathbb{Z}_n^\times \setminus J_n$ and $\overline{QR}_n = J_n \setminus QR_n$, these five sets are related to each other as visualized in Figure 4 (left). Also illustrated is the action of the squaring operation: it is 4:1 from $\mathbb{Z}_n^\times$ to QR_n, 2:1 from J_n to QR_n, and 1:1 (i.e., bijective) from QR_n to QR_n. For reference, we reproduce all number-theoretic details relevant to this paper in the full version [23].

4.1   Sign-Agnostic Quadratic Residues

For an RSA modulus n, it is widely believed that efficiently distinguishing elements in QR_n from elements in $\overline{QR}_n$ is a hard problem. It also seems to be infeasible to sample elements from QR_n without knowing a square root of the samples, or to construct hash functions that map to QR_n and could be modeled as random oracles. However, such properties are a prerequisite in certain applications in cryptography [24], which renders group QR_n unsuitable for such cases. As we see next, by switching from the group of quadratic residues modulo n to the related group of *sign-agnostic quadratic residues* modulo n, sampling and hashing becomes feasible.

The use of sign-agnostic quadratic residues in cryptography is explicitly proposed in [22,24]. However, some aspects of the algebraical structure of this group are concealed in both works by the fact that the group operation is defined to act directly on specific *representations* of elements. In the following paragraphs we use a new and more consistent notation that aims at making the algebraical structure more readily apparent.

Let $(H, \cdot)$ be an arbitrary finite abelian group that contains an element $T \in H \setminus \{1\}$ such that $T^2 = 1$. Then $\{1, T\}$ is a (normal) subgroup in H, that is, quotient group $H/_{\{1,T\}}$ is well-defined, $\psi : H \to H/_{\{1,T\}} : x \mapsto \{x, Tx\}$ is a group homomorphism, and $|\psi(H)| = |H/_{\{1,T\}}| = |H|/2$ holds. Further, for all subgroups $G \leq H$ we have that $\psi(G) \leq \psi(H) = H/_{\{1,T\}}$. In such cases, if G is such that $T \in G$, then $|\psi(G)| = |G/_{\{1,T\}}| = |G|/2$ as above; otherwise, if $T \notin G$, then $|\psi(G)| = |G|$ and thus $\psi(G) \cong G$.

Consider now the specific group $H = \mathbb{Z}_n^\times$, for a Blum integer n. Then $T = -1$ has order 2 in $\mathbb{Z}_n^\times$ and above observations apply, with mapping $\psi : x \mapsto \{x, -x\}$. For any subgroup $G \leq \mathbb{Z}_n^\times$, let $G/_{\pm 1} := \psi(G)$. For subgroup $QR_n \leq \mathbb{Z}_n^\times$, as $-1 \notin QR_n$, we have $QR_n/_{\pm 1} \cong QR_n$ and thus $|QR_n/_{\pm 1}| = \varphi(n)/4$. Moreover, as $J_n \leq \mathbb{Z}_n^\times$ and $-1 \in J_n$, we have $|J_n/_{\pm 1}| = |J_n|/2 = \varphi(n)/4$. Similarly we see $|\mathbb{Z}_n^\times/_{\pm 1}| = \varphi(n)/2$. After setting $\overline{QR}_n/_{\pm 1} := (\mathbb{Z}_n^\times/_{\pm 1}) \setminus (QR_n/_{\pm 1})$ we finally obtain $|\overline{QR}_n/_{\pm 1}| = \varphi(n)/4$.

Note that we just observed $QR_n/_{\pm 1} \leq J_n/_{\pm 1} \leq \mathbb{Z}_n^\times/_{\pm 1}$ and $|QR_n/_{\pm 1}| = \varphi(n)/4 = |J_n/_{\pm 1}|$. The overall structure is hence $QR_n/_{\pm 1} = J_n/_{\pm 1} \lneq \mathbb{Z}_n^\times/_{\pm 1}$, as illustrated in Figure 4 (right). After agreeing on notations $\{\pm x\} = \{x, -x\}$ and $\{\pm x\}^2 = \{\pm(x^2)\}$ we obtain the following (proven in the full version [23]):

Lemma 3. *Let n be a Blum integer, then* $QR_n/_{\pm 1} = \{\{\pm x\}^2 : \{\pm x\} \in \mathbb{Z}_n^\times/_{\pm 1}\}$.

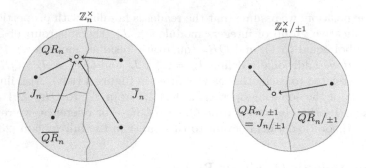

Fig. 4. Illustration of $\mathbb{Z}_n^\times$ and $\mathbb{Z}_n^\times/{\pm 1}$ (for Blum integers n), and subgroups QR_n, J_n, and $J_n/{\pm 1} = QR_n/{\pm 1}$. Also visualized is the action of the squaring operation.

Moreover, by exploiting identity $QR_n/{\pm 1} = J_n/{\pm 1}$, we directly get the following characterizations of $QR_n/{\pm 1}$ and $\overline{QR}_n/{\pm 1}$. Observe that the sets are well-defined since $\left(\frac{x}{n}\right) = \left(\frac{-x}{n}\right)$ for all $x \in \mathbb{Z}_n^\times$.

$$QR_n/{\pm 1} = \left\{ \{\pm x\} \in \mathbb{Z}_n^\times/{\pm 1} : \left(\tfrac{x}{n}\right) = +1 \right\} \tag{1}$$

$$\overline{QR}_n/{\pm 1} = \left\{ \{\pm x\} \in \mathbb{Z}_n^\times/{\pm 1} : \left(\tfrac{x}{n}\right) = -1 \right\} . \tag{2}$$

Many facts on the structure of $\mathbb{Z}_n^\times$ can be lifted to $\mathbb{Z}_n^\times/{\pm 1}$. This holds in particular for the following five lemmas and corollaries, which we prove in the full version [23]. We stress that the following results do not appear in [22, 24].

Lemma 4 (Square roots in $\mathbb{Z}_n^\times/{\pm 1}$). *Let n be a Blum integer. Every element $\{\pm y\} \in QR_n/{\pm 1}$ has exactly two square roots in $\mathbb{Z}_n^\times/{\pm 1}$. More precisely, there exist unique $\{\pm x_0\} \in QR_n/{\pm 1}$ and $\{\pm x_1\} \in \overline{QR}_n/{\pm 1}$ such that $\{\pm x_0\}^2 = \{\pm y\} = \{\pm x_1\}^2$. The factorization of n can readily be recovered from such pairs $\{\pm x_0\}, \{\pm x_1\}$: non-trivial divisors of n are given by $\gcd(n, x_0 - x_1)$ and $\gcd(n, x_0 + x_1)$. Square roots in $\mathbb{Z}_n^\times/{\pm 1}$ can be efficiently computed if the factors of $n = pq$ are known.*

Corollary 1 (Squaring in $\mathbb{Z}_n^\times/{\pm 1}$, $QR_n/{\pm 1}$, $\overline{QR}_n/{\pm 1}$). *Let n be a Blum integer. The squaring operation $\mathbb{Z}_n^\times/{\pm 1} \to QR_n/{\pm 1} : \{\pm x\} \mapsto \{\pm x\}^2$ is a 2:1 mapping. Moreover, squaring is a 1:1 function from $QR_n/{\pm 1}$ to $QR_n/{\pm 1}$ and from $\overline{QR}_n/{\pm 1}$ to $QR_n/{\pm 1}$. These relations are illustrated in Figure 4 (right).*

Lemma 5 (Computing square roots in $\mathbb{Z}_n^\times/{\pm 1}$ is hard). *Let n be a Blum integer. Computing square roots in $\mathbb{Z}_n^\times/{\pm 1}$ is as hard as factoring n.*

Lemma 6 (Samplability and decidability). *Let n be a Blum integer and $t \in \mathbb{Z}_n^\times$ be fixed with $\left(\frac{t}{n}\right) = -1$. The algorithm that samples a $\leftarrow_R \mathbb{Z}_n$ and returns $\{\pm a\}$ generates a distribution that is statistically indistinguishable from uniform on $\mathbb{Z}_n^\times/{\pm 1}$. If the algorithm is modified such that it returns $\{\pm a\}$ if $\left(\frac{a}{n}\right) = +1$ and $\{\pm ta\}$ if $\left(\frac{a}{n}\right) = -1$, then the output is statistically indistinguishable from uniform on $QR_n/{\pm 1}$. $\overline{QR}_n/{\pm 1}$ can be sampled correspondingly. Sets $QR_n/{\pm 1}$ and $\overline{QR}_n/{\pm 1}$ are efficiently decidable (within $\mathbb{Z}_n^\times/{\pm 1}$) by equations (1) and (2).*

Lemma 7 (Indifferentiable hashing into $QR_n/_{\pm 1}$). *Let $H' : \{0,1\}^* \to J_n$ denote a hash function that is indifferentiable from a random oracle (see the full version [23] on how to construct one). Consider auxiliary function $G : J_n \to QR_n/_{\pm 1} : y \mapsto \{\pm y\}$ and let $H = G \circ H'$. Then $H : \{0,1\}^* \to QR_n/_{\pm 1}$ is indifferentiable as well.*

Remark 1 (Representation of elements). An efficient and compact way to represent elements $\{\pm x\} \in \mathbb{Z}_n^\times/_{\pm 1}$ is by the binary encoding of $\overline{x} = \min\{x, n - x\} \in [1, (n - 1)/2]$, as proposed by [22]. The decoding procedure is $\overline{x} \mapsto \{\overline{x}, -\overline{x}\}$.

4.2   Constructing a 2:1-TDF from Sign-Agnostic Quadratic Residues

We use the tools from Section 4.1 to construct a factoring-based extractable 2:1-TDF, which will map $\mathbb{Z}_n^\times/_{\pm 1} \to QR_n/_{\pm 1}$. While the Apply algorithm corresponds to squaring, extractability is possible given distinct square roots of an element.

Construction 1 (Blum-2:1-TDF). *Define algorithms* Blum-2:1-TDF = (TdGen, Apply, Reverse, Decide, Extract) *as follows:*

- TdGen(1^λ): *Pick random Blum integer $n = pq$ of length λ such that $p < q$. Pick $t \in \mathbb{Z}_n^\times$ with $\left(\frac{t}{n}\right) = -1$. Return* pub $\leftarrow (n, t)$ *and* td $\leftarrow (p, q)$. *We will use sets $A_0(\text{pub}) := QR_n/_{\pm 1}$, $A_1(\text{pub}) := \overline{QR}_n/_{\pm 1}$, $A(\text{pub}) := \mathbb{Z}_n^\times/_{\pm 1}$, and $B(\text{pub}) := QR_n/_{\pm 1}$.*
- Apply(pub, $\{\pm a\}$): *Return $\{\pm b\} \leftarrow \{\pm a\}^2$.*
- Reverse(td, $\{\pm b\}, d$): *By Lemma 4, element $\{\pm b\} \in QR_n/_{\pm 1}$ has exactly two square roots: $\{\pm a_0\} \in QR_n/_{\pm 1}$ and $\{\pm a_1\} \in \overline{QR}_n/_{\pm 1}$. Return $\{\pm a_d\}$.*
- Decide(pub, $\{\pm a\}$): *Return 0 if $\{\pm a\} \in QR_n/_{\pm 1}$; otherwise return 1.*
- Extract(pub, $\{\pm a_0\}, \{\pm a_1\}$): *Both $\gcd(n, a_0 - a_1)$ and $\gcd(n, a_0 + a_1)$ are non-trivial factors of $n = pq$. Return* td$^* \leftarrow (p, q)$ *such that $p < q$.*

These algorithms are all efficient. Correctness of Blum-2:1-TDF and the security properties follow straightforwardly from the number-theoretic facts established in Sections 4.1; a formal proof appears in the full version [23]. Observe that the samplability of sets A, A_0, A_1, B is warranted by Lemma 6.

Theorem 1 (Security and extractability of Blum-2:1-TDF). Blum-2:1-TDF *is (second) preimage resistant (Def. 9) under the assumption that factoring is hard, and extractable (Def. 8).*

Remark 2 (Choice of element t). In Construction 1, public element t can be any quadratic non-residue; small values likely exist and might be favorable for storage efficiency. Observe that, if $p \equiv 3 \bmod 8$ and $q \equiv 7 \bmod 8$, for $t = 2$ we always have $\left(\frac{t}{n}\right) = -1$, so there is not need to store t at all.

5   DAPS Construction Based on Extractable 2:1-TDF

We now come to the central result of this paper, a DAPS scheme generically constructed from any extractable 2:1 trapdoor function, such as the factoring-based Blum-2:1-TDF from the previous section.

$$\mathsf{KGen}(1^\lambda) : \text{Return } (\mathsf{sk}, \mathsf{vk}) = (\mathsf{td}, \mathsf{pub}) \text{ where } (\mathsf{td}, \mathsf{pub}) \leftarrow_R \mathsf{TdGen}(1^{\lambda_2})$$

Sign(sk, subj, msg) :	Ver(vk, subj, msg, σ) :
1. $s \leftarrow \mathsf{Reverse}(\mathsf{td}, H_{\mathsf{pub}}(\mathsf{subj}), 0)$	1. Parse $(s, a_1, \ldots, a_{\lambda_h}) \leftarrow \sigma$
2. $(d_1, \ldots, d_{\lambda_h}) \leftarrow H^{\#}(\mathsf{subj}, s, \mathsf{msg})$	2. If $\mathsf{Decide}(\mathsf{pub}, s) \neq 0$, return 0
3. For $1 \leq i \leq \lambda_h$:	3. If $\mathsf{Apply}(\mathsf{pub}, s) \neq H_{\mathsf{pub}}(\mathsf{subj})$, return 0
(a) $b_i \leftarrow H_{\mathsf{pub}}(\mathsf{subj}, s, i)$	4. $(d_1, \ldots, d_{\lambda_h}) \leftarrow H^{\#}(\mathsf{subj}, s, \mathsf{msg})$
(b) $a_i \leftarrow \mathsf{Reverse}(\mathsf{td}, b_i, d_i)$	5. For $1 \leq i \leq \lambda_h$:
4. Return $\sigma \leftarrow (s, a_1, \ldots, a_{\lambda_h})$	(a) If $\mathsf{Apply}(\mathsf{pub}, a_i) \neq H_{\mathsf{pub}}(\mathsf{subj}, s, i)$, return 0
	(b) If $\mathsf{Decide}(\mathsf{pub}, a_i) \neq d_i$, return 0
	6. Return 1

Fig. 5. Double-authentication-preventing signature scheme 2:1-DAPS

Construction 2 (DAPS from extractable 2:1-TDF). *Let λ denote a security parameter, and let λ_2 and λ_h be parameters polynomially dependent on λ. Let $X = (\mathsf{TdGen}, \mathsf{Apply}, \mathsf{Reverse}, \mathsf{Decide})$ be an extractable 2:1 trapdoor function and let $H^{\#} : \{0,1\}^* \to \{0,1\}^{\lambda_h}$ be a hash function. For each pub output by TdGen, let $H_{\mathsf{pub}} : \{0,1\}^* \to B(\mathsf{pub})$ be a hash function. Double-authentication-preventing signature scheme 2:1-DAPS consists of the algorithms specified in Figure 5.*

The basic idea of the signing algorithm is as follows. From any given subject, the signer derives message-independent signing elements $b_1, \ldots, b_{\lambda_h} \in B$.[6] The signer also hashes subject and message to a bit string $d_1 \ldots d_{\lambda_h}$; for each bit d_i, she finds the preimage a_i of the signing element b_i which is in the d_i partition of A; either in A_0 or A_1. The signature σ is basically the vector of these preimages. Intuitively, the scheme is unforgeable because it is hard to find preimages of signing elements b_i without knowing the trapdoor. The scheme is extractable because the signing elements b_i are only dependent on the subject, so the signatures of two different messages for the same subject use the same b_i; if $H^{\#}$ is collision resistance, at least one different d_i is used in the two signatures, so two distinct preimages of b_i are used, allowing recovery of the trapdoor.

5.1 Security of Our Construction

We next establish existential unforgeability of 2:1-DAPS (cf. Definition 3). The proof proceeds by changing the EUF simulation so that it performs all operations without using the signing key and without (noticeably) changing the distribution of verification key and answers to $\mathcal{A}$'s oracle queries. From any forgery crafted by adversary $\mathcal{A}$, either a preimage or second preimage of X, or a collision of $H^{\#}$ can be extracted. Observe that, by Lemma 1, it suffices to require second preimage resistance of X in Theorem 2. The proof appears in the full version [23].

Theorem 2 (2:1-DAPS is EUF). *In the setting of Construction 2, if X is second preimage resistant, $H^{\#}$ is collision-resistant, and H_{pub} is a random oracle, then double-authentication-preventing signature 2:1-DAPS is existentially*

---

[6] For rationale on why the subj-dependent value s is required see the full version [23].

unforgeable under adaptive chosen message attacks. More precisely, for any efficient EUF algorithm $\mathcal{A}$ making at most q_1 queries to $H_{\mathsf{pub}}(\cdot)$ and q_S queries to $\mathcal{O}_{\mathsf{Sign}}$ oracle, there exist efficient algorithms $\mathcal{B}_1$, $\mathcal{B}_2$, and $\mathcal{C}$ such that

$$\mathbf{Succ}_{\text{2:1-DAPS},\mathcal{A}}^{\text{EUF}}(\lambda) \leq q_1 \mathbf{Succ}_{X,\mathcal{B}_1}^{\text{INV-1}}(\lambda_2) + 2q_S\lambda_h \, \mathbf{Succ}_{X,\mathcal{B}_2}^{\text{INV-2}}(\lambda_2) + \mathbf{Succ}_{H^\#,\mathcal{C}}^{\text{CR}}(\lambda_h),$$

where $\mathbf{Succ}_{H^\#,\mathcal{C}}^{\text{CR}}(\lambda_h)$ is the success probability of algorithm $\mathcal{C}$ in finding collisions of hash function $H^\#$.

Assuming collision resistance of $H^\#$, two signatures for different messages but the same subject result in some index i where the hashes $H^\#(\mathsf{subj}, s, \mathsf{msg}_1)$ and $H^\#(\mathsf{subj}, s, \mathsf{msg}_2)$ differ. The corresponding ith values a_i in the two signatures can be used to extract the signing key. This is the intuition behind Theorem 3; the proof appears in the full version [23].

Theorem 3 (2:1-DAPS is DSE*). *In the setting of Construction 2, if X is extractable and $H^\#$ is collision-resistant, then double-authentication-preventing signature 2:1-DAPS is double-signature extractable with trusted setup.*[7]

5.2   Efficiency of Our Construction

Table 1 shows the size of verification keys, signing keys, and signatures, and the cost of signature generation and verification for the 2:1-DAPS based on Blum-2:1-TDF, with abstract results as well as for 1024- and 2048-bit keys. We assume the element representation from Remark 1, the verification key optimization from Remark 2, and an implementation of H_{pub} as in Lemma 7.

We also report the results of our implementation of DAPS using the libgcrypt cryptographic library.[8] As libgcrypt does not have routines for square roots or Jacobi symbols, we implemented our own, and we expect that there may be space for improvement with optimized implementations of these operations. Timings reported are an average of 50 iterations, performed on a 2.6 GHz Intel Core i7 (3720QM) CPU, using libgcrypt 1.5.2, compiled in x86_64 mode using LLVM 3.3 and compiler flag -O3. Source code for our implementation is available online at http://eprints.qut.edu.au/73005/.

With 1024-bit signing and verification keys, a signature is about 20 KiB in size, and takes about 0.341 s to generate and 0.105 s to verify. While less efficient than a regular signature scheme, we believe these timings are still tolerable; this holds in particular if our scheme is used to implement CA functionality where signature generation happens rarely and verification results can be cached.

6   Applications

DAPS allows applications that employ digital signatures for establishing unique bindings between digital objects to provide self-enforcement for correct signer

---

[7] See the full version [23] for how to achieve double-signature extractability without trusted setup using zero-knowledge proofs.

[8] http://www.gnu.org/software/libgcrypt/

Table 1. Efficiency of 2:1-DAPS based on sign-agnostic quadratic residues

	General analysis	libgcrypt implementation	
λ_h	—	160	160
λ_2 (size of n in bits)	—	1024	2048
Key generation time	—	0.097 s	0.759 s
Signing key size (bits)	$\log_2 n$	1024	2048
Verification key size (bits)	$\log_2 n$	1024	2048
Signature generation cost	$(\lambda_h + 1) \cdot$ Jac, $(\lambda_h + 1) \cdot$ sqrt	0.341 s	1.457 s
Signature size (bits)	$(\lambda_h + 1) \log_2 n$	$164\,864 = 20\,\text{KiB}$	$329\,728 = 40\,\text{KiB}$
Signature verification cost	$(2\lambda_h + 1) \cdot$ Jac, $(\lambda_h + 1) \cdot$ sqr	0.105 s	0.276 s

Legend: Jac: computation of Jacobi symbol modulo n; sqrt: square root modulo n; sqr: squaring modulo n.

behaviour, and resistance by signers to coercion. Whenever the verifier places high value on the uniqueness of the binding, it may be worthwhile to employ DAPS instead of traditional digital signatures, despite potential increased damage when signers make mistakes.

It should be noted that use of DAPS may impose an additional burden on honest signers: they need to maintain a list of previously signed subjects to avoid double signing. Some signers may already do so, but the importance of the correctness of this list is increased with DAPS. As noted below, signers may wish to use additional protections to maintain their list of signed subjects, for example by cryptographically authenticating it using a message authentication code with a key in the same hardware security module as the main signing key.

In this section, we examine a few cryptographic applications involving unique bindings and discuss the potential applicability of DAPS.

Certificate authorities. DAPS could be used to ensure that certification authorities in the web PKI behave as expected. For example, by having the subject consist of the domain name and the year, and the message consist of the public key and other certificate details, a CA who signs one certificate for "www.example.com" using DAPS cannot sign another for the same domain and time period without invalidating its own key. A CA using DAPS must then be stateful, carefully tracking the previous subjects signed and refusing to sign duplicates. In commercial CAs, where signing is done on a hardware security module (HSM), the list of subjects signed should be kept under authenticated control of the HSM.

A DAPS-based PKI would need to adopt an appropriate convention on validity periods to accommodate expiry of certificates without permitting double-signing. For example, a DAPS PKI may use a subject with a low-granularity non-overlapping validity period ("www.example.com‖2014") since high-granularity overlapping validity periods in the subject give a malicious CA a vector for issuing two certificates without signing the exact same subject twice ("www.example.com‖20140501-20150430" versus "www.example.com‖20140502-20150501").

Furthermore, a DAPS-based PKI could support revocation using standard mechanisms such as certificate revocation lists. Reissuing could be achieved by including a counter in the DAPS subject (e.g., "www.example.com‖2014‖0") and using DAPS-based revocation to provide an unambiguous and unalterable auditable chain from the initial certificate to the current one.

One of the major problems with multi-CA PKIs such as the web PKI is that clients trust many CAs, any one of which can issue a certificate for a particular subject. A DAPS-based PKI would prevent one CA from signing multiple certificates for a subject, but not other CAs from also signing certificates for that subject. It remains a very interesting open question to find cryptographic constructions that solve the multi-CA PKI problem.

Time-stamping. A standard approach to preventing time-stamping authorities from "changing the past" is to require that, when asserting that certain pieces of information x exist at a particular time t, the actual message being signed must also include the (hash of) messages authenticated in the previous time periods. The authority is prevented from trying to change the past and assert that $x' \neq x$ existed at time t because the signatures issued at time periods $t + 1, t + 2, \ldots$ chain back to the original message x.

DAPS could be used to alternatively discourage time-stamping authority fraud by having the subject consist of the time period t and the message consist of whatever information x is to be signed at that time period. A time-stamping authority who signs an assertion for a given time period using DAPS cannot sign another for the same time period without invalidating its own key. Assuming an honest authority's system is designed to only sign once per time period, the signer need not track all signed subjects, since time periods automatically increment.

Hybrid DAPS + standard signatures. DAPS could be combined with a standard signature scheme to provide more robustness in the case of an accidental error, but also provide a clear and quantifiable decrease in security due to a double signing, giving users a window of time in which to migrate away from the signer.

We can achieve this goal by augmenting a generic standard signature scheme with our factoring-based DAPS as follows. The signer publishes a public key consisting of the standard signature's verification key, the 2:1-DAPS verification key n, and a verifiable Rabin encryption under key n of, say, the first half of the bits of the standard scheme's signing key. The hybrid DAPS signature for a subject/message pair would consist of the standard scheme's signature on subject and message concatenated, and the DAPS signature on separated subject and message. If two messages are ever signed for the same subject, then the signer's DAPS secret key can be recovered, which can then be used to decrypt the Rabin ciphertext containing the first half of the standard scheme's signing key. This is not quite enough to readily forge signatures, but it substantially and quantifiably weakens trust in this signer's signatures, making it clear that migration to a new signer must occur but still providing a window of time in which to migrate. As the sketched combination of primitives exhibits non-standard dependencies between different secret keys, a thorough cryptographic analysis would be required.

7 Conclusions

We have introduced a new type of signatures, *double-authentication-preventing signatures*, in which a subject/message pair is signed. In certain situations, DAPS can provide greater assurance to verifiers that signers behave honestly since there is a great disincentive for signers who misbehave: if a signer ever signs two different messages for the same subject, then enough information is revealed to allow anyone to fully recover the signer's secret key. Although this leads to less robustness in the face of accidental errors, it also provides a mechanism for *self-enforcement* of correct behaviour and gives trusted signers such as CAs an argument to resist coercion and the compelled certificate creation attack.

Our construction is based on a new primitive called *extractable 2:1 trapdoor functions*. We have shown how to instantiate this using an algebraic reformulation of sign-agnostic quadratic residues modulo Blum integers; the resulting DAPS is unforgeable assuming factoring is hard, with reasonable signature sizes and computation times.

We believe DAPS can be useful in scenarios where trusted authorities are meant to make *unique* bindings between identifiers and digital objects, such as certificate authorities in PKIs who are supposed to make unique bindings between domain names and public keys, and time-stamping authorities who are supposed to make unique bindings between time periods and pieces of data.

Besides the practical applications of DAPS, several interesting theoretical questions arise from our work. Are there more efficient constructions of DAPS? How else can extractable 2:1 trapdoor functions be instantiated? Given that DAPS and double-spending-resistant digital cash use similar number-theoretic primitives, can DAPS be used to generically construct untraceable digital cash? Can these techniques be applied to key generation in the identity-based setting? Can DAPS be adapted to provide assurance in a multi-CA setting?

References

1. Soghoian, C., Stamm, S.: Certified lies: Detecting and defeating government interception attacks against SSL (short paper). In: Danezis, G. (ed.) FC 2011. LNCS, vol. 7035, pp. 250–259. Springer, Heidelberg (2012)
2. Fox-It: Black tulip: Report of the investigation into the DigiNotar certificate authority breach (2012)
3. Google Online Security Blog: An update on attempted man-in-the-middle attacks (2011)
4. Dwork, C., Lotspiech, J.B., Naor, M.: Digital signets: Self-enforcing protection of digital information (preliminary version). In: 28th ACM STOC, pp. 489–498. ACM Press (1996)
5. Camenisch, J.L., Lysyanskaya, A.: An efficient system for non-transferable anonymous credentials with optional anonymity revocation. In: Pfitzmann, B. (ed.) EUROCRYPT 2001. LNCS, vol. 2045, pp. 93–118. Springer, Heidelberg (2001)

6. Jakobsson, M., Juels, A., Nguyên, P.Q.: Proprietary certificates. In: Preneel, B. (ed.) CT-RSA 2002. LNCS, vol. 2271, pp. 164–181. Springer, Heidelberg (2002)
7. Kiayias, A., Tang, Q.: How to keep a secret: leakage deterring public-key cryptosystems. In: Sadeghi, A.R., Gligor, V.D., Yung, M. (eds.) ACM CCS 2013, pp. 943–954. ACM Press (2013)
8. Chor, B., Fiat, A., Naor, M.: Tracing traitors. In: Desmedt, Y.G. (ed.) CRYPTO 1994. LNCS, vol. 839, pp. 257–270. Springer, Heidelberg (1994)
9. Goyal, V.: Reducing trust in the PKG in identity based cryptosystems. In: Menezes, A. (ed.) CRYPTO 2007. LNCS, vol. 4622, pp. 430–447. Springer, Heidelberg (2007)
10. Chaum, D., Fiat, A., Naor, M.: Untraceable electronic cash. In: Goldwasser, S. (ed.) CRYPTO 1988. LNCS, vol. 403, pp. 319–327. Springer, Heidelberg (1990)
11. Lamport, L.: Constructing digital signatures from a one way function. Technical Report CSL-98, SRI International (1979)
12. Merkle, R.C.: A certified digital signature. In: Brassard, G. (ed.) CRYPTO 1989. LNCS, vol. 435, pp. 218–238. Springer, Heidelberg (1990)
13. Waidner, M., Pfitzmann, B.: The dining cryptographers in the disco: Unconditional sender and recipient untraceability with computationally secure serviceability. In: Quisquater, J.-J., Vandewalle, J. (eds.) EUROCRYPT 1989. LNCS, vol. 434, pp. 690–690. Springer, Heidelberg (1990)
14. van Heyst, E., Pedersen, T.P.: How to make efficient fail-stop signatures. In: Rueppel, R.A. (ed.) EUROCRYPT 1992. LNCS, vol. 658, pp. 366–377. Springer, Heidelberg (1993)
15. van Heijst, E., Pedersen, T.P., Pfitzmann, B.: New constructions of fail-stop signatures and lower bounds (extended abstract). In: Brickell, E.F. (ed.) CRYPTO 1992. LNCS, vol. 740, pp. 15–30. Springer, Heidelberg (1993)
16. Barić, N., Pfitzmann, B.: Collision-free accumulators and fail-stop signature schemes without trees. In: Fumy, W. (ed.) EUROCRYPT 1997. LNCS, vol. 1233, pp. 480–494. Springer, Heidelberg (1997)
17. Pedersen, T.P., Pfitzmann, B.: Fail-stop signatures. SIAM Journal on Computing 26, 291–330 (1997)
18. Mashatan, A., Ouafi, K.: Forgery-resilience for digital signature schemes. In: Proc. 7th ACM Symposium on Information, Computer and Communications Security (ASIACCS 2012), pp. 24–25. ACM (2012)
19. Krawczyk, H., Rabin, T.: Chameleon signatures. In: NDSS 2000. The Internet Society (2000)
20. Shamir, A., Tauman, Y.: Improved online/offline signature schemes. In: Kilian, J. (ed.) CRYPTO 2001. LNCS, vol. 2139, pp. 355–367. Springer, Heidelberg (2001)
21. Ateniese, G., de Medeiros, B.: Identity-based chameleon hash and applications. In: Juels, A. (ed.) FC 2004. LNCS, vol. 3110, pp. 164–180. Springer, Heidelberg (2004)
22. Goldwasser, S., Micali, S., Rivest, R.L.: A digital signature scheme secure against adaptive chosen-message attacks. SIAM J. Comput. 17, 281–308 (1988)
23. Poettering, B., Stebila, D.: Double-authentication-preventing signatures (full version). Cryptology ePrint Archive, Report 2013/333 (2014)
24. Hofheinz, D., Kiltz, E.: The group of signed quadratic residues and applications. In: Halevi, S. (ed.) CRYPTO 2009. LNCS, vol. 5677, pp. 637–653. Springer, Heidelberg (2009)

Statistical Properties of Pseudo Random Sequences
and Experiments with PHP and Debian OpenSSL

Yongge Wang[1] and Tony Nicol[2]

[1] UNC Charlotte, USA
[2] University of Liverpool, UK
yongge.wang@uncc.edu, tonynicol@inbox.com

Abstract. NIST SP800-22 (2010) proposed the state of the art statistical testing techniques for testing the quality of (pseudo) random generators. However, it is easy to construct natural functions that are considered as GOOD pseudorandom generators by the NIST SP800-22 test suite though the output of these functions is easily distinguishable from the uniform distribution. This paper proposes solutions to address this challenge by using statistical distance based testing techniques. We carried out both NIST tests and LIL based tests on the following pseudorandom generators by generating more than 200TB of data in total: (1) the standard C linear congruential generator, (2) Mersenne Twister pseudorandom generator, (3) PHP random generators (including Mersenne Twister and Linear Congruential based), and (4) Debian Linux (CVE-2008-0166) pseudorandom generator with OpenSSL 0.9.8c-1. As a first important result, our experiments show that, PHP pseudorandom generator implementation (both linear congruential generators and Mersenne Twister generators) outputs completely insecure bits if the output is not further processed. As a second result, we illustrate the advantages of our LIL based testing over NIST testing. It is known that Debian Linux (CVE-2008-0166) pseudorandom generator based on OpenSSL 0.9.8c-1 is flawed and the output sequences are predictable. Our LIL tests on these sequences discovered the flaws in Debian Linux implementation. However, NIST SP800-22 test suite is not able to detect this flaw using the NIST recommended parameters. It is concluded that NIST SP800-22 test suite is not sufficient and distance based LIL test techniques be included in statistical testing practice. It is also recommended that all pseudorandom generator implementations be comprehensively tested using state-of-the-art statistically robust testing tools.

Keywords: pseudorandom generators, statistical testing, OpenSSL, the law of the iterated logarithm.

1 Introduction

The weakness in pseudorandom generators could be used to mount a variety of attacks on Internet security. Heninger et al [6] surveyed millions of TLS and SSH servers and found out that 0.75% of TLS certificates share keys due to poor implementation of pseudorandom generators. Furthermore, they were able to recover RSA private keys for 0.50% of TLS hosts and 0.03% of SSH hosts because their public keys shared non-trivial common factors (due to poor implementation of pseudorandom generators), and

M. Kutyłowski and J. Vaidya (Eds.): ESORICS 2014, Part I, LNCS 8712, pp. 454–471, 2014.

DSA private keys for 1.03% of SSH hosts because of insufficient signature randomness (again, due to poor implementation of pseudorandom generators). It is reported in the Debian Security Advisory DSA-1571-1 [3] that the random number generator in Debian's OpenSSL release CVE-2008-0166 is predictable. The weakness in Debian pseudorandom generator affected the security of OpenSSH, Apache (mod_sl), the onion router (TOR), OpenVPN, and other applications (see, e.g., [1]). These examples show that it is important to improve the quality of pseudorandom generators by designing systematic testing techniques to discover these weak implementations in the early stage of system development.

Statistical tests are commonly used as a first step in determining whether or not a generator produces high quality random bits. For example, NIST SP800-22 Revision 1A [12] proposed the state of art statistical testing techniques for determining whether a random or pseudorandom generator is suitable for a particular cryptographic application. In a statistical test of [12], a significance level $\alpha \in [0.001, 0.01]$ is chosen for each test. For each input sequence, a P-value is calculated and the input string is accepted as pseudorandom if P-value $\geq \alpha$. A pseudorandom generator is considered good if, with probability α, the sequences produced by the generator fail the test. For an in-depth analysis, NIST SP800-22 recommends additional statistical procedures such as the examination of P-value distributions (e.g., using χ^2-test). In section 3, we will show that NIST SP800-22 test suite has inherent limitations with straightforward Type II errors. Furthermore, our extensive experiments (based on over 200TB of random bits generated) show that NIST SP800-22 techniques could not detect the weakness in the above mentioned pseudorandom generators.

In order to address the challenges faced by NIST SP800-22, this paper designs a "behavioristic" testing approach which is based on statistical distances. Based on this approach, the details of LIL testing techniques are developed. As an example, we carried out LIL testing on the flawed Debian Linux (CVE-2008-0166) pseudorandom generator based on OpenSSL 0.9.8c-1 and on the standard C linear congruential generator. As we expected, both of these pseudorandom generators failed the LIL testing since we know that the sequences produced by these two generators are strongly predictable. However, as we have mentined earlier, our experiments show that the sequences produced by these two generators pass the NIST SP800-22 test suite using the recommended parameters. In other words, NIST SP800-22 test suite with the recommended parameters has no capability in detecting these known deviations from randomness. Furthermore, it is shown that for several pseudorandom generators (e.g., the linear congruential generator), the LIL test results on output strings start off fine but deteriorate as the string length increases beyond that which NIST can handle since NIST testing tool package has an integer overflow issue.

The paper is organized as follows. Section 2 introduces notations. Section 3 points out the limitation of NIST SP800-22 testing tools. Section 4 discusses the law of iterated logarithm (LIL). Section 5 reviews the normal approximation to binomial distributions. Section 6 introduces statistical distance based LIL tests. Section 7 reports experimental results, and Section 8 contains general discussions on OpenSSL random generators.

2   Notations and Pseudorandom Generators

In this paper, N and R^+ denotes the set of natural numbers (starting from 0) and the set of non-negative real numbers, respectively. $\Sigma = \{0, 1\}$ is the binary alphabet, Σ^* is the set of (finite) binary strings, Σ^n is the set of binary strings of length n, and Σ^∞ is the set of infinite binary sequences. The length of a string x is denoted by $|x|$. For strings $x, y \in \Sigma^*$, xy is the concatenation of x and y, $x \sqsubseteq y$ denotes that x is an initial segment of y. For a sequence $x \in \Sigma^* \cup \Sigma^\infty$ and a natural number $n \geq 0$, $x{\restriction}n = x[0..n-1]$ denotes the initial segment of length n of x ($x{\restriction}n = x[0..n-1] = x$ if $|x| \leq n$) while $x[n]$ denotes the nth bit of x, i.e., $x[0..n-1] = x[0]\ldots x[n-1]$.

The concept of "effective similarity" (see, e.g., Wang [14]) is defined as follows: Let $X = \{X_n\}_{n \in N}$ and $Y = \{Y_n\}_{n \in N}$ be two probability ensembles such that each of X_n and Y_n is a distribution over Σ^n. We say that X and Y are computationally (or statistically) indistinguishable if for every feasible algorithm A (or every algorithm A), the total variation difference between X_n and Y_n is a negligible function in n.

Let $l : N \to N$ with $l(n) \geq n$ for all $n \in N$ and G be a polynomial-time computable algorithm such that $|G(x)| = l(|x|)$ for all $x \in \Sigma^*$. Then G is a polynomial-time pseudorandom generator if the ensembles $\{G(U_n)\}_{n \in N}$ and $\{U_{l(n)}\}_{n \in N}$ are computationally indistinguishable.

3   Limitations of NIST SP800-22

In this section, we show that NIST SP800-22 test suite has inherent limitations with straightforward Type II errors. Our first example is based on the following observation: for a function F that mainly outputs "random strings" but, with probability α, outputs biased strings (e.g., strings consisting mainly of 0's), F will be considered as a "good" pseudorandom generator by NIST SP800-22 test though the output of F could be distinguished from the uniform distribution (thus, F is not a pseudorandom generator by definition). Let $\text{RAND}_{c,n}$ be the sets of Kolmogorov c-random binary strings of length n, where $c \geq 1$. That is, for a universal Turing machine M, let

$$\text{RAND}_{c,n} = \{x \in \{0, 1\}^n : \text{ if } M(y) = x \text{ then } |y| \geq |x| - c\}. \tag{1}$$

Let α be a given significance level of NIST SP800-22 test and $\mathcal{R}_{2n} = \mathcal{R}_1^n \cup \mathcal{R}_2^n$ where

$$\mathcal{R}_1^n \subset \text{RAND}_{2,2n} \text{ and } |\mathcal{R}_1^n| = 2^n(1 - \alpha)$$
$$\mathcal{R}_2^n \subset \{0^n x : x \in \{0, 1\}^n\} \text{ and } |\mathcal{R}_2^n| = 2^n \alpha.$$

Furthermore, let $f_n : \{0, 1\}^n \to \mathcal{R}_{2n}$ be an ensemble of random functions (not necessarily computable) such that $f(x)$ is chosen uniformly at random from $\mathcal{R}_{2n}$. Then for each n-bit string x, with probability $1 - \alpha$, $f_n(x)$ is Kolmogorov 2-random and with probability α, $f_n(x) \in \mathcal{R}_2^n$. Since all Kolmogorov 2-random strings are guaranteed to pass NIST SP800-22 test at significance level α (otherwise, they are not Kolmogorov 2-random by definition) and all strings in $\mathcal{R}_2^n$ fail NIST SP800-22 test at significance level α for large enough n, the function ensemble $\{f_n\}_{n \in N}$ is considered as a "good" pseudorandom generator by NIST SP800-22 test suite. On the other hand, a similar proof as in Wang [14] can be used to show that that $\mathcal{R}_{2n}$ could be efficiently distinguished from the uniform distribution with a non-negligible probability. Thus $\{f_n\}_{n \in N}$ is not a cryptographically secure pseudorandom generator.

The above example shows the limitation of testing approaches specified in NIST SP800-22. The limitation is mainly due to the fact that NIST SP800-22 does not fully realize the differences between the two common approaches to pseudorandomness definitions as observed and analyzed in Wang [14]. In other words, the definition of pseudorandom generators is based on the indistinguishability concepts though techniques in NIST SP800-22 mainly concentrate on the performance of individual strings. In this paper, we propose testing techniques that are based on statistical distances such as root-mean-square deviation or Hellinger distance. The statistical distance based approach is more accurate in deviation detection and avoids above type II errors in NIST SP800-22. Our approach is illustrated using the LIL test design.

4 Stochastic Properties of Long Pseudorandom Sequences

The law of the iterated logarithm (LIL) describes the fluctuation scales of a random walk. For a nonempty string $x \in \Sigma^*$, let

$$S(x) = \sum_{i=0}^{|x|-1} x[i] \quad \text{and} \quad S^*(x) = \frac{2 \cdot S(x) - |x|}{\sqrt{|x|}}$$

where $S(x)$ denotes the *number* of 1s in x and $S^*(x)$ denotes the *reduced number* of 1s in x. $S^*(x)$ amounts to measuring the deviations of $S(x)$ from $\frac{|x|}{2}$ in units of $\frac{1}{2}\sqrt{|x|}$.

The law of large numbers states that, for a pseudo random sequence ξ, the limit of $\frac{S(\xi \restriction n)}{n}$ is $\frac{1}{2}$, which corresponds to the frequency (Monobit) test in NIST SP800-22 [12]. But it states nothing about the reduced deviation $S^*(\xi \restriction n)$. It is intuitively clear that, for a pseudorandom sequence ξ, $S^*(\xi \restriction n)$ will sooner or later take on arbitrary large values (though slowly). The law of the iterated logarithm (LIL), which was first discovered by Khinchin [7], gives an optimal upper bound $\sqrt{2 \ln \ln n}$ for the fluctuations of $S^*(\xi \restriction n)$. It is shown in [13] that p-random sequences satisfy common statistical laws such as the law of the iterated logarithm. Thus it is reasonable to expect that pseudorandom sequences produced by pseudorandom generators satisfy these laws also.

5 Normal Approximations to S_{lil}

In this section, we provide several results on normal approximations to the function $S_{lil}(\cdot)$ that will be used in following sections. The DeMoivre-Laplace theorem is a normal approximation to the binomial distribution, which states that the number of "successes" in n independent coin flips with head probability $1/2$ is approximately a normal distribution with mean $n/2$ and standard deviation $\sqrt{n}/2$. We first review a few classical results on the normal approximation to the binomial distribution.

Definition 1. *The normal density function with mean μ and variance σ is defined as*

$$f(x) = \frac{1}{\sigma\sqrt{2\pi}} e^{-\frac{(x-\mu)^2}{2\sigma^2}}; \tag{2}$$

For $\mu = 0$ and $\sigma = 1$, we have the standard normal density function $\varphi(x)$ and the standard normal distribution function $\Phi(x)$:

$$\varphi(x) = \frac{1}{\sqrt{2\pi}} e^{-\frac{x^2}{2}} \quad and \quad \Phi(x) = \int_{-\infty}^{x} \varphi(y) dy \qquad (3)$$

The following DeMoivre-Laplace limit theorem is derived from the approximation theorem on page 181 of [4].

Theorem 1. *For fixed x_1, x_2, we have*

$$\lim_{n \to \infty} Prob\left[x_1 \le S^*(\xi \lceil n) \le x_2\right] = \Phi(x_2) - \Phi(x_1). \qquad (4)$$

The growth speed for the above approximation is bounded by $\max\{k^2/n^2, k^4/n^3\}$ where $k = S(\xi \lceil n) - \frac{n}{2}$.

In this paper, we only consider tests for $n \ge 2^{26}$ and $x_2 \le 1$. That is, $S^*(\xi \lceil n) \le \sqrt{2 \ln \ln n}$. Thus $k = S(\xi \lceil n) - \frac{n}{2} \simeq \frac{\sqrt{n}}{2} S^*(\xi \lceil n) \le \sqrt{2n \ln \ln n}/2$. Hence, we have $\max\left\{\frac{k^2}{n^2}, \frac{k^4}{n^3}\right\} = \frac{k^2}{n^2} = \frac{(1-\alpha)^2 \ln \ln n}{2n} < 2^{-22}$

By Theorem 1, the approximation probability calculation errors in this paper will be less than 2^{-22} which is negligible. Unless stated otherwise, we will not mention the approximation errors in the remainder of this paper.

6   Snapshot LIL Tests and Random Generator Evaluation

The distribution S_{lil} defines a probability measure on the real line R. Let $\mathcal{R} \subset \Sigma^n$ be a set of m sequences with a standard probability definition on it. That is, for each $x_0 \in \mathcal{R}$, let $Prob[x = x_0] = \frac{1}{m}$. Then each set $\mathcal{R} \subset \Sigma^n$ induces a probability measure $\mu_n^{\mathcal{R}}$ on R by letting

$$\mu_n^{\mathcal{R}}(I) = Prob\left[S_{lil}(x) \in I, x \in \mathcal{R}\right]$$

for each Lebesgue measurable set I on R. For $U = \Sigma^n$, we use μ_n^U to denote the corresponding probability measure induced by the uniform distribution. By definition, if $\mathcal{R}_n$ is the collection of all length n sequences generated by a pseudorandom generator, then the difference between μ_n^U and $\mu_n^{\mathcal{R}_n}$ is negligible.

By Theorem 1, for a uniformly chosen ξ, the distribution of $S^*(\xi \lceil n)$ could be approximated by a normal distribution of mean 0 and variance 1, with error bounded by $\frac{1}{n}$ (see [4]). In other words, the measure μ_n^U can be calculated as

$$\mu_n^U((-\infty, x]) \simeq \Phi(x \sqrt{2 \ln \ln n}) = \sqrt{2 \ln \ln n} \int_{-\infty}^{x} \phi(y \sqrt{2 \ln \ln n}) dy. \qquad (5)$$

Figure 1 shows the distributions of μ_n^U for $n = 2^{26}, \cdots, 2^{34}$. For the reason of convenience, in the remaining part of this paper, we will use $\mathcal{B}$ as the discrete partition of the real line R defined by

$$\{(\infty, 1), [1, \infty)\} \cup \{[0.05x - 1, 0.05x - 0.95) : 0 \le x \le 39\}.$$

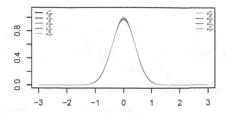

Fig. 1. Density functions for distributions μ_n^U with $n = 2^{26}, \cdots, 2^{34}$

Table 1. The distribution μ_n^U induced by S_{lil} for $n = 2^{26}, \cdots, 2^{34}$ (due to symmetry, only distribution on the positive part of real line R is given)

	2^{26}	2^{27}	2^{28}	2^{29}	2^{30}	2^{31}	2^{32}	2^{33}	2^{34}
[0.00, 0.05)	.047854	.048164	.048460	.048745	.049018	.049281	.049534	.049778	.050013
[0.05, 0.10)	.047168	.047464	.047748	.048020	.048281	.048532	.048773	.049006	.049230
[0.10, 0.15)	.045825	.046096	.046354	0.04660	.046839	.047067	.047287	.047498	.047701
[0.15, 0.20)	.043882	.044116	.044340	.044553	.044758	.044953	.045141	.045322	.045496
[0.20, 0.25)	.041419	.041609	.041789	.041961	.042125	.042282	.042432	.042575	.042713
[0.25, 0.30)	.038534	.038674	.038807	.038932	.039051	.039164	.039272	.039375	.039473
[0.30, 0.35)	.035336	.035424	.035507	.035584	.035657	.035725	.035850	.035850	.035907
[0.35, 0.40)	.031939	.031976	.032010	.032041	.032068	.032093	.032115	.032135	.032153
[0.40, 0.45)	.028454	.028445	.028434	.028421	.028407	.028392	.028375	.028358	.028340
[0.45, 0.50)	.024986	.024936	.024886	.024835	.024785	.024735	.024686	.024637	.024588
[0.50, 0.55)	.021627	.021542	.021460	.021379	.021300	.021222	.021146	.021072	.020999
[0.55, 0.60)	.018450	.018340	.018234	.018130	.018029	.017931	.017836	.017743	.017653
[0.60, 0.65)	.015515	.015388	.015265	.015146	.015032	.014921	.014813	.014709	.014608
[0.65, 0.70)	.012859	.012723	.012591	.012465	.012344	.012227	.012114	.012004	.011899
[0.70, 0.75)	.010506	.010367	.010234	.010106	.009984	.009867	.009754	.009645	.009541
[0.75, 0.80)	.008460	.008324	.008195	.008072	.007954	.007841	.007733	.007629	.007530
[0.80, 0.85)	.006714	.006587	.006466	.006351	.006241	.006137	.006037	.005941	.005850
[0.85, 0.90)	.005253	.005137	.005027	.004923	.004824	.004730	.004640	.004555	.004474
[0.90, 0.95)	.004050	.003948	.003851	.003759	.003672	.003590	.003512	.003438	.003368
[0.95, 1.00)	.003079	.002990	.002906	.002828	.002754	.002684	.002617	.002555	.002495
[1.00, ∞)	.008090	.007750	.007437	.007147	.006877	.006627	.006393	.006175	.005970

With this partition, Table 1 lists values $\mu_n^U(I)$ on $\mathcal{B}$ with $n = 2^{26}, \cdots, 2^{34}$. Since $\mu_n^U(I)$ is symmetric, it is sufficient to list the distribution in the positive side of the real line.

In order to evaluate a pseudorandom generator G, first choose a list of testing points $n_0, \cdots, n_t$ (e.g., $n_0 = 2^{26+t}$). Secondly use G to generate a set $\mathcal{R} \subseteq \Sigma^{n_t}$ of m sequences. Lastly compare the distances between the two probability measures $\mu_n^{\mathcal{R}}$ and μ_n^U for $n = n_0, \cdots, n_t$.

A generator G is considered "good", if for sufficiently large m (e.g., $m \geq 10,000$), the distances between $\mu_n^{\mathcal{R}}$ and μ_n^U are negligible (or smaller than a given threshold). There are various definitions of statistical distances for probability measures. In our analysis, we will consider the total variation distance [2]

$$d(\mu_n^{\mathcal{R}}, \mu_n^U) = \sup_{A \subseteq \mathcal{B}} \left| \mu_n^{\mathcal{R}}(A) - \mu_n^U(A) \right| \tag{6}$$

Hellinger distance [5]

$$H(\mu_n^{\mathcal{R}}\|\mu_n^{U}) = \frac{1}{\sqrt{2}}\sqrt{\sum_{A\in\mathcal{B}}\left(\sqrt{\mu_n^{\mathcal{R}}(A)} - \sqrt{\mu_n^{U}(A)}\right)^2} \qquad (7)$$

and the root-mean-square deviation

$$\mathrm{RMSD}(\mu_n^{\mathcal{R}}, \mu_n^{U}) = \sqrt{\frac{\sum_{A\in\mathcal{B}}\left(\mu_n^{\mathcal{R}}(A) - \mu_n^{U}(A)\right)^2}{|\mathcal{B}|}}. \qquad (8)$$

7 Experimental Results

As an example to illustrate the importance of LIL tests, we carried out both NIST SP800-22 tests [9] and LIL tests on the following commonly used pseudorandom bit generators: The standard C linear congruential generator, Mersenne Twister generators, PHP web server random bit generators (both MT and LCG), and Debian (CVE-2008-0166) random bit generator with OpenSSL 0.9.8c-1. Among these generators, linear congruential generators and Debian Linux (CVE-2008-0166) pseudorandom generators are not cryptographically strong. Thus they should fail a good statistical test. As we expected, both of these generators failed LIL tests. However, neither of these generators failed NIST SP800-22 tests which shows the limitation of NIST SP800-22 test suite.

It should be noted that NIST SP800-22 test suite [9] checks the first 1,215,752,192 bits ($\approx$145MB) of a given sequence since the software uses 4-byte $\mathtt{int}$ data type for integer variables only. For NIST SP800-22 tests, we used the parameter $\alpha = 0.01$ for all experiments. For each pseudorandom generator, we generated 10,000$\times$2GB sequences. The results, analysis, and comparisons are presented in the following sections.

7.1 The Standard C Linear Congruential Generator

A linear congruential generator (LCG) is defined by the recurrence relation

$$X_{n+1} = aX_n + c \quad \mod m$$

where X_n is the sequence of pseudorandom values, m is the modulus, and $a, c < m$. For any initial seeding value X_0, the generated pseudorandom sequence is $\xi = X_0 X_1 \cdots$ where X_i is the binary representation of the integer X_i.

Linear congruential generators (LCG) have been included in various programming languages. For example, C and C++ functions drand48(), jrand48(), mrand48(), and rand48() produce uniformly distributed random numbers on Borland C/C++ rand() function returns the 16 to 30 bits of

$$X_{n+1} = \mathtt{0x343FD} \cdot X_n + \mathtt{0x269EC3} \mod 2^{32}.$$

LCG is also implemented in Microsoft Visual Studio, Java.Util.Random class, Borland Delphi, and PHP. In our experiments, we tested the standard linear congruential generator used in Microsoft Visual Studio.

In our experiments, we generated $10,000 \times 2GB$ sequences by calling Microsoft Visual Studio stdlib function rand() which uses the standard C linear congruential generator. Each sequence is generated with a 4-byte seed from www.random.org [11]. For the $10,000 \times 2GB$ sequences, we used a total of $10,000 \times 4$-byte seeds from www.random.org. The rand() function returns a 15-bit integer in the range [0, 0x7FFF] each time. Since LCG outputs tend to be correlated in the lower bits, we shift the returned 15 bits right by 7 positions. In other words, for each rand() call, we only use the most significant 8 bits. This is a common approach that most programmers will do to offset low bit correlation and missing most significant bits (MSB).

Since linear congruential generator is predictable and not cryptographically strong, we expected that these 10,000 sequences should fail both NIST SP800-22 tests and LIL tests. To our surprise, the collection of 10,000 sequences passed NIST SP800-22 [9] testing with the recommended parameters. Specifically, for the randomly selected 10 sequences, all except one of the 150 non-overlapping template tests passed the NIST test (pass ratio = 0.965). In other words, these sequences are considered as random by NIST SP800-22 testing standards. On the other hand, these sequences failed LIL tests as described in the following.

Table 2. Total variation and Hellinger distances for Standard C LCG

n	2^{26}	2^{27}	2^{28}	2^{29}	2^{30}	2^{31}	2^{32}	2^{33}	2^{34}
d	.061	.097	.113	.156	.176	.261	.324	.499	.900
H	.064	.088	.126	.167	.185	.284	.387	.529	.828
RMSD	.004	.006	.008	.010	.011	.017	.021	.031	.011

Based on snapshot LIL tests at points $2^{26}, \cdots, 2^{34}$, the corresponding total variation distance $d(\mu_n^{cLCG}, \mu_n^U)$, Hellinger distance $H(\mu_n^{cLCG} \| \mu_n^U)$, and the root-mean-square deviation RMSD(μ_n^{cLCG}, μ_n^U) at sample size 1000 are calculated and shown in Table 2. It is observed that at the sample size 1000, the average distance between μ_n^{cLCG} and μ_n^U is larger than 0.10 and the root-mean-square deviation is large than 0.01. It is clear that this sequence collection is far away from the true random source.

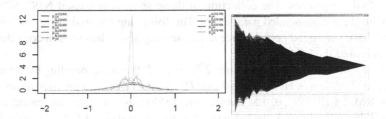

Fig. 2. Density functions for distributions μ_n^{cLCG} with $n = 2^{26}, \cdots, 2^{34}$ (first) and LIL curves for the standard C LCG (second) for $10,000 \times 2GB$ strings

The first picture in Figure 2 shows that the distributions of μ_n^{cLCG} for $n = 2^{26}, \cdots, 2^{34}$ are far away from the expected distribution in Figure 1. Furthermore, the second picture in 2 shows the LIL-test result curves for the 10,000 sequences. For a good random bit generator, the LIL curves should be distributed within the y-axis interval $[-1, 1]$

through the entire x-axis according to the normal distribution. For example, a good curve should look like the third picture in the following Figure 3. However, LIL curves for the standard C LCG generated sequences in the second picture of Figure 2 start reasonably well but deteriorate as the string length increases.

7.2   Mersenne Twister Generators

Mersenne Twister (MT) is a pseudorandom generator designed by Matsumoto and Nishimura [8] and it is included in numerous software packages such as R, Python, PHP, Maple, ANSI/ISO C++, SPSS, SAS, and many others. The commonly used Mersenne Twister MT19937 is based on the Mersenne prime $2^{19937} - 1$ and has a long period of $2^{19937} - 1$. The Mersenne Twister is sensitive to the seed value. For example, too many zeros in the seed can lead to the production of many zeros in the output and if the seed contains correlations then the output may also display correlations.

In order to describe the pseudorandom bit generation process MT19937, we first describe the tempering transform function $t(x)$ on 32-bit strings. For $x \in \Sigma^{32}$, $t(x)$ is defined by

$$
\begin{aligned}
y_1 &:= x \oplus (x >> 11) \\
y_2 &:= y_1 \oplus ((y_1 << 7) \text{ AND } \text{0x9D2C5680}) \\
y_3 &:= y_2 \oplus ((y_2 << 15) \text{ AND } \text{0xEFC60000}) \\
t(x) &:= y_3 \oplus (y_3 >> 18)
\end{aligned}
$$

Let $x_0, x_2, \cdots, x_{623} \in \Sigma^{32}$ be $32 \times 624 = 19968$ bits seeding values for the MT19937 pseudorandom generator. Then the MT19937 output is the sequence $t(x_{624})t(x_{625})t(x_{626})$ $\cdots$ where for $k = 0, 1, 2, 3, \cdots$, we have $x_{624+k} = x_{397+k} \oplus (x_k[0]x_{k+1}[1..31])A$ and A is the 32×32 matrix

$$
A = \begin{pmatrix} 0 & I_{31} \\ a_{31} & (a_{30}, \cdots, a_0) \end{pmatrix}
$$

with $a_{31}a_{30} \cdots a_0 = \text{0x9908B0DF}$. For a 32 bit string x, xA is interpreted as multiplying the 32 bit vector x by matrix A from the right hand side.

Using the source code provided in Matsumoto and Nishimura [8], we generated $10,000 \times 2\text{GB}$ sequences. The collection of these sequences passed NIST SP800-22 [9] test with the recommended parameters. The following discussion shows that these sequences have very good performance in LIL testing also. Thus we can consider these sequences passed the LIL test.

Based on snapshot LIL tests at points $2^{26}, \cdots, 2^{34}$, the corresponding total variation distance $d(\mu_n^{MT19937}, \mu_n^U)$, Hellinger distance $H(\mu_n^{MT19937} \| \mu_n^U)$, and the root-mean-square deviation $\text{RMSD}(\mu_n^{MT19937}, \mu_n^U)$ at sample size 1,000 (resp. 10,000) are calculated and shown in Table 3. In Table 3, the subscript 1 is for sample size 1,000 and the subscript 2 is for sample size 10,000.

Figure 3 shows the distributions of $\mu_n^{MT19937}$ for $n = 2^{26}, \cdots, 2^{34}$ where the curves are plotted on top of the expected distribution in Figure 1. Furthermore, the third picture in Figure 3 shows the LIL-test result curves for the 10,000 sequences. The plot in the third picture of Figure 3 is close to what we are expecting for a random source.

Table 3. Total variation and Hellinger distances for MT19937

n	2^{26}	2^{27}	2^{28}	2^{29}	2^{30}	2^{31}	2^{32}	2^{33}	2^{34}
d_1	.057	.068	.084	.068	.063	.075	.073	.079	.094
H_1	.056	.077	.072	.069	.065	.083	.074	.080	.081
$RMSD_1$	.004	.004	.005	.004	.004	.005	.005	.005	.006
d_2	.023	.025	.026	.021	.020	.025	.026	.027	.020
H_2	.022	.022	.024	.021	.021	.026	.024	.023	.020
$RMSD_2$	.001	.002	.002	.001	.001	.002	.002	.002	.001

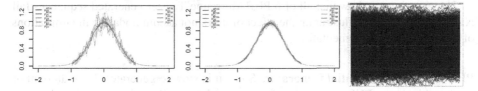

Fig. 3. Density functions for distributions $\mu_n^{MT19937}$ at $n = 2^{26}, \cdots, 2^{34}$ with 1000 (first) and 10,000 (second) strings and LIL plot for Mersenne Twister MT19937 with 10,000×2GB strings (third)

7.3   PHP Web Server Random Bit Generators

PHP is a server side processing language and its random number generator is very important for guaranteeing Web server security. In the experiments, we installed an Apache web server together with PHP v5.3.5. By default, PHP supports rand(), which is a linear congruential random bit generator, and m_rand() which is a Mersenne Twister random bit generator. The random bit outputs from these two generators are tested in the experiments. By modifying php.ini script in PHP 5.3, one may also use the OpenSSL pseudorandom generator via the openssl_random_pseudo_bytes() function call.

PHP Mersenne Twister. In Section 7.2, we showed that the output of the correctly implemented Mersenne Twister pseudorandom generators has very good performance and passes both the NIST and LIL testing. However, if the Mersenne Twister in PHP implementation is not properly post-processed, it generates completely non-random outputs. This is illustrated by our experiments on the PHP Mersenne Twister implementation.

Since the PHP server script is slow in generating a large amount of pseudorandom bits, we only generated 6 × 2GB random bit strings from hte PHP Mersenne Twister m_rand() function call. It is estimated to take 2 years for our computer to generate 10, 000×2GB random bit strings since each 2GB sequence takes 90 minutes to generate.

As discussed earlier, it is expected that LIL values stay within the interval $[-1, 1]$. However, LIL curves for the 6 PHP MT generated sequences display a range from 0 to -2000. This indicates that these sequences are overwhelmed with zeros which get worse as the sequence gets longer.

By checking the rand.c code in PHP 5.3.27, it seems that programmers are prepared to make arbitrary changes with arbitrary post-processing. In particular, for the PHP Mersenne Twister, it will output an integer in the range $[0, 0x7FFFFFFF]$ each time while the source code in Matsumoto and Nishimura [8] that we used in Section 7.2

outputs an integer in the range [0, 0xFFFFFFFF] each time. This difference is not realized by some PHP implementers as illustrated in the following comments of PHP rand.c. Thus it is important to use the LIL test to detect these weak implementations.

```
/* Melo: hmms.. randomMT() returns 32 random bits...
 * Yet, the previous php_rand only returns 31 at most.
 * So I put a right shift to loose the lsb. It *seems*
 * better than clearing the msb.
 * Update:
 * I talked with Cokus via email and it won't ruin
 * the algorithm */
```

The experiments show that all of 6 PHP Mersenne Twister generated sequences fail NIST SP800-22 tests, illustrating the effect of users not accommodating the limitations of the PHP 31 bit implementation.

PHP Linear Congruential Generator. Since it is slow to generate a large amount of random bits using PHP script, we only generated $6 \times 2\text{GB}$ sequences using the PHP rand() function call (similarly, it is estimated to take 2 years for our computer to generate $10,000 \times 2\text{GB}$ random bits). All of the sequences have similar LIL curves as shown in the first picture of Figure 4. The second picture in Figure 4 shows that the distributions of μ_n^{phpLCG} at $n = 2^{26}, \cdots, 2^{34}$ are far away from the expected distribution in Figure 1. One may also compare the second picture in Figure 4 against the density distributions by the standard C linear congruential generator in Figure 2. In summary, the PHP implementation of the linear congruential generator comprehensively failed NIST and LIL tests.

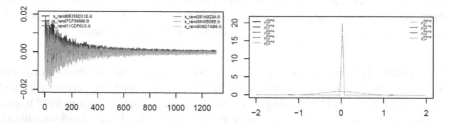

Fig. 4. LIL curves for PHP LCG generated sequences (first) and density functions for distributions μ_n^{phpLCG} (second) of $6 \times 2\text{GB}$ PHP LCG sequences with $n = 2^{26}, \cdots, 2^{34}$

7.4 Flawed Debian's OpenSSL package

It is reported in Debian Security Advisory DSA-1571-1 [3] that the random number generator in Debian Linux (CVE-2008-0166) pseudorandom generator based on OpenSSL 0.9.8c-1 is predictable since the following line of code in md_rand.c has been removed by one of its implementors.

MD_Update(&m, buf, j); /* purify complains */

Note that the code `MD_Update(&m,buf,j)` is responsible for adding the entropy into the state that is passed to the random bit generation process from the main seeding function. By commenting out this line of codes, the generator will have small number of states which will be predictable.

We generated $10,000 \times 2\text{GB}$ sequences using this version of the flawed Debian OpenSSL with multi-threads (the single thread results are much worse). The snapshot LIL test result for this flawed Debian OpenSSL implementation is shown in Figure 5, where the first picture is for the sample size of 1,000 and the second picture is for the sample size of 10,000. In particular, Figure 5 shows the distributions of μ_n^{Debian} for $n = 2^{26}, \cdots, 2^{34}$ where the curves are plotted on top of the expected distribution in Figure 1. As a comparison, we carried out snapshot LIL test on the standard OpenSSL pseudorandom generator [10]. We generated $10,000 \times 2\text{GB}$ sequences using the standard implementation of OpenSSL (with single thread). The snapshot LIL test result for this standard OpenSSL implementation is shown in Figure 6, where the first picture is for the sample size of 1,000 and the second picture is for the sample size of 10,000. In particular, Figure 6 shows the distributions of $\mu_n^{OpenSSL}$ for $n = 2^{26}, \cdots, 2^{34}$ where the curves are plotted on top of the expected distribution in Figure 1.

The results in Figures 5 and 6 indicate that the flawed Debian pseudorandom generator has a very large statistical distance from the uniform distribution while the standard OpenSSL pseudorandom generator has a smaller statistical distance from the uniform distribution. In other words, statistical distance based LIL tests could be used to detect such kinds of implementation weakness conveniently.

While the Debian Linux implementation of openSSL pseudorandom generator fails the LIL test obviously, the experiments show that the collection of the 10,000 sequences passed the NIST SP800-22 testing with the recommended parameters.

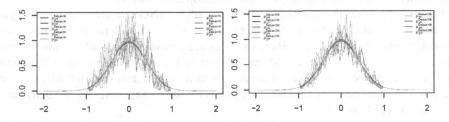

Fig. 5. Density functions for distributions μ_n^{Debian} with $n = 2^{26}, \cdots, 2^{34}$

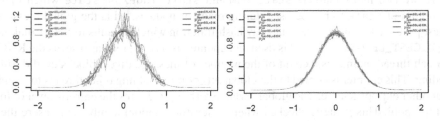

Fig. 6. Density functions for distributions $\mu_n^{OpenSSL}$ with $n = 2^{26}, \cdots, 2^{34}$

7.5   Summary of Experiments

As a summary, Table 4 lists the results of both NIST SP800-22 testing and LIL testing on commonly used pseudorandom generators. In the table, we listed the expected testing results for MT19937 as "pass" since MT19937 was designed to be k-distributed to 32-bit accuracy for every $1 \leq k \leq 623$. In other words, the output of MT19937 is uniformly distributed and should pass all statistical tests even though the output is not cryptographically strong. The results in Table 4 show that the LIL testing techniques always produce expected results while NIST SP800-22 test suite does not.

Table 4. NIST SP800-22 and LIL testing results

Generator	NIST SP800-22	LIL	expected result
Standard C LCG	pass	fail	fail
MT19937	pass	pass	pass
PHP LCG	fail	fail	fail
PHP MT19937	fail	fail	fail
flawed Debian openSSL	pass	fail	fail
standard openSSL	pass	pass	pass

8   General Discussion on OpenSSL Random Generators

It is noted in [1] that the serious flaws in Debian OpenSSL had not been noticed for more than 2 years. A key contributor to this problem was the lack of documentation and poor source code commenting of OpenSSL making it very difficult for a maintainer to understand the consequences of a change to the code. This section provides an analysis of the OpenSSL default RNG. We hope this kind of documentation will help the community to improve the quality of OpenSSL implementations.

Figure 7 illustrates the architecture of the OpenSSL RNG. It consists of a 1023 byte circular array named `state` which is the entropy pool from which random numbers are created. `state` and some other global variables are accessible from all threads. Crypto locks protect the global data from thread contention except for the update of `state` as this improves performance. Locked access, direct access to data from threads, and the mapping of global to local variables (e.g., `state_num` to `st_num`, `md` to `local_md`) are illustrated in Figure 7.

`state` is the entropy pool that is a declared array of of 1023+ `MD_DIGEST_SIZE` bytes. However the RNG algorithm only uses `state[0..1022]` in a circular manner. There are two index markers `state_num` and `state_index` on `state` which mark the region of `state` to be accessed during reads or updates. `md` is the global message digest produced by the chosen one-way hash function which defaults to SHA1 making `MD_DIGEST_LENGTH = 20`. `md` is used and updated by each thread as it seeds the RNG.

Each thread maintains a count of the number of message digest blocks used during seeding. This counter is copied to the global `md_count` enabling other threads to read it as another entropy source. The global variable `entropy` records the entropy level of the entropy pool. This value is checked when generating random numbers to ensure they are based on sufficient entropy. `initialized` is a global flag to indicating seed status. If not initialized, entropy collection and seeding functions are called.

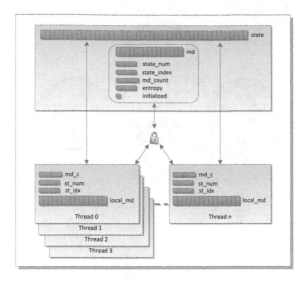

Fig. 7. High Level view of OpenSSL RNG

8.1 OpenSSL Entropy Collection

Entropy data is required to seed the RNG. OpenSSL caters for a number of entropy sources ranging from its default source through to third party random bit generators. This section discusses the OpenSSL library-supplied entropy collection process. Once entropy data is collected, it is passed to `ssleay_rand_add` or `ssleay_rand_seed` to be added into the RNG's entropy pool.

RAND_poll is the key entropy collection function. Default entropy data sources for Windows installations are illustrated in Figure 8. A check is made to determine the operating system and if Windows 32 bit, ADVAPI32.DLL, KERNEL32.DLL and NE-TAPI32.DLL are loaded. These libraries include Windows crypto, OS, and network functions. Following is an overview of the default entropy collection process.

1. Collect network data using `netstatget(NULL, L"LanmanWorkstation", 0, 0, &outbuf)`. By using `LanmanWorkstation`, it returns a `STAT_WORKSTATION_0` structure in `outbuf` containing 45 fields of data including: time of stat collection, number of bytes received and sent on LAN, number of bytes read from and written to disk etc. Each field is estimated as 1 byte of entropy. `netstatget` is also called with `LanmanServer` to obtain another 17 bytes of entropy in `STAT_SERVER_0`.

2. Collect random data from the cryptographic service provided by ADVAPI32. Use the default cryptographic service provider in `hProvider` to call `CryptGenRandom` and obtain 64 bytes of random data in `buff`. the `RAND_add` function is passed 0 as the entropy estimate despite this data coming from an SHA-based crypto RNG so presumably the OpenSSL programmer does not trust this source. An attempt is made to access the processor's on-chip RNG and if successful 64 bytes of random data are passed to `RAND_add` with a 100% entropy value.

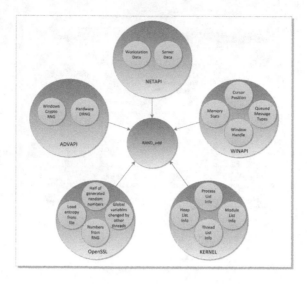

Fig. 8. OpenSSL entropy sources on Windows

3. Get entropy data from Windows message queue, 4-byte foreground window handle, and 2-byte cursor position. However, dynamically tracing these operations identified an OpenSSL coding error discussed in Section 8.2.
4. Get kernel-based entropy data by taking a snapshot of the heap status then walking the heap collecting entropy from each entry. Similarly walk the process list, thread list and module list. The depth that each of the four lists is traversed is determined as follows: the heap-walk continues while there is another entry and either the good flag is false OR a timeout has not expired AND the number or iterations has not exceeded a max count. This ensures loop termination in a reasonable time. However, setting the good flag is suspicious as it is set if random data is retrieved from the Microsoft crypto library or from the hardware DRNG. This is odd as zero was assigned as the entropy value for the crypto library numbers and data from the DRNG may be unavailable yet the good flag is still set which limits the amount of kernel data collected.
5. Add the state of global physical and virtual memory. The current process ID is also added to ensure that each thread has something different than the others.

8.2   Potential Bugs in OpenSSL Entropy Collection

```
418.            CURSORINFO ci;
419.            ci.cbSize = sizeof(CURSORINFO);
420.            if (cursor(&ci))
421.                RAND_add(&ci, ci.cbSize, 2);
```

In above OpenSSL code, a static trace implies that all 20 bytes of CURSOR_INFO are added into the entropy pool as $ci.cbsize$ is set to the size of the CURSORINFO structure. The programmer has decided that this data is worth an entropy value of 2 which is passed to RAND_add. However, a dynamic code trace shows that ci.cbsize is set to zero after the call to cursor(&ci), where cursor is defined as:

```
395.        cursor = (GETCURSORINFO) GetProcAddress(user, "GetCursorInfo");
```

user is the DLL module handle containing function GetCursorInfo. GetCursorInfo that returns true on success and ci.cbsize is initialized to sizeof (CURSORINFO) before the call. However, MSDN does not promise to maintain the fields in this structure on return yet the OpenSSL code relies on it. Our experiments show the ci.cbsize is zero yet is attributed an entropy value of 2.

RAND_add calls ssleay_rand_add. The local variables in ssleay_rand_add are shown in the following.

```
static int ssleay_rand_add(const void *buf, int num, double add)
    {
    int i,j,k,st_idx;
    long md_c[2];
    unsigned char local_md[MD_DIGEST_LENGTH];
    EVP_MD_CTX m;
    int do_not_lock;
```

According to the code, the ssleay_rand_add function increments the global entropy value by 2 if there is not enough current entropy. However, in the Windows environment, the ci.cbsize is always 0 yet it has 2 bytes of entropy added and if timing causes this to happen multiple times due to other threads also incrementing the entropy counter, there could potentially be a situation where there is substantially less entropy than that reported. Specifically, once the entropy threshold of 32 is reached, entropy is no longer updated.

8.3 Seeding the RNG

To seed the RNG, RAND_add is called and the collected entropy data, its length and an entropy estimate are passed in as function parameters. For flexibility, this function is a wrapper for the actual entropy addition function to enable alternatives to be chosen by RAND_get_rand_method so the function binding is dynamic through a pointer to meth->add. RAND_get_rand_method returns the addresses of the preferred functions. For example, it checks for an external device and if not found it returns the address of the default functions in a structure of type RAND_METHOD which holds pointers to the functions. Of the five functions now available, RAND_add() calls meth->add() which in this case (default) points to the physical function ssleay_rand_add. Studying ssleay_rand_add reveals that the entropy data passed to it is hashed directly into the RNG's state.

```
static void ssleay_rand_add(const void *buf,int num,double add)
```

A byte buffer buf of length num containing data, ideally from a good entropy source, is passed to this function to be mixed into the RNG. add is the entropy value of the data in buff estimated by the programmer. For system generated entropy, the value is not calculated but presumably estimated by the OpenSSL developers. RAND_add is available to the caller to add more or better entropy if required. In a summary, Figure 9 describes the seeding flowchart for OpenSSL random number generators.

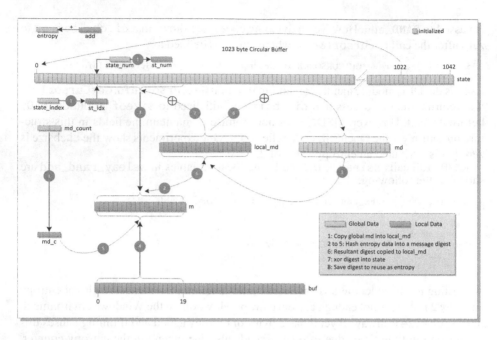

Fig. 9. Seeding the OpenSSL Random Number Generator

OpenSSL provides a second function `ssleay_rand_seed` to seed the RNG, but this simply calls `ssleay_rand_add`, providing the buffer size as the entropy value, i.e., it assumes 100% entropy.

8.4   OpenSSL Documentation Error

If a user requests secure random numbers but the entropy is inadequate, an error message is generated pointing them to: http://www.openssl.org/support/faq.html. The FAQ under "Why do I get a 'PRNG not seeded' error message?" states: "As of version 0.9.5, the OpenSSL functions that need randomness report an error if the random number generator has not been seeded with at least 128 bits of randomness". Yet in the code, entropy is defined in `rand_lcl.h` as 32 (bytes) which is 256 bits.

9   Conclusion

This paper proposed statistical distance based LIL testing techniques. This technique has been used to identify flaws in several commonly used pseudorandom generator implementations that have not been detected by NIST SP800-22 testing tools. It is concluded that the LIL testing technique is an important tool and should be used for statistical testing. We also provided a detailed documentation on OpenSSl random generators and described several potential attacks.

References

1. Ahmad, D.: Two years of broken crypto: debian's dress rehearsal for a global pki compromise. IEEE Security & Privacy 6(5), 70–73 (2008)
2. Clarkson, J.A., Adams, C.R.: On definitions of bounded variation for functions of two variables. Tran. AMS 35(4), 824–854 (1933)
3. Debian. Debian security advisory dsa-1571-1, http://www.debian.org/security/2008/dsa-1571
4. Feller, W.: Introduction to probability theory and its applications, vol. I. John Wiley & Sons, Inc., New York (1968)
5. Hellinger, E.: Neue begründung der theorie quadratischer formen von unendlichvielen veränderlichen. J. für die reine und angewandte Mathematik 136, 210–271 (1909)
6. Heninger, N., Durumeric, Z., Wustrow, E., Halderman, J.A.: Mining your ps and qs: Detection of widespread weak keys in network devices. In: Proc. 21st USENIX Security Symposium, vol. 2 (2012)
7. Khinchin, A.: Über einen satz der wahrscheinlichkeitsrechnung. Fund. Math. 6, 9–20 (1924)
8. Matsumoto, M., Nishimura, T.: Mersenne twister: a 623-dimensionally equidistributed uniform pseudo-random number generator. ACM TOMACS 8(1), 3–30 (1998)
9. NIST. Test suite (2010), http://csrc.nist.gov/groups/ST/toolkit/rng/
10. OpenSSL. Openssl implementation from http://www.openssl.com/
11. RANDOM.ORG. Random.org, http://www.random.org/
12. Rukhin, A., Soto, J., Nechvatal, J., Smid, M., Barker, E., Leigh, S., Levenson, M., Vangel, M., Banks, D., Heckert, A., Dray, J., Vo, S.: A Statistical Test Suite for Random and Pseudorandom Number Generators for Cryptographic Applications. NIST SP 800-22 (2010)
13. Wang, Y.: Resource bounded randomness and computational complexity. Theoret. Comput. Sci. 237, 33–55 (2000)
14. Wang, Y.: A comparison of two approaches to pseudorandomness. Theoretical computer science 276(1), 449–459 (2002)

Efficient Hidden Vector Encryption with Constant-Size Ciphertext

Tran Viet Xuan Phuong, Guomin Yang, and Willy Susilo*

Centre for Computer and Information Security Research
School of Computer Science and Software Engineering
University of Wollongong, Australia
tvxp750@uowmail.edu.au, {gyang,wsusilo}@uow.edu.au

Abstract. A Hidden Vector Encryption (HVE) scheme is a special type of anonymous identity-based encryption (IBE) scheme where the attribute string associated with the ciphertext or the user secret key can contain wildcards. In this paper, we introduce two constant-size ciphertext-policy hidden vector encryption (CP-HVE) schemes. Our first scheme is constructed on composite order bilinear groups, while the second one is built on prime order bilinear groups. Both schemes are proven secure in a selective security model which captures plaintext (or payload) and attribute hiding. To the best of our knowledge, our schemes are the first HVE constructions that can achieve constant-size ciphertext among all the existing HVE schemes.

Keywords: Hidden vector encryption, Ciphertext policy, Constant-size ciphertext, Viète's Formulas.

1 Introduction

Embedding policy-based access control into modern encryption schemes is an interesting but challenging task that has been intensively studied by the cryptologic research community in recent years. Typical examples of such encryption schemes include Attribute-based Encryption (ABE) [1–4] and Predicate Encryption [5, 6] schemes, which can be treated as special instances of a more general notion called Functional Encryption which was formalized by Boneh, Sahai, and Waters [7].

As a special type of functional encryption, Hidden Vector Encryption (HVE) schemes [5, 6, 8, 9] allow wildcards to appear in either the encryption attribute vector associated with a ciphertext or the decryption attribute vector associated with a user secret key. Similar to ABE schemes, we name the former Ciphertext Policy (CP-) HVE schemes and the latter Key Policy (KP-) HVE schemes. The decryption will work if and only if the two vectors match. That is, for each position, the two vectors must have the same letter (defined in an alphabet Σ)

---

* This work is partially supported by Australian Research Council Discovery Project (DP130101383).

M. Kutyłowski and J. Vaidya (Eds.): ESORICS 2014, Part I, LNCS 8712, pp. 472–487, 2014.

unless a wildcard symbol '⋆' appears in one of these two vectors at that position. In this paper, we focus on the construction of CP-HVE schemes.

Related Works. All the recent development on functional encryptions can be traced back to the earlier work on identity-based encryption which was introduced by Shamir [10] and first realized by Boneh and Franklin [11] and Cocks [12]. One important extension of IBE is hierarchical IBE (HIBE) [13], which allows users at a level to issue keys to those on the level below.

The notion of Anonymous IBE was introduced by Boneh et al. [14] and later formalized by Abdalla et al. [15]. Compared with the normal IBE, anonymous IBE supports the additional feature of identity/attribute hiding. That is, except the user holding the correct decryption key, no one is able to link a ciphertext with the identity string used to create that ciphertext.

In [16], Abdalla et al. also proposed another extension of IBE called Wild-carded IBE (or WIBE for short). WIBE is closely related to CP-HVE except that the former does not consider the property of identity/attribute hiding when it was introduced in [16]. Abdalla et al. proposed several WIBE constructions based on the Waters HIBE [17], the Boneh-Boyen HIBE [18], and the Boneh-Boyen-Goh HIBE [13]. Recently, to address the identity hiding problem, Abdalla et al. also proposed an anonymous WIBE in [19].

In a predicate encryption system [5, 6] for a (polynomial-time) predicate P, two inputs (besides some public parameters) are required in the encryption process, one is the message M to be encrypted, and the other one is an index string i. A decryption key is generated based on a master secret and a key index k. The decryption key can successfully decrypt a valid encryption of (i, M) if and only if $P(k, i) = 1$. IBE can be treated as a special type of predicate encryption where the predicate function simply performs an equality test, while for HVE the predicate function will ignore the positions where wildcard symbols '⋆' have occurred when doing an equality test.

After the notion of hidden vector encryption was first proposed by Boneh and Waters in [5], several HVE schemes [6, 8, 9, 20–23] have been proposed, most of which are key policy based (i.e., the wildcards '⋆' appear in the decryption attribute vector). One common drawback in many early HVE schemes (e.g. [5, 6, 21, 22]) is that the ciphertext size and the decryption key size are large (linear in the length of the vector). In [8], Sedghi et al. proposed an HVE scheme that has constant decryption key size and short (but still not constant-size) ciphertext. In [9], Hattori et al. introduced a formal definition for CP-HVE and proposed a CP-HVE scheme based on the anonymous HIBE proposed in [24] and the wildcarded IBE proposed in [16]. Hattori et al.'s CP-HVE scheme also has a linear cipertext size. To the best of our knowledge, there is no HVE scheme proposed in the literature that can achieve constant-size ciphertext.

Our Contributions. We propose two ciphertext policy hidden vector encryption schemes with constant-size ciphertext.

- Our first proposed scheme (CP-HVE1) is constructed on bilinear groups with a composite order $n = pq$ where p, q are prime numbers. The security of the scheme is proven in the standard model under three complexity assumptions: the Decisional L-composite Bilinear Diffie-Hellman Exponent (L-cBDHE) assumption, the L-composite Decisional Diffie Hellman (l-cDDH) assumption, and the Bilinear Subspace Decision (BSD) assumption.

- Additionally, we also construct our second scheme (CP-HVE2), which is built on bilinear groups with a prime order. We note that our second scheme is more efficient compared to the scheme converted from CP-HVE1 by applying the conversion tool from a composite order to a prime order bilinear group. Our second scheme is proven under the Decisional L-Bilinear Diffie-Hellman Exponent (L-BDHE) assumption.

We highlight the differences between our schemes and the previous HVE schemes in Table 1. A more detailed comparison among these schemes is given in Sec. 7.

Table 1. A Comparison on Ciphertext Size and Key Size among HVE Schemes

Scheme	Type	Constant Ciphertext Size	Constant Key Size
Katz et al. [6]	Key Policy	No	No
Shi, Waters [20]	Key Policy	No	No
Ivovino and Persiano [21]	Key Policy	No	No
Sedghi et al. [8]	Key Policy	No	Yes
Lee and Dong [25]	Key Policy	No	Yes
Park [23]	Key Policy	No	Yes
Hattori et al. [9]	Ciphertext Policy	No	No
Ours	Ciphertext Policy	Yes	No

2   Preliminaries

2.1   Bilinear Map on Prime Order Groups

Let $\mathbb{G}$ and $\mathbb{G}_T$ be two multiplicative cyclic groups of same prime order p, and g a generator of $\mathbb{G}$. Let $e : \mathbb{G} \times \mathbb{G} \to \mathbb{G}_T$ be a bilinear map with the following properties:

1. Bilinearity : $e(u^a, v^b) = e(u^b, v^a) = e(u, v)^{ab}$ for all $u, v \in \mathbb{G}$ and $a, b \in \mathbb{Z}_p$.
2. Non-degeneracy : $e(g, g) \neq 1$

Notice that the map e is symmetric since $e(g^a, g^b) = e(g, g)^{ab} = e(g^b, g^a)$.

Decision L-BDHE Assumption. The Decision L-BDHE problem in $\mathbb{G}$ is defined as follows: Let $\mathbb{G}$ be a bilinear group of prime order p, and g, h two independent generators of $\mathbb{G}$. Denote $\overrightarrow{y}_{g,\alpha,L} = (g_1, g_2, \ldots, g_L, g_{L+2}, \ldots, g_{2L}) \in \mathbb{G}^{2L-1}$ where $g_i = g^{\alpha^i}$ for some unknown $\alpha \in \mathbb{Z}_p^*$. We say that the L-BDHE assumption holds in $\mathbb{G}$ if for any probabilistic polynomial-time algorithm A

$$|\Pr[A(g, h, \overrightarrow{y}_{g,\alpha,L}, e(g_{L+1}, h)) = 1] - \Pr[A(g, h, \overrightarrow{y}_{g,\alpha,L}, T) = 1]| \leq \epsilon(k)$$

where the probability is over the random choive of g, h in $\mathbb{G}$, the random choice $\alpha \in \mathbb{Z}_p^*$, the random choice $T \in \mathbb{G}_T$, and $\epsilon(k)$ is negligible in the security parameter k.

2.2   Bilinear Map on Composite Order Groups

Let p, q be two large prime numbers and $n = pq$. Let $\mathbb{G}, \mathbb{G}_T$ be cyclic groups of order n, We say $e : \mathbb{G} \times \mathbb{G} \to \mathbb{G}_T$ is bilinear map on composite order groups if e satisfies the following properties:

1. Bilinearity : $e(u^a, v^b) = e(u^b, v^a) = e(u, v)^{ab}$. for all $u, v \in \mathbb{G}$ and $a, b \in \mathbb{Z}_p$.
2. Non-degeneracy : $e(g, g) \neq 1$

Let $\mathbb{G}_p$ and $\mathbb{G}_q$ be two subgroups of $\mathbb{G}$ of order p and q, respectively. Then $\mathbb{G} = \mathbb{G}_p \times \mathbb{G}_q$, $\mathbb{G}_T = \mathbb{G}_{T,p} \times \mathbb{G}_{T,q}$. We use g_p and g_q to denote generators of $\mathbb{G}_p$ and $\mathbb{G}_q$, respectively. $e(h_p, h_q) = 1$ for all elements $h_p \in \mathbb{G}_p$ and $h_q \in \mathbb{G}_q$ since $e(h_p, h_q) = e(g_p^a, g_q^b) = e(g^{qa}, g^{pb}) = e(g, g)^{pqab} = 1$ for a generator g of $\mathbb{G}$.

Below are three complexity assumptions defined on composite order bilinear groups: the decisional L-composite bilinear Diffie-Hellman exponent (L-cBDHE) assumption, the L-composite Decisional Diffie-Hellman (L-cDDH) assumption, and the bilinear subspace decision (BSD) assumption.

The Decisional $L-$cBDHE Assumption

$$\text{Let } g_p, h \overset{R}{\leftarrow} \mathbb{G}_p, g_q \overset{R}{\leftarrow} \mathbb{G}_q, \alpha \overset{R}{\leftarrow} \mathbb{Z}_n$$
$$Z = (g_p, g_q, h, g_p^\alpha, \ldots, g_p^{\alpha^L}, g_p^{\alpha^{L+2}}, \ldots, g_p^{\alpha^{2L}}),$$
$$T = e(g_p, h)^{\alpha^{L+1}}, \text{ and } R \leftarrow \mathbb{G}_{T,p}$$

We say that the decisional $L-$cBDHE assumption holds if for any probabilistic polynomial-time algorithm A

$$|\Pr[A(Z, T) = 1] - \Pr[A(Z, R) = 1]| \leq \epsilon(k)$$

where $\epsilon(k)$ denotes an negligible function of k.

The $L - c$DDH Assumption

$$\text{Let } g_p \overset{R}{\leftarrow} \mathbb{G}_p, g_q, R_1, R_2, R_3 \overset{R}{\leftarrow} \mathbb{G}_q, \alpha, \beta \overset{R}{\leftarrow} \mathbb{Z}_n$$
$$Z = (g_p, g_q, g_p^\alpha, \ldots, g_p^{\alpha^L}, g_p^{\alpha^{L+1}} R_1, g_p^{\alpha^{L+1}\beta} R_2)$$
$$T = g_p^\beta R_3, \text{ and } R \leftarrow \mathbb{G}$$

We say that the $L - c$DDH assumption holds if for any probabilistic polynomial-time algorithm A

$$|\Pr[A(Z, T) = 1] - \Pr[A(Z, R) = 1]| \leq \epsilon(k)$$

where $\epsilon(k)$ denotes an negligible function of k.

The BSD Assumption

$$\text{Let } g_p \leftarrow \mathbb{G}_p, g_q \leftarrow \mathbb{G}_q$$
$$Z = (g_p, g_q)$$
$$T \leftarrow \mathbb{G}_{T,p}, \text{ and } R \leftarrow \mathbb{G}_{T,p}$$

We say that the BSD assumption holds if for any probabilistic polynomial-time algorithm A

$$|\Pr[A(Z,T) = 1] - \Pr[A(Z,R) = 1]| \le \epsilon(k)$$

where $\epsilon(k)$ denotes an negligible function of k.

2.3   The Viète's Formulas

Both of our schemes introduced in this paper are based on the Viète's formulas [8] which is reviewed below. Consider two vectors $\vec{v} = (v_1, v_2, \ldots, v_L)$ and $\vec{z} = (z_1, z_2, \ldots, z_L)$. Vector v contains both alphabets and wildcards, and vector z only contains alphabets. Let $J = \{j_1, \ldots, j_n\} \subset \{1, \ldots, L\}$ denote the positions of the wildcards in vector $\vec{v}$. Then the following two statements are equal:

$$v_i = z_i \vee v_i = * \text{ for } i = 1 \ldots L$$

$$\sum_{i=1, i \notin J}^{L} v_i \prod_{j \in J} (i - j) = \sum_{i=1}^{L} z_i \prod_{j \in J} (i - j). \tag{1}$$

Expand $\prod_{j \in J} (i - j) = \sum_{k=0}^{n} a_k i^k$, where a_k are the coefficients dependent on J, then (1) becomes:

$$\sum_{i=1, i \notin J}^{L} v_i \prod_{j \in J} (i - j) = \sum_{k=0}^{n} a_k \sum_{i=1}^{L} z_i i^k \tag{2}$$

To hide the computations, we choose random group elemen H_i and put v_i, z_i as the exponents of group elements: $H_i^{v_i}, H_i^{z_i}$. Then (2) becomes:

$$\prod_{i=1, i \notin J}^{L} H_i^{v_i \prod_{j \in J}(i-j)} = \prod_{k=0}^{n} (\prod_{i=1}^{L} H_i^{z_i i^k})^{a_k} \tag{3}$$

Using Viète's formulas we can construct the coefficient a_k in (2) by:

$$a_{n-k} = (-1)^k \sum_{1 \le i_1 < i_2 < \ldots < i_k \le n} j_{i_1} j_{i_2} \ldots j_{i_k}, \ 0 \le k \le n. \tag{4}$$

where $n = |J|$. If we have $J = \{j_1, j_2, j_3\}$, the polynomial is $(x - j_1)(x - j_2)(x - j_3)$, then:

$$a_3 = 1$$
$$a_2 = -(j_1 + j_2 + j_3)$$
$$a_1 = (j_1 j_2 + j_1 j_3 + j_2 j_3)$$
$$a_0 = -j_1 j_2 j_3.$$

3   Ciphertext-Policy Hidden Vector Encryption

A ciphertext-policy hidden vector encryption (CP-HVE) scheme consists of the following four probabilistic polynomial-time algorithms:

- **Setup**$(1^k, \Sigma, L)$: on input a security parameter 1^k, an alphabet Σ, a vector-length L, the algorithm outputs a public key PK and master secret key MSK.
- **Encryption**$(PK, \overrightarrow{v}, M)$: on input a public key PK, a message M, a vector $v \in \Sigma_L^*$ where Σ^* denotes $\Sigma \cup \{*\}$, the algorithm outputs a ciphertext CT.
- **KeyGen**$(MSK, \overrightarrow{x})$: on input a master secret key MSK, a vector $\overrightarrow{x} \in \Sigma_L$, the algorithm outputs a decryption key SK.
- **Decryption**(CT, SK): on input a ciphertext CT and a secret key SK, the algorithm outputs either a message M or a special symbol $\perp$.

Security Model. The security model for a CP-HVE scheme is defined via the following game between an adversary A and a challenger B.

- **Init:** The adversary A chooses two target patterns,

$$\overrightarrow{v_0^*} = (v_{0,1}, v_{0,2}, \ldots, v_{0,L}) \text{ and } \overrightarrow{v_1^*} = (v_{1,1}, v_{1,2}, \ldots, v_{1,L})$$

under the restriction that the wildcards '*' must appears at the same positions.
- **Setup:** The challenger B run **Setup**(k, Σ, L) to generate the PK and MSK. PK is then passed to A.
- **Query Phase 1:** A adaptively issues key queries for $\overrightarrow{\sigma} = (\sigma_1, \ldots, \sigma_L) \in \Sigma_L$ under the restriction that $\overrightarrow{\sigma}$ does not match $\overrightarrow{v_0^*}$ or $\overrightarrow{v_1^*}$. That is, there exist $i, j \in \{1, \ldots, L\}$ such that $v_{0,i}^* \neq * \wedge v_{0,i}^* \neq \sigma_i$, and $v_{1,j}^* \neq * \wedge v_{1,j}^* \neq \sigma_j$. The challenger runs **KeyGen**$(MSK, \overrightarrow{\sigma})$ and returns the corresponding decryption key to A.
- **Challenge:** A outputs two equal-length messages M_0^*, M_1^*. B picks $\beta \leftarrow \{0, 1\}$ and runs Encrypt$(PK, \overrightarrow{v_\beta^*}, M_\beta^*)$ to generate a challenge ciphertext C^*. B then passes C^* to A.
- **Query Phase 2:** same as Learning Phase 1.
- **Output:** A outputs a bit β' as her guess for β.

Define the advantage of A as

$$\mathbf{Adv}_A^{\mathsf{CP-HVE}}(k) = \Pr[\beta' = \beta] - 1/2.$$

4 CP-HVE Scheme 1

In this section, we present our first CP-HVE under composite order bilinear groups. Let $\overrightarrow{v}$ denote the attribute vector associated with the ciphertext and $\overrightarrow{z}$ the attribute vector associated with the user secret key. The expression of these two vectors is designed based on the idea The Viète's formulas. To do encryption, we represent each component of the vector $\overrightarrow{v}$ by $(g^{v_i})^{\prod\limits_{j \in J}(i-j)}$ where J denotes all the wildcard positions and is attached to the ciphertext. Notice that $\prod\limits_{j \in J}(i-j) = \sum\limits_{k=0}^{n} a_k i^k$ according to the Viète's formulas. In the decryption process, based on

J, the decryptor can reconstruct the coefficients a_k, and generate $\prod_{j \in J} g^{z_i i^k a_k} = (g^{z_i})^{\prod_{j \in J}(i-j)}$ for each component of $\vec{z}$. In this way, whether $v_i = z_i$ will not affect the decryption if $i \in J$.

▶ **Setup**$(1^k, \Sigma, L)$: The setup algorithm first chooses $N << L$ where N is the maximum number of wildcards that are allowed in an encryption vector. It then picks large primes p, q, generates bilinear groups $\mathbb{G}, \mathbb{G}_T$ of composite order $n = pq$, and selects generators $g_p \in \mathbb{G}_p, g_q \in \mathbb{G}_q$. After that, it selects random elements:

$$g, f, v, v', h_1, \ldots, h_L, h'_1, \ldots, h'_L, w \in \mathbb{G}_p,$$
$$R_g, R_f, R_v, R_{v'}, R_{h_1}, \ldots, R_{h_L}, R_{h'_1}, \ldots, R_{h'_L} \in \mathbb{G}_q,$$

and computes :

$$G = gR_g, F = fR_f, V = vR_v, V' = v'R_{v'},$$
$$H_1 = h_1 R_{h_1}, \ldots, H_L = h_L R_{h_L},$$
$$H'_1 = h'_1 R_{h'_1}, \ldots, H'_L = h'_L R_{h'_L},$$
$$E = e(g, w).$$

Then it creates the public key and master secret key as:

$$PK = \{g_p, g_q, G, F, V, V', (H_1, \ldots, H_L), (H'_1, \ldots, H'_L), E\},$$
$$MSK = \{p, q, g, f, v, v', (h_1, \ldots, h_L), (h'_1, \ldots, h'_L), w\}.$$

▶ **Encrypt**$(PK, M, \vec{v} = (v_1, \ldots, v_L) \in \Sigma_L^*)$: Suppose that $\vec{v}$ contains $\tau \leq N$ wildcards which occur at positions $J = \{j_1, \ldots, j_\tau\}$. The encryption algorithm first chooses:

$$s \in_R \mathbb{Z}_n, \text{ and } Z_1, Z_2, Z_3, Z_4 \in_R \mathbb{G}_q.$$

Using formulas (3) and (4), compute a_k for $k = 1, 2, \cdots, \tau$, and $t = a_0$. Then set:

$$C_0 = M \cdot E^s, C_1 = G^{\frac{s}{t}} Z_1, C_2 = F^s Z_2,$$
$$C_3 = ((\prod_{i=1}^{L} VH_i^{v_i})^{\prod_{k=1}^{\tau}(i-j_k)})^{\frac{s}{t}} \cdot Z_3, C_4 = ((\prod_{i=1}^{L} V'(H'_i)^{v_i})^{\prod_{k=1}^{\tau}(i-j_k)})^{\frac{s}{t}} \cdot Z_4,$$
$$J = \{j_1, j_2, \ldots, j_\tau\},$$

and ciphertext $CT = \{C_0, C_1, C_2, C_3, C_4, J\}$.

▶ **KeyGen**$(MSK, \vec{z} = (z_1, \ldots, z_L) \in \Sigma_L)$: The key generation algorithm chooses r_1, r'_1, r_2 randomly in Z_n, and computes:

$$K_1 = g^{r_1}, K_2 = g^{r'_1}, K_3 = g^{r_2}, \begin{pmatrix} K_{4,0} = w(\prod_{i=1}^{L} h_i^{z_i} v)^{r_1}(\prod_{i=1}^{L} (h'_i)^{z_i} v')^{r'_1} f^{r_2}, \\ K_{4,1} = (\prod_{i=1}^{L} h_i^{z_i} v)^{ir_1}(\prod_{i=1}^{L} (h'_i)^{z_i} v')^{ir'_1}, \\ \cdots \\ K_{4,N} = (\prod_{i=1}^{L} h_i^{z_i} v)^{i^N r_1}(\prod_{i=1}^{L} (h'_i)^{z_i} v')^{i^N r'_1} \end{pmatrix}.$$

The secret key is $SK = \{K_1, K_2, K_3, K_{4,0}, \ldots, K_{4,N}\}$.

► **Decrypt**(CT, SK): The decryption algorithm first applies the Viète's formulas to compute

$$a_{\tau-k} = (-1)^k \sum_{1 \le i_1 < i_2 < \ldots < i_k \le \tau} j_{i_1} j_{i_2} \ldots j_{i_k}, 0 \le k \le \tau$$

and then outputs:

$$M = \frac{e(K_1, C_3) \cdot e(K_2, C_4) \cdot e(K_3, C_2)}{e(\prod\limits_{k=0}^{\tau} K_{4,k}^{a_k}, C_1)} \cdot C_0.$$

Correctness

$$e(K_1, C_3) = e(g^{r_1}, ((\prod_{i=1}^{L} VH_i^{v_i})^{\prod_{k=1}^{\tau}(i-j_k)})^{\frac{s}{a_0}} \cdot Z_3)$$

$$= \prod_{i=1}^{L} e(g, v)^{\frac{sr_1 \prod_{k=1}^{\tau}(i-j_k)}{a_0}} \cdot e(g, h_i)^{\frac{sr_1 \prod_{k=1}^{\tau}(i-j_k)v_i}{a_0}}.$$

$$e(K_2, C_4) = e(g^{r_1'}, ((\prod_{k=1}^{L} V'(H')_i^{v_i})^{\prod_{k=1}^{\tau}(i-j_k)})^{\frac{s}{a_0}} \cdot Z_4)$$

$$= \prod_{i=1}^{L} e(g, v')^{\frac{sr_1' \prod_{k=1}^{\tau}(i-j_k)}{a_0}} \cdot e(g, h_i')^{\frac{sr_1' \prod_{k=1}^{\tau}(i-j_k)v_i}{a_0}}.$$

$$e(K_3, C_2) = e(g^{r_2}, F^s Z_2) = e(g, f)^{r_2 s}.$$

$$e(\prod_{k=0}^{\tau} K_{4,k}^{a_k}, C_1) = e(w^{a_0}(\prod_{k=0}^{\tau}\prod_{i=1}^{L} v^{i^k a_k} h_i^{z_i i^k a_k} v^{i^k a_k})^{r_1}(\prod_{k=0}^{\tau}\prod_{i=1}^{L}(h_i')^{z_i i^k a_k} v'^{i^k a_k})^{r_1'} f^{r_2 a_0}, G^{\frac{s}{a_0}} Z_1)$$

$$= e(g, w)^{\frac{sa_0}{a_0}} \cdot e(g, f)^{\frac{sr_2 a_0}{a_0}} \cdot \prod_{i=1}^{L} e(g, h_i)^{\frac{sr_1 \prod_{k=1}^{\tau}(i-j_k)z_i}{a_0}} e(g, v)^{\frac{sr_1 \sum_{k=0}^{\tau} i^k a_k}{a_0}}$$

$$\cdot \prod_{i=1}^{L} e(g, h_i')^{\frac{sr_1' \prod_{k=1}^{\tau}(i-j_k)z_i}{a_0}} e(g, v')^{\frac{sr_1' \sum_{k=0}^{\tau} i^k a_k}{a_0}}$$

$$= e(g, w)^s \cdot e(g, f)^{sr_2} \cdot \prod_{i=1}^{L} e(g, v)^{\frac{sr_1 \prod_{k=1}^{\tau}(i-j_k)}{a_0}} \cdot e(g, h_i)^{\frac{sr_1 \prod_{k=1}^{\tau}(i-j_k)z_i}{a_0}}$$

$$\cdot \prod_{i=1}^{L} e(g, v')^{\frac{sr_1' \prod_{k=1}^{\tau}(i-j_k)}{a_0}} \cdot e(g, h_i')^{\frac{sr_1' \prod_{k=1}^{\tau}(i-j_k)z_i}{a_0}}.$$

Then we have

$$\frac{e(K_1, C_3) \cdot e(K_2, C_4) \cdot e(K_3, C_2)}{e(\prod\limits_{k=0}^{\tau} K_{4,k}^{a_k}, C_1)}$$

$$= \frac{\prod\limits_{i=1}^{L} e(g,v)^{\frac{sr_1 \prod_{k=1}^{\tau}(i-j_k)}{a_0}} \cdot e(g,h_i)^{\frac{sr_1 \prod_{k=1}^{\tau}(i-j_k)v_i}{a_0}} \cdot \prod\limits_{i=1}^{L} e(g,v')^{\frac{sr_1' \prod_{k=1}^{\tau}(i-j_k)}{a_0}} \cdot e(g,h_i')^{\frac{sr_1' \prod_{k=1}^{\tau}(i-j_k)v_i}{a_0}}}{\prod\limits_{i=1}^{L} e(g,v)^{\frac{sr_1 \prod_{k=1}^{\tau}(i-j_k)}{a_0}} \cdot e(g,h_i)^{\frac{sr_1 \prod_{k=1}^{\tau}(i-j_k)z_i}{a_0}} \cdot \prod\limits_{i=1}^{L} e(g,v')^{\frac{sr_1' \prod_{k=1}^{\tau}(i-j_k)}{a_0}} \cdot e(g,h_i')^{\frac{sr_1' \prod_{k=1}^{\tau}(i-j_k)z_i}{a_0}}}$$

$$\cdot e(g, w)^s \cdot e(g, f)^{sr_2},$$

and can recover message M by:

$$\frac{e(K_1, C_3) \cdot e(K_2, C_4) \cdot e(K_3, C_2)}{e(\prod_{k=0}^{\tau} K_{4,k}^{a_k}, C_1)} \cdot C_0 = \frac{e(g, f)^{r_2 s} \cdot M \cdot e(g, w)^s}{e(g, w)^s \cdot e(g, f)^{s r_2}} = M.$$

Theorem 1. *Our CP-HVE Scheme 1 is secure if the Decisional $L-cBDHE$ assumption, the $L - cDDH$ assumption, and the BSD assumption hold.*

We prove Theorem 1 by the following sequence of games.

$$Game_0 : [C_0, C_1, C_2, C_3, C_4]$$
$$Game_1 : [C_0 \cdot R_p, C_1, C_2, C_3, C_4]$$
$$Game_2 : [R_0, C_1, C_2, C_3, C_4]$$
$$Game_3 : [R_0, C_1, C_2, R_3, C_4]$$
$$Game_4 : [R_0, C_1, C_2, R_3, R_4],$$

where R_p is a randomly chosen from $\mathbb{G}_{T,p}$, R_0 is uniformly distributed in $\mathbb{G}_T$, and R_0, R_3, R_4 are uniformly distributed in $\mathbb{G}$.

We will prove the following Lemmas. Notice that in $Game_4$ the challenge ciphertext is independent of the message and the encryption vector, which means the adversary has no advantage in winning the game over random guess.

Lemma 1. *Assume that the Decisional $L-cBDHE$ assumption holds, then for any PPT adversary, the difference between the advantages in $Game_0$ and $Game_1$ is negligible.*

Lemma 2. *Assume that the BSD assumption holds, then for any PPT adversary, the difference between the advantages in $Game_1$ and $Game_2$ is negligible.*

Lemma 3. *Assume that the $L-cDDH$ assumption holds, then for any PPT adversary, the difference between the advantages in $Game_2$ and $Game_3$ is negligible.*

Lemma 4. *Assume that the $L-cDDH$ assumption holds, then for any PPT adversary, the difference between the advantages in $Game_3$ and $Game_4$ is negligible.*

(The proof is given in the full version of the paper).

5   CP-HVE Scheme 2

One straightforward approach to obtain a new CP-HVE scheme under prime-order bilinear groups is to apply the conversion technique introduced by Lewko [26]. In this section, we present a new prime-order CP-HVE scheme that is more efficient than the converted scheme.

▶ **Setup**$(1^k, \Sigma, L)$: The setup algorithm chooses $N << L$ to be the maximum number of wildcards that are allowed in an encryption vector. Then it generates other system parameters including:

$$e : \mathbb{G} \times \mathbb{G} \to \mathbb{G}_T,$$
$$L + 1 \text{ random elements } V, H_1, \ldots, H_L \in_R \mathbb{G},$$
$$\text{Then chooses randomly generator } g, w, f \in \mathbb{G},$$
$$Y = e(g, w).$$

The public key and master secret key are set as:

$$PK = (Y, V, (H_1, \ldots, H_L), g, f, p, \mathbb{G}, \mathbb{G}_T, e),$$
$$MSK = w.$$

▶ **Encrypt**$(PK, M, \vec{v} = (v_1, \ldots, v_L) \in \Sigma_L^*)$: Assume that $\vec{v} = (v_1, \ldots, v_L)$ contains $\tau \leq N$ wildcards which occur at positions $J = \{j_1, \ldots, j_\tau\}$. The encryption algorithm chooses $s \in_R \mathbb{Z}_p$, and computes using Viete's formulas $t = a_0$. It then computes:

$$C_0 = MY^s, C_1 = g^{\frac{s}{t}}, C_2 = f^s, C_3 = (\prod_{i=1}^{L} VH_i^{v_i})^{\frac{\Pi_{k=1}^{\tau}(i-j_k)s}{t}},$$

and set the ciphertext $CT = (C_0, C_1, C_2, C_3, J = \{j_1, j_2, \ldots, j_\tau\})$.

▶ **Key Generation**$(MSK, \vec{z} = (z_1, \ldots, z_L) \in \Sigma_L)$: given a key vector $\vec{z} = (z_1, \ldots, z_L)$, the key generation algorithm chooses $r, r_1 \in_R \mathbb{Z}_p$, then it creates secret key SK as:

$$K_1 = g^r, K_2 = g^{r_1}, \begin{pmatrix} K_{3,0} = w(\prod_{i=1}^{L}(H_i^{z_i}V)^r f^{r_1} \\ K_{3,1} = (\prod_{i=1}^{L} H_i^{z_i}V)^{ir} \\ \ldots \\ K_{3,N} = (\prod_{i=1}^{L} H_i^{z_i}V)^{i^N r} \end{pmatrix}.$$

▶ **Decrypt**(CT, SK): The decryption algorithm first applies the Viete formulas on $J = \{j_1, \ldots, j_\tau\}$ included in the ciphertext to compute:

$$a_{\tau-k} = (-1)^k \sum_{1 \leq i_1 < i_2 < \ldots < i_k \leq \tau} j_{i_1} j_{i_2} \ldots j_{i_k}, \text{ for } 0 \leq k \leq \tau$$

and then outputs:

$$M = \frac{e(K_1, C_3) \cdot e(K_2, C_2)}{e(\prod_{k=0}^{\tau} K_{3,k}^{a_k}, C_1)} \cdot C_0.$$

Correctness

$$e(K_1, C_3) = e(g^r, ((\prod_{i=1}^{L} VH_i^{v_i})^{k=1}^{\prod_{k=1}^{\tau}(i-j_k)})^{\frac{s}{a_0}})$$

$$= \prod_{i=1}^{L} e(g, V)^{\frac{sr\prod_{k=1}^{\tau}(i-j_k)}{a_0}} \cdot e(g, H_i)^{\frac{sr\prod_{k=1}^{\tau}(i-j_k)v_i}{a_0}}.$$

$$e(K_2, C_2) = e(g^{r_1}, f^s) = e(g, f)^{r_1 s}$$

$$e(\prod_{k=0}^{\tau} K_{3,k}^{a_k}, C_1) = e(w^{a_0}(\prod_{k=0}^{\tau}\prod_{i=1}^{L} H_i^{z_i i^k a_k} V^{i^k a_k})^r f^{r_1 a_0}, g^{\frac{s}{a_0}})$$

$$= e(g, w)^{\frac{s a_0}{a_0}} \cdot e(g, f)^{\frac{s r_1 a_0}{a_0}} \cdot \prod_{i=1}^{L} e(g, V)^{\frac{sr\prod_{k=1}^{\tau}(i-j_k)}{a_0}} e(g, H_i)^{\frac{sr\prod_{k=1}^{\tau}(i-j_k)z_i}{a_0}}$$

$$= e(g, w)^s \cdot e(g, f)^{s r_1} \cdot \prod_{i=1}^{L} e(g, V)^{\frac{sr\prod_{k=1}^{\tau}(i-j_k)}{a_0}} \cdot e(g, H_i)^{\frac{sr\prod_{k=1}^{\tau}(i-j_k)z_i}{a_0}}.$$

Then we have:

$$\frac{e(K_1, C_3) \cdot e(K_2, C_2) \cdot C_0}{e(\prod_{k=0}^{\tau} K_{3,k}^{a_k}, C_1)} = \frac{M \cdot e(g, w)^s \cdot \prod_{i=1}^{L} e(g, V)^{\frac{sr\prod_{k=1}^{\tau}(i-j_k)}{a_0}} \cdot e(g, H_i)^{\frac{sr\prod_{k=1}^{\tau}(i-j_k)v_i}{a_0}} \cdot e(g, f)^{r_1 s}}{e(g, w)^s \cdot e(g, f)^{s r_1} \cdot \prod_{i=1}^{L} e(g, V)^{\frac{sr\prod_{k=1}^{\tau}(i-j_k)}{a_0}} \cdot e(g, H_i)^{\frac{sr\prod_{k=1}^{\tau}(i-j_k)z_i}{a_0}}} = M.$$

6   Security Proof of CCP-HVE2 Scheme

Theorem 2. *Assume decision L-BDHE assumption holds in* $\mathbb{G}$, *then our CP-HVE Scheme 2 is secure.*

Proof. Suppose that there exists an adversary A which can attack our scheme with non-negligible advantage ϵ, we construct another algorithm B which uses A to solve the decision L-BDHE problem. On input $(g, h, \overrightarrow{y}_{g,\alpha,L} = (g_1, g_2, \ldots, g_L, g_{L+2}, \ldots, g_{2L}), T)$, where $g_i = g^{\alpha^i}$ and for some unknown $\alpha \in \mathbb{Z}_p^*$. The goal of B is to determine whether $T = e(g_{L+1}, h)$ or not.
In the rest of the proof, we denote $W(\overrightarrow{v}) = \{1 \le i \le L | v_i = *\}$ and $\overline{W}(\overrightarrow{v}) = \{1 \le i \le L | v_i \ne *\}$, and $W(\overrightarrow{v})|_j^k$ as $\{i \in W(\overrightarrow{v}) | j \le i \le k\}$.
B simulates the game for A as follows:

- **Init:** A declares two challenge alphabet vectors $\overrightarrow{v_0^*} \in \Sigma_L^*$ and $\overrightarrow{v_1^*} \in \Sigma_L^*$ under the restriction that $W(\overrightarrow{v_0^*}) = W(\overrightarrow{v_1^*})$. B flips a coin $\mu \in \{0, 1\}$. For simplicity we denote $\overrightarrow{v_\mu^*} = (v_1^*, v_2^*, \cdots, v_L^*)$.
- **Setup:** B chooses $N \ll L$, and random values $\gamma, y, \psi, u_1, \ldots, u_L \in_R \mathbb{Z}_p$ and sets

$$Y = e(g^\alpha, g^{\alpha^L} g^\gamma), f = g^\psi,$$
$$V = g^y \prod_{i \in \overline{W}(\overrightarrow{v_\mu^*})} g^{\alpha^{L+1-i} v_{\mu,i}^*},$$
$$\{H_i = g^{u_i - \alpha^{L+1-i}}\}_{i \in \overline{W}(\overrightarrow{v_\mu^*})}, \{H_i = g^{u_i}\}_{i \in W(\overrightarrow{v_\mu^*})}.$$

The master key component w is $g^{\alpha^{L+1}+\alpha\gamma}$. Since B does not have $g^{\alpha^{L+1}}$, B cannot compute w directly.

- **Query Phase 1:** A queries the user secret key for $\vec{\sigma_u} = (\sigma_1, \sigma_2, \ldots, \sigma_u)$ that does not match the challenge patterns. Let $k \in \overline{W}(\vec{v_\mu^*})$ be the smallest integer such that $\sigma_k \neq v_{\mu,k}^*$.

B needs to simulate the user key generation process. We start from $K_{3,i}$.

$$K_{3,0} = w(\prod_{i=1}^{L} H_i^{\sigma_i} V)^r f^{r_1}$$

$$= g^{\alpha^{L+1}+\alpha\gamma}(\prod_{\overline{W}(\vec{v_\mu^*})|_1^k} g^{u_i - \alpha^{L+1-i}} \cdot \prod_{W(\vec{v_\mu^*})|_1^k} (g^{u_i}))^{\sigma_i} \cdot g^{y + \sum_{\overline{W}(\vec{v_\mu^*})} \alpha^{L+1-i} v_{\mu,i}^*})^r f^{r_1}.$$

$$\stackrel{def}{=} g^{\alpha^{L+1}+\alpha\gamma}(g^X)^r f^{r_1}$$

where

$$X = \sum_{\overline{W}(\vec{v_\mu^*})} \alpha^{L+1-i} v_{\mu,i}^* + y + \sum_{\overline{W}(\vec{v_\mu^*})|_1^k} (u_i - \alpha^{L+1-i})\sigma_i + \sum_{W(\vec{v_\mu^*})|_1^k} u_i \sigma_i.$$

Since

$$\sum_{\overline{W}(\vec{v_\mu^*})|_1^k} (u_i - \alpha^{L+1-i})\sigma_i + \sum_{W(\vec{v_\mu^*})|_1^k} u_i \sigma_i = \sum_{\overline{W}(\vec{v_\mu^*})|_1^k} (-\alpha^{L+1-i}\sigma_i) + \sum_{i=1}^{k} u_i \sigma_i$$

and recall $\sigma_i = v_{\mu,i}^*$ for $i \in \overline{W}(\vec{v_\mu^*})|_1^{k-1}$ and $\sigma_k \neq v_{\mu,k}^*$. Hence, we have

$$X = \alpha^{L+1-k}\Delta_k + \sum_{\overline{W}(\vec{v_\mu^*})|_{k+1}^L} \alpha^{L+1-i} v_{\mu,i}^* + \sum_{i=1}^k x_i \sigma_i + y$$

where $\Delta_k = v_{\mu,k}^* - \sigma_k$. Then we choose $\hat{r}, r_1$ randomly in $\mathbb{Z}_n$, and set $r = \frac{-\alpha^k}{\Delta_k} + \hat{r}$. $K_{3,0}$ can be represented as

$K_{3,0}$

$$= g^{\alpha^{L+1}+\alpha\gamma} \cdot g^{-\alpha^{L+1}} \cdot g^{\sum_{i\in\overline{W}(\vec{v_\mu^*})|_{k+1}^L} \frac{-\alpha^{L+1-i+k} v_{\mu,i}^*}{\Delta_k}} \cdot g^{\alpha^k(-\frac{\sum_{i=1}^k x_i\sigma_i+y}{\Delta_k})} \cdot (V\prod_{i=1}^k h_i^{\sigma_i})^{\hat{r}} \cdot f^{r_1}$$

$$= g^{\alpha\gamma} \cdot g^{\sum_{i\in\overline{W}(\vec{v_\mu^*})|_{k+1}^L} \frac{-\alpha^{L+1-i+k} v_{\mu,i}^*}{\Delta_k}} \cdot g^{\alpha^k(-\frac{\sum_{i=1}^k x_i\sigma_i+y}{\Delta_k})} \cdot (V\prod_{i=1}^k H_i^{\sigma_i})^{\hat{r}} \cdot f^{r_1}.$$

For $\hat{k} = 1$ to N, we compute

$$K_{3,\hat{k}} = (g^{y + \sum_{\overline{W}(\vec{v_\mu^*})} \alpha^{L+1-i} v_{\mu,i}^*} \cdot (\prod_{\overline{W}(\vec{v_\mu^*})|_1^{k-1}} g^{u_i - \alpha^{L+1-i}} \cdot \prod_{W(\vec{v_\mu^*})|_1^{k-1}} (g^{u_i})^{\sigma_i})^{\frac{-\alpha^k i^{\hat{k}}}{\Delta_k} + \hat{r}i^{\hat{k}}}.$$

Table 2. Performance Comparison

Scheme	Group Order	Ciphertext Size	Decryption Cost	Assumption
Katz et al. [6]	pqr	$(2L+1)\lvert\mathbb{G}\rvert+1\lvert\mathbb{G}_T\rvert$	$(2L+1)$p	c3DH
Shi–Waters [20]	pqr	$(L+3)\lvert\mathbb{G}\rvert+1\lvert\mathbb{G}_T\rvert$	$(L+3)$p	c3DH
Ivovino–Persiano[21]	p	$(2L+1)\lvert\mathbb{G}\rvert+1\lvert\mathbb{G}_T\rvert$	$(2L+1)$p	DBDH + DLIN
Sedghi et al. [8]	p	$(N+3)\lvert\mathbb{G}\rvert+1\lvert\mathbb{G}_T\rvert$	3p	DLIN
Lee–Dong [25]	pqr	$(L+2)\lvert\mathbb{G}\rvert+1\lvert\mathbb{G}_T\rvert$	4p	cBDH BSD c3DH
Park [23]	p	$(2L+3)\lvert\mathbb{G}\rvert+1\lvert\mathbb{G}_T\rvert$	5p	DBDH+DLIN
Hattori et al. [9]	pq	$(2L+3)\lvert\mathbb{G}\rvert+1\lvert\mathbb{G}_T\rvert$	3p	$L-w$DBDHI BSD $L-c$DDH
CP-HVE1	pq	$4\lvert\mathbb{G}\rvert+1\lvert\mathbb{G}_T\rvert$	4p	$L-c$BDHE BSD $L-c$DDH
CP-HVE2	p	$3\lvert\mathbb{G}\rvert+1\lvert\mathbb{G}_T\rvert$	3p	L-BDHE

Other elements in the key can also be simulated:

$$K_1 = g^r = (g^{\alpha_k})^{-1/\Delta_k} \cdot g^{\hat{r}}, K_2 = g^{r_1}.$$

- **Challenge:** A sends to message M_0, M_1 to B, then sets using Viete formulas

$$a_{\tau-k} = (-1)^k \sum_{i \le i_1 < i_2 < \ldots < i_k \le \tau} j_{i_1} j_{i_2} \ldots j_{i_k}, 0 \le k \le \tau.$$

Let $t = a_0$. It creates ciphertext as:

$$C_0 = M_b \cdot T \cdot e(g^\alpha, h)^\gamma, C_1 = h^{1/t}, C_2 = h^\psi, C_3 = ((h^{y+\sum_{i=1}^{L} u_i v_{\mu,i}^*} \prod_{k=1}^{\tau} (i-j_k))^{\frac{1}{t}}$$

If $T = e(g,h)^{\alpha^{L+1}}$, the challenge ciphertext is a valid encryption of M_b. On the other hand, when T is uniformly distributed in $\mathbb{G}_T$, the challenge ciphertext is independent of b.

- **Query Phase 2:** Same Phase 1.
- **Guess:** A output $b' \in \{0,1\}$. If $b' = b$ then B outputs 1, otherwise outputs 0.

If $b' = 0$, then the simulation is the same as in the real game. Hence, A will have the probability $\frac{1}{2} + \epsilon$ to guess b correctly. If $b' = 1$, then T is random in $\mathbb{G}$, then A will have probability $\frac{1}{2}$ to guess b correctly. Therefore, B can solve the decision L-BDHE assumption also with advantage ϵ.   □

7 Performance Comparison

We give a detailed comparison among all the HVE schemes in Table 2. The schemes are compared in terms of the order of the underlying group, ciphertext size, decryption cost, and security assumption. In the table, p denotes the pairing operation, L the length of the vector, and N denotes the maximum number of wildcards.

Remark: In Table 2, we do not count the wildcard positions when measuring the ciphertext size. To indicate those wildcard positions, a naive way is to use an L-bit string, which has the same size as several group elements when L is linear in the security parameter. When $N \ll L$, then a more efficient way is to use the index for the first wildcard position and the offsets for the remaining wildcard positions.

8 Conclusion

We proposed two efficient ciphertext policy Hidden Vector Encryption schemes in this paper. Both of our encryption schemes can achieve constant ciphertext size, which forms the major contribution of this work. We proved the security of our schemes in a selective security model which captures both plaintext and attribute hiding properties. One of our future work is to extend our schemes so that they can achieve adaptive security.

References

1. Goyal, V., Pandey, O., Sahai, A., Waters, B.: Attribute-based encryption for fine-grained access control of encrypted data. In: Proceedings of the 13th ACM Conference on Computer and Communications Security, CCS 2006, pp. 89–98. ACM, New York (2006)
2. Lewko, A., Okamoto, T., Sahai, A., Takashima, K., Waters, B.: Fully secure functional encryption: Attribute-based encryption and (Hierarchical) inner product encryption. In: Gilbert, H. (ed.) EUROCRYPT 2010. LNCS, vol. 6110, pp. 62–91. Springer, Heidelberg (2010)
3. Waters, B.: Ciphertext-policy attribute-based encryption: An expressive, efficient, and provably secure realization. In: Catalano, D., Fazio, N., Gennaro, R., Nicolosi, A. (eds.) PKC 2011. LNCS, vol. 6571, pp. 53–70. Springer, Heidelberg (2011)
4. Lewko, A., Waters, B.: New proof methods for attribute-based encryption: Achieving full security through selective techniques. In: Safavi-Naini, R., Canetti, R. (eds.) CRYPTO 2012. LNCS, vol. 7417, pp. 180–198. Springer, Heidelberg (2012)
5. Boneh, D., Waters, B.: Conjunctive, subset, and range queries on encrypted data. In: Vadhan, S.P. (ed.) TCC 2007. LNCS, vol. 4392, pp. 535–554. Springer, Heidelberg (2007)
6. Katz, J., Sahai, A., Waters, B.: Predicate encryption supporting disjunctions, polynomial equations, and inner products. In: Smart, N.P. (ed.) EUROCRYPT 2008. LNCS, vol. 4965, pp. 146–162. Springer, Heidelberg (2008)

7. Boneh, D., Sahai, A., Waters, B.: Functional encryption: Definitions and challenges. In: Ishai, Y. (ed.) TCC 2011. LNCS, vol. 6597, pp. 253–273. Springer, Heidelberg (2011)

8. Sedghi, S., van Liesdonk, P., Nikova, S., Hartel, P., Jonker, W.: Searching keywords with wildcards on encrypted data. In: Garay, J.A., De Prisco, R. (eds.) SCN 2010. LNCS, vol. 6280, pp. 138–153. Springer, Heidelberg (2010)

9. Hattori, M., Hirano, T., Ito, T., Matsuda, N., Mori, T., Sakai, Y., Ohta, K.: Ciphertext-policy delegatable hidden vector encryption and its application to searchable encryption in multi-user setting. In: Chen, L. (ed.) IMACC 2011. LNCS, vol. 7089, pp. 190–209. Springer, Heidelberg (2011)

10. Shamir, A.: Identity-based cryptosystems and signature schemes. In: Blakely, G.R., Chaum, D. (eds.) CRYPTO 1984. LNCS, vol. 196, pp. 47–53. Springer, Heidelberg (1985)

11. Boneh, D., Franklin, M.K.: Identity-based encryption from the weil pairing. In: Kilian, J. (ed.) CRYPTO 2001. LNCS, vol. 2139, pp. 213–229. Springer, Heidelberg (2001)

12. Cocks, C.: An identity based encryption scheme based on quadratic residues. In: Honary, B. (ed.) Cryptography and Coding 2001. LNCS, vol. 2260, pp. 360–363. Springer, Heidelberg (2001)

13. Boneh, D., Boyen, X., Goh, E.J.: Hierarchical identity based encryption with constant size ciphertext. In: Cramer, R. (ed.) EUROCRYPT 2005. LNCS, vol. 3494, pp. 440–456. Springer, Heidelberg (2005)

14. Boneh, D., Di Crescenzo, G., Ostrovsky, R., Persiano, G.: Public key encryption with keyword search. In: Cachin, C., Camenisch, J.L. (eds.) EUROCRYPT 2004. LNCS, vol. 3027, pp. 506–522. Springer, Heidelberg (2004)

15. Abdalla, M., Bellare, M., Catalano, D., Kiltz, E., Kohno, T., Lange, T., Malone-Lee, J., Neven, G., Paillier, P., Shi, H.: Searchable encryption revisited: Consistency properties, relation to anonymous ibe, and extensions. J. Cryptology 21(3), 350–391 (2008)

16. Abdalla, M., Catalano, D., Dent, A., Malone-Lee, J., Neven, G., Smart, N.: Identity-based encryption gone wild. In: Bugliesi, M., Preneel, B., Sassone, V., Wegener, I. (eds.) ICALP 2006. LNCS, vol. 4052, pp. 300–311. Springer, Heidelberg (2006)

17. Waters, B.: Efficient identity-based encryption without random oracles. In: Cramer, R. (ed.) EUROCRYPT 2005. LNCS, vol. 3494, pp. 114–127. Springer, Heidelberg (2005)

18. Boneh, D., Boyen, X.: Efficient selective-ID secure identity-based encryption without random oracles. In: Cachin, C., Camenisch, J.L. (eds.) EUROCRYPT 2004. LNCS, vol. 3027, pp. 223–238. Springer, Heidelberg (2004)

19. Abdalla, M., De Caro, A., Phan, D.H.: Generalized key delegation for wildcarded identity-based and inner-product encryption. IEEE Transactions on Information Forensics and Security 7(6), 1695–1706 (2012)

20. Shi, E., Waters, B.: Delegating capabilities in predicate encryption systems. In: Aceto, L., Damgård, I., Goldberg, L.A., Halldórsson, M.M., Ingólfsdóttir, A., Walukiewicz, I. (eds.) ICALP 2008, Part II. LNCS, vol. 5126, pp. 560–578. Springer, Heidelberg (2008)

21. Iovino, V., Persiano, G.: Hidden-vector encryption with groups of prime order. In: Galbraith, S.D., Paterson, K.G. (eds.) Pairing 2008. LNCS, vol. 5209, pp. 75–88. Springer, Heidelberg (2008)

22. Blundo, C., Iovino, V., Persiano, G.: Private-key hidden vector encryption with key confidentiality. In: Garay, J.A., Miyaji, A., Otsuka, A. (eds.) CANS 2009. LNCS, vol. 5888, pp. 259–277. Springer, Heidelberg (2009)

23. Park, J.H.: Efficient hidden vector encryption for conjunctive queries on encrypted data. IEEE Trans. on Knowl. and Data Eng. 23(10), 1483–1497 (2011)

24. Seo, J., Kobayashi, T., Ohkubo, M., Suzuki, K.: Anonymous hierarchical identity-based encryption with constant size ciphertexts. In: Jarecki, S., Tsudik, G. (eds.) PKC 2009. LNCS, vol. 5443, pp. 215–234. Springer, Heidelberg (2009)

25. Lee, K., Lee, D.H.: Improved hidden vector encryption with short ciphertexts and tokens. Des. Codes Cryptography 58(3), 297–319 (2011)

26. Lewko, A.B.: Tools for simulating features of composite order bilinear groups in the prime order setting. In: Pointcheval, D., Johansson, T. (eds.) EUROCRYPT 2012. LNCS, vol. 7237, pp. 318–335. Springer, Heidelberg (2012)

Enabling Short Fragments for Uncoordinated Spread Spectrum Communication

Naveed Ahmed[1], Christina Pöpper[2], and Srdjan Capkun[3]

[1] DTU Copenhagen, Denmark
naah@dtu.dk
[2] HGI Ruhr-University Bochum, Germany
christina.poepper@rub.de
[3] ETH Zurich, Switzerland
srdjan.capkun@ethz.ch

Abstract. Uncoordinated spread spectrum (USS) protocols have been proposed for anti-jamming communication in wireless settings without shared secrets. The existing USS protocols assume that fragments of hundreds of bits can be transmitted on different channels in order to identify fragments that belong to the same message. However, such long transmissions are susceptible to reactive jamming. To address this problem, we present a protocol that allows the use of short fragments of a few bits only. This makes our scheme resilient to a large class of reactive jammers. We prove that reassembling the fragmented message is not only feasible but also efficient: it can be completed in polynomial time in the size of the message, even if the jammer is computationally resourceful. We demonstrate the protocol efficiency by simulating the reassembly process at the link layer under different design parameters.

Keywords: Anti-jamming, Spread-spectrum Communication, Wireless Security.

1 Introduction

The primary countermeasure against jamming attacks on wireless communication is spread spectrum (SS) communication. Traditional (coordinated) SS communication between two parties requires shared secrets, however, establishing the secret key is a challenge in itself [1]. If two parties are unknown to each other, such as in wireless ad-hoc communication, emergency alert broadcast, or the dissemination of navigation signals [2], pre-sharing secrets is not feasible. Jamming-resistant key establishment is not only a bootstrapping problem but it reoccurs during re-keying if the old keys have been compromised.

A few years ago, a technique for uncoordinated spread spectrum (USS) communication, which does not require pre-shared secrets, was proposed at the US Air Force Academy [3]. Since then the interest in USS has grown, both for civilian [1,4,5] and military applications [6]. In effect, a USS transmitter transmits a long message as a sequence of shorter, fixed-size encoded fragments (frames) on randomly selected channels. A channel here corresponds to a frequency channel in frequency hopping spread spectrum (FHSS) or a chip code (or sequence of chip codes) in direct sequence spread spectrum (DSSS).

M. Kutyłowski and J. Vaidya (Eds.): ESORICS 2014, Part I, LNCS 8712, pp. 488–507, 2014.

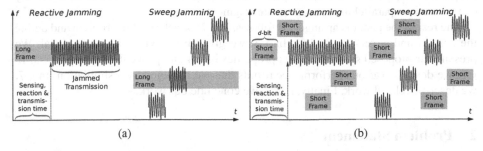

Fig. 1. Long and short frame transmissions. (a) Long frames are an easy target for jammers. Reactive jammers will have sufficient time to sense an ongoing transmission and then react to jam the used channel. Sweep (non-reactive) jammers have a high probability of hitting the channel where a long frame is transmitted. (b) Short frames reduce the risk of successful jamming attacks for both reactive and non-reactive sweep jammers.

The frame size is a key parameter of USS communication because it determines how fast a transmitter can switch the transmission channel. Clearly, if the frames are long then the respective channel will remain active for a long time, which makes it easy for a reactive adversary to locate and jam the channel and which results in high jamming probabilities for sweep jammers, as illustrated in Fig. 1-(a). If the switching frequency is high enough (see Fig. 1-(b)) then the adversary does not get enough time to react.

The feasibility of real-time, reactive radio jamming has recently been demonstrated using software-defined radio equipment [7, 8] with reaction times on the order of few symbol durations for 802.15.4 communication. Although error correction schemes can be used to repair some errors, these schemes are not effective against reactive jammers that can jam the channel if the frames are long. Thus, a USS protocol that supports short frames is highly desirable. Existing USS protocols, however, depend on long frames in order to transmit "linking information" that is used to identify parts that belong to the same message (we further elaborate on this in § 3 and § 7). This identification problem exists due to trivial pollution attacks at the link layer, in which a large number of well-designed fake frames are broadcasted to overburden the reassembly process at a legitimate receiver.

In this paper, we challenge the current assumption that long frames are indeed a necessary requirement for USS schemes. The idea of our solution is based on two insights. First, the payload and the message link do not need to be in the same fragment – instead they can be decoupled. This allows to independently transmit the payload and the link as shorter fragments. Second, if the function that computes a link is secure against a computationally unbounded adversary, then the size of the link can be reduced to a few bits. Using these insights, our protocol is the *first scheme for USS communication that allows for short fragments–down to a few bits*.

In more details, consider a reactive adversary who can jam frames longer than d-bit. To circumvent this reactive jamming, we disassemble a long message into m fragments of d-bit each, which are cryptographically linkable. As we will show, our protocol enables a USS receiver to reassemble the original message in a time that is polynomial in

m, provided $z(z + 1) < 2^d$, where z is the number of fake fragments that an adversary can transmit in parallel to each legitimate fragment.

The rest of the paper is arranged as follows. In § 2, we clarify the problem and define the system and adversary models. In § 3, we give an overview of our proposal. We present our proposed solution and its properties in § 4 and prove its security in § 5. In § 6, we describe various performance results that we obtained by a simulation. In § 7, we describe related work. Finally, in § 8, we conclude our work.

2   Problem Statement

Problem Formulation: A number of message fragmentation schemes [1,9–11] for USS communication were proposed (see § 7). The current approaches face a dilemma.

First, the required fragment size is too long to be practical against reactive jamming at the physical layer. That is, the proposed schemes apply linking techniques that not only require embedded linking information within the fragment but also the linking information must be hundred bits long for adequate cryptographic security.

Second, shortening the fragments (to provide more resistance to reactive jammers) conflicts with the schemes' very resistance against computationally powerful adversaries. For instance, the minimum fragment size of hash-based solutions [9] is mainly given by the length of the hash values used in the frame encoding; if the length of the hash values is reduced to make the scheme resistant to faster jammers then the hash function may no longer be second pre-image resistant. A computationally powerful adversary will then be able to break the linking function and introduce exponential complexity in the reassembly process—with the effect of a DoS-attack.

The goal of this work is to identify a way that allows to significantly reduce the frame size compared to prior proposals.

System Model: We consider an environment in which the communication bandwidth is given by a set of channels C, where $|C| = n$. For instance, $c \in C$ can be a frequency channel or a spreading code (or a short sequence of chippings codes) that encodes d bits. We consider ad-hoc communication between pairs of devices or from a transmitter T to unknown receivers in its transmission range (broadcast). T transmits d-bit fragments, encoded in frames, on randomly selected channels. We do not assume any shared secrets in the system and all protocol specifications are public and known to the receivers.

A receiver R is located in the transmission range of T and can receive on all or a subset of channels in parallel (broadband or partial-band receiver). R does not need to be time synchronized with T at the fragment level but is assumed to be in reception mode while the sender is transmitting. There can be a large number of receivers, but we do not assume any inter-receiver communication. We do not consider point-to-point communication, i.e., we do not require headers with physical address information.

Adversary Model: The aim of an adversary A is to prevent R from reassembling a legitimate message sent by T. The adversary can mount attacks at two different levels.

First, at the radio level, A can try to jam T's transmission. We assume that, due to limitations of radio equipments (e.g., required time for sensing and synthesizing the frequency of the carrier wave), A cannot deterministically jam transmissions of fragments of a few bits. Similar to conventional SS communication, $\mathcal{A}$ can jam a frame probabilistically by guessing as was, e. g., analyzed for longer frames in [1]. Therefore, as typical for conventional SS, we assume that $\mathcal{A}$ can only jam a limited portion of the available bandwidth. We note that number of channels where the attacker can jam may also be larger than the number of receiving channels at the receiver (which increases reception time accordingly).

Second, at a computational level, an all-powerful $\mathcal{A}$ tries to exploit our protocol at the data link layer. To this end, $\mathcal{A}$ transmits fake fragments to make it infeasible for $\mathcal{R}$ to identify legitimate fragments. The adversary may be located within the transmission range of $\mathcal{T}$ and her fake fragments can be a function of the legitimate fragments.

We synthesize the above discussion in two assumptions:

Assumption 1 (Minimum Reaction Time). *The reaction time of $\mathcal{A}$, i. e., the time required to sense an ongoing transmission on a channel and then jam that channel, is longer than the time required to transmit a frame containing a d-bit fragment ($d \geq 1$).*

In short, we assume that communication using conventional FHSS with fragments of d bits would resist the considered reactive attacker $\mathcal{A}$ (but cannot be used due to the lack of shared secrets). The reaction time depends on $\mathcal{A}$'s distance to $\mathcal{T}$ and to $\mathcal{R}$ and on the response times of $\mathcal{A}$'s radio equipments; channel switching can easily account for tens of microseconds [7, 12] and channel sensing by energy detection may be up to an order of milliseconds [13]. Given the bit rates of common wireless standards for comparison (e. g., 11 Mbit/s for 802.11b or 5-15 Mbit/s in 3G-UMTS) and the resulting bit duration of around one μs, it is reasonable to assume that the combined attack time is longer than the frame transmission time for a d-bit fragment when d is small.

Assumption 2 (z-channel Adversary). *$\mathcal{A}$'s transmission power is limited to $z < n$ channels (on which $\mathcal{A}$ can transmit in parallel) such that $z(z + 1) < 2^d$.*

Assumption 2 limits the bandwidth on which the adversary can transmit; e. g., our proposed scheme will work efficiently for $d = 5$-bit fragments if the attacker transmits on up to $z = 4$ channels in parallel. Note that unlimited computation power cannot be used to overcome the limitations of the communication hardware.

The effect of non-reactive jamming strategies (e.g., sweep jamming) on $\mathcal{R}$ is the same as randomly corrupting some of the fragments, because $\mathcal{T}$ sends the fragments on randomly selected channels; for UFH, random selection is the optimum strategy [9]. In principle, error-correcting schemes [14] can be used to counter random errors. Traditional error correction increases the frame size, though. Therefore, we propose a scheme based on the repetition of fragments in order to tolerate random errors.

Clearly, $\mathcal{A}$'s attacks are not effective at the radio level given the design parameters, z and d, correctly capture the capabilities of $\mathcal{A}$'s radio equipment. Next, we introduce the details of our protocol and show that $\mathcal{A}$, even with infinite computational power, cannot devise a jamming strategy that exploits our protocol at the data link layer.

3   Solution Overview

In this section, we provide an overview of our protocol, which we call the collision detection protocol (CDP or CD protocol). In the CDP, a message $\mathbf{T}_m^{\mathcal{T}}$ to be broadcasted

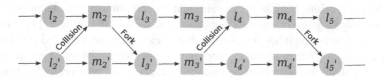

Fig. 2. Collisions and forks among paths significantly increase the number of paths that $\mathcal{R}$ must reassemble. Although forks and collisions are unavoidable for short fragments, collisions can be detected, which suffices to efficiently decode a legitimate message.

by transmitter $\mathcal{T}$ is assembled as a list of m message fragments (M-fragments), each of which is d bits long: $\mathbf{T}_m^{\mathcal{T}} = m_1, \ldots, m_m$. We define $\mathbf{T}_m^{\mathcal{T}}[i \to j] = m_i, \ldots, m_j$, where $1 \leq i \leq j \leq m$. Each M-fragment is sent on a randomly selected SS channel. Since an adversary can transmit fake fragments, we link the M-fragments together, so that the CDP receiver $\mathcal{R}$ can reassemble the original message. For this purpose, we use a link certificate $\mathbf{T}_l^{\mathcal{T}}$, which consists of m linking fragments (L-fragments) each of size d bits. The i-th L-fragment is computed from the message fragments using a CDP linking function: $l_i = link(\mathbf{T}_m^{\mathcal{T}}[1 \to i])$; we specify this function in § 4.1. We then interleave the L-fragments and the M-fragments, to obtain a transmission schedule: $\mathbf{T}^{\mathcal{T}} = m_1, l_2, m_2, \ldots, l_m, m_m$. The schedule $\mathbf{T}^{\mathcal{T}}$ is followed by $\mathcal{T}$ who sends fragments sequentially on randomly selected channels.

Since an L-fragment is a function of prior M-fragments, $\mathcal{R}$ can perform an online verification of the incoming L-fragments. A *path* is a plausible reconstruction of the transmission schedule $\mathbf{T}^{\mathcal{T}}$ and it consists of a list of interleaved L-fragments and M-fragments upon which the linking function can be verified. We say that $\mathcal{R}$ is tracking a path at an index i if the online verification of the i-th L-fragment l_i succeeds for the path $m_1 \to l_2 \to \cdots \to l_i \to m_i$. A path is complete, when the tracking terminates successfully with the verification of the m-th L-fragment.

A z-channel adversary can simultaneously transmit on z channels, and thus $\mathcal{R}$ may receive $z + 1$ fragments at each time instant. In this case, finding the path of the original message (consisting of m fragments) involves searching among $(z + 1)^m$ plausible paths, which can be infeasible, e. g., with $m = 128$ and $z = 2$. In this paper, we show that if an appropriate linking function is used then the number of paths are significantly reduced, which enables $\mathcal{R}$ to efficiently reassemble a legitimate message. Ideally, if $z + 1$ fragments are received per time unit then no more than $z + 1$ paths should be tracked by $\mathcal{R}$. In reality, however, the number of trackable paths could be more than $z + 1$ due to a combination of *collisions* and *forks*. We say that a collision occurs when two paths merge together (at an L- or M-fragment) and a fork occurs when a path splits into different paths, as illustrated in Fig. 2. Ideally, one would expect that the linking function can resist both collisions and forks in order to limit the number of paths, however, this may be impossible to achieve; e. g., if $d = 4$ then the probability that two random paths will have the same subsequent L-fragment is at least 2^{-4}.

Fortunately, the following two insights lead to a technique that reduces the number of search paths for short fragments. First, by preventing collisions only, we can avoid an exponential number of plausible paths. If there are no collisions then $\mathcal{R}$ never tracks more than $z + 1$ paths when receiving $z + 1$ fragments per time unit. Without collisions, the search space for tracking can be visualized as a tree-shaped structure (due to the forks), which will have less than $z + 1$ complete paths. Second, a linking function that only takes the current and the previous fragment into account (such as a hash chain in [1]) is not sufficient to detect collisions, because if a collision is not detected in the first link that arrives after the collision then the collision will remain undetected in the subsequent tracking. Hence, the number of paths would be high for such a function.

We propose a linking function that takes all (or a large number of) the previous fragments into account, which enables to detect collisions in the subsequent tracking (hence the name *collision detection protocol*). Although an adversary may be able to create collisions between her path and the legitimate path, these collisions can be detected once the tracking progresses with the arrival of more fragments. Towards the end of the legitimate path, collisions are less likely to be detected, but this does not exponentially increase the message reassembly time, since only few fragments are concerned.

4 Collision Detection Protocol

We next present our proposed scheme on the sender (§ 4.1) and receiver (§ 4.2-4.3) side.

4.1 Sender Side: Message Transmission

Let the message $\mathbf{T}_m^{\mathcal{T}}$ to be sent by $\mathcal{T}$ come from a uniformly distributed encoding of the message payload, making $\mathbf{T}_m^{\mathcal{T}}$ unpredictable for the adversary, e.g., $\mathbf{T}_m^{\mathcal{T}}$ can be computed by a symmetric encryption function: $\mathbf{T}_m^{\mathcal{T}} \leftarrow \mathcal{E}_K\left(N_{\mathcal{T}}, \mathcal{M}, \mathcal{S}_{Sk_{\mathcal{T}}}(\mathcal{M})\right)$. Here, K is a publicly known key, $N_{\mathcal{T}}$ is a secretly generated nonce used to randomize $\mathbf{T}_m^{\mathcal{T}}$, $\mathcal{M}$ is the payload, and $\mathcal{S}_{Sk_{\mathcal{T}}}(\mathcal{M})$ is the signature[1] computed on $\mathcal{M}$ using $\mathcal{T}$'s private key $Sk_{\mathcal{T}}$. The payload may contain a time-stamp to provide freshness of $\mathbf{T}_m^{\mathcal{T}}$.

Assuming the encryption function has pseudo-random properties [15], the output $\mathbf{T}_m^{\mathcal{T}}$ is uniformly distributed for the adversary until $\mathbf{T}_m^{\mathcal{T}}$ is transmitted. This randomization is required in order to make the value of a fragment unpredictable for the adversary before the fragment is actually transmitted (details will follow later). The signature $\mathcal{S}_{Sk_{\mathcal{T}}}$ is required so that $\mathcal{R}$ can distinguish a legitimate message from fake messages.

As described in § 3, $\mathcal{T}$ assembles $\mathbf{T}_m^{\mathcal{T}}$ as a list of M-fragments, computes the link certificate $\mathbf{T}_1^{\mathcal{T}}$, and interleaves it with $\mathbf{T}_m^{\mathcal{T}}$: $\mathbf{T}^{\mathcal{T}} = \left[\mathbf{T}_1^{\mathcal{T}}[i], \mathbf{T}_m^{\mathcal{T}}[i] : 1 \leq i \leq m\right]$. The i-th fragment $\mathbf{T}^{\mathcal{T}}[i]$ is transmitted at the i-th time instant t_i on randomly selected channels.

Resilience to Fragment Loss. To tolerate possible fragment loss (due to, e.g., adversarial jamming or channel noise), the front-end of $\mathcal{T}$ operates with a repetition factor of ρ: each fragment $\mathbf{T}^{\mathcal{T}}[i]$ is repeated ρ times between time instants t_i and $t_i + \Delta T$ on randomly selected channels, as illustrated in Fig. 3. Here, ΔT is the window size in which $\mathcal{R}$ senses the incoming signals for data. The period size ΔT is fixed but $\mathcal{R}$ may not know the start and end of a period.

---

[1] Existing digital signature schemes (DSS) are only secure against computationally bounded adversaries, but this does not affect the security of the link layer, which is responsible for re-assembling the message from received fragments.

Properties of the Linking Function.
The core of our scheme is the linking of message fragments using a linking function: $\mathcal{H} : \{0,1\}^* \rightarrow \{0,1\}^d$. This function is computed on the current fragment and all prior fragments. We require the following property to hold for $\mathcal{H}(\cdot)$ in order to efficiently identify the legitimate message $\mathcal{T}_m$ at $\mathcal{R}$.

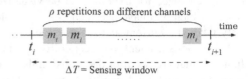

Fig. 3. Repetitions enable $\mathcal{R}$ to tolerate fragment losses, as common for USS techniques

Property 1. *Let x_l, x_l' and x_h be three bit strings such that $x_l \neq x_l'$, $|x_l| = |x_l'| \leq md$, and $|x_h| = d$. Let x_l be known to the adversary, x_l' be chosen by the adversary, and x_h comes from the uniform distribution. The function $\mathcal{H}(\cdot)$ is a linking function if $\mathcal{H}(x_l) = \mathcal{H}(x_l') \Rightarrow \mathcal{H}(x_l, x_h) = \mathcal{H}(x_l', x_h)$ only holds with probability 2^{-d}.*

As an intuition, x_h stands for the current fragment of a transmitted message, which is connected to all prior fragments x_l using the link $\mathcal{H}(x_l, x_h)$. Similarly, x_l' stands for all prior fragments of an adversarial message. $\mathcal{A}$ may well compute x_l' such that $\mathcal{H}(x_l) = \mathcal{H}(x_l')$ holds for $x_l' \neq x_l$, which results in a collision of the two search paths in the decoding process on $\mathcal{R}$. This collision, however, is likely to be detected during the consideration of the next fragment x_h, because the corresponding links, $\mathcal{H}(x_l, x_h)$ and $\mathcal{H}(x_l', x_h)$, can only be equal with a low probability (2^{-d}). This probability is further decreased when more fragments arrive: Property 1 not only specifies the collision detection probability with the current fragment x_h, but also with all subsequent fragments of the message.

Instantiation of the Linking Function. A simple instantiation of $\mathcal{H}(\cdot)$ is a cryptographic hash function, such as SHA-256. For this purpose, one can treat ',' as string concatenation, pad the resultant string to make it compliant to the hash function, and truncate the digest to d-bit. $\mathcal{H}(\cdot)$ can also be constructed using a set of random tables (especially if d is a few bit long), or using the truncated output of an encryption or signature function. The bitwise XOR function however, does *not* satisfy Property 1 and collisions will propagate (i. e., remain undetected) with probability 1.

If SHA-256 type hash function is used, then new fragments must be prepended to the existing string of fragments. We explain this requirement in the following. Due to the Merkle-Damgård construction, SHA-256 computes the digest from an input iteratively, by taking 512-bit at a time. Let s_1 and s_2 be two bit strings that are multiples of 512-bit[2] with $s_1 \neq s_2$. Let s_3 be another bit string of arbitrary length. If a collision occurs, namely $\mathcal{H}(s_1) = \mathcal{H}(s_2)$, then we also get another collision $\mathcal{H}(s_1, s_3) = \mathcal{H}(s_2, s_3)$. Therefore, to avoid this problem and to cause re-computation of the whole chain of compression functions inside SHA-256, new fragments must be prepended.

Note that Property 1 does not imply one-wayness, second pre-image resistance, or conventional collision-resistance of $\mathcal{H}(\cdot)$. This is important because, for the link layer, we consider a computationally unbounded adversary, for whom these assumptions may not hold. With a small value of d, such as 4 bits, the standard assumptions of a hash function are not even realistic for a computationally limited adversary.

---

[2] The internal "chunk size" of SHA-256 and SHA-512 is 512 bit.

If the fragments are very short and the adversary can introduce a large number of parallel fragments, a single link certificate may not be enough to detect collisions efficiently. This problem can be addressed by using $\alpha > 1$ link certificates; we call α *amplification factor*. With $\alpha = 2$, the encoding becomes: $m_1, l_2, l'_2, m_2, \ldots, m_m$. Each additional link certificate uses a different linking function. When we describe the receiver side, we assume $\alpha = 1$, but the results can be extended for $\alpha > 1$ and we investigate its impact on the performance of the CDP in § 6.

4.2 Receiver Side: Reception of Fragments

Handling of Fragment Loss and Fake Fragments. The CDP tolerates a situation in which up to a certain threshold of the transmitted fragments—typically half of them—get corrupted or lost due to adversarial jamming or channel characteristics. To achieve time synchronization, $\mathcal{R}$ uses a sliding-window technique to get alignment for the ΔT window, which can be achieved by repeating the decoding process $\rho/2$ times, possibly in parallel. To illustrate the decoding process, we consider two special cases of a receiver antenna. In both cases, the purpose is to make sure that a z-channel adversary can only make $\mathcal{R}$ accept, at most, one value per adversarial channel.

First, we consider a broadband antenna, namely $\mathcal{R}$ can receive data on all channels in parallel. In this case, the top $z + 1$ values that occur the most in ΔT are marked as received. Clearly, a z-channel adversary cannot make $\mathcal{R}$ to ignore the legitimate transmission, because for doing so the adversary would need to transmit $z + 1$ different values, such that each of them occurs at least ρ times.

In the second case, the receiver antenna is narrow-band, namely $\mathcal{R}$ can only receive on one or a few channels. In this case, our solution is very similar to the technique from [2, 9]: $\mathcal{R}$ listens on randomly selected channels. The probability that $\mathcal{R}$ listens on the correct channel(s) (where a fragment is being transmitted) is n'/n, where n is the total number of channels and n' is the number of channels where $\mathcal{R}$ can listen on in parallel. Since a fragment is repeated ρ times, $\mathcal{R}$ is expected to receive $\rho n'/n$ fragments. With an argument similar to the first case, the top $z + 1$ values occurring the most are marked as received. To make this scheme work, we further require $\rho \gg n/n'$ such that $\rho n'/n$ is sufficiently large (such as 32).

Receiver's Search Space. The described handling of arriving fragments during ΔT results in at most $z + 1$ fragments. In this way, $\mathcal{R}$ gets up to $z + 1$ fragments for each t_i. We use capital letters to denote variables corresponding to received fragments, e. g., M_1 where the first M-fragment is expected. Note that $\mathcal{R}$ does not have a-priori knowledge about the type of fragments it receives. The set of *received* fragments between t_i and $t_i + \Delta T$ is called the i-th *reception set*, denoted by σ_i. For a z-channel adversary, the size of a reception set is $|\sigma_i| \leq z + 1$, in which up to z fragments can be from the adversary. In the following, we denote the adversary's transmission schedule as $\mathbf{T}^{\mathcal{A}}$, where $\mathbf{T}^{\mathcal{A}}[i]$ is the set of M/L-fragments transmitted by $\mathcal{A}$ in the i-th time period.

To achieve fragment alignment, $\mathcal{R}$ makes a random guess to mark odd time instants for the reception of L-fragments and even time instants for the reception of M-fragments. The guess is correct if it matches the position of legitimate fragments. If the decoding fails, $\mathcal{R}$ switches the role of even and odd fragments. In this way, two

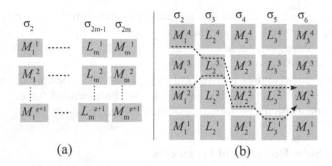

Fig. 4. (a) The search space $\mathcal{S}$ for a CDP receiver $\mathcal{R}$ (b) Two example paths: $\Pi_3 = M_1^2, L_2^3, M_2^4, L_3^1, M_3^2$ and $\Pi_3' = M_1^4, L_2^3, M_2^2, L_3^2, M_3^2$

decoding attempts are enough to achieve correct alignment. All received fragments are arranged in a search space:

Definition 1 (Search Space). *The search space is* $\mathcal{S} = [\sigma_1, \ldots, \sigma_{2m}]$, *where* $\sigma_{2i} = \mathbf{T}_m^{\mathcal{T}}[i] \cup \mathbf{T}_m^{\mathcal{A}}[i]$, *and* $\sigma_{2i-1} = \mathbf{T}_1^{\mathcal{T}}[i] \cup \mathbf{T}_1^{\mathcal{A}}[i]$, *for* $1 \leq i \leq m$.

As illustrated in Fig. 4-(a), reception sets on each odd index correspond to L-fragments and sets on each even index correspond to M-fragments. Certainly, an adversary does not need to abide by the rule and can transmit an L-fragment where an M-fragment is expected (and vice versa). This, however, does not help her because the linking function that connects L- and M-fragments is not symmetric, namely if $1_i = link(\mathbf{m}_1, \ldots, \mathbf{m}_i)$ holds then $\mathbf{m}_i \neq link(1_2, \ldots, 1_i)$.

4.3   Receiver Side: Decoding Algorithm

The receiver's goal is to efficiently identify the fragments of the legitimate transmission from the search space. For this purpose, we next introduce the notion of a *path*:

Definition 2 (Path). *Let* $L_i \in \sigma_{2i-1}$ *and* $M_i \in \sigma_{2i}$. *A path of length j is* $\Pi_j = M_1, L_2, \ldots, L_j, M_j$, *which is a sequence of j interleaved M-fragments and L-fragments, such that all the linking functions in Π_j can be verified.*

Two example paths are shown in Fig. 4-(b), one being $\Pi_3 = M_1^2, L_2^3, M_2^2, L_3^1, M_3^2$. The path Π_3 is tracked by verifying the relations $L_2^3 = \mathcal{H}(M_1^2, M_2^2)$ and $L_3^1 = \mathcal{H}(M_1^2, M_2^2, M_3^2)$. A complete path, Π_m, represents an entire CDP transmission, which is then considered as a candidate for the legitimate transmission $\mathbf{T}^{\mathcal{T}}$. A candidate message on which the signature verification succeeds represents $\mathbf{T}^{\mathcal{T}}$.

Algorithm. The CDP decoding algorithm—denoted by $search(\mathcal{S}, Pk_{\mathcal{T}})$—reassembles the legitimate message from all received fragments. Its inputs are the search space $\mathcal{S}$ and the sender's public key $Pk_{\mathcal{T}}$. The algorithm is based on a recursive depth-first search and terminates within a time polynomial in m and z, which we will prove in § 5.

Each of the M-fragments of $\mathcal{S}$ is associated with a visited-counter (v-counter), initialized to zero. Let θ be a constant representing the threshold (maximum) of the v-counters. Its value will be determined in § 5 in the security analysis.

The function $search(\cdot)$ consists of the following steps:

1. By exhaustive search, find the *roots* of all paths in $\mathcal{S}$. A root is a path of type $\Pi_2 = M_1, L_2, M_2$, where $L_2 = \mathcal{H}(M_1, M_2)$ for $M_1 \in \sigma_2$, $L_2 \in \sigma_3$, and $M_2 \in \sigma_4$.
2. Start a depth-first search (*dfs*) from each root path Π_2 found in Step 1 by calling a recursive function $b = dfs(\Pi_2)$ (defined below). If $b = 1$ then the legitimate message has been found, so terminate $search(\cdot)$ successfully. If $b = 0$, repeat Step 2 with a new root.
3. Terminate $search(\cdot)$ with an error signal.

The recursive function $b = dfs(\Pi_i)$ is defined as follows:

1. From the path Π_i of length i, compute a new *extended* path $\Pi_{i+1} = \Pi_i, L_{i+1}, M_{i+1}$, where $L_{i+1} = \mathcal{H}(M_1, \ldots, M_{i+1})$ for $L_{i+1} \in \sigma_{2i+1}$, and $M_{i+1} \in \sigma_{2i+2}$. If no such new pair (L_{i+1}, M_{i+1}) can be found then return 0.
2. If the v-counter associated with the new M-fragment M_{i+1} is equal to θ then backtrack to the path Π_i, i.e., go back to Step 1.
3. If the v-counter of M_{i+1} is less than θ then increment the v-counter. If $i + 1 = m$ go to Step 4; otherwise make a recursive call to compute b: $b = dfs(\Pi_{i+1})$. If the returned value b is 0 (indicating a failure to find the legitimate message) then backtrack, i.e., go back to Step 1. If $b = 1$ then return 1.
4. The path is complete. Extract the message from path Π_m. Verify the signature of the message. If the signature verification fails then backtrack to Step 1. If the signature verification succeeds (meaning that this is a legitimate path) then return 1.

Running Time. We derive an upper bound on the running time of the decoding algorithm $search(\cdot)$. Let T_l be the time to compute the hash function $\mathcal{H}(\cdot)$. In $\mathcal{S}$, an upper bound on the number of root paths is $(z + 1)^2$. Each root path requires one computation of the hash function. Therefore, in Step 1 of $search(\cdot)$, the upper bound on the time to compute all root paths is $(z + 1)^2 T_l$.

For Step 2 of $search(\cdot)$, each M-fragment in $\mathcal{S}$ is associated with a v-counter that is upper-bounded by θ. Therefore, each M-fragment can cause at most θ computations of the hash function. The total number of M-fragments in $\mathcal{S}$ is $m(z + 1)$. Hence, the time to compute Step 2 of $search(\cdot)$ is $m\theta(z + 1)T_l$. Due to our repetition scheme (Fig. 3), the decoding process may need to be repeated ρ times. An upper bound on the running time of the algorithm is, therefore, as follows:

$$\tau_r < \rho\big(m\theta(z + 1) + (z + 1)^2\big)T_l. \tag{1}$$

Since the hash function is efficiently computable, T_l represents a polynomial time. If θ is polynomial in m then the running time of the decoding algorithm, τ_r, has an upper bound that is polynomial in z and m, as given by Eq. 1.

Clearly, if we do not set a threshold, i.e., $\theta = \infty$, then the decoding algorithm reduces to an exhaustive search, which may require an exponential amount of time. On the other hand, if the number of fake paths is small then θ can be set to a small number. In the next section, we show that there is indeed a limit on the number of fake paths, which allows us to determine the value of θ, thus guaranteeing that the legitimate message can be reassembled efficiently.

5   Security Analysis

We now show that our protocol cannot be successfully attacked on the link layer.

5.1   Definitions

Security of the CDP is defined as adversary's inability to jam a legitimate transmission.

Definition 3 (Security of CDP). *The CDP protocol is secure if a z-channel adversary, under Assumptions 1-2, cannot prevent the CDP receiver $\mathcal{R}$ from receiving and reassembling a legitimate message, consisting of m fragments, within an amount of time that is polynomial in m and z.*

As described earlier, with an appropriate value of d, radio level jamming by $\mathcal{A}$ can be prevented. At the link layer, however, $\mathcal{A}$ may prevent $\mathcal{R}$ from reassembling a legitimate message. To show the link layer security, namely the efficiency of reassembly process, the notion of collision is important, and in the following we formally define this notion. Let $\Pi_{i \to j}$, with $i < j$, denote a partial path from L_i, M_i to L_j, M_j.

Definition 4 (Collision). *Consider two paths Π_j and Π'_j in a search space. We can write the two paths as $\Pi_j = \Pi_i, \Pi_{i+1 \to j}$ and $\Pi'_j = \Pi'_i, \Pi'_{i+1 \to j}$, for $i < j$. The path Π'_j is said to generate a (i, Π_j)-collision in Π_j if $\Pi_{i+1 \to j} \overset{m}{=} \Pi'_{i+1 \to j}$ and $\Pi_i \overset{m}{\neq} \Pi'_i$, where $\overset{m}{=}$ means that the corresponding M-fragments in two paths are equal.*

For example, in Fig. 4, the two paths are $\Pi_3 = M_1^2, L_2^3, M_2^2, L_3^1, M_3^2$ and $\Pi'_3 = M_1^4, L_2^3, M_2^2, L_3^2, M_3^2$. The path Π'_3 creates a $(1, \Pi_3)$-collision in Π_3, and the path Π_3 creates a $(1, \Pi'_3)$-collision in Π'_3. From Def. 4 it is clear that a (i, Π_j)-collision implies (i, Π_{i+1})-, ..., (i, Π_{j-1})-collisions, e.g., in Fig. 4 the $(1, \Pi_3)$-collision implies the $(1, \Pi_2)$-collision. If one of the (i, Π_{i+1})-, ..., (i, Π_{j-1})-collisions does not occur then a (i, Π_j)-collision cannot occur. This fact is later used in the security proof.

In Def. 4, a (i, Π_j)-collision can be generated due to an adversarial strategy or purely by chance. When the subsequent pair of fragments are added to the path, i.e., Π_j grows to Π_{j+1}, the (i, Π_j)-collision can only propagate to the (i, Π_{j+1})-collision with a probability that is negligible in d. This happens due to Property 1 of our linking function $\mathcal{H}(\cdot)$, and we formally prove this fact. The low probability of collision propagation is exemplified below.

Example 1. *Consider a legitimate path, $\Pi_2 = M_1, L_2, M_2$, and a 1-channel adversary who generates a $(1, \Pi_2)$-collision. For this purpose, she computes M'_1, L'_2, such that $M'_1 \neq M_1$ and $L'_2 = \mathcal{H}(M'_1, M_2)$. In this way, her fake path merges into Π_2, but a propagation of the $(1, \Pi_2)$-collision to a $(1, \Pi_3)$-collision requires $L_3 = \mathcal{H}(M'_1, M_2, M_3)$. Since M_3 was not sent by $\mathcal{T}$ when the $(1, \Pi_2)$-collision was generated, M_3 was unknown to her for $(1, \Pi_2)$-collision. Due to Property 1, she can only guess the value of L_3 (or M_3) with probability 2^{-d}. Hence, L_3 cannot be used by the adversary to generate a $(1, \Pi_2)$-collision. The probability of a successful propagation of the $(1, \Pi_2)$-collision to a $(2, \Pi_3)$-collision is thus 2^{-d}. The probability of propagation decreases further as more L-fragments are added to the legitimate path.* ∎

On the other hand, $\mathcal{A}$ can create both collisions and forks between her own z paths, which may result in an exponential number of fake paths. Therefore, our decoding algorithm (§ 4.3) uses v-counters for the M-fragments when exploring the search space. Each time a path from the search space is decoded, the v-counters associated with the path are incremented. If a counter reaches the threshold θ, the associated M-fragment is not used in the subsequent decoding process. In this way, the M-fragments of the adversary start becoming unavailable as the decoding proceeds.

We proceed in two steps. First, we model a *benign adversary*, who relies on the transmission of random messages as attack strategy, and quantify an upper bound on the probability of collisions in the search space (Claims 1 and 2). Later we quantify the advantage of a computationally unbounded adversary over the benign adversary (Claim 3), which brings us finally to argue on the security of our protocol (Claim 4).

Definition 5 (Random Transmission). *The random transmission of a benign adversary is* $\mathbf{T}^{rnd} = [\mathbf{T}_l^{rnd}[i], \mathbf{T}_m^{rnd}[i] : 1 \leq i \leq m]$, *where* $\mathbf{T}_m^{rnd}[i]$ *is a set consisting of* z *(uniformly distributed) d-bit random strings and* $\mathbf{T}_l^{rnd}[i]$ *is a set consisting of the i-th L-fragments of the link certificates of* $\mathbf{T}_m^{rnd}$.

Claim 1. *Let* Π_j^T *be the path of the legitimate transmission. For a z-channel benign adversary under Assumption 2 (i. e., with $z(z+1) < 2^d$), the following relation holds for $i < j \leq m$ and $\eta = (1+z)2^{-d}$:*
$$\text{Number of } (i, \Pi_j^T)\text{-collisions} \leq 2z\eta^{j-i}.$$

Claim 2. *The total number of collisions in a partial legitimate path Π_j^T in the presence of* $\mathbf{T}^{rnd}$ *is* $\aleph_j^{rnd} < 2z\eta(j-1)$.

Claim 3. *The total number of collisions in a partial legitimate path Π_j^T in the presence of* $\mathbf{T}^{\mathcal{A}}$, *which is due to a computationally unbounded adversary $\mathcal{A}$, is* $\aleph_j^{\mathcal{A}} \leq \aleph_j^{rnd} + z$.

The proofs of Claims 1, 2, and 3 can be found in Appendix A.

Claim 4. *The transmission* $\mathbf{T}^T$ *of the CD protocol as specified in § 4.1 is secure as per Def. 3.*

Proof. From Eq. 1, we know that an upper bound on the running time of the decoding algorithm is $\rho(m\theta(z+1) + (z+1)^2)T_l$. The term T_l (the time to compute a link) is polynomial in m, due to our choice of a hash function as a linking function. The only unknown value is the threshold θ, which we determine in the following.

Using Claim 3, we can calculate an upper bound on the number of collisions into a legitimate full path Π_m. A fragment on a path Π_m can be visited by the decoding algorithm not only by full-length fake paths but also by partial fake paths (of length less than m). Therefore, an upper bound on the threshold θ is the total number of paths that can pass through a legitimate fragment:

$$\theta \leq \sum_{j=2}^{m} \aleph_j^{\mathcal{A}} + 1 = 2z\eta[1 + 2 + \cdots + (m-1)] + z + 1 = z\eta m(m-1) + z + 1. \quad (2)$$

Here, the constant 1 is due to the legitimate path itself. Clearly, the upper-bound is polynomial in m and z. Hence, with $\theta = z\eta m(m-1) + z + 1$ the decoding is guaranteed to succeed in polynomial time in the adversarial environment.

6 Performance Evaluation

We evaluate the theoretical results by a simulation that addresses the link-layer reassembly process on the receiver side. Physical-layer issues, such as signal strengths, modulation types, and the actual transmission of the signals are not part of this simulation.

Setup. The simulation code is written in C and is parameterizable for the adversarial power (z), length of fragments (d), number of fragments (m), and amplification factor (α). The simulation randomly generates a legitimate message consisting of m fragments and mixes the message with z other random messages to simulate the benign adversary[3]. The resulting search space has $(z+1)^m$ plausible combinations to search for a legitimate message. For a typical set of values, say $z = 2$ and $m = 128$, the infeasibility to explore this search space is clear.

The CDP protocol makes the search of the legitimate message tractable. To demonstrate this, we encode the legitimate message as per the CDP protocol. The linking function in the simulation is the truncated output of SHA-256. The CDP decoder efficiently reassembles all CDP messages from the search space. The output consists of one legitimate message, z adversarial messages, and a small number of accidental messages formed by pure chance. In the simulation, this whole process is called a *run*.

Metrics. We consider three metrics to demonstrate the performance of the CDP. The first one is Ω, the number of fake paths per legitimate path in a given search space. This metric is independent of the computer and language used to implement the CDP. The second metric is the running time τ_r of the decoding algorithm, which depends on the computer used for the simulation; in our case, it is a Thinkpad T400s laptop with 3GB memory and P9400 Intel Core 2 processor at 2.4GHz clock. This measure is machine specific and should be interpreted in a relative sense. The third metric is the maximum value of θ (see § 4.3), which determines the theoretical upper bound on the running time of the decoding algorithm, as per Eq. 1.

To get statistically significant measurements, each of the presented results is based on 10,000 independent simulation runs. We report three values over these 10,000 samples: the minimum value Ω_{min}, the arithmetic mean Ω_{avg}, and the maximum value Ω_{max}. Alongside, we also report the values of the standard deviation (SD) and the 95% confidence intervals (CI).

Results. The first set of results shown in Table 2a indicates the variation of Ω with respect to z. In this set, the message size is 768-bit, which is divided into 128 fragments of 6 bits. In these simulation runs, one link certificate is used $(\alpha = 1)$. The results show that Ω increases with z, but it remains tractable as long as the threshold $z(z + 1) < 2^d$ (cf. Assumption 1) is respected, which occurs at $z = 7$ in this case. Furthermore, the value of θ is consistent with the theoretical upper bound of Eq. 2.[4]

---

[3] From Claim 3, we know that a reactive adversary can generate at most z additional fake paths compared to the benign adversary. Hence, we can limit the simulation to the benign adversary for the performance evaluation and there from derive the results for the worst-case adversary.

[4] The upper bound of θ in Eq. 2 is large when compared to the actual value of θ reported in Table 2a. This is due to the extensive use of over-approximations in our security analysis.

Table 1. Performance results

z	0	1	2	3	4	5	6	7
Ω_{min}	1	2	3	4	5	6	8	37
Ω_{avg}	1	2.067	3.329	4.98	7.435	11.9	23.3	132.34
Ω_{max}	1	4	7	11	17	24	56	351
SD	0	0.256	0.565	0.997	1.637	2.81	5.94	44.968
95% CI	1–1	2–3	3–5	4–7	5–11	7–18	13–36	63–234
θ	1	2	3	4	5	6	9	32
τ_r [ms]	0.57	1.71	3.71	6.68	11.68	21.17	47.59	261.75

α	1	2	3	4	5	6
Ω_{min}	33	8	8	8	8	8
Ω_{avg}	131.66	8.8751	8.0943	8.0104	8.0011	8.0002
Ω_{max}	419	14	10	9	9	9
SD	46.228	0.9221	0.3082	0.1014	0.0331	0.0141
95% CI	62–238	8–11	8–9	8–8	8–8	8–8
θ	30	3	2	2	1	1
τ_r [ms]	308.75	177.17	289.0	437.667	562.5	711

(a) z =variable, $d = 6$, $m = 128$, $\alpha = 1$ (b) α =variable, $d = 6$, $m = 128$, $z = 7$

The second set of results is shown in Table 2b and indicates the variation of Ω with respect to the amplification factor α, for a 7-channel adversary. Once again, the message size is 768-bit divided into 128 fragments of 6-bit each. Ideally, there should be 8 paths, i. e., $\Omega = 8$, corresponding to one legitimate and 7 adversarial paths. As expected, the value of Ω quickly converges to 8 with an increase in α. In this particular configuration, $\alpha = 2$ is optimum for the decoding time. These simulation runs demonstrate that the use of additional link certificates can improve the security level of the CDP, however, increasing α too much can in turn degrade the decoding time, due to software overhead.

The third set of results is shown in Table 2 and indicates the variation of Ω with respect to the fragment size d. In these simulation runs, we use a 7-channel adversary and one link certificate. The message size is $128d$, which is formatted as 128 fragments of d bits. The results show that increasing d also increases the security level, namely the number of fake paths decreases. This is due to the

Table 2. Performance results for d =variable, $\alpha = 1$, $m = 128$, $z = 7$

d	6	7	8	9	10	11	12	13
Ω_{min}	37	8	8	8	8	8	8	8
Ω_{avg}	132.339	14.674	10.291	9.007	8.467	8.223	8.113	8.053
Ω_{max}	351	28	17	15	12	11	11	10
SD	44.9682	2.9075	1.5322	1.0103	0.6836	0.467	0.339	0.233
95% CI	63–234	10–21	8–14	8–11	8–10	8–9	8–9	8–9
θ	32	6	4	3	3	2	2	2
τ_r [ms]	261.75	34.9	33.867	30.788	29.457	29.0	28.67	28.64

fact that by increasing d the threshold on z also increases, due to the relation $z(z+1) < 2^d$. We also note that the machine we use for testing has a 32-bit architecture, which means increasing d from 6 to 13 does not significantly increase the software overhead, because each fragment is internally stored as a 32-bit memory word. Therefore, the decrease in τ_r is almost entirely due to a decrease in the number of fake paths.

Security Performance Trade-Off. The CD protocol allows trade-offs between security and performance by changing d, α, and the linking function. As a typical design flow, consider a reactive adversary who takes at least $10\mu s$ to sense and jam an active SS channel. If each of the channels supports a data rate of $800\text{-}kbps$ or more then it is safe to assume that 8 bits cannot be deterministically jammed within a $1\text{-}\mu s$ window, which implies $d \leq 8$-bit. From the threshold $z(z+1) < 2^d$, we can derive the maximum value of z to be $z \leq 15$. Since z is the ratio of the absolute power (in Watts) of the adversary's antenna to that of $\mathcal{T}$'s antenna, $\mathcal{T}$'s transmission power can be changed to an optimal level that meets the constraint of $z \leq 15$, as proposed by Xu et al. [16].

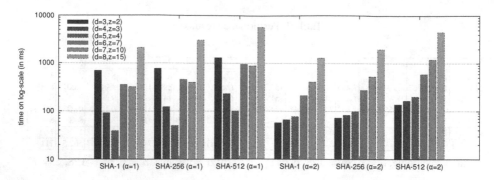

Fig. 5. Visualization of security and performance trade-offs. For the left three sets of data, $\alpha = 1$, for the right three, $\alpha = 2$. The parameters d and z respectively model the levels of protection against reactive and pollution attacks (the smaller d and the larger z, the more protection the scheme provides). The decoding times are specific for our implementation; they must be interpreted in a relative sense. The message size in all these cases is about 1024-bit: for instance, $m = 128$ for $d = 8$, and $m = 171$ for $d = 6$.

The next step is the design of a CDP receiver with $z \leq 15$ and $d \leq 8$. Fig. 5 shows how different linking functions and values of α change the decoding time in our simulation. The best decoding time is achieved with SHA-1, $\alpha = 1$, $d = 5$ for a 4-channel adversary with a $1ms$ reaction time. Fig. 5 also shows that the use of more than one link ($\alpha \geq 2$) is beneficial if the fragment length d is very small and that the selection of the hash-function may have a non-negligible impact on overall running time.

7   Related Work

Many protocols have been proposed for uncoordinated anti-jamming communication. Many of these protocols [17–19] assume that packets of arbitrary size can be received with a certain probability, which, however, is only realistic if the jammer is non-reactive or the combined transmission power of senders is greater than that of the jammer.

The first scheme for keyless anti-jamming broadcast was proposed in 2007 by Baird *et al.* [3] using concurrent codes. Its security depends on the pre-image resistance of the hash function and the adversary's inability to delete or overshadow 1s in transmitted packets. For impulse radios employing time hopping [20], this scheme is promising; for DSSS and FHSS, however, it requires specialized radio transceivers.

Strasser *et al.* [1] propose a scheme for UFH using the hash function to achieve anti-jamming key-establishment. The fragment sizes of this scheme are in the order of hundreds of bits, e. g., SHA-1 based fragments are to be longer than 160 bits. Since the security of this scheme depends on the computational power of the adversary, a truncated hash of a small size, such as 16 bit, will make the scheme insecure.

To make the solutions more efficient, Strasser *et al.* [9], Slater *et al.* [10], and Pöpper *et al.* [2] propose alternatives to the hashes, but the fragment size remains a limiting factor. For example, for the scheme using short signatures based on bilinear maps [9], the linking information is $4k$-bit, where k is the security level, again resulting in packets of few hundred bits (even for short-term security levels). The decoding of messages in these schemes is (partially) offline. The decoding process in our protocol is online, i. e., the decoding can start as soon as fragments are arriving. Wang *et al.* [21] model UFH transmissions as a multi-armed bandit problem. Since they assume the same verification schemes as proposed by Strasser *et al.* [1, 9], this scheme is vulnerable to reactive jamming due to long packets. In our protocol, the requirement $z(z + 1) < 2^d$ implies the fragment size to be $2log_2(z + 1)$-bit (e.g., 2-bit for $z = 1$). This means that a single hop in FHSS systems or a sequence of codes in DSSS systems is used to transmit only $2log_2(z + 1)$ bits, thus allowing a higher switching frequency.

As an alternative to UFH, Pöpper *et al.* [22] propose a UDSSS scheme that transmits messages of fixed length without splitting them into fragments; large messages and reactive jammers are also a problem for this scheme. Jin *et al.* [23] propose a DSSS-based scheme using time-reversed message extraction and key scheduling. This scheme can only be applied for a known receiver, it requires offline decoding, and the size of the first fragment is half of the full message size. Liu *et al.* propose a UDSSS protocol based on the theory of finite projective planes [24] and another protocol called randomized differential (RD)-DSSS [4]. Both are quite robust against reactive jammers, but cannot directly be applied to FHSS-based communication. RD-DSSS assumes a computationally bounded adversary, as opposed to our CDP.

Xu *et al.* [25] propose the use of timing-based covert channels for anti-jamming transmission. They, however, assume that the transmission power of an adversary is comparable to that of a legitimate transmitter, i. e., $z \approx 1$. To cope with insertion or pollution attacks, where an adversary transmits fake packets, the authors assume shared secrets. Xiao *et al.* [5] propose a UFH-based broadcast scheme that assumes collaboration of receivers, namely after having received a message the receiver helps to broadcast it to other receivers. This is orthogonal to our work. Strasser *et al.* [26] propose a complementary technique to detect jamming attacks using received signal strength. If the presence of a jammer is detected then the receiver can take additional countermeasures, such as changing the location to reduce the strength of the jamming signals. In contrast to BitTrickle proposed by Liu *et al.* [12], our protocol does not rely on physical-layer authentication approaches to verify individual bits nor on specific hardware.

Xu *et al.* [16] propose an adaptive protocol for point-to-point UFH transmission, which is modelled as a game played between a sender, a receiver, and a jammer. The transmission power of the transmitter and jammer may vary. As compared to our solution, the jammer is assumed to be weaker, not being able to jam in the current time-slot. The authors assume bi-directional, time-slotted communication between the sender and receiver, in which the sender can always receive acknowledgement (ACK) from the receiver in the same time-slot and frequency channel.

8   Conclusion

Avoiding DoS-threats is important for all dependable wireless networks. USS protocols are link-layer protocols that are required in situations where parties who do not share a secret need to communicate under the threat of (reactive) jamming attacks. Existing USS protocols, however, are not effective enough against fast reactive jammers due to their dependency on long fragments. In this context, the presented protocol is the first USS protocol that supports short fragments of a few bits. Our protocol uses the idea of collision detection to efficiently link legitimate fragments, even when the jammer pollutes the communication channels with a large number of fake fragments using concurrent transmissions. We hope that the presented protocol will serve as an important technique for bootstrapping spread spectrum communication in cases where shared secrets do not exist or have been compromised.

References

1. Strasser, M., Pöpper, C., Capkun, S., Cagalj, M.: Jamming-resistant key establishment using uncoordinated frequency hopping. In: Proc. of S&P, pp. 64–78. IEEE (2008)
2. Pöpper, C., Strasser, M., Capkun, S.: Anti-jamming broadcast communication using uncoordinated spread spectrum techniques. IEEE Journal on Selected Areas in Communications 28(5), 703–715 (2010)
3. Baird, L., Bahn, W., Collins, M., Carlisle, M., Butler, S.: Keyless jam resistance. In: Information Assurance and Security Workshop (IAW), pp. 143–150. IEEE (2007)
4. Liu, Y., Ning, P., Dai, H., Liu, A.: Randomized differential DSSS: Jamming-resistant wireless broadcast communication. In: Proceedings of INFOCOM, pp. 1–9. IEEE (2010)
5. Xiao, L., Dai, H., Ning, P.: Jamming-resistant collaborative broadcast using uncoordinated frequency hopping. IEEE Trans. on Information Forensics & Security 7(1), 297–309 (2012)
6. Hamilton, S., Hamilton, J.: Secure jam resistant key transfer: Using the DOD CAC card to secure a radio link by employing the BBC jam resistant algorithm. In: Military Communications Conference (MILCOM), pp. 1–7. IEEE (2008)
7. Wilhelm, M., Martinovic, I., Schmitt, J., Lenders, V.: Short paper: Reactive jamming in wireless networks. In: Proc. of WiSec, pp. 47–52. ACM (2011)
8. Wilhelm, M., Martinovic, I., Schmitt, J., Lenders, V.: Wifire: a firewall for wireless networks. In: Proceedings of the ACM SIGCOMM Conference, pp. 456–457. ACM (2011)
9. Strasser, M., Pöpper, C., Capkun, S.: Efficient uncoordinated FHSS anti-jamming communication. In: Proc. of MobiHoc, pp. 207–218. ACM (2009)
10. Slater, D., Tague, P., Poovendran, R., Matt, B.J.: A coding-theoretic approach for efficient message verification over insecure channels. In: Proc. of WiSec, pp. 151–160. ACM (2009)
11. Slater, D., Poovendran, R., Tague, P., Matt, B.J.: Tradeoffs between jamming resilience and communication efficiency in key establishment. SIGMOBILE Mobile Computing and Communications Review 13, 14–25 (2009)
12. Liu, Y., Ning, P.: BitTrickle: Defending against broadband and high-power reactive jamming attacks. In: Proceedings of INFOCOM, pp. 909–917. IEEE (2012)
13. Cabric, D., Tkachenko, A., Brodersen, R.W.: Experimental study of spectrum sensing based on energy detection and network cooperation. In: Proc. of TAPAS. ACM (2006)
14. Bhargava, V.: Forward error correction schemes for digital communications. IEEE Communications Magazine 21(1), 11–19 (1983)
15. Goldwasser, S., Micali, S.: Probabilistic encryption. Journal of Computer and System Sciences 28(2), 270–299 (1984)
16. Xu, K., Wang, Q., Ren, K.: Joint UFH and power control for effective wireless anti-jamming communication. In: Proceedings of INFOCOM, pp. 738–746. IEEE (2012)
17. Awerbuch, B., Richa, A., Scheideler, C.: A jamming-resistant MAC protocol for single-hop wireless networks. In: Proc. of PODC, pp. 45–54. ACM (2008)
18. Dolev, S., Gilbert, S., Guerraoui, R., Newport, C.: Gossiping in a multi-channel radio network. In: Pelc, A. (ed.) DISC 2007. LNCS, vol. 4731, pp. 208–222. Springer, Heidelberg (2007)

19. Dolev, S., Gilbert, S., Guerraoui, R., Newport, C.: Secure communication over radio channels. In: Proc. of ACM Symp. on Principles of Distributed Computing, pp. 105–114 (2008)
20. Win, M., Scholtz, R.: Impulse radio: How it works. IEEE Communications Letters 2(2),
36–38 (1998)
21. Wang, Q., Xu, P., Ren, K., Li, X.: Towards optimal adaptive UFH-based anti-jamming wireless communication. Journal on Selected Areas in Communications 30(1), 16–30 (2012)
22. Pöpper, C., Strasser, M., Capkun, S.: Jamming-resistant broadcast communication without
shared keys. In: Proceedings of the USENIX Security Symposium, pp. 231–247 (2009)
23. Jin, T., Noubir, G., Thapa, B.: Zero pre-shared secret key establishment in the presence of
jammers. In: Proc. of MobiHoc, pp. 219–228. ACM (2009)
24. Liu, A., Ning, P., Dai, H., Liu, Y., Wang, C.: Defending DSSS-based broadcast communication against insider jammers via delayed seed-disclosure. In: Proceedings of the 26th Annual
Computer Security Applications Conference, pp. 367–376. ACM (2010)
25. Xu, W., Trappe, W., Zhang, Y.: Anti-jamming timing channels for wireless networks. In:
Proceedings of Wireless Network Security (WiSec), pp. 203–213. ACM (2008)
26. Strasser, M., Danev, B., Capkun, S.: Detection of reactive jamming in sensor networks. ACM
Transactions on Sensor Networks (TOSN) 7(2), 16 (2010)

A   Proofs of Claims

A.1   Proof of Claim 1

Proof. Let p_j be the probability of a $(i, \Pi_j^{\mathcal{T}})$-collision due to one fake path Π_i'. Let q_i be the total number of fake paths of length i; each of the q_i paths can cause a $(i, \Pi_j^{\mathcal{T}})$-collision. Therefore, we have

$$\text{Number of } (i, \Pi_j^{\mathcal{T}})\text{-collisions} \le p_j q_i. \tag{3}$$

We next determine the values of p_j and q_i.

Value of p_j: According to Def. 4, a $(i, \Pi_j^{\mathcal{T}})$-collision occurs if a fake path Π_j' merges into the legitimate path $\Pi_j^{\mathcal{T}}$ after index i, i.e., $\Pi_{i+1 \to j}' = \Pi_{i+1 \to j}^{\mathcal{T}}$. By definition, a $(i, \Pi_j^{\mathcal{T}})$-collision implies $(i, \Pi_{i+1}^{\mathcal{T}})$, $\ldots$, $(i, \Pi_j^{\mathcal{T}})$-collisions. The required conditions corresponding to these collisions, $\Re_{i+1} \ldots \Re_j$ are as follows:

$$\Re_{i+1} \stackrel{\text{def}}{=} \exists L_{i+1} \in \sigma_{2i+1} : L_{i+1} = \mathcal{H}(M_1, \ldots, M_{i+1}) = \mathcal{H}(M_1', \ldots, M_i', M_{i+1})$$
$$\vdots \tag{4}$$
$$\Re_j \stackrel{\text{def}}{=} \exists L_j \in \sigma_{2j-1} : L_j = \mathcal{H}(M_1, \ldots, M_j) = \mathcal{H}(M_1', \ldots, M_i', M_{i+1}, \ldots, M_j).$$

Here, $\{M_i, M_i'\} \subseteq \sigma_{2i}$ and $\{M_j\} \subseteq \sigma_{2j}$. Let $p_{i+1}, \ldots, p_j$ be the probabilities corresponding to the $(i, \Pi_{i+1}^{\mathcal{T}}), \ldots, (i, \Pi_j^{\mathcal{T}})$-collisions. First we claim that $p_{i+1} \le \eta$ because a path Π_i' can use any of the L_{i+1} in σ_{2i+1} to cause a $(i, \Pi_{i+1}^{\mathcal{T}})$-collision. For a given value of L_{i+1}, the collision probability is 2^{-d} due to Property 1 of the linking function. We have $|\sigma_{2i+1}| = z + 1$, therefore, $p_{i+1} \le (z+1)2^{-d} = \eta$. On the next pair of fragments, once again for $z + 1$ values of L_{i+2}, we have $Pr[(i, \Pi_{i+2}^{\mathcal{T}})\text{-collision}| (i, \Pi_{i+1}^{\mathcal{T}})\text{-collision}] \le \eta$. Thus, $p_{i+2} = p_{i+1} \cdot Pr[(i, \Pi_{i+2}^{\mathcal{T}})$

Table 3. Maximum number (#) of fake paths along the legitimate path

Index i	1	2	3	$\mid\ldots\mid$	$j-1$
q_i (max. # of fake paths of length i)	z	$\leq z + \frac{1}{2}z = \frac{3}{2}z$	$\leq z + \frac{3}{4}z = \frac{7}{4}z$	$\ldots$	$\leq (\frac{2^{j-1}-1}{2^{j-2}})z$
Prob. of (i, Π_{i+1})-collision per fake path	$p_{i+1} \leq \eta \leq \frac{1}{2}$	$p_{i+1} \leq \eta \leq \frac{1}{2}$	$p_{i+1} \leq \eta \leq \frac{1}{2}$	$\ldots$	$p_{i+1} \leq \eta \leq \frac{1}{2}$
Total # of (i, Π_{i+1})-collisions	$\leq \eta z = \frac{1}{2}z$	$\leq \frac{3}{4}z$	$\leq \frac{7}{8}z$	$\ldots$	$\leq (\frac{2^{j-1}-1}{2^{j-1}})z$

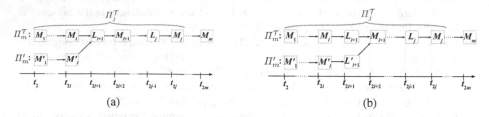

(a)   (b)

Fig. 6. Long and short fragment transmissions. (a) Long fragments are an easy target for jammers. Reactive jammers will have sufficient time to sense an ongoing transmission and then react to (deterministically) jam the used channel. Sweep (non-reactive) jammers have a high probability of hitting the channel where a long fragment is transmitted. (b) Short fragments reduce the risk of successful jamming attacks for both reactive and non-reactive sweep jammers.

-collision$|$ (i, Π_{i+1}^{T})-collision$] \leq \eta^2$. Re-applying the above arguments until index j, we get this result:

$$p_j \leq \eta^{j-i}. \tag{5}$$

Value of q_i: We assume $z(z + 1) < 2^d$, which implies $\eta \leq 1/2$.[5] Table 3 shows upper bounds on the value of q_i (the number of fake paths of length i). For the first pair of fragments, there are no collisions, but there are z adversarial paths due to $\mathcal{T}^{rnd}$, thus $q_1 = z$. Next, q_2 is the sum of the number of $(1, \Pi_2)$-collisions and the number of adversarial paths (z). Repeating this procedure, we can calculate the rest of the table. For convenience, we use a simpler expression $2z$ to represent an upper bound on q_i:

$$q_i \leq (\frac{2^{j-1} - 1}{2^{j-2}})z < 2z. \tag{6}$$

Substituting Eq. 5 and Eq. 6 in Eq. 3 proves the claim.

---

[5] Solving η from $z(z + 1) < 2^d$ results in $\eta < 1/z$. Clearly, for $z > 1$, we have $\eta \leq 1/2$. For the remaining two values, $z = 1$ and $z = 0$, the minimum values of d that satisfy the relation $z(z + 1) < 2^d$ are 1 and 2 respectively, which implies that $\eta = 1/2$ for these two values.

A.2   Proof of Claim 2

Proof. An upper bound on $\aleph_j^{rnd}$ is obtained by summing up all collisions on path $\Pi_j^{\mathcal{T}}$:

$$\aleph_j^{rnd} \leq \sum_{i=1}^{j-1} \text{Number of } (i, \Pi_j^{\mathcal{T}})\text{-collisions} = \sum_{i=1}^{j-1} q_i p_j \quad \text{(using Claim 1)}$$

$$< \sum_{i=1}^{j-1} 2z\eta^{j-i} = 2z\eta^j \left[\eta^{-1} + \eta^{-2} + \cdots + \eta^{-(j-1)} \right]$$

$$< 2z\eta^j \left[\eta^{-(j-1)} + \cdots + \eta^{-(j-1)} \right] = 2z\eta(j-1).$$

This completes the proof.

A.3   Proof of Claim 3

Proof. The proof is based on the following observation: The adversary is constrained by the fact that she must send her fragment at t_i before receiving $\mathcal{T}$'s fragment at t_{i+1} because fragments are transmitted in order. The conditions to create collisions are the same as in Eq. 4. There are two cases of collisions, which we analyze in the following.

First, we consider case (a) of the $(i, \Pi_j^{\mathcal{T}})$-collision as shown in Fig. 6-(a). Here, the fragment M_{i+1} is unknown before t_{2i+1} and, hence, the output of the linking function, L_{i+1}, appears as a random value to the adversary. Before t_{2i+1}, there is no strategy to generate $[M_1', \ldots, M_i']$ deterministically in such a way that a collision can be created.

Next, we consider case (b) of the collision, as in Fig. 6-(b). We analyze the situation at t_{2i+1} when $\mathcal{T}$ transmits L_{i+1}. On reading L_{i+1}, the adversary's task is to generate L_{i+1}' such that the condition $\Re_{i+1}$ holds. The condition $\Re_{i+1}$ can be satisfied by computing a new L_{i+1}', but a z-channel adversary cannot generate more than z values of L-fragments at a time. Therefore, $\mathcal{A}$ can only create z number of $(i, \Pi_{i+1}^{\mathcal{T}})$-collisions.

If the adversary is not active at t_{2i+3}, a $(i, \Pi_{i+1}^{\mathcal{T}})$-collision cannot deterministically propagate to a $(i, \Pi_{i+2}^{\mathcal{T}})$-collision because, at t_{2i+1}, the value of M_{i+2} (required to compute L_{i+2}) is still unknown. If the adversary is active at t_{2i+3}, the above arguments for $\Re_{i+1}$ can be applied to $\Re_{i+2}$ to generate either a new $(i+1, \Pi_{i+2}^{\mathcal{T}})$-collision or make a $(i, \Pi_{i+1}^{\mathcal{T}})$-collision propagate as a $(i, \Pi_{i+2}^{\mathcal{T}})$-collision. The same arguments can be applied for the rest of the conditions up to $\Re_j$.

Therefore, we conclude that the best $\mathcal{A}$ can do is to create z number of $(i, \Pi_j^{\mathcal{T}})$-collisions. Creating z collisions, however, does not affect the number of collisions that are inherently present in the search space due to random transmission, because any attack strategy can be considered as an instance of random transmissions in which the adversary provides the output of coin tosses. Hence, the total number of collisions is $\aleph_j^{\mathcal{A}} \leq \aleph_j^{rnd} + z$. This completes the proof.

Fingerprinting Far Proximity from Radio Emissions

Tao Wang, Yao Liu, and Jay Ligatti

University of South Florida, Tampa, FL 33620, USA
taow@mail.usf.edu, {yliu,ligatti}@cse.usf.edu

Abstract. As wireless mobile devices are more and more pervasive and adopted in critical applications, it is becoming increasingly important to measure the physical proximity of these devices in a secure way. Although various techniques have been developed to identify whether a device is close, the problem of identifying the *far proximity* (i.e., a target is at least a certain distance away) has been neglected by the research community. Meanwhile, verifying the far proximity is desirable and critical to enhance the security of emerging wireless applications. In this paper, we propose a secure far proximity identification approach that determines whether or not a remote device is far away. The key idea of the proposed approach is to estimate the far proximity from the unforgeable "fingerprint" of the proximity. We have validated and evaluated the effectiveness of the proposed far proximity identification method through experiments on real measured channel data. The experiment results show that the proposed approach can detect the far proximity with a successful rate of 0.85 for the non-Line-of-sight (NLoS) scenario, and the successful rate can be further increased to 0.99 for the Line-of-sight (LoS) scenario.

Keywords: Far proximity, channel impulse response, wireless fingerprinting.

1 Introduction

As mobile platforms are more and more pervasive and adopted in critical applications, it is becoming increasingly important to measure the physical proximity of mobile devices in a secure way. For example, Implantable Medical Devices (IMDs) like pacemakers may grant access to an external control device only when that device is close enough [25]. As another example, contactless-payment systems (like Google Wallet), which enable users to make payments by placing a mobile device in the close proximity of a payment terminal, may require the mobile devices to be within several centimeters or even millimeters of the payment terminals.

Thus, verifying the *close proximity* has triggered significant attention and activity from the research community, and multiple techniques have been proposed to achieve the efficient identification of close proximity (e.g., [5, 7, 11, 12, 16, 24, 29]), including the well-known distance bounding protocols and their variants (e.g., [5, 24, 29]).

Although various techniques have been developed to identify whether a device is close, the problem of identifying the *far proximity* (i.e., a target is at least a certain distance away) has been neglected by the research community. Meanwhile, verifying the far proximity is desirable and critical to enhance the security of emerging wireless applications. By enforcing far proximity, in addition to traditional access control

M. Kutyłowski and J. Vaidya (Eds.): ESORICS 2014, Part I, LNCS 8712, pp. 508–525, 2014.

and cryptographic approaches, we can enhance the security of various critical wireless applications, such as satellite communication, long-haul wireless TV, radio, and alarm broadcasting, and Marine VHF radio for rescue and communication services [2].

For example, GPS devices receive signals, presumably from satellites in space, to determine their locations. Ideally, the GPS devices could verify that received signals are from far-away sources, to avoid being deceived by a nearby adversary's signals. In cellular networks, mobile phones may at times expect to receive signals from particular cell towers. It has been demonstrated that adversaries can set up a fake short-range cell tower to fool nearby mobile phones [21, 31]. To avoid being deceived by such a fake cell tower, it is desirable that mobile phones can authenticate that the signals they receive originate from a tower at an expected, further distance away.

Existing close proximity identification techniques (e.g., [7, 11, 16]) qualitatively decide whether or not a target is nearby, but they cannot be directly extended to address the far proximity identification problem. The qualitative decision that a target is not nearby doesn't quantitatively guarantee that the target is at least a certain distance away (i.e., in the far proximity).

Distance bounding protocols (e.g., [5, 24, 29] demonstrated their success in quantitatively estimating the distance between two wireless devices. However, they cannot be directly applied to enforce far proximity identification. In distance bounding protocols, a local device sends a challenge to a remote device, and the remote device replies with a response that is computed as a function of the received challenge. The local device then measures the round-trip time between sending its challenge and receiving the response, subtracts the processing delay from the round-trip time, and uses the result to calculate the distance between itself and the remote device. However, by delaying its response to a challenge, a dishonest remote device can appear to be arbitrarily further from the local device than it actually is.

In this paper, we develop a secure far proximity identification approach that can determine whether a remote device is far away. The key idea of the proposed approach is to estimate the proximity from the unforgeable "fingerprint" of the proximity. We develop a technique that can extract the fingerprint of a wireless device's proximity from the physical-layer features of signals sent by the device. The proximity fingerprints are closely related to the distance between the local and remote devices. They are easy to extract but difficult to forge. We also develop a novel technique that uses the proximity fingerprint to identify the lower bound of the distance between the local and the remote devices.

The contributions of this paper are: (1) we develop a novel fingerprinting technique that enables the local device to extract the fingerprint of a wireless device's proximity from the physical-layer features of signals sent by the device; (2) we discover the theoretical relationship between the proximity and its fingerprint, and we developed a technique that can use such a relationship to estimate the lower bound of the distance between the local and remote devices; and (3) we validate and evaluate the effectiveness of the proposed far proximity identification method through experiments on the real-world data. The experiment results show that the proposed approach can detect the far proximity with a success rate of 0.85 for the non-Line-of-sight (NLoS) scenario, and the success rate can be further increased to 0.99 for the Line-of-sight (LoS) scenario.

The rest of the paper is organized as follows. Section 2 describes our assumptions and system and threat models. Section 3 presents the proposed far proximity identification techniques. Sections 4 and 5 discuss the experimental evaluation and related work. Section 6 concludes this paper.

2   System and Threat Models

To facilitate the presentation, we refer to the local device, which verifies the proximity, as the *verifier* and the remote device, whose proximity is being verified, as the *prover*. The verification system consists of a verifier and a prover. Both are equipped with radio interfaces that can transmit and receive wireless signals.

The verifier aims to determine whether or not a prover is at least a certain distance away, and it analyzes the signals emitted by the prover to achieve this goal. The verifier can work in both *active* or *passive* modes. In the active mode, the verifier sends a message to the prover to initialize the proximity identification, and the prover cooperates with the verifier by sending wireless signals back to the verifier to enable the verification. In the passive mode, instead of actively sending out signals, the verifier monitors the wireless channel to capture the prover's signal. Once the prover's signals are captured, the verifier can identify the prover's proximity.

We assume that the prover is untrusted. The prover may provide the verifier with fake messages and wrong configuration information regarding its hardware and software settings, such as device type, signal processing delay, and protocols in use. The prover may intentionally delay its replies to the verifier's messages or send bogus replies at any time to mislead the verifier. However, we assume that the verifier can receive wireless signals sent by the prover. We assume that there are no metal shields on the straight line between the verifier and the prover to block wireless signals from the prover.

3   Far Proximity Verification

A simple and naive method to identify whether a prover is far away is to examine the received signal strength (RSS). A signal decays as it propagates in the air. Thus, it seems that strong RSS indicates a short signal propagation length and a close transmitter, whereas weak RSS strength implies a far-away transmitter. However, a dishonest prover can increase or decrease its transmit power to pretend to be close to, or far from, the verifier. The root reason for the failure of the naive method is that RSS can be easily forged. In this paper, we discover unforgeable and unclonable *fingerprints* of the proximity and propose techniques that can identify the far proximity based on these fingerprints.

3.1   Proximity Fingerprints

Because of the multipath effect [9], a signal sent by the prover generally propagates to the verifier in the air along multiple paths due to reflection, diffraction, and scattering. Each path has an effect (e.g., distortion and attenuation) on the signal traveling on it [23]. A *channel impulse response* characterizes the overall effects imposed by the multipath propagation, and it reflects the physical feature of a wireless link [9]. Because it is difficult to change the physical feature, channel impulse responses have been used as "**link signatures**" to uniquely identify the wireless link between a wireless transmitter and a receiver [6, 23, 33].

Figure 1 (a) shows a simple example of multipath propagation. The signal sent by the prover is reflected by an obstacle (i.e., a building), and thus it travels along Path 1 (the direct path from the prover to the verifier), and Path 2 (the reflection path). The signal copy that travels along one path is usually referred to as a *multipath component* [9]. Let $r1$ and $r2$ denote the multipath components that travel along Path 1 and Path 2 respectively. Figure 1 (b) is an example of the corresponding channel impulse response, which shows that $r1$ arrives at the verifier first and the peak of the signal amplitude of $r1$ is A_{r1}, and $r2$ arrives after $r1$, and its peak is A_{r2}.

Intuitively, if the prover increases (decreases) the transmit power, both A_{r1} and A_{r2} will increase (decrease), but the prover cannot adjust its transmit power such that it arbitrarily manipulates only one of A_{r1} and A_{r2}, because it is difficult for the prover to identify and modify the physical paths over which multipath components propagate [23]. On the other hand, the length of the signal propagation path is closely related to the amplitude of the received signal. A far-away prover results in weaker A_{r1} and A_{r2} than a close prover. Based on this intuition, we give the definition of proximity fingerprint below.

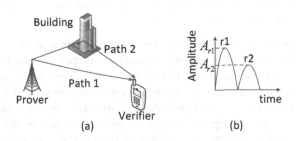

Fig. 1. An example of the multipath effect

Definition 1 (Proximity Fingerprint) *Let A_{r1} and A_{r2} be the amplitudes of the first and the second received multipath components, respectively. The proximity fingerprint f is the ratio of A_{r1} to A_{r2}, i.e., $f = \frac{A_{r1}}{A_{r2}}$.*

Key Features of Proximity Fingerprints: It appears that an attacker (i.e., a dishonest prover or a third-party adversary against benign provers) could affect the proximity fingerprint by intentionally placing a reflector nearby the prover to generate a fake path, in addition to the direct signal path from the prover to the verifier.

However, at the verifier's view, the direct and fake paths are still one unresolvable path if the difference between the arrival times of the signals traveling on both paths is much smaller than the symbol duration, which is the transmission time of a wireless physical-layer unit [9]. To be successful, an attacker has to place the reflector far enough away from the prover (i.e., δc meters, where δ is the symbol duration and c is the speed of light [9]), such that the difference between the two path arrival times is resolvable at the verifier. More crucially, at this distance the attacker must make sure that the prover's signal can exactly hit his reflector and be bounced back to the target verifier. However, it is quite uncertain for the prover's signal to be delivered to the reflector, then reflected by the reflector to the verifier due to the random scattering effect caused by long distance propagation [9].

For example, GPS satellites have a typical symbol duration of 0.01 second [1]. It is impractical for the satellite's signal to exactly hit a reflector that is 3,000,000 meters away, and moreover be reflected by the reflector to hit a target GPS navigation device on earth.

To summarize, proximity fingerprints are caused by wireless reflections somewhere, which the verifier does not need to know and identify. The verifier can easily extract A_{r1} and A_{r2} from the channel impulse response and compute the proximity fingerprint as A_{r1}/A_{r2}. Note that estimating the channel impulse responses is a must-have function for most modern wireless systems [9, 20]. But in order for the attacker to be successfully, the attacker has to know (1) how to pinpoint a far-away place to put a reflector or an active wireless device, and (2) exactly where to direct the reflector to shoot a needle in a haystack. Thus, significant practical hurdles exist for attacking proximity fingerprints. In this way, verifiers can easily extract proximity fingerprints, but it is difficult for attackers to forge or manipulate a specific fingerprint.

The attacker may also launch active attacks to undermine the verification of proximity fingerprints. In later section (3.4), we will discuss these active attacks and the corresponding countermeasures.

Impact of Directional Antennas: When directional antennas are used, the multipath effect may be reduced. However, directional antennas cannot provide perfect laser-like radio signals. For example, the beamwidth of a 3-element Yagi Antenna, the most common type of directional antenna, is 90 degrees in the vertical plane and 54 degrees in the horizontal plane [14]. Thus, it is not possible to completely eliminate the multipath effect, and accordingly the multipath propagation has been also considered in designing wireless communication systems equipped with directional antennas (e.g., [28, 32]). The proximity fingerprint can be calculated based on a very limited number of paths (i.e., two paths), and thus it is compatible to wireless systems with directional antennas in use.

3.2 Far Proximity Identification Using Proximity Fingerprints

Based on the study of proximity fingerprint, we now reveal the relationship between the proximity fingerprint and the actual proximity, and we propose far proximity identification techniques that can provide fine granularity and lower bounds on proximity (i.e., the prover is at least a certain distance away from the verifier) using the proximity fingerprint.

Far Proximity Identification. To calculate the proximity of the prover, we first model the fingerprint of the proximity. We consider signal propagation in two typical wireless environments, i.e., the outdoor and the indoor environments.

Outdoor Signal Propagation: One of the most common models for outdoor signal propagation in urban, suburban, and rural areas is the Okumura Model [9]. According to the Okumura model, the signal path loss in decibels (dB) in urban areas can be modeled as

$$L(\text{dB}) = 69.55 + 26.16 \log_{10}(f_c) - 13.82 \log_{10}(h_{te})$$
$$- a(h_{re}, f_c) + (44.9 - 6.55 \log_{10}(h_{te})) \log_{10}(d),$$

where d is the length of the path along which the signal propagates from the transmitter to the receiver, f_c is the central frequency, h_{te} and h_{re} are the transmitter's and the receiver's antenna heights respectively, and $a(h_{re}, f_c)$ is a correction factor computed using h_{re} and f_c [9]. Based on the Okumura Model, we give Lemma 1

Lemma 1. *The proximity fingerprint in the outdoor environment is $\sqrt{(\frac{d_2}{d_1})^{\frac{\gamma}{10}}}$, where d_1 and d_2 are the lengths of the paths along which the first and the second received multipath components travel respectively, $\gamma = 44.9 - 6.55 \log_{10}(h_{te})$, and h_{te} is the transmitter's antenna height.*

Proof: The received signal power P_r can be represented as $P_r(\text{dB}) = P_t(\text{dB}) - L (\text{dB})$, where P_t is the transmit power. To facilitate the calculation, we change the unit of P_r from dB to watt (W). Thus, $P_r(\text{W}) = 10^{\frac{1}{10}(P_t(\text{dB}) - L(\text{dB}))} = \frac{P_t(\text{W})}{L(\text{W})}$, and $L(\text{W}) = 10^{\frac{1}{10}L(\text{dB})} = 10^{\frac{1}{10}(\beta + \gamma \log_{10}(d))}$, where $\beta = 69.55 + 26.16 \log_{10}(f_c) - 13.82 \log_{10}(h_{te}) - a(h_{re}, f_c)$ and $\gamma = 44.9 - 6.55 \log_{10}(h_{te})$. The amplitude of a signal is the square root of the received signal power. Accordingly, $A_{r1} = \sqrt{P_{r1}(\text{W})} = \sqrt{\frac{P_t(\text{W})}{10^{\frac{1}{10}(\beta + \gamma \log_{10}(d_1))}}}$ and $A_{r2} = \sqrt{P_{r2}(\text{W})} = \sqrt{\frac{P_t(\text{W})}{10^{\frac{1}{10}(\beta + \gamma \log_{10}(d_2))}}}$, where d_1 and d_2 are the lengths of the paths along which the first and the second received multipath components travel respectively. Note that both multipath components have the same values for γ and β, because they are from the same signal source (i.e., the prover) and exhibit the same frequency f_c. Thus, the proximity fingerprint f can be written as $f = \frac{A_{r1}}{A_{r2}} = \sqrt{(\frac{d_2}{d_1})^{\frac{\gamma}{10}}}$. According to the Okumura Model, the signal path loss models in suburban and rural areas are $L_{suburban}(\text{dB}) = L(\text{dB}) - 2[\log_{10}(f_c/28)]^2 - 5.4$ and $L_{rural}(\text{dB}) = L(\text{dB}) - 4.78[\log_{10}(f_c)]^2 + 18.33 \log_{10}(f_c) - K$, respectively, where K ranges from 35.94 (countryside) to 40.94 (desert). By using the same analysis, we can obtain similar result that f in the suburban and rural areas is $\sqrt{(\frac{d_2}{d_1})^{\frac{\gamma}{10}}}$.   □

Indoor Signal Propagation: The path loss in the indoor environment can be usually represented by the ITU Indoor Propagation Model [20] as shown below

$$L(\text{dB}) = 20 \log f_c + \lambda \log d + P_f(N_f),$$

where λ is the empirical path loss at the same floor, N_f denote the number of floors between the transmitter and receiver, and $P_f(N_f)$ denotes the floor penetration loss. Based on the ITU indoor model, we give Lemma 2

Lemma 2. *The proximity fingerprint in the indoor environment is* $\sqrt{(\frac{d_2}{d_1})^{\frac{\lambda}{10}}}$, *where* d_1 *and* d_2 *are the lengths of the paths along which the first and the second received multipath components travel respectively, and* λ *is the empirical floor penetration loss factor.*

Proof: As discussed earlier, the received signal power P_r can be represented as P_r(dB) $= P_t$(dB) - L (dB). By converting the unit of P_r from dB to W, we can obtain P_r(W) $=$ $\frac{P_t(\text{W})}{L(\text{W})} = \frac{P_t(\text{W})}{10^{\frac{1}{10}(20\log f_c + \lambda \log d + P_f(N_f))}}$. The proximity fingerprint, the ratio of A_{r1} to A_{r2}, can be written as $f = \frac{\sqrt{P_{r1}(\text{W})}}{\sqrt{P_{r2}(\text{W})}} = \sqrt{(\frac{d_2}{d_1})^{\frac{\lambda}{10}}}$ □

Far Proximity Identification: Assume there are no large metallic obstacles that can significantly block the signal propagation between the verifier and the prover. The path that the first received multipath component usually travels along (i.e., Path 1) is roughly straight between the verifier and the prover due to penetration and diffraction-around-obstacles features of wireless signals [9]. Thus, d_1 approximately equals to the distance between the verifier and the prover. The lower bound of d_1 is given in Lemma 3.

Lemma 3. *Let* d *be the distance between the prover and the verifier. We have* $d \geq$ $\frac{c}{B(f^{\frac{2}{\alpha}}-1)}$, *where* c *is the speed of light,* B *is the bandwidth of the communication system,* α *is the path loss exponent, and* f *is the proximity fingerprint.*

Proof: Let t denote the time at which the prover's signal starts to propagate to the verifier. Let t_1 and t_2 denote the arrival times of the first and the second received multipath components, respectively. Therefore, $d_1 = (t_1 - t)c$ and $d_2 = (t_2 - t)c = (t_1 - t)c + (t_2 - t_1)c = d_1 + \Delta c$, where $\Delta = t_2 - t_1$. From Lemmas 1 and 2, we know that for both the outdoor and indoor environments, the proximity fingerprint f can be generalized by the same expression $f = \sqrt{(\frac{d_2}{d_1})^{\alpha}}$, where α equals to $\frac{\gamma}{10}$ and $\frac{\lambda}{10}$ for the outdoor and indoor propagation respectively. The first received multipath component travels along the straight line between the verifier and the prover. Hence, the distance d between the verifier and the prover is equal to d_1. According to [9], for re-solvable multiple path components, $\Delta \geq \frac{1}{B}$, where B is the bandwidth of the wireless communication system. Thus, $f = \sqrt{(\frac{d_2}{d})^{\alpha}} = \sqrt{(\frac{d+\Delta c}{d})^{\alpha}} \geq \sqrt{(\frac{d+\frac{c}{B}}{d})^{\alpha}}$ and we have $d \geq \frac{c}{B(f^{\frac{2}{\alpha}}-1)}$.   □

Choosing α**:** For the outdoor signal propagation, according to the Okumura model, $\gamma = 44.9 - 6.55 \log_{10}(h_{te})$, where h_{te} is the height of the transmitter's antenna. If the verifier has specific types of targets, for example, the verifier aims to verify the proximity of a satellite, a cellular base station, or a TV tower, then the verifier can directly compute γ by looking up the typical values of h_{te} from the corresponding wireless device handbooks. Alternatively, the verifier can also get an estimate of γ by using the typical transmitter antenna height in the outdoor environment (e.g., the typical transmitter antenna height ranges between 1 to 200 meters [20], and thus γ approximately lies between 44.9 and 29.83). After obtaining γ, the verifier can compute $\alpha = \frac{\gamma}{10}$. For the indoor signal propagation, $\alpha = \frac{\lambda}{10}$, where λ is the indoor path loss factor that doesn't rely on the antenna height and it can be obtained through empirical experiments.

Note that the path loss exponent α for both outdoors and indoors can be actually regarded as an attenuation factor that reflects the attenuation caused by the propagation path. Previous studies have performed extensive empirical experiments to measure typical values of such an attenuation factor in different wireless environments [9]. For example, the attenuation factor is 2.0 for vacuum free space, 2.7–3.5 for urban areas, 3.0–5.0 for suburban areas, and 1.6–1.8 for indoors [9]. In the following discussion, without loss of generality, we use these typical empirical values of the attenuation factor as the example α. Nevertheless, the verifier can obtain α empirically using existing readily-available approaches (e.g., [3, 19]), and a real-measured attenuation factor can help to improve the accuracy of the proximity lower bound estimation.

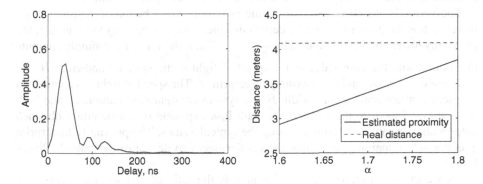

Fig. 2. An example of the real-measured channel impulse response obtained from the CRAWDAD data set

Fig. 3. Estimated lower bound v.s. the real distance

Experimental Examples. Figure 2 shows an example of a real-measured channel impulse response obtained from the CRAWDAD data set [27], which contains channel impulse responses collected in an indoor environment with obstacles (e.g., cubicle offices and furniture) and scatters (e.g., windows and doors). The channel impulse response was measured when the distance between the transmitter and the receiver is 4.09 meters. From Figure 2, we can see that each received multipath component leads to a triangle in shape with a peak [23]. The second multipath component arrives at the receiver about 75 nanoseconds after the arrival of the first one. The proximity fingerprint is 5.6499. The channel impulse response was measured indoors, and thus α ranges between 1.6 and 1.8.

We use Lemma 3 to estimate the lower bound of the proximity of the transmitter, and Figure 3 shows the result. We can observe that the estimated lower bound increases as α increases. However, when α reaches the maximum value (i.e., 1.8) of the indoor environment, the real distance is still bounded by (i.e., greater than) the estimated lower bound. Specifically, when $\alpha = 1.8$, the lower bound of the proximity is 3.84 meters. This means the transmitter should be at least 3.84 meters away from the receiver. The actual distance between the transmitter and the receiver is 4.09 meters, which is slightly greater than the lower bound 3.84 meters.

Note that long-haul communications may desire a much relaxed tightness of the proximity lower bound. For example, GPS satellites running on the Low Earth Orbit have an altitude of approximately 2,000,000 meters (1,200 miles). With a proximity lower bound of 1,000,000 meters (i.e., the bound is less than the actual proximity by 50%), it would be possible to prevent most attackers from impersonating the satellites, because it is usually very difficult for the attacker to achieve such a long transmission range.

3.3   System Design

In what follows, we show how the theoretical result of Lemma 3 can be used in a practical communication system to achieve the far proximity identification.

The verifier's objective is to find out the proximity lower bound of the prover, i.e., to verify that the prover is at least a certain distance away. According to Lemma 3, the proximity lower bound is computed by $\frac{c}{B(f^{\frac{2}{\alpha}}-1)}$. Thus, the verifier can simply compute this bound with the knowledge of the speed of light c, the system bandwidth B, the path loss exponent α, and the proximity fingerprint f. The speed of light c is a universal physical constant and the bandwidth B is a system configuration parameter, and both of them are known to the verifier. The path loss exponent α can be either obtained empirically, or can be determined using the typical values. The proximity fingerprint f is the only remaining factor that the verifier needs to decide to compute the lower bound.

As we discussed earlier, the fingerprint f is the ratio of A_{r1} to A_{r2}, where A_{r1} and A_{r2} are the amplitudes of the first and the second received multipath components. A_{r1} and A_{r2} can be extracted from the channel impulse response. A wireless packet is usually preceded by a preamble, a special data content that indicates the beginning of an incoming packet. When the prover sends a packet to the wireless channel, the verifier will first capture the preamble using the match filtering technique [10]; then the verifier knows that there is an incoming packet and continues to receive the payload. The preamble not only enables packet capture, but also enables the estimation of the channel impulse response at the verifier.

After receiving the preamble, the verifier can use existing channel estimation techniques (e.g., least-square (LS) and linear minimum mean squared error (LMMSE) estimators [4]) to estimate the channel impulse response from the preamble, and thereby obtain the values of A_{r1} and A_{r2} and the proximity fingerprint $f = A_{r1}/A_{r2}$. It is worth pointing out that using the preamble is not the only way to obtain A_{r1} and A_{r2}. The verifier can also use blinding estimation methods (e.g., [30]) to estimate the channel impulse response from the entire content of the preamble and the payload. In addition, the verifier can use hybrid methods (e.g., [13]) that combine preamble-based estimation and blind estimation together to improve the estimation accuracy. After obtaining the proximity fingerprint f and demodulating the payload and authentication information, the verifier then verifies the prover's proximity using Lemma 3.

3.4 Dealing with Jam-and-Replay Attacks

To fool the verifier, the attacker may try to create a fake second path by using another active wireless device to send signals from a different direction. In this case, the attacker must make sure that there is no multipath effect for the signals traveling on the direct path (i.e., the path from the prover to the verifier) and the fake path (i.e., the path from the active wireless device to the verifier). Otherwise, the attacker cannot control and guarantee that the fake path is exactly the second received path at the verifier side. Eliminating the multipath effect completely is normally regarded as infeasible.

However, the attacker may alternatively launch Jam-and-replay attacks to deceive the far proximity identification system. In the jam-and-replay attack, the attacker replays an intercepted signal from the prover at the attacker's own location, such that the verifier is fooled into taking the attacker's proximity as the prover's proximity. At the same time, the attacker jams the transmission to prevent the verifier from receiving the original signal from the prover; hence, traditional anti-replay mechanisms such as sequence numbers do not work.

A common method of addressing jam-and-replay attacks is to explore timestamps (e.g., [16]). In such a method, the sender includes a timestamp in the transmitted message, which indicates the time when a particular bit or byte called the anchor (e.g., the start of the message header) is transmitted over the air. Upon receiving a frame, the receiver can use this timestamp and its local message receiving time to estimate the message traverse time. An overly long time indicates that the message has been forwarded by an intermediate attacker.

Timestamps-based method requires clock synchronization between the sender and the receiver, but it generally has a low synchronization requirement in common wireless applications. For example, in an 11 Mbps 802.11g wireless network, the transmission of a typical 1500-byte TCP message requires 1.09 (i.e., $\frac{1500*8}{11 \times 10^3}$) milliseconds. Thus, the attacker at least doubles the transmission time of the message to 2.18 milliseconds. As long as the verifier and the prover have coarsely synchronized clocks that differ in the order of milliseconds, the verifier can detect jam-and-replay attacks. Note that the synchronization requirement can be further relaxed in GPS applications. GPS satellites have a transmission rate ranging between 20 bits/s and 100 bits/s [1]. The transmission of a standard 1500-bits GPS navigation message [1] takes 15 − 75 seconds, and accordingly the synchronization accuracy can be reduced to the order of seconds.

In addition, to launch jam-and-replay attacks, the attacker must send jamming signals to jam the wireless transmission. Jamming attacks have been extensively studied in the literature, and various techniques regarding jamming detection and countermeasures have been proposed (e.g., [9, 15, 26]). The prover and the verifier can also use existing jamming detection or anti-jamming techniques to discover the presence of jam-and-replay attacks, or to defend against such attacks.

4 Experimental Evaluation

4.1 Experiment Setup

Wireless propagation can be either line-of-sight (LoS) or non-LoS (NLoS). In LoS scenarios, there exist no major or very few obstacles residing between the transmitter and receiver, and thus LoS scenarios usually feature better signal quality. In NLoS scenarios, there exist a number of major obstacles between the transmitter and receiver, and NLoS scenarios are more complicated with higher signal distortion and sharper changes in signal strength.

Far proximity identification often applies to long-haul wireless communications (e.g., GPS) in outdoor environments, which are usually open and have a much stronger feature in LoS than NLoS. Compared to outdoor environments, indoor environments like offices, residential homes, and shops, are more complicated due to the frequent occurrences of walls, people, furniture, cubicles, etc. Thus, indoor environments usually have a fairly large number of NLoS propagation paths. In our experiment, we choose the more challenging indoor environment for our evaluation to examine the worst-case performance of the proposed method.

We validate the proposed far proximity identification technique using the CRAW-DAD data set [22], which contains more than 9,300 real channel impulse response measurements (i.e., link signatures) in a 44-node wireless network [27]. The measurement environment is an indoor environment with obstacles (e.g., cubicle offices and furniture) and scatters (e.g., windows and doors). More information regarding the CRAWDAD data set can be found in [22, 27].

We herein use *error rate* and *tightness of the bound* as metrics to evaluate the performance of the proposed technique in the real world. In addition, the proximity lower bound is computed based on a key factor, the proximity fingerprint. Thus, the proximity fingerprints plays a vital role in proximity identification. To further validate the the feasibility of using proximity fingerprints for proximity identification, we also perform experiments to reveal the relationship between the real distance and the proximity fingerprints. Our evaluation metrics are summarized below.

- **Error rate:** The error rate is the ratio of the number of failed trials (i.e., error happens in the trail) to the total number of trials.
- **Tightness of the bound:** Tightness is the normalized difference between the estimated lower bound and the real distance (i.e., $\frac{d-\beta}{d}$, where β is the estimated proximity lower bound, and d is the real distance between the verifier and the prover).
- **Proximity Fingerprints:** The proximity fingerprint is the ratio of the amplitude of the first received multipath component to that of the second one.

4.2   Experiment Results

Based on the CRAWDAD data set, we perform experiments under both LoS and NLoS scenarios to show the error rate, tightness of the bound, and the relationship between the proximity fingerprint and the distance.

We distinguish two types of channel impulse responses: if a LoS path exists and there are no obstacles between the transmitter and the receiver, we mark the corresponding channel impulse responses as LoS channel impulse responses. Otherwise, we mark them as NLoS channel impulse responses. Thus, we obtain two sets of data. The first set is formed by all LoS channel impulse responses, and the second one is formed by all NLoS channel impulse responses. We perform our experiments using both sets.

Error Rate Error Rate vs. Pathloss: To obtain the error rate, we experiment as follows. Let N_{LoS} denote the number of channel impulse responses in the LoS data set. For each channel impulse response in the data set, we compute the proximity fingerprint and the corresponding proximity lower bound using Lemma 3. We also compute the real distance between the transmitter and the receiver based on their coordinates. If the lower bound is less than the real distance, we mark the trial as successful. Otherwise, we mark the trial as failed. Accordingly, the error rate is calculated as $\frac{N_f}{N_{LoS}}$, where N_f is the number of failed trails and N_{LoS} is the total number of trials. We perform the experiment again using the NLoS data set and obtain the corresponding error rate for the NLoS scenario.

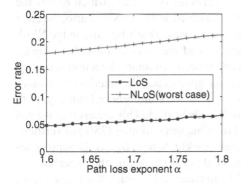
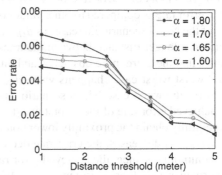

Fig. 4. Error rate as a function of pathloss exponent α

Fig. 5. Error rate as a function of the distance threshold $d_{threshold}$ in the LoS scenario

The channel impulse responses are collected from an indoor environment, and the corresponding pathloss exponent α empirically ranges between 1.6 and 1.8. Thus, we perform our experiment for different values of α in this range. Figure 4 plots the error rate as a function of α. The pathloss exponent α reflects how a signal is distorted and attenuated during its propagation, and a large α can result in higher signal distortion and attenuation. Accordingly, from Figure 4 we can observe that the error rate increases as α increases. However, when α reaches the maximum value for indoor environments, the achieved error rate in the LoS scenario is as low as 0.075. For the minimum α of 1.6, the proposed approach has a reduced error rate of 0.05.

For the NLoS scenario, we can still achieve an error rate between 0.17 and 0.22. Note that NLoS scenarios are the worst-case scenarios. Far proximity identification is typically used in outdoor environments, which have the stronger LoS feature. As shown in Figure 4, the error rate of LoS scenarios is much lower than that of the NLoS scenarios.

Error Rate vs. Distance: We then perform experiments to examine how the real distance affects the error rate. For each channel impulse response in the LoS data set, we compute the distance between the corresponding transmitter and the receiver. Let d_{max} and d_{min} denote the maximum and minimum distance among all computed distances. We calculate the error rate using the set formed by channel impulse responses whose corresponding distance are larger than a threshold value $d_{threshold}$. We start from $d_{threshold} = d_{min}$ and increase $d_{threshold}$ each time until $d_{threshold}$ reaches d_{max}. We perform the experiments again using the NLoS set.

Figure 5 shows the error rate as a a function of $d_{threshold}$ in the LoS scenario. The error rate decreases as $d_{threshold}$ increases. The obvious reason is that a larger $d_{threshold}$ indicates a longer distance between the transmitter and the receiver, and thus a higher chance that the estimated proximity lower bound is less than the distance. When $d_{threshold}$ approaches the maximum distance between the sender and the receiver, the corresponding error rate is 0.01. When $d_{threshold}$ approaches the minimum distance, the error rate slightly increases but it is still a small rate that ranges between 0.05 and 0.07 for different α.

Figure 6 plots the error rate of the NLoS scenario for $\alpha = 1.80$, which results the worst error rate as compared to other values of α. Contrary to the LoS scenario, the error rate of the NLoS scenario increases as $d_{threshold}$ increases. That's because in the NLoS scenario a longer distance between the transmitter and the receiver indicates a higher chance that there are more obstacles, and thus a reduced proximity detection accuracy. The "worst worst case" happens when $d_{threshold}$ approaches the maximum distance d_{max} for the worst case NLoS scenario. However, as we can observe from Figure 6, the achieved error rate of the "worst worst case" is about 0.25. This means that we can successfully obtain the proximity lower bound for a majority number (75%) of verifiers. As $d_{threshold}$ decreases, the error rate decreases quickly. When $d_{threshold}$ approaches the minimum distance, the achieved error rate is about 0.15. Again, the experiment is performed in an indoor environment (e.g., WiFi and Bluetooth), which has a short signal propagation distance. Outdoor wireless applications (e.g., space communications and TV broadcasting) usually have the stronger LoS feature, and therefore can substantially benefit from the proposed method in terms of significantly reducing the error rate.

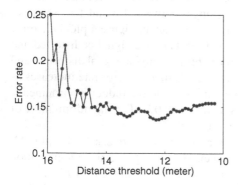

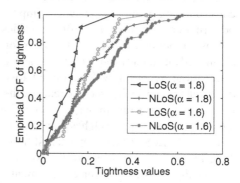

Fig. 6. Error rate as a function of the distance threshold $d_{threshold}$ in the NLoS scenario

Fig. 7. The empirical CDFs of the tightness

Tightness of the Proximity Bound. Our second evaluation metric is the tightness of the bound. To evaluate the tightness, we perform the following experiments using LoS and NLoS data sets. In all experiments, the pathloss exponent α is set to the minimum and maximum values of 1.6 and 1.8. For each channel impulse response in the LoS data set, we compute the distance between the corresponding transmitter and the receiver and the proximity lower bound. Based on the bound and the actual distance, we can calculate the tightness of the bound. We then sort all the tightness values and compute the empirical cumulative distribution function (CDF) for them. We perform the experiment again using NLoS data set and obtain the CDFs of the NLoS tightness values.

Figure 7 shows the CDF curves of the tightness computed using channel impulse responses collected in LoS and NLoS scenarios. For the LoS scenario with $\alpha = 1.8$, we can observe that 95% of the tightness values are less than 0.2. The indoor environment typically features a short propagation path, and thus a 0.2 tightness indicates a small absolute difference in distance. For example, if the distance between the transmitter and receiver is 5 meters, the achieved tightness can be around 1 meter. In particular, the maximum distance d_{max} between the transmitter and the receiver is about 11 meters, and the corresponding proximity bound is 9.56 meters, which is very close to the actual distance.

For the NLoS scenario with $\alpha = 1.8$, we can observe from Figure 7 that 90% of the tightness values are less than 0.3. Compared to the LoS Scenario, the NLoS scenario has a reduced performance due to the existence of obstacles. Again, the experiment is conducted based on short-range communications, and a 0.3 tightness still suggests a small absolute difference in distance. When α decreases to 1.6, the achieved tightness increases. That's because the corresponding estimated proximity lower bound decreases, and a decreased bound grows the difference between the bound and the real distance, and thus augments the tightness. However, for $\alpha = 1.6$, we can still observe that a great majority of the tightness values are fairly small, e.g., 95% and 80% of the tightness values are less than 0.25 and 0.3 in the LoS and the NLoS (worst-case) scenarios respectively. As we have discussed, such tightness of the bound is usually sufficient to prevent attackers from impersonating the transmitters in typical long-haul outdoor wireless applications.

Proximity Fingerprint vs. Distance. The proximity fingerprint is an important parameter in computing the proximity lower bound. According to Lemma 3, the theoretical proximity lower bound is calculated as $\frac{c}{B(f^{\frac{2}{\alpha}}-1)}$. From this formula, we can easily derive that as the proximity fingerprint f increases (other parameters remain the same), the proximity lower bound decreases and vice versa. Note that the proximity lower bound reveals the least distance between the verifier and the prover. Thus, the increase of the proximity fingerprint f may also indicate the decrease of the real distance and vice versa. We plot the proximity fingerprint as a function of the distance in Figure 8. We can see that the proximity fingerprint in the NLoS scenario slightly differs from that of the LoS scenario in magnitude due to the reflection loss. However, for both scenarios, their proximity fingerprints exhibit the same tendency, i.e., they both decrease as the distance increases. This observation is consistent with our theoretical result.

5   Related Work

Related work falls into the following two areas.

(a) Distance Bounding Protocols: Distance bounding protocols are a class of protocols that determine an approximate distance between a local device and a remote device.

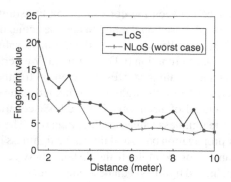

Fig. 8. Relationship between the distance and the proximity fingerprint

(e.g., [5, 24, 29]). Distance bounding protocols and their variants are based on the common observation that the distance between the local and the remote devices is equal to the product of the speed of electromagnetic wave and the one-way signal propagation time. The approximate distance is obtained from a series of wireless packets exchanged between the local device and the remote device. Specifically, the local device sends a challenge to the remote device, which then replies with a response that is generated based on the challenge. The local device measures the round-trip time between sending the challenge and receiving the response, subtracts the processing delay from the round-trip time, and uses the result to compute the distance. Because the response is generated based on the challenge, the distance bounding protocol can prevent the remote device from pretending to be closer than it actually is by sending a fake response before it receives the challenge.

However, by delaying its response to a challenge, a remote device can appear to be arbitrarily further from the local device than it actually is. Hence, distance-bounding protocols cannot enforce lower bounds on proximity (i.e., requirements that the remote device be *at least* a certain distance from the local device). For this reason, the GPS-device and mobile-phone examples used for motivation in Section 1 cannot be enforced by distance-bounding protocols.

(b) Close Proximity Identification: There also exist traditional close proximity detection techniques (e.g., [8, 17]) that can detect the presence of nearby objects without any physical contact. These techniques use electromagnetic field changes to identify a close object. A proximity sensor generates an electromagnetic field or a beam of electromagnetic radiation (e.g., infrared). If an object moves into the field range of the sensor, a field change can result, and thus the sensor senses the presence of the object. For example, a sound alert is triggered when a vehicle moves into the close proximity of a worker or an obstacle. However, traditional techniques cannot identify the proximity of a specific object, because the proximity sensor reports all nearby objects as long as those objects are in the field range.

Researchers later developed techniques that identify the close proximity of an individual target if the target can emit wireless signals (e.g., [7, 11, 18]). For example, based on the observation that a strong received signal usually indicates a close transmitter, Macii et al developed approaches that determine the proximity of the remote wireless device by measuring received signal strength [18]. However, the use of signal strength to determine proximity was found to be insecure, as a dishonest remote device can easily pretend to be close to the local device by boosting its transmit power.

More recent efforts overcome this drawback with the assistance of special hardware [7,11]. Cai et al. proposed a scheme that identifies the presence of a close wireless device by using multiple antennas [7]. Halevi et al. proposed to use ambient sensors to detect whether a Near-Field-Communication (NFC) device is nearby or not [11]. Although those approaches can prevent attackers manipulating transmit power to deceive the local device, they cannot be directly extended to address the far proximity identification problem. They output a decision regarding whether a target is nearby, but such a decision cannot guarantee that the target is at least a certain distance away. Also, the requirement of special hardware such as multiple antennas and ambient sensors introduces extra cost and may reduce their compatibility.

Liu et al. proposed a new close proximity identification approach that does not rely on special hardware [16]. By using the wireless physical features that uniquely identify a wireless link between a transmitter and a receiver, the proposed technique enables the local device to distinguish between a nearby and a far-away remote device. An attacker cannot manipulate such physical features to pretend to be close to the local device. However, similar to all previous approaches, this approach is a decision-based, i.e. outputs a simple "yes" or "no" to indicate whether the remote device is very close or not. Hence, it does not provide the quantitative lower bound of the proximity, which is the primary contribution of this paper.

6 Conclusion

In this paper, we proposed a far proximity identification approach that determines the lower bound of the distance between the verifier and the prover. The key idea of the proposed approach is to estimate the proximity lower bound from the unforgeable fingerprint of the proximity. We have examined the proposed approach through experimental evaluation using the CRAWDAD data set.

References

1. Gps signals, http://en.wikipedia.org/wiki/GPS_signals (accessed July 27, 2013)
2. Marine vhf radio, http://en.wikipedia.org/wiki/Marine_VHF_radio (accessed July 13, 2013)
3. Alam, N., Balaie, A.T., Dempster, A.G.: Dynamic path loss exponent and distance estimation in a vehicular network using doppler effect and received signal strength. In: Proceedings of 2010 Vehicular Technology Conference Fall (VTC 2010-Fall), pp. 1–5 (2010)
4. Biguesh, M., Gershman, A.B.: Training-based mimo channel estimation: A study of estimator tradeoffs and optimal training signals. IEEE Transaction on Signal Processing 54(3), 884–893 (2006)
5. Brands, S., Chaum, D.: Distance bounding protocols. In: Helleseth, T. (ed.) EUROCRYPT 1993. LNCS, vol. 765, pp. 344–359. Springer, Heidelberg (1994)

6. Brik, V., Banerjee, S., Gruteser, M., Oh, S.: Wireless device identification with radiometric signatures. In: Proceedings of the 14th ACM International Conference on Mobile Computing and Networking (MobiCom 2008), pp. 116–127 (2008)
7. Cai, L., Zeng, K., Chen, H., Mohapatra, P.: Good neighbor: Ad hoc pairing of nearby wireless devices by multiple antennas. In: Proceedings of the Annual Network and Distributed System Security Symposium (NDSS 2011) (2011)
8. Chen, Z., Luo, R.C.: Design and implementation of capacitive proximity sensor using micro-electromechanical systems technology. IEEE Transactions on Industrial Electronics 45(6), 886–894 (1998)
9. Goldsmith, A.: Wireless Communications. Cambridge University Press, New York (2005)
10. Gunnam, K., Choi, G., Yeary, M., Zhai, Y.: A low-power preamble detection methodology for packet based rf modems on all-digital sensor front-ends. In: Proceedings of the IEEE Instrumentation and Measurement Technology Conference (2007)
11. Halevi, T., Ma, D., Saxena, N., Xiang, T.: Secure proximity detection for NFC devices based on ambient sensor data. In: Foresti, S., Yung, M., Martinelli, F. (eds.) ESORICS 2012. LNCS, vol. 7459, pp. 379–396. Springer, Heidelberg (2012)
12. Hancke, G.P., Kuhn, M.G.: An RFID distance bounding protocol. In: Proceedings of SecureComm 2005, pp. 67–73 (2005)
13. Jinho, C.: Equalization and semi-blind channel estimation for space-time block coded signals over a frequency-selective fading channel. IEEE Transactions on Signal Processing 52(3), 774–785 (2004)
14. Kuechle, L.B.: Selecting receiving antennas for radio tracking, http://www.atstrack.com/PDFFiles/receiverantrev6.pdf
15. Liu, A., Ning, P., Dai, H., Liu, Y., Wang, C.: Defending DSSS-based broadcast communication against insider jammers via delayed seed-disclosure. In: Proceedings of the 26th Annual Computer Security Applications Conference, ACSAC 2010 (December 2010)
16. Liu, Y., Ning, P., Dai, H.: Authenticating primary users' signals in cognitive radio networks via integrated cryptographic and wireless link signatures. In: Proceedings of 2010 IEEE Symposium on Security and Privacy (S&P 2010), pp. 286–301 (May 2010)
17. Lo, P.H., Hong, C., Lo, S.C., Fang, W.: Implementation of inductive proximity sensor using nanoporous anodic aluminum oxide layer. In: Proceedings of 2011 International Solid-State Sensors, Actuators and Microsystems Conference (TRANSDUCERS), pp. 1871–1874 (2011)
18. Macii, D., Trenti, F., Pivato, P.: A robust wireless proximity detection technique based on rss and tof measurements. In: Proceedings of 2011 IEEE International Workshop on Measurements and Networking (M&N 2011), pp. 31–36 (2011)
19. Mao, G., Anderson, B.D.O., Fidan, B.: Path loss exponent estimation for wireless sensor network localization. The International Journal of Computer and Telecommunications Networking 51(10), 2467–2483 (2007)
20. Molisch, A.F.: Wireless Communications, 2nd edn. Wiley India Pvt. Limited (2007)
21. Paget, C.: Practical cellphone spying. In: DEF CON 18 (2010)
22. Patwari, N., Kasera, S.K.: CRAWDAD utah CIR measurements, http://crawdad.cs.dartmouth.edu/meta.php?name=utah/CIR
23. Patwari, N., Kasera, S.K.: Robust location distinction using temporal link signatures. In: MobiCom 2007: Proceedings of the 13th Annual ACM International Conference on Mobile Computing and Networking, pp. 111–122. ACM, New York (2007)
24. Rasmussen, K.B., Čapkun, S.: Realization of rf distance bounding. In: Proceedings of the USENIX Security Symposium (2010)
25. Rasmussen, K.B., Castelluccia, C., Heydt-Benjamin, T.S., Čapkun, S.: Proximity-based access control for implantable medical devices. In: Proceedings of the 16th ACM Conference on Computer and Communications Security (CCS 2009) (2009)

26. Scholtz, R.A.: Spread Spectrum Communications Handbook. McGraw-Hill (2001)
27. SPAN. Measured channel impulse response data set, http://span.ece.utah.edu/pmwiki/pmwiki.php?n=Main.MeasuredCIRDataSet
28. Sud, S.: A low complexity spatial rake receiver using main beam multipath combining for a cdma smart antenna system. In: Proceedings of 2007 IEEE Military Communications Conference (MILCOM), pp. 1–6 (2007)
29. Tippenhauer, N.O., Čapkun, S.: ID-based secure distance bounding and localization. In: Backes, M., Ning, P. (eds.) ESORICS 2009. LNCS, vol. 5789, pp. 621–636. Springer, Heidelberg (2009)
30. Tsatsanis, M.K., Giannakis, G.B.: Blind estimation of direct sequence spread spectrum signals in multipath. IEEE Transactions on Signal Processing 5(45), 1241–1252 (1997)
31. Weinmann, R.: The baseband apocalypse. In: BlackHat DC (2011)
32. Yu, L., Liu, W., Langley, R.J.: Robust beamforming methods for multipath signal reception. Digital Signal Processing 20(2), 379–390 (2007)
33. Zhang, J., Firooz, M.H., Patwari, N., Kasera, S.K.: Advancing wireless link signatures for location distinction. In: MobiCom 2008: Proceedings of the 14th ACM International Conference on Mobile Computing and Networking. ACM, New York (2008)

A Cross-Layer Key Establishment Scheme in Wireless Mesh Networks

Yuexin Zhang[1], Yang Xiang[1], Xinyi Huang[1,2,*], and Li Xu[2]

[1] School of Information Technology, Deakin University
Burwood, VIC 3125, Australia
[2] Fujian Provincial Key Laboratory of Network Security and Cryptology
School of Mathematics and Computer Science, Fujian Normal University
Fuzhou, 350108, China
{yuexinz,yang.xiang}@deakin.edu.au, {xyhuang,xuli}@fjnu.edu.cn

Abstract. Cryptographic keys are necessary to secure communications among mesh clients in wireless mesh networks. Traditional key establishment schemes are implemented at higher layers, and the security of most such designs relies on the complexity of computational problems. Extracting cryptographic keys at the physical layer is a promising approach with information-theoretical security. But due to the nature of communications at the physical layer, none of the existing designs supports key establishment if communicating parties are out of each other's radio range, and all schemes are insecure against man-in-the-middle attacks. This paper presents a cross-layer key establishment scheme where the established key is determined by two partial keys: one extracted at the physical layer and the other generated at higher layers. The analysis shows that the proposed cross-layer key establishment scheme not only eliminates the aforementioned shortcomings of key establishment at each layer but also provides a flexible solution to the key generation rate problem.

Keywords: Key establishment, Cross-layer, Coding, Channel phase, Wireless mesh networks.

1 Introduction

Wireless mesh networks (hereinafter, WMNs) becomes a research hotspot due to its low costs for deployment, easy expansion, and capability of self organization and self configuration. WMNs consists of two types of entities: mesh routers and mesh clients [1]. Mesh clients are stationary or mobile devices, and mesh routers form the mesh backbone for mesh clients. Each node (including mesh clients and mesh routers) in WMNs serves as a host and as a router, but mesh clients are not as powerful as mesh routers. As shown in Fig. 1, mesh clients can access the networks through mesh routers or meshing with other mesh clients directly [1].

---

* Corresponding author.

M. Kutyłowski and J. Vaidya (Eds.): ESORICS 2014, Part I, LNCS 8712, pp. 526–541, 2014.

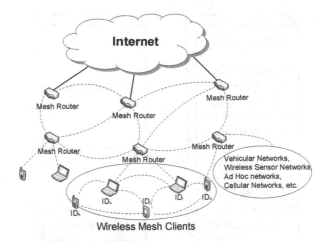

Fig. 1. Hybrid WMNs [1]

To secure wireless communications among clients, cryptographic keys are needed to provide confidentiality, integrity and authentication services. As a fundamental problem, key establishment has been extensively and intensively studied. Existing designs can be classified into two main types: asymmetric key establishment schemes and symmetric key establishment schemes. Most of them are implemented at higher layers (Fig. 2 shows the system model). However, there are some disadvantages in those schemes. For example, a large portion of them rely on the intractability of computational problems, and some of those problems will become tractable on quantum computers. Specifically, costly computation operations are needed to be executed in asymmetric key based schemes. In symmetric key based schemes, e.g., key pre-distribution schemes, considerable memory spaces are used to pre-load secrets.

To obtain communication keys with information-theoretical security, there is an increasing interest in extracting keys by exploiting the wireless channel. In the typical multipath environments, the wireless channel between two clients (e.g., Alice and Bob) experiences a time-varying, stochastic mapping between the transmitted and received signals. This mapping (commonly termed fading) is unique, location-specific and reciprocal, namely, the fading is invariant within the channel coherence time whether the signals are transmitted from Alice to Bob or vice-versa. In wireless communications, coherence time is a statistical measure of the time duration over which the channel impulse response is essentially invariant. Based on communication theory [2], the fading decorrelates over distances of the order of half a wavelength, λ. Thus, the signals transmitted between Alice and Bob and the signals transmitted between Alice (or Bob) and the eavesdropper (who is at least $\lambda/2$ away from the clients) experience independent fading. For instance, at 2.4 GHz used in IEEE 802.11b and 802.11g, these properties ensure that the eavesdropper cannot get useful information as long as it is roughly $\lambda/2 = 6.25$ cm away from Alice and Bob.

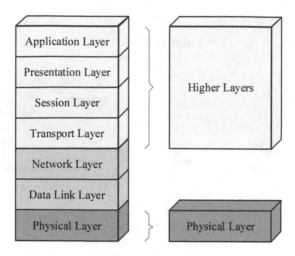

Fig. 2. The system model

But as a coin always has two sides, physical layer based key extraction schemes cannot establish communication keys securely when two clients are out of each other's radio range. It is due to the fact that the two clients must forward the fluctuated states to untrusted relay devices. Besides, the key generation rate of those schemes is quite slow (about 1 bit/sec, and more details will be given in Section 2.2), which constraints their applications.

Our Contribution. Many schemes have been proposed to extract secret keys from the wireless channel at the physical layer (a brief review of closely related works shall be given in Section 2), but few of them can securely and efficiently extract keys when two clients are out of each other's communication range. Facing the practical requirement, this paper presents a cross-layer key establishment scheme by employing the characteristics of the physical layer and higher layers corporately. Our scheme possesses the following properties:

1. Our scheme is specifically designed for assisting two remote mesh clients, who are out of each other's radio range, to establish a secure communication key;
2. In this paper we propose a cross-layer key establishment scheme. The channel phase is employed by clients to extract a partial key at the physical layer, and XOR coding is used to obtain another partial key at higher layers. The communication key is determined by these two partial keys;
3. The security of our scheme is guaranteed by two-fold: a partial key generated by coding at higher layers and the other partial key extracted via the wireless fading channel at the physical layer. Security analysis shows that our scheme is secure against man-in-the-middle attacks and node capture attacks; and
4. According to the needs of practical applications, e.g., security concerns and environmental conditions, the proposed design provides a flexible solution to

key generation rate problem. Clients in our scheme can dynamically adjust the length of the generated partial key (extracted at the physical layer). Definitely, a shorter partial key (extracted at the physical layer) will contribute to a higher key generation rate.

Organization of This Paper. The remainder of this paper is organized as follows. We present a brief overview on the related work in Section 2. Section 3 reviews the preliminaries required in this paper. The proposed scheme is described in Section 4, and its security and performance analysis is given in Section 5. Section 6 concludes this paper.

2   Related Work

A number of key establishment schemes were presented, for example, the Diffie-Hellman protocol allows two clients to establish a shared secret key over an insecure channel without prior knowledge. Symmetric key pre-distribution schemes, on the other hand, need to pre-load keys or secrets at clients. Due to restrictions on length, in this section we only focus on the closely related works.

2.1   Establish Keys Using XOR Coding

At higher layers, XOR coding technology was employed to establish secret keys in [3], where a mobile device S was used to bootstrap networks. In key pre-distribution phase, system authority: (a). produces a Vernam cipher R^1, generates a large key pool P, and computes XOR coding blocks $\{K_i \oplus R\}$s; (b). stores mobile device S with coding blocks $\{K_i \oplus R\}$s and corresponding identifiers; and (c). selects r keys and key identifiers from key pool P for each sensor node. After deployment, S broadcasts $HELLO$ messages and neighbor nodes A and B respond by sending their key identifiers. Upon receiving the identifiers id_A and id_B from node A and B respectively, mobile device S computes $K_i(A) \oplus R \oplus K_i(B) \oplus R$ and broadcasts $K_i(A) \oplus K_i(B)$. Based on the received XOR coding $K_i(A) \oplus K_i(B)$, A and B can easily recover each other's key (A owns $K_i(A)$, computes $K_i(A) \oplus K_i(A) \oplus K_i(B)$, and obtains $K_i(B)$. B can obtain $K_i(A)$ by executing similar operations). Then they can negotiate a communication key using $K_i(A)$ and $K_i(B)$. Liu et al. improved and applied it to a cluster-based hierarchical network in [5].

2.2   Extract Keys Using the Wireless Fading Channel

It is possible to extract secret bits from the physical layer, and the fundamental bounds are pointed out in [6, 7]. However, the authors of [6, 7] only provided theoretical results without giving explicit constructions. But it motivates other

---

[1] A Vernam cipher R is a binary sequence introduced in [4]. It is randomly generated according to a Bernoulli (1/2) distribution and its size is equal to the key size.

schemes using the attenuation of amplitude, deviation of phase or decline of other physical quantities to extract secret bits at the physical layer.

The attenuation of amplitude was employed to extract secrets in [8–11]. Mathur et al. used the crucial characteristics in [8] that the received signals at the receiver are modified by the channel in a manner unique to the transmitter-receiver pair. In Mathur et al.'s scheme, two wireless devices evaluated the envelope of multipath fading channel between them by probing a fixed test frequency, and quantized the evaluation into secret bits. Furthermore, the authors validated their algorithm using the 802.11a packet preamble on a FPGA-based 802.11 platform. They showed that it is possible to achieve key establishment rates of 1 bit/sec in a real indoor wireless environment. In [9], Received Signal Strength (RSS) was used as a channel statistic. By exploiting quantization, information reconciliation and privacy amplification, Jana et al. evaluated the effectiveness of secret key extraction from RSS variations in a variety of environments and settings. Besides, Vehicle-to-Infrastructure communication keys and Vehicle-to-Vehicle communication keys were extracted in [10]. In [11], an environment adaptive secret key generation scheme was proposed.

Deviation of phase (or phase offset) was used to extract secret bits in [12–15]. To increase the key bit generation rate, Zeng et al. exploited multiple-antenna diversity in [12] to generate secret keys for wireless nodes and implemented it on off-the-shelf 802.11n multiple-antenna devices. Pairwise key generation approach and group key generation approach were presented in [13] by utilizing the uniformly distributed phase information of channel responses under narrowband multipath fading models. A cooperative key generation protocol was proposed in [14] to facilitate high rate key generation in narrowband fading channels with the aid of relay node(s). Zhuo et al. [15] presented a multihop key establishment scheme based on the assumption that the network is biconnected, and the security of [15] is guaranteed against adversaries in a single path.

It is also proved in [16, 17] that decline of other physical quantities are available to extract secret bits. Liu et al. came up with a novel idea to extract cryptography keys in [16]. Noticing that the fading exhibited in RSS measurements follows similar increasing or decreasing trend despite of the mismatch of absolute values, they proposed a fading trend based secret key extraction scheme. Liu et al. presented another idea in [17] to mitigate the non-reciprocity component by learning the channel response from multiple Orthogonal Frequency-Division Multiplexing (OFDM) subcarriers.

However, there are some practical requirements that schemes [8–17] failed to securely fulfill. For example, (1). It is a practical requirement in WMNs that two remote clients should establish a secret key to secure their communications. The schemes in [15, 16] provide solutions to fulfill this requirement, but some problems still exist in their schemes. The proposed scheme in [15] is based on the assumption that the network is biconnected, i.e., there are at least two disjoint paths between any pair of nodes. This assumption limits its practicality. In [16], a collaborative key extraction scheme is designed under the assistance of relay nodes. However, the extracted key is not secure as it is known by one of the relay nodes; (2). Designed schemes should be secure against man-in-the-middle attacks. Until now, the existing physical layer based key extraction schemes failed to secure against this kind of attacks. Realizing that it is possible to utilize the characteristics of the physical layer and higher layers cooperatively to meet foregoing requirements, in this paper we present a cross-layer key establishment scheme. At higher layers, we use coding to gain partial secrets; At the physical layer, we employ the channel phase to extract other partial secrets. The details of our scheme will be described in Section 4.

3 Preliminaries

This section presents some preliminaries required in this paper.

3.1 Extract Secret Bits from the Wireless Fading Channel

The characteristic of the wireless channel between two wireless devices provides them an access to extract secret keys, even in the presence of an eavesdropper [8, 9]. An example is given in Fig. 3.

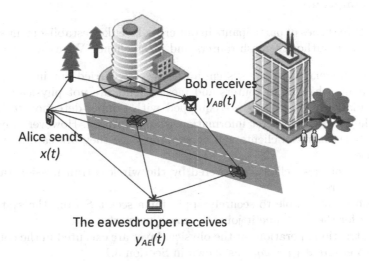

Fig. 3. An example of fading

In Fig. 3, Alice sends a sinusoidal signal $x(t) = A \sin(w_c t + \phi_0)$ to Bob. Here A is the amplitude, w_c is the angular frequency, and ϕ_0 is the initial phase. Due to the multipath environment, noise, and/or mobile environment, the sinusoidal signals received at Bob and the eavesdropper are different. Let $y_{AB}(t)$ and $y_{AE}(t)$ denote the signals received by Bob and the eavesdropper, and they can be written as:

$$y_{AB}(t) = A_{AB} \sin(w_c t + \phi_0 + \phi_{AB}) + n_{AB}(t),$$
$$y_{AE}(t) = A_{AE} \sin(w_c t + \phi_0 + \phi_{AE}) + n_{AE}(t).$$

Here, A_{AB} and A_{AE} are the modulated amplitudes, and they are functions of path loss and shadowing; ϕ_{AB} and ϕ_{AE} are the deviated phases, and they are depend on delay, Doppler, and carrier offset [2]. $n_{AB}(t)$ and $n_{AE}(t)$ denote the additive white Gaussian noise.

Upon receiving $y_{AB}(t)$, Bob sends the signal $x(t) = A\sin(w_c t + \phi_0)$ back to Alice in the coherence time. Similarly, Alice and the eavesdropper will receive $y_{BA}(t)$ and $y_{BE}(t)$, and they can be written as:

$$y_{BA}(t) = A_{BA}\sin(w_c t + \phi_0 + \phi_{BA}) + n_{BA}(t),$$
$$y_{BE}(t) = A_{BE}\sin(w_c t + \phi_0 + \phi_{BE}) + n_{BE}(t).$$

By assuming that key extraction operations are executed in the coherence time, we have $\phi_{AB} = \phi_{BA}$. If the eavesdropper is more than $\lambda/2$ away from Alice and Bob, it cannot extract any useful secrets by making use of his received signals. Taking Fig. 3 as an example, ϕ_{AE} and ϕ_{AB} (ϕ_{BE} and ϕ_{BA}) are statistically independent as long as the eavesdropper is more than $\lambda/2$ away from Bob (Alice).

3.2   Assumptions

There are three types of participants in our cross-layer key establishment scheme, i.e., the system authority, mesh routers and mesh clients. We assume that:

1. Operations related to the system authority are carried out in a secure environment, while mesh routers and mesh clients are not physically secure. Particularly, mesh routers are equipped with tamper-detection technology and they can erase secret information when captured. However, any secret data stored in mesh clients will be exposed once they are captured by adversaries;
2. The area of mesh clients is covered by the wireless transmission radius of mesh routers;
3. A mesh client is able to securely apply for a secret S from the system authority for the first time it joins the mesh networks; and
4. Key extraction operations at the physical layer are executed in the coherence time to ensure $\phi_{AB} = \phi_{BA}$ as shown in Section 3.1.

3.3   Adversary Model

As assumptions made in [8–17], the adversary is at least $\lambda/2$ away from legitimate clients, and it can eavesdrop the communications among clients. We also assume that the adversary knows the key establishment scheme and it can perform phase estimation during key generation process. In addition, the adversary aims to derive the secret keys generated between legitimate mesh clients, and

---

[2] Path loss, shadowing, delay, Doppler, and carrier offset are components in analysis of a communication system. Please refer to [2] for more information.

it is not interested in interrupting the key generation scheme by jamming the communications. Different from the schemes in [8, 9, 13], we assume that relay clients are not fully trusted, and node capture attacks and man-in-the-middle attacks are considered in this paper.

4   A Cross-Layer Key Establishment Scheme in WMNs

This section is devoted to the description of our cross-layer key establishment scheme for two mesh clients who are beyond each other's communication range.

4.1   Overview

As shown in Fig. 4, the scheme consists of five phases, and details of each phase will be followed in Section 4.2.

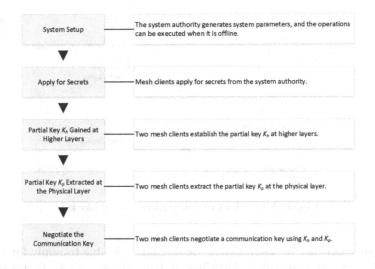

Fig. 4. Five phase of our cross-layer key establishment scheme

4.2   A Cross-Layer Key Establishment Scheme

System Setup: Assume that the population of residents in a community is P. For each individual, there are about Q devices (like PCs or phones) may serve as mesh clients and access the WMNs through mesh routers or directly meshing with other mesh clients. It means that there are about $M = PQ$ mesh clients in this area. During the system setup phase, the system authority

- Chooses N independent secrets $S_1, S_2, ..., S_N$ from a finite field GF_q, for $N \geq M$. Let id_i be the identifier of secret S_i;

- Computes $S_i^2, S_i^3, \ldots, S_i^e$, for $i = 1, 2, \ldots, N$. e is the expected times that secret S_i be used to establish communication keys;
- Chooses a secure hash function $H(x)$;
- Produces Vernam cipher R_{ij}s, i.e., binary sequences drawn randomly according to a Bernoulli $(\frac{1}{2})$ distribution. Here $i = 1, 2, \ldots, N$, $j = 1, 2, \ldots, N$, and $i \neq j$. The generated R_{ij}s should possess the characteristic that $R_{ij} = R_{ji}$;
- Computes coding blocks $\{H(S_i^k) \oplus R_{ij}\}$s, for $2 \leq k \leq e$; and
- Loads $\{id_i, k : H(S_i^k) \oplus R_{ij}\}$s at mesh routers.

To facilitate understanding, we provide a flowchart of computing coding blocks in Fig. 5. Note that R_{ij}s possess the characteristic $R_{ij} = R_{ji}$.

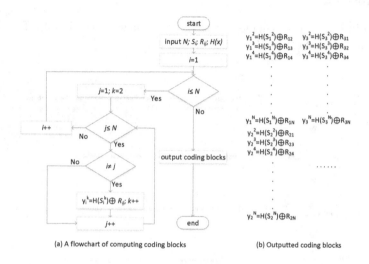

(a) A flowchart of computing coding blocks   (b) Outputted coding blocks

Fig. 5. A flowchart of computing coding blocks

Apply for Secrets: We assume that mesh client i is able to apply for a secret S_i and the corresponding secret identifier id_i from the system authority securely for the first time it joins the mesh networks.

Partial Key K_h Gained at Higher Layers: When two mesh clients u and v want to establish a communication key, they should execute following operations:

- Say $HELLO$ to each other and exchange secret identifiers id_u, id_v. This operation can be completed by employing forward function of multiple relay clients; and
- Send a request, $\{req: id_u, id_v\}$, to mesh routers.

Upon receiving the request, mesh routers retrieve the stored coding blocks $\{id_i, k : H(S_i^k) \oplus R_{ij}\}$s and reply mesh clients u, v with $\{id_u, x; id_v, y : H(S_u^x) \oplus H(S_v^y) = H(S_u^x) \oplus R_{uv} \oplus H(S_v^y) \oplus R_{vu}\}$ publicly.

Then, mesh clients u and v:

- Compute $H(S_v^y)$ and $H(S_u^x)$, separately. Taking client u as an example, it owns S_u, computes $H(S_u^x)$ and $H(S_u^x) \oplus H(S_u^x) \oplus H(S_v^y)$, and obtains $H(S_v^y)$. Client v can obtain $H(S_u^x)$ by executing similar operations;
- Negotiate the partial key K_h using $H(S_u^x)$ and $H(S_v^y)$. For example, client u and v can compute $K_h = H(H(S_u^x) \| H(S_v^y))$. Here, $\|$ is the connection operation.

Partial Key K_p Extracted at the Physical Layer: The basic idea of key extraction algorithms at the physical layer is to employ the inherent channel randomness associated with distinct pairwise links, i.e., the sinusoidal signal transmitted back and forth between two mesh clients will experience the same phase variation over the coherence time period. We assume that there are x relay clients between u and v, denoted as $r_1, r_2, \ldots, r_x$. As depicted in [13], the key extraction scheme contains $|K_p|/\log_2(q)$ round, and there are two time slots $(ST_1$ and $ST_2)$ in each round. Here $|K_p|$ is the length of K_p. In ST_1:

- Mesh client u chooses ϕ_1 uniformly at random from $[0, 2\pi]$, and sends the sinusoidal signal $x(t) = A \sin(w_c t + \phi_1)$ to relay client r_1;
- Relay client r_i forwards the signal to relay client r_j, where r_i, $r_j \in \{r_1, r_2, \ldots, r_x\}$ and $1 \le i < j \le x$;
- Relay client r_x forwards the signal to mesh client v.

The steady-state portion of the beacon received at mesh client v can be written as

$$y_{u \to v}(t) = A' \sin(w_c t + \phi_1 + \phi_{ur_1} + \phi_{r_1 r_2} + \cdots + \phi_{r_x v}) + n'(t),$$

where $n'(t)$ denotes the additive white Gaussian noise, and ϕ_{ij} denotes the phase offset when the signal is transmitted from client i to client j. After ST_1, client v gets $\phi_{u \to v} = \phi_1 + \phi_{ur_1} + \phi_{r_1 r_2} + \cdots + \phi_{r_x v}$. In ST_2:

- Mesh client v chooses ϕ_2 uniformly at random from $[0, 2\pi]$ and sends the sinusoidal signal $x(t) = A \sin(w_c t + \phi_2)$ to relay client r_x;
- Relay client r_j forwards the signal to relay client r_i, where r_i, $r_j \in \{r_1, r_2, \ldots, r_x\}$ and $1 \le i < j \le x$;
- Relay client r_1 forwards the signal to mesh client u.

Similarly, the steady-state portion of the beacon received at mesh client u can be written as

$$y_{v \to u}(t) = A'' \sin(w_c t + \phi_2 + \phi_{vr_x} + \phi_{r_x r_{x-1}} + \cdots + \phi_{r_1 u}) + n''(t).$$

After ST_2, client u obtains $\phi_{v \to u} = \phi_2 + \phi_{vr_x} + \phi_{r_x r_{x-1}} + \cdots + \phi_{r_1 u}$.

At the end of first round, both client u and v can compute the phase components Φ_1

$$\text{client } u: \quad \Phi_1 = \phi_{v \to u} + \phi_1 \bmod 2\pi,$$
$$\text{client } v: \quad \Phi_1 = \phi_{u \to v} + \phi_2 \bmod 2\pi.$$

As shown in [13], we can map Φ_1 into the quantization inter/index using the formula:

$$Q_x = k \quad if \ \ x \in [\frac{2\pi(k-1)}{q}, \frac{2\pi k}{q}),$$

for $k = 1, 2, \ldots, q$. Thus, the quantization of phase value generates $\log_2(q)$ bits secret. To extract the partial key K_p with length $|K_p|$, mesh clients u and v need to repeat the operations (presented in ST_1 and ST_2) for $|K_p|/\log_2(q)$ round.

Due to the presence of noise and interference, manufacturing variations, half-duplex mode of communication and estimation errors, *secure sketch* can be applied to reconcile the differences in the bit streams (refer to [13] for details).

Negotiate the Communication Key: After completing the aforementioned operations, mesh clients u and v obtain shared partial keys K_h and K_p. Then they can negotiate the communication key K using K_h and K_p. For example, the communication key can be computed as: $K = H(K_h \| K_p)$.

This completes the description of our cross-layer key establishment scheme.

5 Security and Performance Analysis

In this section, we analyze the security and performance of our cross-layer key establishment scheme.

5.1 Security Analysis

The security of our proposed cross-layer key establishment scheme is guaranteed by two-fold: the partial key K_h generated at higher layers and the partial key K_p extracted at the physical layer.

At higher layers, coding is employed to ensure the security of the partial key K_h. Under the assumption that a mesh client is able to apply for a secret S from system authority securely for the first time it joins the mesh networks, any pair of clients can compute and obtain K_h. Take **Partial Key K_h Gained at Higher Layers** as an example, only clients u and v can decode $H(S_u^x) \oplus H(S_v^y)$, obtain $H(S_v^y)$ and $H(S_u^x)$, and compute $K_h = H(H(S_u^x) \| H(S_v^y))$ correctly.

At the physical layer, it is widely assumed that an adversary cannot obtain the identical channel response for key generation if it is at least $\lambda/2$ away from communicating clients [8–17], and this has been validated in real experiments in [8, 9]. During **partial key K_p extracted at the physical layer** phase, the adversary will experience independent channel variations as long as it is more than 6.25 cm away from the communicating nodes. Here we let the carrier frequency be 2.4 GHz. In our scheme, the communicating nodes include clients u, v and relay clients $r_1, r_2, \ldots, r_x$.

Resilience against Man-in-the-Middle Attacks. When the fading channel is employed to extract secret keys, Mathur et al. pointed out in [8] that two clients will suffer from man-in-the-middle attacks if they are not within each other's communication range. Just as other physical layer based schemes, the partial key K_p extracted from the wireless fading channel are vulnerable to man-in-the-middle attacks. But the communication key K generated in our scheme is secure against such kind of attacks. The reason is that the communication key in our scheme is computed as: $K = H(K_h \| K_p)$. Recall that K_h is computed by coding at higher layers. Without secret S_u or S_v, an attacker cannot compute K_h correctly. So it cannot cheat the communicating clients. The cross-layer key establishment design makes the scheme resist against man-in-the-middle attacks when two clients are beyond each other's radio range.

Resilience against Node Capture Attacks. Our cross-layer key establishment scheme is secure against node capture attacks. Assume that the adversary obtains a secret S_w by capturing client w. It can impersonate client w and try to establish communication key with legitimate client v. The adversary can obtain $H(S_v^y)$ after mesh routers replied $H(S_w^x) \oplus H(S_v^y)$. However, it cannot obtain $H(S_v^{y-1})$ or $H(S_v^{y+1})$ by using $H(S_v^y)$ due to the one way hash function. Furthermore, it cannot obtain those clients' secrets who established communication keys with client v, because client v establishes communication keys with different clients using different secret codings. For coding $H(S_v^y) \oplus R_{vw}$, it is only used between clients w and v. So, the leak of a secret in our scheme will not contribute to other secrets' insecurity.

5.2   Performance Analysis

Probability of Successful Partial Key Generation. During **partial key K_p extracted at the physical layer** phase, each node (source node and destination node) generates an initial phase randomly. As assumed in [13], all observations in different time slots or at different nodes are affected by independent noise realizations. Let T_0 be the observation time, f_s be the sampling rate and N be the number of samples in the observation. The estimation errors converge to zero-mean Gaussian random variables with variances σ_ϕ^2 when N increases, and it can be lower-bounded by the Cramer-Rao bounds (CRB) [18]. Recall that the amplitude of the transmitted sinusoid signal is A, when estimating it in white noise with Power Spectral Density (PSD) $\frac{N_0}{2}$, the CRBs for the variance of the phase estimate is given as (refer to schemes [13, 18] for details)

$$\sigma_\phi^2 \geq \frac{2f_s N_0 (2N-1)}{A^2 N(N+1)} \approx \frac{4N_0}{A^2 T_0} \qquad (1)$$

When N is sufficiently large, $\frac{f_s}{N} = \frac{1}{T_0}$. As described in **Partial key K_p Extracted at the Physical Layer**, there are x relay nodes. Thus, the variance of the accumulated estimation errors across $x + 2$ nodes is $\sigma_{(x+2)}^2 = (x + 2)\sigma_\phi^2$. Wang et al. present the average probability of quantization index agreement P_{QIA} in [13] as

$$P_{QIA} = \int_{\frac{2\pi i}{q}}^{\frac{2\pi(i+1)}{q}} P_{QIA}(\phi)\frac{q}{2\pi}d\phi \approx \int_{\frac{2\pi i}{q}}^{\frac{2\pi(i+1)}{q}} P_i^{(x+2)}(\phi)\frac{q}{2\pi}d\phi \qquad (2)$$

where $P_i(\phi) = \int_{\frac{2\pi i}{q}}^{\frac{2\pi(i+1)}{q}} \frac{1}{\sqrt{2\pi}\sigma_{(x+2)}} e^{-\frac{(y-\phi)^2}{2\sigma^2_{(x+2)}}} dy$.

Randomness of Key. To extract high entropy secret bits from wireless fading channel, most of the related schemes rely on node mobility or channel variations. In a static environment the adversary has the ability to predict the changes of channel phase when clients u and v are stationary (it is pointed out in [9, 17]). However, our cross-layer key establishment scheme can provide communication keys with sufficient randomness even in a static environment. In our scheme, ϕ_1 and ϕ_2 are chosen uniformly at random from $[0, 2\pi]$ by clients u and v respectively, which contributes to the randomness of the partial key K_p. Besides, secrets S_u, S_v are generated randomly by the system authority, the partial key K_h is obtained by $K_h = H(H(S_u^x)\|H(S_v^y))$, and the communication key is computed as $K = H(K_h\|K_p)$. Due to the randomness of K_p and K_h, our scheme can provide random communication keys in the dynamic or static environment.

Key Rate. Due to the fact that in the time slots where the channel changes slowly, a limited number of key bits can be generated. It has been investigated by previous work in [8] that two wireless clients can generate a communication key at about 1 bit/sec by using off-the-shelf 802.11a hardware. This constraint significantly limits their practical applications [14]. The cross-layer key establishment scheme provides a flexible solution to this limitation. In practical applications, clients in our scheme can dynamically adjust the length of the generated partial key K_p based on actual application requirements, e.g., security concerns and environmental conditions. Definitely, a short partial key K_p will save the partial key generation time at the physical layer, and this will contribute to a high key generation rate. Our cross-layer key establishment scheme will degrade to XOR coding based scheme when the length of partial key K_p is "0".

Storage, Communication and Computation Complexities. We consider the storage, communication and computation costs of our scheme from two parts: the partial key K_h generated at higher layers and the partial key K_p extracted at the physical layer. To obtain the partial key K_h, client u needs to: (a). apply a secret S_u and the corresponding secret identifier id_u from the system authority; (b). exchange identifiers id_u, id_v with client v and send request {req: id_u, id_u} to mesh routers; (c). compute K_h using S_u after receiving $\{id_u, x; id_v, y : H(S_u^x) \oplus H(S_v^y)\}$. To extract partial key K_p, client u needs to repeat the operations (presented in ST_1 and ST_2) for $|K_p|/log_2^{(q)} = 16$ rounds when $|K_p| = 64$ bits and $q = 16$.

Specifically, our cross-layer key establishment scheme will degrade to XOR coding based scheme when $|K_p| = 0$. In this case, our scheme has the same security level as [3, 5]. Recall that each node needs to pre-load r keys and $N - 1$ coding blocks in [3] and [5], respectively. So, our scheme has a significant advantage over [3, 5] from the aspect of storage costs at clients. The light storage costs at mesh clients are achieved by migrating all coding blocks to mesh routers (recall that mesh routers have much more storage space than clients). To establish communication keys, clients need to exchange identifiers. Obviously, communication costs of clients in our scheme are the same with [3, 5]. However, comparing with schemes [3, 5], computation costs are higher in our scheme. Because client u in [3, 5] only needs to execute XOR coding, but it needs to compute S_u^x, $H(S_u^x)$, and XOR coding in our scheme.

We now compare the computation cost of our cross-layer key establishment scheme (consumed at higher layers when computing S_u^x) with the technique of asymmetric key cryptography. To achieve a security level of 80-bit, our scheme shall require one modular exponentiation with the length of 40-bit when $|K_h| = |K_p| = 40$, while it requires at least one modular exponentiation with the length of 1024-bit using asymmetric key techniques such as the RSA.

Take sensor node MICAz mote as an example, it is equipped with an 8-bit AVR processor (the ATmega128) and has only 4 kB of RAM and 128 kB flash memory [19]. To the best of our knowledge, the fastest software implementation of modular multiplication (mod-mul) for such 8-bit AVR processors roughly requires 240 clock cycles for operand with a length of 40-bit and roughly 220596 clock cycles for a 1024-bit operand. It means that the costs of performing a 1024-bit modular multiplication equal to 920 times of performing a 40-bit modular multiplication. It is the same case for modular squaring (mod-sqr). Thus, we have

$$\text{mod-mul-1024} = 920 \times \text{mod-mul-40}, \text{and}$$

$$\text{mod-sqr-1024} = 920 \times \text{mod-sqr-40}.$$

The basic method to perform modular exponentiation (mod-exp) is called "square-and-multiply" method. Take an n-bit modular exponentiation as an example, the computation costs for the modular exponentiation roughly need n times modular squaring and $n/2$ times modular multiplication operations. In this case, the computation costs of modular exponentiation are

$$\text{mod-exp-1024} = 1024 \times \text{mod-sqr-1024} + 512 \times \text{mod-mul-1024}$$

$$= (1024 \times 920 \times 0.8 + 512 \times 920) \times \text{mod-mul-40}$$

$$= 1224704 \times \text{mod-mul-40}, \text{and}$$

$$\text{mod-exp-40} = 40 \times \text{mod-sqr-40} + 20 \times \text{mod-mul-40}$$

$$= 52 \times \text{mod-mul-40}.$$

$$(\text{mod-sqr} = 0.8 \times \text{mod-mul})$$

So, one 1024-bit modular exponentiation is at least 20000 times more expensive than one 40-bit modular exponentiation.

We can accelerate the 1024-bit modular exponentiation using hardware acceleration technologies: The implementation of modular multiplication for a 1024-bit operand can be accelerated to $3\mu s$ with a hardware accelerator [20]. Together with micro controllers running at a frequency of 8MHz, a 1024-bit modular multiplication only requires $3\mu s \times 8M = 24$ clock cycles. This can also meet the practical requirement[3]. But in wireless mesh networks, mesh clients consist of various devices, including laptap/desktop PC, pocket PC, PDA, IP phone, RFID reader, BACnet (building automation and control networks) controller and tiny wireless sensor nodes. Assuming each device with hardware acceleration would be too strong to hold in certain situations. It is obvious that an efficient protocol without the need of hardware acceleration, such as the one proposed in this paper, can better suit the nature of wireless mesh networks.

6   Conclusion

As a fundamental security technology, key establishment has been widely studied in wireless mesh networks. Many key establishment schemes are proposed, and they are implemented at the physical layer or higher layers. However, due to the characteristics of these layers, there are some inherent disadvantages in those schemes. This paper presents a cross-layer key establishment scheme, with which the communication key is determined by two partial keys: one extracted at the physical layer and the other generated at higher layers. The analysis shows that the proposed cross-layer key establishment scheme not only eliminates the shortcomings of key establishment at each layer but also provides a flexible solution to the key generation rate problem.

Acknowledgement. The authors would like to thank anonymous reviewers for their helpful comments, and Dr. Zhe Liu (from the University of Luxembourg) for his generous sharing of simulation data.

Xinyi Huang is supported by Distinguished Young Scholars Fund of Department of Education, Fujian Province, China (JA13062), Fok Ying Tung Education Foundation (Grant NO. 141065), National Natural Science Foundation of China (Grant NO. 61202450), Ph.D. Programs Foundation of Ministry of Education of China (Grant NO. 20123503120001) and Fujian Normal University Innovative Research Team (NO. IRTL1207).

References

1. Akyildiz, I.F., Wang, X., Wang, W.: Wireless mesh networks: A survey. Computer Networks 47(4), 445–487 (2005)
2. Goldsmith, A.: Wireless communications. Cambridge University Press (2005)
3. Oliveira, P.F., Barros, J.: A network coding approach to secret key distribution. IEEE Transactions on Information Forensics and Security 3(3), 414–423 (2008)
4. Vernam, G.: Cipher printing telegraph systems: For secret wire and radio telegraphic communications. Journal of the A.I.E.E. 45(2), 109–115 (1926)

---

[3] To be more precise, a 1024-bit modular multiplication with hardware acceleration is roughly 10 times more efficient than a 40-bit modular multiplication without hardware acceleration.

5. Liu, J., Sangi, A.R., Du, R., Wu, Q.: Light weight network coding based key distribution scheme for MANETs. In: Lopez, J., Huang, X., Sandhu, R. (eds.) NSS 2013. LNCS, vol. 7873, pp. 521–534. Springer, Heidelberg (2013)
6. Maurer, U.M.: Information-theoretically secure secret-key agreement by not authenticated public discussion. In: Fumy, W. (ed.) EUROCRYPT 1997. LNCS, vol. 1233, pp. 209–225. Springer, Heidelberg (1997)
7. Maurer, U.M., Wolf, S.: Secret-key agreement over unauthenticated public channels I: Definitions and a completeness result. IEEE Transactions on Information Theory 49(4), 822–831 (2003)
8. Mathur, S., Trappe, W., Mandayam, N.B., Ye, C., Reznik, A.: Radio-telepathy: Extracting a secret key from an unauthenticated wireless channel. In: MOBICOM, pp. 128–139. ACM (2008)
9. Jana, S., Premnath, S.N., Clark, M., Kasera, S.K., Patwari, N., Krishnamurthy, S.V.: On the effectiveness of secret key extraction from wireless signal strength in real environments. In: MOBICOM, pp. 321–332. ACM (2009)
10. Zan, B., Gruteser, M., Hu, F.: Key agreement algorithms for vehicular communication networks based on reciprocity and diversity theorems. IEEE Transactions on Vehicular Technology 62(8), 4020–4027 (2013)
11. Premnath, S.N., Jana, S., Croft, J., Gowda, P.L., Clark, M., Kasera, S.K., Patwari, N., Krishnamurthy, S.V.: Secret key extraction from wireless signal strength in real environments. IEEE Transaction on Mobile Computing 12(5), 917–930 (2013)
12. Zeng, K., Wu, D., Chan, A.J., Mohapatra, P.: Exploiting multiple-antenna diversity for shared secret key generation in wireless networks. In: INFOCOM, pp. 1837–1845. IEEE (2010)
13. Wang, Q., Su, H., Ren, K., Kim, K.: Fast and scalable secret key generation exploiting channel phase randomness in wireless networks. In: INFOCOM, pp. 1422–1430. IEEE (2011)
14. Wang, Q., Xu, K., Ren, K.: Cooperative secret key generation from phase estimation in narrowband fading channels. IEEE Journal on Selected Areas in Communications 30(9), 1666–1674 (2012)
15. Hao, Z., Zhong, S., Yu, N.: A multihop key agreement scheme for wireless ad hoc networks based on channel characteristics. The Scientific World Journal 2013 (2013)
16. Liu, H., Yang, J., Wang, Y., Chen, Y.: Collaborative secret key extraction leveraging received signal strength in mobile wireless networks. In: INFOCOM, pp. 927–935. IEEE (2012)
17. Liu, H., Wang, Y., Yang, J., Chen, Y.: Fast and practical secret key extraction by exploiting channel response. In: INFOCOM, pp. 3048–3056. IEEE (2013)
18. Rife, D.C., Boorstyn, R.: Single tone parameter estimation from discrete-time observations. IEEE Transactions on Information Theory 20(5), 591–598 (1974)
19. Liu, Z., Großschädl, J., Wong, D.S.: Low-weight primes for lightweight elliptic curve cryptography on 8-bit AVR processors. In: INSCRYPT 2013. LNCS. Springer (2013)
20. Lin, W.C., Ye, J.H., Shieh, M.D.: Scalable montgomery modular multiplication architecture with low-latency and low-memory bandwidth requirement. IEEE Transactions on Computers 63(2), 475–483 (2014)

Author Index